From Far East to Asia Pacific

De Gruyter Studies in Military History

―

Edited by
Jörg Echternkamp and Adam Seipp

Volume 4

From Far East to Asia Pacific

Great Powers and Grand Strategy 1900–1954

Edited by
Brian P. Farrell, S.R. Joey Long, and David J. Ulbrich

DE GRUYTER
OLDENBOURG

ISBN 978-3-11-152165-7
e-ISBN (PDF) 978-3-11-071871-3
e-ISBN (EPUB) 978-3-11-071877-5
ISSN 2701-5629

Library of Congress Control Number: 2022935571

Bibliographic information published by the Deutsche Nationalbibliothek
The Deutsche Nationalbibliothek lists this publication in the Deutsche Nationalbibliografie;
detailed bibliographic data are available on the internet at http://dnb.dnb.de.

© 2024 Walter de Gruyter GmbH, Berlin/Boston
This volume is text- and page-identical with the hardback published in 2022.
Cover image: "Japan I see your cruisers and raise you a dreadnought!", Illus. in: Puck, v. 66, no. 1699 (1909 September 22), cover. Illustrator: Glackens, L. M. (Louis M.), 1866–1933. Copyright 1909 by Keppler & Schwarzmann.
Typesetting: Integra Software Services Pvt.

www.degruyter.com

Acknowledgements

The co-editors and contributors wish to thank the National University of Singapore for the research grant funding that enabled us to run the conference which initiated this volume. We also wish to thank the staff of Singapore History Consultants Pte. Ltd., and the Rise of Asia Museum, for their co-sponsorship of, and fundamental assistance with, that conference. We are also grateful to Associate Provost Karen Hinkle, Dean William Clements, Professor Lea Williams, and the Faculty Development Committee at Norwich University for underwriting some production costs for this volume. Finally, our thanks to the editorial and publications staff at De Gruyter Academic for their support for and assistance in realizing this volume.

Figure A.1: December 2019 Conference in Singapore.

Figure A.2: Rise of Asia Museum, Singapore.

Contents

Acknowledgements —— V

List of Maps —— XI

List of Figures —— XIII

List of Tables —— XV

Notes on Contributors and Acknowledgements —— XVII

Sources: List of Abbreviations used in Citations —— XXI

Glossary: Names and Spelling —— XXIII

Brian P. Farrell
From Far East to Asia Pacific: Great Powers and Grand Strategy, 1900–1954 —— 1

Section One

Brian P. Farrell
Follow the Money: E for Economics and Grand Strategy —— 15

Shannon A. Brown
Grand Strategy by Other Means: US Foreign Policy, Public-Private Collaboration, and "Employing all Proper Methods in China," 1895–1914 —— 19

Yamamoto Fumihito
Follow the Money: The Manchurian Incident, Economic Recovery and Japan's Policy Change in the 1930s —— 49

Section Two

David J. Ulbrich
Military Power in Grand Strategy, 1900–1954 —— 81

David J. Ulbrich
Facing the Rising Sun in the Pacific: Grand Strategy, the US Marine Corps and Amphibious Capabilities, 1900–1941 —— 85

Brian P. Farrell
Twilight in China: Great Powers and the Defence of Shanghai, 1925–1937 —— 113

Charles Burgess
"To Treat China as a Great Power": Great Britain, Southeast Asia, and American Grand Strategy for the Defeat of Japan, 1941–1945 —— 151

Karl Hack
Grand Strategy and Its Layers: Britain and Southeast Asia, 1946–1954 —— 183

Section Three

S.R. Joey Long
Diplomacy, (Hot and Cold) War, and Grand Strategy, 1940–1954 —— 217

Jeremy A. Yellen
What Grand Strategy? Japan, 1931–1945 —— 221

Andrea Benvenuti
Frustrating the Americans and Befriending the Communists: Nehru's Policy in the Early Asian Cold War, 1947–1954 —— 251

Lauriane Simony
The British Council and Its Rivals: Great Powers' Cultural Competition in Post-Independence Burma, 1948–1955 —— 281

S.R. Joey Long
Adversaries, Allies and the Shaping of US Grand Strategy: The Eisenhower Administration and the 1954 Geneva Conference —— 309

Marek W. Rutkowski
Expanding the Area of Peace: India and the Geneva Conference of 1954 —— 339

Coda

Brian P. Farrell
On Two Doorsteps: Middle Powers and Grand Strategy —— 363

Peter Dean
Managing Great Power Allies: Australian Grand Strategy in Asia, 1900–1954 —— 365

Brian P. Farrell
Reflections: Making Sense of and Shaping Order in the Asia-Pacific 1900–1954 —— 393

Index —— 397

List of Maps

Map 1.1 Railways in China, circa 1911
Source: Brian P. Farrell, adapted from a map found in Lee En-Han, *China's Quest for Railroad Autonomy, 1904-1911* (Singapore: Singapore University Press, 1977) —— **38**

Map 3.1 War Plan ORANGE envisioned as the American naval campaign to defeat Japan in the early 20th century
Source: Matthew S. Muehlbauer and David J. Ulbrich, *Ways of War: American Military History from the Colonial Era to the Twenty-First Century*, 2nd ed. (London: Routledge, 2018) —— **89**

Map 4.1 Treaty Ports and Principal British Enclaves 1918
Source: Brian P. Farrell, adapted from an original in Robert Bickers, *Out of China: How the Chinese Ended the Era of Western Domination* (London: Allen Lane, 2017) —— **133**

Map 4.2 Shanghai and area in 1932 with the highlighted 1927 Cordon Line
Source: Brian P. Farrell, adapted from an original in Lionel Curtis, *The Capital Question of China* (London: Macmillan, 1932) —— **135**

Map 4.3 Shanghai International Settlement and the 1927 Cordon Line
Source: Brian P. Farrell, adapted from an original in Charles W. Gwynn, *Imperial Policing* (London: Macmillan, 1939) —— **141**

Map 4.4 Outline for Plan N, April 1927
Source: Brian P. Farrell, adapted from an original in NAUK, WO106/85, Duncan to WO, 7 April 1927 —— **144**

Map 5.1 China and Southeast Asia in late 1943. The extent of Japanese occupation and the "Hump" Air Freight Route from India to China
Source: Charles Burgess —— **158**

Map 6.1 The Songhkla Position in the 1950s
Source: Karl Hack, adapted from NAUK, DEFE5/44, COS(53)99, 17 February 1953, Appendix B —— **186**

Map 6.2 The British Defence Coordination Council (Far East), Malayan and ANZAM (Australia, New Zealand and Malaya) Planning Areas in the early 1950s
Source: Karl Hack, adapted from an original in NAUK, DEFE11/97 —— **191**

Map 6.3 British Malaya and Its Administrative Divisions in 1941
Source: Karl Hack (maps use old Malayan spelling, eg Johore not Johor) —— **193**

Map 7.1 The Empire of Japan in early 1942
Source: Jeremy A. Yellen —— **223**

Map 12.1 Map of the Asia-Pacific Region in the 21st Century
Source: Australian National University —— **366**

List of Figures

Figure A.1　December 2019 Conference in Singapore
　　　　　　Credit: Singapore History Consultants Pte. Ltd —— V
Figure A.2　Rise of Asia Museum, Singapore
　　　　　　Credit: RoAM, Singapore —— VI
Figure 1.1　Willard Straight, U.S Consul-General, Mukden (1906–1909)
　　　　　　Credit: Library of Congress, USA —— 24
Figure 2.1　Takahashi Korekiyo, Finance Minister of Japan, 1931–1936
　　　　　　Credit: National Diet Library, Japan —— 58
Figure 2.2　Japan's first mass-produced car: Datsun Type 14 (1935) manufactured by Nissan
　　　　　　Credit: TAKA@P.P.R.S - The 43rd Tokyo Motor Show 2013_PENTAX K-3_088 —— 65
Figure 2.3　Japan's first electronic refrigerator: Shibaura SS-1200 (1933)
　　　　　　Credit: Toshiba Science Museum —— 66
Figure 2.4　Canon's first camera with its lenses manufactured by Nippon Kōgaku: Hanza Canon (1936)
　　　　　　Credit: Canon Inc —— 66
Figure 2.5　Imperial Japanese Navy Battleship *Musashi* with its gigantic rangefinder manufactured by Nippon Kōgaku on top of its superstructure (Laid down in 1938, commissioned in 1942). Photo taken from the bow, August 1942
　　　　　　Credit: World War II Database (https://ww2db.com/image.php?image_id=1593) —— 67
Figure 3.1　Process of American grand strategy flowing down to U.S. Marine Corps doctrine, force structure, and equipment, together with the feedback loop back up to strategy and grand strategy
　　　　　　Credit: Marine Corps University Press —— 87
Figure 3.2　Senior American leaders observing a joint Marine Corps-Army amphibious exercise at New River, North Carolina, in July 1941
　　　　　　Credit: Marine Corps University Press —— 108

List of Tables

Table 2.1 Gross Domestic Product Growth Rate: Long-Term: 1900–1950
           Credit: All graphs in Chapter 2 developed by Yamamoto Fumihito —— 51
Table 2.2 Total GDP: 1900–1950 —— 52
Table 2.3 Per Capita GDP: 1918–1945 —— 53
Table 2.4 GDP Growth in the 1930s —— 61
Table 2.5 Japanese Military Spending: 1930–1937 —— 62
Table 2.6 Ripple Effects of Takahashi's Economics —— 62
Table 2.7 Japanese-Manchurian Trade —— 69
Table 2.8 Shares of Japanese and British Cotton Products in Third Countries —— 71

Notes on Contributors and Acknowledgements

Andrea Benvenuti is an Associate Professor in International Relations at the University of New South Wales in Sydney, Australia. Educated at Florence University, Monash University, and Oxford University, Benvenuti currently teaches Twentieth-Century International History and Diplomacy at both undergraduate and postgraduate levels. His research interests lie in post-1945 International History with a strong focus on the Cold War in both Asia and Europe. In 2017, he published *Cold War and Decolonisation: Australia's Policy towards Britain's End of Empire in Southeast Asia* with NUS Press. He is currently working on two major research projects: a co-authored monograph on China's foreign policy since 1949 and a single-authored book on India's Asia policy in the 1950s.

Shannon A. Brown is a Senior Lecturer and Master's Degree Program Director at the Center for Homeland Defense and Security at the Naval Postgraduate School (NPS) in Monterey, California. As a member of the Department of National Security Affairs faculty at NPS, he provides graduate instruction to cohorts of defense and security professionals from the U.S. Navy, U.S. Marine Corps, Department of Homeland Security, and representatives of state, local, territorial, and tribal governments. His academic specialties include public policy, international relations, and the history of technology. He is an experienced policy analyst with an extensive background in academic management and graduate course and program development, having served as the Dean of Faculty and Academic Programs and the Chairman of the Department of National Security Studies at the Eisenhower School for National Security and Resource Strategy, one of the National Defense University postgraduate professional military education (PME) colleges in Washington, D.C. His academic interests include industrial policy, specifically the study of arms manufacturing, arms trafficking, and comparative export policies; technology policy; and surveillance studies. He holds a Doctor of Philosophy degree in history from the University of California at Santa Cruz.

Charles J. Burgess is a Postdoctoral Fellow at the National University of Singapore, where he also earned his PhD in 2020. His research focuses on Western military power in Asia in the twentieth century, particularly the interactions between national policy, grand strategy, and the operational level of war. He is currently working on a book manuscript that will examine Allied grand strategy and anti-Japanese resistance forces in Southeast Asia during WWII. Prior to embarking on his PhD studies, Charles spent nearly 15 years working for the US government in various Asia-focused analytical and operational positions.

Professor **Peter J. Dean** is Chair of Defence Studies and Director of the UWA Defence and Security Institute. He is a Senior Fellow at the Perth USAsia Centre and a Visiting Fellow at the Strategic and Defence Studies Centre (SDSC) at The Australian National University. Peter has an extensive background in military and defence studies. He specialises in Australian defence policy and strategy, the US-Australia Alliance, military operations in the Indo-Pacific and amphibious/archipelagic warfare. He is the author of eight books with two more, *Fighting Australia's Cold War: The nexus of strategy and operations in a multipolar Asia, 1945–1965,* ANU Press (with Tristan Moss) and *Australia in the Second World War,* University Press of Kentucky (with Karl James), in press for 2022. He has previously been a Fulbright Fellow and Endeavour Research Scholar in Australia-United States Alliance Studies, as well as a fellow with the Centres for Strategic and International Studies (CSIS) and Australia, New Zealand and Pacific Studies at Georgetown University in Washington D.C.

Brian P. Farrell is Professor of Military History at the National University of Singapore, where he has been teaching since 1993. He is the principal investigator of the research project which spawned this edited volume. His current research interests include imperial defence and the British Empire, and the Western military experience in Asia, both in the nineteenth and twentieth centuries. Major publications include *The Basis and Making of British Grand Strategy 1940–1943: Was There a Plan?* 2 vols. (1998), *The Defence and Fall of Singapore 1940–1942* (2015) [2005], *Between Two Oceans: A Military History of Singapore*, 2nd edition (2010) [1999], and *Empire in Asia: A New Global History*, 2 vols. (2018).

Karl Hack is Professor of History at The Open University in the UK, having previously taught at the Nanyang Technological University, Singapore. His books include: *Defence and Decolonisation in Southeast Asia* (2001); *Did Singapore Have to Fall?* (2004 with Kevin Blackburn); *Dialogues with Chin Peng* (2004, with C.C. Chin); *War Memory and the Making of Modern Malaysia and Singapore* (2012 with Kevin Blackburn); and *The Malayan Emergency: Revolution and Counterinsurgency at the end of empire* (2022).

S.R. Joey Long is Associate Professor of History at the National University of Singapore and co-principal investigator on the project which spawned this edited volume. He received his PhD in history from the University of Cambridge. He is the author of *Safe for Decolonization: The Eisenhower Administration, Britain, and Singapore* (2011), and a number of articles on the Cold War in Southeast Asia, the history of Singapore, and Asia-Pacific security.

Marek W. Rutkowski is Lecturer in Global Studies at Monash University Malaysia. His research focuses on Cold War politics in Asia with a particular interest in middle power diplomacy, development, and Eastern European involvement. Marek received his PhD in History from the National University of Singapore in 2017. He has published research on Poland's Cold War foreign policy in Asia and is currently working on a book manuscript exploring the role of the International Control Commission (ICC) in Vietnam in the period leading up to the Second Indochina War.

Lauriane Simony is a Teaching Assistant at Sorbonne Nouvelle University in Paris, where she completed her Ph.D. in British History in November 2020. Her research focuses on the British Council in post-independence Burma, and issues of cultural diplomacy in the double historical context of decolonisation of the British Empire and the Cold War. She presented papers at several conferences and workshops, including the English Studies Society Conference at Paris Nanterre University in June 2018 and the ASEAS-UK Conference at the University of Leeds in September 2018. She also co-organised the "Cultural diplomacy in the world since 1945: prestige, influence, cooperation" international conference that was held at Sorbonne Nouvelle University in May 2019. She was awarded a research grant by the English Studies Society in France to conduct research at the National Archives in Myanmar in February-March 2019. She is currently working on an article for a special issue of *Contemporary British History*, looking at the British Council's "diplomatic departure" from Burma during the military dictatorship in the 1960s.

David J. Ulbrich is Associate Professor and Director of the online Masters of Arts in History and Military History Programs at Norwich University, USA. He previously served as a civilian historian at the U.S. Army Engineer School. Ulbrich earned his doctorate in history at Temple University. Ulbrich's books include the award-winning *Preparing for Victory: Thomas Holcomb and the Making of the Modern Marine Corps 1936–1943* (Naval Institute Press, 2011), the co-authored *Race and Gender in Modern Western Warfare* (De Gruyter, 2019), and the co-authored *World War II: A Global History* (6th ed., Routledge, 2021). Ulbrich's future projects include a co-edited anthology on amphibious warfare in world history.

Yamamoto Fumihito is an author, historian, and book translator (English to Japanese). Born in Paris, brought up in Tokyo and educated in Japan and Singapore, his research interests lie in the international history of the twentieth century, especially in Anglo-Japanese history. He received his PhD from the National University of Singapore, and his MA and BA from Dokkyo University, Saitama Japan. He published a research monograph in Japanese, *Nichiei Kaisen Eno Michi: Igirisu No Shingapōru Senryaku To Nihon No Nanshin No Shinjitsu* (The Road to the Anglo-Japanese War: Truths of the British Singapore Strategy and Japan's Southbound Policies) (2016). He also co-edited three volumes of studies in Japanese, *Kensho Taiheiyo Senso to so no Senryaku* (Studies of the Pacific War and Its Strategies) (2013). His translation works include Kishore Mahbubani's *The Great Convergence: Asia, the West and the Logic of One World*, Niall Ferguson's *Empire: How Britain Made the Modern World*, and Paul Kennedy's *The Rise and Fall of British Naval Mastery*. He also co-translated Azar Gat's *War in Human History*.

Jeremy A. Yellen is a historian of modern Japan and an Associate Professor in the Department of Japanese Studies at the Chinese University of Hong Kong. His research focuses on modern Japan's international, diplomatic, and political history during the 1930s and 1940s, with specific focus on questions of empire, international order, and war. He is the author of *The Greater East Asia Co-Prosperity Sphere: When Total Empire Met Total War* (Cornell University Press, 2019).

Sources: List of Abbreviations used in Citations

Rather than repeat across chapters the full names of repositories or publications from where we drew sources for multiple citations, we present here in one list the abbreviations used to identify said repository or publication, as cited in our footnotes.

Abbreviation	Repository or Publication
AHEC	U.S. Army Heritage and Education Centre, Carlisle Barracks, Carlisle PA
BL	The British Library, London
CWIHP	The Cold War International History Project, The Woodrow Wilson International Center for Scholars, Washington DC
DCER	*Documents on Canadian External Relations:* multi-volume edited collection, annual volumes. Published by the Department of Foreign Affairs, Trade and Development, Canada, on an ongoing basis, began in 1967 (documents dating back to 1909).[1]
DDEL	Dwight D. Eisenhower Presidential Library and Museum, Abilene KS
FDR Library	Franklin Delano Roosevelt Presidential Library and Museum, Hyde Park NY
FRUS	*Papers Relating to the Foreign Relations of the United States:* multi-volume edited collection, annual volumes (multiple and or by subject where warranted). Published by the Office of the Historian, Department of State, United States Government, ongoing, began in 1861.
GPO	Government Printing Office, Washington DC
HIA	Hoover Institution Archives, The Hoover Institution on War, Revolution and Peace, Stanford University, Stanford CA
HMSO	Her Majesty's Stationery Office, London
LOC	Library of Congress, Washington DC
MCS	Marine Corps Schools, Quantico VA
MCUA	Marine Corps University, Quantico VA
NAA	National Archives of Australia, Canberra

---

[1] The current federal government of Canada declared in November 2015 that for public communications purposes the department would be referred to as Global Affairs Canada. But the legal title remains as above and the minister is still identified as the Minister of Foreign Affairs. The editorial management of the series is much more coherent than current government management of the name of the department.

(continued)

Abbreviation	Repository or Publication
NADB	National Archives Department (Burma), Rangoon[2]
NARACP	National Archives and Records Administration (USA), College Park MD repository
NARADC	National Archives and Records Administration (USA), Washington DC repository
NAUK	The National Archives (UK), Kew
NIDS	National Institute of Defence Studies (Japan), Tokyo
NMML	The Nehru Memorial Museum and Library, New Delhi
NDL	The National Diet Library (Japan), Tokyo

---

[2] The military junta currently wielding power refers to the country and thus the archives as Myanmar and the metropolis as Yangon.

Glossary: Names and Spelling

Asian history written in English for a global readership always raises the problem of transliteration and the spelling of names of people and places. Chinese linguists developed the *Hanyu pinyin* system, based on but amending older forms of romanization of Chinese words. Since the 1980s it has been widely accepted as the global standard for such romanization. We largely use it here. In most such cases, the first time we wrote the name we included the older Wade-Giles or conventional spelling in brackets next to the pinyin transliteration.[1] But some names became so widely recognized under older systems of romanization – such as Wade-Giles – and were so widely reproduced, in not only the primary sources of the time but also decades of secondary sources, that we made some exceptions, to assist international readers less familiar with pinyin. These are noted below. Robert Bickers eloquently captured the dilemmas posed by these problems in his brief "Pronunciation Guide" in *Out of China: How the Chinese ended the Era of Western Domination* (London: Allen Lane, 2017). We also remind readers that we have adopted the East Asian custom of placing the surname first when writing out the names of individuals, Chinese, Japanese and Korean, with a single exception: Syngman Rhee, for the same reason of entrenched familiarity noted above.

Hanyu pinyin		Wade-Giles or conventional
Aihui		Aigun
Beijing	[city]	Peking, or Peiping, or Beiping
[The city was renamed Beiping/Peiping in June 1928 by the Guomindang, then restored to current spelling in October 1949 by the Chinese Communist Party]		
Chen Youren		Eugene Chen [spelling used here]
Chongqing	[city]	Chungking [spelling used here]
Guangdong	[province]	Canton
Guangzhou	[city]	Canton, or Kwangchow
Guomindang	[political party]	Kuomintang

---

[1] There are in addition names such as Manchuria, Shanghai, and Wuhan, among others, whose English spelling has not been changed in transliteration.

(continued)

Hanyu pinyin		Wade-Giles or conventional
Hai	[river]	Pei-ho
Hankou	[city]	Hankow
Huguang	[province]	Hukuang [spelling used here]
Huangpu	[river]	Whangpoo
Jiang Jieshi		Chiang Kai-shek [spelling used here]
Jinan	[city]	Tsinan [spelling used here]
Jinzhou	[city]	Chinchow
Lüshun	[city]	Port Arthur
Nanjing	[city]	Nanking
Qing	[dynasty]	Ch'ing, or Manchu
Qingdao	[city]	Tsingtao, or Tsingtau
Rehe	[province]	Jehol
Shandong	[province]	Shantung
Shenyang	[city]	Mukden [spelling used here]
Sun Yixian		Sun Yat-sen [spelling used here]
Tianjin	[city]	Tientsin
Wusung	[creek]	Woosung
Xinhai	[city]	Hsin-hai
Xinjiang	[province]	Sinkiang
Yangzi	[river]	Yangtze [spelling used here]
Zhabei	[urban district]	Chapei [spelling used here]
Zhang Zuolin		Chang Tso-lin [spelling used here]

Brian P. Farrell
From Far East to Asia Pacific: Great Powers and Grand Strategy, 1900–1954

There was a low point, a rock bottom, to the "century of humiliation" the People's Republic of China (PRC) describes as the dominant theme of the Chinese national experience from the 1840s to the 1940s. It was marked in a document, a Protocol, signed on 7 September 1901 by 12 parties. Its formal title was "very nineteenth century": *Austria–Hungary, Belgium, France, Germany, Great Britain, Italy, Japan, The Netherlands, Russia, Spain, United States and China – Final Protocol for the Settlement of the Disturbances of 1900*. Our less verbose era now refers to it as simply the *Boxer Protocol*. The imperial government of Qing China was a signatory, and in a way signed its own death certificate. The multinational military suppression of the "Boxer Rebellion" in the summer of 1900 motivated the Great Powers to impose on the Qing a tighter, much better coordinated and more strictly enforced regime of imposed globalization than the sprawling array of privileges conceded, one agreement at a time, by the "unequal treaties" the Qing signed, with various powers, from 1842 onwards. Qing China now had little state agency left. It was integrated by coercion into systems of geopolitical and economic order designed by others and imposed on it. China's weakness was the cardinal fact around which geopolitics and regional order revolved, in an extended region from Vladivostok to Rangoon. That weakness shaped the ways in which that region was connected to what was now a global order, built by "high imperialism."

More than half a century later another diplomatic moment marked – by symbol and substance – the end of the era launched by the Boxer Protocol. But this time the cardinal fact was China's resurgence. And the marker was a Final Declaration, not a Protocol – and the main point was what it omitted, not what it included. In spring 1954, the Great Powers met in Geneva to try to resolve two military conflicts that threatened to turn the Cold War into an open war, in both North and Southeast Asia. Both were civil wars in which Great Powers intervened against each other: in Korea, and in French Indochina, principally Vietnam. The PRC was heavily involved in both conflicts. Its Foreign Minister, Zhou Enlai, caused a global sensation by attending, sometimes dominating, the Geneva Conference. For the first time in more than a century, a senior representative of the government of China sat at a conference table of Great Powers not as their victim, or supplicant, but as a principal. China was far from recovered from the multiple traumas it suffered after a generation of total and civil wars;

but it was unified once again, and led by an effective national government. That government immediately began to push its way back into the constant struggle to reorder the region and the world. Due to its sheer size alone, the Great Powers had no choice but to start treating this reinvigorating China as a rising and serious power. China could not dictate the outcome of the Geneva Conference in 1954. But it could, and did, prevent anyone else from imposing any settlement either.

The central argument this book will make is that these events "bookended" a distinct period in the international and strategic histories of the area the Western Powers once called the Far East. We shall refer to it as the Asia Pacific, by which we mean an area that almost equates to the "pre-modern" Sinic World Order: the regions marked by the centrality, or at least the presence, of Chinese influence, ranging from Southeast Asia to Vladivostok and further north. The Boxer Protocol and the Final Declarations of Geneva periodize an era in Asia Pacific history that was defined by a paramount theme: this region was unique in the histories of efforts to build a global order, for reasons that coalesced around 1900 and began to unravel around 1954. The main reason was a structural problem. The region could not be reordered unless either China or the Great Powers drove or supported it; but neither China nor the Great Powers could reorder anything on their own. They needed each other. Our unpacking of that theme rests on three premises.

The first is that Great Powers exercised formidable agency in world history, but this has been too frequently overlooked as a result of fads and trends in the study of military and international history. The second is that geopolitics and the reordering of regions were essential features in international and military history – and in the construction, over several generations, of a global order that subsumed the Asia Pacific. The third is that the dimension in which Great Powers sought to bring about geopolitical reordering can best be understood by exploring how they formulated and applied their grand strategies – which, by default, makes it necessary to understand grand strategy.

The interaction of three themes also frames the chapters of the book and the volume as a whole: Great Powers; grand strategies; and the centrality of China and Japan, whether weak or strong. The collection of chapters in this book aims therefore, as a volume, to do three things: to explain why China and Japan were so central yet so constrained; to explain why Great Powers mattered, yet so rarely got what they wanted; and to explain why exploring grand strategies can provide such clear insights into this distinct period in the larger story of efforts to build – and to order – a "Global Asia Pacific." In 1901, the Great Powers dictated to China the terms of its place in the global order. In 1954, China helped to prevent the Great Powers from defining anything more than a new set of "rules of engagement," for yet another struggle to determine how the Asia Pacific would be globalized, and by whom. These chapters will analyze a number of different ways in which various powers, at various times, and in different contexts, used grand strategies to address the questions that connected all these problems: what was China to be, and how would it relate to the rest of the world?

The volume emerges from an international conference held in Singapore in December 2019. That conference was titled *Great Powers and Grand Strategies in the Asia Pacific 1900–1954*. It was held in a brand new and fitting venue, the newly opening Rise of Asia Museum, itself located on the grounds of an equally appropriate, older and more familiar public site in Singapore, Haw Par Villa. This placed us at a contemporary site looking back, in retrospect, at an important chapter in the current Asian story. The conference summarized its intentions as follows:

> This period in international history was ultimately defined by the combination of Chinese weakness and instability and Great Power attempts to "manage" that situation. From that starting point, this conference aims to evaluate grand strategies pursued by Great Powers – including the British Empire, France, the United States of America, Russia/Soviet Union, and especially China and Japan – to try to manage not only the region but also each other, and to consider the impact all this had on regional and global states systems and order.

The volume expresses the exchanges produced at, and reflections generated by, the conference. It is therefore timely to lay down some conceptual definitions.

Although scholars in general and historians in particular are quite capable of arguing about how to define anything at all until the literal end of time, defining Great Power, historically, need not overtax us here. Our goal is a workable and robust definition, not the elusive hare that captures everything and fully satisfies everyone. We may define a Great Power by using these three criteria: a state generally accepted by other states as a Great Power; a state capable of projecting meaningful hard power in some form – military, economic, or political – beyond its own immediate neighbourhood; a state that needed to be taken into consideration in any geopolitical effort to reorder a region. An effective Great Power displayed all three. For the region we analyze here, during the era we analyze, we may identify several Great Powers – but in doing so we note that neither the concept, nor their status, was unchanging, or even stable.

There were two powers with a claim to the status located entirely within the region itself: China and Japan. China was not capable of projecting power beyond its own boundaries – and often not even within – until the last stage of this era, from 1950 onwards. But its sheer size, weight, centrality and importance made it always a power to be reckoned with – and often the power that determined events one way or the other, Great or not. Japan visibly emerged as a Great Power at the start of this era, and eventually dominated the agenda by seeking to reorder the region by itself, according to its own designs – but was destroyed militarily in 1945, then forced to reinvent itself under foreign occupation. Neither China nor Japan could reorder the region to its desires – but no other powers could do so without taking at least one of them, usually both, squarely into account. There was one power with a significant part of its own national territory located in the region, yet it was still seen as an "external" Great Power, whose centre of gravity lay far away: Russia, at first Imperial, then Soviet. At the beginning of this era, then again in the 1920s, finally again from 1945, Russian power and/or ambitions played significant roles in reordering the region. Russian ambitions focused always on China and or Japan, and while far from failure, fell constantly well short of full realization. But its sheer size, mass, and position generally kept it squarely within the array of powers contesting the region. By virtue of its general status in the world, and its status inside the European states system, France – simultaneously Imperial and Republican in this part of the world – was treated as a Great Power, despite having a relatively modest presence and leverage in the wider region. The French remained active but in the end exerted more influence by military defeat, at home in 1940, and in the region in 1954, than by anything else. For at least some part of this era, Italy, Austria–Hungary and Germany were all seen as Great Powers with some presence and influence in the region, particularly Germany, even if not themselves significant inside it. Germany remained an active player in various ways in regional affairs into the Second World War, but after the Great War was not really treated as a regional Great Power. That leaves two.

Nearly as significant as the two regionally embedded Great Powers were the two leading externally oriented ones – states whose centre of gravity was not located in the region but became, undeniably, prime movers within it. These two Great Powers acquired this status in the region because they were, or became, the leading power in the global order of political economy: the British Empire and the United States of America (USA). Into the early years of the Second World War the British Empire remained by far the most significant "Western" power in the wider region, with visible and significant political, economic, and territorial interests ranging from North China to Burma. It also remained, until well into the Great War, the leading power in building and reshaping what became a truly global order of economics and geopolitics. Resting on economic and maritime power, the British vital interest became to manage the global order itself – and the British task in the region became either to integrate it into that global order, or keep it there on congenial terms. But while British power was fundamental to geopolitics in the region, it had real limits. The region was never first in British global priorities, nor in British economic interests, and the many calls on British power always constrained the leverage it could exert in the region. The USA became the driving power in succession to the British Empire, both globally and in the region – but only took the lead during, and as a result of, the Second World War. Despite the fact that American economic strength overtook British in many ways even before the Great War, and despite a flurry of American ambition from 1919-1922, the USA did not try to supplant the British as the principal "external" power in the region until total war with Japan provoked it to do so. American entry onto the world stage as an undeniably Great Power was a major marker of the beginning of the era that concerns us, and it took place in the region on which we focus. And the relationships between the USA and China became and remained pivotal to our entire story, from start to finish. But the USA did not begin this story either as the "Greatest Power" or with any intention to become that.

Together these Great Powers, whose individual fortunes and agendas waxed, waned, oscillated and spun, tried to reorder this wider region, and to integrate it effectively into a wider global order. That wider order did not stand still either – shaken to its core by the Great War; suffering a false start in 1919; rebooted to only partial effect in the region in 1922; shaken again by the Great Depression and what became the Second World War, escalating from a conflict that broke out in China in 1937. While at times they thought they had forged a viable new order – 1901, 1919, 1922, 1945 – none of these wider agreements were ever really consolidated. Nor at any time was any Great Power, or any combination of them, able to impose their own preferred design on the region to any lasting effect. There were "negative victories." The Great Powers found a way in 1922 to delay the clash over the cardinal questions: what was China to be and how was it to relate to the rest of the world? And from 1941-1945 they fought successfully to prevent Japan from answering those questions by itself. But no "vision," neither Wilsonian, Washington, or San Francisco, provided any design on which the wider region could be reordered to any lasting effect by Great Powers. Yet nothing could be done without them either. Powers of lesser stature, and sub or non-state actors, very often exercised significant agency. The internal divisions and weaknesses of Republican China did not prevent it from becoming a true driver of geopolitical change. Nationalist ambitions and anticolonial frustrations with the prevailing "imperial" order were volatile drivers of geopolitics. "Middle" powers – for example Australia as an adjunct to friendly Great Powers, or a reborn Korea as a battleground that divided them – played more than minor roles. But the heavy lifting came from the heavyweights, through whom the profound forces of the era – economic, ideological, technological – expressed geopolitical sway.

The problem often comes from perspective. It may be compared to the widespread and long lasting perception of the Great War as having been "futile" – fought in a futile manner for a futile cause, or for no cause other than greed and power. The twin origins of this "futility myth" were the massive death toll and staggering pain and suffering inflicted by the war and the overheated rhetoric used to fight it to a finish. Claims such as "the war to end all wars" and "the war to make the world safe for democracy" were never going to be realized. So they were always going to provoke anger and disillusion if taken literally, especially given the palpable human cost of the conflict. But just because the Great War failed to solve everything for all time did not mean that it never "solved" anything at any time, or that it did not change the course of global history. It may be ideologically and rhetorically satisfying to argue that "war never solves anything," but historically it is absolute nonsense to say so – to conflate "everything" with "nothing" is to invite failure to understand. We may apply similar analysis to how Great Power has been understood. Being a Great Power never meant this or that state or empire could do what it wanted, or get what it desired, or prevent what it opposed. It meant the three things we identified above: recognition of larger stature, agency beyond self, and acceptance of standing. No more – but no less either. The Great War was largely not fought in Asia; but it changed Asia. Great Powers did not reorder the Asia Pacific to their liking; but no reordering unfolded without them either, and they drove the reordering that did transpire. Their efforts during the period "bookended" by the dynamic status of China are the focus of this volume.

Grand strategy is the other principal theme of this volume, because we argue that analyzing grand strategy is the best way to understand those efforts by Great Powers to build, and rebuild, a globalized Asia Pacific. It is frankly easier to define grand strategy as a concept, as something that exists and can be understood and applied, when the context is direct and clear: conducting military operations while waging open war. In that context, I defined grand strategy as follows:

> Grand strategy is dependent on national war policy: the determination of the objectives for which the nation went to war, the nature of the sacrifices it is prepared to make to pursue them, and the conditions under which it will accept an enemy's submission. These are the ends; grand strategy is the means. It is an art, not a science, and a constant process: the art of relating the organization and application of power to the pursuit of national objectives.[1]

---

[1] Brian P. Farrell, *The Basis and Making of British Grand Strategy 1940–1943: Was There a Plan?* (Lewiston NY: Edwin Mellen Press, 1998), 2 vols.

That definition was applied to a study of the British central direction of war during the Second World War, but I remain confident that it applies to the concept more generally. Since I wrote that definition, grand strategy as a concept has resurfaced as a high-profile topic of controversy in overlapping public discussions of international relations, current affairs, security and strategic studies, and military history. This is partly due to the constant global obsession with anything related to the USA. The Americans have rediscovered the topic, so the rest of us must now follow suit. The fading of the Cold War, the onset of the "War on Terror," and the "rise of China" all provoked relentless discussion about whether the USA had, or could have, or should have, a grand strategy – or whether such a thing was even possible, or ever existed. As is always the case with such broad discussions, contributions range from profound to puerile.[2] But along the way several interesting features emerged.

One is the tendency to overreact to the word "grand." This often seems to be understood as suggesting that any such strategy must be both comprehensive, a true "master plan," and successful – or at least manifestly sensible and viable. This discounts the possibility that a state might have an unwise or even outlandish grand strategy, and while that metric might be useful in evaluating quality it does not help us understand sheer existence. Another is the tendency to confuse the relationship between defining policy and implementing strategy. Entwined as they invariably are, national policy, strategic foreign policy, and grand strategy are not the same thing. To use a contemporary example: to "contain the rise of China" is a policy objective, but it is not a grand strategy. That must involve a specific programme for how to achieve that objective. And still another is the inherent difficulty of applying the concept to situations other than open war, something that certainly seemed evident during the "War on Terror." But from all that confusion we can extract an understanding that can focus this volume.

To be "grand" strategy, the exercise in question should at least directly involve, if not emanate from, the summit of authority. Definitions that explain grand

---

[2] Recent notable examples include Hal Brands, *What Good is Grand Strategy? Power and Purpose in American Statecraft from Harry S. Truman to George W. Bush* (Ithaca: Cornell University Press, 2014); Eliot A. Cohen, *The Big Stick: The Limits of Soft Power and the Necessity of Military Force* (New York: Basic Books, 2017); John Lewis Gaddis, *On Grand Strategy* (New York: Penguin, 2018), distilled from a seminar course the author co-taught for years. One panel of papers at the 2021 Society for Military History Annual Meeting was titled "A Decade about Something: American Society, Warfare, and Grand Strategy in the 1990s." Kings College London maintains a research centre, supported by four departments, titled The Centre for Grand Strategy.

strategy to be an art of relating means to ends without stipulating that the qualifying adjective "grand" should only be applied to an overarching exercise, connected to the summit of authority, fail to explain what therefore makes this different from any other such exercise, at any other level. In the American context that seems to have settled in as our basis for discussion, this is not challenging to identify. Does the exercise connect in any significant way to the National Command Authority? Is the President involved, at least to sign off? Yes? Then it might be grand strategy. No? Then it is not. Can grand strategy be applied to activities other than geopolitics, statecraft and war? Of course. Can companies have grand strategies? Yes. Can individuals? Why not? But for our purpose here, we focus on grand strategy as an implement of geopolitics and statecraft. However, while we may argue that at its core defining grand strategy in the abstract is not as difficult as the literature has made it seem, there is no doubt that grand strategy involves layers of complication, overlap, entanglement, nuance, and plural expressions that are anything but straightforward.

That problem can also be tackled by starting with two important but not terribly complicated premises. First, it is easier to identify and explain grand strategy when it involves implementing a program driven by the use of military force to achieve objectives, but grand strategy is present whether that is the case or not. The qualifying condition for the definition presented above indicates why: "This [carrying out grand strategy] can only be done effectively through the intimate cooperation of military and political leaders." This stipulates two permanently operating factors: the need to embed military power within a broader range of capabilities in order to pursue national objectives – whether waging open war or not – and the need to supervise the pursuit of those objectives at a level of authority that can direct, and ideally coordinate, all those capabilities. That point is underlined by the second premise: the Second World War experience. The Second World War was in fact an outlying anomaly in global military history, something that becomes very clear when one examines Allied grand strategy. Allied grand strategy became both brutalist and starkly essential: apply every possible erg of power and leverage, by any means necessary, in order to destroy the military and national power of the Axis Powers and compel their unconditional surrender.[3] Nothing before or after has been that simple, certainly not for Great Powers. So how can grand strategy be defined, let alone applied, in circumstances nowhere near so stark and clear cut?

This volume explores a variety of ways by which to address that question. One theme explored by most chapters is the interplay between agents at various

---

3 Farrell, *passim*.

levels of command executing grand strategy – while sometimes also trying to shape it – and the summit of command, as it defined, revisited, or tried to implement grand strategy. Another theme is the problem of defining and implementing grand strategy that involved using or being ready to use military force in circumstances other than open war, usually in the hope that could be prevented. Several chapters unpack the theme of a particular national understanding of and approach to grand strategy, one informed by such factors as history, purpose, structure, and system. Another common theme is the impact of contingency and circumstances on the definition and execution of grand strategy. Some chapters discuss the importance of personality, others focus more on profound forces. Some identify methods other than military force by which Great Powers attempted to craft and execute grand strategy, including what we now call "soft power."[4] Others argue that profound forces, especially economic growth and or national feeling, played decisive roles in shaping grand strategy efforts to reorder the region. Most chapters take pains to remind us that grand strategy does not take place and therefore cannot be studied in a silo – that as with all aspects of war and statecraft the clash of dynamic and unpredictable opposing wills, as well as the element of friction, must never be ignored. And while all chapters agree that grand strategy must involve a programme of actions by which an objective can be achieved or denied, beyond that they do not agree unanimously on how best to understand what grand strategy was, let alone how it shaped the Asia Pacific. But they all agree that it did.

There are two things this volume does not try to do. The first is to present a detailed evaluation of the Chinese experience by focusing directly on Chinese agents and Chinese sources. This has been addressed comprehensively in recent years;[5] we seek to understand how Great Powers tried to globalize China, not to add another voice to the strong chorus already studying China's own agency as their principal focus. The second is to explore in critical depth the strategic studies and international relations theories related to grand strategy and or Great Powers. This is not to suggest such work is not relevant; our own work is frequently informed in important ways by drawing from such discussions.

---

4 Joseph Nye, *Soft Power: The Means to Success in World Politics* (New York: PublicAffairs, 2004), is the standard work that defines this concept.
5 Standard studies include Hans van de Ven, *War and Nationalism in China 1925–1945* (London: Routledge Curzon, 2003); Jonathan Fenby, *The Penguin History of Modern China: The Fall and Rise of a Great Power 1850 to the Present* (3rd Edition) (London: Penguin, 2019 [2008]); Odd Arne Westad, *Restless Empire: China and the World Since 1750* (New York: Basic Books, 2015); Robert Bickers, *Out of China: How the Chinese Ended the Era of Western Domination* (London: Allen Lane, 2017).

But our purpose is to do what historians enjoin each other to do: go back and look again at the primary sources, engage directly with them, and interpret what they have to say – driven especially by our constant concern for contingency and particularity. There is nevertheless one quasi-theoretical method we do identify as a tool which most chapters used, to greater or lesser extent, to "speak to the common brief." This is yet another American-dominated methodology: the so-called DIME model.

Diplomacy – Intelligence (or Information) – Military – Economic Theory as an analytical tool has an established lineage across a wide array of disciplines.[6] The basic idea is that any study that seeks to analyze decision-making – in this case grand strategy – should evaluate the questions it poses about a time, place and problem by ascertaining what role and influence diplomatic, intelligence, military and economic conditions, circumstances, actions, policies etc. had on the experience and the outcome. While more influential in American discussion than anywhere else, and more apparent in the realm of American professional military education than in any other conversation, DIME theory has attracted interest from such diverse disciplines as cyberwarfare, neurology and decision making, and public policy, in addition to national security and strategic studies. Some variant of the method is often of course used without necessarily applying, or even working consciously under, the acronym itself. But it can be useful as a framing device for an analytical approach that, such as this one, combines a roster of different studies into one collected brief. Volumes such as this one need a common organizing theme around which the reader can see the larger patterns of discussion unfold; the DIME model was one way we built that theme.

Finally, the literature devoted to the study of grand strategy, historical and otherwise, is deep as well as broad. The field-shaping decision by the British Official History project *The History of the Second World War* to produce a six volume sub-series simply titled *Grand Strategy* dates back to the 1950s. Paul Kennedy's landmark edited book *Grand Strategies in War and Peace* was published in 1991.[7] This volume does not pretend it can overturn our understanding of the concept, nor aspire to. But we do think our approach can shed important

---

6 The literature is too vast to survey here, but illustrative examples include John G. Krenson, "On Strategy: Integration of DIME in the Twenty-First Century," US Army War College, 2012; Joint Chiefs of Staff, USA, *Joint Doctrine Note 1–118, Strategy*, 2018; Thorsten Kodalle et al., "DIME: A General Theory of Influence in a DIME/PMESII/ASCOP/IRC2 Model," in *Journal of Information Warfare*, Vol. 20, 1, 2020.

7 Various authors, *Grand Strategy*, Vols. I–VI (London, HMSO, 1956–1976); Paul Kennedy, editor, *Grand Strategies in War and Peace* (New Haven: Yale University Press, 1991).

light both on grand strategy per se and on Great Powers and how they used it to try to reorder the Asia Pacific. The volume presents a selected roster of chapters that aim to illustrate the main problems involved in efforts by Great Powers to reorder the Asia Pacific, from 1900–1954, by digging more deeply into specific experiences, examples, and themes, rather than by presenting any comprehensive narrative. The collected chapters offer breadth and range of perspective when combined, depth of archival research within each one. This breadth includes discussions of economic approaches to and influence on grand strategy; diplomacy and statecraft; the problems of managing allies, both at war and in hopes of preventing war; the difficulty of using force to prevent war; efforts by agents other than Great Powers to influence the region; planning for and waging open war; and, of course, whether or not 1954 really did mark the end of an era in regional and global order. If it prompts readers to consider such questions with more interest, we shall be well content.

Section One

Brian P. Farrell
Follow the Money: E for Economics and Grand Strategy

In 1987, Paul Kennedy published a monograph with an unusually accurate title: *The Rise and Fall of the Great Powers: Economic Change and Military Conflict from 1500 to 2000*. The book made a significant if controversial impact on the academic world, but found its real audience in the much larger world of the interested general reader. The book found its way into discussions that ranged from the coffeeshop to the policy makers conference table. A competent study that delivered a critical analysis of just what the title promised, it owed its outsize influence to timing and context – as well as marketing. This ambitious, wide-ranging historical tour de horizon promised to explain the problem of imperial overstretch – of why Great Powers tried and failed to adjust to winds of change and hold on to interests they accumulated in times of plenty, but eventually became too weak to sustain. The public audience which made the book celebrated was the American general reader; the agenda was the question of whether or not Kennedy's analysis suggested a present or future dilemma for the United States of America (USA). Kennedy made a pointed argument: the foundations of military power and the ability to maintain military strength lay always in the economic base from which such power must be raised, trained, and maintained. The underpinning of national power, and thus of grand strategy, was economic strength.

This academic statement of the generally obvious was not without merit. Historians too frequently rush past economic questions, problems, and issues, for a variety of reasons – foremost among which must be a widespread lack of numeracy and grasp of the subject. Military and international historians, the former in particular, are among the most egregious offenders. For example, one of the half dozen most important studies of the Second World War is the landmark study edited by Mark Harrison, *The Economics of World War II: Six Great Powers in International Comparison*, published in 2000. But you are likely to find only a minority of sophisticated students of the Second World War identifying the book as of that stature; campaigns, battles, strategy, command, leadership, turning points, mistakes, and even technology all consistently attract more attention. The balance is not well struck. This volume begins therefore to address that problem by devoting its first section to two papers that focus entirely on economic aspects of the theme before us: Great Powers, Grand Strategy, and the Asia Pacific, from 1900–1954.

Shannon Brown identifies the focus of his chapter in a powerful phrase: "grand strategy by other means." Brown analyzes American approaches to the "Far East" in the period between the end of the First Sino-Japanese War in 1895 and the outbreak of the Great War in 1914. He argues that these approaches cannot be understood without situating them where nearly all were conceived, and from which they were pursued: the relationships between commerce, trade, investment, and economic power on the one hand, and statecraft and regional order on the other. But this is not just a study in "dollar diplomacy." Brown argues that economic leverage became the central instrument in American grand strategy towards the region as the result of a prolonged discussion ignited by the presidencies of William McKinley and Theodore Roosevelt, a discussion over how the USA should manage its evident new status as a Great Power in the region. Grappling with the annexation of the Philippines after victory in the Spanish-American War, and the national debate over the implications for American foreign policy writ large, Brown argues that the key factor was the emergence of a partnership. Strong and expanding private sector economic interests forged a working partnership with a state apparatus, for managing foreign policy and grand strategy, that was only beginning to develop the capability to project truly great power. Pursuing a grand strategy that sought to prevent any one power from dominating the region, the USA used financial and economic strength to try to manage the volatile interplay between a declining Qing China, a rising Imperial Japan, and ever more ambitious European Great Powers. But this partnership faced not only the limits of what capital could accomplish on the ground in Northeast Asia, in the face of territorially defined spheres of influence, but even more important the vagaries of American domestic politics. The effort to make the Open Door policy a reality on the ground by using American money as a weapon in the scramble to globalize China ran into the hostility of the Wilson administration, and the upheaval of the Great War. Yet while "grand strategy by other means" did not achieve what its principal authors aspired to do, it made the USA an active Great Power in the region, with an increasingly visible stake and expanding leverage.

While Brown discusses the use of economic power as a means of grand strategy, Yamamoto Fumihito analyzes an example of fundamental changes in economic structure and capabilities that prompted what became a decisive change in grand strategy. The familiar argument is that the Great Depression was a decisive turning point in Japanese and thus regional and global history because it did fatal damage to the Japanese political economy. That provoked an irreversible turn towards a national policy of imperial expansion by military conquest, driven by a collective military dictatorship. Weakness, fear and desperation poisoned the politics of Japan, giving militarist imperialists the chance to take over the national agenda and turn towards the imperial path. Yamamoto begs to differ on a structural level. He argues that historians have too often overlooked the fundamental importance of the management of the Japanese economy, in favour of more closely examining military and political problems. They have therefore misunderstood what happened to Japan economically, and the influence this had on the turn towards a path of imperial expansion by military conquest. Yamamoto argues that Takahashi Korekiyo decisively altered the national experience during his tenure as Finance Minister of Japan, from December 1931 until he was assassinated in February 1936, by army extremists launching an attempted coup. This "Keynes of Japan," known as "the man who rescued the country from the Great Depression," implemented economic policies that were so successful they not only pulled Japan out of the Depression earlier than most other Great Powers but also altered the very structure of the Japanese economy. Japan quickly went from an economy relying on export-driven light industries and primary products to one being expanded by the rapid development of a true heavy industrial manufacturing sector. Japan had palpably lacked the heavy industrial strength on which any power must rely in order to wage modern war; Takahashi, priming the pump by measures that included heavy but targeted military spending, developed that strength. This in turn had a decisive effect on the pre-existing and escalating argument, within Japanese political and military circles, about what strategic foreign policy the nation should adopt – and by what grand strategy it should pursue it. Rather than being driven to wars of conquest by economic desperation, Yamamoto identifies a Japan that turned towards military expansion, at the risk of major war, from newfound strength and confidence in its hard power capabilities. Here, economic strength proved to be an enabler of grand strategy. Frankly, twas ever thus.

Shannon A. Brown
Grand Strategy by Other Means: US Foreign Policy, Public-Private Collaboration, and "Employing all Proper Methods in China," 1895–1914

What is the appropriate role of the private sector in the formulation and execution of foreign policy? This question must be explored if American grand strategy in the Asia-Pacific region is to be understood as something more than historians' reductionist characterizations of Theodore Roosevelt's sweeping understanding of power politics in Asia at the turn of the twentieth century, and his role, with like-minded politicians and naval officers, in driving the United States toward international engagement.[1] The intellectual and conceptual roots of American grand strategy most certainly emerged during the last decade of the nineteenth century, and the application of nascent grand strategic concepts – end, ways and means, and the recognition of diplomatic, informational, military, and economic instruments of national power – can be seen in the developments that led to the Spanish-American War, as well as that conflict's imperial outcomes in both Southeast and Northeast Asia. Though scholars of international relations have argued that public opinion, domestic constituency lobbying, and a free hand given to ambitious (if not always well-informed) agents of influence do little to inform the grand strategy of a state, it is apparent from examining the period from 1895 to 1914 that these externalities did indeed shape American policy and strategy vis-a-vis China, Japan, and Russia.[2] These externalities were put on full display with the inconsistent foreign policy approaches that characterized the Roosevelt, Taft, and Wilson administrations, whip-sawing from permissive private-sector engagement in Manchuria, to close collaboration between the state and commercial interests, and then to a

---

[1] An excellent overview of Roosevelt's grand strategic approach to the Pacific can be found in Michael J. Green, *By More Than Providence: Grand Strategy and American Power in the Asia Pacific Since 1783* (New York: Columbia University Press, 2017), 78–108.
[2] A critique of international security studies and political science can be found in Kevin Narizny, *The Political Economy of Grand Strategy* (Ithaca: Cornell University Press, 2007), 1–2; 8–11. The author acknowledges that an intersectional approach to the analysis of American grand strategy is a fraught undertaking that involves setting up disciplinary straw men, but the point Narizny makes is important to consider: why treat the state as a contained unit of analysis, holding internal considerations *ceteris paribus* (other things being equal)?

withdrawal of government support for private-sector entanglements in 1913. Although immature at the turn of the nineteenth century, American tools of statecraft – the economic and diplomatic instruments of power – were nonetheless shaped in Northeast Asia, with contributions to their development made by constituencies trying to reconcile ambitious (if not entirely unrealistic) commercial visions with a weak and ill-resourced US policy, one that would eventually organize in accordance with a grand strategy that could be reduced to a few key objectives: "Leave the door open, rehabilitate China, and satisfy Japan."[3]

In the last decade of the nineteenth century, members of the American political elite demonstrated a growing awareness of Northeast Asia's *eventual* economic importance as both a market for American goods, and, more immediately, as a geostrategic stage for the diplomatic and military machinations of states that were in open competition in the region. This is not to say that there were ready indications that American political interests were tied to quantifiable overseas investments or reliable export markets. But for many Americans looking east, commercial competition became the rationale for engagement with China, as laissez-faire involvement on the continent before the 1890s was superseded by the Cleveland Administration's focus on using "personal and official influence" in Beijing to promote a strategy that enhanced American "commercial enterprise" – language that featured prominently in a memorandum from Secretary of State Richard Olney to Charles Denby, the US Chargé d'Affaires in Beijing, in late 1896.[4] This was perhaps the first official suggestion to recommend blending public and private efforts to establish a firm American foothold in China, as part of a larger strategy that eventually came to include the economic and political development of the Philippines after the Spanish-American War; engagement with Japan on the matter of wartime finance during that state's war with Russia; and syndicate investment with other Great Powers' banks in Manchuria. Instructions to Denby were explicit in the 1896 memorandum: "You should employ all proper methods for the extension of American commercial interests in China, while refraining from advocating the projects of any one firm to the exclusion of others."[5] This was *grand strategy by other means,* according to which the American public and private sectors functioned as collaborators, rather than as superior and subordinate or agent and principal, in the pursuit of presumed national interests. This approach to

---

[3] Colonel Edwin House, Green, *By More Than Providence*, 116.
[4] Quoted in Thomas McCormick, "Insular Imperialism and The Open Door: The China Market and the Spanish-American War," *Pacific Historical Review* 32 (May 1962), 156.
[5] *FRUS*, 1896, Olney to Denby, 19 December 1896.

grand strategy formulation was the product of strong personalities emerging in the public and private sectors, vying to engage in a discourse that sought to *define* national interests, and chart a course to achieve political and economic objectives in China and elsewhere in the Pacific region, at a time when actual US interests were limited, and on-the-ground engagement was hobbled by a paucity of resources.

This chapter explores the roles of some of those key personalities and analyzes events that yielded in two policy approaches, internationalization and neutralization, promoted with limited effectiveness by the US government in the years before the outbreak of the Great War. These policy approaches exemplified the blend of public and private measures that were intended to support a larger American grand strategy, albeit one that was limited in scope, informed by speculation about the value of markets and the intentions of competitors in the region, and poorly resourced because of the low priority given to regional affairs by the executive branch. That strategy ultimately failed because of poor bureaucratic coordination, inconsistencies in US foreign policy that reflected the preferences of a succession of presidents and their subordinates, and grave misjudgments about the viability of ambitious plans that required the open support of competing states – and their private-sector proxies – seeking to promote their own national interests and preserve their respective economic imperatives.

Translating Politics into Policy

The introduction and acceptance of several core concepts – national interest, mercantilism, and the connections between economic and military strength – that supported the development of grand strategy by American diplomatic, political, and business elites is owed in part to the publication of The *Influence of Seapower Upon History* by Alfred Thayer Mahan in 1890. Mahan's insistence on the connections between access to sea lanes and national power appealed to American industrialists who saw the world as a stage for vigorous economic competition, and his framing of long-term struggles between nations similarly resonated both with American politicians and with leading figures associated with the private-sphere interest groups that sought to influence US foreign policy. Some of these interest groups were – and remain – well known: the Navy League, the US Chambers of Commerce, and the National Association of Manufacturers, each of which published journals and maintained an active schedule of public events to promote their respective institutional views on overseas expansion and trade. Other groups were more obscure, often organized around focused religious or political agendas, but there were often overlaps in membership between these lesser-known entities and the more active lobbies that coalesced around military and economic policy promotion.[6]

Interest group associations were not unique in their pursuit of influence in Washington. Investment banks – J.P. Morgan and the firm of Kuhn, Loeb & Company, perhaps the better-known examples – took an active role in publicly encouraging economic engagement in Asia and influencing American outreach to the government of China. Though sometimes at cross-purposes with official US policy, these financial institutions also worked with the governments of France, Russia, Germany, and Japan during the first decade of the twentieth century. During the Russo-Japanese War, Kuhn, Loeb & Company head Jacob Schiff achieved some notoriety for his efforts to prevent the Tsarist government from obtaining war financing, an intervention ascribed to Schiff's anger over Russia's anti-Semitic policies; more than just an obstructionist, Schiff took sides in a very public way, meeting Takahashi Korekiyo, deputy governor of the Bank of Japan, in April 1904 to arrange a $200 million war loan for the Japanese government.[7] Other Americans, like Edward H. Harriman, President of the Union Pacific and Southern Pacific Railroads, also took an interest in the region, entertaining overtures from Japanese investors who sought to acquire his stake in the Pacific Mail Steamship Company, all the while developing his own commercial grand strategy that, if realized, would have linked rail freight, ocean-going cargo, and banking operations in the Asia-Pacific region, all under the banner of an American consortium.[8]

Men like Loeb and Harriman were not politicians, but they understood domestic politics; they were not statesmen, but they successfully appealed to the vanity of men responsible for carrying out US foreign policy in Northeast Asia, namely Willard Straight, William Woodville Rockhill, and Lloyd C. Griscom,

---

6 Thomas J. McComick, a member of the Wisconsin School of diplomatic history, developed a model of interest group involvement in the foreign policy processes that shape grand strategy; refer to McCormick, "The State of American Diplomatic History," in Herbert J. Bass, ed., *The State of American History* (Chicago: Quadrangle Books, 1970), 119–41.

7 Charles Vevier, *The United States and China, 1906–1913* (New York: Greenwood Press, 1968), 25. For more detail about the efforts of Jacob Schiff to force the Tsarist government to moderate some of its more troubling anti-Semitic policies and behaviours, refer to Susie J. Pak, *Gentleman Bankers: The World of J.P. Morgan* (Cambridge, MA: Harvard University Press 2013), 92–93.The definitive study on the role of Jacob Schiff in war financing during the Russo-Japanese War is Adam Gower, *Jacob Schiff and the Art of Risk: American Financing of Japan's War with Russia (1904–1905)* (London: Palgrave Macmillan, 2018).

8 Vevier, *The United States and China*, 21.

diplomats working in the region who held strong views on the role of American firms in policy and strategy. Straight, who has been the focus of considerable historical scholarship, emerged as a player in the development of hybrid public-private foreign policy while serving at Mukden [Shenyang] in Manchuria as the US Consul-General.[9] He and Griscom were identified by Harriman (among others) as useful interlocutors in China. Griscom was an enthusiastic mercantilist stationed in China, while Straight spoke the language, claimed to understand Manchuria's politics, and had extensive contacts first cultivated during his tenure as a journalist and later as vice consul in the Kingdom of Korea. Griscom, the son of a financier and shipbuilder, was drawn to government service at a young age and took leadership roles at the US legations in Turkey, Persia, and Japan during the Roosevelt administration.[10] Rockhill, an experienced polyglot diplomat who had spent years in Tibet and Mongolia before taking positions at the Beijing legation and in the Cleveland State Department, later served Theodore Roosevelt as US Minister to China from 1905 until 1909. Straight, Griscom and Rockhill all straddled the line between the public and private sectors, and at various moments saw their roles in China and Manchuria as brokers for the markets, interlocutors for the powerful, and vocal champions for Asian investment. Using both official and private channels, each of these agents argued that establishing a foothold in Manchuria and China, either commercial or financial, was in the national interest of the United States.[11]

---

9 Perhaps because of his connections to the American financial elite, or the fact that he left behind a voluminous collection of private papers and diaries, Willard Straight has been the focus of many academic treatments by scholars of Northeast Asia. Representative examples include Harry N. Scheiber, "World War I as Entrepreneurial Opportunity: Willard Straight and the American International Corporation," *Political Science Quarterly* 84 (September 1969), 486–511; Eric Rauchway, "Willard Straight and the Paradox of Liberal Imperialism," *Pacific Historical Review* 66 (August 1997), 363–97; Straight features prominently in George T. Mazuzan, "'Our New Gold Goes Adventuring': The American International Corporation in China," *Pacific Historical Review* 43 (May 1974), 212–32; Priscilla Roberts, "Willard D. Straight and the Diplomacy of International Finance During the First World War," *Business History* 40 (July 1998), 16–47; and Priscilla Roberts, "Willard Straight, World War I, and 'Internationalism of All Sorts': The Inconsistencies of an American Liberal Interventionist," *Australian Journal of Politics and History* 44 (December 1998), 493–511. The Willard Straight Papers, held by Cornell University and available online at https://ecommons.cornell.edu/handle/1813/22047, are cited in this chapter.
10 Salvatore Prisco, "Progressive Era Diplomat: Lloyd C. Griscom and Trade Expansion," *Diplomacy and Statecraft* 18 (2007), 542.
11 George T. Mazuzan, "'Our New Gold Goes Adventuring': The American International Corporation in China," *Pacific Historical Review* 43 (May 1974), 216.

Figure 1.1: Willard Straight, U.S Consul-General, Mukden (1906–1909).

Adjacent to these government officials were men like commercial booster John Foord who had a key role in founding the American Asiatic Association (AAA). Foord, as an industry advocate, served as a direct link between the manufacturing elite of the United States and the federal government. Starting his career as a writer and editor with the New York-based *Journal of Commerce*, he spent the 1890s publishing on business topics and helping to organize businessmen, especially exporters and trade agents who served markets in the Asia-Pacific region. These efforts led to the formation of the Committee on American Interests in China in January 1898, an organization that Foord used to more directly align business interests with sympathetic legislators on Capitol Hill.[12] In June 1898, the committee was superseded with the founding of the AAA, which Foord and others organized against a backdrop of "renewed European threats in

---

[12] Foord's emergence as a leading figure in promoting American business interests in China is detailed in James J. Lorance, "Organized Business and the Myth of the China Market: The American Asiatic Association, 1898–1937," *Transactions of the American Philosophical Society* 71 (1981), 13–15.

China and the reality of war with Spain."[13] Foord was very influential in the years to come, aggressively promoting expansionist trade policy as part of what he believed to be a larger American grand strategic framework – informed by his own sense of what was in the national interest – through the *Journal of the American Asiatic Association*, the mouthpiece of an organization with an explicit charter: "to foster and safeguard the trade and commercial interests of the citizens of the United States, and others associated therewith, in the Empires of China, Japan, and Korea, and in the Philippine Islands, and elsewhere in Asia or Oceania."[14] The primacy of the "China market" to the economic fortunes of the United States was a recurring theme in publications and events sponsored by the AAA.

The China Market and the National Interest

Was the fabled "China market," which promised salvation from industrial overproduction, a myth that informed Hamiltonian foreign policy around the turn of the nineteenth century?[15] The notion that endless Chinese appetites for finished goods from the United States and Europe could stave off industrial overproduction's cyclical economic disruptions in the West seemed, at first glance, like a rational basis for American involvement in Manchuria and China, as champions of commercial expansion, like the Chambers of Commerce, demanded. The notion of a China market myth that rejected the conventional wisdom of a generation of American politicians active before the Great War was first advanced in the academic history literature by Walter LeFeber and Paul Varg in the 1960s. The former notably called out China enthusiasts who supported mercantile and diplomatic measures for chasing a "long dream" that yielded few results, while the latter demonstrated that American missionary and diplomatic activities in Manchuria and elsewhere in China in the decades following the "Open Door" were, in fact, exaggerated in their effectiveness and

---

13 Lorance, 17.
14 "Extract from the Constitution of the Association," *Journal of the American Asiatic Association* 1 (June 1899), 45.
15 The "China market" debate is well beyond the scope of this chapter, but for in insightful reframing of the debate, see John R. Eperjesi, *The Imperialist Imaginary: Visions of Asia and the Pacific in American Culture* (Hanover, NH: Dartmouth College Press, 2005).

value.[16] Through careful analysis of commercial records and statistics, the work of Issacs, Divine, and Neumann extended Varg's assessment of American involvement and demonstrated that economic activity was similarly limited despite the rhetoric of China advocates who were plying their lobbying trade a generation or two earlier.[17]

Nonetheless, mythmaking was key to fostering domestic American awareness of China's potential – and long-term value – to the United States as a regional partner, and mythology was instrumental in promoting the idea that involvement in China was in the national interest of the United States. There was evidence from the field, after all, that American complacency in China before the Russo-Japanese War had created conditions that might have hobbled US corporations' access to Manchuria. A scramble for concessions, rights and political influence had been underway before the first shots of the Russo-Japanese War were fired. The competition for railway concessions in China that followed the 1895 cessation of the Sino-Japanese War was a competition for foreign financing, and it was during this period (1895–1899) that some of the earliest internationalization schemes naturally emerged: competing foreign banks, usually operating with the blessing of their home governments, signed documents to divide their shares in Chinese railway rights, and many foreign companies organized to do business in China signed bilateral agreements to carve up territories and markets.[18] Once those kinds of agreements were in place, the British and Germans, in 1898 and 1899, negotiated supplementary railway agreements that sceptics felt were likely to increase costs for American exporters looking to move goods from the coast to Manchuria and northern China (essentially practising cartel-style price fixing). These accords followed the Russians

---

[16] Walter LeFeber, "America's Long Dream in Asia," *Nation* 205 (Nov 6, 1967), 456–59; Paul Varg, "The Myth of the China Market, 1890–1914," *American Historical Review* 73 (February 1968), 742–58.

[17] For early examples of these claims, see Harold Issacs, *Scratches on Our Minds: American Images of China and India* (New York, 1958); Robert Divine, *The Illusion of Neutrality* (Chicago, 1962); and William L. Neumann, "Determinism, Destiny and Myth in the American Image of China," in *Issues and Conflicts – Studies in Twentieth Century American Diplomacy*, ed. George L. Anderson (Lawrence, KS: University of Kansas Press, 1959), 1–22. Other important studies include Paul A. Varg, *The Making of a Myth: The United States and China, 1897–1912* (East Lansing, MI: The Michigan State University Press, 1968); Ernest R. May, *Imperial Democracy: The Emergence of the United States as a Great Power* (New York: Harcourt, Brace, and World, Inc., 1961); and Thomas J. McCormick, *China Market: America's Quest for Informal Empire, 1893–1901* (Chicago: Quadrangle Books, 1967).

[18] Lee En-Han, *China's Quest for Railway Autonomy, 1904–1911: A Study of the Chinese Railway-Rights Recovery Movement* (Singapore: University Press, 1977), 16–17.

and Germans establishing monopolies over railway routes in Manchuria and Shandong [Shantung]. The British carved out their own sphere of control in the Yangtze [Yangzi] Valley.[19] Reports from US consular officials on these matters, combined with the difficulties that American financiers had in securing a foothold in China, led American business leaders and diplomats to worry that the United States might be missing out; Denby, reporting from Beijing in early 1897, lamented the fact that Chinese officials "conceded on all hands that the work of developing China should be conceded to Americans, because the United States had and could have no ulterior designs on Asiatic territory," yet baulked at seriously considering offers from American financiers to award concessions.[20]

In 1895, this fear of missing out had led to the creation of the American China Development Company, a private firm organized for the purpose of investing in Chinese rail and resource development projects. This first attempt at penetrating the market yielded mixed results, as the Americans soon discovered that they were participating in a "battle of concessions" that pitted European firms against each other and with a newly created Chinese railway administrative bureaucracy. Despite this Chinese bureaucracy's attempts, on behalf of the company, to reassure Beijing that the Americans were not of a "covetous spirit," an initial attempt to secure the rights for the railway line between Lukouchiao and Hankou [Hankow] and to provide capital for the construction of the track fell flat. In short order, the company found itself with only a single railway concession – between Hankou and Guangzhou [Canton] – in part because of the interventions of Secretary of State John Sherman (Olney's successor), who disliked the idea of using government leverage to benefit a private sector firm.[21] After years of engagement in pursuit of additional projects, the end result was that the American China Development Company lost out on another concession – a line between Lukouchiao and Hankou – to a Belgian syndicate. Despite the Olney State Department's initial efforts to improve the company's standing by encouraging (and, by implication, threatening) Chinese government officials to facilitate access to the concessions being awarded to foreign firms, Secretary Sherman derailed this first formal attempt at grand strategy by other means – the introduction of American capital and technical expertise with limited expectations for the right to

---

[19] McCormick, "Insular Imperialism and the Open Door," *Pacific Historical Review* 32 (May 1962), 165.
[20] *FRUS*, 1897, Denby to Olney, 10 January 1897, 57–58.
[21] Charles S. Campbell, "American Business Interests and the Open Door in China," *The Far Eastern Quarterly* 1 (November 1941), 45.

manage rail lines.²² The private sector, smarting from this initial defeat, took notice and began to politically organize in the United States.

The strategic importance of the so-called "battle of concessions" was not lost on the political leadership of China, who began to consider the possibility that their country might be broken up as major powers carved out spheres of influence and laid claim to mining, lumber, port and rail rights. Chinese authorities, despite their reticence to meet the terms and conditions that were offered by the American China Development Company on matters of railway financing and administration, nonetheless continued to lobby for additional capital investment, in part as a hedge against foreign domination of key rail lines that were being contemplated.²³ These Chinese overtures aligned with the sentiments of Secretary of State William Day (Sherman's successor), Charles Denby (the Chargé d'Affaires in Beijing), and E.H. Conger (Denby's successor), all of whom believed that an expansion of the American financial presence would, in turn, lead to opening Asian markets to American exporters, and that these developments might serve both the economic and strategic interests of the United States. These discussions were an early effort to craft a regional strategy that balanced the influence of foreign powers in China and inextricably linked the fortunes of China with the United States. The chosen instruments of this strategy were banks and merchants. Formalizing the strategy required better strategic communications, such as diplomatic announcements informed by an intellectual underpinning that would find favour among policymakers in Washington. The first steps in this direction included the so-called Large Policy, followed by the Open Door Notes.

Nascent Grand Strategy and the "Large Policy"

A January 1898 letter addressed to President William McKinley from the New York Chamber of Commerce reflected demands that the signatories hoped to see translated into policy and, over time, integrated into the country's grand strategy: "that the trade of the United States to China is now rapidly increasing . . . with the further opening of that country, [will] assume large proportions unless arbitrarily barred by the action of foreign governments . . . such proper steps be taken as will

---

22 *FRUS*, 1897, Denby to Olney, 10 January 1897, 57–58; see also William R. Braisted, "The United States and the American China Development Company," *The Far Eastern Quarterly* 11 (February 1952), 149.
23 Lee En-Han, 16.

commend themselves to your wisdom for the prompt and energetic defense of the existing treaty rights of our citizens in China, and for the preservation and protection of their important commercial interests in that Empire."[24] The context for this appeal to the President is important. Secretary John Hay's predecessor, John Sherman, was openly hostile to linking American business interests with official diplomatic efforts, and thought that private sector interventions might be counterproductive for American policy; in an interview with the *Philadelphia Press* newspaper in January 1898, Sherman famously suggested that a formal partition of China by foreign powers might actually be beneficial to US commercial interests, as "the powers would gladly seize the opportunity to trade with us."[25] In Sherman's conservative view, the mythic China Market would exist regardless of political conditions in China, and alarmists like John Foord (along with Clarence Clary, who was once sent abroad to negotiate for railway concessions as a representative of the American China Development Company) were overstating the need for direct intervention using the diplomatic instrument of national power to promote private sector interests. Sherman's interview was published on 3 January 1898; three days later, Foord and Clary called to order the first meeting to incorporate the Committee on American Interests in China, which six months later evolved into the American Asiatic Association, its memberships' sights fixed on China.[26]

China market mythology notwithstanding, US interest in Manchuria (and elsewhere in the Pacific) emerged as a logical extension of the "Large Policy" that became associated with the McKinley administration and was an outgrowth of the Spanish-American War. Historians credit Henry Cabot Lodge, a close friend of Theodore Roosevelt and part of the inner circle of policymakers and strategists that included Hay and Mahan, with formally articulating this very abstract approach to American imperialism, a policy that one historian has suggested "was no secret to anyone who had read attentively American periodical literature or the pages of the *Congressional Record* during the preceding decade" before war between Spain and the United States erupted.[27] Lodge wrote to Roosevelt as the Rough Riders colonel was assembling his regiment in Tampa: "We ought to take Porto Rico as we have taken the Philippines and then close in on Cuba. Let us get the outlying things first. The Administration I believe to be

---

24 *The American Asiatic Association* (New York: The Lehmaier Press, 1900), 16–17.
25 Quoted in Campbell, "American Business Interests and the Open Door in China," 47.
26 *American Asiatic Association* (Privately published pamphlet, 1899), 10.
27 Julius W. Pratt, "The 'Large Policy' of 1898," *The Mississippi Valley Historical Review* 19 (September 1932), 222.

doing very well following out a large policy."²⁸ Lodge, a senator from Massachusetts, had long since established himself as a proponent of imperial expansion, having served on Capitol Hill when the United States was contemplating the annexation of Hawaii (1897), the construction of a canal in Nicaragua, and the development of policies intended to drive European influence from the western hemisphere.²⁹ The Large Policy was an articulation of ideas and demands that had already found an audience in the United States, including the aforementioned commercial and industrial interests that coalesced around John Foord.³⁰ Far from being a proper grand strategy, the Large Policy nonetheless opened the aperture to the idea of overseas conquest followed by more informal methods of overseas engagement (to include commercial linkages), all of which were predicated on assumptions about American altruism and a responsibility to the international community.³¹

The Large Policy took form in the two Open Door Notes that Secretary of State Hay issued in 1899 and 1900. The Notes were the products of consultations between Hay and William Woodville Rockhill, who served as Hay's advisor on East Asian politics, and Alfred Hippisly, an employee of the Chinese Maritime Customs service and a staunch proponent of open trade.³² Alfred T. Mahan also had a role in the conceptualization of the Notes; in corresponding with Hay, Mahan highlighted the importance of maritime power in connection with the commercial interests that the United States hoped to advance in the years to come.³³ A *North American Review* article published shortly after the second Open Door note in the summer of 1900 captured Mahan's thoughts on the China trade and on the US role in the region.³⁴ Other influences on the notes included American cotton manufacturers, who had spent years demanding that the State Department consider the importance of cotton exports to the Pacific and insisting that diplomats promote equality of access for American

---

28 *Selection from the Correspondence of Theodore Roosevelt and Henry Cabot* Lodge, *1884–1914*, Volume I (New York: Charles Scribner's Sons, 1925), 302.
29 Pratt, "Large Policy," 231–32.
30 Vevier, 10.
31 William. C. Widenor, *Henry Cabot Lodge and the Search for an American Foreign Policy* (Berkeley: University of California Press, 1980), 113–14.
32 Vevier, 10.
33 Lorence, 8.
34 A.T. Mahan, "Effects of Asiatic Conditions Upon International Policies," *North American Review* 528 (November 1900).

textile interests.[35] It is also worth noting that there were direct linkages between these cotton interests and the senior leadership of the American China Development Company, whose leadership had their own ongoing dialogue with Secretary Hay.[36]

The Open Door Notes served two purposes. The first of the notes, circulated among the European powers in August 1899, aligned with the formal demand that the Chamber of Commerce (and others) had made a year earlier, namely, that American individuals and firms be guaranteed access to markets in China. The second note, not circulated to the governments of other powers in advance of publication in July 1900, was a statement of a longer-term objective that Hay and the administration hoped to obtain with assurances from the other states with influence over Chinese affairs: a guarantee of territorial integrity for China. This demand did not emerge from a political or intellectual vacuum; diplomats like Lloyd Griscom, who spent years in Turkey and Persia representing the State Department, had firsthand knowledge of the strategies used by Russia and Great Britain to secure trade and customs concessions from weaker states in exchange for financing infrastructure projects.[37] Early private sector entrants to those markets could use diplomatic leverage to exclude other firms from industrial and financial opportunities, and Hay used the Open Door Notes to signal to the world's imperial powers that the United States would not tolerate exclusionary behaviour in Asia.

Hay's stated positions aligned with the strategic thinking of Theodore Roosevelt. With his focus on maritime power and engagement with the Great Powers of the region, specifically the combatants Russia and Japan, Roosevelt saw Manchuria as a stage for – rather than an actor in – regional power politics.[38] By the time of his election to the presidency, American commercial

---

[35] For a brief summation of the role of cotton industry lobbyists in promoting free trade with China – and the presumed linkages between the southern economy of the United States, domestic railway interests, and the Panama Canal project – see John Barrett, "America and Asia: A Survey of Present Critical Conditions in the Trade of the United States with the Far East," (Unpublished pamphlet, Trans-Mississippi Congress, 1905), 21–24.

[36] Campbell, 45.

[37] Prisco, "Progressive Era Diplomat," 541.

[38] Roosevelt's views on Manchuria have been the source of considerable historiographical debate, a partial summary of which can be found in Charles E. Neu, "Theodore Roosevelt and American Involvement in the Far East, 1901–1909," *Pacific Historical Review* 4 (Nov. 1966), 433–35. At the heart of this debate is the "free hand" thesis: that Roosevelt's grand strategy included "trading" Korea to Japan in 1905 and overlooking events in Manchuria in order to facilitate US-Japanese discussions about the security of the Philippines. For an updated assessment of the historiographical debate, see also John Edward Wilz, "Did the United States Betray Korea in 1905?" *Pacific Historical Review* 54 (August 1985), 243–70.

interests had long been busy on the ground in China, seeking favour from local politicians and looking for opportunities in an environment already occupied by British, Belgian, German, French, Japanese, and Russian agents, all of them acting with some degree of state sanction and the implied (if not de facto) support of their respective diplomatic services. The diplomatic and economic instruments of American national power were weak on the Asian continent: US consular staffs were small, and despite rhetoric coming from Washington about the practical importance of the Open Door, best understood as "freedom of opportunity," the US presence was underwhelming and American influence was minor.[39] Internationalizing investment and neutralizing markets were policy ideas that predated the 1905 Treaty of Portsmouth, which reinforced Russian and Japanese claims in Manchuria and provided the impetus for American commercial agents to revisit these approaches to the geopolitical realignment that appeared to be unfolding in China, Manchuria, and Korea. These approaches were, in fact, the tools of a weak state, part of an emerging grand strategy with a questionable national interest underpinning, and limited resources committed to achieving, long-term foreign policy goals.

That said, the internationalization and neutralization of markets, assets, and resources emerged as an economic practice for two reasons, both linked to risk mitigation. The first, predicated on the assumption that certain governments were unable or unwilling to make capital available for economic development, or incapable of guaranteeing returns on bonds, meant that consortia of foreign bankers entered the market with pooled money and collaborated on terms for loans, in negotiations that were not always favourable for a government seeking external support. In this connection, foreign governments could apply diplomatic pressure, working in lockstep with financial houses, to add leverage to negotiations. It was not always the case that governments and financial institutions worked hand-in-glove, however, as bankers had their own agendas and pursued policies that could undermine diplomatic goals. Herein lies a complication with defining the national interest, and how political elites thought about the connections that were forged by financial agents: did the flag follow or lead capital, and would violations of financial agreements – or other disruptions to the status quo – result in armed intervention by one or more interested parties?

From these questions emerged the second presumed benefit of neutralization: reduced likelihood of armed conflict over assets or resources. Contracts

---

[39] Raymond A. Esthus, "The Changing Concept of the Open Door, 1899–1910," *The Mississippi Valley Historical Review* 46 (December 1959), 437.

between banks and political elites formalized shared financial risk, and the leverage of a group of states' diplomatic instruments of power could, in theory, be applied to correct any party's attempts to undermine the economic and political order. The private and public sectors could pursue national interests using finance as the vehicle, as long as both the bank and the host government's leadership agreed on the significance of the investment relationship. In the case of the Open Door, internationalization was a logical approach for American banks to take in order to enhance their position in China. This approach was the result of hard-won experience after 1899, when American bankers discovered that in Asia and the Caribbean they were at a disadvantage compared to the British and French, who had already built local relationships and created financial dependencies that proved hard to disrupt. The Open Door and the Large Policy were about freedom and access to opportunity, but new frameworks and corporate structures had to be developed for Americans to truly enjoy access to China if mercantile dreams about Asian markets were ever to be realized.

The International Banking Corporation (IBC), founded in 1901, was a first attempt to create an American financial institution that could compete on an equal footing with the British Hong Kong and Shanghai Banking Corporation and the French Banque D'Orsay, and perhaps contribute to a reordering of the global financial system by encouraging internationalized investment that included American representation. The IBC was the product of a reimagining of US law; under the National Bank Act of 1863, American banks were subject to regulation by the federal government, and there were strict rules prohibiting the establishment of overseas branch banks. In 1898, after considering numerous petitions from interested parties hoping to establish financial institutions in Latin America and Asia, the Treasury Department encouraged Congress to consider a reform to banking laws and allow for the creation of "intercolonial" banks.[40] These pleas fell on deaf ears, but the organizers of the IBC found a loophole and created a foreign trust, incorporated in Connecticut (well known for lax banking laws), with a charter that permitted its agents to conduct business "without restriction, in any place."[41] The US government had been reluctant to allow bankers to operate as independent agents overseas, perhaps fearing the foreign policy and grand strategic implications of American capital

---

[40] US Department of the Treasury, Comptroller of the Currency, *Annual Report of the Comptroller of the Currency to the Third Session of the Fifty-Fifth Congress of the United States*, 5 December 1898 (Washington, DC: GPO, 1898), 1: XLIV.

[41] Peter James Hudson, *Bankers and Empire: How Wall Street Colonized the Caribbean* (Chicago: University of Chicago Press, 2017), 64–65.

going adventuring abroad, but the IBC deployed to the Caribbean, Philippines, and China nonetheless. In China, the IBC obtained a contract with the Qing government to advance an indemnity payment.[42] The experiences of the IBC in the Philippines (where the British and the Catholic Church dominated banking in the archipelago) and in Panama (where the IBC had to compete with British banks in connection with the isthmian canal project) reinforced the view among some American bankers that international syndicates were the best approach to foreign development investment.[43]

Other factors drove the engagement of American business in foreign policy matters, although this engagement was sometimes more reactive than proactive, focused on preserving reputations and access rather than expanding the influence of firms overseas. John Hay's death, and the looming threat of a China boycott brought on by racist immigration policies on the West Coast of the US, forced a reconsideration of American foreign policy. Hay's successor, Secretary of State John Foster, sounded the alarm that a prolonged boycott of American goods in China, the result of immigration policies and anti-Chinese sentiment experienced by visiting students and merchants, could provoke "an effective stop to all American enterprises in China," and that the Open Door might close for many years.[44] Foster's concerns acknowledged an important element of grand strategy: the role of the public and of popular opinion in developing and supporting grand strategy and the policies required to achieve short- and long-term goals. It was in this connection that the hard realities of American immigration politics collided with and jeopardized the China market fantasies and regional "imaginaries" that informed the popular imagination of Americans, who saw the so-called "Far East" as part of the country's destiny.[45]

This concept of the "imaginary" is an important element of grand strategy by other means. Loosely defined as an abstract imperial fantasy or "geographical discourse" informed by a wide range of academic and popular sources that shaped the public's understanding of the geography and polity of a distant locale, the first decade of the twentieth century saw the emergence of an "American Pacific" imaginary that found expression in American claims about China's potential, the dangers posed by Japan, and the risks to abstract American interests if other Great Powers came to dominate the region. The imaginary aligned the views and expectations of bankers, merchants, and farmers on the matter of

---

[42] *FRUS*, 1905, Rockhill to Secretary of State, 25 July 1905. Hudson, 66.
[43] Hudson, 68, 70–71.
[44] Jerry Israel, "For God, For China, and For Yale – The Open Door in Action," *The American Historical Review* 75 (February 1970), 797.
[45] Eperjesi, *The Imperialist Imaginary*, 4.

keeping China "open" – it was a popularization of the China Market discourse that had its origins in the late nineteenth-century publications of trade groups and missionary associations, expanded to include the geopolitical tensions of the region.[46] The annexation of the Philippines, the Boxer Rebellion and Protocol, and the Russo-Japanese War were key events that shaped American public perceptions of the Asia-Pacific region – indeed, even the geographic bounding of "Asia" – and the *Journal of the American Asiatic Association*, under the editorship of John Foord, played an important role informing domestic audiences about events in Asia; but more importantly, it took on an advocacy role echoed by investors, merchants, and others with material interests in US relationships with China, Japan and Russia. To this end, Foord was influential in foreign policy circles, and the journal became an instrument for communicating opposition to Chinese immigration restrictions on the West Coast, a position that aligned with its function in the domestic discourse to promote the free movement of people with a transactional frame of reference for policy and courtesy. Better immigration laws, and a better experience for immigrants in the United States, might lead to less violence against American merchants, and a better mutual understanding that could inform elite opinions.[47]

The American Pacific imaginary was not limited to the lay person or the casual reader of popular press books and newspapers. Edward Harriman and Jacob Schiff maintained their own versions of the imaginary that linked the United States with distant points in Asia, and they pursued policies that were, at their heart, mercantilist, and often worked at cross-purposes with official US policy.[48] Schiff was an overt supporter of the Japanese, working to raise capital for the war effort, and expecting to reap long-term benefits from an association that was very publicly antagonistic toward the Russian government. While Roosevelt arranged the Treaty of Portsmouth to terminate the Russo-Japanese War and rebalance power between the Japanese and Russians with an eye on the military presence that both powers had on the ground in Manchuria and coastal China, Harriman was pursuing his own agenda in Japan, concerned that the terms of the Portsmouth Treaty might be the prelude to the closing of the Open Door.[49]

---

46 Ibid, xii.
47 John Eperjesi, "The American Asiatic Association and the Imperialist Imaginary of the American Pacific," *boundary 2* 28 (Spring 2001), 207–08.
48 An overview assessment of Harriman's grand designs can be found in George Kennan, *E.H. Harriman's Far Eastern Plans* (New York: Country Life Press, 1917).
49 Prisco, "Progressive Era Diplomat," 544–45.

"We'll Girdle the Earth": Private Sector Mercantile Grand Strategy

Harriman was an empire builder and had his own mercantile grand strategy, contemplating projects that spanned the greater Asia-Pacific region and extended across the globe. In the immediate aftermath of the Russo-Japanese War, he travelled to Japan to secure the operating rights for the South Manchurian Railway, which Russia had awarded Japan at the 1905 Portsmouth Conference as part of the war termination treaty. From Harriman's perspective, this railway link fit into a larger plan to connect China, Japan, the Philippines, Hawaii, and the west coast of the United States, in an integrated transportation and communications network that maximized the efficiency of the rolling stock and steamships already under his control. His vision also included an investment stake in the Trans-Siberian Railway; obtaining concessions from Japan in order to get access to rail rights-of-way in China was just one segment of his larger scheme to "girdle the earth."[50] The result of these discussions was the Katsura-Harriman Agreement, drafted in mid-October and nearly ratified before the Japanese government withdrew from the plan.[51] Harriman then pressed for a vague neutralization plan, promoting the idea of shared management of the railway as a cost-savings for the government of Japan and the firms associated with its management, but these overtures were also rebuffed.[52]

The reasons for the rejection of Harriman's schemes are complicated. On the one hand, the Japanese government expressed concerns that the terms of the railway control agreement might be looked upon unfavourably by the Japanese public, who had already expressed outrage over the terms of the Portsmouth treaty by rioting.[53] The "founding fathers" (*genro*) of the Meiji government were also openly dismissive of the proposal. Members of the Japanese government were also consulting separately with other Americans, among them Samuel M. Roosevelt, an elder cousin of the President, who suggested that he could independently arrange

---

[50] Lloyd C. Griscom, *Diplomatically Speaking* (New York: Little, Brown and Co., 1940), 263. Harriman's interest in the Trans-Siberian Railway is briefly described in Edward H. Zabriskie, *American-Russian Rivalry in the Far East: A Study in Diplomacy and Power Politics, 1895–1914* (Philadelphia: University of Pennsylvania Press, 1946), 134.
[51] Richard T. Chang, "The Failure of the Katsura-Harriman Agreement," *The Journal of Asian Studies* 21 (November 1961), 65.
[52] Prisco, "Progressive Era Diplomat," 545.
[53] Chang, 67. Harriman was present in Tokyo when the Hibiya Park Incident took place, preparing to meet with representatives of the Japanese government about the Manchuria railway. This is described in Kennan, 13–14.

financial assistance to cover the cost of repairing and upgrading the railway. Roosevelt also seemed interested in stymying Harriman's efforts; he is alleged to have told Baron Kaneko in late 1905: "If you let Mr Harriman take the whole charge of the South Manchuria Railway, the full gains of your war with Russia will never be reaped by Japan."[54] Beyond popular opinion, nationalism informed by Japan's own grand strategic designs in the region might have also led to the collapse of the agreement and a rejection of the internationalization (cost-sharing) proposal. Baron Komura Jutaro, Japan's Foreign Minister, went on record insisting that southern Manchuria – and especially the railway, considered the spoils of war – remain under direct Japanese control.[55] The Japanese government ultimately distanced itself from Harriman, who nevertheless shifted his attention to other railways in Manchuria, looking to secure other concessions or create the conditions for more favourable access to those lines of transportation. Importantly, after these discussions Harriman recognized the folly of bilateral negotiations that did not include the US government, and changed his approach to more actively involve the State Department.[56]

It was in this connection that Harriman began to work with Willard Straight, who, in 1906, was serving as Consul General at Mukden in Manchuria. Straight shared Harriman's vision of mercantile interests tying China closer to the United States. Undaunted by the failure of his proposal to acquire Japanese assets in Manchuria, Harriman and Straight persisted and a plan to create a new Manchuria bank was floated – and ultimately rejected – by Harriman; the news from Harriman came in the form of a telegraph: "Unsettled money conditions make it impracticable – Harriman."[57] Straight persisted, however, interpreting the railway executive's response as a deferral, rather than a rejection, of the plan, and he continued his dialogues with local Chinese officials on the matter.

---

54 S.M. Roosevelt, quoted in Chang, 71.
55 Richard Chang's 1961 article on the Katsura-Harriman agreement cites the work of Japanese historians who emphasize the role of Baron Komura in the collapse of the discussions. Chang also notes that there is little evidence to support the claims made by historians and biographers of members of the Roosevelt family that S.M. Roosevelt actually had the contacts to arrange for external financial assistance to recapitalize the railway. The exact reasons for the sudden withdrawal of the Japanese government from the agreement have never been conclusively explained.
56 Kennan, 43–44.
57 Cornell University, Willard Straight Papers, Reel 2 Segment 1, Harriman to Straight, Telegram, 5 October 1907, see also Millar to Straight, 5 October 1907.

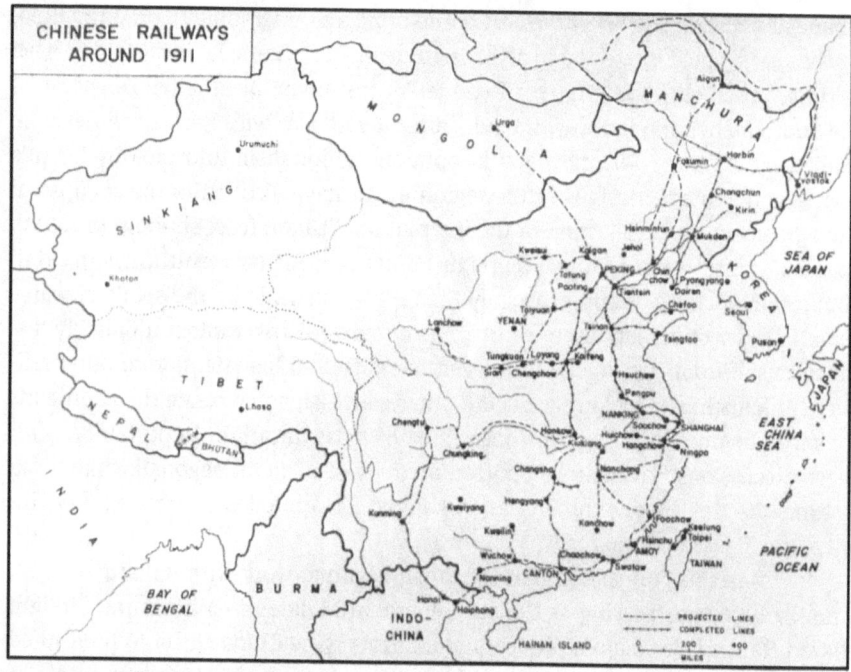

Map 1.1: Railways in China, circa 1911.

Not Empire Building ... Empire Shaping

Although the Manchuria Bank concept was delayed by the "unsettled conditions" in American capital markets, Harriman's greater vision of a neutralized railway system was quietly supported by the Russian government. In 1907, agents of the Russian government approached several American bankers associated with the railway magnate and suggested that the China Eastern Railway that ran across northern Manchuria might be available for purchase if the Japanese agreed to dispose of the South Manchuria Railway. Straight, encouraged by the possibilities, wrote to an associate: "We, the Americans, are favoured above all others and that ours is the opportunity to befriend China ... mind you, once we had established ourselves in Manchuria we would be in a position to ... do a tremendous work in furthering the Chinese Renaissance. The task of not empire building, but of empire shaping could with proper handling be ours."⁵⁸ These private acquisition discussions continued through 1908, using both commercial and diplomatic channels.⁵⁹ Japanese resistance to the idea of an outright purchase of the southern railway gave additional impetus to Straight – representing Harriman's financial interests while working as Consul General – to present the Manchuria Bank idea to the senior leadership of the United States at the earliest opportunity. That opportunity presented itself in short order.

At the direction of President Roosevelt, Secretary of War William Howard Taft made a Pacific tour in late 1907. After stops in the Philippines and Japan, he visited Vladivostok and met Willard Straight, who had been summoned in advance of the Secretary's arrival in Russia. Taft wanted information about the state of affairs in Manchuria, and Straight used the opportunity to present his own thoughts on empire-shaping, presenting this assessment of Japanese efforts to create a regional order and how the US might contravene these efforts.

Straight's memorandum was very thorough and called attention to patterns of Japanese behaviour that might jeopardize the Open Door, or even position the Japanese as the dominant power on the continent. First among his observations was the fact that many sections of Manchuria remained closed to foreign traders, even after the formal end of the military occupation in April 1907.⁶⁰ He noted that the terms of the 1905 Peking Agreement, which called for the return of confiscated Chinese land and property following the withdrawal of Japanese occupation forces, had thus far been ignored, calling into question the willingness of the Japanese to observe China's sovereign claims over the region.⁶¹ "Foreign financial and commercial interests, particularly, regard Japanese activities in Manchuria as a menace to Chinese sovereignty; They fear that Japanese are endeavouring to use their political influence to establish themselves as the intermediaries between foreigners and Chinese."⁶² Several "service enterprises" were identified in Straight's report; these were Japanese firms that were establishing de facto monopolies over finance and certain trade goods. These included the Yokohama Specie Bank, Mitsui Bussan Kaisha, "the agent for the Japanese Cotton Exporters Association . . . virtually controls the export of beans to

---

58 Cornell University, Willard Straight Papers, Reel 2 Segment 1, Straight to Phillips, 8 September 1907.
59 Willard Straight, "China's Loan Negotiations," *The Journal of Race Development* 3 (April 1913), 379.
60 Cornell University, Willard Straight Papers, Reel 2 Segment 1, Memorandum on Manchurian Affairs, 3, 20 November 1907.
61 Ibid, 6–7.
62 Ibid, 9.

Japan from Manchuria," and the Okura Company, "a firm of large contractors, now operates Penhsisu coal and iron mines, and has built roads in Mukden."[63] Straight asserted that the president of the South Manchurian Railway Company, Baron Goto, was actively lobbying his government in Tokyo "to acquire from the Foreign Office control of Japanese international relations in Manchuria," thereby creating a very overt public-private policy hybrid. From Straight's perspective, Japan had a grand strategy, and Tokyo was actively working towards accomplishing several key goals to this end: excluding foreign trade and investment from Manchuria, a blatant disregard of the Open Door Notes; committing systemic erosions of Chinese sovereignty, in violation of treaties that were widely known; and encouraging – if not subsidizing – the development of a mercantilist policy that would complicate entry for any foreign power or foreign firm looking to do business in the region.[64]

Straight used the opportunity of this meeting with the Secretary of War to discuss the creation of a Manchuria bank, backed with US capital, or guaranteed with the Boxer Indemnity. Without some kind of new approach to financing projects in Manchuria, Straight surmised, it was entirely possible that the Japanese would succeed in shutting out foreign capital excepting those arrangements that benefited their sphere of influence in the region. If nothing else, Straight suggested, a joint US-Chinese financial venture that made between $20 million and $30 million available for Manchurian economic development would demonstrate an American commitment to the region – promoting a "Chinese Renaissance" – with the effect that "trade with this empire and our influence on the Pacific should be vastly augmented."[65]

Although Taft was unresponsive to Straight's pleas for support of an American-sponsored Manchuria bank, he acknowledged the threat the Japanese posed to American interests in Asia, and after his election to the presidency in

---

[63] Ibid, 4. A detailed discussion of the organization and practices of large Japanese firms operating in China can be found in William D. Wray, "Japan's Big-Three Service Enterprises in China, 1896–1936," in Peter Duus, Ramon H. Myers and Mark Peattie, *The Japanese Informal Empire in China, 1895–1937* (Princeton, NJ: University Press, 1989), 31–64.

[64] The heavy-handed nature of Japan's administration of the region, and a description of subsidies provided to specific firms organized into cartels, was noted by Ambassador Wright, serving in Tokyo, in a dispatch to the Secretary of State. See *FRUS*, 1906, Ambassador Wright to Secretary of State, Tokyo, 5 June 1906. Enclosed with this report was a translated clipping from the *Jiji Shimpo* newspaper, dated 31 May 1906, that highlighted the crucial role of banking and the Mitsui Bussan Kaisha, "sole agent in Manchuria for the five companies that have formed an export union." See also Cornell University, Willard Straight Papers, Reel 2 Segment 1, Memorandum on Manchurian Affairs, 11–12.

[65] Ibid, 14.

1908, upon taking office he modified Roosevelt's grand strategic approach by putting renewed policy emphasis on China through the use of "promotional capitalism" as a foreign policy tool. This approach was a re-imagining, or perhaps a re-interpretation, of the Open Door: the long-standing objective of "freedom of opportunity" for American business was supplanted by "freedom of investment."[66] American business thus became the "chosen instruments" of the administration. Entrepreneurs and bankers were encouraged by the Taft administration to seek out opportunities for wealth creation and political involvement. This approach was a departure from Roosevelt's careful Great Power engagement in the Asia-Pacific region, openly challenging the Japanese position in Manchuria and giving the impression to American agents operating on the continent that they were free to pursue their own interests.

Promotional capitalism might have been the favoured technique for the Taft administration, but Huntington Wilson, in a letter to Willard Straight, noted that fundamental problems inhibited the ability of the US government to support any commercial ventures, real or projected: the diplomatic instrument was lacking. The American missions in Asia suffered from a lack of qualified translators, poor communications between consular officials and offices, no coordinated policies for the region, and no consistency in the quality of reports sent back to the State Department in Washington. Wrote Wilson: "I have for years been impressed with the fact that the lack of inter-communication has been one of the weakest spots in our foreign service."[67] Despite the best of intentions, and a public communications effort that encouraged American investment in the region, there simply was no well-developed diplomatic infrastructure in place to closely assist American businessmen looking to enter the market, nor was there a systematic effort to collect data and make it available to the private sector in order to raise awareness of opportunities in the market, in part because of the shortage of qualified personnel.[68]

---

66 Green, *By More Than Providence*, 121.
67 Cornell University, Willard Straight Papers, Reel 2, 000715, Huntington Wilson to Straight, 19 August 1907.
68 Article I of the American Asiatic Association's constitution explicitly referred to promotion of "the creation and maintenance of a consular service of the United States in Asia and in Oceania, which shall be founded upon the principles of uniform selection for proved fitness, of regular promotion, security of tenure during good service, and adequate compensation" as a promotional objective of the Association. See "Extract from the Constitution of the Association," *Journal of the American Asiatic Association* 1 (June 1899), 45.

Infrastructure and Neutralization

Taft's election resulted in a significant change to US foreign policy vis a vis China and Japan. The new administration took the Open Door seriously and saw the injection of private American capital as one tool of order-making, promoting internationalization and neutralization as policies to undermine Japanese and Russian power on the continent.[69] Whereas the American Pacific imaginary was a chauvinistic set of fantasies about the future of America – and Americans – in Asia, the "community of interest" was a corollary to a different kind of imaginary that positioned the US – and American capital – as the lynchpin for management schemes that would greatly reduce the risk of a war in Asia over infrastructure and resource concessions. The "community of interest" emerged as a shorthand for international cooperation between and among public and private sector leaders who claimed to share a collective understanding of how best to manage the instruments of power in the Asia-Pacific region. The most ambitious of these proposals was the Manchuria neutralization scheme, advanced by Secretary of State Philander Knox in 1909.

There were precedents for Knox's neutralization proposal: the "community of interest" model – or rationale – that grew out of the Northern Securities Company trust controversy in the United States, as well as a colonial consortium finance model that was coalescing in the Caribbean. Supporters of the Northern Securities Company insisted that modern industrial enterprises were more efficient when combined into monopolies; this was held to be especially true for infrastructure. The trust arrangement was, according to proponents, purpose-built to prevent stock raids that created speculative bubbles and destabilized financial markets. Business combines could increase efficiencies, and reassure owners that the railway lines were operating profitably and without the risk of an economic disruption creating havoc on the pricing for goods and services, as competing lines reduced prices to the point of unprofitability. More than an ownership arrangement or a profit-maximization method, the Northern Securities Company was a governance model that allowed competitors to share risk and benefits.[70] In the proposed neutralization scheme, competitors who might be inclined to engage in cutthroat behaviors in pursuit of their own companies' survival interests formed a "community of interest" wherein the benefits of

---

69 E.S. Rosenberg, *Financial Missionaries to the World: The Politics and Culture of Dollar Diplomacy* (Durham, NC: University of North Carolina Press, 2003), 61–62.
70 James Wilford Garner, "The Northern Securities Case," *The Annals of the American Academy of Political Science*, 24 (July 1924), 146–47.

shared risk and ownership outweighed the disadvantages that came with surrendering a measure of sovereignty over assets.[71]

The neutralization scheme – which would have gone beyond control of the railways and extended to other resource concessions – emerged from two unsuccessful internationalization attempts by the Taft administration to assert the Open Door. The first of these was a project developed by a joint group of American and British bankers who had secured from China the rights to construct the Chinchow-Aigun [Jinzhou-Aihui] Railway; among those participating in the negotiations was Willard Straight, who had resigned from the State Department and was now working for the American banking group.[72] The second was actually an American demand to be included in an international consortium of financial institutions that had formed the Hukuang [Huguang] Railway Loan consortium. There were three participants in the financial arrangement, terms of which were nearly completed in June 1909 when Secretary Knox, acting at the direction of President Taft, began to apply pressure to the Chinese government to halt the finalization of the loan, while diplomats and American bankers made overtures to their European counterparts to become the fourth member of the consortium. The Chinese government and the consortium members acquiesced, and the American Group – consisting of J.P. Morgan & Company, Kuhn, Loeb & Company, First National Bank and National City Bank – joined Hong Kong and Shanghai Banking Corporation, Deutsche-Asiatische Bank, and Banque de l'Indo-Chine as partners in the loan.[73]

In late 1909, Secretary Knox advanced a formal proposal to neutralize the railways of Manchuria. The idea had been under consideration for some time in Washington, as a logical approach to the "Manchuria problem," and a method to ensure the Open Door remained so; indeed, the proposal built upon efforts

---

[71] K.K. Kawakami, "Manchuria: The Crux of Chino-Japanese Relations," *Foreign Affairs* 6 (April 1928), 392. Kawakami's editorial – that features a conspicuous reference to the "community of interest" that existed between Russia and Japan in Manchuria – is given context in a review article that attempts to highlight the state of great power relationships in Manchuria; see "In the Orient View: A Survey of the Periodical Press of China and Japan," *Pacific Affairs* 1 (June 1928), 32. See also "The Commercial Neutralization of Manchuria," *The Advocate of Peace* 72 (March 1910), 52–53.

[72] E.W. Edwards, "Great Britain and the Manchurian Railways Question, 1909–1910," *The English Historical Review* 81 (October 1966), 747. See also Cornell University, Willard Straight Papers, Reel 3 Segment 2, Davison to Straight, 6 November, Straight to J.P. Morgan and Company, 29 October 1909, Straight to J.P. Morgan and Company, 10 January 1910.

[73] Cornell University, Willard Straight Papers, Reel 3, "Draft of September 8th, 1909, Hukuang Railway Loan of 1909."

undertaken by Harriman and his associates.[74] Allegations of favouritism shown to Japanese customers using railway lines controlled by Japanese firms were among the reasons offered as justification for the Knox plan: rebates and subsidies were, after all, not in the spirit of the Open Door.[75] The neutralization plan was deceptively simple in concept, but fraught in its realization: all powers with an interest in Manchuria would sign on to an international financial consortium to loan funds to China to not only construct new railways, but also purchase existing rail lines from Japan and Russia. Each power would own a stake in the consortium and would be due payments for outstanding loans and royalties for the efficient management of existing lines.[76]

The concept was not well received in Japan, where metropolitan newspapers pointed out that Edward Harriman's earlier proposals to neutralize the Japanese railways had also failed to win support from the various sovereign and commercial actors with an interest in Manchuria. Baron Goto, speaking on record to the *Nichi Nichi Shimbun*, suggested that "Mr Straight, he thinks, *fons et origo mali*" ("the source and origin of evil") for the Knox proposal: "Joining hands with the discontented group of English capitalists to have made a failure in the Fakumen Railway business, he has succeeded in forming a combination strong enough to enlist the active support of the Washington Cabinet."[77] Although Taft and Knox saw the neutralization plan as a technique to promote American national interests in China – guaranteeing additional "freedom of investment" – and further promoting the notion that the United States could serve as a neutral interlocutor, the Japanese saw the concept as directly opposed to their own national interests. Japanese resistance to the plan was logical; why would the government in Tokyo, or one of its proxies in Manchuria, sell off assets that were part of a larger ongoing economic development effort in northeast Asia?

The neutralization plan was also given a cold reception by British diplomats who were already frustrated by the insistence of the US government that the Americans be given a seat at the table in the late-stage Hukuang Loan dis-

---

74 Straight, "China's Loan Negotiations," 380.
75 "The Commercial Neutralization of Manchuria," *The Advocate of Peace* 72 (March 1910), 52.
76 *FRUS*, 1910, P. Knox statement to Press, 6 January 1910, 243–44.
77 "The Manchurian Railway Proposal: A Statement by Baron Goto," *The New York Times*, Tuesday, 18 January 1910. Copy in Cornell University, Willard Straight Papers, Reel 3. Baron Goto Shinpei, the article notes, was first approached by representatives of H.L. Harriman after the baron became president of the South Manchuria Railway Company in 1906. He rebuffed the proposal, noting that such an arrangement would embarrass the Japanese.

cussions with the Chinese government, a move that was supposed to reinforce the Taft administration's commitment to China, but ended up alienating key players in both the British government and the finance community.[78] Ultimately, the neutralization plan failed, not because of its irrationality – indeed, Huntington Wilson, Assistant Secretary of State, noted that the proposal was an entirely "practical policy" – but because no leverage could be applied to the various powers to disrupt their existing treaties and agreements with the targets of the scheme, Russia and Japan.[79]

On 10 January 1910, Secretary Knox appeared before the Congressional Committee on Foreign Affairs to discuss recent foreign policy efforts and address questions about pending civil service reforms that might reshape the State Department. In his comments, one observer noted that "Mr Knox insisted very strongly on the fact that the Department of State was undermanned; that there were far too few men in the department." Echoing remarks captured in the private correspondence of Willard Straight, Knox formally and publicly acknowledged that the diplomatic arm of the federal government was under-resourced for the grand strategic challenges that lay ahead in Asia.[80] The failure of the Manchuria neutralization plan could be judged to be a failure of sense-making: the policy, supported by ambitious commercial agents, was detached from the geopolitical reality on the ground in Asia. Knox and his fellow diplomats overestimated the receptiveness of the Great Powers and their commercial proxies to any scheme or program that required the surrender of rights or assets.

While the neutralization plan could be understood as an attempt to buttress the US government's "conservation" policy, protecting the territorial integrity of China and the administrative rights of the imperial government, the proposal had an ironic outcome. American lobbying for the neutralization of Manchuria and the preservation of the Open Door had, in fact, created a new community of interest – between Japan and Russia. The two competitors, concerned about the interventionism of the Taft administration and how American meddling might undermine their relationships with the other Great Powers, signed an agreement on 4 July 1910, pledging to "safeguard their respective interests in

---

[78] LOC, Manuscript Division, Philander C. Knox Papers, Box 8, Department of State Memo, 30 September 1909; *FRUS*, 1909, P. Knox to W. Rockhill, 24 May 1909, 144–45; see also E.W. Edwards, *British Diplomacy and Finance in China, 1895–1914* (London: Oxford University Press, 1987), 147.
[79] Charles Vevier, "The Open Door in Action, 1906–1913," *Pacific Historical Review* 24 (February 1955), 59.
[80] Charles Johnston, "The Foreign Policy of the United States," *North American Review* 192 (July 1910), 36–37.

Manchuria – an arrangement which, though undoubtably a natural one, was not . . . calculated to assure to China herself the right to develop this territory."[81]

After the failure of the neutralization plan, the US government and American financiers turned their attention away from Manchuria to focus on China. The 1911 uprisings that led to the formation of the Chinese Republic presented a new opportunity for bankers, and the Four Power consortium that emerged from the contentious Hukuang Loan discussions began to organize for a comprehensive "reorganization loan" to support the new government. In the spirit of international cooperation, the Japanese and Russians were admitted to the loan consortium, but the Chinese government cast a suspicious eye on the composition and intentions of the group.[82] Debates over whether to admit Japanese and Russian financial institutions to the consortium roiled the members; at least one American member of the American Group quit in protest over Russian participation, only to rejoin a day later. By late 1912, American participation in the consortium was in jeopardy, and the impending presidential election cast a shadow over the future of the arrangement.[83]

Republican Chinese political intrigue, combined with waning enthusiasm on the part of the American Group participants, led to the collapse of the Six Power consortium, and brought an end to this stage of internationalization as a form of policy and strategy. Between December 1912 and February 1913, different members of the American Group expressed concerns about the solvency of the Chinese government and the ability of the international financial markets to absorb additional Chinese bonds. Shortly after Woodrow Wilson was inaugurated on 4 March 1913, representatives of the American Group met with the new Secretary of State, William Jennings Bryan, to present a series of requests and demands that included an assurance that no other American banks be permitted to join the group; that the security of the loan be linked to Chinese government revenues; and that the US government commit to using force to compel the Chinese government to comply with the terms of the loan.[84] Wilson, surprised by the American Group's demands, kneecapped the Six Power Consortium by demanding that US financial institutions withdraw from China; Wilson

---

[81] E.W. Edwards, "Great Britain and the Manchurian Railways Question," 762; Straight, "China's Loan Negotiations," 380.
[82] The controversy over the admission of Russia and Japan to the consortium is described from the perspective of a participant in Willard Straight, *The Politics of Chinese Finance: Address Delivered by Mr Willard Straight at the Dinner of the East Asiatic Society of Boston*, 2 May 1913 (New York 1913), 9.
[83] Charles Vevier, "The Open Door in Action," 60.
[84] Ibid, 62.

"rejected the bankers' arguments that they were pursuing political and patriotic goals rather than economic advantage," effectively reining in an instrument of national power that had, for over a decade, been trying to move American foreign policy in a specific direction.[85]

Conclusion

During the period under consideration in this chapter, the US economic and diplomatic instruments of power were in their early stages of development in the Asia-Pacific region, despite the grand strategic intentions of Theodore Roosevelt and his successors. Reporting from Mukden, Willard Straight lamented the limited abilities and poor communication that characterized the State Department's work in China and Manchuria at a time when political conditions were moving in the direction of armed confrontation between Russia and Japan, with the Chinese caught in the middle. The ability of the US government to apply economic leverage to any of the significant players in Manchuria was also limited, despite the best efforts of American financiers to promote internationalization and neutralization as risk-management and risk mitigation methods.

The fact that American finance had a presence in China was a function of the inconsistent foreign policies of the McKinley, Roosevelt, and Taft administrations. J.P. Morgan, Jacob Schiff, E.H. Harriman and many others aspired to take a piece of the "China market," and in doing so, attempted to commit the US government to an evolving grand strategy that was also being shaped in part by lobbying organizations like the American Asiatic Association. Financiers, merchants and other enthusiasts had their part in the struggle to define the national interest, and these different constituencies promoted visions of a US-China relationship that did not necessarily comport with geopolitical realities. At times, the "American Pacific imaginary" informed private sector decisions and actions that actually antagonized other powers and their commercial proxies in Manchuria. President Wilson, recognizing the risks that came with creating private-sector financial commitments, moved quickly after his election to stop further designs that might damage relations with Japan and Russia.

Grand strategy by other means was ultimately a failure, perhaps because there was no agreement about what was the national interest of the United States. With no clearly defined national interest underpinning foreign policy in

---

[85] Clarence B. Davis, "Financing Imperialism: British and American Bankers as Vectors of Imperial Expansion in China, 1908–1920," *Business History Review* 56 (Summer 1982), 260.

Asia, American diplomatic and economic engagement in China and Manchuria was marked by changing presidential administrations: Roosevelt had a strong sense of interest and policy, and he communicated that sense to his Cabinet and their subordinates, but his focus on Japan resulted in the poor resourcing of the diplomatic instrument of power in China and Manchuria, ensuring that any broad grand strategic vision would not persist after his departure from office. The Taft administration saw China as a state to be salvaged and backstopped – "conserved" – with American capital but the government offered inconsistent support and guidance to interested parties. The Wilson administration, when confronted by an American consortium of bankers seeking guarantees that seemed more imperial than conservationist, immediately disengaged financiers from any involvement in Chinese statecraft. There simply was no single unifying vision of what the US role in China should be, or whether Manchuria was, in fact, a viable place for American capital to compete with other powers – and do so without upsetting the tenuous balance that emerged after the Treaty of Portsmouth was signed. Similarly, there was no government consensus on whether American firms' attempts to influence foreign governments in Manchuria and China were an appropriate instrument for promoting American interests abroad.

An observer of Asian affairs and Great Power politics noted the following in 1910, as the Manchuria neutralization proposal was collapsing: "The first stage of world-politics was the struggle for territory . . . The second stage of world politics was the struggle for markets. The third, on which we are now entering, is the contest, not so much for territory or even for markets, as for fields of development; for the introduction of organizing power and capital, rather than merchandise, into new regions."[86] What remained unsettled after the period under review in this chapter was whether the "third stage" – fields of development – would be the bailiwick of the public or private sector, but it was clear by 1914 that the US government would trump industry in all matters connected to the formulation and execution of grand strategy in Northeast Asia.

---

86 Johnston, "The Foreign Policy of the United States," 37.

Yamamoto Fumihito
Follow the Money: The Manchurian Incident, Economic Recovery and Japan's Policy Change in the 1930s

One widespread and long-standing belief is that the Great Depression had such a devastating impact on the politics and economy of Imperial Japan that it created a national climate of fear which enabled militarists to seize power, and launch an imperial policy of military aggression. Panic fostered political extremism and this drove Japan to wage war. This supposedly began with the Manchurian Incident, triggered by rogue elements of the Kwantung Army in September 1931. But this chapter argues otherwise. Its purpose is not to discuss the Manchurian Incident itself, but rather to situate it within a very different context of political history: one shaped by spectacular economic recovery. It argues that this economic recovery, not Great Depression-induced panic, drove the policy change from the "democratic" 1920s to the "militaristic" 1930s.

A principal source for this study and its argument is the Madison Project Database of the University of Groningen, a database of historical economic statistics calculated by a team of economic historians. This large-scale ambitious project aimed to produce accurate statistics that would help establish such things as national gross domestic products (GDPs) in different eras.[1] Needless to say, governments in the 1930s did not announce such sophisticated economic data, much of which was not then practically collectible. In other words, the decision makers of the past did not use these particular statistics when making policies. But these statistics shed important light on economic conditions of the past. Economists and economic historians calculate and use these kinds of data, but political historians who study Japanese history in the 1930s have not yet seriously engaged them. To make international and historical comparisons easier, the Madison Project statistics are based on the 2011 US Dollar, not on local currency or the monetary values of the past. Some may therefore doubt the accuracy of such data. These concerns are understandable. But the economic data calculated by the Madison Project based on 2011 US Dollar does not in fact differ greatly from data calculated by Japanese economists based on

---

[1] For an outline of the Madison Project, see Jutta Bolt, Robert Inklaar, Hermande Jong and Jan Luitenvan Zanden, *Rebasing "Madison": New Income Comparisons and the Shape of Long-Run Economic Development* (University of Groningen: Groningen Growth and Development Centre, January 2018) https://www.rug.nl/ggdc/html_publications/memorandum/gd174.pdf

the Japanese Yen, and largely matches the economic conditions of the past that can be ascertained by critical reading of such sources as periodicals, newspapers and magazines.[2] Of course, we have to bear in mind that the general population living in the 1930s did not see these statistics either. But such data clearly shows that, as the Manchurian Incident unfolded, Japan achieved a V-shaped recovery from the Great Depression. The point here is how this fact of economic recovery affected Japan's strategic foreign policy, and therefore the choices it could make in grand strategy, at that time.

Economic Trends 1900–1950: General Views

Before discussing the time of the Manchurian Incident, we first need briefly to explain long-term economic trends.[3] In the first half of the twentieth century, state economic policies did not play as great a role in stabilizing a national economy than became common after the Second World War; as a result, economic fluctuations were more volatile. In other words, economic booms and slumps appeared sharper than they do now. Table 2.1 indicates the long-term transition of GDP growth rate, which tells us several important points. First, during the first half of the twentieth century, Japan experienced around 15 per cent growth three times: first, in 1915–1916, during the Great War; second, in 1938–1939, during the Second Sino-Japanese War; and third, in 1947–1948, during the early postwar reconstruction period. The peak of the Japanese economy before the Second World War was 1939. Second, Japan experienced minus 50 per cent growth from 1944 to 1945. This shows us the degree of devastation Allied bombing inflicted on the Japanese economy. Third, the impact of the Great Depression was less severe on the Japanese economy than on the US economy, and Japan achieved a rapid V-shaped recovery from it.

---

[2] As for economic data determined by Japanese economists based on the Japanese Yen, see Miwa Ryoichi and Hara Akira, eds, *Kingendai Nihon Keizaishi Yōran, Kaitei-ban (The Documents and Statistics of Japanese Economic History since the 1850s (Revised with Corrections))* (Tokyo: University Press, 2010). This book is the most substantial compilation of economic data regarding modern Japanese history.

[3] The Madison Project Database 2018 can be accessed at: https://www.rug.nl/ggdc/historical development/maddison/releases/maddison-project-database-2018?lang=en

The database only provides per capita GDP and the country's population of that particular year. But we can easily determine the total GDP by multiplying per capita GDP by population. We can also figure out the growth rate by calculating the increase or decrease rate from the total GDP of the previous year.

Table 2.1: Long-Term GDP Growth Rate 1900–1950.

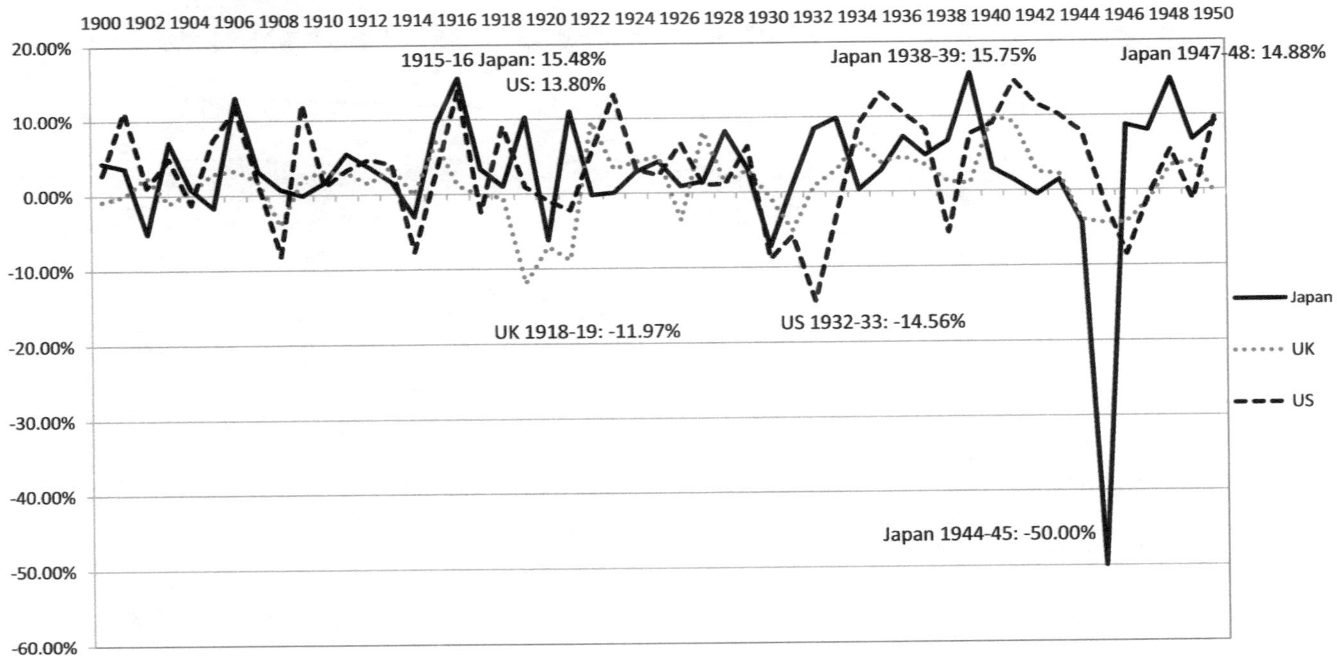

Made by the author using statistics found in the Madison Project Database 2018.

Table 2.2: Total GDP 1900–1950.

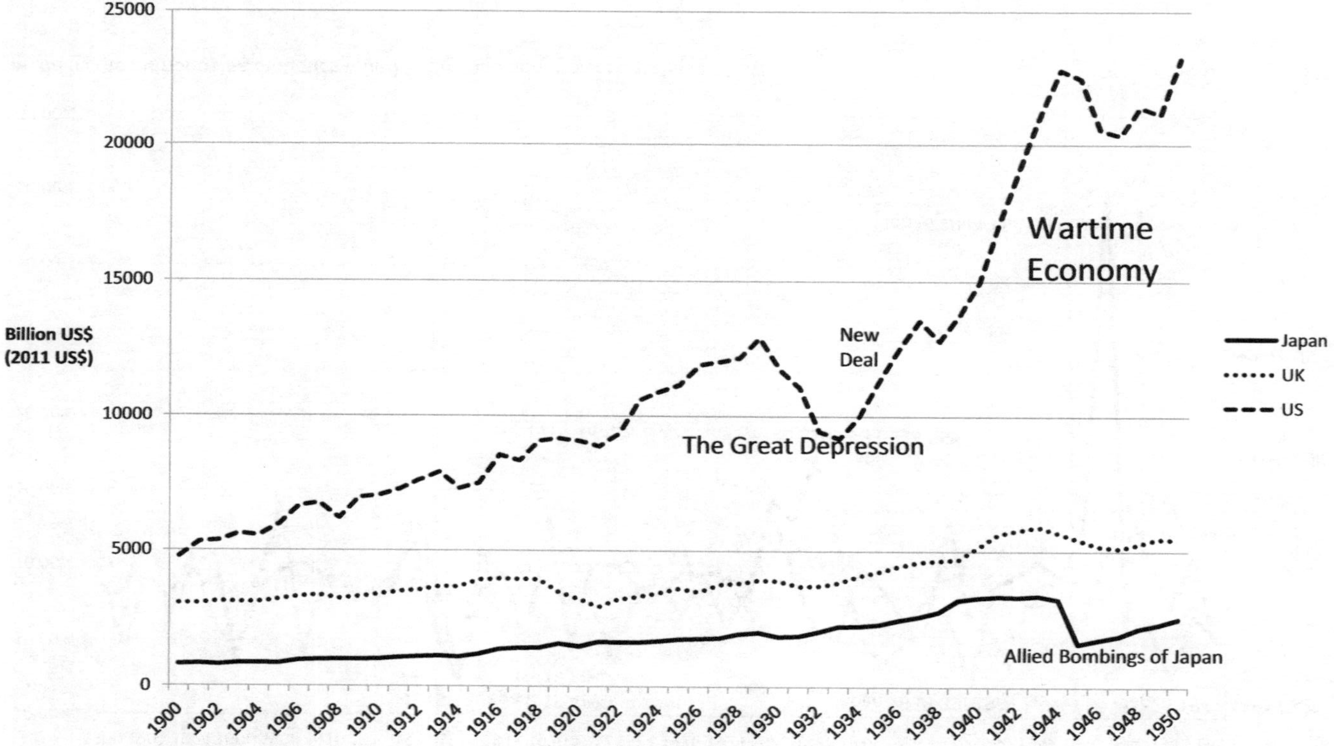

Made by the author using statistics found in the Madison Project Database 2018.

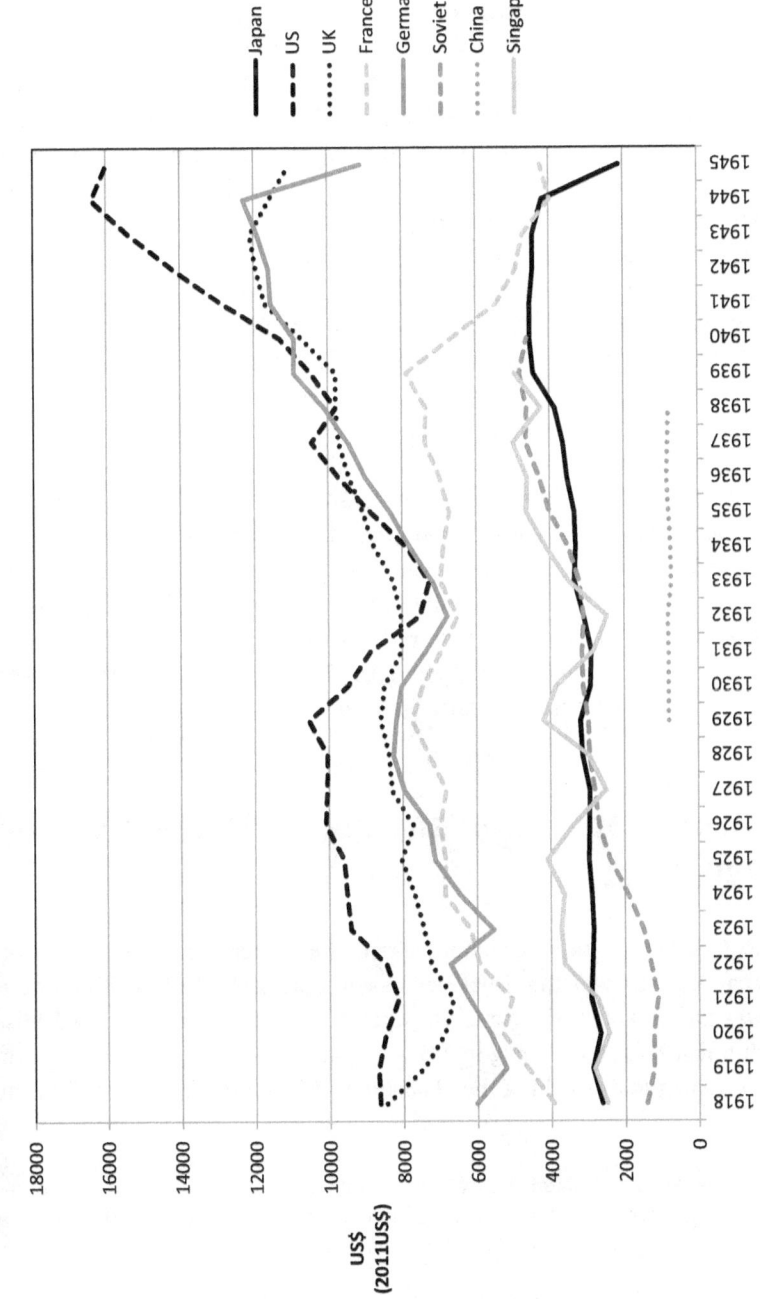

Table 2.3: Per Capita GDP 1918–1945.

Made by the author using statistics found in the Madison Project Database 2018.

Table 2.2 indicates the transition of total GDP during the first half of the twentieth century. It clearly shows us how rich the American economy was but also the severity of its suffering as a result of the Great Depression. After launching the New Deal in late 1933, the American economy started recovering, but only in 1937 did it return to the level of 1929. In other words, the American people suffered for eight years. This table also indicates the phenomenal growth of the American economy in the 1940s. In fact, it was during the Second World War that the United States became the global economic super power.

Table 2.3 indicates per capita GDP from 1918 to 1945. Unfortunately, the data on Singapore is only available until 1939, the Soviet Union until 1940, and China between 1929 and 1938. These all show us the living standard of each and its long-term transition. What stimulates our interest first is that in the 1930s the economic living standards of Japan, Singapore, and the Soviet Union were on roughly the same level.[4] It is very likely that, compared to Singapore, the living standards of Japanese big cities like Tokyo and Osaka were higher but those of rural areas were much lower. Second, the living standard of Japan was still much lower than Western countries but much higher than China. Third, the Second World War had a massive impact on the living standards of ordinary people in many countries. During the German occupation of France, people suffered severely; but on the other side of the Atlantic, the living standards of the American people rose higher and higher. And in the last year of the war, people in Japan and Germany suffered catastrophically.

The Great Depression and the Shōwa Depression of 1930–1931

From 1929 to 1931, a severe economic depression struck Japan. This was rooted in two causes. One was the Great Depression that began in New York and the other was the mismanaged economic policies implemented by Finance Minister Inoue Junnosuke of the Hamaguchi Osachi Cabinet. On 2 July 1929, new Prime Minister Hamaguchi Osachi of the *Minseitō* party[5] formed his Cabinet. This new

---

4 The Madison Project Database also made more clear economic conditions during the Soviet Era: they were much lower than hitherto believed: The Madison Project Database 2018: https://www.rug.nl/ggdc/historicaldevelopment/maddison/releases/maddison-project-database-2018?lang=en

5 The *Minseitō* was one of the two main parties of the late 1920s. The other was the *Seiyūkai*. Political historians tend to describe the diplomacy of *Minseitō* as internationalistic while that

Cabinet set two big policy agendas. First, Japan would return to the gold standard at the pre-Great War price of gold. For this purpose, Hamaguchi chose Inoue Junnosuke as Finance Minister. Second, Japan would participate in the London Naval Conference and enact agreements on auxiliary warships which were not restricted by the Washington Naval Treaty: cruisers, destroyers, and submarines. There is no need to discuss the London Naval Conference here. But as for the gold standard, like most other powers Japan left it during the Great War, on 12 September 1917. This was to prevent the outflow of gold. Since then, returning to the gold standard had always been a major item on the political agenda. At first, Japanese governments saw the detachment as a temporary measure. But the chance to return to the gold standard did not come as economic conditions did not allow it. After the economic boom driven by the Great War ended, the Japanese economy fell into a long-term recession. Then the Great Kantō Earthquake hit the Greater Tokyo area on 1 September 1923. This made an already bad economy much worse. The chance to rejoin the gold standard thus did not arrive until Hamaguchi formed his Cabinet in 1929. It should be noted that the Japanese economy did begin to improve under the Seiyūkai party,[6] during the premiership of Tanaka Giichi from 1927–1929. Two Finance Ministers in Tanaka's Cabinet, Takahashi Korekiyo and Mituchi Chūzō, succeeded in turning the economy around. But the consensus in the *Seiyūkai* party was that the Japanese economy was not robust enough to rejoin the gold standard. Also, before the economy fully recovered, the government changed again from the *Seiyūkai* party to the *Minseitō*.

When *Minseitō* regained power, the exchange rate stood at 100 Yen to 44.6 Dollars. To return to the gold standard at the pre-war parity – 100 Yen to 49.875 Dollars – Inoue had to value the Yen upwards by about 10 per cent. For this purpose, he adopted austerity policies. He cut government spending and naval disarmament became the symbol of this. But these austerity policies had an adverse influence on the economy. The general trend of the Japanese economy in the 1920s was deflation but Inoeu's measures made it worse. The economy deteriorated again. Hamaguchi and Inoue explained to Japanese citizens that this downturn would be temporary, and the economy would pick up in the long run. They asked the nation to persevere for a short while. But then, on 24 October 1929

---

of *Seiyūkai* was nationalistic. While this was true to some degree, the differences were not clear-cut. Their differences were more obvious in economic and fiscal policies. The *Minseitō* maintained fiscal discipline by reducing governmental spending. In contrast, the *Seiyūkai*, under the strong influence of Takahashi Korekiyo, increased governmental spending to expand the economy.

6 See footnote 5.

the Great Depression began in New York. Yet Hamaguchi and Inoue did not change their goals even after they witnessed the collapse of the stock exchange in New York. The Japanese government announced on 22 November 1929 that Japan would rejoin the gold standard on 11 January 1930. The global economy had already started sinking and the Japanese government announced that Japan would hop on board this sinking ship! The government could not have chosen a worse time to make such a move. Deflation became unstoppable, and exports to the United States plummeted. This all further shrank the economy. The Shōwa Depression of 1930–1931 thus began.

In 1930 and 1931, the situation became still worse. Investors and speculators, including major banks such as National City Bank, Hong Kong and Shanghai Banking Corporation, Sumitomo Bank, Mitsui Bank, and Mitsubishi Bank, sold the Yen and bought Dollars. On the understanding that Japan could not maintain the gold standard in the long term, they thought they could profit by buying back the Yen later. This made the downward trend of the economy unstoppable but Inoue stuck to his policies. Amid this serious economic situation, ratifying the London Naval Treaty became a big political issue. Meanwhile in autumn 1930, the harvest of rice was very good, but at this time this actually made things worse. The prices of agricultural products had already started to tumble due to the bad economy. The surplus of rice spurred this downward trend further. To make matters worse, next year, in 1931, a cold summer struck northern Japan. The rice harvest was bad but the price of rice did not recover. During this period, regardless of the harvest, rice farmers suffered greatly.

Against this gloomy and stagnated atmosphere, on 14 November 1930, Prime Minister Hamaguchi was shot by a nationalist at Tokyo Station. Nationalist extremists were angry about the ratification of the London Naval Treaty, but we should not overlook economic motives as well. Under Hamaguchi and Inoue, economic conditions were becoming worse and worse. Hamaguchi died from his wounds on 26 August 1931.[7] Wakatsuki Reijirō had succeeded him as Prime Minister on 14 April 1931. Inoue stayed in the Cabinet as Finance Minister and there was no change in economic and fiscal policies. Then suddenly on 18 September 1931, the Manchurian Incident broke out. The Manchurian Incident was planned and instigated by Ishiwara Kanji, a middle-echelon officer of the Kwantung Army, the Imperial Japanese Army (IJA) command and garrison stationed in Manchuria. It was not planned in Tokyo. But, as this chapter will examine below, this incident became the catalyst that fundamentally changed

---

7 Inoue Junnosuke was also assassinated on 29 February 1932.

the character of Japan. Three days later, on 21 September, the United Kingdom abandoned the gold standard. These two incidents combined to topple the *Minseitō* government. On 11 December 1931, Wakatsuki's Cabinet resigned en masse.[8]

Takahashi Economics

On 13 December 1931, Inukai Tsuyoshi of the Seiyūkai party formed a new Cabinet, and chose Takahashi Korekiyo as his Finance Minister. Takahashi had served as Prime Minister twice for a short while, first from 13 November 1921 to 12 June 1922, and then in May 1932. But he was better known as Governor of the Bank of Japan, from 1911–1913, and especially as Finance Minister. He is sometimes called "Japan's Keynes." What is interesting is that Takahashi is evaluated very differently by political and economic historians. Overall, political, diplomatic and military historians tend to describe him as no more than a supporting actor in Japanese modern history.[9] But to economic historians, he is a giant, the most influential figure of modern Japanese history. He is regarded as the man who rescued Japan from the Great Depression. There is broad consensus among economic historians that Japan recovered from the Great Depression faster than other major powers. The discussion among economic historians is over which, among various policies Takahashi implemented during this period, was the most effective, and how they worked. They disagree on this point. I am a diplomatic and military historian and will not dive into this discussion. The problem is that political, diplomatic, and military historians have almost totally ignored what turn out to be accurate economic and industrial factors when they examine the transition from the "democratic" 1920s to the "militaristic" 1930s.

---

[8] As for the Shōwa Depression and the impact of the Great Depression on the Japanese economy, see Nakamura Takafusa, *Shōwa Kyōkō to Keizai Seisaku* (*The Shōwa Depression and Economic Policies*) (Tokyo: Kodansha, 1994). This book is a classic study of the Shōwa Depression. Its first edition was published in 1978.

[9] For example, the following works just briefly mention the achievements of Takahashi Korekiyo. Kitaoka Shinichi, *The Political History of Modern Japan: Foreign Relations and Domestic Politics* (London: Routledge, 2018) and Kitaoka Shinichi, *From Party Politics to Militarism in Japan, 1924–1941* (Boulder: Lynne Rienner, 2020).

Figure 2.1: TAKAHASHI Korekiyo, Finance Minister of Japan, 1931–1936.

As is seen in the excellent biography by economic historian Richard J. Smethurst, Takahashi's life was remarkable.[10] He was born in Edo (later Tokyo) in 1854, and spent his boyhood during the turbulent last years of the Edo period and Meiji Restoration. He lacked a formal education and taught himself. Luckily for him, he learnt spoken English from Americans in his boyhood years in Yokohama, and later in San Francisco. He went to San Francisco as a domestic servant boy and was there when Edo became Tokyo. Hearing news of political change in Japan, he hurriedly returned. He then moved from job to job mostly as an English teacher, interpreter and translator. But later he came to stand out as an international banker, working for the Bank of Japan and the Yokohama Specie Bank, and then as a financier, using his fluency in English as a weapon to move up the ladder. His language skills and personal interactions with the City of London and Wall Street in New York became reflected in his ways of thinking. Unlike diplomats-turned-politicians, his connections with Westminster or Washington were less strong. He was far more a pragmatist than an ideologue. He always put economic development first.

---

10 Richard J. Smethurst, *Takahashi Korekiyo, Japan's Keynes: From Foot Soldier to Finance Minister* (Cambridge MA: Harvard University Press, 2007).

When Takahashi became Finance Minister in the Inukai cabinet, he was already in his late 70s. But this experienced financier went on to rescue Japan from the Great Depression and the Shōwa Depression. In fact, Japan recovered from the Great Depression far more quickly than other major powers. The bottom year of the Great Depression in the United States was 1933, but by that year Japan was already in recovery. Takahashi made use of the conditions he faced, especially those shaped by the Manchurian Incident, to turn the economy around. He resorted to drastic measures. First, on the day he took office, he took Japan off the gold standard. Second, he greatly increased military spending, which helped the IJA in the Manchurian Incident. Third, he implemented the Rural Relief Package (*Jikyoku Kyūkyū Jigyō*). This was an economic stimulus package which poured a large amount of central as well as local government funds into public construction in rural areas, such as roads, ports, and flood prevention works, to increase employment and stimulate demand. Fourth, he encouraged lower interest rates to stimulate investment in the private sector. Fifth, to protect domestic industries, he raised tariffs. Sixth, to finance military spending and public construction, he issued a large amount of government bonds, and ordered the Bank of Japan to buy them. To do so, the Bank of Japan printed money, which increased the money supply. An increased money supply made the Japanese Yen weaker against other currencies, but Takahashi let the Yen become weaker and weaker. He considered that a weaker Yen should boost Japanese exports. In December 1931, the exchange rate stood at 100 Yen to 49 Dollars. This fell to 28 Dollars a year later and 25 Dollars in 1933. In the end, it stabilised at around 29–30 Dollars. In short, the Yen became 40 per cent weaker against the US Dollar. Also, Japanese exporters lost western markets, especially in the United States, during the Great Depression. However, the Manchurian Incident opened up new markets for Japanese manufacturers and Japanese exports to Asian markets grew rapidly in this period. As Takahashi expected, Japanese exports grew dramatically.[11] As a result of these measures, the Japanese economy recovered swiftly.

There are similarities between Takahashi's economic policies and the economic policies later known as "Keynesian Economics." John Maynard Keynes' famous work, *The General Theory of Employment, Interest and Money*, was published in 1936. It has been said that Keynes came up with the ideas in this book in the summer of 1932 at the earliest. So "Takahashi Economics" preceded "Keynesian Economics." But considering his personal connections with American and British banking and financial worlds, there is a high possibility that

---

[11] Ibid, 238–98.

Takahashi knew Keynes' earlier works, probably indirectly, and got some ideas from them.[12] If so, Japan was the first country to adopt "Keynesian Economics."

As Table 2.4 shows, while other major powers were still struggling amid the Great Depression, the Japanese economy rapidly recovered. The growth rate from 1931–1932 reached about 8 per cent, and from 1932–1933 around 10 per cent. Japanese economic growth between 1931 and 1933 was by far the best in the world. There was an economic slump in 1934 but this was due to bad weather and a natural disaster. The 1934 summer in northern Japan was cold, and so the rice harvest that year was poor. Also, in September that year the Muroto Typhoon hit the Japanese archipelago. The damage it caused was catastrophic, especially in western Japan. About 3,000 people died, 15,000 were injured, and 200,000 lost their homes. The economic damage exceeded US$300 million (1934).[13] The damage to the agricultural sector was severe and it took two years to recover fully. But the industrial sector continued to recover during this period.

In the National Budget of the 1932 fiscal year,[14] Takahashi increased military spending – the IJA budget plus the Imperial Japanese Navy (IJN) budget – by 32.1 per cent from the previous fiscal year. The reason was that he expected ripple effects from military spending. At that time, military spending took up a large share of the national budget, about 30 per cent, and around 3.5 per cent of gross national product (GNP). Takahashi expected to create general economic demand by boosting military spending. The share of military spending jumped to about 35 per cent of the national budget and 5.2 per cent of GNP in the 1932 fiscal year. In the 1933 fiscal year, it reached nearly 39 per cent of the national budget and 5.8 per cent of GNP.[15] Actually, Takahashi's theory worked and we can confirm this by looking at economic statistics.

Table 2.6 shows that expanded military and non-military government spending functioned as an economic stimulus package. In 1932, government spending on facilities, machinery, and equipment jumped, especially spending on military equipment, that is weapons. The IJA and IJN placed orders with arms manufacturers who in turn placed orders with steel companies. As a result of these measures, private sector investment clearly increased from 1933 to 1936. In other words, increased military spending on the Manchurian Incident functioned as an economic stimulus package. Table 2.6 also shows that exports had already recovered by 1932.

---

12 Ibid, 305–06.
13 The Wikipedia article on the 1934 Muroto Typhoon is quite good: https://en.wikipedia.org/wiki/1934_Muroto_typhoon
14 The Japanese fiscal year is from 1 April to 31 March next year.
15 Takeda Haruhito, *Nihon Kēzai-shi (Japan's Economic History)* (Tokyo: Yuhikaku, 2019), 248.

Table 2.4: GDP Growth in the 1930s.

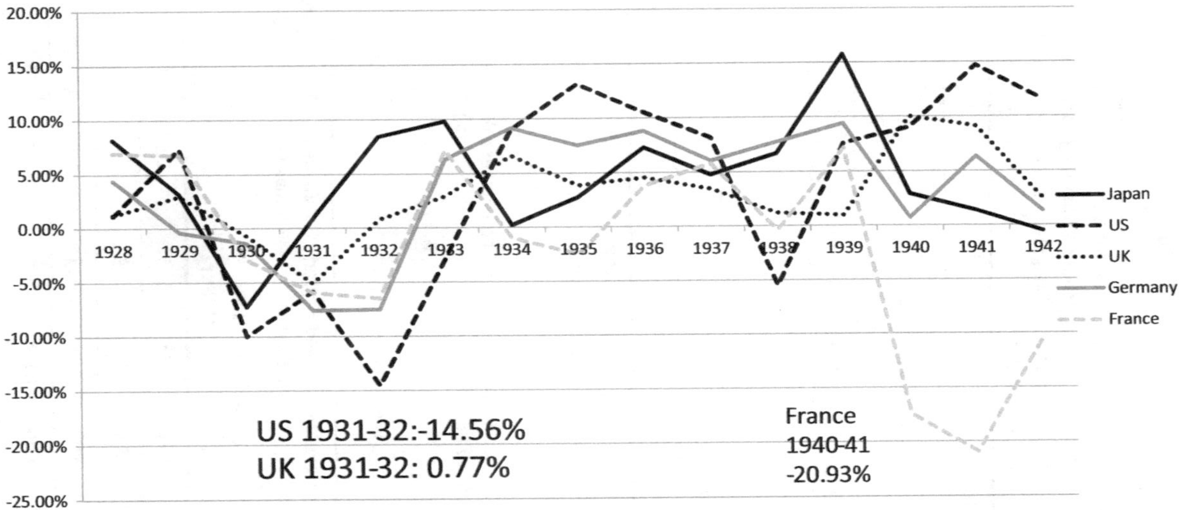

US 1931-32: -14.56%
UK 1931-32: 0.77%
France 1940-41: -20.93%

Japan's Growth Rate			
1929-30	-7.27%	1934-35	2.76%
1930-31	0.83%	1935-36	7.27%
1931-32	**8.39%**	1936-37	4.77%
1932-33	**9.82%**	1937-38	6.68%
1933-34	0.20%	1938-39	15.75%

Made by the author using statistics found in the Madison Project Database 2018.

Table 2.5: Japanese Military Spending in the early to mid-1930s.

	Army Budget (Million Yen)	Navy Budget (Million Yen)	Share of Total Military Spending in the National Budget	Percent Change of Total Military Spending from the previous year	Total Military Spending as a percentage of GNP
1930	200	242	28.4%	−10.3	3.0%
1931	227	227	30.8%	−5.2	3.5%
1932	**373**	**312**	**35.2%**	**32.1**	**5.2%**
1933	462	409	38.7%	15.6	5.8%
1934	458	483	43.6%	−4.1	5.6%
1935	496	536	46.8%	2	5.7%
1936	510	567	47.2%	3.4	5.6%
1937	591	645	45.7%	18.4	12.8%

Reference: Today's Defence Spending as a percentage of GDP:
US, around 3%; Russia, around 4%; Singapore, around 3%;
Japan, around 1%; China, around 2%.
Source: Takeda, *Nihon Kēzai-shi*, 247.
Military spending in 1937 includes a special budget for the Sino-Japanese War – 2,034 million Yen – adding to Army Budget and Navy Budget.

Table 2.6: Ripple Effects of Takahashi's Economics.

	Personal Expenditure Consumption	Private Fixed Capital Formation	Government-fixed Capital Formation		Government Purchases	Export	Gross Demand
			Military	Non-Military			
1930	11,325	946	978	173	805	1,624	2,046	16,919
	92.1	86.5	78.4	98.9	75	93.5	72.3	**88.1**
1931	10,198	697	908	175	733	1,939	1,628	15,370
	90	73.7	92.8	101.2	91.1	119.4	79.6	**90.8**
1932	10,154	570	1,255	353	902	2,217	2.047	16,243
	99.6	81.8	**138.2**	**201.7**	**123.1**	114.3	**125.7**	105.7
1933	11,228	859	1,332	355	977	2,464	2,632	18,515

Table 2.6 (continued)

Year	Personal Expenditure Consumption	Private Fixed Capital Formation	Government-fixed Capital Formation		Government Purchases	Export	Gross Demand
			Military	Non-Military			
	110.6	150.7	106.1	100.6	108.3	111.1	128.6	114.0
1934	12,515	1,218	1,329	452	877	2,421	3,011	20
	111.5	141.8	99.8	127.3	89.8	98.3	114.4	110.7
1935	13,081	1.501	1.43	472	958	2,637	3,648	22,297
	104.5	123.2	107.6	104.4	109.2	108.9	115.2	108.8
1936	13,722	1,838	1,490	532	958	2,273	3,724	23,497
	104.9	122.5	104.2	112.7	100.0	103.3	107.4	105.4
1937	15,583	1,849	2,961	1,965	996	4,714	4,405	29,512
	113.6	100.6	198.7	369.4	104.0	173.1	118.3	125.6

The Upper: Million Yen
The Bottom: Per Cent change from the previous year
Source: Takeda, *Nihon Kēzai-shi*, 247.

But the fruits of Takahashi Economics were not only limited to economic recovery. Even more important, from 1931 to 1936, the economic and industrial structure of Japan changed fundamentally. Before the Manchurian Incident, Japan was still a light industrial country. Its main products were raw silk, cotton textiles, and silk textiles. The main export product was raw silk and the main market was the United States. In those days, stockings made with Japanese silk were quite popular among American women. However, to make cotton products, Japan had to import raw cotton from the United States and British India. Overall, in the 1920s, the Japanese economy depended structurally on the United States. In the late 1920s, raw silk made up 36 per cent of total Japanese exports. Of all raw silk produced in Japan, 85 per cent was exported, of which 98 per cent was exported to the United States. But the Great Depression, the Manchurian Incident, and the economic recovery changed this structure completely. During the Great Depression, the export of raw silk to the United States plummeted. The value of raw silk exports in 1930 was a mere 12.8 per cent of that in 1925.[16] In the 1920s,

---

[16] Matsumoto Takashi, *Kyōkō ni Tachimukatta Otoko: Takahashi Korekiyo* (*The Man Who Fought Against the Depression: Takahashi Korekiyo*) (Tokyo: Chuokoron Shinsha, 2012), 260.

manufacture of raw silk was an important source of revenue in rural areas of Japan. Revenues from agricultural products fluctuated greatly depending on weather, but revenue from sericulture was stable. For this reason, farmers raised silkworms as a side business to stabilise their income. In fact, 40 per cent of Japanese farmers raised silkworms. This income from sericulture collapsed after the Great Depression started in New York. These farmers suffered severely. To rescue these rural areas, Takahashi implemented the Rural Relief Package to pour governmental funds into public construction in these areas. This created jobs temporarily. But, at the same time, a far greater change took place.

Boosted military spending worked as a stimulus to create and grow new industries. These were iron and steel, electrical, automobiles, machines, optical, heavy industry, chemicals, papermaking, and rubber. Military spending also revived shipbuilding. In addition, to strengthen the shipbuilding and shipping industry, Takahashi subsidised the replacement of merchant vessels. The shipbuilding industry, which had grown earlier, especially during the Great War, but stagnated in the 1920s, was revived by these measures. These new industries absorbed workers, and Japan achieved almost full employment by 1936. Not only that, but these industries greatly enhanced Japan's war potential and soon became its key industries.

Many of Japan's global brands today were born or grew greatly during this period. The roster is impressive: Nissan, Toyoda (the predecessor of Toyota), Mitsubishi Denki (Mitsubishi Electric), Hitachi, Shibaura Seisakujo and Tokyo Denki (these two merged and became Toshiba in 1939), Matsushita Denki Kigu (the predecessor of Panasonic), Nippon Kōgaku (the predecessor of Nikon), Canon, Takachiho Seisakujo (the predecessor of Olympus), Fujifilm, Tōyō Rayon (the predecessor of Toray), and Bridgestone. In fact, the years from 1931 to 1936 were the epoch-making era in Japanese industrial history. Nissan started mass production of cars in 1935, Toyoda in 1936. In 1933, Shibaura, Hitachi, and Mitsubishi started making self-designed electronic refrigerators (earlier in 1930, Shibaura made the first prototype of the electronic refrigerator, copying the General Electric product). In those days, electronic refrigerators were the latest gadget. Matsushita started making radios in 1931 and light bulbs in 1936. Canon and Takachiho started making cameras in 1936. Nippon Kōgaku (Nikon), which made optical devices for the government, especially the IJN, provided lenses, viewfinders and rangefinders for the first Canon camera.[17] They became rivals later but

---

17 The lenses for Canon's first camera were the photographic lenses Nippon Kōgaku made for civilian purposes for the first time. Without the history of the IJN, Nikon cameras would not exist. Nippon Kōgaku was established during the Great War in 1917 as a supplier of optical devices to the IJN. As a result of the Washington Conference in 1921–1922, orders from the IJN

collaborated then. Takachiho used the brand name Olympus for its first cameras. Nippon Kōgaku started producing lenses for aerial photographs in 1933. Fujifilm was established as a company producing photograph films in 1934. Tōyō Rayon expanded greatly as the manufacturer of "artificial silk," or rayon, in this period. And Bridgestone began mass production of tyres in 1934. The point is that, without the Manchurian Incident and Takahashi Economics, this industrial boom would not have occurred. Before the Manchurian Incident, Japan was still a light industrial country; within half a decade, the foundation of Japan as an industrial power had taken shape.

Figure 2.2: Japan's first mass-produced car: Datsun Type 14 (1935) manufactured by Nissan.

The company which expanded most phenomenally in this period was Mitsubishi Shipbuilding & Engineering. Originally a shipbuilding company based in Nagasaki, it expanded enormously with the great volume of orders from the IJN and the IJA. In 1934, it was renamed Mitsubishi Heavy Industries. Its core business was manufacturing ships and aeroplanes, but it also made railway cars, and various types of heavy machinery for both military and civilian use. Later it became the largest private firm in Japan producing and manufacturing various kinds of weapons, including the famous *Zero* fighter, the bombers *Nell* and

---

were reduced so greatly that, to survive, Nippon Kōgaku started supplying its products to the IJA and civil sectors of the government. Perhaps best known products Nippon Kōgaku made for the IJN were the large rangefinders mounted on top of the superstructure of *Yamato*-class battleships. The IJN ceased to exist in 1945 and Nippon Kōgaku became a manufacturer of optical devices for civilian use. During the Korean War, the performance of its photographic lenses became known to the world. In the 1960s, Nikon cameras became a global brand.

Figure 2.3: Japan's first electronic refrigerator: Shibaura SS-1200 (1933).

Figure 2.4: Canon's first camera with its lenses manufactured by Nippon Kōgaku: Hanza Canon (1936).

Betty which sunk HMS *Prince of Wales* and HMS *Repulse* in 1941, and the battleship *Musashi*, the second ship of *Yamato* class. The history of Mitsubishi Heavy Industries clearly indicates that military spending in the 1930s turned Japan from a light industrial into a heavy industrial country. *Nell* started flying in July 1935 and its successor *Betty* in October 1939. The company started preliminary design work on developing the *Zero* in May 1937, and the keel of the

Musashi was laid down on 29 March 1938. The aviation technology of Japan was clearly behind other major powers until the time of the Manchurian Incident, but was catching up with them fast in the mid-1930s.[18]

Figure 2.5: Imperial Japanese Navy Battleship Musashi with its gigantic rangefinder manufactured by Nippon Kōgaku on top of its superstructure (Laid down in 1938, commissioned in 1942). Photo taken from the bow, August 1942.

The advent of the aluminium industry kept pace with the rapid evolution of aircraft. The production of aluminium in Japan started in 1934. Until then, the supply of aluminium depended on imports from North America and Europe. At first, Japanese metal companies tried to produce aluminium from raw material found within the Japanese territories, so they used alunite produced in Korea. But aluminium made from alunite was too flimsy to be used in aircraft manufacture. The solution was bauxite imported from Bintan Island in the Dutch East Indies, just south of Singapore. Bauxite from Bintan was ideal. In 1936, Nippon Aluminium started producing aluminium in its factory in Takao, Taiwan, using bauxite imported from Bintan. Nippon Aluminium was a new company established in 1935 to produce aluminium from bauxite produced in Bintan. Takao in Taiwan was chosen for its factory because it was halfway between Bintan and mainland Japan and was abundant in electricity. After the success of Nippon Aluminium, soon almost all metal companies changed their

---

18 Mitsubishi Jūkōgyō Kabushikigaisha (Mitsubishi Heavy Industry, Ltd.) (ed.), *Mitsubishi Jūkōgyō Kabushikigaisha Shashi* (*The History of Mitsubishi Heavy Industry, Ltd.*), (Tokyo: Mitsubishi Heavy Industry, Ltd., 1967). See also the website of Mitsubishi Heavy Industry: https://www.mhi.com/company/aboutmhi/outline/history.html

raw material to imported bauxite. They imported bauxite from Bintan Island, British Malaya, or Batam Island, just next to Bintan. Mass production of aluminium in Japan thus began and provided materials for industry, especially aircraft.[19] Raw material from Southeast Asia made this possible. Japan had no bauxite, so production of aluminium depended completely on imported bauxite from the Dutch East Indies and British Malaya.

The Japanese metal industry produced one of the most advanced aluminium alloys in the world – 7075 aluminium alloy. It is famous as the material used in the *Zero* fighter. The *Zero* was known for its excellent manoeuvrability, but this was only possible due to its ultra-light weight but very solid material. It was secretly invented by Sumitomo Metal Industries in 1936 as a cutting-edge alloy. The invention of 7075 aluminium alloy indicated that Japan was catching up with advanced countries technologically quite rapidly. This alloy is widely used in various industries even today.[20] Sumitomo Metal itself was born in the previous year in 1935 with the merger of Sumitomo Copper Works and Sumitomo Steel Works. It was one of the two largest metal firms in Japan. The other was Nippon Steel, established in 1934 by the merger of several metal companies. In the mid-1930s, Japan's iron and steel companies were consolidated into these two big firms.[21] The birth of two big metal companies enhanced Japan's metal industry greatly. In the 1920s, Japan had had to import a large amount of steel from the United States. Now, these two companies provided steel for Japanese manufacturers.

What is also important in this period is that Japan's trading partners diversified. During the 1920s, the United States was its most important trading partner by far. In 1926, the United States took 42 per cent of Japanese exports. But this dwindled to 18 per cent by 1934[22] while Japanese exports more than doubled from 1931 to 1936.[23] The newly established puppet state of Manchukuo grew greatly and rapidly as a market for Japanese products. In 1926, Manchuria

---

[19] Kibata Michiko, "*Senzen Taiwan ni okeru Aluminium Seirengyō ni tuite* (A Study of the Aluminium Smelting Industry in Taiwan during the Japanese Colonial Era)," *The Keizai Ronshu (The Economic Review of Kansai University)*, Vol. 64–1 (June 2014), 27–46.

[20] For today's application of 7075 aluminium alloy, see the 7075 aluminium alloy page of the Wikipedia: https://en.wikipedia.org/wiki/7075_aluminium_alloy

[21] In 2012, about eight decades later, these two firms merged into Nippon Steel & Sumitomo Metal Corporation. In 2019, it was renamed Nippon Steel Corporation.

[22] Tanaka Akihiko and Kawashima Shin, eds., *20 Seiki no Higashi-Ajia Kankeishi 1 Kokusai-kankei Gairon (20th Century East Asia: A New History 1, Introduction to the History of International Relations)* (Tokyo: University of Tokyo Press, 2020), 88.

[23] Nakamura Munetoshi, *Tekisuto Gendai Nihon Keizai-shi (Contemporary Economic History of Japan)* (Tokyo: Gakubun-sha, 2018), 43.

only took 4 per cent of Japanese exports but this grew to 17 per cent by 1934.[24] Now, as a market for Japanese products, Manchuria matched the United States. What was more, as Table 2.7 shows, Manchuria, unlike the United States, became a market for Japan's heavy-industrial sectors.

Table 2.7: Japanese-Manchurian Trade.

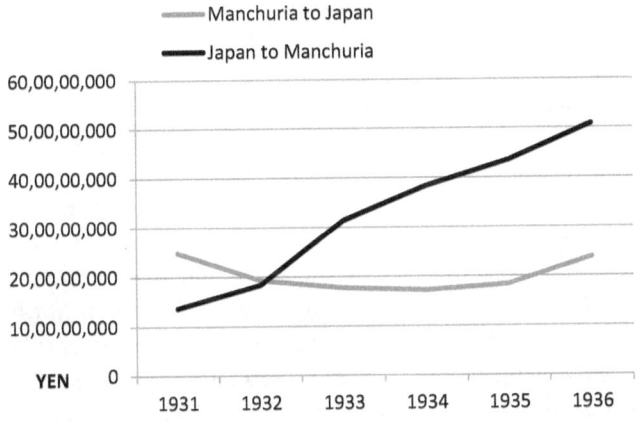

Japan to Manchuria (1934–36)		
Item	Percentage among Items	Proportion of Japan
Cotton textiles	15.2%	93.5%
Steel	9.3%	82.7%
Vehicles and Vessels	7.3%	87.7%
Machines and Tools	5.9%	76.6%
Wheat	5.6%	54.1%

---

24 The Kwantung Leased Territory (Dalian and Lüshun [Port Arthur]) 13 per cent, plus Manchukuo 4 per cent. Ikeda Michiko, *Tainichi Keizai Fuusa (Embargoes Against Japan)* (Tokyo: Nihon Keizai Shinbun, 1992), 30.

Table 2.7 (continued)

Manchuria to Japan (1934–36)		
Item	Percentage among Items	Proportion of Japan
Soybean	22.5%	26.3%
Soymeal	19.0%	72.4%
Coal	14.2%	71.6%

Source: Takeda, *Nihon Kēzai-shi*, 247.
The graph is made by the author using statistics in Takeda, *Nihon Kēzai-shi*, 247.

In the 1920s, Manchuria was the source of agricultural products such as soybeans. Now, Manchuria helped Japan's heavy-industrialisation. Japan's heavy-industrial sectors were still in early stages of development and lacked international competitiveness. They could not easily export their products to North American and European markets. Manchuria as a new market contributed greatly to the rapid development of Japan's heavy-industrial sectors. In addition, the newly established Manchukuo needed steel, vehicles, vessels, machines and tools for its own development. This forged what looked to many like an array of "win-win relationships" between Japan's heavy-industrial sectors and Manchukuo.

Japanese trading relations also diversified in this period. From 1926 to 1934, many countries raised their share of Japanese exports: Egypt from 1 to 3 per cent; British India from 7 to 11 per cent; Dutch East Indies from 3 to 7 per cent; Latin American countries from 0.5 to 2 per cent; United Kingdom from 2 to 5 per cent; Philippines from 1.3 to 1.6 per cent; and African countries (except Egypt) from almost 0 to 4.1 per cent.[25] There is an impression that Japan became isolated during and after the Manchurian Incident. This may be true politically and diplomatically but definitely not economically. In the 1920s, Japanese trading partners were limited to the United States and several other countries; by the mid-1930s, they had expanded across the world. During the era of Takahashi Economics, Japanese traders, boosted by favourable exchange rates, cultivated new markets in Africa, the Middle East, and Latin America, and exported cotton products, rayon and other goods. To Egypt, Japan exported various textile products and imported raw cotton and phosphate ore.[26] Now Japan traded almost all over the globe.

---

25 Ibid.
26 Inoue Toshikazu, *Senzen Nihon no "Globalism": 1930-nendai no Kyōkun (Japan's "Globalisation" Before the War: What Can We Learn from the 1930s?)* (Tokyo: Shinchosha, 2011), 151–59.

As a result of this expanded Japanese trade, the share of Japanese cotton in various countries increased. Table 2.8 indicates this.

Table 2.8: Shares of Japanese and British Cotton Products in Third Countries.

	Japan			Britain	
	1929	1931	1935	1929	1931
Straits Settlements	13.9%		37%	55.8%	
India	29.9%	45.2%	52.4%	65.7%	49.9%
Dutch East Indies	30.1%	47.3%	75.7%	25.4%	12.3%
Egypt	18.0%	58.5%	63%	45.2%	3.4%
Argentina	4.0%	6.3%		52.9%	28.3%
Australia	3.4%	6.8%	18.0%	90.5%	87.3%
Kenya and Uganda	29.0%		77%	26.0%	
Tanganyika	24.9%	37.4%	77%	26.4%	17.4%
The Philippines	15.6%	30.8%	30%	11.9%	7.5%
Turkey	15.5%	31.2%		17.0%	10.1%
South Africa	6.9%		12.0%	61.1%	
Thailand	23.2%	37.0%	65.2%	27.3%	11.2%

Source: Takeda, *Nihon Kēzai-shi*, 247.
Statistics of India and Thailand are based on volume; those of other countries are based on value.

By 1935, the share of Japanese cotton products dramatically increased in India, the Dutch East Indies, Egypt, Kenya, Uganda, Tanganyika (now Tanzania), and Thailand. Japanese cotton products eroded these markets where British cotton products previously had a large share. This resulted in trade conflicts between Britain and Japan. Again, there is an impression that Japan in the 1930s was economically isolated, and this prompted Japan eventually to fight the Western powers in the early 1940s to break the status quo. But the picture is not that simple. In reality, Japanese economic expansion, boosted by free trade, rather than economic blocs, generated new sources of conflict.[27]

It is true that Japan created the Yen Bloc, which consisted of Japan, Taiwan, Korea, and Manchuria, by incorporating Manchukuo into it. This Yen Bloc became

---

[27] Japanese historian Inoue Toshikazu points out this. See Ibid, 151.

the prime market for growing Japanese heavy industry. Yet one should not ignore the fact that Japan's free-trade fields expanded dramatically at the same time. What is more, the newly created Yen Bloc was not self-sufficient. Growing heavy industry required resources[28] such as oil, tin,[29] bauxite, rubber, and iron ore,[30] since the Yen Bloc could not provide these. The more Japan became heavy-industrialised the more it needed these resources. These resources were to be found in the United States, the Dutch East Indies, and British Malaya. Southeast Asia was quite rich in these resources so naturally, in the mid-1930s, Southeast Asia drew attention from Japan, especially Japanese businessmen. Japan now had to import crucial resources from this region.

The economic recovery pushed Takahashi Korekiyo up to the pinnacle of power. In the mid-1930s, he became more influential than the Prime Minister. The Prime Minister often changed – including Takahashi himself. After the assassination of Inukai in May 1932, Takahashi was Prime Minister for 10 days. But he remained in the post of Finance Minister most of the time during this period. Understandably, the business community backed him strongly. Remarkably, moderate non-communist labour unions also came to support him. The leaders of *Sōdōmei*, a federation of labour unions which comprised around two-thirds of organised workers, gave him their support. Under the "prestige" of Takahashi, effective tripartite relations between labour unions, employers, and the government were formed. These "win-win relations" pushed up the economy even further. Furthermore, Takahashi largely controlled the budgets of the IJA and IJN. For the fiscal years of 1932 and 1933, he greatly expanded military spending, but once the economy started to pick up, he came to control the IJN and IJA budgets. In fact, he slightly reduced the IJA budget for the 1934 fiscal year. For the fiscal years of 1934, 1935, and 1936, the IJA and IJN budgets were far smaller than the services initially demanded. Takahashi considered that further expansion of military spending would now harm the Japanese economy and international relations. By imposing fiscal caps, he controlled the IJA and IJN. As the Finance Minister who had brought economic boom, his

---

[28] The author referred to the following book for information on various natural resources: Fujii Hisashi, *"Rea Metalu" no Taiheiyō Sensō ("Rare Metals" and the Pacific War)* (Tokyo: Gakken, 2013).

[29] Tin was needed to make ball bearings, and without ball bearings it was impossible to make moving machines including tanks, aircraft, and ships. Japan imported tin from British Malaya. The United States also imported tin from British Malaya and the Dutch East Indies.

[30] Japan's self-sufficient ratio of iron ore in 1936 was only 16.7 per cent. Moreover, iron ore produced in Japan contained too much sulphur and phosphorus to satisfy industrial requirements. Therefore, Japan had to import a large amount of iron ore to satisfy industrial as well as military needs. The largest source of imported iron ore was British Malaya.

prestige and popularity among the people were so high that even the IJA and IJN could do nothing but accept his budgetary controls. Araki Sadao, Army Minister in 1932–1934, bitterly debated the IJA budget with Takahashi every year, but personally Araki respected him greatly. Within the IJA, the mainstream was also quite supportive. This was especially true in the case of General Hayashi Senjūrō, Army Minister in 1934–1935, and Major-General Nagata Tetsuzan, the leader of the most influential faction, the *Tōseiha*. Nagata believed that to prepare for large-scale wars in the future, it was necessary to put effort into heavy-industrialisation, and so Japan should not start a new war in the immediate future. Unfortunately, Nagata was assassinated by a radical of the rival faction, the *Kōdō*, on 12 August 1935.

All in all, in the mid-1930s, under the strong influence of Takahashi, there was a loose consensus among the Cabinet, the business community, and the IJA that, in the immediate future, Japan should focus on its own economic development and the development of Manchukuo, and should not seek further expansion.[31]

The End of Takahashi Economics

Takahashi regarded the Rural Relief Package and increased military spending as temporary measures to stimulate the economy. He had no intension to continue them after achieving economic recovery. Since 1933, he repeatedly explained in Parliament that these were temporary measures and would end before long. He considered that too long continuation of the Rural Relief Package would deprive communities of the spirit of self-help, while too much expansion of military spending would harm the economic balance and international relations. First, he terminated the Rural Relief Package with the end of the 1934 fiscal year (31 March 1935). Second, in 1935, he rejected the further expansion of military spending, and tried to reduce the IJA and IJN budgets for the 1936 fiscal years. In autumn 1935, his determination to reduce the IJA and IJN budgets and tough negotiations with Army and Navy Ministers were reported in newspapers.

---

[31] Matsuura Masataka, "*Takahashi Korekiyo to 'Kyokoku-icchi' Naikaku: Seitō Houkaigo no Seiji Keizai*" ("Takahashi Korekiyo and the 'National Unity' Cabinet: the Political and Economic Conditions after the Collapse of the Party Politics"), in Kitaoka Shinichi and Mikuriya Takeshi, eds., *Sensō, Fukkō, Hatten: Shōwa Seiji- ki ni okeru Kenryoku to Kōsō* (*War, Recovery and Development: Power and Visions in Shōwa Political History*) (Tokyo: University Press, 2000), 63–105; Matsumoto, *Kyōkō ni Tachimukatta Otoko: Takahashi Korekiyo*, 342.

Reading these papers, the young and radical military officers who had not met Takahashi got angry. Ministers and senior officers who knew Takahashi respected him so that, no matter how bitterly they discussed the budgets, these discussions did not affect personal relations. But some radical junior officers who had never met him went much further.

In fact, for these radicals, Takahashi was the embodiment of evil. He was not only a politician but also a representative of the "corrupted" financial community. As the politician who prioritised industrial development, he did not pay attention to poverty in rural areas. Even though the cold summer and the 1934 Muroto Typhoon devastated the rural areas in 1934, Takahashi terminated the Rural Relief Package with the end of the 1934 fiscal year. On the other hand, the financial community made a great deal of money "cheatingly" during the transition period from Inoue Economics to Takahashi Economics, by selling and buying back Japanese Yen. Takahashi "utilised" the position of Finance Minister "to help his friends" do this. Among these naïve and radical officers, these views had validity. Actually, economic discrepancy between cities and rural areas was still quite wide. The economy of rural areas recovered, but urban areas not only recovered more quickly but also expanded quite rapidly. During Takahashi Economics, the economic gap between the agricultural and industrial sectors widened.[32] It was only after the outbreak of the Second Sino-Japanese War in 1937 that the agricultural sector fully recovered. Further economic demands to fight the war finally brought benefits to rural areas.[33] For those from agricultural communities in rural areas of Japan, the modern and prosperous life in mid-1930s Tokyo was unimaginable. They came to believe that Takahashi and "a privileged few" in Tokyo "manipulated" this. For these reasons, he became one of the most important targets when the radical junior officers of the IJA attempted a coup on 26 February 1936. This was the 26 February Incident. In the early morning, Takahashi was assassinated at his house in Aoyama, Tokyo, at the age of 81.

---

[32] For the attitudes of radical younger officers towards Takahashi, Takahashi Economics and economic discrepancy, see the following books: Suzaki Shinichi, *Nī Nī Roku Jiken: Seinen Shōkō No Shinri To Ishiki (February 26 Incident:The Views and Minds of Radical Younger Officers)* (Tokyo: Yoshikawa-kōbunkan, 2003); Inoue Toshikazu, *Ronten Betsu Shōwa-shi: Sensō Heno Michi (Issues of Showa History: The Road to the War)* (Tokyo: Kōdan-sha, 2019); Kita Hiroaki, *Nī Nī Roku Jiken Zenkenshō (February 26 Incident: Fully Re-examined)* (Tokyo: Asahi Shinbun-sha, 2003); Hayashi Shigeru ed., *Nī Nī Roku Jiken Hiroku 1 (Documents on February 26 Incident, Vol.1)* (Tokyo: Shōgaku-kan, 1971).

[33] Kobayashi Youhei "Sekai-Kyōkō ka no Nihon (Japan During the Great Depression)" in Tsutsui Kiyotaka, ed., *Shōwa-shi Kōgi 2 (Lectures of Shōwa History 2)* (Tokyo: Chikuma-shobō, 2016), 76.

The assassination of Takahashi Korekiyo inflicted irreparable damage on Japan. After the assassination, no Finance Minister tried to cut the IJA budget. Thus the IJA and IJN budgets skyrocketed uncontrollably. Furthermore, his assassination eliminated the centre of power and gravity from Japanese national politics. In the mid-1930s, he was that centre of power. But no one replaced him since his power base lay in the prestige he acquired through the economic recovery. After that, the IJA gained a much more free hand to pursue its own policies more independently. Thus Japanese external policies became more "militaristic." One year later, the Second Sino-Japanese War broke out. Four years later, Japan opened hostilities against the Western Allies.

Conclusion

During the period from the Manchurian Incident in September 1931 to the 26 February Incident in 1936, the economic character of Japan changed fundamentally. The Manchurian Incident was the catalyst for this. Before the incident, Japan was a light industrial country. Today, Japan is known as the manufacturer of cars, various kinds of electronic appliances, and cameras. But it was no such thing before the Manchurian Incident. Japanese technology had not yet produced such products. The Japanese made a living exporting raw silk, cotton textiles, and silk textiles. In other words, the life of the Japanese people was sustained by American women wearing stockings, South Asian women wearing saris, and Southeast Asian people wearing sarongs. Among them, American women were the most valuable customers, since American stockings made of Japanese silk were very popular and no strong competitor existed in the American market. Japan could supply the raw material of raw silk and silk textiles, but to make cotton textiles it had to import raw cotton from the United States and British India. Under this economic structure, it was impossible to adopt confrontational policies towards the United States and Britain. Naturally, Japan adopted conciliatory foreign policies towards these countries. It is impossible to find the origins of the Pacific War in 1920s Japan. Needless to say, there was no industrial base in 1920s Japan to sustain a large-scale war.

The economic recovery from the Great Depression, and the heavy-industrialisation during and after the Manchurian Incident, changed this structure completely. As we saw in this chapter, Finance Minister Takahashi Korekiyo did an excellent job during the period from 1931 to 1936. He achieved the V-shaped recovery from the Great Depression partly by expanding military spending on the Manchurian Incident. During this time, expanded military spending increased economic demand, and this economic demand in turn created new industries. Within half a decade, Japan turned from a light-industrial to a heavy-industrial country. The origin of post-war Japan as the manufacturer of cars, various kinds of electronic appliances, and cameras, can be traced back to this era. In other words, without the Manchurian Incident and Takahashi Economics, Japan could not have achieved the "economic miracle" of the 1950s and 1960s.

The V-shaped recovery Japan achieved on its own gave the Japanese people self-confidence or even over-confidence. Many Japanese felt that, since the Manchurian Incident, living conditions had become better and better. The Manchurian Incident and the economic boom cleared away the gloomy and sombre atmosphere of the Shōwa Depression. The Manchurian Incident, and the Shanghai Incident in 1932, greatly tarnished the international image of Japan, but most Japanese did not care about international opinion. Foreign voices which criticised Japan still struggled amid the Great Depression. Japanese newspapers which supported the Taishō Democracy in the 1920s now earnestly supported the Manchurian Incident and Japanese withdrawal from the League of Nations. Clearly, the atmosphere of society became more nationalistic and militaristic than the "democratic" 1920s.[34] But while this was influenced to some degree by distress in rural Japan, which was indeed politically exploited by radical army officers, the more important drivers of changing attitudes were this newfound national economic confidence, shaped by this changing economic structure.[35]

We can also explain the origins of the Pacific War through the heavy-industrialisation of this era. As the result of this heavy-industrialisation, the resources Japan required most by import changed from raw cotton to oil, tin, bauxite, rubber, and iron ore. Without these natural resources, Japanese heavy-industrial sectors could not operate because the Japanese archipelago and the Yen Bloc did not produce them. The Yen Bloc functioned as the main markets for Japan's expanding heavy-industrial sectors but it was not a self-sustainable economic bloc. Quite naturally, Southeast Asia now attracted the attention of the Japanese people as an accessible region enormously rich in these resources.

In the latter half of the 1930s, Japan imported tin, bauxite, rubber, and iron ore, from British Malaya and the Dutch East Indies. But Anglo-Japanese relations

---

[34] See Chapter 7 by Jeremy Yellen, in this volume, for further discussion of changing Japanese foreign policies from 1931.

[35] It could be argued that until 1932, before the economic boom, the main drive of "militaristic" Japan was distress in rural areas, which resulted in the May 15 Incident in 1932 and, to some degree, in the February 26 Incident in 1936. But from the mid-1930s onwards, the main driver was economic confidence. This was especially true after heavy-industrial sectors offered the prospect of producing more advanced weapons.

deteriorated, partly due to expanded Japanese exports, mainly due to expanded military operations in China. After Germany occupied much of continental Europe in the early summer of 1940, the view suddenly appeared within the IJA that Japan could forcibly capture oil, tin, bauxite, rubber, and iron ore, in Southeast Asia. This was an opportunity to take action, which could help Japan end its war in China. The colonial master of the Dutch East Indies was occupied by the Germans. The colonial master of British Malaya was occupied by the fight against the Germans. Eventually in December 1941, Japan opened hostilities against the United Kingdom, the Netherlands, and the United States, to seize this opportunity.[36] The expanded industrial base, and the weapons produced by the heavy-industrial sectors, gave Japanese leaders the means to fight against these countries, reasons to do so, and the confidence that they could pull it off.

But the economic and industrial base of the Allies was far greater. Furthermore, the Second World War created huge economic demand for the American economy, and this economic demand expanded the American economy phenomenally. During the war, the United States turned this economic and industrial power into military power. This military power defeated Japan by the summer of 1945. However, Japanese industry survived the defeat. Although factories and production facilities were destroyed by Allied bombing, technology and know-how the Japanese manufacturers had honed since the 1930s survived. Many of the Japanese brands which were born or grew during the era of Takahashi Economics became global brands by the 1970s. Ironically, the Japanese surrender to the Allies opened markets for Japanese products. The rapid economic growth of Japan in the post-war era has been called the "Japanese economic miracle." But as we saw in this chapter, the starting point of this economic miracle was not the Japanese surrender in 1945. It was the Manchurian Incident in 1931. And the driver of subsequent military expansion was not panic – it was confidence.

---

36 Brian P. Farrell, *The Defence and Fall of Singapore 1940–1942* (Stroud: Tempus, 2005); Yamamoto Fumihito, *Nichiei Kaisen Eno Michi: Igirisu No Shingapōru Senryaku To Nihon No Nanshin No Shinjitsu (The Road to the Anglo-Japanese War: Truths of the British Singapore Strategy and Japan's Southbound Policies)* (Tokyo: Chuokoron Shinsha, 2016).

Section Two

David J. Ulbrich
Military Power in Grand Strategy, 1900–1954

Whereas "diplomacy," "intelligence," and "economic" elements of the DIME model receive due attention in other sections of this anthology, this second section focuses on the relationship of "military" elements to grand strategy. The threat of military force, let alone its kinetic application, can provide the foundation for other options such as deterrence or soft power diplomacy.[1] In some ways, each of this section's four chapters is *sui generis* in time and place, as well as author expertise. Yet in other important ways, the chapters highlight patterns of how and why national motivations were intertwined with planning and executing military operations to pursue grand strategic goals.[2] In addition, the authors point to intense competition for hegemony in the Asia Pacific by Great Powers and regional nations, whose grand strategies not only affected, but were likewise affected by, military considerations. Meanwhile, regional nations exercised agency, albeit restricted, that limited Great Powers' abilities to attain their goals.

David J. Ulbrich takes a bottom-up approach in his chapter on the US Marine Corps and interwar plans and preparations to fight Japan. He demonstrates how the Marines aligned their doctrines, force structures, and equipment with what they concluded were operational and strategic needs of the US Navy. The Navy's needs were, in turn, nested within the nation's grand strategy in the Asia-Pacific. The American process of grand strategizing proved to be messy because the civilian government never set down unqualified goals for the use of military force. As a unique political system, America's constitutional federal republic with its democratic-based system neither looked nor functioned like the other Great Powers or regional nations. During the 1920s, the anti-military Republican Party directed a 90 percent reduction in American armed forces mobilized for the Great War. Then the 1930s saw increasing isolationism of the Great Depression that imposed more fiscal restrictions on the US military. Even so, the Marines never lost sight of their necessary contributions at the operational level of warfare: island base seizure and advanced base defence. The seizure of

---

1 See Chapter 2 on "Strategic Ends and Means" and Chapter 3 on "Strategic Ways" in Joint Chiefs of Staff, USA, *Joint Doctrine Note 1–18, Strategy*, 2018.
2 See Carl von Clausewitz, *On War*, ed. and trans. Michael Howard and Peter Paret (Princeton, NJ: University Press, 1984), 87.

https://doi.org/10.1515/9783110718713-005

enemy bases took precedence in offensive campaigns; and the holding of American island bases against enemy attack became a priority on the defensive side. Thus, looking up from the Marine Corps' operational focus to American strategy and grand strategy helps to elucidate those higher levels of warfare. Ulbrich's case study of operational perspectives also highlighted the muddled, and hence impotent, grand strategy of the United States in the Asia Pacific.

Brian P. Farrell's chapter concentrates on Great Power and especially British perspectives in China during the uncertain interwar years. That post-Qing nation spiralled deeper into bloody civil warfare among warlords, communists, and nationalists in the 1920s. Even so, these groups also wanted to expel all outsiders from China. Farrell uses the crisis in Shanghai in 1927 as a touchstone to explore factors that shaped British grand strategy in China. He points to Shanghai, rather than Hong Kong, as the key city due to its location at the mouth of the Yangtze River. The British prioritized protecting their citizens, possessions, and interests in Shanghai. Nevertheless, like the United States at the time, the British Army's demobilization after the Great War left the nation, and by extension its empire, with limited military strength. Consequently, any British operations on the ground in China needed to be carefully considered and executed. When in January 1927 Chinese forces under Chiang Kai-shek's nominal control threatened Shanghai, the pressure to hold the city prompted the British to deploy the Shanghai Defence Force. The reinforcements eventually increased to nearly 20,000 soldiers later that year. Farrell argues that, by safeguarding a presence in Shanghai, the British successfully averted a major conflict involving the Great Powers in China, while still maintaining that city as a platform from whence they could manage the evolving situation in the war-torn East Asia nation. The British thus employed limited means – using concentrated military power in Shanghai – to achieve a grand strategic goal. The short-lived success, however, fell apart when hostilities erupted in Manchuria in 1931 and China in 1937. By the later date, the British could merely watch from afar, powerless to defend Shanghai, let alone impede the expanding conflict.

China remained a hotly contested battleground during the Second World War as shown by Charles Burgess in his chapter. He dissects the ways that American and British grand strategy converged in China and Southeast Asia. By 1941, the US Navy at Pearl Harbor and the US Army in the Philippines posed nominal deterrent threats to Japanese aggression in the Asia Pacific. Then Japan's attack on Pearl Harbor suddenly and rudely thrust the US into a global conflict without grand strategy goals or military means in East Asia. During their mad scramble to adjust, American civilian and military leaders decided to use China and Southeast Asia as critical theatres in the fight against Japan and, more significantly, to dictate grand strategy in the evolving Anglo-American alliance. Burma could become the logistical lifeline to China, which could be home to major operating bases for future Anglo-American ground and air operations against Japanese forces fighting there. China could likewise support an invasion of Japan's home islands. Meanwhile, Anglo-American interests diverged as the British favoured limiting offensive operations in Burma to support the Chinese. This scenario seemingly elevated China to Great Power and ally status, retaining prominence in American eyes through 1943. After that, the two-pronged American campaigns in the Central and Southwest Pacific theatres turned into offensive juggernauts that drew American attention away from previously planned commitments in China. The tides of war relegated China as an ancillary theatre. Burgess notes that fighting the Chinese diverted most of the Imperial Japanese Army units from the western Pacific.

Jumping to the post-war era, Karl Hack's chapter uses the British plan in 1941 to defend Malaya against a Japanese invasion as a historical analogue for the proposed British defence of that same nation from communist attacks in early 1950s. Both operational plans called for British and Commonwealth units to hold the narrow Kra Isthmus against enemy advances southward through Thailand towards Malaya. This defensive scheme would, the British hoped, protect Malaya and safeguard the landward approaches to the all-important port of Singapore on the far southern tip of the Malayan peninsula. Maintaining the British presence in that port city remained a priority of British grand strategy in the region. Formulated in 1941, mishandling Plan Matador resulted in a spectacular British defeat in Malaya and then Singapore, from December 1941 into February 1942. The pre-war plan bore witness to British naivete, as it required a willingness to abrogate Thailand's neutrality well before any major power attacked – but the British were not so willing. The operation was aborted very late, which disrupted all other defence plans. Hack then devotes the bulk of his chapter to the 1950s when British war plans called for a strikingly similar defence of the Songkhla (Singora) line running from the city of the same name southwest across the Kra Isthmus. The British remained uncertain if China's People's Liberation Army units would make that invasion. Meanwhile, communist insurgencies undermined stability in Malaya and French Indochina, magnifying British fears in the region. The plan to defend the Songkhla Line ceased to be a viable option in 1957 due to British success against the Malayan insurgency, the establishment of an independent Malaya, the growing American commitment in South Vietnam, and the creation of the Southeast Asia Treaty Organization. Taken together, these considerations reduced the perceived threats to the Malayan peninsula and de-emphasized the nation in British grand strategy.

One final point to note is the centrality of military force in grand strategy writ large. This section forms effective pivot points to the other two that will help readers engage the broader concept. The theme of China may serve as the exemplar. Ulbrich discusses American preparations for a war that would be fought about China, Farrell and Burgess portray the Chinese as active, if not autonomous, players in the unfolding grand strategic considerations in East Asia, and Hack focuses on an early British and Western response to a new threat from a new China. These discussions can all help amplify the economic dimensions identified in Section One, discussing China as a crucial forum for economic expansion, and the diplomatic pressures analyzed in Section Three, ranging from China as a theatre of total war to China as a threat, an adversary, or even a potential ally. In important ways, military force and power can be seen as the binding agent in considerations of grand strategy, this time and place being a notable example.

David J. Ulbrich
Facing the Rising Sun in the Pacific: Grand Strategy, the US Marine Corps and Amphibious Capabilities, 1900–1941

The concept of "grand strategy" is most often associated with Otto von Bismarck, B.H. Liddell Hart, George Kennan, or others, who grasped the connections between national ends and military means as instruments of power. Europeans and Asians seem to grasp and apply the term better than has the United States. Their national military priorities have been dictated in large part by neighbouring friends and foes alike. For the United States, grand strategy is a squishy term in military history and military affairs. When visible, American national military priorities appear less steadfast during peacetime and then grow more frantic during wartime. For purposes of this chapter, strategic studies scholar Edward Luttwak offers a layered definition that best applies to the United States:

> All states have a grand strategy, whether they know it or not. That is inevitable because grand strategy is simply the level at which knowledge and persuasion, or in modern terms intelligence and diplomacy, interact with military strength to determine outcomes in a world of other states with their own "grand strategies."[1]

Those states cannot exist in a vacuum when friends and foes alike possess competing national goals. This can be seen during the Second World War in dramatically different grand strategies for the United States, the United Kingdom and the Soviet Union, yet they shared common enemies and similar exigencies to reach their respective goals. Once the conflict ended, so too did their commonalities.

Asia-Pacific scholar Michael J. Green adds more nuance to American grand strategy by showing how pluralistic political factors caused tensions and contradictions in that grand strategy. Problems can be seen in the plans for, execution during, and aftermath of conflicts. In recent decades, the Vietnam War and

---

[1] Edward Luttwak, *The Grand Strategy of the Byzantine Empire* (Cambridge MA: Belknap Press of Harvard University Press, 2009), 409.

Note: Portions of this chapter are outgrowths of the author's "The US Marine Corps, Amphibious Capabilities, and Preparations for War with Japan," *Marine Corps University Journal* 6 (Spring 2015), 71–106; and *Preparing for Victory: Thomas Holcomb and the Making of the Modern US Marine Corps, 1936–1943* (Annapolis MD: Naval Institute Press, 2011).

the Global War on Terror come to mind as examples. Nevertheless, Green can identify an evolving grand strategy in Asia and the Pacific that incorporated many factors and encompassed more than two centuries. He argues that the United States could not abide another nation asserting hegemony and implementing exclusionary policies vis-à-vis American interests and presence in the region.[2]

Acquiring the Philippines, Guam and Wake Islands after victory in the Spanish-American War in 1898 gave the United States a presence in East Asia and the Pacific Ocean. These new territories marked a watershed in American history because they gave the United States a tangible presence in East Asia and the Western Pacific Ocean. China represented an enticing commercial resource as American industries sought expanded markets and hoped to maintain "Open-Door" trade with that nation's large population. The commercial interests and requisite diplomatic machinations and military force to protect them affected American grand strategies in Asia and the Pacific.

The protection of American interests employing diplomacy and by projecting force constituted grand strategy. These factors put the United States at loggerheads with Japan, the other rising power with territorial ambitions in East Asia and the Western Pacific Ocean. As time passed, their mirrored grand strategies impeded each nation from achieving their respective goals. This mirror analogy, albeit not always symmetric but rather sometimes fuzzy or misshapen, provides a useful way of analyzing American military force's relationships to national strategies between 1900 and 1941. To put it another way, grand strategies have rationales rooted in perceived realities of military power, geography, ideology, resources and the like; however, those grand strategies were not always rational, especially when analyzed in retrospect.[3]

Green's explanation and Luttwak's definition serve as springboards for analyzing the US Marine Corps' role in American grand strategy. This chapter traces how and why grand strategy affected strategic and operational levels of war and vice versa. The Japanese threat in the Asia-Pacific required the military to prepare for potential conflict. During the process of formulating American strategic plans to fight Japan, missions were dispensed downward from the civilian-run government to the US Navy to the Marine Corps. American grand strategic and strategic priorities provided the impetus for the Marines to review their operational doctrines, force structures, and equipment procurement in

---

[2] Michael J. Green, *By More than Providence: Grand Strategy and American Power in the Pacific Since 1783* (New York: Columbia University Press, 2017), 1–18.
[3] Robert Gesbrink, "The Enduring Grand Strategy of the United States Represented as a Mirror Strategy," National Defense University, MA Thesis, 2016), 4–8; and Colin S. Gray, "National Style in Strategy: The American Example," International Security 6, No. 2 (Fall 1981), 22.

the 1920s and 1930s. The advanced base defence and amphibious assault missions allowed the Marine Corps to match its operational capabilities to the Navy's higher-level needs in the Pacific, thereby fulfilling the nation's highest-level goals. Indeed, those amphibious missions also affected the American strategic planning process, thereby creating a fluid model where ideas moved up and down the levels of warfare (Figure 3.1). This matched grand strategy as defined in Brian P. Farrell's introduction to this anthology: "a constant process: the art of relating the organization and application of power to the pursuit of national objectives."[4] That the Marines grasped these connections would later bear fruit in the Second World War. Neither the US Army nor the Navy could boast such success in the pre-war years.

Figure 3.1: American Grand Strategy, Strategy, Operations, and the U.S. Marine Corps, 1900–1933.

As early as 1900, senior admirals in the US Navy argued that American power needed to be projected across the vast Pacific Ocean. A few years later in 1905, victory in the Russo-Japanese War turned Japan into a regional power. Moreover, due to severe deficiencies in their island nation's natural resources, Japanese leaders coveted the raw materials and agricultural production of the Asian mainland. Any southward or westward expansion would inevitably bring this rising power into conflict with America's strategic and commercial interests. The US Navy's planners focused their attention on the Pacific Ocean and Japan, otherwise known by the colour designation "Orange." American strategists prepared several scenarios with potential allies and enemies designated by colors.

---

4 Brian P. Farrell, *The Basis and Making of British Grand Strategy 1940–1943: Was There a Plan?* (Lewiston NY: Edwin Mellen Press, 1998), 2 vols.

The resulting American "War Plan Orange" spanned the next several decades until 1938. All its iterations shared several tenets. American strategists expected that the Japanese would launch a pre-emptive strike, likely without a formal declaration of war. That attack would presumably be directed against American bases in the Philippines and Guam. Following the initial Japanese onslaught, the US Fleet would sortie from Hawaii and sail across the Pacific. The US Fleet would either relieve besieged American forces in the Philippines or liberate the archipelago, if it already had fallen. Meanwhile, as the US Fleet menaced the Japanese home islands, American planners hoped that the Imperial Japanese Navy (IJN) would contest the American offensive. As assumed in versions of War Plan Orange and the US Navy's war games, this ensuing naval battle would result in a decisive American victory. Alternatively, if the Japanese chose not to fight, the US Fleet would blockade their home islands. Regardless, the American victory would consign Japan to the status of a diminished, isolated regional power.[5]

War Plan Orange's answer to the Japanese menace in the Asia-Pacific region marked the genesis of two operational missions for the US Marine Corps: amphibious assault and island defence. During the anticipated offensive campaign, the Marines would seize and hold "temporary advanced bases in cooperation with the Fleet and . . . defend such bases until relieved by the Army."[6] The newly captured bases would subsequently function as coaling stations, safe anchorages, repair facilities, supply depots, and eventually aircraft bases.

The US Marines made positive strides in developing amphibious capabilities from 1900 to 1915. Marines specializing in this new type of warfare created an Advanced Base School, where they studied operational issues important to any base defence such as artillery placement, communications, logistics, and staff organization. Academic study and practical experience coalesced in 1914 with a simulated assault on Culebra, a small island near Puerto Rico in the Caribbean. Warships from the US Atlantic Fleet attacked 1,700 Marines defending the island. The Marine Advanced Base Brigade succeeded beyond expectations

---

5 See Edward S. Miller, *War Plan Orange: The US Strategy to Defeat Japan, 1897–1945* (Annapolis MD: Naval Institute Press, 1991); and Mark R. Peattie and David C. Evans, *Kaigun: Strategy, Tactics and Technology in the Imperial Japanese Navy, 1887–1941* (Annapolis MD: Naval Institute Press, 1997).
6 Holland M. Smith, *The Development of Amphibious Tactics in the US Navy* (Washington DC: History and Museums Division, Headquarters US Marine Corps, 1992), 22.

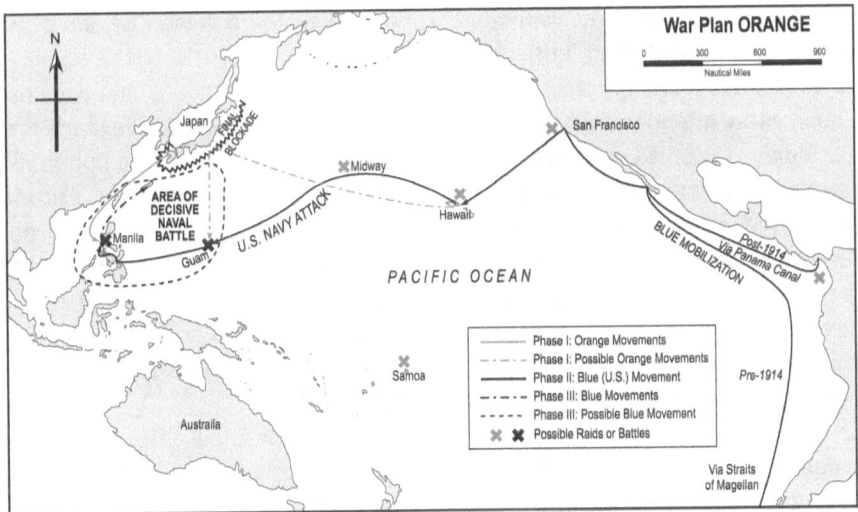

Map 3.1: War Plan ORANGE envisioned as the American naval campaign to defeat Japan.
Source: M.S. Muehlbauer and D.J. Ulbrich, *Ways of War: American Military History from the Colonial Era to the Twenty-First Century*, 2nd ed. (London: Routledge, 2018), 306, map 10.1.

by quickly fortifying the island, harassing the Navy warships and repulsing amphibious assaults.[7]

In his role as the Marine Corps' Assistant Commandant, Colonel John A. Lejeune created an ad hoc war plans committee in 1915. He and three promising Marine captains serving at Headquarters Marine Corps – Ralph S. Keyser, Earl "Pete" Ellis and Thomas Holcomb – comprised the committee. Of these, Ellis emerged as the premier amphibious warfare theorist until his untimely death in 1923. Naval officers like Rear Admiral Clarence Stewart Williams, in his role as head of the Navy's War Plan Division, also recognized the Corps' potential as an amphibious force supporting naval strategy.

Among other issues, Lejeune's war plans committee set to work examining the Navy's evolving strategic needs and determining how the Marine Corps could best fulfil them. By 1916, however, it was not the spectre of a war with Japan or the possibility of amphibious operations in the Pacific that absorbed the Marines' energies. Instead, it was the bloody conflict raging in Europe.

---

[7] Graham A. Cosmas and Jack Shulimson, "The Culebra Manoeuvre and the Formation of the US Marine Corps' Advance Base Force, 1913–1914," in *Changing Interpretations and New Sources in Naval History*, ed. Robert William Love Jr (New York: Garland Press, 1980), 293–306.

Lejeune and his war plans committee worked diligently to determine how new weapons technology and battlefield tactics might affect their service's combat capabilities. Mobilizing and fighting the Great War in France demanded the Corps' entire attention. Although Marines gained invaluable combat experience and enjoyed positive publicity, the war did little to help the Corps maintain its reputation as the nation's amphibious assault and base defence forces. Consequently, Marines worried that their service could be seen as a second American land army that could be disbanded during the postwar demobilization. Why, for example, would the United States need additional ground forces to achieve strategic, let alone grand strategic, objectives? The US Army could play these roles with much larger units and more resources, and so the Marine Corps seemed to be redundant.[8]

Following the armistice that ended hostilities in November 1918, the former belligerent nations tried to return to a normal prewar existence. The physical and psychological scars left indelible marks on those nations. Few families in Europe escaped the loss or maiming of loved ones among 20 million military casualties in the Great War. Meanwhile, the US military suffered a fraction of the other nation's losses with 116,000 Americans killed and 300,000 wounded. Nevertheless, during the 1920s and 1930s, most Americans, whether Republicans or Democrats, recoiled from the bloody experience in France. They did not want to maintain sizeable armed forces because they saw a large military as a precursor to American involvement in future wars. The American people and their elected leaders reduced manpower and budgets of the nation's armed services to prewar levels.[9]

Demobilization saw the US Army and Navy's wartime personnel totals of 3.7 million and 430,000 men reduced by more than 80 percent. Expenditures dropped from $9 billion in 1918 to $1 billion in 1920 and even lower to $250 million in 1925. The US Marine Corps also shrank precipitously from 75,101 men in 1918 to 17,047 in 1920. Many units were deactivated. Among these was the Marine Advanced Base Brigade that had simulated the defence of Culebra during manoeuvres before the war. The Corps' officer cadre fell from 2,462 in wartime to 962 in 1920. Despite postwar anxieties in the 1920s, however, the Marine Corps did survive as an institution. The Marines did not move in the direction of specialized, small unit roles like the British Royal Marines. Instead, recently promoted Major General John A. Lejeune worked to solidify the Corps' place in American naval

---

8 Ulbrich, *Preparing for Victory*, 14–27.
9 See William E. Leuchtenberg, *The Perils of Prosperity, 1914–1932* (Chicago: University Press, 1958).

strategy when he became commandant in 1920. These two lines of efforts were mutually inclusive.[10]

At Lejeune's behest, then-Major Pete Ellis authored two definitive reports on amphibious operations that very next year. His "Navy Bases: Their Location, Resources and Security" and "Advanced Base Operations in Micronesia" served as primers on how advanced bases could support fleet operations. Two decades before the American entry into the Second World War, Ellis predicted with uncanny accuracy the base defence and amphibious assault operations of a coming conflict with the Japanese.[11] Because Japan was "the only purely Pacific world power," Ellis saw it as the only first-rate threat to the United States. His report "Navy Bases" anticipated that Japan would take the offensive and try to capture outlying American island bases. These bases would then form a strategic defence-in-depth.[12] His other report, "Advanced Base Operations," stood as a companion work to "Navy Bases." It outlined a strategy for seizing and defending various Pacific islands, including the Marianas, Marshalls, and Carolines, which the Japanese already controlled. Imagining a potential campaign in the Pacific, Ellis outlined targets for amphibious assaults and anticipated certain naval battles. He suggested that Marines receive simultaneous training for the offensive and defensive components of their mission. Knowledge of how to defend an island against an enemy amphibious assault could only improve the attackers' abilities to make a successful assault in the future, and vice versa.[13]

Both of Ellis' reports cast the Marine Corps in operational roles mandated at the strategic level by War Plan Orange. Later in 1926, the interservice report, "Joint Action of the Army and Navy," similarly called for training, supply and maintenance of Marine units for the following priorities: "For land operations in support of the fleet for the initial seizure and defence of advanced bases and for such limited auxiliary land operations as are essential to the prosecution

---

10 Allan R. Millett, *Semper Fidelis: The History of the United States Marine Corps: The Revised and Expanded Edition* (New York: Free Press, 1991), 654; Matthew S. Muehlbauer and David J. Ulbrich, *Ways of War: American Military History from the Colonial Period to the Twenty-first Century* (New York: Routledge, 2018), 301–04.

11 Dirk A. Ballendorf and Merrill L. Bartlett, *Pete Ellis: Amphibious Warfare Prophet, 1880–1923* (Annapolis, MD: Naval Institute Press, 1997).

12 Earl H. Ellis, *Navy Bases: Their Location, Resources, and Security* (1921; repr., Washington DC: GPO, 1992), 3–6, 10–23, 30, 48.

13 Earl H. Ellis, *Advanced Base Operations in Micronesia* (1921; repr., Washington DC: GPO, 1992), 39–50.

of the naval campaign."[14] The missions constituted the Marine Corps' strategic *raison d'être*, as well as the ongoing keys to survival during an era of restricted resources. In this way, military necessity blended with institutional pragmatism.[15]

Although the Corps' new missions were distilled, two obstacles remained. First was the continued emphasis and commitment to "banana wars" in Latin America. A powerful clique among Marine officers remained dedicated to constabulary security as the Corps' primary role. Lejeune, Russell, Holcomb and others needed to break this internal resistance against amphibious development. Second and external to the Corps, obtaining the resources and writing the doctrine to fulfil that mandate became Lejeune's primary goals in his final years as commandant. Reductions in budgets and personnel, however, persisted throughout the 1920s, despite his best efforts. The Corps was not alone in experiencing these years of famine. The US Army and Navy also suffered from steeply declining budgets.[16]

Then the stock market crashed in the United States in October 1929, and a severe economic downturn engulfed the nation. The Great Depression caused even greater military downsizing of the US military than occurred during the 1920s. The fiscal assault came at the hands of the isolationists, a loose coalition of American politicians and citizen groups with a grand strategy that, for them, was rational. They believed that because the United States erred by entering the Great War, their nation should henceforth remain insulated from military and political entanglements worldwide. Isolationist influence increased during the 1930s. Their message resonated with most Americans, who worried more about feeding, clothing, and housing themselves than about happenings in faraway Asia or Europe. Congress responded to isolationism's political power by slashing personnel levels in the Marine Corps by 25 percent and the Navy by 6 percent, between 1931 and 1934.[17]

In addition to ruining the American economy and choking the military, the stock market crash of 1929 set off a chain reaction that created a global economic depression. Among the nations affected was Japan. Rising unemployment and

---

14 "Joint Army and Navy Basic War Plan – Orange," 6 October 1920, quoted in Frank J. Infusino, "US Marines and War Planning, 1940–1941," (M.A. thesis, San Diego State University, 1974), 145.
15 Allan R. Millett and Jack Shulimson, eds., *Commandant of the Marine Corps* (Annapolis MD: Naval Institute Press, 2004); and Leo J. Daugherty III, *Pioneers in Amphibious Warfare, 1898–1945: Profiles of Fourteen American Military Strategists* (Jefferson, NC: McFarland, 2009).
16 Ulbrich, *Preparing for Victory*, 38–42.
17 Robert Dallek, *Franklin D. Roosevelt and American Foreign Policy, 1932–1945*, rev. ed. (New York: Oxford University Press, 1995), 70, 86; Robert Debs Heinl Jr., *Soldiers of the Sea: The United States Marine Corps, 1775–1962* (1962; repr., Baltimore, MD: Nautical and Aviation Publishing, 1991), 668–69; Gray, "National Style in Strategy," 22.

declining exports put unbearable pressure on the nation's moderate government. The Japanese people reacted in 1930 by electing a militarist government dedicated to an expansionist foreign policy. From the perspectives of watchful Americans at the time, the apparent need for natural resources heightened Japanese ambitions and contributed to Japan's developing grand strategy vis-à-vis the Asian mainland. The Japanese military then invaded Manchuria in 1931. This conquest would, Japanese military and political leaders hoped, bolster the home islands' prosperity, provide outlets for colonists, and reduce European and American influence in the region.[18]

Although the subjugation of Manchuria, or Manchukuo as the Japanese renamed their new territory, defied tenets of the League of Nations, the League could do nothing to stop their advance. In the United States, President Herbert Hoover could merely condemn Japanese aggression. To threaten American military action would have been electoral suicide because isolationists in Congress would never support any decisive response. So even as American military planners, including Marines, tried to lay strategic and operational foundations for a conflict against the Japanese, the political reality in the United States left the American military languishing in worse conditions during the 1930s, and at a time when Japan began asserting hegemony in the Asia Pacific. The US military lacked the means – projecting military force – to stop Japanese expansionism or support the grand strategic end – protecting American influence and interests – in the region. A sizeable majority of the American people lacked the political will to support increasing American military power. This self-inflicted impotence meant that the United States possessed reactive and passive grand strategy by default – thus conceding the initiative to Japan, whose leaders ignored criticisms by both Hoover and the League of Nations.[19]

During the lean years of the Great Depression, the Marines tried to make the most of the resources and expertise within the Corps. They put a premium on military education for officers, to include studying the highest levels of warfare at the Navy and Army schools. These opportunities allowed Marine officers

---

18 See Michael A. Barnhart, *Japan Prepares for Total War: The Search for Economic Security* (Ithaca, NY: Cornell University Press, 1987); Louise Young, *Japan's Total Empire: Manchuria and the Culture of Wartime Imperialism* (Berkeley: University of California Press, 1998); and Yoshihisa Tak Matsusaka, *The Making of Japanese Manchuria, 1904–1932* (Cambridge MA: Harvard University Asian Center, 2001), 312–411. See also Chapter 2 by Yamamoto Fumihito, and Chapter 7 by Jeremy Yellen, in this volume.
19 Robert A. Divine, *The Illusion of Neutrality* (Chicago: University Press, 1962), 23–30; and Fred Greene, "The Military View of American National Policy: 1904–1940," *American Historical Review* 66 (January 1961): 355–77.

to consider operations, strategy and grand strategy in systematic ways, and interact with peers from the Army and Navy. Among the Marines who leveraged the military education was Colonel Thomas Holcomb. As a highly decorated veteran of the Great War, a member of Lejeune's war plans committee in 1915, and a rising star among Marine officers, Holcomb applied past experiences to his studies at the Naval War College in 1930–1931. He exemplified the type of professional development advocated by Neville and Lejeune. Holcomb's year at the Army War College from June 1931 to June 1932 proved to be still more fertile in his development as a senior officer. He worked with other students to formulate plans for attacking enemy nations and defeating enemy forces in fabricated and realistic scenarios. In one course project, Holcomb played the role of naval commander of an American force conducting an amphibious assault on Halifax, Nova Scotia. This assignment reinforced his conviction that a successful landing operation required planning down to the minutest details. Another career officer, Army Major George S. Patton Jr, also worked on this group project with Holcomb. These academic exercises helped Patton during amphibious operations a decade later in the European Theatre of Operations.[20]

Additionally, while working independently at the Army War College in 1932, Holcomb wrote a special report titled "The Marine Corps' Mission in National Defence, and Its Organization for a Major Emergency." He asked an important question about the Corps: "What should be the most suitable organization for a major emergency?" His lengthy answer outlined the principles of seizing and defending advanced bases, and he discussed all aspects of training and supplying Marine units. Amphibious operations represented the Corps' future role in the nation's war plans. No longer did Holcomb see the Marine Corps as a constabulary force fighting small wars, or "other minor operations" as he called them. He instead firmly placed the Corps at the operational level of war and argued that Marines should contribute to strategic requirements in any conflict.[21]

Although Holcomb's report drew on existing ideas and documents, its significance as an original endeavour should not be discounted. In an appendix, he also anticipated the creation of the Fleet Marine Force next year in 1933, the end of the Corps' constabulary duties in Central America in 1934, the creation of a triangular Marine division-sized unit, and lastly the publications of doctrinal manuals – on amphibious assault operations in 1934 and base defence

---

20 AHEC, File Number 386–6, "Report of Committee No 6. Subject: Plans and Orders for the Seizure of Halifax," 29 March 1932, and File Number 388–5, "Analytical Studies, Synopsis of Report, Committee No 5," 2 March 1932.
21 AHEC, File 387–30, Thomas Holcomb, "The Marine Corps' Mission in National Defense, and Its Organization for a Major Emergency," 30 January 1932, 1–4.

operations in 1936. The degree to which Holcomb's report circulated beyond the Army War College's confines is not clear. However, his report did constitute an unofficial blueprint for the Corps' future that he himself followed later in the 1930s and during the war years.[22]

After graduating from the Army War College in 1932, Holcomb's critical academic study and practical experiences prepared him for his next duty station in the Navy Department, where he served as the senior Marine officer on the Navy's War Plans Division and offered advice on amphibious operations and strategic planning relating to War Plan Orange. The Marine units could play offensive or defensive roles as needs arose. In this position, Holcomb embedded his service's operational capabilities in American strategic plans. In so doing, his efforts coincided with the direction that Major General Ben H. Fuller, then serving as commandant, wanted the Marine Corps to go.[23]

Codifying Amphibious Doctrine, Creating Force Structures and Procuring Equipment, 1933–1938

Following Franklin D. Roosevelt's election as president in 1932, the Marine Corps' fortunes slowly began to improve. Roosevelt looked sympathetically on the plights of the Marine Corps and the Navy Department as a whole. This connection dated back to President Woodrow Wilson's administration from 1913 to 1921, when Roosevelt served as Assistant Secretary of the Navy and frequently interacted with the junior officers who later rose to flag officers during the 1930s and 1940s. Other political allies of the US military also assumed leadership roles in Congress. Among the most influential was Carl Vinson, Democrat from Georgia and chairman of the Naval Affairs Committee in the US House of Representatives.

Despite the best efforts of Roosevelt, Vinson and a few others, the US military's funding slipped to low levels. The Marines felt this crunch as their annual expenditures ran between $15 and $25 million from 1935 to 1939 (in then-year dollars). Nevertheless, the decade of famine also saw the flourishing of force

---

22 AHEC, File 387-30, Holcomb, "[Appendix] Discussion of the Marine Corps' Mission in National Defense, and Its Organization for a Major Emergency," 30 January 1932, 13.
23 Miller, *War Plan Orange*, 36, 181, 183, 329, 377–78; Merrill L. Bartlett, "Ben Hebard Fuller and the Genesis of the United States Marine Corps, 1891–1934," *Journal of Military History* 69 (January 2005), 73–92.

structure improvements, doctrinal developments, technological adaptations, and operational planning.[24]

In 1933, the creation of the Fleet Marine Force gave the Corps a platform, albeit modest in size, to support amphibious assault and base defence units. With an amphibious force structure on paper, the Marine Corps needed to codify the amphibious doctrines employed by the Fleet Marine Force in future conflicts. Much work was already underway at the Marine Corps Schools in the mid-1920s when Brigadier General Robert H. Dunlap was commandant. His ideas and efforts and the ideas outlined by Ellis formed the foundations for the *Tentative Manual for Landing Operations* (1934) and the *Tentative Manual for Defence of Advanced Bases* (1936), produced by the faculty and students.[25] The two "tentative" surveys looked to the future, while a separate doctrinal survey titled the *Small Wars Manual* (1935 and 1940) enumerated past lessons from Marine deployments as constabulary units in Latin America.

Classes at the Marine Corps Schools were suspended from November 1933 to May 1934, so faculty and students could compile the *Tentative Manual for Landing Operations*. They completed their work in June 1934. Not only did this resulting document outline lessons learned from past amphibious operations, it also anticipated challenges in future operations. Despite the British amphibious fiasco at Gallipoli during the Great War, for example, American Marines postulated that careful planning, adequate training, and proper equipment could overcome the tactical advantages enjoyed by an enemy defending a shoreline. This document created a rational framework that would facilitate American amphibious assault operations in the Second World War. This process of systematic analysis regarding practical lessons of the past likewise demonstrated the institutional adaptability that has been the hallmark of the Marine Corps.[26]

The *Tentative Manual for Landing Operations* solidified one part of the Corps' mission and fit nicely into War Plan Orange's strategic priorities. Nevertheless,

---

24 NARADC, RG 127, Personnel Department General Correspondence (PDGC) 1933–38, Box 135, File 1975-10, Major General Commandant to Chief of Naval Operations (CNO), "Expeditionary Force," 17 August 1933.

25 MCUA, MCS, *Tentative Manual for Landing Operations*, 1934, History Amphibious File 39; NARADC, RG 127, Box 7, Entry 246, Marine Corps Schools, *Tentative Manual for Defence of Advanced Bases*, 1936, War Plans and Related Material 1931–1944; and Daugherty, *Pioneer of Amphibious Warfare*, 194–212.

26 MCUA, MCS, *Tentative Manual for Landing Operations*, 1934, paragraphs 1.1, 1.2, 1.5, 1.8, 1.22, 3.120; Donald F. Bittner, "Taking the Right Fork in the Road: The Transition of the US Marine Corps from an 'Expeditionary' to an 'Amphibious' Corps, 1918–1941," *Battle Near and Far: A Century of Overseas Deployment – The Chief of Army Military History Conference 2004*, eds. Peter Dennis and Jeffrey Grey (Canberra, Australia: Army History Unit, 2005), 124–25.

this document made no detailed examination of advanced base defence complexities. The landing manual likewise failed to account, in any detail, for the need to defend a captured base. At the same time, Thomas Holcomb received his first star and became commandant of the Marine Corps Schools in February 1935. He supervised the completion of a doctrinal manual on base defence. Because of his previous work on war plans and his military studies, Holcomb brought especially significant knowledge about amphibious warfare to the writing of the Corps' new base defence manual.[27] Although no documents cite Holcomb by name, his tacit influence can be seen in the following lines in the *Tentative Manual for Defence of Advanced Bases*: "Defence of advanced bases will involve the combined employment of land, air and sea forces. Depending on the nature of the hostile attacks against a base, one arm or service may play the major role, but in the event of a general landing attack, the land forces will constitute the basic element of the defence. In any case, the ultimate success of the defence will depend upon the closest cooperation and coordination between the naval defence forces, the shore defence forces and the aviation forces."[28]

This indicated a clearly defined place for the Marine Corps within the US military. Holcomb and the Marines looked up from the operational and tactical levels to the Navy's strategic and the nation's grand strategic objectives. They then formulated operational and tactical doctrines to attain those objectives.

In 1936, Holcomb was promoted to become Commandant of the Marine Corps. He jumped over several more senior Marine generals for several reasons. He maintained a friendship with President Roosevelt dating back to the Great War. He also fitted a particular political profile inside the Corps that placed him in the ascendant clique. He favoured the new dual mission of amphibious assault and base defence over the outmoded mission of constabulary security in small wars. Indeed, his interest in amphibious doctrine and strategic planning dated back 20 years to his membership on Lejeune's ad hoc war plans committee in 1915.[29]

With the Fleet Marine Force established and amphibious doctrines codified, the next stage of readying the Corps for amphibious operations entailed conducting several "Fleet Landing Exercises" between 1934 and 1941. Known as FLEXs, these simulated amphibious assaults and base defences gave the Marine Corps and Navy several opportunities to experiment with doctrines, troubleshoot problems, and field test equipment. The Navy performed several types of

---

[27] David J. Ulbrich, "Document of Note: The Long-Lost *Tentative Manual for Defence of Advanced Bases* (1936)," *Journal of Military History* 71, No 4 (October 2007), 889–901.
[28] MCS, *Tentative Manual for Defence of Advanced Bases*, Preface, no pagination.
[29] Ulbrich, *Preparing for Victory*, 38–42.

long-range shore bombardment, including counter-battery and interdiction fire. The Marines tested existing weapons and vehicles which they might employ in an actual amphibious assault, and they established a defensive position against possible counterattacks from land or sea. In so doing, the Marines discovered deficiencies in the Navy's landing craft. Only with great difficulty could Navy whaleboats or motor launches transport troops from ships through the surf to the beach. These craft offered little protection to their occupants, moved too slowly, lacked seaworthiness in rough surf, and failed to traverse coral reefs. The Marines also found such weaknesses as combat loading, which would need careful consideration to ensure that transport vessels might be packed so that equipment could be off-loaded more efficiently. It became abundantly clear that existing Navy vessels, although essential as weapons platforms, were not ideal for moving men or equipment. It took several years before the Corps found suitable landing craft and the money to pay for them, in part because the Navy would not fund these efforts. Eventually, however, the Marines identified two ideal civilian designs for landing craft – Andrew Jackson Higgins' "Eureka" boat and Daniel Roebling's "Alligator" amphibian tractor. Both could be adapted to military use, and both surpassed anything in the Navy or Marine Corps' existing inventory. Nevertheless, the Corps financial situation did not improve significantly even in the fiscal year 1938. At barely 20,000 officers and men, the Marines could not field a full 16,000-man division.[30]

Most federal expenditures still went to domestic projects. With unemployment rates rising from 16 percent in 1935 to almost 20 percent in 1937, the American public opposed increasing military appropriations. Security threats in Europe and East Asia were either mistakenly assessed or ignored altogether. The isolationists' political power was nowhere more evident than in the passage of the Neutrality Act in May 1937. They tenaciously held onto the belief that a militarily powerful and internationally active United States would provoke a future conflict. That Act maintained most of the stringent restrictions of the previous 1935 and 1936 versions, such as bans on arms shipments and loans to belligerent nations. Consequently, large appropriations were hard to come by, not only for the Marine Corps, but also for the Army and the Navy.[31]

---

[30] MCUA, History Amphibious File 73, "A History of the US Fleet Landing Exercises," report by B.W. Galley, 3 July 1939; Smith, *The Development of Amphibious Tactics*, 25–38.

[31] Robert A. Divine, *Reluctant Belligerent: American Entry into World War II*, 2nd ed. (New York: John Wiley & Sons, 1979), 42–47; and David M. Kennedy, *Freedom from Fear: The American People in Depression and War, 1929–1945* (New York: Oxford University Press, 1999), 355–58.

Meanwhile, tensions in East Asia grew more acute. The same year 1937 represented a watershed because Japanese forces invaded China. The cities of Beijing, Shanghai and Nanjing [Nanking] quickly fell to Japan's control. Unbridled Japanese brutality emerged most vividly in Nanjing in December. They committed unspeakable atrocities against civilian men, women and children living in the city. Chinese men, combatants and non-combatants alike, were executed in the streets. Japanese soldiers raped and murdered Chinese women and girls by the tens of thousands. When their actions brought condemnation from the United States and nations around the globe, the official Japanese position flatly denied any wrongdoing.[32] These conquests did not, however, bring Japan victory in this Second Sino-Japanese War in 1938. Instead, the fighting dragged on and cost more than 1.5 million Japanese casualties between 1937 and 1945. Thus, the quest for natural resources as one component of Japan's grand strategy turned into an endless, winless quagmire.

Over in Europe, Nazi Germany steadily expanded its territory by annexing Austria and occupying the Sudetenland in 1938. Neither France nor Britain stopped Germany. Instead, they appeased the Germans at Munich in September and allowed them to occupy the Sudetenland and then the rest of Czechoslovakia. Their acquiescence emboldened the German dictator, Adolf Hitler, to move still further toward his goal of dominating Europe. The fluid situations in East Asia and Europe reduced the utility of War Plan Orange. The new set of threats dictated that the United States prepare for several unfavourable strategic scenarios, including conflicts with multiple allies and multiple enemies. Herein lay part of the American problem: the grand strategic objective had become muddled over the decades, so as to hardly exist at all. This listlessness, in turn, emboldened the Japanese and Germans.[33]

Nevertheless, yet another iteration of the outmoded war plan appeared in 1938. American strategists, especially in the Navy, remained locked in the mindset that the United States would face Japan as a single adversary. Other assumptions remained consistent with earlier Orange Plans. A "period of strained relations" between the two nations would be accompanied by mobilization of military forces. "Active hostilities" would begin before any declaration of war. The 1938 version presumed that the superiority of the US Navy over the IJN "will be adequate to permit operations by the United States Fleet

---

[32] See Yuki Tanaka, *Hidden Horrors: Japanese War Crimes in World War II* (Boulder CO: Westview Press, 1997); and Joshua E. Fogel, ed., *The Nanjing Massacre in History and Historiography* (Berkeley: University of California Press, 2000).
[33] Mark R. Peattie, *Ishiwara Kanji and Japan's Confrontation with the West* (Princeton NJ: University Press, 1975), 295–308.

to the westward of Oahu." These operations would be the "defeat of Orange through military and economic pressure, made progressively more severe until the national objective [of victory over Japan] is attained." Several pages of the 1938 version then outlined the defence of the Alaska-Hawaii-Panama frontier. In the likely event of a Japanese first strike, American forces in the Philippines and on other islands in the western Pacific would fight holding actions until the US Fleet launched a counterattack and swept across the Pacific to relieve them.[34]

The Japanese, for their part, also planned for a possible war with the United States. Military historians Mark R. Peattie and David C. Evans argue that the Japanese had long followed a "wait-and-react" strategy. The Japanese anticipated three phases for naval operations during the conflict:

> First, searching operations designed to seek out and annihilate the lesser American naval forces . . . in the western Pacific; second, attritional operations against a westward-moving American main battle force coming to assist in the relief or reconquest of American territories there; and third, a decisive encounter in which the American force would be crushed and the Americans forced to negotiate.[35]

American planners conceded that the Japanese would capture American-held advanced island bases in the western Pacific. The Japanese expected to use their bases in the Marshalls, Marianas and other Micronesian islands in offensive and defensive operations. Construction of airfields began on these islands as early as 1934 and accelerated military building programmes thereafter. The Japanese plan to defeat the US Fleet mirrored the American Orange Plan. It seems that each side was playing into the other's hands. Japan's wait-and-react strategy remained intact until 1940, when such priorities as natural resources and such realities as American naval expansion caused the Japanese to shift toward an offensive mindset.[36]

In the United States, however, the outmoded War Plan Orange did not affect the Marine Corps, which continued to play critical roles in the last Orange Plan as well as in subsequent war plans. Because the Corps' contributions were tactical and operational rather than strategic or grand strategic, the Marines kept their focus on defending friendly bases and attacking enemy-held bases.

---

34 NARACP, Microfilm 1421 (M1421), Reel 10, "Joint Army and Navy Basic War Plan – Orange (1938)," Joint Board No 325, Serial 618, 1–18.
35 Peattie and Evans, *Kaigun*, 464.
36 Ibid., 465–73; and D. Clayton James, "American and Japanese Strategies in the Pacific War," in *Makers of Modern Strategy from Machiavelli to the Nuclear Age*, ed. Peter Paret (Princeton NJ: University Press, 1986), 710, 717.

They adapted to the evolving contingencies in 1938.[37] Two significant measures confirmed that year that the US Navy accepted the Marine Corps as its amphibious assault and base defence force. First, the Navy adapted the *Fleet Training Publication 167 (FTP–167)* as its schema for amphibious operations. *FTP–167* drew heavily on the Marine Corps' own *Tentative Manual for Landing Operations* completed in 1934. With some minor modifications, *FTP–167* carried the seaborne service into the Second World War.[38]

Second, US Secretary of the Navy Claude Swanson created a board of naval officers to assess the strategic value of Guam, Wake, Midway and other islands in the light of Japanese threats in the Pacific. By December 1938, the so-called "Hepburn Board" (named for its head Admiral Arthur J. Hepburn) prioritized the Pacific's advanced bases based on their benefits for aircraft, submarines, and surface warships in a potential war with Japan. The board stated that Guam should become a "Major Advanced Fleet Base" for operations supporting American forces in the Philippines and the Western Pacific. Wake and Midway Islands should become patrol plane or supply bases for defensive and offensive actions. The Hepburn Board recommended that construction start as soon as possible on those islands. Apart from recommendations regarding the bases proper, the board directed the Marine Corps to create "defence detachments" to safeguard the island bases against Japanese attacks. This new force structure was the culmination of doctrines outlined in the *Tentative Manual for Defence of Advanced Bases* of 1936.[39]

Other steps raised the Marines' operational readiness in 1938. American entrepreneurialism provided the technological means for effective ship-to-shore transportation during an amphibious operation. The American military possessed no landing craft capable of providing speed, durability and seaworthiness during this transit. Furthermore, any craft needed to be able to land on a beach and extract itself from that beach with relative ease. The commercial designs "Alligator" amphibian tractor and "Eureka" boat provided vessels to meet

---

37 NARADC, RG 127, Marine Corps Budget Estimate FY 1936–1943, Box 1, Entry 248, Commander-in-Chief US Fleet to CNO, 27 July 1937.
38 Allan R. Millett, "Assault from the Sea: The Development of Amphibious Warfare between the Wars – The American, British and Japanese Experiences," in *Military Innovations in the Interwar Period*, ed. Williamson Murray and Allan R. Millett (Cambridge: University Press, 1996), 74–77.
39 NARACP, RG38, Box 50, Strategic Plans Division War Plans Division, Series III, Misc. Subject File, "Report of the Board to Investigate and Report Upon the Need, for Purposes of National Defence, for the Establishment of Additional Submarine, Destroyers, Mine and Naval Air Bases on the Coasts of the United States, Its Territories and Possessions," (hereafter Hepburn Report) 1 December 1938; and David J. Ulbrich, "Clarifying the Origins and Strategic Mission of the US Marine Corps Defense Battalion, 1898–1941," *War and Society* 17, No 2 (October 1999): 90–91.

performance specifications. Both found enthusiastic supporters among Marine officers. Even so, subsistence-level budgets restricted the Marines from supporting the two boat builders. The opportunistic Higgins and Roebling spent their own money to modify their civilian designs to fit the amphibious assault applications.[40]

Looking Up from the Operational to the Strategic Level, 1939-1941

The rising anxieties about Japanese aggression in China and the grim future in Europe made War Plan Orange obsolete in 1939. Yet, no clearly defined connection between American grand strategy and military strategy existed in 1939. This situation left military planners with too many unanswered questions about who the United States' adversaries would be, how a conflict might start, where fighting would mostly likely occur, and what the objectives of the war might be. The final question goes to the heart of grand strategy. And, the stubbornly isolationist American people and US Congress impeded answers from coming from on high.

American strategists reacted by formulating the more realistic Rainbow Plans with five versions addressing possible wartime circumstances that might confront the United States. Rainbow Plan 1 called for a unilateral American defence of the Western Hemisphere north of the Caribbean and Panama Canal Zone. American forces would avoid conflicts in Europe or Asia. Rainbow 2 anticipated that the United States, together with Britain and France as allies, would concentrate their military power in the Pacific against Japan. Europe would remain a lesser strategic priority. Rainbow 3 echoed the ORANGE War Plans, with the United States launching a unilateral offensive against the Japanese in the western Pacific. Rainbow 4, building on Rainbow 1, expected the United States to defend the Western Hemisphere against enemy threats from Europe and East Asia. Lastly, Rainbow 5 envisioned American, British, and French conducting offensive operations to defeat Germany as quickly as possible. The United States, meanwhile, would maintain a strategic defensive in the Pacific against Japan. With Germany defeated, American and Allied forces could shift to

---

40 Timothy Moy, *War Machines: Transforming Technologies in the US Military, 1920-1940* (College Station TX: Texas A&M University Press, 2001), 117-18, 150-57; and Jerry E. Strahan, *Andrew Jackson Higgins and the Boats that Won World War II* (Baton Rouge LA: Louisiana State University Press, 1994), 24-39.

crush Japan. As a result of these new scenarios, the US Army shifted its strategic emphasis towards defence of the Western Hemisphere or war in Europe but away from Japan and the Pacific Ocean. This protective stance resembled something of a grand strategy, but not quite complete. East Asia held little or no interest among most Army planners, except for those who agreed with General Douglas MacArthur's delusional belief that he could defend the Philippines in a war with Japan.[41]

Unlike the Army, however, American seaborne services would fight in all five Rainbow Plans. Marines recognized that they would play active operational roles in the Pacific. It mattered little what the Navy did at the strategic level or the United States did at the grand strategic level. If the US Fleet launched an offensive campaign against the Japanese, then the Marines would capture enemy bases in support of the fleet and defend them against possible counter-attack. Or, if the US Fleet stood on the defensive, then the Marines would also be called upon to hold American bases and recapture any bases taken by the Japanese. This realization, that higher-level decisions would not affect their missions, came as relief to the Marines. After fortifying an island, defence battalions afforded American naval, aviation, and amphibious forces with bases for ongoing operations. The defence battalions therefore fitted the Navy's strategic and the Corps' doctrinal moulds perfectly. The units became part of the Fleet Marine Force and complemented the amphibious assault units therein. As a force structure, the defence battalion represented the culmination of the *Tentative Manual for Defence of Advanced Bases* in 1936.[42]

As American strategies shifted to meet new threats, Marines practised their amphibious assault doctrines and improved their landing craft in additional FLEXs in 1939. The force structure for the other half of the two missions also began to take shape during that summer with the unveiling of the Marine Corps' "defence battalion."[43] As envisioned on paper, this 1,000-man unit boasted an impressive array of weapons: 12 Navy 5-inch artillery pieces, 12 3-inch antiaircraft artillery guns, 48 .50-calibre machine guns, and 48 .30-calibre machine guns. All units would also receive high-intensity searchlights and radar systems. Some defence battalions might even receive larger 7-inch artillery pieces

---

[41] NARACP, JB 325, Serial 642, M1421, Reel 11, "Joint Army and Navy Basic War Plans, Rainbow No 1, 2, 3, 4, and 5," 9 April 1940; Henry G. Gole, *The Road to Rainbow: Army Planning for Global War, 1934–1940* (Annapolis MD: Naval Institute Press, 2003), 108–09, 177–81; Unsigned editorial, "The Idea of the Fleet Marine Force," *Marine Corps Gazette* 23, no. 6 (June 1939): 61.
[42] Ulbrich, "Document of Note," 889–901.
[43] MCUA, Holcomb Papers, Box 6, Hepburn Report, pp. 1–6, 62–70, 87–89; and Chief of Naval Operations to Major General Commandant, 16 February 1939; 1–2.

and aviation resources. The heavy weaponry surpassed that of the typical Marine light infantry unit. Indeed, the defence battalion's firepower rivaled that of a US Navy light cruiser.[44]

Despite the fact that global war appeared ever more likely in 1939, the United States armed forces remained ill-prepared for any conflict. During that summer, the Navy conducted a detailed self-assessment to answer the question, "Are We Ready?" The final report answered "no." According to Chief of Naval Operations Admiral Harold R. Stark, both seaborne services suffered from "critical deficiencies" in manpower, equipment, and weaponry. Of relevance to the Corps was "the lack of Pacific bases west of Hawaii." Stark highlighted the inability of the Navy and the Marine Corps to seize enemy island bases or protect those bases once they had been secured. He did everything he could to alleviate these deficiencies.[45]

The Marine Corps enjoyed an unwavering advocate in Admiral Stark. Knowing the threats, he began deploying Marine units to island bases in the Pacific. He also directed the Corps to created four new defence battalions. This task, however, caused severe strains on Marine personnel. Not only was the Corps still too small to field a full-strength division, but the existing units lacked sufficient supplies. Stark proposed that the Army supply the new units with ammunition. The topic entered the discussion at one of Roosevelt's Cabinet meetings in late August 1939.[46] The Army, itself experiencing shortages, could not satisfy the Navy's needs. The Army's acting chief of staff, Major General George C. Marshall, replied to Stark that furnishing the Corps with sufficient ammunition:

> will impair the efficiency of mobile units of the Regular Army, whose prompt employment may loom as important as those of the [defence] battalions of the Marine Corps under consideration. This applies particularly to .50-calibre armour-piercing ammunition, of which 40 percent of the entire Army stock is requested, and [3-inch antiaircraft] shells, 25 percent of our stock being involved.[47]

---

44 NARACP, RG127, Box 4, Division of Plans and Policies War Plans Section General Correspondence 1926–1942, Unsigned memorandum, "Material Requirements for Four Defence Battalions," 15 August 1939.
45 Ernest J. King, *The US Navy at War, 1941–1945: Official Reports to the Secretary of the Navy* (Washington DC: Department of the Navy, 1946), 37.
46 NARACP, RG127, Box 4, Division of Plans and Policies War Plans Section General Correspondence 1926–42, Stark to Holcomb, 7 August, Marshall to the President, 11 August, and George V. Strong to Marshall, 11 August 1939.
47 NARACP, RG127, Box 4, Division of Plans and Policies War Plans Section General Correspondence 1926–42, Marshall to Stark, 18 August 1939.

The limited stockpiles of ammunition for these two essential weapons caused great concern to Marshall, Stark, Commandant Thomas Holcomb, and the military planners.

Shifting American Strategies, Adaptable Marine Missions, 1939–1941

When German forces invaded Poland on 1 September 1939, the governments of France and Britain quickly declared war on Germany. That same month, President Roosevelt reacted by declaring a "limited national emergency" with two goals in mind: "safeguarding" American neutrality and "strengthening our national defence within the limits of peacetime authorizations."[48] Roosevelt's goal represented a strategy and drew closer to being a grand strategy.

War in Europe caused a rapid succession from Rainbow War Plan 2 with its focus on Japan, to War Plan 3 with its focus on Germany, and finally to War Plan 4. This last change occurred when France surrendered to Germany in June 1940. The strategic situation degenerated to the point that the United States and beleaguered Great Britain opposed the Axis powers of Germany, Italy and Japan. War Plan 4 reduced the United States to secure the western hemisphere against potential Axis incursions. American forces in the Pacific would set up a defensive perimeter from the Panama Canal Zone west to Hawaii and north to Alaska.[49]

The new seminal questions concerned how much and how fast the United States could mobilize and prepare for a conflict. President Roosevelt adopted a short-of-war strategy. The Marine Corps exercised little influence over the changes in strategic plans or processes, so the Marines worked to create combat-ready units adequate to meet those expectations of fighting on one or even two oceans in 1940 and thereafter. Marine units participated in FLEX 6 from January to March 1940. The simulated attacks showed the most significant improvements and achieved the highest level of realism to date, though limitations and deficiencies in equipment and manpower still plagued the Americans. Doctrine intersected with practice as the Marines recognized the following principles as essential to successful assaults: naval gunfire and aviation close air support could be combined with Marine forces to effect an amphibious assault; logistical capabilities could be

---

48 F. Roosevelt, "The 577th Press Conference (Excerpts)," 8 September 1939, in *The Public Papers and Addresses of Franklin D. Roosevelt, 1939*, Vol. 8, (New York: Macmillan, 1941), 483–84.
49 NARACP, Joint Board No. 325, Serial 642, M1421, Reel 11, Joint Army and Navy Basic War Plans, Rainbow Nos. 1, 2, 3, 4, and 5, 9 April 1940.

expanded to supply those troops on shore; and specially trained and equipped defence battalions could secure islands against counterattacks by enemy forces. The Eureka boats and Alligator tractors proved themselves superior to all competitors. Their respective designers, Higgins and Roebling, finally received large contracts for the Eureka and Alligator; and the boat and the tractor would become respectively known as the "Landing Craft, Vehicle, Personnel" (LCVP) and the "Landing Vehicle Tracked" (LVT-1). Even so, funds took a long time to be disbursed to contractors, and the manufacturers procured new materials at an interminably slow pace. This sluggishness vexed Marine leaders like Holcomb and Holland M. Smith.[50]

The final months of 1940 showed that the United States could expect only the British to be a major ally. In the Pacific, token resistance by British and Dutch forces could not hope to halt determined Japanese expansion. Not even Rainbow Plan 5 accounted for the complexity or flexibility of the new circumstances. Stark, Marshall, and other senior military leaders wrestled with a strategic question: how could the United States sustain war efforts of epic proportions against Japan in the Pacific and against Germany and Italy in Europe?[51]

As a possible answer, Stark laid out the United States' future military options in his so-called "Stark Memorandum" of 12 November 1940. He had to balance the Navy's natural strategic emphasis in the Pacific with Europe's growing crisis. "The present situation of the British Empire is not encouraging," he observed. "I believe it is easily possible, lacking active American military assistance, for that empire to lose the war."[52] This set the stage for the rest of his report that outlined the United States' strategic problems, muffled internal debates among naval officers, and encouraged President Roosevelt to state national objectives and choose a grand strategy. The Stark Memorandum rested on two realistic assumptions: American entry in the war was all but inevitable; and Europe constituted the more immediate threat to the United States.[53]

---

50 Strahan, *Andrew Jackson Higgins*, 42–50; and Moy, *War Machines*, 159–60.
51 Stetson Conn, "Changing Concepts of National Defence in the United States, 1937–1947," *Military Affairs* 28, No 2 (Spring 1964): 5–6; and Jonathan G. Utley, "Franklin Roosevelt and Naval Strategy, 1933–1941," in *FDR and the US Navy*, ed. Edward J. Marolda (New York: St Martin's Press, 1998), 53–57.
52 MCUA, Stark, summary notes, Box 142, memorandum for SecNav, p4, 12 November 1940 (hereafter Stark Memorandum).
53 Stark Memorandum, 2–3, 21–24. See Mark M. Lowenthal, "The Stark Memorandum and the American National Security Process, 1940," in *Changing Interpretations and New Sources in Naval History*, ed. Robert W. Love (New York: Garland, 1980), 355–56.

Consequently, the United States adopted a "Germany First" strategy. In so doing, Stark conceded to what the Army's strategic planners wanted when he formulated Plan DOG. In this newest scheme, the war in Europe would be dominated by the Army, leaving the Navy in a subordinate role. The seaborne services would play a larger, albeit defensive, role in the Pacific against Japan. Plan DOG formed the nucleus for the United States' eventual wartime grand strategy.[54]

Although the Marines remained observers of Plan DOG and successive war plans, this did not mean that the Corps was ignored. Stark and the Navy concentrated on strategic and higher objectives, which only concerned the Corps in terms of mobilization timetables and resource allocations, but mattered very little to it in terms of the Marines' missions. Both base defence and amphibious assault fitted the operational requirements of Plan DOG, because they concerned the prosecution of the war. With help from the Marines, the US Fleet would hold the defensive perimeter from Alaska to Hawaii to Central America against Japanese incursions. American forces would maintain communication lines from the Hawaii through Australia, and to British-held Singapore and Malaya. Stark hoped that the Marines could hold Wake, Midway, Guam and other islands for future American operations. Japanese-held island bases would have to be assaulted and defended in turn. Any American islands taken by the Japanese would need to be recaptured by American forces. In sum, the Navy would conduct limited operations utilizing its air, surface, and amphibious forces to maintain the strategic *status quo* in the Pacific. With Germany defeated, the United States could turn its full weight against Japan. In this way, Plan DOG resembled Rainbow Plan 5. In any event, Marines could expect to defend island bases and conduct amphibious assaults in either plan and the preceding War Plan Orange.[55]

Because naval campaigns outlined in the war plans would require larger amphibious assault units, the Corps received authorization to create more viable, larger division-sized units of about 18,000 Marines capable of seizing enemy-held islands. The creation of two paper divisions in the Fleet Marine Force occurred in early February 1941. In July, elements of the US Army's 1st Infantry Division, the 1st Marine Division, and the US Atlantic Fleet made simulated amphibious landings in the Caribbean and at New River, North Carolina. The new force structures and exercises followed the doctrinal principles laid down in the *Tentative Manual for Landing Operations* from 1934 and the *FTP–167*

---

54 Stark Memorandum, 14–15, 23–26; and Lowenthal, "The Stark Memorandum," 358–59.
55 Stark Memorandum; and George W. Baer, *One Hundred Years of Sea Power: The US Navy, 1890–1990* (Stanford CA: University Press, 1994), 154–57.

from 1938. Although these exercises suffered some setbacks, the participating Marines, soldiers and sailors learned what *not* to do.[56] This Marine Corps emphasis on amphibious warfare took on another element as well – institutional survival.

Figure 3.2: Senior American leaders observing a joint Marine Corps-Army amphibious exercise at New River, North Carolina, in July 1941. From left to right: Major General Holland M. "Howlin Mad" Smith of the 1st Marine Division; Major General Commandant Thomas Holcomb; Secretary of the Navy Franklin Knox (looking through binoculars); and then-Colonel Teddy Roosevelt, Jr., of the U.S. Army 1st Infantry Division. These men embodied operational, strategic, and grand strategic perspectives. Courtesy: U.S. Marine Corps University.

During 1941, events propelled the United States towards aligning with the United Kingdom, China, and eventually the Soviet Union, and thus closer to war with the Axis powers. More than 80 million Americans listened to the radio on 27 May as Roosevelt declared a state of "unlimited national emergency." Thousands of kilometres of ocean could no longer guarantee the nation's security. Roosevelt believed that the United States must step up its material aid to Britain. In June, Germany launched Operation Barbarossa against the Soviet Union, and Japan made further inroads into China and greedily eyed resource-

---

56 MCUA, Holcomb Papers, Box 27, H. Smith to Chief of Naval Operations via Major General Commandant, 10 September, Holland M. Smith to Ernest King, 14 November, and Deputy Chief of Staff of the US Army to Chief of Naval Operations, 10 October 1941.

rich Southeast Asia. Because the situation looked so grim in these regions, Congress followed the president's lead by extending the Selective Service Act in August and creating a manpower pool of 46 million men from which to draw for military service. Federal money in 1941 also insured growth of the US military, and the Marine Corps expanded from 38,648 to 50,087 Marines.[57] The weakened isolationists could not stop conscription and appropriations. They could only amend the law to stipulate that American draftees could only be stationed in the Western Hemisphere. The isolationists remained politically active for the rest of the year. Their message, however, fell on increasingly deaf ears. Most Americans accepted preparedness for war as a given in 1941, though they did not necessarily favour their nation's entry into war.[58]

Wartime Epilogue and Conclusions

The last few months of peace in late 1941 passed very quickly. The Marines struggled to ready themselves on far-flung Pacific islands while mobilizing back in the United States. Commandant Holcomb's efforts to meet expectations resembled robbing-Peter-to-pay-Paul as he ordered units with full complements to be split apart to create cadres for separate units. The US Navy and Army's senior leaders experienced similar problems in matching resources to needs.[59]

Although the prewar focus remained Europe, Plan DOG did not relegate American forces to a purely static defence in the Pacific. The Marine Corps and the Navy could do more than protect a line stretching from the Panama Canal to Hawaii to Alaska. The plan allowed much latitude in interpreting what "strategic defence" actually meant at the operational and tactical levels. As part of limited offensive operations, Marine amphibious assault units would move from San Diego to Hawaii and "make preparations and train for landing attacks on Japanese bases in the Marshalls for purposes of capture or demolition, with particular emphasis on plans for the capture of Eniwetok."[60] Marine defence battalions would hold bases on Wake, Midway, Palmyra, Johnston, Samoa, and Guam against potential Japanese attacks, or alternatively bait the Japanese into

---

[57] Dallek, *Roosevelt and American Foreign Policy*, 262–70; and Kennedy, *Freedom from Fear*, 482–85.
[58] Dallek, *Roosevelt and American Foreign Policy*, 309–11.
[59] Ulbrich, *Preparing for Victory*, 92–102.
[60] NARACP, RG38, Box 84, US Navy and Related Operational, Tactical and Industrial Publications 1918–1970, "US Pacific Fleet Operating Plan – Rainbow 5," July 1941, 30.

battle over their control.⁶¹ The US Pacific Fleet could react to Japanese operations in these or other areas, effectively using the bases as bait to draw the IJN into a decisive battle.

While American planners anticipated Japanese attacks on the Philippines, Guam, or Wake, the idea of a massive air attack against the main US Navy and Army bases at Pearl Harbor seemed too far-fetched to be plausible. Sadly, underestimating Japanese skill and audacity resulted in dire consequences on Sunday morning 7 December 1941. On that infamous day, the Japanese caught the Americans unawares and launched a pre-emptive strike that destroyed the US Fleet's battleship component, and laid waste to the ground-based aircraft on Oahu in Hawaii.

In the hours, days and months thereafter, the Japanese launched attacks against Wake, Guam, the Philippines, Midway, Singapore, and the Dutch East Indies. Elements of a defence battalion on Wake Island proved its mettle for more than a fortnight before succumbing to overwhelming Japanese force in late December 1941. Although attacked, Midway was not captured by the Japanese. It was later the scene of a decisive naval battle in June 1942. Indeed, Marines in two defense battalions held Midway against Japanese aerial attacks. Their anti-aircraft fire downed 10 Japanese planes during their aerial assault, which did not destroy Midway's ground defences in anticipation of an amphibious assault in the coming days. It is also worth noting that a defence battalion opposed daily Japanese aerial bombing raids and frequent Japanese Navy bombardments on Guadalcanal, from August to February 1943. These units' performances on Wake, Midway, and Guadalcanal validated the operational missions, force structures and doctrines laid down in the *Tentative Manual for Defence of Advanced Bases* years earlier. Marine tactical successes on Midway and Guadalcanal also fed into operational and strategic objectives.⁶²

The *Tentative Manual for Landing Operations* also proved effective in the island-hopping and leapfrogging campaigns in the Pacific, though not without halting progress, necessary revisions, and heavy casualties. At Guadalcanal, the 1st Marines made an unopposed landing on 7 August 1942. The real challenge came not in the Marines defending their tenuous beachhead and all-important airfield against Japanese air, land, and sea incursions, but rather in the Navy maintaining supply lines to the island. Although suffering severe

---

61 Miller, *War Plan Orange*, 271–72, 284; Baer, *One Hundred Years of Sea Power*, 156–57, 171.
62 See Charles D. Melson, *Condition Red: Marine Defence Battalions in World War II* (Washington DC: History and Museums Division, Headquarters Marine Corps, 1996).

losses in men, aircraft, and ships, the US Navy succeeded in this logistical mission and destroyed the Japanese supply system.[63]

More than a year after the amphibious operation on Guadalcanal, the US Navy's long-anticipated drive across the Central Pacific began in November 1943. The Marines' bloody assault against Tarawa stood as one example of how, even with the soundest doctrines, more logical force structures, and the best available equipment, the fog and friction of war can conspire to bring about near disaster. The hard-won victory on Tarawa provided the Marines and their Navy counterparts with lessons that created a learning curve. The Americans adapted to overcome the corresponding Japanese evolution of tactics in their defensive efforts on Peleliu, Saipan, Iwo Jima, and Okinawa, in 1944 and 1945.

The value of the Marine Corps' doctrines, force structure and equipment extended well beyond the Central Pacific into the Southwest Pacific and to the European Theatres, where the US Army and Navy conducted several large-scale amphibious assaults. The ideas outlined in the *Tentative Manual for Landing Operations* (1934) found their way into Navy's *FTP–167* (1938) and subsequently to the War Department and Army in FM 31–5 *Basic Field Manual – Landing Operations on Hostile Shores* (1941). This Army document's preface stated that it "is based to large extent on the Landing Operations Doctrine, US Navy, 1938. The arrangement of subject matter is similar to the Navy publication and many illustrations are taken from it." The US Army's Chief of Staff General George C. Marshall's name appeared on the signature block "by order of the Secretary of War."[64]

The operational and tactical applications of amphibious assault and base defence in the Pacific and European Theatres remained means to strategic ends as determined by the senior Allied leaders. Although untested in the 1920s and 1930s, the Marine Corps amphibious doctrines laid out in the tentative manuals, new force structures, and equipment procurement proved to be remarkably forward-looking in fulfilling the US Navy's strategic needs in the Pacific and Europe. Looking up from the operational level of warfare, the Marines took their cues from the American strategic plans and adapted their missions to fit. The late military historian Russell F. Weigley saw great value in this process: "Simply by defining the specific problems into which amphibious operations divided themselves, the Marine Corps made it evident that the problems most

---

63 Richard B. Frank, *Guadalcanal: The Definitive Account of the Landmark Battle* (New York: Random House, 1990); and David J. Ulbrich, "Thomas Holcomb, Alexander Vandegrift and Reforms in Amphibious Command Relations," *War and Society* 28, No 1 (May 2009): 113–47.
64 US War Department, FM 31–5 *Basic Field Manual – Landing Operations on Hostile Shores* (Washington DC: GPO, 1941), II.

likely were not insoluble; and the Corps went on to delineate many of the solutions."[65] The Marines helped the Navy achieve its strategic objectives, which in turn made reaching grand strategic objectives possible. Foreign affairs scholar Walter Russell Mead argued that American grand strategy reflects the ever-shifting interests, coalitions, ideologies, and voices in the United States. This mirror analogy, not necessarily symmetric but rather sometimes fuzzy or misshapen, provides a useful way to analyze the relationships of American military force to grand strategy in the interwar years.[66]

---

[65] Russell F. Weigley, *The American Way of War: A History of United States Military Strategy and Policy* (1973; repr., Bloomington IN: Indiana University Press, 1977), 264.
[66] Gesbrink, "The Enduring Grand Strategy of the United States," 4–8.

Brian P. Farrell
Twilight in China: Great Powers and the Defence of Shanghai, 1925–1937

In April 1923, the British Army General Staff informed the British government that in its considered opinion the Army was dangerously small. There was nothing new about this argument, laid out in a memorandum titled *Future Size of Our Regular Army*, which no doubt accounted for the stipulation that "only essential protective requirements have been considered." The paper argued that "the limit of policy reductions in fighting troops has been reached" – the Army should be spared any further economy-seeking reductions. In a *tour de horizon* that analyzed current and possible future requirements in no less than eight locales, including the British Isles, the possibility that it might one day be necessary to send reinforcements to China was barely noted. Trouble with Japan, or a Chinese attack on Hong Kong, were deemed "easily imaginable . . . though remote." In any such case, "these possibilities must be left to be dealt with by emergency measures, if and when they arise."[1] In January 1927, exactly that did "arise." The British government decided to send to China more than a full division of British and Indian troops, plus substantial naval reinforcements and air support. Their mission was to defend not Hong Kong but Shanghai, or at least British interests there. During the far from peaceful interwar years, only the Palestine Revolt of 1936–1939 drew in more British Army reinforcements to meet an emergency. Sending in what became the Shanghai Defence Force (SDF) was expensive and – at the time – controversial, condemned by some as impulsive or aggressive. The controversy was understandable, but the accusation was not fair.

The close call of 1927 in Shanghai, which saw nothing more than minor skirmishing between foreign and Chinese forces, was later overshadowed by serious fighting there between Chinese and Japanese forces in early 1932 – and even more by what in retrospect must be seen as the first major battle of the Second World War, the Japanese conquest of the city in autumn 1937. The battle that did not occur in 1927, due in part to British policy, did however directly influence the chain of events that exploded 10 years later into open war in China – by which time the Great Powers entangled in China had become adversaries, rather than ostensible partners. This was certainly more a China-Japan story than anything else. But crucial and revealing light can be shed on why and how that story led to open war by looking back to Shanghai in 1927,

---

[1] NAUK, CAB24/59/100, CP(200)23, 17 April 1923.

and more closely at the Great Power that, in so many ways, was the man in the middle: the British Empire. The British decision to defend their presence in Shanghai in 1927 by deploying a strong combat force of all arms was part of a wider and carefully orchestrated grand strategy – one that aimed at clearly defined ends, was implemented by calibrated means, and managed by an impressive combination of flexibility and determination. It can in fact be seen as an important answer to an open question: is it possible to have a "grand strategy" if you are not waging open war?

This chapter will address that question. It will explain why the British deployed strong combat forces to Shanghai in 1927, how this fitted into what became a coherent British grand strategy regarding China, and how this affected Great Power relations regarding China and foreign interests therein. It will make three arguments. First, the principal drivers of change were the Chinese themselves, organized and disorganized, military, political, economic, and diplomatic. Second, while it is fair to say that Shanghai 1927 was a military success for the Great Powers, it must also be said that it triggered – and exposed – what eventually became a fatal parting of the ways regarding China. Finally, British policy in 1927 must be seen in the end as more success than failure, and the root of this success lay in the aim to which it was devoted: not to hold any line, or die in any ditch, but rather to manage what could no longer be prevented: change.

As noted in the introduction to this volume, which spells out the definition of grand strategy used in this chapter, the straightforward circumstances of total war – destroy the enemy – were an anomaly outside the world wars. So how could grand strategy be defined, let alone applied, in circumstances nowhere near so clear cut? The problems posed by the need to defend Shanghai in 1927 provide an important example of just that dilemma. The British government did not seek war in China, not on any scale, nor did they aim to destroy anyone. But they decided it was necessary to deploy significant military power, and be ready to use it, in circumstances, they realized, that even in the best-case scenario they could only influence, not determine nor impose. To achieve a good outcome, they required as clear a national policy as they could define; and to realize that policy they had to implement a general programme of action – a grand strategy. The Great Powers, and Chinese political-military forces, clashed in various ways in China in 1927; that clash peaked around Shanghai, and triggered important consequences for the issue at hand: the political arrangements by which all sought to include China in wider agreements to define both regional and global order. Using British experiences as the principal vantage point, working mainly through the so-called DIME model – as also defined in the volume introduction – this chapter will explain how the British forged a coherent grand strategy regarding China in 1927, why it should be seen as more success than failure, and what all that can tell us.

The real root of the problem that erupted over Shanghai in 1927 was that in the 1920s there was no effective central government in China. The most glaring reason for this was the volatile interaction between a declining China and ever more powerful and ambitious foreign Great Powers, from the 1840s onwards. There is no room here for a comprehensive review of what the People's Republic of China (PRC) refers to as the "century of humiliation,"[2] but we do need to note the basics, in order to make sense of what happened regarding Shanghai in 1927. Led by the British, who remained the most visible foreign presence in China, the Great Powers militarily coerced first Qing and then nominally "Republican" China into an interlocking array of treaties, the so-called "treaty system." By this system the treaty powers established a dominating position on the commanding heights of the Chinese political economy. This allowed them to control the points of interface between China and the wider world, and influence both China's internal economy and its political relations with the rest of the world. Enclaves of territory sliced away from China on its coastline, and along the great navigable river systems which dominated its vast interior, provided a physical platform from which to exercise such control and influence. The First and Second Opium Wars, the massive upheaval known as the Taiping Rebellion, the Franco-Chinese War, the First Sino-Japanese War, and the so-called Boxer "Rebellion" were all leveraged by the Great Powers to drag China, by the early twentieth century, into a new and now global order of political economy, on their terms.

Multiple Chinese efforts to respond to these developments did not prevent the decline of the Qing Empire, but the Xinhai Revolution of 1911 that toppled the Qing produced a Republic of China only in name. This new China was politically divided from the start, and could not produce a successor state strong enough to destroy the entangling web of the treaty system. The Great Powers worked to develop a multilateral agenda to globalize a China that none felt they could dominate alone, nor afford to allow any other power to do so. Time and again they found ways to reconcile potential clashes of interest by multilateral

---

2 Standard studies include Robert Bickers, *The Scramble for China: Foreign Devils in the Qing Empire 1832–1914* (London: Allen Lane, 2011), and *Out of China: How the Chinese Ended the Era of Western Domination* (London: Allen Lane, 2017); Odd Arne Westad, *Restless Empire: China and the World Since 1750* (New York: Basic Books, 2015); Jonathan Fenby, *The Penguin History of Modern China: The Fall and Rise of a Great Power 1850 to the Present* (3rd Edition) (London: Penguin, 2019 [2008]).

agreement. By applying the so-called "most-favoured nation clause" to many treaties signed with China, the powers wove an interlocking web of rights and privileges. This all created a complicated and delicate array of relationships not only between the Great Powers and China, but also between the Powers themselves regarding China.[3] Then in 1914 the Great War erupted.

The Great War galvanized the situation in four ways. First, it sparked a steady expansion of the Chinese economy, as Great Powers bought everything China could grow, make, mine, and sell, to wage total war. This whetted economic appetites all around. Second, it pitted those Powers against each other, including within China itself. Bound by a bilateral alliance since 1902, a Japanese and British combined expeditionary force conquered the German enclave around the city of Qingdao [Tsingtao] in Shandong province – and the Japanese retained control of the area. Noticing how distracted the European Powers were by what became a general and total war, Japan tried in 1915 to turn the weak and divided Chinese state into a virtual protectorate, by issuing the notorious 21 Demands. British and American pressure forced the Japanese to dilute this ultimatum to some extent. But wartime need for Japanese help prompted both, in 1917, to give expedient nods to Japanese claims that Japan had a special interest in China that must be acknowledged. Yet neither were ready to agree that this give Japan special licence in China, and both were disturbed by this revelation of Japanese ambitions. Third, the outbreak of the Russian Revolution threw all China north of the Great Wall into uproar, destabilizing the entire northern frontier from Xinjiang to the Amur River – especially northern Manchuria, where Russia retained a sphere of influence despite being painfully defeated by Japan in war in 1905. Finally, Republican China joined the war on the Allied side, seeking fair return for making a mildly useful contribution to final victory over the Central Powers in 1918.[4]

The Paris Peace Conference in 1919 brought the problem to a new level. The Republic of China delegation presented a series of demands that amounted to

---

3 The extensive literature on the treaty system can be sampled by, in addition to sources cited in note 2, Robert Nield, *China's Foreign Places: The Foreign Presence in China in the Treaty Port Era, 1840–1943* (Hong Kong: University Press, 2015); Robert Bickers and Isabella Jackson, eds., *Treaty Ports in Modern China: Law, Land and Power* (London: Routledge, 2016).
4 Xu Guoqi, *China and the Great War: China's Pursuit of a New National Identity and Internationalization* (Cambridge: University Press, 2005), and *Asia and the Great War: A Shared History* (Oxford: University Press, 2017); Minohara Toshihiro et al, eds., *The Decade of the Great War: Japan and the Wider World in the 1910s* (Leiden: Brill, 2014); Christopher Arnander and Frances Wood, *Betrayed Ally: China in the Great War* (Barnsley: Pen & Sword, 2016); Robert E. Hannigan, *The Great War and American Foreign Policy 1914–1924* (Philadelphia PA: University of Pennsylvania Press, 2017).

terminating the treaty system, aiming to restore full Chinese state sovereignty in all respects, from extraterritoriality through enclaves. Politically active Chinese hoped this would be sympathetically received because this conference was expected to establish nothing less than a truly new world order, one organized around principles that categorically rejected those on which the treaty system was built. But the champions of that agenda, led by US President Woodrow Wilson, were not prepared for the jarring clash that arose between those new principles and the prevailing realities on the ground in East Asia. The peace conference did establish the League of Nations, a new permanent body through which a new world order would be organized around such principles as national self-determination and collective security. But over China, the new met the old. The Chinese demanded that Japan return directly and immediately to them the occupied areas of Shandong province and accompanying privileges seized during the war from the Germans – whose treaty rights the Allies voided. The Japanese refused, insisting that their special position in China must be respected, and any eventual return must be negotiated multilaterally, within the larger context of the treaty system, not as a special case. Wilson could not persuade them to give way. But without Japan the League could not hope to position Asia within what was supposed to be a global new order. So Wilson gave way, and refused to press the Chinese demand.[5] The reaction in China changed everything forever.

When news of the Shandong decision reached China, it triggered such a massive wave of protests and riots that historians now widely agree this launched a 4 May Movement that must be seen as the beginning of mass Chinese modern political nationalism.[6] The backlash over the Shandong "betrayal" entwined three trajectories that now drove events in China: entanglements with the Great Powers and their treaty system; political fragmentation; and a genuine explosion in national feeling. From the start this new nationalism focused on the highly visible foreign presence in so much of China as its main target and principal grievance. This changed Chinese politics; those who sought to shape a new China now had to champion this new national feeling. But it also brought an existing political fault line into sharp focus. The government recognized by the Great Powers barely

---

[5] Bruce A. Elleman, *Wilson and China: a Revised History of the Shandong Question* (London: M.E. Sharpe, 2002); Erez Manela, *The Wilsonian Moment: Self-Determination and the International Origins of Anticolonial Nationalism* (Oxford,: University Press, 2007); Tang Qi-Hua, *Chinese Diplomacy and the Paris Peace Conference* (New York: Palgrave Macmillan, 2020).
[6] Rana Mitter, *A Bitter Revolution: China's Struggle with the Modern World* (Oxford: University Press, 2004); Xiaoming Chen, *From the 4 May Movement to Communist Revolution* (Albany: SUNY Press, 2007); Paul French, *Betrayal in Paris: How the Treaty of Versailles led to China's Long Revolution* (London: Penguin, 2014).

controlled the capital city of Beijing; since 1915 it had been little more than a pawn in a power struggle triggered by the Xinhai Revolution. The collapse of central government devolved effective political and administrative power to the existing network of regional governors. Many had, or soon secured, command authority over military forces raised in their regions; most of these "armies" came to be organized around a dominant individual leader. These so-called *tuchuns* revived a very old Chinese tradition by jockeying for power and position. Some tried to prevent the construction of an effective central government; some tried to establish such a government; still others tried to promote a more federal system. This created a confusing civil, political, and sometimes military struggle that split the country into competing power centres, a situation often described as a conflict between so-called "warlords."[7] These "warlords" faced a daunting challenge to try to forge any truly national movement from a regional base, but there was one political "party" that aspired to do just that: the *Guomindang* [Kuomintang], or Nationalist Party of China. Led by Dr Sun Yat-sen, it crafted an ideological programme that called for a unified, sovereign and independent China, under a strong central government. From its power base in the southern province of Guangdong [Canton or Kwangtung], the Guomindang declared itself to be the legitimate government of China. All these developments put the treaty powers in a much more difficult situation.

The Great Powers confronted an escalating mass nationalism that focused on destroying the system by which they all related to China, and each other. Politically, they were committed to recognizing a weak regime that was now itself compelled by domestic anger to describe the treaty system as a network of chains enslaving China that must be broken, once and for all. And despite the fact that both Japan and China joined the League, the United States did not – and in any case the League's core principle of self-determination fundamentally challenged the core principle of the treaty system: established treaty rights. Something had to give. This gap in the new world order surfaced in late 1921, at a conference held in Washington, at which the world focused on discussions to prevent a naval arms race.

Two of the principal powers involved, the British and Japanese, tried to prevent the China question from even being discussed at the conference. But American insistence plus the logic of the situation – the object of the conference was nothing less than to build a new security order for the Asia-Pacific

---

7 Hsi-sheng Chi, *Warlord Politics in China 1916–1928* (Stanford CA: University Press, 1976); David Bonavia, *China's Warlords* (Oxford: University Press, 1995). Frank Dikotter, *The Age of Openness: China Before Mao* (Berkeley: University of California Press, 2008), is a strong revisionist critique of the "warlord" construct.

region, something that subsumed naval armaments – placed China on the agenda. There was no avoiding this. The Great Powers worried about a future naval war in the Pacific, but such a conflict would not be about the Pacific. It would be about the question that now threatened to divide them all: the future of China. This gave the Chinese delegation, once again representing a government that barely functioned outside Beijing, the chance to pick up where it left off in Paris.[8] It did so, to decisive effect.

The Chinese delegation identified 10 objectives, including the immediate return of Shandong province and the progressive dismantling of the treaty system as soon as possible, as "national demands." They exploited a glaring loophole: unless the Powers could reach a viable agreement regarding how to respond to new pressures in China, any other security agreements they made would not prevent, sooner or later, a major war over the future of East Asia.[9] The point was fundamental. Japan reluctantly agreed to return Shandong, but to get a workable agreement the Powers had to make promises in bad faith that now created a new, and very fraught, hostage to fortune. In what became known as the Nine Power Treaty the signatory powers, including China, agreed to respect the territorial integrity and sovereignty of the Republic of China, preclude any further impositions on it, and negotiate the eventual termination of the treaty system, starting with extraterritorial privileges and foreign control over tariffs. This resembled the "Open Door" policy the United States had been espousing since 1899, which called on all Powers not to carve out exclusive political and economic privileges in any part of China. And it did commit the Powers in principle to ending the treaty system. But on the other hand, the Powers pointedly noted that until China had an effective central government that could suppress "warlordism," and pull China together, the final agreements by which the treaty system would be terminated could not be concluded – there would be no one to enforce them. And Japan refused to renounce the claim it had a special position regarding China that must be respected come what may. The Washington Conference ended in February 1922 with that most dangerous

---

[8] NAUK, FO412/118, General Survey of Political Situation in Pacific and Far East with Reference to the Forthcoming Washington Conference, 20 October 1921; *Documents on British Foreign Policy, 1919–1939, 1st Series, Vol. XIV, Far Eastern Affairs, 1920–22*, (London: HMSO, 1966); *FRUS*, 1921, Vol. 1; Yamato Ichihashi, *The Washington Conference and After* (Stanford CA: University Press, 1928).

[9] *FRUS*, 1922, Vol. 1; *League of Nations Second Year Book 1 January 1921–6 February 1922*, 257–61; W.W. Willoughby, *China at the Conference: A Report* (Baltimore MD: The Johns Hopkins Press, 1922); A.E. Kane, *China, the Powers and the Washington Conference* (Shanghai: The Commercial Press, 1937).

type of diplomatic agreement: one that could be, and was, read in different ways by different parties.[10]

The Washington Agreements actually made the whole situation worse. Chinese opinion in general took the Nine Power Agreement as a promise by the Powers to move in good faith towards ending the treaty system. But China remained fragmented, indeed sank into a multiparty civil war. The notional government in Beijing had to press for the promised treaty revision negotiations, but the signatory Powers – egged on by their nationals living and working in China – made it obvious that none really intended to move towards negotiating in good faith. Each, at best, hid behind China's escalating civil war to justify stalling their commitment.[11] In this volatile context, a decisive factor now emerged, one that henceforth set the pace: the Guomindang launched a determined bid to unify China under its leadership.

In several ways the Guomindang resembled the various *tuchun* forces, being a quite loose coalition of regional leaders grouped around a rather shaky power base in Guangdong. But Sun Yat-sen had higher national stature than any other leader, and the platform he presented as the party agenda focused squarely on national goals. This did not impress the Western Powers very much. They saw Sun and the party not as a potential central government but as yet another contending regional force – posing a potentially radical threat to their own interests, marked by erratic, unreliable, and bickering leadership. So they rejected repeated appeals by Sun for support for his national agenda. That created an opportunity. It was seized in 1923 by an old rival now dressed in new clothes: Revolutionary Russia, now the Soviet Union. The new Bolshevik state was frozen out of both the Paris and Washington Conferences by the other Powers, which saw it, with good reason, as a clear and present danger to the wider global order. Struggling to survive, seeking to distract the Great Powers by causing them problems elsewhere, the Soviets identified China as a region where they could profitably pursue both goals. Long discussions led to a breakthrough, shaped by Soviet tactical goals. The Soviets renounced all the old treaties between

---

10 NAUK, FO412/116, Conference Records, Vol II, Pacific and Far Eastern Questions, November 1921-March 1922; *FRUS*, 1922, Vol. 1; Erik Goldstein and John Maurer, eds., *The Washington Conference 1921–1922: Naval Rivalry, East Asian Stability and the Road to Pearl Harbor* (London: Routledge, 1994).
11 NAUK, FO412/118, The Results of the Washington Conference, 27 March 1922; *FRUS*, 1923, Vol. 1; Stanley K. Hornbeck, "Principles and Policies in Regard to China," *Foreign Affairs*, Vol. 1, No. 2, 1922; Tsurumi Yusuke, "The Difficulties and Hopes of Japan," *Foreign Affairs*, Vol. 3, No. 2, 1924; Akira Iriye, *After Imperialism: The Search for a New Order in the Far East 1921–1931* (Cambridge MA: Harvard University Press, 1965), Introduction, Chs. 1–2.

the Russian Empire and China, pledging to return all territorial concessions and end all extraterritorial privileges. They accepted Sun's argument that national re-unification must come before social revolution in China. So, through the Comintern, they directed the young and small but dynamic Communist Party of China to form an alliance with the Guomindang, as a subordinate partner in a new "United Front." And they provided concrete assistance to help Sun complete a "National Revolution," to unify a sovereign China.[12]

Soviet assistance ranged from funds, munitions, and equipment to transportation, intelligence, and propaganda. But their most important contributions were advice and leadership, provided by two individuals in particular. Mikhail Markovich Borodin, an experienced political agent, arrived in October 1923 to lead the Comintern mission. He was reinforced the following October by an experienced senior Red Army officer, General Vasily Konstantinovitch Blyukher – who became widely known by the alias Galin – sent to help develop the military power of the "National Revolution." The mission these two men led helped turn the Guomindang from a disorganized and motley collection of squabbling individuals and factions, that could not make any forward progress, into something that began to look like a semi-organized and partly disciplined organization working collectively on a common plan – from a movement into a party, with some structure, focus and direction. Borodin steered the Chinese Communists into the new coalition and inspired the Guomindang to develop a more radical programme, build a wider urban network of support, and launch an aggressive anti-foreign propaganda campaign, to tap into, and harness, rising national feeling. He also helped establish the Whampoa Military Academy in May 1924, to train the leaders of a new national military force. Blyukher took on the task of helping to build what became in May 1925 the National Revolutionary Army (NRA). The "grand strategy" of the National Revolution had already been defined by Sun: launch an all-out "Northern Expedition," by which the Guomindang would literally march north from its base in Guangdong, defeat or digest regional forces that it could not co-opt, and unify China under its direction. The Soviet advisers could not prevent Sun from launching several false starts, but did help the party consolidate its position in the south, and build up the strength it needed to carry out any such design.[13]

---

12 Iriye, Part One; Dan Jacobs, *Borodin: Stalin's Man in China* (Cambridge MA: Harvard University Press, 1981); Alexander Pantsov, *The Bolsheviks and the Chinese Revolution, 1919–1927* (Honolulu: University of Hawaii Press, 2000).
13 NAUK, CAB24/174/40, CP341(25), 9 July 1925; *FRUS*, 1924, Vol. 1; Iriye, Part One; Jacobs, Chs. 10–13; Arthur Waldron, *From War to Nationalism: China's Turning Point, 1924–1925* (Cambridge:

Then in March 1925 Sun died of cancer. That left the party divided about how to move forward, and under whose direction. Events soon provided some answers.

The Great Powers were now seriously worried about the situation in China. The Soviet intervention provoked suspicion and rising alarm, fuelled by intelligence reports about Borodin and Blyukher. The growing intensity of Chinese national feeling, the expansion of the Guomindang, and long delays in launching the promised treaty negotiations all made the situation combustible. The British, the most visible foreign presence in China, came under the most intense pressure, ranging from strikes and riots to a long boycott of trade, in and around Guangzhou and Hong Kong. At the same time the British identified themselves, with reason, as the principal target of Soviet efforts to foment trouble around the globe. They became inclined to see the Guomindang as a Soviet proxy being built up to stampede them and the other Powers out of China, by detonating a social revolution. This volatile situation blew up in May 1925, when a labour dispute in a Japanese-owned cotton mill in Shanghai erupted after a Japanese foreman shot and killed a Chinese demonstrator. One thing led to another, and on 30 May British subjects serving in the Shanghai Municipal Police (SMP) fired into a huge crowd of Chinese demonstrators protesting the cotton mill incident, killing 12. This triggered the chain of events that led to crisis over Shanghai in 1927.[14]

The challenge the British had to face down in 1927 was multifaceted, but was driven by the Guomindang. The eruption of national anger over the 30 May Incident gifted the United Front propaganda material that it skilfully exploited to foment an intense anti-foreign mood that, this time, did not "die down." Carried by this political wave, squabbling, feuding and bickering, but also building up military forces and ratcheting up its propaganda offensive, the Guomindang finally launched the real Northern Expedition on 9 July 1926. Their first phase objective was the great Yangtze River and its system of tributaries, the principal artery of trade and movement within China and the great line of division between north and south. The possibly 100,000 troops moving north were in principle

---

University Press, 1995); Bruce A. Elleman, *Modern Chinese Warfare, 1795–1989* (London: Routledge, 2001), Ch. 10.

14 NAUK, CAB24/176/17, CP518(25), 28 November 1925; 24/181/3, CP303(26), 28 July 1926; Nicholas Roosevelt, "Russia and Great Britain in China," *Foreign Affairs*, Vol. 5, No. 1, 1926; William Roger Louis, *British Strategy in the Far East 1919–1939* (Oxford: Clarendon Press, 1971), Ch. IV; Meyrick Hewlett, *Forty Years in China* (London: Macmillan, 1944); Edmund S.K. Fung, *The Diplomacy of Imperial Retreat: Britain's South China Policy, 1924–1931* (Oxford: University Press, 1991), Ch. 3; Phoebe Chow, *Britain's Imperial Retreat from China, 1900–1931* (London: Routledge, 2017), Chs. 4–5.

outnumbered at least five to one by the combined forces of the even more fractious coalitions of "warlords" opposing them, operating nominally on behalf of the notional national government. But these forces were stronger north of the Yangtze, and in any case the advance unfolded amidst much confusion all around. Military encounters took place here and there, but the rising tide of nationalism stirred by the United Front did much to sweep the way clear, subverting, imploding, and hollowing out opposition. Regional commanders switched sides, cities "fell" with little fighting. By October the NRA overran the strategically pivotal riverport tri-city junction of Wuhan – combining the port cities Wuchang, Hankou and Hanyang – and moved in growing strength into the Central Yangtze Valley.[15]

This raised the alarm. Central China was the principal area of British interest, and the Yangtze system was the hub of the entire treaty port network. Alarm became emergency on 3 January 1927 when a huge crowd of angry civilians besieged the small British Concession at Hankou. Guomindang troops at first seemed to try to keep them under control, but on 5 January appeared to join forces with the "mob," using them as a weapon to storm the Concession in massive numbers. The small contingent of British Royal Marines sent as a landing party by warships, to protect British lives and property, decided not to resist this onslaught, but rather to evacuate their nationals and abandon the enclave. The British government endorsed this decision after the fact, but now confronted a moment of truth.[16] Coming from three directions, the NRA was advancing towards the cornerstone of the British presence in China: Shanghai.

The crisis over Shanghai ran from January into July 1927; its repercussions lasted much longer. The grand strategy the British applied to manage the crisis featured three defining characteristics. First, it was determined by a clear national policy, which was itself crafted after a careful review of the geopolitical situation. Second, it was implemented along complementary lines of diplomacy, military intervention, and political management. These were all informed by multiple channels of intelligence that evaluated political, military, and economic considerations. Finally, it was directed by a flexible chain of command and decision-making system that harnessed political, military, and diplomatic officials,

---

15 Donald A. Jordan, *The Northern Expedition: China's National Revolution of 1926–1928* (Honolulu: University Press of Hawaii, 1976); Iriye, Ch. III; Jacobs, Ch. 14; Hans van de Ven, *War and Nationalism in China 1925–1945* (London: Routledge Curzon, 2003).
16 NAUK, CAB23/54/1, Cabinet Minutes, 12 January 1927; FO371/12449, Correspondence, China, January 1927; H.R. Isaacs, *The Tragedy of the Chinese Revolution* (Stanford: University Press, 1961 (1938)), Chs. 5–7; Louis, Ch. IV; Jordan, Chs. 9–11; Jacobs, Chs. 14–15.

on the spot in China and at home in the United Kingdom, to work in tandem to achieve national goals. Naturally there were shortcomings. Political intelligence was often dangerously incomplete; recurring arguments arose over what to do next and how; some important aims were not achieved, some capabilities were not fit to purpose. But in the end this was a success story, due more than anything else to a cardinal insight: the clear understanding of what the British Empire could not achieve and therefore should not attempt.

National policy was determined before the explosion at Hankou, and not revised. It revolved around the most important insight of all: China was going to change fundamentally. Therefore the best the British could hope to do was try to manage that change as much as they could, to preserve their established position for as long as possible and then to revise that position as favourably as they could. This insight involved evaluating not only the situation in China and its likely direction, especially British relations with China, but also the impact of both on the Great Powers, and their relationships with each other regarding China. By 1926 the problem became defined by four perceptions. First, the civil war in China now seemed likely to burst its bonds, and anti-foreign sentiment, focused on the British, was certain to intensify. Second, the Powers could not forge any common position on how to cope with growing pressure to implement the promises made in Washington in 1922. Third, this all made it possible that change in China might provoke another major war between Great Powers, as it had in 1904. Finally, this therefore threatened the most fundamental of all British national interests: the stability of the global order. British interests in China itself were useful, and supported by a vocal domestic lobby. But they were not by themselves fundamental to British security. But global stability was. The British Empire was a satisfied power. Its overriding strategic interest was to prevent any violent challenge to the global political economic order it did so much to build. Major war between Great Powers, or social revolution in an important country, were therefore by definition threats to the security of the Empire. And in the mid-1920s the region of the globe that seemed most likely to trigger one of those threats was China.

The British decision-making system that formulated national policy and grand strategy was quite likely at that time the most effective in the world, all things considered. At the pinnacle was collective government by a Cabinet of ministers, answerable to Parliament, led by a Prime Minister with largely undefined authority. Much depended on what the individual made of the office, but the convention was government by shared Cabinet responsibility and deliberation. The Cabinet of the day led a Conservative party government that enjoyed a large majority in Parliament, helmed by Prime Minister Stanley Baldwin, whose principal interest and expertise lay in domestic affairs. But he led a strong and experienced team of ministers, and had the self-confidence and political strength to allow them to take the lead in foreign affairs. They included Winston Churchill as Chancellor of the Exchequer, former Prime Minister Arthur Balfour – by now an elder statesman, but also the British plenipotentiary who negotiated the Washington Agreements in 1922 – and Austen Chamberlain as Foreign Secretary. These men wanted to preserve strong British interests in China for as long as possible, but were also crystal clear on the global fundamentals of the British position, and on the need to manage change. Chamberlain and his department, the Foreign Office (FO), which boasted a number of experienced officials well informed about China, played the lead role in driving British policy towards China. The FO proactively led a collective effort to handle the crisis in China, consulting constantly and working effectively with other interested parties, from Cabinet level downwards.

The most important interested party was the military. No Royal Air Force (RAF) units were stationed in China. In 1925, the British Army presence there was small, only three infantry battalions. Two were deployed to garrison Hong Kong, and one, as per the Boxer Protocol, to protect specific privileges: the Legation in Beijing, the Concession in Tianjin [Tientsin] – the nearest port to the capital – and the lines of communication between the two, along the Hai [Pei-ho] River. The Royal Navy (RN) took the lead in the region, making the Vice Admiral in command of the China Station the principal British military officer in China. His flotilla comprised both riverine gunboats and blue water warships, including seven cruisers.[17] These "men on the spot" were deployed to protect the British presence in the region; that was understood to mean treaty rights, British-owned property, and persons. In "normal" times they relied on their presence as a deterrent, reinforced by small-scale shows of force when necessary. They reported to the service ministries in London. But through an important innovation launched in 1923, the integration of professional military advice and direction into national policy now ran through a more coordinated chain of command. The professional heads of the three armed forces were combined into a standing subcommittee of the Cabinet, the Chiefs of Staff Committee (COS), tasked to provide coordinated military advice to the Prime Minister and Cabinet, and implement government directions. The innovation quickly bore fruit, at least in part because it reinforced the existing tendency to organize around collective deliberation. The Cabinet could also call on the Committee of Imperial Defence (CID), established in 1902, comprising the Prime Minister and whomever he saw fit to co-

---

17 Initial reinforcements were en route when the Hankou Incident erupted: one infantry battalion from Gibraltar and one cruiser squadron from the Mediterranean. NAUK, CAB53/12/6, COS19(25), 25 June 1925; WO106/83, Chronology of Events in connection with the despatch of troops to China, December 1926-April 1927, 30 April 1930.

opt, for advice on defence-related problems. This was intended to ensure that any issue concerning imperial defence was addressed by all branches of the state that might be affected – within a framework that upheld the supremacy of civil government, but enabled it to draw continuously on considered professional advice. By long-standing convention, the FO took the lead to define the policy that any resulting grand strategy was formulated to achieve. And by long-standing practice, the FO also consulted closely with its own "men on the spot," ranging from the British Ambassador to China – the senior British executive officer in the region – through the network of Consuls stationed at the treaty ports. Finally, the chains of command led by the Ambassador and the Commander-in-Chief China Station usually consulted closely with each other.[18]

This was how the system was designed to operate. As with any such system, in the end everything depended on how it was used in practice. No design can rule out problems such as personality clashes, bureaucratic turf wars, painfully slow response time, wishful or group thinking, deliberate disobedience – the list is long. But this British system gave the government the chance to formulate policy, and implement grand strategy, that emerged from a multi-layered evaluation of all relevant considerations by all interested parties. Its challenge was to combine the strengths of collective deliberation and careful consultation with the ability to be realistic, responsive, flexible, and clear. That ultimately made the men, not the machine, the crucial factor; and attitude, not structure, the vital dynamic.

As noted, British national policy towards China was publicly redefined before the Hankou evacuation triggered a major crisis. It emerged through a FO review of the political situation, triggered, in summer 1926, by two things: the Northern Expedition, and the Chinese backlash against the failure of negotiations to restore control over tariffs to China, as pledged in the Nine Power Agreement.[19] Cabinet agreed that a dramatic public change in British intentions towards China was now necessary. The policy was announced to the world in December, earning it the label "the Christmas Memorandum." The British government preferred to try to manage the treaty system in step with the other Great Powers, to work with the rising powers in China to slowly dismantle it – just as the Powers worked together to build it in the first place. But Chinese nationalism, aimed at the British, now seemed well ahead of multilateral efforts

---

18 Louis, Ch. IV; Norman Gibbs, *Grand Strategy: Volume 1: Rearmament Policy* (London: HMSO, 1976); Fung, Introduction.
19 NAUK, CAB24/181/8, CP308(26), 30 July, 24/182/5, CP380/26, 4 November 1926; FO371/11653, Correspondence, China: Special Tariff Conference, July 1926; Lionel Curtis, *The Capital Question of China* (London: Macmillan, 1932); Louis, Chs. IV–V.

to respond. To safeguard British interests, the British decided they must carve out a new middle position between these two forces, from which they might be able to keep both in play. The memorandum reaffirmed the British commitment to the Washington promises to negotiate the end of the treaty system. While it repeated that this could only be accomplished by working with a stable and effective central government of China, it also promised to treat all relevant Chinese requests as sympathetically as possible, in order to help build such a government. More provocatively, it invited the other Powers to join the British in declaring that "they desire to go as far as possible towards meeting the legitimate aspirations of the Chinese nation."[20]

This was a change in tone, but a decisive change. The Americans sympathized with the commitment to the Washington process, but were annoyed by what looked like a grandstand play, and inclined to keep their own counsel. The French and Japanese resented what they saw as a ploy to curry favour with the Chinese at their expense, one that might disrupt the treaty system. And most British residents in China reacted in outrage, condemning the policy as a complete surrender – which ironically made it appear more sincere.[21] The British Empire now had a policy: provided it could be done by agreement and in measured steps, it would help bring about the promised changes in China, hopefully with as much multilateral management as possible. That policy had two clear objectives. First, it aimed to preserve existing British interests for as long as possible, and to enable them to be adapted to a new China as advantageously as possible. Second, it aimed to ensure that change unfolded without provoking a level of political or military violence that might trigger a social revolution or a major war. The flip side to this definition of political objectives through diplomatic expression was the question of military protection. The military response closely resembled the political: the British wanted to avoid being wrong-footed by fast-paced change in China, and had already identified their military "bottom line."

When anti-British sentiment exploded in China in summer 1925, the COS reviewed military options regarding the defence of British Empire interests in the country. Admiral of the Fleet David Beatty, First Sea Lord, expressed their fundamental evaluation: if the preponderant weight of national power in China, organized or otherwise, launched a determined campaign to destroy the treaty

---

20 NAUK, CAB24/182/28, CP403(26), 30 November 1926; Curtis, Ch. XX; Louis, Chs. IV–V; Chow, Ch. 6.
21 NAUK, FO371/12449, Correspondence, China, January 1927; *FRUS*, 1927, Vol 2; Louis, Ch. V; Fung, Ch. 5; Goto-Shibata Harumi, *Japan and Britain in Shanghai, 1925–1931* (London: Macmillan, 1995); Bickers, *Out of China*, Ch. 2.

system, and evict the foreign enclaves from which it operated, the only way the treaty powers could stop this was if Japan intervened in great force to protect it. No other power had the military capability to intervene with enough force to prevent such an outcome. While the FO reviewed the political situation in autumn 1926, the COS considered military plans to defend British interests in central China. They assumed it would be necessary to combine any British reinforcements sent to the country within a larger multinational formation, led ideally by the Japanese. When the evacuation of Hankou triggered a crisis, the Cabinet called on the COS to appreciate the situation, with particular reference to Shanghai. They began by reiterating their advice of July 1925:

> Offensive action in China on a large scale is not possible for the British Empire acting alone, and finality could not be hoped for from any operation within our capacity. Offensive action on a large scale can only be international, and even on that basis it would probably be unprofitable, except possibly for Japan, who must be the predominant partner.

The situation since then had deteriorated, and regarding Shanghai the main point was clear:

> We wish to emphasize that it is impossible for Great Britain to undertake the defence of the Settlement single-handed . . . Even if it were possible we should greatly deprecate isolated action except as the very last resort, as it would inevitably involve us in a war in which, in all probability, the whole of China would be united against us, with disastrous results to our vast interests throughout the East.

To preclude all doubt the COS presented a one-sentence general conclusion: "The importance of securing international cooperation in any action against China, whether economic or military, cannot be too strongly emphasized."[22]

This appeared to connect the national policy objective – engineer slow, controlled and beneficial change – to the diplomatic strategy – tilt towards the greater pressure of Chinese nationalism while not burning multilateral bridges – with the military strategy – assemble a coalition of the treaty powers, to prevent the situation from escalating beyond control. But appearances were not only slightly deceiving, events were also moving very fast. Cabinet considered this COS paper of 11 January 1927 the next day; that same day, they received a telegram from Vice-Admiral Reginald Tyrwhitt, Commander-in-Chief China Station, warning that the threat was escalating so rapidly the only way to prevent a repeat at Shanghai of what happened in Hankou was to send powerful reinforcements to the city, led by at least a full division of ground combat forces. The plan the COS were crafting

---

22 NAUK, CAB53/12/6, COS19(25), 25 June 1925; CAB24/184/4, CP4(27) Revise, 15 January 1927.

was to commit perhaps a brigade of British reinforcements to an international force of at least one division in strength; but this called for a massive increase in that commitment, and made a crucial point: the clock was ticking. The Guomindang advance now seemed to be escalating in violence and accelerating in speed, which would make the threat dire: because the nearest British reinforcements could only come from India, unless strong forces were set in motion quickly they might not arrive in time to prevent an onslaught into Shanghai. Cabinet realized this was a moment of decision and deliberated long and hard. Signals on the ground were mixed: the other Powers showed some concern about the threat to Shanghai, and their men on the spot inclined to a stronger response, but the home governments seemed less determined. Cabinet directed the FO and its diplomats on the spot to try to forge a coalition of the powers, considered the utility of imposing an economic blockade on the Guomindang, but also directed the COS to prepare for possible troop movements to the area, and agreed to review developments after consulting the British Ambassador in China, Miles Lampson. Lampson backed the COS report, but also supported Tyrwhitt's warning that the situation was about to escalate beyond control. This now triggered the assumption that Chamberlain directed the COS to adopt, when preparing their report: "that we should approach this subject on the assumption that Shanghai is to be held in all circumstances."[23]

Cabinet made the cardinal decisions at its next meeting on 17 January. Relying on an economic blockade could not be effective, it would hurt British interests more than the Guomindang. Conversations about military cooperation must continue, especially with the Japanese, but such cooperation could not be relied on. Given that more than 80,000 NRA troops might close in on Shanghai before the end of the month, and Shanghai was so important to the entire treaty system that British military and civilian officials on the spot all agreed it must not be abandoned, Cabinet drew the line:

> That regard for the protection of British lives no less than the disastrous effect which the surrender of Shanghai to violence would have on the British position in China, Japan, India and throughout the East, precluded the possibility of basing any policy either on the evacuation (even if that were possible) or on the surrender of Shanghai.

The Guomindang should now be informed:

> that we were prepared to go a very long way towards meeting their desires in regard to treaty revision, provided that they in turn were prepared to negotiate a settlement. But if they refused to negotiate, and insisted on recovering the concessions by force, whether

---

[23] NAUK, CAB23/54/1, Cabinet Minutes, 12 January 1927; FO371/12449, Correspondence, China, January 1927; C.W. Gwynn, *Imperial Policing* (London: Macmillan, 1939), Ch. VIII.

by mob violence or by troops, [they] should be told that we should take such steps as we thought fit. In that event we should hold Shanghai, preferably in concert with other Powers, but in the last resort with British forces only.[24]

This was in fact a decisive change in policy. Up to this point the British were only prepared to resist any disorganized mob onslaught into their territorial enclaves; to avoid being dragged into the Chinese civil war they had until now been willing, in principle, to give way to any attempt to enter in force by an organized military formation. That was now partly set aside. At Shanghai, British reinforcements would be deployed to protect British lives and property, and preserve the International Settlement, by denying entry to "any Chinese force, organized or disorganized." Smaller concessions might have to be abandoned if pressured; but at Shanghai, by themselves if necessary, the British would fight to prevent the treaty system from being crushed by a Chinese military-political stampede. Having said all that, the FO carried the day to frame what would remain a calibrated grand strategy. The rules of engagement restricted British forces to defending British lives, property, and international enclaves only, and the League of Nations would be so informed. British movements as well as intentions would be communicated openly with the other Powers. And the ultimate objective of defending Shanghai would be kept publicly front and centre:

> While making clear that there could be no surrender to violence and that the military dispositions had the object of carrying out the Government's pledges to defend the lives of British subjects in China, emphasis should be laid on the fact that the Government's policy was primarily one of conciliation and a settlement by agreement.[25]

This policy, and the grand strategy to achieve it, were contested several times, both in London and China. One Cabinet faction, led by Winston Churchill, pressed for stronger military action in China, as did Lampson and Tyrwhitt. Chamberlain and the FO, with the important support of the COS, successfully defended the more cautious approach. They were more impressed by the force of Chinese feeling and the limits to British military power, and their design framed British crisis management. Four complications deserve some attention: the unique situation at Shanghai itself; the practical problems of military strategy on the spot; the challenges of securing and leveraging accurate intelligence; and the difficulties of trying to bring the treaty system powers together. At the time and on the spot

---

24 NAUK, CAB23/54/2, Cabinet Minutes, 17 January 1927; Gwynn, Ch. VIII.
25 NAUK, CAB23/54/2, Cabinet Minutes, 17 January, 23/54/4, 26 January, 23/54/8, 7 February 1927; CAB24/184/41, CP41(27), 3 February 1927; Gwynn, Ch. VIII.

they unfolded together and influenced each other; in the interest of analytical clarity, we will evaluate them in succession here.

No one thought the treaty system could survive the "fall" of Shanghai because the city was unique. It was the biggest and most important treaty port, cornerstone of the treaty system, fundamental to the national interests of not only China but also three Great Powers regarding China: the British and Japanese Empires, and the United States. But its political, demographic, economic, military, and geographic circumstances all made it a complicated place to manage, for everyone. Location, location, location: Shanghai means "by the sea," and is the gateway to one of the most densely populated and economically important regions on the planet, then and now: the Yangtze River tributary system. It was one of the first five treaty ports in which the Qing were compelled to allow first the British, then other foreign powers, to trade freely. By the 1920s the British were present in 49 such ports, spread along both the ocean coastline and the great riverine systems that penetrated deep into the interior. Shanghai connected the ocean to the greatest of them all, the Yangtze being navigable for nearly 2,000km upriver and connecting to several major tributaries. Before the British arrived, it consisted of an old walled town, a minor fishing port, along the banks of the Huangpu River [Whangpoo], a man-made tributary, barely 30km upriver from the mouth at which the Yangtze flows into the East China Sea. They chose an anchorage along the Huangpu just north of that old town, in 1845, and declared their intentions: "There our navy can float, and by our ships, our power can be seen and, if necessary, promptly felt. Our policy is the thorough command of this great river."[26]

Over the next 75 years that is what unfolded. The RN China Station became the principal British defence force in China because it could exercise "gunboat diplomacy," using blue water and riverine forces to patrol the waterways of commerce and protect trade, deep in the Chinese interior. The other powers not only followed suit, they all carved out arrangements that enabled them to exploit the treaty port enclaves to spur trade and commerce. The most important such arrangement was extraterritoriality, excluding foreign nationals and businesses from the jurisdiction of Chinese courts and placing them under a system of consular courts, set up by the treaty powers, that applied their own legal codes. The treaty powers also took effective control of the Imperial (later Chinese) Maritime Customs Service, which became the mainstay of Chinese state

---

26 NAUK, CAB53/12/6, COS19(25), 25 June 1925; Sterling Seagrave, *The Soong Dynasty* (London: Sidgwick & Jackson, 1985), 4–6; Isabella Jackson, *Shaping Modern Shanghai: Colonialism in China's Global City* (Cambridge: University Press, 2018).

finance, and the crucial platform by which China's trade was connected to the global economy. And the enclaves themselves were divided into concessions and settlements, nicely defined by the FO:

> The only difference between a concession and a settlement is that in the former the land was leased direct by the Chinese Government to a foreign Government, which then granted titles (such as our Crown leases) to lot-holders, whereas in a settlement the Chinese Government merely granted the right to set up a municipal administration, leaving it to the individual foreigner to acquire such land as he needed from the individual native owner.[27]

Shanghai included both: a separate French Concession, administered directly by a Consul, and the International Settlement, formed initially from British and American leased areas but by the 1920s incorporating a number of nationalities, and administered by the Shanghai Municipal Council (SMC), a body elected by local ratepayers. Hong Kong was the only British colonial territory in the region; Guangzhou, Nanjing – the old imperial capital upriver from Shanghai – Hankou and Tianjin were also significant British enclaves; but Shanghai, despite the fact it was not directly administered by the British state, was the hub of them all.[28]

By the 1920s Shanghai was the fourth busiest port in the world, by far the largest port and most important industrial, manufacturing, banking and financial centre in China, the dominant site for publishing in China, the base for the extensive network of foreign missions and missionaries spread all over China, and a pivotal location for Chinese politics, business, industry, trade and commerce. The success of the treaty system created these facts, not least by providing spaces physically, legally, and economically safer in which to reside and from which to do business – as a result, from the 1850s onwards, very large numbers of Chinese, from the poorest labourers to the wealthiest tycoons, flocked into settlements and concessions to do just that. Demographically, by far the majority of residents in the enclaves were Chinese. Shanghai became the largest and most important of all. The British community was no longer the largest foreign population, yet remained dominant in the SMC, as well as in property, business, finance, trade and commerce; American interests were

---

27 NAUK, CAB24/184/15, CP15(27), 18 January 1927; Donna Brunero, *Britain's Imperial Cornerstone in China: The Chinese Maritime Customs Service, 1854–1949* (New York: Routledge, 2017); Bickers and Jackson, *Treaty Ports*; Douglas Clark, *Justice by Gunboat: Warlords, Lawlords, and the Making of Modern China and Japan* (Hong Kong: Earnshaw, 2017).
28 By the late 1920s still more than three quarters of British investments in China were located in Shanghai: NAUK, WO106/79, MI2, British Interests in Shanghai, 19 June 1929; Fung, Introduction.

Map 4.1: Treaty Ports and Principal British Enclaves 1918.

important, and Japanese interests grew rapidly after 1914, securing them a seat on the council. The enclave faced military threats since the 1850s, and maintained two multinational forces: the Shanghai Volunteer Corps (SVC) and the SMP. But against a large organized field army the enclave had to rely on the treaty powers for protection. And that complicated things. The SMC could not defend the settlement itself, but did not answer directly to the treaty powers, and could confuse any efforts to defend the city. The "Shanghailanders" were a vocal lobby in British politics. Most were hard-line opponents of any policy to accept change in China, and pressed for strong military support in order to stubbornly defend all existing "treaty rights."[29] All this put the British government and armed forces in an awkward position. They were by default the leading power intending to defend Shanghai, and their nationals still dominated its local administration, but neither could act as a free agent – both must not only work with each other but also with other powers, at both levels. And all this must be done in a city which to the Chinese was now the focal point of their struggle to determine whether or not the Guomindang, or anyone else, would build an effective national government – and towards which powerful Chinese military, political, and business elements were gravitating, to fight it out.

These singular characteristics of Shanghai made it more difficult to defend against military invasion. The decision to send serious reinforcements framed the strategic problem on the spot: how best to use these forces to deter or if necessary defeat any serious physical attack on Shanghai – without escalating the Chinese civil war, or being dragged into that conflict, or provoking a backlash from other powers. This required the makers of grand strategy to stay on top of fast moving and unpredictable questions: where should the reinforcements go, and who should decide whether or not they should engage anyone, anywhere, for any reason? The first decision was what to send. Cabinet briefly delayed, hoping for a positive Japanese response, but after the Japanese government declared on 25 January that it would not send ground forces to China it gave the green light.[30] Three brigades of infantry, comprising 12 battalions, were embarked for China – one from India, two from units combined from the

---

[29] NAUK, CAB24/186/41, CP142(27), 6 May 1927; WO106/79, British Interests in Shanghai, 19 June 1929; Stella Dong, *Shanghai: The Rise and Fall of a Decadent City*, (New York: Harper Collins, 2001); Bickers, *Out of China*, Ch. 2; Jackson, *Shaping Modern Shanghai*. The leading newspaper of the Shanghailanders, the *North China Daily News*, reliably expressed this "hard line" majority. See also note 52.

[30] NAUK, CAB24/54/3, Cabinet Minutes, 21 January, 23/54/4, 26 January 1927; FO371/12449–12450, Correspondence, China, January 1927; Fung, Ch. 7; Goto-Shibata, Ch. 3; Chow, Ch. 7.

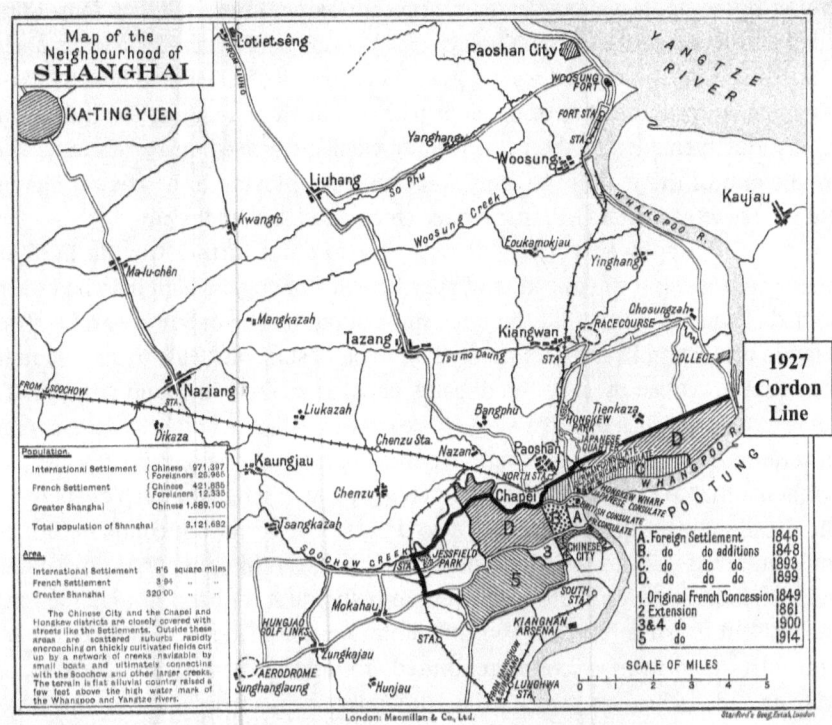

Map 4.2: Shanghai and area in 1932. The 1927 Cordon Line is highlighted.

UK and the Mediterranean – to constitute the Shanghai Defence Force (SDF). Major-General John Duncan, a widely-travelled officer with Great War experience of divisional command, was appointed General Officer Commanding, which upon arrival made him the senior British Army officer in China; that was itself a deliberately public signal of intent. While this amounted to a division-sized force, because it had to be concentrated in haste it was not complete. Some battalions had to be brought to full strength by recalling troops from the Reserve. Half the normal artillery complement of a division could not be sent in time. The terrain outside the city was mainly wet farmland broken up by small streams spanned by bridges deemed too weak to carry tanks, so the War Office decided to send an armoured car company instead. After some discussion about whether it would do more harm than good by provoking a backlash, the RAF sent out an Army Cooperation Squadron, to provide reconnaissance and light ground attack support. And the China Station was powerfully reinforced, by a second additional cruiser squadron, two aircraft carriers, and supporting vessels.[31] It took some humming and hawing to settle the deployment. Various parties raised concerns about Chinese and Japanese reactions, or practical problems of where and how to house the force, and suggested holding all or part of it at Hong Kong, to await developments. But events forced the pace; leading elements arrived on 14 February, and by the end of the month the main forces were deploying in or around Shanghai – three weeks before NRA main force elements closed on the city.[32]

The SDF deployed very publicly, to try to deter further trouble by their mere presence. But the question of specific rules of engagement also had to be settled. The stipulation that the force must stand on the defensive and restrict itself to protecting lives and property had to be fleshed out. This was the dimension that provoked most of the debates between makers of grand strategy. To some extent this was unsurprising. It is easier to delegate authority to use force to commanders on the spot when you are waging declared and open war; governments that are using force to try to prevent war will tend to push deeper into the details. But in this case it was also dangerous, because incomplete British understandings of the political dynamics around the Guomindang – discussed below – made London more reactive than it should have been. It took too long to spell out the absolute limits to the military mission. Tension and confrontation with Guomindang factions continued around the Pearl River delta area, as well as along the Yangtze, as the NRA advanced north. Serious questions pressed: should British nationals be evacuated from the interior to Shanghai? If more violence occurred, should British forces respond? Would negotiations to resolve the incident at Hankou produce any result? Would "warlord" forces in the region delay or stop NRA efforts to cross the Yangtze and advance on Shanghai? Should British combat power push upriver to intervene for any reason, or remain concentrated around Shanghai? Geography played some role. Seasonal variations in the depth of the Yangtze meant that many upriver ports could not be protected by China Station fleet units during the winter months; should they be held anyway, or evacuated? Would other Powers cooperate in any

---

[31] NAUK, CAB23/54/25, Cabinet Minutes, 7 April 1927; CAB53/13/4, COS69(27), 29 March 1927; WO106/83, Chronology of Events in connection with the despatch of troops to China, December 1926-April 1927, 30 April 1930; FO371/12449–12451, Correspondence, China, January-February 1927; Gwynn, *Imperial Policing*, Ch. VIII.

[32] NAUK, CAB23/54/7, Cabinet Minutes, 4 February, 23/54/8, 7 February, 23/54/9, 10 February 1927; WO106/83, Chronology of Events in connection with the despatch of troops to China, December 1926-April 1927, 30 April 1930; FO371/12449–12451, Correspondence, China, January-February 1927; Harry Moses, *For Your Tomorrow: A History of the 2nd Battalion Durham Light Infantry 1919–1955* (Durham: The Memoir Club, 2013), Ch. 3. "Shanghai 1927: 2nd Battalion Gloucestershire Regiment," http://www.redcoat.info/shanghai1927.htm.

military response? These questions were discussed repeatedly and at length within and between the FO, the COS, the CID, the Cabinet, and with the "men on the spot." Decisions emerged one at a time, only really filling in all the blanks by early May. But they were in the end a sensible effort to balance control with responsiveness – in effect, an understanding brokered by the FO and COS. The minimal mission – to protect lives and property, and avoid wider involvement – was spelt out with finality. The Commander-in-Chief China Station was directed to restrict any action to the minimum necessary force, aimed directly at wherever the trouble was occurring, and carried out as quickly as possible in direct response to whatever provoked it. But Vice-Admiral Tyrwhitt was confirmed as having the final decision on whether to use force.[33]

The issue of whether or not to remain concentrated around Shanghai was not easily resolved. It became urgent after NRA forces entered Nanjing and, on 24 March, attacked foreign consulates and other prominent foreign properties in the city, killing at least seven civilians, including two Britons. American and British naval forces bombarded the city, to protect landing parties evacuating foreign nationals.[34] This clash provoked a flash of anger among the treaty Powers, which prompted the COS to recommend the most aggressive military strategy the British considered during the crisis. Powerful foreign naval forces deployed upriver, led by three cruisers and eight destroyers of the China Station. Tyrwhitt and his foreign counterparts discussed specific operations they might carry out to respond to this NRA escalation. In that context, the COS suggested that a window of opportunity now presented itself. The "northern" forces of the "warlords" had now been driven north of the Yangtze. This, plus seasonal deep water, and international anger, opened that window. British forces could now blockade Guangzhou, seize the Guomindang navy, and block all crossings along the Yangtze, to prevent any further northward advance by the NRA. British nationals would have to be evacuated, and while the British could do all this alone it was far more likely to be strategically effective – to halt the NRA without dragging the British into the war – if such a campaign were carried out by the much-desired international coalition, or at least with its blessing. The COS presented this recommendation on 29 March; Cabinet decided to consult Tyrwhitt and Lampson but also authorized preparations, in

---

33 NAUK, CAB23/54/11, Cabinet Minutes, 17 February, 23/54/19, 28 March, 23/54/23, 4 April, 23/54/27, 13 April, 23/55/2, 19 May 1927; CAB24/186/16, CP111(27), 31 March, 24/186/27, CP128 (27), 17 April, 24/186/29, CP130(27), 20 April 1927; FO371/12453–12454, Correspondence, China, April 1927.

34 NAUK, CAB23/54/19, Cabinet Minutes, 28 March, 23/54/20, 30 March 1927; CAB24/186/9, CP110(27), 29 March 1927; FRUS, 1927, Vol. 2; Louis, Ch. IV.

case it decided to proceed. And on 1 April Cabinet agreed to send a fourth brigade to China, with the balance of the divisional artillery and supporting engineers. But the COS stressed the cardinal point: the need to move quickly if at all, before any favourable conditions changed and the window closed. After much discussion, Cabinet put Tyrwhitt on standby on 12 April, pending one more effort to secure Japanese and American support for aggressive action up-river.[35] But events in Shanghai that same day soon moved the whole situation in a very different direction, one that made this proposal the "high water mark" for British military preparations during the crisis. Those events also vindicated the cautious decision to wait before opening the window.

The COS reaction to the clash at Nanjing and the NRA advance highlighted the crux of the problem: for the British to connect what they wanted to achieve with what they decided to do they required accurate intelligence, political and military – intelligence about the other Powers, to be sure, but especially about the Chinese. And intelligence was not always accurate, rarely complete, and not always effectively digested or applied. But the challenges were formidable. The military capabilities of the various Chinese armies were reasonably well understood. That was not the case with their political alignments, intentions, and likely behaviour. To start with, in China and at home British authorities drifted into sloppy shorthand labelling. The "northerners" or "warlord" armies were broadly seen as anti-Guomindang, mostly anti-communist, and more likely to protect foreign interests than threaten them. But their ability to translate numbers and equipment into effective action was overestimated, as was their political stability. The Japanese were perhaps the only treaty power not surprised by how successful Guomindang campaigns to disrupt and subvert many of these forces were, although by February 1927 the British were learning fast. Conversely, most British tended to refer to the Guomindang as the "southerners" or "Cantonese," and, at least at first, overlook how volatile the frictions inside the nationalist movement really were. They also overestimated the impact of their Christmas Memorandum on the Guomindang, many of whom dismissed it as a smoke screen. But above all, they did not quite understand how crucial the webs of social, commercial, and political networks in and around urban China were in shaping Guomindang intentions and capabilities. The "government" that set itself up at Wuhan to negotiate with the British was dominated by more radical elements of the party, working closely with the Soviet advisers. They

---

35 NAUK, CAB23/54/19, Cabinet Minutes, 28 March, 23/54/22, 1 April, 23/54/23, 4 April, 23/54/26, 12 April 1927; CAB24/186/9, CP110(27), 29 March 1927; CAB53/13/4, COS69(27), 29 March 1927; FO371/12453–12454, Correspondence, China, April 1927; WO106/83, Chronology of Events in connection with the despatch of troops to China, December 1926-April 1927, 30 April 1930.

rapidly built up powerful communist-dominated labour organizations in Shanghai and other central Chinese cities, rejected any compromise over the Hankou incident, and used the arrival of foreign military reinforcements to stir up even more popular anger. The confrontation in Nanjing convinced many British officials they were about to launch an all-out assault on the foreign presence. That view was reinforced that same week by the arrival of vanguard NRA forces in Shanghai, as well as a dramatic communist-led takeover of the municipal administration of some Chinese districts of the city, as "warlord" units retreated in confusion. Yet at the same time British diplomats and intelligence sources, military and commercial, began to see indications that tensions inside the Guomindang might soon boil over.[36]

This was not wrong. And it was driven by many of those urban networks, deeply embedded within settlements and concessions. The development of a modern globalized economy in China was in fact a partnership between the treaty powers and Chinese business and commercial circles, which operated mainly out of foreign enclaves, especially Shanghai. These powerful vested interests regarded the United Front with alarm, and moved against it; the independent China they wanted was not to be formed by social revolution. Their principal allies were non-communist nationalists concentrated in much of the NRA, under the effective leadership of Chiang Kai-shek – a protégé of Sun Yat-sen – with longstanding ties to Chinese business leaders in Shanghai. He emerged in 1925 as principal leader of the party factions opposed to the radical left, and the dominant military commander within the NRA. Indications that Chiang and his supporters were now at odds with the radical leadership in Wuhan helped persuade the British to wait on developments before trying to block the Yangtze.[37] That turned out favourably for them.

On 6 April, police controlled by the Manchurian *tuchun* Chang Tso-lin [Zhang Zuolin], abetted by the treaty powers, raided the Soviet Legation in Beijing, arrested dozens of Soviet agents and Chinese communist activists, and seized a large amount of documentation. This haul confirmed the extent and

---

36 NAUK, CAB23/54/23, Cabinet Minutes, 4 April 1927; FO371/12449–12454, Correspondence, China, January-April 1927; WO106/79, China (Notes for CIGS use at Imperial Conference), 26 October 1926; Jacobs, Chs. 15–17; Isaac, Chs. 11–13; Louis, Chs. IV–V; Fung, Chs. 5–8; Goto-Shibata, Chs. 2–3.

37 NAUK, CAB23/54/23, Cabinet Minutes, 4 April 1927; FO371/12453–12454, Correspondence, China, March-April 1927; Isaac, Chs. 11–13; Louis, Ch. IV; Jacobs, Chs. 15–17; Jay Taylor, *The Generalissimo: Chiang Kai-shek and the Struggle for Modern China* (Cambridge MA: Harvard University Press, 2009), Ch. 2; Bickers, *Out of China*, Ch. 2.

ambition of Comintern subversion activities in China, aimed at the treaty powers.[38] Emboldened, on 12 April Chiang unleashed NRA units, supported by organized crime elements in Shanghai and other cities, in a massive surprise attack against communist-led groups. This counter-coup provoked a "white terror," escalating to a bloodbath in which several hundred communists, workers, and supporters were summarily executed in Shanghai, and thousands more elsewhere, over the following months.[39] The British quickly identified the potential strategic repercussions of this dramatic turn. On 14 April, the COS argued that fast changing events now made it advisable to watch and wait for a little while, singling out a notable factor:

> The military aspect of this dissension grows, and Chiang Kai-shek apparently feels himself strong enough to adopt an independent attitude rather than to bow to the Hankow communist-extremists – whose power is exercised through the Labour Unions. The army seems loyal to Chiang....

The British duly held their fire and evaluated the situation, as the "counter-coup" unfolded. Chamberlain felt the correlation of forces was clear enough to warrant stepping back from the brink. On 20 April, he opposed any military or naval intervention upriver, insisted on continuing negotiations regarding Hankou and Nanjing, and stated that British forces should stand fast, until the British could be more certain about not only American and Japanese attitudes but also "the immediate result of the struggle a) between Borodin cum Chen and Chiang, and b) between North and South." The debate continued into early May, but died down when Chiang and the NRA forces loyal to him did not disturb the enclaves in Shanghai. By late May the COS advised that it might soon be safe to begin to draw down the reinforcements sent there in such haste.[40]

The draw down of the SDF was caught up in the final factor that influenced the crisis: constant efforts by British authorities at every level to build an effective treaty power coalition, to defend the foreign presence in China in general and Shanghai in particular. When the SDF arrived in Shanghai, parading through the streets of the Settlement, it immediately transformed the situation on the ground. Surviving Chinese archives do not disclose whether or not it actually deterred a deliberate NRA effort to seize the enclave, but it seems fair to assume the force made some difference. The Wuhan "government" denounced the SDF as

---

[38] *FRUS*, 1927, Vol. 2; NAUK, FO371/12454, Correspondence, China, April 1927; Jacobs, Chs. 15–17; Isaac, Chs. 11–13; Iriye, Ch. III; Louis, Ch. IV.
[39] Iriye, Ch. IV; Louis, Ch. IV; Taylor, Ch. 2; Bickers, *Out of China*, Ch. 2; Chow, Ch. 8; Phil Carradice, *The Shanghai Massacre: China's White Terror, 1927* (Barnsley: Pen & Sword, 2018).
[40] NAUK, CAB23/55/2, Cabinet Minutes, 19 May 1927; CAB24/186/26, CP127(27), 14 April, 24/186/29, CP130(27), 20 April, 24/186/32, CP133(27), 25 April 1927.

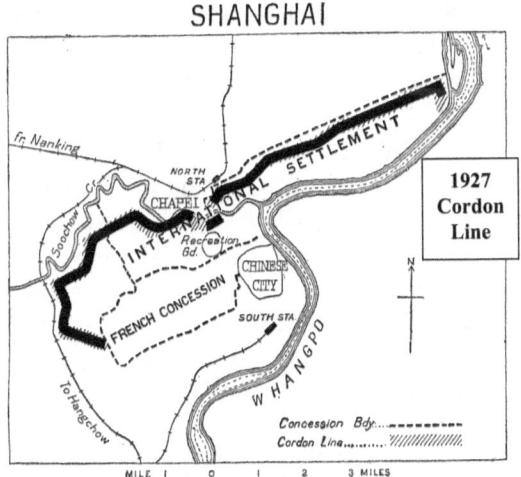

Map 4.3: Shanghai International Settlement and the 1927 Cordon Line.

an "invasion"; but the Guomindang "Foreign Minister," Eugene Chen – a leading Wuhan-based radical – also accepted British assurances that the mission of the force was purely defensive. He agreed to fold this into an accord reached in late February by which the British relinquished the lost concession at Hankou – but warned they would not tolerate any more stampedes into any enclaves. This visible but pointed gesture of good faith indicated the other side of the coin: the Guomindang also faced a fast-moving and complicated situation that challenged its ability to tiptoe through the mines. No Chinese faction could be certain the British would not be reinforced by other powers, so the Guomindang tried to sow divisions between the Americans, Japanese, and British. But the most likely explanation is that the networks that entwined Chinese business interests with Chiang Kai-shek and the "moderates" in the Guomindang were always going to insist the nationalists tread warily regarding Shanghai. The stakes were just too high – this was the beating heart of the entire Chinese national economy, the harbour inside which their own interests were moored, and passions now ran so high that social revolution seemed like a real threat. This "anti-radical" array was in fact just as alarmed by the clash at Nanjing as the treaty powers, and did not dispute a fundamental British concern: if the treaty system collapsed under the impact of a sudden explosion of mass violence, this might well sweep everyone's established interests away.[41]

---

41 NAUK, FO371/12449–12454, Correspondence, China, January-April 1927; Louis, Ch. V; Fung, Ch. 6; Chow, Ch. 7.

So the timely British decision to deploy strong combined forces in Shanghai did something very important: it sharply raised the bar any sort of violent assault on the enclaves must clear in order to succeed. That bought everyone time and space in which to reconsider.

In Shanghai, the raising of the bar was very visible. The SVC – plus supporting international forces provided mostly by naval landing parties – was only strong enough to man a line of defended checkpoints, called the Cordon, laid out to block entry into the enclaves themselves. This Cordon was more than 30km in length and denied entry to both the Settlement and the Concession, forming a horizontal thumb-shaped perimeter with its base on the Huangpu River. But it was almost entirely urban and not naturally strong defensive ground. And these calculations were based only on repelling disorganized mobs, not an organized army. The entire protected space could be shelled by medium artillery from just outside the city. Duncan pushed the SDF, a much stronger force, out beyond the perimeter for much of its length, especially on the western flank. He wanted to exploit more defensible ground and provide more space, to try to avoid fighting in built-up areas. His infantry companies dug in, erecting company defensive positions, preparing fields of fire for their machine guns and supporting artillery. The SDF stood alone; its arrival prompted the SMC to argue there was now no need to mobilize local forces whose businessmen volunteers were needed more urgently at work! But the NRA advance and communist activity in Shanghai finally compelled it in late March to mobilize the SVC, and request the international landing parties to deploy. The relationships between the contingents were never formally clarified at the political level, but on the ground Duncan worked out practical arrangements to cooperate with most of them that stood up under pressure.[42]

Chinese authorities, and the political opposition in the UK, complained about the SDF deploying outside the enclaves.[43] But Duncan insisted this was a

---

[42] NAUK, WO106/81, Defence of Shanghai International Settlement, 3 Febuary 1925; FO371/12452–12453, Correspondence, China, February-March 1927; The Royal Institute of International Affairs, "The Shanghai Crisis," *International Affairs*, Vol 11, No 2, 1932; "Shanghai 1927: 2nd Battalion Gloucestershire Regiment," http://www.redcoat.info/shanghai1927.htm.; Gwynn, Ch. VIII. The French deployed an infantry battalion that cooperated in the overall defensive operation.

[43] NAUK, CAB23/54/4, Cabinet Minutes, 26 January, 23/54/7, 4 February 1927. Chow, Ch. 7, discusses UK domestic political opposition in some detail. The House of Commons discussed the SDF 20 times from early February to late May 1927 but there was only one substantive debate, on 16 March, prompted by a motion to congratulate the government on "prompt action to save British lives in China": UK Parliament, *Hansard*, House of Commons Debates, February-May 1927. Interestingly, while former prime minister David Lloyd George criticized the government in the House, he also agreed that sending the SDF was a responsible decision aiming

military necessity, to protect the international zones and also cover British persons and property located outside the formal boundaries. The SDF carried out patrols to escort British and foreign nationals into the defended area; some of them provoked minor firefights. Duncan was correct; the SDF was too big to billet, let alone fight, strictly inside the enclaves, and the only way to keep the area out of hostile artillery range was to push forward. On 7 April, with tensions running high, Duncan sent the War Office an outline plan titled Operation N (drafted by his GSO1, Colonel John Gort) that proposed to push the defended perimeter out much further. One brigade would occupy the relatively open country north of the Settlement all the way to the junction of the Wusong Creek [Woosung] and Huangpu River; another would push out further west of the Settlement boundary; the third would occupy the central position: the teeming Chinese district of Chapei, just north of the centre of the Settlement. This would have doubled the defended area (but not the perimeter), and involved occupying the most volatile Chinese area of the city. But tensions faded before this plan could be fully considered, so it was never carried out.[44]

London did support Duncan's original perimeter, which enabled the SDF to fight in front of rather than in the enclaves when the challenge came. The SDF repelled several efforts by troops from "northern" forces – sometimes retreating in confusion, sometimes deserting outright – to enter the enclave, to escape the NRA advance (and also kept at bay numerous efforts by civilians to enter). SDF units or patrols came under fire at least a dozen times, and fought one deliberate engagement. On the afternoon of 21 March, NRA forces advancing towards the city overran "northern" troops defending the Shanghai North Railway Station, in Chapei. The SDF perimeter ran only a few hundred metres south of the station. The defeated "northern" forces tried to escape into the Settlement. The Durham Light Infantry stood its ground to repel this onslaught, which became so intense that Duncan had to reinforce them with a company from his force reserve. This

---

to support a sensible new policy: to reach accommodation with nationalism in China. He repeated this in a foreword to a journalist monograph he encouraged, published in September: Arthur Ransome, *The Chinese Puzzle* (London: George Allen & Unwin, 1927), Ch. 2. Lloyd George and Ransome both made the distinction clear: the controversy was over allowing the SDF to move beyond Settlement boundaries, not sending it in the first place.

44 NAUK, WO106/85, Duncan to WO, 7 April 1927; Defence of the Realm, "5th Armoured Car Company in China 1927–1929," https://defenceoftherealm.wordpress.com/2017/05/01/5th-armoured-car-company-in-china-1927-29/; Gwynn, Ch. VIII; J.R. Colville, *Man of Valour* (London: Collins, 1972), 60–63.

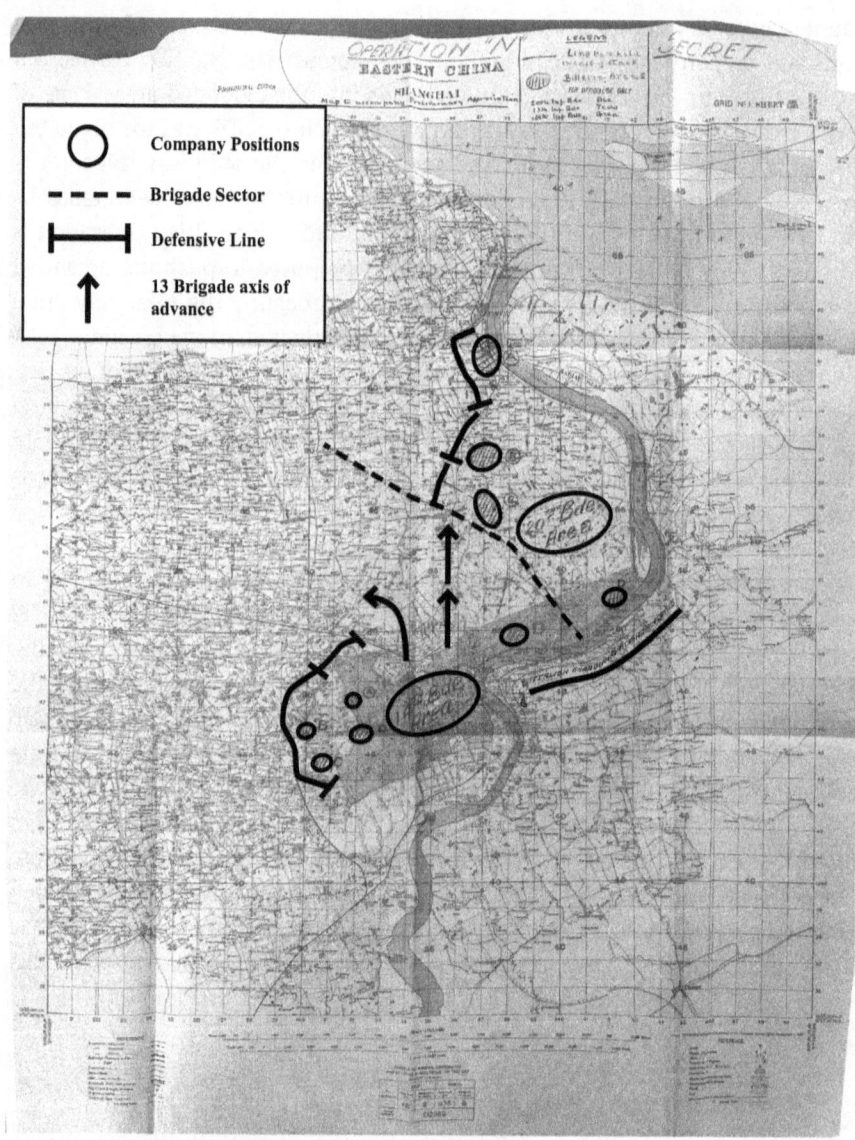

Map 4.4: Outline for Plan N, April 1927.

battalion action cost the SDF two killed and seven wounded, but they killed more than 60 Chinese soldiers and took several hundred prisoners.[45]

Japanese garrison forces manning the sector just east of this position were also attacked by Chinese soldiers seeking refuge, with similar results. But despite the strong desire of most diplomats and military commanders on the spot, and vocal demands from most resident nationals, the American and Japanese governments did not agree to combine forces with the SDF. American diplomats urged their government to send a full division to China to help protect the treaty ports, but Washington refused. Secretary of State Frank Kellogg spelt out a strictly limited policy: American forces would protect American lives in China but nothing more, neither property nor treaty rights. American cruisers were sent to Shanghai, along with, eventually, a full regiment of the US Marine Corps. But the latter, while it deployed in the Settlement, was strictly confined to providing internal security within its boundaries.[46] Their presence did allow Duncan to deploy his combat strength up front. And the powerful concentration of international naval forces at Shanghai certainly made a difference. The China Station alone deployed no less than 13 cruisers at the height of the crisis, always retaining at least four in the Huangpu River. This firepower, plus air support from carrier- and land-based squadrons, offset the shortfall in SDF artillery. Operating to support the prepared defences of the SDF, it would definitely have complicated any serious NRA attack on the Settlement. Nevertheless, obvious international reluctance to act aggressively provoked Shanghailanders as well as the FO. Residents badgered home governments to use the strong forces now deployed to "sort out" the China situation once and for all – by which they meant break the military power of the NRA, and "secure treaty rights" by overpowering force. London rejected such demands, tightening rules of engagement to make sure commanders on the spot did not cross their lines. But perhaps the best answer came from Brigadier Smedley Butler, commanding the US Marine contingent that deployed in Shanghai. Butler pointedly stressed the rules

---

45 Royal Institute of International Affairs, "The Shanghai Crisis"; "Shanghai 1927: 2nd Battalion Gloucestershire Regiment"; Moses, Ch. 3; Gwynn, Ch. VIII. Overall, the SDF disarmed more than 2,000 "northern" troops.

46 A common view among American officials in China was expressed in a summary report by Major John Magruder, US Army, after a tour as US Military Attaché: "I further fear that without some very definite intervention on the part of the United States or Great Britain, or both, Russia may bring about a condition of chaos here compared with which the conditions of today are mild": NARADC, RG38, Records of the Office of Naval Intelligence, C-10-a, Box 455, Impressions, 2 March 1927; FRUS, 1927, Vol. II; Nobuya Bamba, *Japanese Diplomacy in a Dilemma: New Light on Japan's China Policy, 1924–1929* (Vancouver: UBC Press, 1972), Chs. 5–7; Goto-Shibata, Ch. 3.

of engagement laid down by Kellogg. When pressed by foreign media to indicate how many international troops would be needed to invade China in order to break the Guomindang, Butler replied: "Half a million and it would probably require a million more before the end of the first year."[47]

The British government did not disagree with Butler, but were disappointed by the strict limits Washington set on military cooperation. Japanese reluctance to cooperate was, however, a more serious problem. Fundamental British and American approaches to China did not seem irreconcilable; both at least understood the need to respond politically to Chinese nationalism. But the British did hope there was also common ground between them and Japan, at the very least on the premise that the treaty powers should not allow themselves to be stampeded out of China by violence. Yet despite the fact that Foreign Minister Shidehara Kijuro directed a policy that sought to avoid clashes with Chinese nationalism, trying instead to increase trade and commerce, Tokyo demurred. The Japanese government leaned away from the British when they became the target of anti-foreign sentiment. This frustrated many Japanese nationals in China, who agreed with British claims the treaty powers shared common interests that were now under threat, so they should cooperate. Tokyo reacted badly to the Christmas Memorandum, because it put at risk Japanese interests which did not affect the British. The British hoped the importance of Shanghai to everyone would sway Tokyo, and remained convinced that only Japan could provide the military muscle required to mount any determined defence of the treaty system. The FO and its diplomats lobbied the Japanese relentlessly, and the COS offered to place British forces under Japanese command in any large multinational force. Yet Tokyo remained aloof. But the principal reason it did so in 1927 was something the British tracked, through their embassy in Tokyo, but did not fully digest: internal turmoil.[48]

The Japanese government was nearly paralyzed by the Showa financial crisis, the onset of which, from January onwards, seriously compromised efforts to formulate any policy towards the crisis in China. On 20 April, the Wakatsuki government was forced to resign, giving way to a new administration led by Tanaka Giichi. Tanaka changed Japanese policy towards China, shifting from trying to avoid clashes with Chinese nationalism to assertively confronting

---

[47] NAUK, CAB53/13/4, COS69(27), 29 March 1927; FO371/12449–12454, Correspondence, China, January-April 1927; Barbara Tuchman, *Stilwell and the American Experience in China, 1911–1945* (New York: Macmillan, 1971), Ch. 5; Gwynn, Ch. VIII.
[48] NAUK, CAB23/54/28, Cabinet Minutes, 27 April 1927; FO371/12449–12454, Correspondence, China, January-April 1927; Nobuya, Chs. 5–7; Goto-Shibata, Ch. 3.

perceived threats to Japanese interests. The change in government in Tokyo did not at first seem to rule out cooperation. When the British Ambassador assured Tanaka in early May that the UK still hoped to cooperate with Japan, Tanaka replied "although our Alliance no longer existed the spirit of it did, and he hoped to keep it alive with frank conversations"; Chamberlain immediately responded in kind. The FO reached out hopefully, suggesting that if the British and Japanese could now agree on a broad common policy regarding how to respond to Chinese nationalism – while also protecting their existing treaty rights – they might be able to stabilize the whole situation. Tanaka demurred, insisting the situation in China remained too volatile to allow any such broad agreement, so he would rather react problem by problem. This fell far short of what the British needed, so any chance to connect was lost.[49] Despite Japanese complaints, the British were wrong to think that Tokyo refused to cooperate in Shanghai because it wanted British interests to suffer. Disarray, not design, stymied Japanese government policy when the SDF went in. But under Tanaka, that soon changed. Steadily, perceptibly, the focal point of friction between the resumed Northern Expedition and the foreign treaty powers shifted from the British to the Japanese. And Japanese failure to step up at Shanghai prompted London to reconsider in turn.

As the Guomindang advanced into what Japan considered its sphere of influence, the Tanaka government sent reinforcements to Shandong to deter any NRA move against Japanese interests there. Despite efforts to prevent one, the predictable clash occurred in May 1928, in the city of Jinan [Tsinan]. But this time, not only did the British decline to help bolster international defences in northern China, they also now identified the Japanese as the emerging threat to their general interests in China. More than half the reinforcements sent to Shanghai were withdrawn before the end of 1927. But in the annual review of developments affecting the defence of the British Empire in 1928, the Chief of the Imperial General Staff urged that remaining ground forces be retained in China. He argued the threat was now changing, from the prospect of Chinese onslaughts against British enclaves to the possibility of Japanese pressure on British interests – and ground forces were needed to provide more deterrent, to make Tokyo pause. This change of focus was certainly dramatic. And it was influenced by the British decision that same year to recognize the Guomindang, under the leadership of Chiang Kai-shek, as the national government of China,

---

[49] NAUK, CAB23/54/30, Cabinet Minutes, 4 May 1927; Nobuya, Ch. 7; Goto-Shibata, Ch. 3.

and try to work with it along the policy line laid down in December 1926.⁵⁰ But it was also driven in no small measure by British perceptions that the Japanese decision not to support them at Shanghai in 1927 was calculated to exploit British difficulties, and Japanese policy towards China was now becoming aggressive and fraught.

What then to make of British grand strategy to defend Shanghai in 1927? Two things, both pointing to the same conclusion. First, it heavily influenced what happened next in China, not necessarily to the detriment of British interests. Second, it provided an example of how to execute a grand strategy to prevent a crisis from escalating to open war without abandoning the field. Both highlight the central point: British grand strategy avoided disaster and helped manage change because it revolved around a crucial insight: what not to do, and why.

The DIME paradigm can initiate this conclusion. Economically, decision makers in London understood and kept in view the essential point: British interests in China were useful but not fundamental, while British interests in Shanghai were fundamental to any continued British presence in China.⁵¹ Chinese nationalism could and did hurt the British more economically than the British could hurt it; boycott trumped blockade. Militarily, decision makers in London were a bit quarrelsome, and their agents in China wanted a more assertive approach. But the basic axis between the FO and the COS kept British military strategy grounded on the vital point: the British Empire alone could not defend the treaty system in China, and any effort to do so would shatter its presence there – so British military intervention must remain calibrated accordingly. So framed, this kept the fighting power of the China Station and the SDF concentrated around Shanghai, and focused on the minimal mission to deter, deny and protect – to buy time. Diplomacy was to use that time, informed by Intelligence. Intelligence had its shortcomings, not the least of which was heavy pressure from British residents in China, frequently echoed by British officials there, to carry out a more ambitious agenda than London was willing to support.⁵² Nor was it easy to sort out the layers of complications swirling in and

---

50 NAUK, CAB53/14/10, COS140(28), 23 July 1928; CAB23/58/11, Cabinet Minutes, 24 July 1928; Iriye, ch VI; Nobuya, ch 7; Gwynn, ch VIII; Brian Bond, *British Military Policy between the Two World Wars* (Oxford: Clarendon Press, 1980), 89–91.

51 NAUK, CAB24/181/8, CP308(26), 30 July 1926; WO106/79, MI2, British Interests in Shanghai, 19 June 1929; Fung, Introduction.

52 The depth of this difference in attitude between Britons at home and in China was unfolded in N.A. Pelcovits, *Old China Hands and the Foreign Office* (New York: Institute of Pacific Relations, 1948). Ransome captured the intensity of feeling in 1927 in Chapter 3, "The Shanghai Mind," in *The Chinese Puzzle*.

around the Guomindang and the "warlord" forces, and the British overreacted to the presence of the Soviet advisers sent to China.[53] But the basic insight – Chinese nationalism was now too strong to hold back, so the British focus must be to manage change, not resist it – did much to make up for shortcomings in intelligence. So did the decision to rely ultimately on Diplomacy, stiffened by a visible show of force, to steer through the crisis. The cardinal decision, the Christmas Memorandum, made it possible to reinforce the China Station, and deploy the SDF, without provoking any irreparable breach with the Guomindang and Chinese commercial interests entwined with it. But while the British correctly identified the D in DIME, this revealed something they could not stop – and pushed them down the road towards it.

The Guomindang never evolved into a stable and efficient central government of China, but did become an active national government. This intensified the strain on the treaty system. Japan, insisting as always on the special position it required in China, reacted aggressively. This was probably not avoidable. The United States and the British Empire were in a position to accept the fact that one day the Washington promises must be honoured and the treaty system terminated. But for Imperial Japan, the economic stake it had in China looked like an existential interest it could not relinquish. British suspicions of Japanese intentions escalated to alarm in autumn 1931, after elements of the Kwantung Army provoked a Japanese takeover of Manchuria, and a weak government in Tokyo refused to override them. British interests in north China remained minor, and the British government certainly tried to avoid trouble with Japan over this upheaval, but this escalated concerns about Japanese intentions towards China in general. This became alarm when elements of the Imperial Japanese Navy (IJN) provoked a pitched battle with elements of the NRA in Shanghai, in January 1932. This the British could not sidestep. In March, the COS recommended that the so-called Ten Year Rule be terminated. This was the policy – applied since August 1919 and placed on a renew every day basis in 1928 – that British service ministries were to assume, for plans and spending purposes, there would be no major war for at least 10 years. The COS argued it was now obsolete, dangerously so in East Asia where the British were nowhere near strong enough to face any conflict that arose due to, let alone with, the Japanese. Cabinet agreed. Within a year British foreign policy followed suit, after Japan withdrew from the League of Nations to protest being blamed for aggression in Manchuria, and turned towards an imperial

---

53 For example, NAUK, CAB23/54/7, Cabinet Minutes, 4 February 1927; CAB24/185/22, CP73(27), 28 February 1927.

path.[54] These developments were not caused by the crisis in Shanghai in 1927. But that crisis did reveal to the British that any common interest they shared with Japan as treaty powers could not prevent divergence between the two over how to mange change in China. That divergence, for London, began there and then.

This was the final outcome from British grand strategy to defend Shanghai in 1927. The British learned on the ground that they could not defend the treaty system in China by force and should not try, unless Japan took a lead. And they learned by experience that being willing to respond to change in China could help them come to bearable terms with Chinese nationalism. British policies towards China unfolded accordingly. Ultimately, bricks cannot be made without straw. The British could not repeat their military response in 1927; the bolt was shot. When a far greater challenge arose – starting again at Shanghai – in the second half of 1937, it compelled the British Empire to face the limits of its power. Distracted now by trouble in Europe, the British could not do more than try to redeem, finally, the sacrifice they made at Washington in 1922: to secure American military support, to prevent the destruction of British interests east of India. But if anything, this reinforces the argument that grand strategy in 1927 was sound and sober. The British had always been right. The volatility of China posed two threats to global order: it might trigger a Great Power war, and it might erupt into social revolution. Both things did finally happen. By their grand strategy for crisis management in 1927, the British bought themselves time and space to minimize the damage caused by the storm, when it finally broke, to their most fundamental interest. This was to prevent a stable global order from being destroyed by violence. It was never about "holding on." It was always about adapting.

---

[54] Gibbs, *Grand Strategy*, Chs. 2 and 3. See also Chapter 2 by Yamamoto Fumihito and Chapter 7 by Jeremy Yellen in this volume.

Charles Burgess
"To Treat China as a Great Power": Great Britain, Southeast Asia, and American Grand Strategy for the Defeat of Japan, 1941–1945

It took the outbreak of major war for the United States to face its own grand strategic deficit in Asia. To be sure, the United States had considerable interests in Asia, particularly China, in the early twentieth century. Various diplomatic, economic, and cultural initiatives supported those interests, with an overall policy goal of preventing any one power from dominating the Asia Pacific.[1] Even such a personality as Walter Lippmann wrote in 1943 that the "United States has since 1899 been committed to the task of fostering [China's] development."[2] However, US efforts to weave together a grand strategy to achieve its goals were limited, especially in the light of its own politics and a politically revisionist Japan willing to use military force to change the status quo. Again, according to Walter Lippmann, there was "no serious and sustained conviction that American commitments and interests and ideals must be covered by our armaments, our strategic frontiers, and our alliances."[3] Put simply, in the words of this volume's definition of grand strategy, the United States in the early twentieth century did not effectively relate the organization and application of power to the pursuit of national objectives. Indeed, many American strategic efforts were little more than political platitudes echoing the Open Door, itself an aspirational policy statement. The United States did manage more forceful statements of its Asia policy, such as the 1921–1922 Washington Conference. But despite some more forceful last-minute deterrence efforts, such as loans and Lend-Lease to support China, and diplomatic and economic efforts to deter Japan, it was strategically unprepared to wage war when the time came.[4]

---

[1] The "central theme of American strategic culture" relative to East Asia, according to Michael Green, *By More Than Providence: Grand Strategy and American Power in the Asia-Pacific Since 1783* (New York: Columbia University Press, 2016), 5.
[2] Walter Lippmann, *U.S. Foreign Policy: Shield of the Republic* (Boston: Little, Brown and Company, 1943), 156.
[3] Ibid, 8.
[4] This despite the fact that unilaterally and bilaterally, both the United States and Britain had been in the process of amending both unilateral and coalition strategy in the event of war against Japan. See Edward Miller, *War Plan Orange: The US Strategy to Defeat Japan, 1897–1945*

This chapter examines the evolution of American wartime grand strategy against Japan by analysing the strategic dialogue between the United States, China, and Britain over their respective roles and missions relative to Southeast Asia. It argues that grand strategy against Japan was American in flavour and substance from the outset and that the Americans privileged China within that grand strategy above their purported closest ally, Great Britain. Three things allowed the United States to set this strategic agenda. First, prewar sympathy for China and its war against Japan enabled American strategy. Second, a lack of American military power, especially after Pearl Harbor, forced the United States to seize upon China as the only military means available to them. Third, an American desire for China to assume the mantle of Great Power and stand beside them in managing the eventual peace sustained American strategy. These factors defined the relationship that emerged between the United States, Britain, and China. The United States made it clear to Britain that China was the main ally and that Allied operations should conform to that fact, a fact that emerged most clearly via Anglo-American discussions over Southeast Asia.

The United States realized the importance of both Southeast Asia's strategic geography and Britain's strategic position there gave it good reason to push the British to support operations that aligned with American desires to use China. The British had their own plans, centered on Southeast Asia, based on their own strategic interests, strategic logic, and available capabilities; but the Americans always held a veto that forced the British back to supporting China. This aspect of Allied grand strategy against Japan is often overlooked or diminished in the prevailing literature. Most studies use strategy as evidence of an overall pathology in the Anglo-American relationship, or focus on the acerbic General Joseph Stilwell and his arguments with the British and the Chinese.[5] But Anglo-American strategic discussions relative to Southeast Asia became key

---

(Annapolis, MD: Naval Institute Press, 2007). On Anglo-American talks, see David Reynolds, *The Creation of the Anglo-American Alliance, 1937–1941: A Study in Competitive Cooperation* (Chapel Hill, NC: University of North Carolina, 1981). See also William Johnsen, *The Origins of the Grand Alliance: Anglo-American Military Collaboration from the Panay Incident to Pearl Harbor* (Lexington, KY: University Press of Kentucky, 2016).

5 For Anglo-American relations and the war against Japan, see Christopher Thorne, *Allies of a Kind: The United States, Britain and the War Against Japan, 1941–1945* (Oxford: Oxford University Press, 1978). See also Raymond Callahan, *Burma 1942–1945* (London: Davis-Poynter, 1978). On Stilwell, see Barbara Tuchman, *Stilwell and the American Experience in China, 1911–1945* (New York: Macmillan, 1971); Hans van de Ven, *War and Nationalism in China, 1925–1945* (London: Routledge, 2003), especially Ch. 1; Jay Taylor, *The Generalissimo: Chiang Kai-shek and the Struggle for Modern China* (Cambridge, MA, Harvard University Press, 2009), especially Chs. 5 and 6.

considerations in Allied – essentially American – strategy against Japan for most of the war. These discussions and the resulting plans, as well as logistical support to China, and laudatory language about China's present and future, kept it in the war and provided a base for a later, undefined counteroffensive. In effect, the United States used all these ideas to replace the one of a great naval offensive from Hawaii – lost as a result of Pearl Harbor. Of course, China eventually lost its privileged place in American strategic thinking as the war moved in a different direction and American perceptions of China changed. But for much of the war, China was to the forefront in American grand strategy against Japan.

Those perceptions left their own postwar legacy that saw the United States further entrench itself in "the China tangle," as the US attempted to save China from itself.[6] It was, however, wartime American strategic perceptions of China's potential that set the stage for those later problems. Indeed, when the authors of the US Army's official history of the China-Burma-India Theatre asked General George Marshall, the wartime US Army Chief of Staff, what President Franklin Roosevelt's policy towards China was, he responded: "To treat China as a Great Power."[7] Marshall's statement encapsulated American policy toward China reminiscent of the Open Door and the Nine Power Treaty; it also demonstrated that the United States wanted to buttress China as a means of its grand strategy. To be direct: the United States used this rubric to control the strategic discussions with Britain over the war against Japan, so much so that the US dictated China's place in Allied grand strategy via discussions over Southeast Asia.

China and Strategy in the Wake of Pearl Harbor

China emerged as a focal point in American strategy immediately after Pearl Harbor. To be sure, China was already rising in American strategic calculations as the Japanese threat intensified. China was among the first recipients of American Lend-Lease; American pilots received approval at the highest levels to leave the service and join Claire Chennault's "Flying Tigers;" the United States offered China large credits and loans; and China was a major issue in the

---

[6] Herbert Feis, *The China Tangle: The American Effort in China from Pearl Harbor to the Marshall Mission* (Princeton: University Press, 1953).
[7] Charles Romanus and Riley Sunderland, *Stilwell's Mission to China* (Washington: Center for Military History, 1953), 62.

final negotiations between the US and Japan.[8] But only after the outbreak of the Pacific War did China assume a concrete role in American grand strategy.

On 8 December, Generalissimo Chiang Kai-shek [Jiang Jieshi] suggested an alliance between the Soviet Union, China, Britain, and the United States against Japan. Chiang's call intrigued Roosevelt, who suggested he convene meetings in Chungking with American, British, and Chinese officials (the Soviets declined) to discuss a preliminary strategy against Japan for Washington's consideration. Chiang convened the meetings on 22 December. The result was a series of strategic observations based around Burma as the key battlespace, China as the key theatre, and Chinese armies as the key forces.[9] While no specific plan was proposed, this signified that from the start the United States viewed China as central to Allied grand strategy.

In the meantime, the United States consolidated its control over grand strategy against Japan at the Arcadia conference in Washington. This conference, the first of a series between Roosevelt and British Prime Minister Winston Churchill, established much of the wartime grand strategy bureaucracy, including the Combined Chiefs of Staff (CCS). While the CCS' role was to manage strategy and logistics writ large, it emerged from discussions concerning the Allied response to the Japanese offensive. General Marshall suggested a combined command to manage Allied operations in Southeast Asia and nominated General Archibald Wavell, the British commander in India, as its commander. After much discussion, and British objections, the British agreed to the new command and commander. ABDACOM, or the American-British-Dutch-Australia Command, needed a single point of contact among American and British leadership. The conference attendees agreed that an "appropriate joint body" would form such a mechanism and be based in Washington. This joint body became the CCS.[10]

Using this strategic influence, the Americans began to highlight China's role. They insisted on Burma's transfer to ABDACOM from the British India Command. Burma's inclusion therein elevated its status beyond that of simply

---

[8] For an overview, see Michael Schaller, *The US Crusade in China, 1938–1945* (New York: Columbia University Press, 1979), Chs. 3–4. On the negotiations, see Waldo Heinrichs, *Threshold of War: Franklin D Roosevelt and American Entry into World War II* (New York: Oxford University Press, 1990).

[9] HIA, Joseph Stilwell Papers, Box 16, File 1, Section 3, Part 1, Memo No 124 from Chungking to AMMISCA, 25 December 1941. See also Taylor, *The*, 190.

[10] Winston Churchill, *The Grand Alliance*, Vol. III of *The Second World War* (Boston: Houghton Mifflin, 1951), 599 (Hereafter cited as WSC); *FRUS, The Conferences at Washington, 1941–1942 and Casablanca, 1943*, Minutes of meeting between United States and British Chiefs of Staff, 28 December 1941, 138; J.M.A. Gwyer, *Grand Strategy*, Vol. III, Part I (London: HMSO, 1964), 382.

an attachment to India and cemented its importance to the wider war, and China's place in it, because of its role as China's logistical lifeline. Roosevelt also suggested that China be its own theatre with Chiang Kai-shek as its commander. Indeed, the China Theatre would not report to the CCS; it was beholden only to itself.[11] Chiang warmly accepted Roosevelt's elevation of China's strategic status, which quickly enhanced American control over what planners wanted: a China-centred strategy against Japan. In fact, the War Department's War Plans Division noted in early January 1942 that despite quick agreement on ABDACOM that theatre was essentially a stopgap; China was the key theatre. The Allies must secure Burma to develop China into the primary tool to wear down Japanese forces in the Pacific.[12]

Part of the China Theatre's creation was more a more tangible showcase of China's position as an Allied partner. Concurrent with the creation of ABDACOM and the China Theatre, Roosevelt asked his advisers about establishing a committee to support Chiang in his efforts as a theatre commander.[13] Chiang had similar ideas. After he accepted the China Theatre, he asked Roosevelt for an American general officer to serve as his chief of staff.[14]

Secretary of War Henry Stimson and General Marshall set out to find such an officer. They settled initially on Lieutenant General Hugh Drum, then the US Army's senior line officer and one of the few active general officers with combat experience. An officer with Drum's stature and experience would surely be a boon to China's morale and its place as an Allied power. In the end, however, disagreements and misunderstandings between Drum, Stimson, and Marshall over Drum's mission provoked Stimson and Marshall to decide upon a new candidate: Major (later Lieutenant) General Stilwell.[15]

Stilwell immediately detailed his ideas about the mission. He asked Marshall to approve general objectives including the supply and training of a 30-division

---

11 NAUK, PREM 3/166/1, Telegram from Chiefs of Staff to Churchill, undated (late December 1941). See also Romanus and Sunderland, *Stilwell's Mission to China*, 62.
12 HIA, Joseph Stilwell Papers, Box 16, File 1, Section 3, Part 1, Memo from Lt. Col. W. G. Wyman to the Chief of Staff, "Policy in Support of China," 5 January 1942.
13 *FRUS, The Conferences at Washington, 1941–1942 and Casablanca, 1943*, Notes of meeting between President Roosevelt and his military advisers, 28 December 1941, 128–29.
14 HIA, Stilwell Papers, Box 19, File 11, "Washington Preparatory Planning File Memoranda," Folder 19.17, T.V. Soong to Assistant Secretary of War John J. McCloy, 6 January 1942.
15 On the discussions over Drum's mission, see HIA, Stilwell Papers, Memorandum of General Drum's conversation with General Marshall, 2 January 1942; Box 19, File 11, Folder 19.17, "Washington Preparatory Planning File Memoranda," and Box 19, File 11, Folder 19.18, "China Burma India," Drum to Stimson and Marshall, "Strategic and Operational Conception of the US Effort to Assist China," 8 January 1942. See also Tuchman, *Stilwell*, 310–11.

Chinese army, increased deployments of American air power, contingency plans for the continuation of supplies to China via India should the Burma Road be cut, and the immediate supply of various arms and equipment to China. All of this was to support the broad grand strategic goal of preparing China to be the base for the eventual offensive against Japan.[16]

The War Department amended Stilwell's instructions to comport more with the agreement made with the British relative to the China Theatre, at the ongoing conference. This agreement stipulated that Stilwell would supervise all US military aid to China, command all US forces in China as well as any Chinese forces Chiang assigned to him, and represent the United States on any "international war council" in China. Underscoring all this was the importance of Burma, particularly the status of the Burma Road.[17] Marshall instructed Stilwell that his main mission was to increase the combat effectiveness of the Chinese army as well as supervise and improve US defence assistance to China, under the overall policy guidance issued in the Anglo-American report on assistance to China.[18] Operationally, then, all this depended on Burma, because without Burma using China's geography and manpower became moot.

Stilwell arrived in Chungking in early March. Chiang ordered him to take command of the Chinese Fifth and Sixth Armies in Burma and, as a result, he experienced his first disagreements with the Generalissimo over command issues.[19] Stilwell landed in the midst of the Japanese offensive that ended with the Allies ejected from Burma by May. British forces, part of the Chinese force, and Stilwell himself retreated to India while the remainder of the Chinese force retreated to Yunnan.[20]

---

16 HIA, Stilwell Papers, Box 19, File 1, Section 3, Part 5, Folder 17.4, Stilwell to the Chief of Staff, 31 January 1942.
17 HIA, Stilwell Papers, Box 16, File 1, Section 3, Part 1, Folder 16.14, United States-British Chiefs of Staff Report, "Immediate Assistance to China," 10 January 1942.
18 HIA, Stilwell Papers, Box 19, File 11, Folder 19.19, Marshall to Stilwell, 2 February 1942.
19 On these first clashes with the Generalissimo, see Joseph W. Stilwell, *The Stilwell Papers*, ed. Theodore White (New York: Schocken Books, 1948), 64–5; Romanus and Sunderland, *Stilwell's Mission to China*, 95–96; and Tuchman, *Stilwell*, 277–79. Hans van de Ven is curiously silent on these early command issues, instead focusing on the "inexperienced" Stilwell and his mistaken obsession with offensive operations. But the ramifications for later American attitudes are obvious. Hans van de Ven, *War and Nationalism in China*, 30–33.
20 On Stilwell's "walk out" from Burma, see Frank Dorn, *Walkout: With Stilwell in Burma* (New York: Crowell, 1971).

Translating Grand Strategy into Theatre Strategy

After the Allied "hell of a beating," Stilwell began working his ideas for a counter-offensive to retake Southeast Asia.[21] His ideas echoed the China-focused American grand strategy, and revolved around logistical revitalization of the Chinese Army and operations through Burma into broader Southeast Asia. He would reorganize the Chinese Army into a leaner, more offence-focused force, and train those Chinese divisions in India at a purpose-built training centre at Ramgarh. He would then use Chinese, British and, hopefully, American forces to retake Burma and Thailand, then push for the South China Sea at Guangdong. An airfreight operation would support all this by airlifting supplies from India to China, a route later known as the "Hump."[22]

The American Joint Chiefs of Staff (JCS) responded to Stilwell's plan with mixed views. They approved his plans to reorganize and train the Chinese Army, the Ramgarh training programme and the airfreight operation. In addition to the "Hump" airlift, however, they asked Stilwell to plan a ground campaign limited initially to northern Burma to reopen the Burma Road, since the War Department believed the air freight operation alone would be insufficient. Any Burma offensive, however, required British agreement and participation, since Burma was in the British strategic sphere.[23]

The British, for their part, initially agreed with this strategic direction. Churchill even told Wavell after Arcadia that "if I can epitomize in one word the lesson I learned in the United States, it was 'China.'"[24] He got American agreement to the Germany-first principle at Arcadia and felt that supporting China fitted well with the strategy of holding against Japan. This plus the humiliation the British received in Southeast Asia all underscored his near-constant harangue to his Chiefs of Staff (COS) and Wavell, back in India after ABDACOM's short life, to launch a counter-offensive in Burma.[25]

---

21 Stilwell's famous quote was "I claim we got a hell of a beating. We got run out of Burma and it is humiliating as hell. I think we ought to find out what caused it, go back and retake it." See Stilwell, *Papers*, 106.
22 HIA, Stilwell Papers, Box 19–24, Folder China-Burma-India, File 13–13a, Memo, General Gruber to the Generalissimo, "Proposal to Organize and Train a Chinese Force in India," 27 April 1942; Memo, "Reorganization of the Chinese Army," undated (approximately late June 1942); Memo, Clayton Bissell to the Generalissimo, "Two Stage Air Freight Operation," 24 June 1942.
23 Romanus and Sunderland, *Stilwell's Mission to China*, 152.
24 Telegram from Churchill to Wavell, 23 January 1942, in WSC IV, 118–9.
25 See, for example, NAUK, CAB80/63, Churchill minute, Ismay to COS, 18 May 1942.

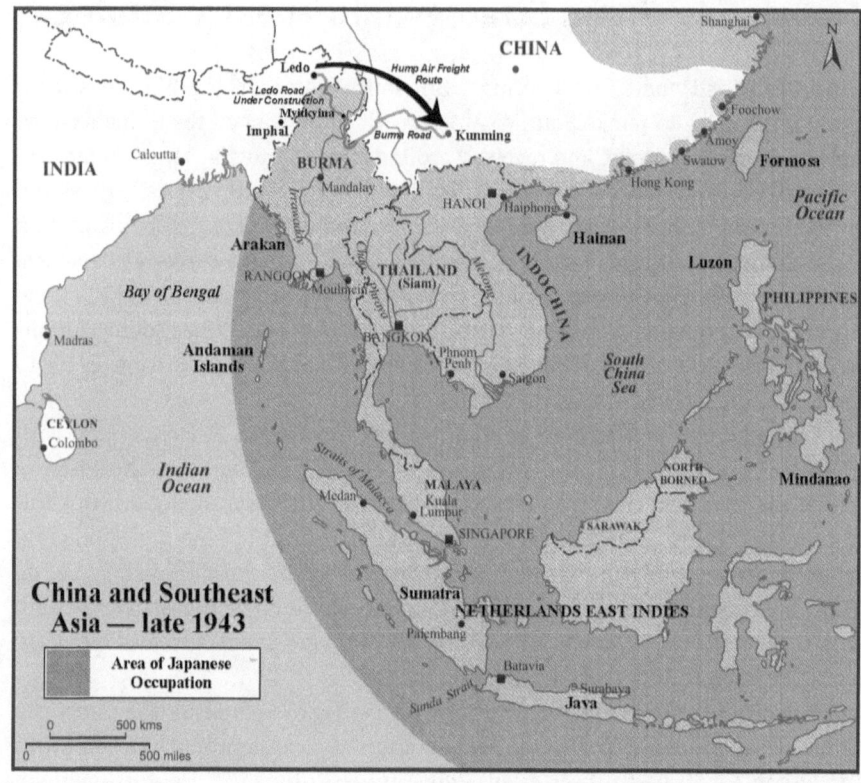

Map 5.1: China and Southeast Asia in late 1943. The extent of Japanese occupation and the "Hump" Air Freight Route from India to China.

The COS and Wavell both assessed counter-offensive possibilities in Burma and the Indian Ocean. Wavell drafted a plan to retake Burma dubbed Anakim. But the prospects looked grim. Competing operations elsewhere and logistical hurdles in India and Burma limited any British activity in support of a China-based grand strategy.[26] A Joint Planning Staff appreciation further dampened overall British, particularly Churchill's, enthusiasm for Burma operations. It stated that the best way to support China was to reopen the Burma Road, but that would require control of the Bay of Bengal and amphibious operations against Rangoon, or a ground campaign from India across northern Burma, all

---

25 See, for example, NAUK, CAB80/63, Churchill minute, Ismay to COS, 18 May 1942.
26 NAUK, CAB80/63, Churchill minute, Ismay to COS, 30 May 1942; Telegram from Wavell to Churchill, 9 June 1942, reprinted in John Connell, *Wavell: Supreme Commander, 1941–1943*, (London: Collins, 1969), 237–38.

of which were then impossible. Moreover, the recapture of Burma itself would contribute little to Japan's defeat. Instead, the British should embark on broader operations in Southeast Asia to interdict Japan's oil supply.[27]

Wavell, however, continued planning operations despite his, and Whitehall's, misgivings. In September, he amended Anakim in the face of logistical realities. New goals included reopening the Burma Road, capturing Akyab and Arakan on the Burma coast, and the Chin Hills in southwest Burma.[28] Churchill was not satisfied. He wanted a broader campaign with the objective of capturing Rangoon and Moulmein, and later Bangkok. This suggested that his support for the initial outline of Allied grand strategy against Japan had already begun to waiver.[29] However, as planning proceeded, and the war progressed, prospects for Burma operations dimmed even more. Force diversions for the North Africa landings (Torch), internal security in India in the wake of anti-British riots in August, and the ongoing monsoon forced Wavell to cancel nearly all plans, except for a limited offensive along the Arakan coast toward Akyab (Cannibal) scheduled for December.

Meanwhile, Stilwell fought for his China-centred plans. He argued with Chiang over the Ramgarh training centre as well as American supply efforts and strategic priorities. Chiang felt more training was unnecessary and, instead, wanted more and newer war materiel, particularly aircraft for Chennault's new China Air Task Force.[30] He was also irritated because China was denied a seat at the CCS table. In response, he issued his so-called "Three Demands." These were: deploy three American divisions to India to work with those Chinese divisions already there to retake Burma; an air combat capability of 500 planes; and 5,000 tons airlifted monthly over the "Hump."[31] In an effort to reassure Chiang about China's role in overall grand strategy, Roosevelt wrote to Chiang in late June: "The United States and our Allies do regard China as a vital part of our common war effort and depend on the maintenance of the China Theatre as an urgent necessity for the defeat of our enemies."[32] He also

---

27 NAUK, CAB79/22/3, JP(42) 537 (Revise), 17 June 1942.
28 Memo from Wavell to General Irwin, 17 September 1942, reprinted in Connell, *Wavell*, 241–42.
29 Michael Howard, *Grand Strategy*, Vol. IV (London: HMSO, 1972), 85.
30 Chennault and the USAAF disbanded the "Flying Tigers" in July 1942. The remaining aircraft and personnel were reorganized as the USAAF 23rd Fighter Group, which, with the 11th Bombardment Squadron, comprised the China Air Task Force.
31 HIA, Stilwell Papers, Box 23, File 56, Folder 23–43, Memo from Generalissimo to Stilwell, 28 June 1942. See also Romanus and Sunderland, *Stilwell's Mission to China*, 172.
32 FDR Library, Map Room Papers, Series 1, Sub-Series 1, Box 10, Roosevelt to Chiang Kai-shek, 27 June 1942.

sent a personal emissary – presidential aide Lauchlin Currie – to China, in response to a request from Chiang.[33]

The Generalissimo finally agreed to the Ramgarh training centre at the end of June, probably because of both Roosevelt's conciliation as well as Stilwell's planning efforts that placed a premium on China's role. Stilwell drafted a campaign plan, dubbed "The Pacific Front," and presented it to Chiang in late July. Its ultimate goal was to open Rangoon port as well as to push for the South China Sea. The crux was that "unless positive action is taken to re-open Burma, the offer of US help to China is meaningless." However, without British help, a Burma campaign would not succeed. Thus, Stilwell recommended that Chiang ask Washington to insist on the following: the British must take control of the Bay of Bengal, invade north Burma toward Mandalay, and take Rangoon by an amphibious operation. Stilwell also wanted a combined British-American-Chinese offensive toward Central Burma from Assam; a Chinese thrust from Yunnan into northern Burma; a "holding attack" south from China towards Hanoi-Haiphong; a northward thrust from Australia into the East Indies, New Guinea, and New Britain; and finally an American drive through the Central Pacific.[34] The Generalissimo liked Stilwell's plan and provided it to Currie, who carried it back for presentation to the JCS.

General Marshall forwarded "The Pacific Front" to the CCS for consideration. He stated that a Chinese collapse was a real possibility, an unacceptable prospect since the Chinese held down about 25 percent of all Japanese ground forces. The best way to support China, then, was an offensive into Burma to re-open the Burma Road. He then recommended that the CCS study a Burma offensive after the monsoon.[35]

The resulting CCS discussions were the first time that body considered strategy in Southeast Asia and China since ABDACOM's dissolution. The result, however, was not much different from the earlier British discussions on the same topic. Since the plan focused on China-based offensives, and Burma was necessary as a strategic rear area to support China, the CCS ordered planners to assess the Burma-focused portions of Stilwell's plan. They concluded that, while in general the plan had merit, there simply was not enough combat

---

[33] FDR Library, Map Room Papers, Series 1, Sub-Series 1, Chiang Kai-shek to Roosevelt, 27 May 1942.
[34] HIA, Stilwell Papers, Box 19–24, File 13–13a China-Burma-India, Folder 19–27, Stilwell to the Generalissimo, 18 July 1942; Box 20, File 21 Proposal, Folder 20–28, Stilwell to the Generalissimo, "The Pacific Front," undated (late July 1942).
[35] NARACP, RG 218, Records of the US JCS, Box 19, Folder CCS 318 Burma 8–25–42, CCS 104, "Retaking of Burma," 25 August 1942; CCS 104/1, "Retaking of Burma," 29 August 1942.

power or logistical capacity to allow for operations into Burma. The necessary forces would not be available until at least April 1943, after Torch. The monsoon, however, would begin soon after, pushing the start date to at least October 1943. Thus, the planners recommended, and the CCS agreed, that General Stilwell inform Chiang the Allies were determined to recapture Burma, and the plan as outlined had merit, but sufficient forces were not then available.[36] In the end, given China's place in US policy and grand strategy, Roosevelt officially informed Chiang. His message focused on Allied efforts to bolster China's defence, such as strengthening "Hump" deliveries, as well as the importance of retaking Burma: "General Stilwell's plan for retaking of Burma which Dr Currie discussed with you is now being developed by the United States Chiefs of Staff and their Planners. Burma must be recaptured in order to establish a practical supply route to China . . . I assure you that the United States will continue to do everything possible to support your forces."[37] Further reassurances came with the Casablanca conference (Symbol) in January 1943. Roosevelt wrote to Chiang just before the conference that he would "take up with the highest possible allied authorities at the earliest possible date the matter of opening the Burma Road without any avoidable delay."[38] A few days later, Roosevelt informed Chiang that he would soon meet Churchill to discuss the details of Burma plans.[39]

Anglo-American Debates over China and Grand Strategy

Symbol's primary objective was to settle European strategy in the wake of the now-successful Torch. However, these discussions also provided the first opportunity since Arcadia to discuss grand strategy against Japan at the highest levels. The British entered this conference with little to say on the subject; they preferred to keep the discussions centred on European strategy. The Americans,

---

36 NARACP, RG 218, Records of the US JCS, Box 19, Folder CCS 318 Burma 8-25-42, CCS 104/2, "Plan for the Recapture of Burma," 9 September 1942.
37 FDR Library, Map Room Papers, Series 1, Sub-Series 1, Box 10, Roosevelt to Chiang Kai-shek, 10 October 1942.
38 FDR Library, Map Room Papers, Series 1, Sub-Series 1, Box 10, Roosevelt to Chiang Kai-shek, 2 January 1943.
39 FDR Library, Map Room Papers, Series 1, Sub-Series 1, Box 10, Roosevelt to Chiang Kai-shek, 9 January 1943.

with General Marshall in the lead, wanted more attention on Burma. After the British COS, led by Chief of the Imperial General Staff Field Marshal Alan Brooke, stated that their proposed plans for Europe precluded Burma operations, Marshall responded that Burma operations were necessary to bolster Chinese morale, and relieve pressure on the Pacific fronts.[40] At a later meeting, American Chief of Naval Operations, Admiral Ernest J. King, stated bluntly, "one of the major British contributions to the defeat of Japan would be to complete the reconquest of Burma and the opening of the Burma Road," highlighting China's place in American views of grand strategy.[41] The British admitted that Burma operations might be worthwhile, but not at the expense of the "Germany-first" principle. The diversion of required supplies from Europe to Burma would jeopardize that tenet of Allied grand strategy.[42] The American chiefs, particularly Marshall, complained to Roosevelt that the British were deliberately avoiding Burma operations because of the difficulties involved and the perilous supply situation, despite ostensible Allied agreement on China's privileged strategic priority.[43]

In the end, with Roosevelt's support, the JCS convinced the British to conduct Anakim by the end of 1943. They did this by bribing the British with the promise of more assault shipping and deployment of additional naval assets to the Atlantic, to allow the British to deploy more naval forces to the Bay of Bengal. In addition, the Americans threatened that if they did not agree to retake Burma, the situation in China might become so severe that the Americans would have to re-evaluate European commitments.[44] Indeed, in the end, General Marshall later admitted that the JCS "booted" the British into agreeing to Anakim.[45]

---

40 *FRUS, The Conferences at Washington, 1941–1942 and Casablanca, 1943*, 541–542 and 545, Minutes of CCS meeting, 14 January 1943, 10.30am. The "Pacific fronts" at this time included only the massive American and Japanese commitment on Guadalcanal as well as operations in New Guinea.
41 *FRUS, The Conferences at Washington, 1941–1942 and Casablanca, 1943*, 590–91, Minutes of CCS meeting, 16 January 1943.
42 NARACP, RG 218, Records of the US JCS, Box 20, Folder CCS 318 Burma 8-25-42, CCS 154, "Operations in Burma, 1943," 17 January 1943.
43 *FRUS, The Conferences at Washington, 1941–1942 and Casablanca, 1943*, 561, Minutes of meetings between Roosevelt and JCS, 15–16 January 1943.
44 NARACP, RG 218, Records of the US JCS, Box 20, Folder CCS 318 Burma 8-25-42, Minutes of 60th CCS meeting, 18 January 1943; *FRUS, The Conferences at Washington, 1941–1942 and Casablanca, 1943*, 603 and 614–616, Minutes of CCS meeting, 16 and 18 January 1943.
45 NARACP, RG 218, Records of the US JCS, Box 20, Folder CCS 318 Burma 8-25-42, JCS Special Meeting, White House, 6 April 1943.

Roosevelt wrote to Chiang immediately to reassure him that China remained foremost in American strategic and political concerns. He reported that he and Churchill agreed "to wage war with an ever-increasing tempo against Japan" and that he was sending Lieutenant General Henry "Hap" Arnold, Commanding General of the US Army Air Forces, as yet another "personal emissary" to brief the Generalissimo, on the Symbol decisions.[46] Roosevelt's dispatch of Arnold – who would also inspect air operations in the China-Burma-India Theatre – was important to American strategy, as increased air operations and supply was close to Chiang's heart. In addition, the trip and its implications followed closely the final agreement between the United States and China, as well as between Britain and China, on their cession of extraterritorial rights in China.[47] All of this served to reinforce to Chiang the high esteem the United States held for China.

In addition to Arnold, Roosevelt sent Lieutenant General Brehon Somervell, the US Army Services of Supply chief, to assess "Hump" supply efforts, while Churchill ordered Field Marshall Sir John Dill, former Chief of the Imperial General Staff and current head of the British Joint Staff Mission in Washington, to give the British imprimatur on the agreed plans. Arnold and Dill met Stilwell and Chiang in Chungking on 6–7 February. While the issues of "Hump" tonnage and the provision of combat aircraft to Chennault and the Chinese Air Force writ large dominated, the discussions satisfied Chiang, who agreed to the Burma campaign decisions. Indeed, given the Allied agreement to provide appropriate naval support in the Bay of Bengal, he ordered Stilwell to "amplify the Chinese preparations" for their portion of the operations.[48]

Chiang wrote to Roosevelt after his meetings with the Arnold group, relaying his gratitude at their visit and the discussion on broader grand strategy and China's place within it. He reiterated requests for more aircraft and "Hump" tonnage, as well as an independent command for Chennault rather than his subordination to the 10th Air Force in India. He offered "personal assurance" that airfields and other ground facilities in support of additional air resources would be made available and that Chinese forces would be ready to undertake

---

[46] FDR Library, Map Room Papers, Box 10, Series 1, Sub-Series 1, Roosevelt to Chiang Kai-shek, 23 January 1943.
[47] The treaty was signed in January and ratified in May but the agreement was concluded on 10 October 1942. See *FRUS, China, 1943*, 690. See also Taylor, *The Generalissimo*, 216.
[48] NARACP, RG 218, Records of the US JCS, Box 20, Folder CCS 318 Burma 8–25–42, Chinese, American, and British Conferences, CCS Memorandum for Information, minutes of meetings, 6–7 February 1943, Chungking Conference, 22 February 1943.

their portion of Anakim.⁴⁹ By early March, Roosevelt acceded to Chiang's requests and ordered a new American air unit for China operations. Roosevelt promoted Chennault to major general and made him commander of the new 14th Air Force. He also promised increased combat aircraft for Chennault and additional "Hump" tonnage.⁵⁰ At the same time, he rejected Marshall's requests to be stern with Chiang, echoing Stilwell's complaints, over his vacillation concerning Chinese participation in Burma operations, and that airpower alone was the solution to China's problems. Roosevelt agreed that Chiang was difficult but respected his hard-won position in China. Moreover, his dual roles as chief executive and commander-in-chief meant that Roosevelt would not treat Chiang like "the Sultan of Morocco." He also reiterated just how important China was to the United States and that Marshall should remind Stilwell and Chennault of that fact.⁵¹

Despite British participation in the meetings with Chiang, the British remained disheartened at the prospects for Burma operations. The Cannibal offensive was going badly because British forces could not cope with the jungle terrain as well as Japanese tactics and tenacity.⁵² Moreover, GHQ India's draft plans continued to highlight the extreme logistical and geographical challenges, including the fact the required men and materiel would probably not be available for Burma's complete reconquest until May 1944.⁵³ Wavell nonetheless agreed to proceed under the Casablanca agreements but quickly fell back into his usual pessimism, concluding that operations in the coming campaign season were too difficult. Thus, in mid-March, Wavell ordered new plans using forces both already in India and earmarked for the theatre focused around operations in the Bay of Bengal, with the goal of landing in northern Sumatra. These operations would allow for Allied attacks against Japanese communications and important resource areas.⁵⁴

---

49 FDR Library, Map Room Papers, Series 1, Sub-Series 1, Box 10, Chiang Kai-shek to Roosevelt, 7 February 1943. See also Taylor, *The Generalissimo*, 226–27.
50 FDR Library, Map Room Papers, Series 1, Sub-Series 1, Box 10, Chiang Kai-shek to Roosevelt, 3 March 1943.
51 Letter from Roosevelt to Marshall, 8 March 1943, reprinted in Romanus and Sunderland, *Stilwell's Mission to China*, 279–80.
52 See the account in Field Marshal Viscount William Slim, *Defeat into Victory* (London: Pan Books, 2009).
53 NARACP, RG 218, Records of the US JCS, Box 20, Folder CCS 318 Burma 8-25-42, Chinese, American, and British Conferences, CCS Memorandum of Information No. 43, minutes of meetings, American-British Conferences New Delhi, India, 22 February 1943, "Reconquest of Burma," Summary of JPS Paper No. 47.
54 Major General S. Woodburn Kirby, *The War Against Japan* (London: HMSO, 1958), I: 362–63.

Cannibal's "lamentable failure and air of feebleness and incompetence" led Churchill to bring Wavell home for consultations.⁵⁵ In anticipation, the Joint Planning Staff studied Wavell's plans and agreed with him that logistical deficiencies, lack of airpower, and the difficulties of taking Rangoon in the face of Japanese strength made operations nearly impossible.⁵⁶ As a result, both Churchill and the COS – already tepid on Burma operations – hardened against them. Churchill began to believe that the best way to defeat Japan was a bomber offensive from China and the Soviet Union, and the best way to support China was via the "Hump" operations. In meantime, however, the British should use their sea power to bypass Burma.⁵⁷

British planners responded to Churchill's call with a document that outlined British views on the war against Japan. Overall, they believed that grand strategy involved five pillars: occupying the resource areas in Korea and North China; cutting communications between those areas and Japan in the Yellow Sea; a bombing offensive against Japanese industry; interdicting maritime communications between the Indies and Japan; and recapturing oil installations in Sumatra and Borneo. The first three options were untenable because they required Soviet participation. The last two options, focused on Southeast Asia, were the most tenable via an advance from the Central Pacific to the Philippines or Formosa, an advance from Australia via New Guinea through Borneo or Mindanao to the South China Sea, or an advance via Sumatra and Singapore to Borneo. Moreover, British planners assessed current and planned operations and stated that, while supporting China via the "Hump" remained politically attractive and should continue, the Americans overestimated the Burma Road's capacity. Moreover, the Chinese appeared unwilling "to play a more active part . . . in the war against Japan." As a result, the British should continue to hold against Japan and plan for a later offensive when forces were available.⁵⁸ Indeed, planners emphasized that the Americans and British should agree that attacking communications between Southeast Asia and Japan and capturing the oil-producing areas there, were the best strategic options against Japan, at that time, and reconquering Burma was essentially useless relative to Japan's defeat.⁵⁹

This change in British views reached the Americans as they were preparing to allocate shipping and combat aircraft to India in anticipation of Anakim. The JCS already planned to redeploy fighter and bomber groups to India after the

---

55 NAUK, PREM3/143/10, Churchill minute, Brigadier Hollis for COS, 9 April 1943.
56 NAUK, PREM3/143/10, JP(43)146 Final, Operation "Anakim," 11 April 1943.
57 NAUK, PREM3/143/7, COS(43) 84th meeting (O), 22 April 1943.
58 NAUK, PREM3/143/7, JP(43)166 (Final), 27 April 1943.
59 NAUK, PREM3/143/7, JP(43)164 (Final), 27 April 1943.

conclusion of the Sicily operation (Husky). Moreover, the United States had already allocated 20 cargo vessels for use in India.[60] Roosevelt, however, noted as early as 6 April that the British were cooling toward Burma.[61] To discuss these simmering strategic issues, the Allies used as an excuse the fact that both Stilwell and Chennault would be in Washington, and Wavell and his air and naval commanders would be in London, to convene a conference in Washington in May.[62]

The British advocated their new strategy at the Trident conference, a strategy with which the Americans disagreed. A back-and-forth ensued between the American and British Chiefs and their respective theatre commanders about Burma and broader Southeast Asia. The British conceded that Burma's reconquest was desirable but was simply too difficult at that time. Any Burma operations should be limited to small operations in northern Burma in support of the Burma Road and the "Hump," with main force operations directed toward Sumatra and Bangkok. Admiral William D. Leahy observed that those operations would not benefit China, which was the whole point of Burma operations. Indeed, discussion became so heated that the CCS had to order the room cleared for private discussions. What emerged represented another victory for American strategic views. The CCS agreed to further development of the "Hump" with the goal of 10,000 tons per month by the end of 1943, "vigorous" air and ground operations from Assam via Ledo and Imphal, as well as a Chinese offensive from Yunnan, to tie down Japanese forces and support the opening of the Burma Road. Finally, they agreed to amphibious operations to capture Akyab and Ramree Island along the Burma coast.[63] The British agreed to this because the Americans agreed to their Mediterranean strategy, namely Husky – the invasion of Sicily – and their low priority for the war in Asia.[64] Indeed, the British had only recently drafted their preferred strategy immediately before Trident,

---

[60] NARACP, RG 218, Records of the US JCS, Box 20, Folder CCS 318 Burma 8–25–42, CCS 198, Status of "Anakim," 13 April 1943; CCS 80th meeting, Supplementary minutes, 16 April 1943.
[61] NARACP, RG 218, Records of the US JCS, Box 20, Folder CCS 318 Burma 8–25–42, minutes of JCS Special Meeting, 6 April 1943.
[62] NAUK, PREM3/143/10, JSM Washington to War Cabinet, 26 April 1943; Churchill to Roosevelt, C–291, 29 April 1943 in Warren Kimball, *Churchill and Roosevelt Correspondence: The Complete Correspondence* (Princeton: University Press, 1987), 2: 202.
[63] *FRUS, Conferences at Washington and Quebec, 1943*, 55–61, Minutes of CCS meeting, 14 May 1943; Field Marshal Lord Alanbrooke, *War Diaries, 1939–1945*, eds. Alex Danchev and Daniel Todman (London: Phoenix Press, 2001), 19–20 May 1943, 406–07 (hereafter cited as *Alanbrooke Diaries*).
[64] A point made in Callahan, *Burma*, 75.

so came unprepared to lobby effectively for it, especially in the light of their European priorities and the strong American China focus.

Even before Trident, however, the British recognized American priorities and began to think of new mechanisms to enhance their lobbying against China's pull factor. For example, the Viceroy of India, Lord Linlithgow, floated the idea of a new Southeast Asia Command to manage British operations in the war against Japan.[65] Trident's results moved this suggestion forward, which then required a similar reorganization in India. Churchill, chagrined at both Wavell and the Indian Army's performance in Arakan, removed Wavell in June as Commander in Chief India and "promoted" him into the viceroyalty after Linlithgow retired.[66] Replacing him at GHQ India was General Sir Claude Auchinleck, whom Wavell had replaced as Commander-in-Chief India in 1941. However, Auchinleck, upon assuming command, came to the same conclusions as Wavell about British capabilities to retake Burma.

Churchill and the COS, eventually forced to agree with Auchinleck, knew the Americans would be apoplectic at yet another delay in Burma operations and the resultant negative impact on Chinese morale. The joint planners agreed: any delay to Burma operations would violate the Trident agreement.[67] Churchill also exploded at the thought of further delays when he wrote to the COS in response to Auchinleck's assessment: "The kind of paper that we have just received from General Auchinleck would rightly excite the deepest suspicions in the United States that we are only playing and dawdling with the war in this theatre." Churchill then recommended increasing air assistance to China, limited operations to keep the pressure on in Burma, and "far-flung" amphibious operations in areas with no monsoonal variables – an obvious reference to the Sumatra operation (Culverin).[68] As a result, they had to come to the table with something. That "something" was actually two items: the creation of a new command in Southeast Asia to manage Churchill's "far-flung" operations in Southeast Asia, and the use of Brigadier Orde Wingate's Long-Range Penetration Groups (LRPGs), also known as the Chindits, to keep the pressure on Burma.[69]

---

65 BL, India Office War Staff files, L-WS-1-1274, Organization of the Higher Command in Southeast Asia, Telegram from Viceroy to Secretary of State for India, 21 April 1943.
66 See Churchill's commentary on the Arakan in NAUK, CAB70/60/19, COS (43) 69th Meeting (O), 8 April 1943. See also, Howard, *Grand Strategy* IV, 542–43.
67 NAUK, CAB84/54/68, JP(43)254 (Final), 16 July 1943.
68 NAUK, PREM3/143/8, Churchill to Ismay, 26 July 1943.
69 Wavell knew Wingate from their time in the Middle East and asked him to come to Burma in 1942 to help in that campaign. The result was Operation Longcloth, a long-range penetration into Burma behind Japanese lines to destroy rail communications and harass Japanese forces. This operation thrilled Churchill, who was weary of British failures in Burma. For background

The upshot was that at the next conference (Quadrant) in August 1943, the British had some kind of plan for operations to support China, just as the Americans desired. The proposed new command and Wingate allowed the British to highlight their interest in Burma. Wingate's operations required no great investment in men and material and could be supplied by air, leaving the new command to concentrate on the preferred British grand strategy of operations into broader Southeast Asia. Churchill believed this approach would ensure that "the Americans will be gratified at the interest we are taking in the Japanese war and at our earnest preparations to undertake it."[70]

Meanwhile, the American position at Quadrant emerged from their own pre-conference discussions about their grand strategy to defeat Japan, which became a CCS paper for discussion at the conference. That paper determined that Japan's final defeat required an invasion of the home islands. Preceding that, China would play a key part as the Allies needed an "overwhelming air offensive from bases in China. This requires the opening of lines of communication to China, which, in turn, involves the early recapture of Burma and the seizure of a port in China. This requires a westward advance by the United States via the Central and South-Southwest Pacific."[71]

Churchill used Wingate, present at Quadrant to impress the Americans, and the soon-to-be created Southeast Asia Command (SEAC), with the American-friendly Admiral Lord Louis Mountbatten chosen as chief, to satisfy these American strategic demands. They were more than happy to unleash Wingate across northern Burma to wreak havoc behind Japanese lines, which would relieve pressure on the Burma Road, but wanted Mountbatten's main forces to occupy northern Sumatra, to interdict Japanese sea and air communications and provide a base for follow on operations. The Americans, however, were unimpressed with Culverin as it did nothing to help China and, after some discussion, were able to temper Churchill's expectations towards that operation.[72]

---

on Wingate, see Christopher Sykes, *Orde Wingate* (London: W. Collins, 1959). For an overview of Wingate's operations from Palestine to Burma, see Simon Anglim, *Orde Wingate and the British Army, 1922–1944* (London: Pickering and Chatto, 2010).
70 NAUK, PREM3/143/8, Churchill to Ismay, 19 July 1943.
71 NARACP, RG 218, Records of the US JCS, Box 128, Folder CCS 381 Japan 8-25-43, Section 6, Plan for the Defeat of Japan, CCS 301, Specific Operations in the Pacific and Far East, 1943–1944, 9 August 1943.
72 LOC, Admiral William D. Leahy Papers, Box 3, Microfilm reel 3, Diary 1943, 19 August, 1943 (hereafter *Leahy Diaries*); *FRUS, Conferences at Washington and Quebec, 1943*, 901–02, Minutes of CCS meeting with Roosevelt and Churchill, 19 August 1943. NARACP, RG 218, Records of the US JCS, Box 128, Folder CCS 381 Japan 8-25-43, Section 6, Plan for the Defeat of Japan, minutes of JCS 107th meeting, 18 August, 1943. The British themselves were not

Wingate's proposed operations, however, satisfied the Americans that operations in Burma were still on the table. Wingate even briefed Roosevelt himself on his project on 18 August.[73] Indeed, the Americans were so impressed that they agreed to form their own LRPG for deployment to Burma to operate under Stilwell's command.[74] In addition, American objections to Culverin successfully removed any serious prospects for it in the near future. China would remain the focus of Allied grand strategy, with an edict that amounted to more of the same: "The main effort should be put into offensive operations with the object of establishing land communications with China and improving and securing the air route." Supporting this were LRPG operations in northern Burma by February 1944 and an amphibious operation like "those contemplated at Trident for the capture of Akyab and Ramree" by spring 1944. In addition, the CCS agreed to increase air attacks against Japan from China with reinforced US and Chinese air forces, supply additional equipment to Chinese ground forces, and improve India's communications, to support SEAC operations.[75]

This agreement ensured some Allied action in Burma. The United States supported SEAC from the beginning for this reason. They believed SEAC was inexorably connected to China operations, with Marshall stating that "it must be remembered that, politically, all US forces in China, or in the Southeast Asia Command, were regarded as being there for the sole purpose of supporting China."[76] Indeed, Stilwell also became SEAC Deputy Supreme Commander, which allowed an American voice in theatre to ensure that Burma operations and support to China remained the priority. In order to entrench American influence over SEAC strategy, the Americans also assigned Major General Al Wedemeyer to SEAC as Mountbatten's Deputy Chief of Staff, and Lieutenant General

---

united on Culverin. Brooke thought Culverin a waste of time and resources and so informed General Marshall.

73 *FRUS, Conferences at Washington and Quebec, 1943*, 908–09, Minutes of CCS Meeting, 20 August 1943.
74 NARACP, RG 493, Records of US Forces in C-B-I, "Eyes Alone" Correspondence of General Joseph W. Stilwell, January 1942–October 1944, Microflim 1419, Roll 2, Marshall to Stilwell, 4 September 1943. The unit was eventually called the 5307th Composite Unit (Provisional), or colloquially "Merrill's Marauders."
75 *FRUS, Conferences at Washington and Quebec, 1943*, 1127, Enclosure to CCS 319/5, QUADRANT: Report to the President and Prime Minister of the final agreed summary of the conclusions reached by the Combined Chiefs of Staff, 24 August 1943.
76 *FRUS, Conferences at Washington and Quebec, 1943*, 883, Minutes of CCS meeting, 18 August 1943.

Raymond Wheeler, as the chief logistical officer, principally to oversee construction of the Burma Road.[77]

On 24 August 1943, Mountbatten received his appointment, though Churchill did not formally publish his orders until October. It outlined the quasi-convergence of American and British strategy achieved at Quadrant. It directed Mountbatten to engage Japanese forces "as closely and continuously as possible" to divert them from the Pacific advance. Of equal importance, however, was "to maintain and broaden our contacts with China" via the "Hump" as well as using "suitably organized, air-supplied ground forces of the greatest possible strength," an obvious reference to LRPGs. Lastly, and this was the key to the British strategy, Mountbatten should use "air and sea power" to capture strategic locales and compel the Japanese to disperse their forces, as well as provide a launching point for follow-on operations, which could be interpreted as either a reference to Culverin (Churchill's preferences) or the Burma coast (the American and Chinese preference).[78]

Meanwhile, Roosevelt dutifully informed Chiang of the conference results immediately upon its conclusion. Foremost was SEAC's creation, which was to "vitalize" operations in Burma. Other issues included reinforcing the "Hump" as well as the India airfields and rail networks, and the proposed offensive operations, including the Chindits. Information on Chiang's Holy Grail – an amphibious operation in the Bay of Bengal – was limited, however, as Roosevelt left the details to Mountbatten.[79]

The British were satisfied that SEAC's creation and Wingate's operations would buy them time in the face of the American push for Burma operations and aid to China. Churchill, however, was loath to sit on his laurels and began to push his broader Southeast Asia agenda with his COS. Continued debates resulted in the conclusion that the only operation they could undertake in line with Churchill's ideas of an "amphibious circus" was a landing in the Andaman Islands (Buccaneer). Underscoring this was information from Mountbatten's trip to meet the Generalissimo. While by all accounts a cordial meeting, Chiang again fell back on his demand for an amphibious operation in the Bay of Bengal.[80] As a result, in the first concept of operations he sent to Whitehall, Mountbatten

---

[77] See Albert C. Wedemeyer, *Wedemeyer Reports!* (New York: Henry Holt & Co, 1958), Ch 19.
[78] NAUK, PREM3/147/4, Directive by the Prime Minster and the Minister of Defence to Admiral Mountbatten, 21 October 1943. See also WSC V: 109.
[79] FDR Library, Map Room Papers, Box 10, Series 1, Sub-Series 1, Roosevelt to Chiang Kai-shek, 25 August 1943.
[80] NAUK, WO203/6453, Report to the Combined Chiefs of Staff by the Supreme Allied Commander Southeast Asia 1943–1946, page 34. See also Louis Mountbatten, *Personal Diary of*

agreed that Buccaneer was the most practical amphibious operation given extant resources, while also advocating the usual advance into north Burma with British and Chinese forces.[81] A strategic stalemate ensued among the British. The COS wanted to limit operations in Asia as much as possible, Churchill wanted his Southeast Asia offensive, and Mountbatten, whose command existed, according to the Americans, primarily to support China, was caught in the middle.

China's Apogee at Cairo

This unsettled strategic atmosphere underscored the discussions at the next Allied conference in Cairo at the end of November. It was here that Asia grand strategy loomed large, especially since Chiang Kai-shek attended. The Americans had pushed hard for some grand strategic consensus relative to the war against Japan, as well as China's role in it beyond the Quadrant agreements, and brought a draft plan for the defeat of Japan, which the British, Americans and Chinese would discuss at Cairo. This plan began the US move away from the focus on China's military role against Japan, because it promoted a Pacific-focused main effort.[82]

Despite this new strategic approach, Roosevelt was excited to meet Chiang. He wrote to him on 27 October expressing his eagerness to meet.[83] Certainly, the gregarious Roosevelt wanted to meet the figure with whom he had exchanged much correspondence but he also had practical reasons. For example, Roosevelt informed Chiang on 10 November that the US would soon begin strategic bombing operations against Japan and asked that Chiang supply bases in southwest China for this purpose.[84] This new strategic variable plus the Four Power Declaration, which the United States, Britain, the Soviet Union and China signed in Moscow just before Cairo, combined to provide further evidence of

---

Admiral the Lord Louis Mountbatten, ed. Philip Ziegler (London: Collins, 1988), 10–16 (hereafter *Mountbatten Diaries*).
81 NAUK, PREM3/148/1, Armindia to Air Ministry, SEACOS 19, 10 November 1943.
82 NARACP, RG 218, Records of the US JCS, Box 129, Folder CCS 381 Japan, Plan for the Defeat of Japan, CCS 417, Overall Plan for the Defeat of Japan, 2 December 1943.
83 FDR Library, Map Room Papers, Box 10, Series 1, Sub-Series 1, Roosevelt to Chiang Kai-shek, 27 October 1943.
84 FDR Library, Map Room Papers, Box 10, Series 1, Sub-Series 1, Roosevelt to Chiang Kai-shek, 10 November 1943. See also Wesley Craven and James Cate, *The Army Air Forces in World War II, Vol. 5, The Pacific: Matterhorn to Nagasaki, June 1944–August 1945* (Washington: Office of Air Force History, 1983), 13–32.

China's wartime role as well as its postwar potential. The Four Power Declaration stated that the signatories would "work together for the organization and maintenance of peace and security."[85] The Declaration was itself an extension of Roosevelts' "Four Policemen" concept he first espoused in 1941 and included China.[86] Delighted at the invitation as well as China's inclusion in the Four Power Declaration, Chiang wrote to Roosevelt that the pact was a "splendid success" and would be among "the greatest contributions to peace and security in the Post War World" and that "China is proud to have taken part in the consummation of the Declaration."[87]

The first Cairo Conference (Sextant) did not run smoothly.[88] The British were unhappy at Chinese attendance and the strategic problems it wrought. Churchill wanted the talks limited to Anglo-American participants because he felt China and its role in the global war was only of minor importance.[89] Brooke also commented, after a particularly laborious CCS meeting with the Chinese staff, that it was a "ghastly affair" and blamed the Americans for inviting them and forcing the attendees to suffer their "distressing interlude."[90] The Chinese were there nonetheless and the Americans were eager to include them in the discussions. Primarily, they wanted finally to gain Chiang's acceptance of Burma operations. To accomplish this, Mountbatten took centre stage and used the opportunity to present outline plans for Burma operations as well as other "far-flung" operations, such as Culverin and Buccaneer. Burma plans remained largely the same: an advance in January into northern Burma with General Stilwell's Chinese forces, and the use of Wingate's Chindits in February to disrupt Japanese communications, while the main forces advanced. Mountbatten added another Arakan advance as well, all intended to disperse the Japanese in Burma and allow the Allies to open the Burma Road and shorten the flight over the "Hump."[91]

---

85 Officially called the "Declaration of Four Nations on General Security." The text is in *FRUS, General, 1943*, I: 755–56.

86 On the "Four Policemen," see Warren Kimball, *The Juggler: Franklin Roosevelt as Wartime Statesmen* (Princeton: Princeton University Press, 1991), 83–105. On China and the "Four Policemen," see Robert Dallek, *Franklin D. Roosevelt and American Foreign Policy, 1932–1945* (New York: Oxford University Press, 1979), 389–90.

87 FDR Library, Map Room Papers, Box 10, Series 1, Sub-Series 1, Chiang Kai-shek to Roosevelt, 2 and 3 November 1943.

88 The Cairo conference was split into two sessions so the Anglo-American delegation could meet Josef Stalin in Tehran.

89 WSC V: 289–290.

90 *Alanbrooke Diaries*, 478–80.

91 *FRUS, The Conferences at Cairo and Tehran, 1943*, 312–15, Plenary meeting, 23 November 1943.

The Generalissimo, however, demurred as he felt this was not enough. He believed that retaking Burma was the key to the entire war against Japan, since retaking Burma would finally allow the Chinese army to march and retake all of China. Indeed, Stilwell, in an attempt to satisfy Chiang, as well as operate within broader American policy about China's importance, submitted to the CCS a memo that outlined his views on China's place in the war. It advocated continued supply operations, Burma's full clearance, and strategic bombing of Japan from China, all culminating in Chinese and American ground advances towards Hong Kong and Shanghai by November 1945.[92] Chiang agreed with the added stipulation that Chinese troops would not advance into Burma without both naval superiority in the Bay of Bengal and an accompanying amphibious operation, with Buccaneer an acceptable option. He also remained insistent on 10,000 tons per month over the "Hump." To assuage Chiang's fears, Churchill promised that – after the Italian fleet's surrender in September – the British could achieve naval superiority in the Bay of Bengal, though the Allies could not promise to time an amphibious operation with the planned land campaign in Burma because of operational and logistical considerations.[93]

As the first Cairo conference ended and the principal attendees adjourned to Tehran or Chungking, the Allies remained in a quandary over Burma operations. The CCS asked Mountbatten to draft a memo to Chiang to seek his agreement on those operations. Since the Generalissimo's plan was too risky and logistically infeasible, Mountbatten asked him to agree to his original plan to clear north Burma. Chiang at first agreed to the operations as outlined, even somewhat mollified by Churchill's statement on the Bay of Bengal, only to change his mind later in the afternoon. Roosevelt, Churchill, and Madam Chiang all approached the Generalissimo and regained his acceptance of Mountbatten's plan. Just before his departure, however, he changed his mind one last time and ordered Stilwell not to agree.[94]

---

92 FRUS, *The Conferences at Cairo and Tehran, 1943*, 371–72, CCS 405, "Role of China in Defeat of Japan," 22 November 1943.
93 FRUS, *The Conferences at Cairo and Tehran, 1943*, 338, Minutes of Combined Chiefs of Staff meetings, 24–25 November 1943.
94 FRUS, *The Conferences at Cairo and Tehran, 1943*, 430, CCS 411/2, 26 November 1943. See also *Mountbatten Diaries*, 34–36 and Stilwell, *The Stilwell Papers*, 246–47. Jay Taylor speculates that these reversals were, in fact, not reversals, and that Chiang had agreed to Mountbatten's ideas from the beginning. Instead, they were misunderstandings amongst the stakeholders and misrepresentations by Stilwell. While this may be true, it misses the point. Roosevelt, Churchill, Mountbatten, the CCS, and especially Stilwell all believed that Chiang was indecisive, which undoubtedly affected later discussions as well as attitudes toward Chiang and the Chinese in general. See Taylor, *The Generalissimo*, 250–252.

Upon their return from Tehran – where Roosevelt and Churchill pledged to Joseph Stalin that they would invade France in May 1944 (Overlord) and Stalin agreed to enter the war against Japan within three months of Germany's defeat – the United States and Britain needed to finalize their grand strategy against Japan within this new strategic context. First on the agenda was Buccaneer, some version of which Churchill had promised to Chiang days before. Churchill was no fan of Buccaneer, preferring Culverin and related follow-on operations towards Singapore. In addition, the Soviet pledge to enter the war changed the strategic picture. Soviet territory would provide much better bases than China from which to launch attacks on Japan proper and, thus, the need for Burma operations was now even lower. Likewise, now that Overlord was officially on the books, the staffs should reexamine all Southeast Asia operations in that context. King and Marshall countered that Buccaneer was necessary, both to disperse Japanese forces in preparation for the planned offensives in the Pacific as well as to guarantee Chinese participation in Burma operations. Roosevelt agreed, and stated that the Allies could not abandon the operation because of promises to Chiang. In the end, Buccaneer was necessary but so was Overlord. Mountbatten should proceed with Buccaneer with the understanding that he would receive no additional forces.[95]

This disagreement continued between the British and American Chiefs in their own discussions. The British Chiefs believed, taking their cue from Churchill, that Buccaneer was not militarily useful. In addition, the amount of amphibious lift required for Buccaneer, scheduled for March 1944, adversely affected the margins required for Overlord. The Americans vehemently disagreed. They fell back on the promise to Chiang of an amphibious operation as down payment for their participation in reconquering Burma. According to Leahy, "the enemy must be engaged in Burma, since unless this were done, they would be able to stop the supply route to China." Brooke disagreed because he felt the Americans overestimated Chinese fighting prowess, not to mention willingness, and that the Japanese could no longer seriously threaten the air route, since the Indian airfields were secure and the Allies could threaten Japanese airbases in Burma. In the end, this debate became so acrimonious that both sides agreed to refer the decision to Roosevelt and Churchill.[96]

Once Churchill and Roosevelt entered the fray, the debate over Buccaneer boiled down to landing craft availability. A long, heated argument erupted over

---

[95] FRUS, *The Conferences at Cairo and Tehran, 1943*, 676–81, Minutes of Combined Chiefs of Staff meeting with Roosevelt and Churchill, 4 December 1943.
[96] FRUS, *The Conferences at Cairo and Tehran, 1943*, 687–88 and 700–04, Minutes of Combined Chiefs of Staff meetings, 4 and 5 December 1943; *Alanbrooke Diaries*, 5 December 1943, 491.

landing craft, the required lift for Overlord – and its cousin Anvil, the landings in southern France – and the number of troops that the diversion of Buccaneer's craft to those European operations would allow. Finally, the British Chief of Air Staff, Air Chief Marshal Charles Portal, recommended that instead of Buccaneer, the Allies launch a series of naval-supported commando raids along the Burma coast.[97] Portal's suggestion apparently offered Roosevelt a way out of the deadlock. On 5 December, Roosevelt told the JCS to give up on the project and sent a short note to Churchill that read, "Buccaneer is off."[98] He sent a message to the Generalissimo the same day stating that the meetings with Stalin produced an agreement on operations that would end the war against Germany in 1944 but those operations required a heavy logistical commitment. Thus, it was "impractical" to launch amphibious operations concurrent with the Burma offensive. Instead, he asked Chiang to proceed with the offensive and offered naval control of the Bay of Bengal, Portal's idea of naval and commando raids on the Burma coast, and strategic bombing operations against Bangkok.[99]

Chiang left Cairo elated, but his elation was short-lived. He felt China's inclusion in the conference had finally showed the world that China had indeed achieved Great Power status. Moreover, the Cairo Declaration, signed 1 December by the United States, Britain, and China, affirmed that all territories Japan had taken from China would be returned, including Manchuria and Formosa. This further enhanced China's reputation and its morale, with Chiang even commenting on such in a message to Roosevelt on 9 December.[100] In the same note, however, Chiang accepted the new Allied strategy as Roosevelt outlined but expressed fear that, without his strategy, including Buccaneer's cancellation, China might collapse. Thus, he asked for a loan of US$1 billion in gold, a doubling of both the size of the Chinese Air Force as well as the American air deployment in China, and 20,000 tons per month "Hump" transport.[101] Roosevelt responded with mollifying, but understated, language. He thanked

---

97 *FRUS, The Conferences at Cairo and Tehran, 1943*, 705–12, Minutes of Combined Chiefs of Staff meeting with Roosevelt and Churchill, 5 December 1943.
98 *FRUS, The Conferences at Cairo and Tehran, 1943*, 726–27, Roosevelt meeting with Joint Chiefs of Staff, 5 December 1943; WSC V, 364; *Alanbrooke Diaries*, 6 December 1943, 492.
99 *FRUS, The Conferences at Cairo and Tehran, 1943*, 803–04, Roosevelt to Churchill, 5 December 1943; FDR Library, Map Room Papers, Series 1, Sub-Series 1, Box 10, Roosevelt to Chiang Kai-shek, 5 December 1943.
100 FDR Library, Map Room Papers, Series 1, Sub-Series 1, Box 10, Chiang Kai-shek to Roosevelt, 9 December 1943. The Declaration's text is in *FRUS, The Conferences at Cairo and Tehran, 1943*, 449. For a discussion of the conference's effects on Chiang and China, see Taylor, *The Generalissimo*, 254.
101 Ibid.

the Generalissimo for agreeing to his outline strategy and reminded him of the strategic bombing operations that would "do much to heighten the morale of both our countries." However, he also reminded Chiang that Burma was the key to China's war. It needed clearing to ensure enough supplies for China's ground forces as well as Chennault's air forces, and he hoped Chiang would commit his forces to the planned offensives. Lastly, he shrugged off the question of the loan, stating that the Treasury department would study the issue.[102]

The reason for Roosevelt's understated response is the new role the United States envisioned for China as well as the history of American perception of China's actions since Pearl Harbor. The new grand strategy the Allies agreed to at Cairo called for the main effort to run through the Philippines and the Pacific.[103] The China-based strategic bombing campaign was a supporting operation, a situation that the American JCS confirmed in March 1944.[104] This new strategic situation effectively allowed Roosevelt to change American grand strategy on the fly. When he cancelled Buccaneer – an act so abrupt that the JCS were unaware of it until it happened – China lost its privileged position in American grand strategy.[105] To be sure, China's geography and manpower remained important factors in American grand strategy. Bases for strategic bombers and millions of Chinese troops holding down hundreds of thousands of Japanese troops were no small things. But with Roosevelt's decision, the idea of an American-led, Chinese-resourced grand counter-offensive against Japan effectively died.

Underscoring this change was Roosevelt's fatigue at not only fighting with Churchill over European strategy, and waning respect for China and its role in the war against Japan, but also his desire to reap the rewards of a loyal postwar Chinese ally. Roosevelt cancelled Buccaneer because he and Stalin had effectively bullied Churchill into agreeing to Overlord, and giving in on Buccaneer

---

102 FDR Library, Map Room Papers, Series 1, Sub-Series 1, Box 10, Roosevelt to Chiang Kai-shek, 20 December 1943.
103 NARACP, RG 218, Records of the US JCS, Box 129, Folder CCS 381 Japan, Plan for the Defeat of Japan, CCS 417, Overall Plan for the Defeat of Japan, 2 December 1943.
104 NARACP, RG 218, Records of the US JCS, Box 129, Folder CCS 381 Japan 8-25-42, Plan for the Defeat of Japan, 1, JCS to MacArthur, Richardson and Nimitz, 2 March 1944; see also Box 21, Folder CCS 381 Burma 8-25-42, Retaking of Burma 7, Correspondence from 2-25-44 to 4-20-44, Handy to Stilwell and Sultan, 26 March 1944.
105 As of 5 December 1943, the JCS were still pushing the British to launch Buccaneer in deference to Chinese wishes. See *FRUS, The Conferences at Cairo and Tehran, 1943*, 687–88 and 700–04, Minutes of CCS meetings, 4 and 5 December 1943.

was an easy way to repay that political debt.[106] However, Roosevelt also was acutely aware of Stilwell's troubles with the Generalissimo, the debate over Chennault's air strategy and Stilwell's ground strategy, Chiang's constant demands for more "Hump" tonnage and, generally, more US and Allied acceptance that China was the key to winning the war against Japan. Despite Roosevelt's desire not to treat Chiang like the "Sultan of Morocco," his frustration was beginning to show. Roosevelt told his son Elliott, who was present at Cairo, that he had met Chiang but could not understand why his troops were not fighting, why Chiang fought against Stilwell's plan to train troops at Ramgarh, and why Chiang wasted so much military potential bottling up the Communists.[107] These thoughts echoed reports he received from Stilwell, the War Department, and Embassy officials. Roosevelt also later told Stilwell that he did not believe Congress would approve the loan, with the implication that he would not lobby for it. Despite this, he still wanted a strong postwar China. Harry Hopkins, echoing Roosevelt's own thoughts, stated at a meeting between Roosevelt and Stilwell that "China will need our help in rehabilitation. Communication – river, coastal and oceanic. How far should we go in helping on communications. Industry, the same thing. The Far East is going to be the most important zone in our foreign affairs."[108] This later perception is important. Buccaneer's cancellation was not the end of China's place in American strategic thinking, though now it was focused on what it could become rather than what it could do. Indeed, what it could do was fast becoming a liability.

Denouement: China and Britain in American Grand Strategy

Because of 14th Air Force's increased attacks on Japanese communications and nascent strategic bombing operations that began in spring 1944, Japan launched Operation Ichi-Go against Chinese airfields in southern China. At the same time, they launched Operation U-Go to eliminate the British threat from India, including

---

106 Roosevelt told Stilwell he had been "stubborn as a mule" over China's place in Allied strategy in general, and Buccaneer was a manifestation of that, but felt he owed it to Churchill because of the more important Overlord. See Stilwell, *The Stilwell Papers*, 251.
107 Elliott Roosevelt, *As He Saw It* (New York: Duell, Sloan & Peirce, 1946), 142.
108 Harry S. Truman Memorial Library, John Paton Davies Papers, Folder John P. Davies Chronological File, 1942–45 (2 of 3), Box 11, 6 December 1943. See also Stilwell, *The Stilwell Papers*, 251–52.

the airfields supplying China.[109] In the midst of these offensives, Stilwell's relationship with Chiang finally broke. Stilwell undiplomatically fought with Chiang over his possible command of Chinese ground forces, which Stilwell considered essential given the need to protect Chinese airfields with those ground forces as the air offensives proceeded, and to support the now underway campaign to clear north Burma. Indeed, that spring he gave up arguing with Chiang, either ignoring him or responding with typically derisive language, and spent most of his time in north Burma supervising the offensive against Myitkyina.[110] But by October, as the Ichi-Go offensive threatened to become a steamroller, the question of Stilwell's command over Chinese troops finally came to a head when Chiang formally requested Stilwell's relief. Roosevelt agreed and wrote to Chiang that the situation had become so bad on the ground that the "United States Government should not assume the responsibility involved in placing an American officer in command of your ground forces throughout China." Stilwell's recall was the conclusion of the events set in motion by Buccaneer's cancellation. This American grand strategy decision removed any vestiges of American support for any Chinese offensive role in the grand strategy to defeat Japan; it would now be limited to pinning Japanese troops.[111] Indeed, Major General Wedemeyer, Stilwell's replacement, was a career staff officer with no combat or command experience, suggesting the United States was no longer interested in China's potential for counter-offensive. Moreover, despite the fact that his new position was effectively a promotion, he was not promoted to lieutenant general until January 1945, suggesting that the position was no longer as important as it once was. By November, even China's role as a base for US strategic bombers waned; by January, Wedemeyer recommended it be stopped.[112]

---

109 On Ichi-Go, see Hara Takeshi, "The Ichigō Offensive," in *The Battle for China: Essays on the Military History of the Sino-Japanese War of 1937–1945*, eds. Mark Peattie, Edward Drea and Hans van de Ven (Stanford: University Press, 2010), 392–402. On U-Go, also called the Imphal-Kohima Offensive, see Raymond Callahan, *Triumph at Imphal-Kohima: How the British Army Finally Stopped the Japanese Juggernaut* (Lawrence, KS: University of Kansas Press, 2017).
110 Stilwell and "Merrill's Marauders" captured the airfield in May, thus relieving the Japanese air threat to the "Hump."
111 FDR Library, Map Room Papers, Series 1, Sub-Series 1, Box 10, Roosevelt to Chiang Kai-shek, 18 October 1944.
112 As of November 1944, the JCS already planned that no additional B-29s would deploy to the India-Burma Theater. By January 1945, Wedemeyer asked the JCS to remove XX Bomber Command from China due to logistics difficulties. General Arnold agreed and recommended its move to the Marianas. See NARACP, RG 218, Records of the US JCS, Box 116, Folder CCS 373.11, Japan

Meanwhile, the British in the wake of Cairo entered into a long strategic discussion that lasted most of 1944 over their role in the grand strategy to defeat Japan. These discussions, oftentimes venomous between Churchill and the COS, centered on the questions of operations in Southeast Asia, from Sumatra to Singapore and into the South China Sea, a British expeditionary force based in Australia for operations through Borneo, or joining the American naval offensive toward Japan. Underscoring these discussions was the political question as to their purpose. Churchill, who consistently lost the fight that his preferred Southeast Asia strategy was the best contribution that Britain could make, now abandoned that argument in favour of recovering British prestige and lost imperial possessions. The COS, instead, favoured using a newly reformed British Pacific Fleet to accompany the American offensive. The Americans had little interest in these discussions as their offensive became a steamroller and China's place in the grand strategy, the whole reason for their interest, was now limited to ancillary operations. By October, the COS finally convinced Churchill to accept their views; the Americans agreed at the second Quebec conference in October.[113]

In the meantime, the Indian Army broke U-Go, which finally enabled their counterattack into Burma. The result was the final reconquest of Burma by May 1945, culminating with the British Indian 14th Army's much vaunted charge through Burma as well as an amphibious landing near Rangoon.[114] In northern Burma, however, the Allied re-opening of the Burma Road in January 1945 finally accomplished the political objective, the only objective left after Cairo, of supplying China. Thus, the campaign to reconquer all of Burma became what one historian aptly labeled a "private war between [the 14th Army] and the Japanese" that, in the end, contributed little to the overall defeat of Japan.[115]

8–20–43, Section 8, Air Plan for the Defeat of Japan, JCS 1190/4, Movement of XX Bomber Command from China, 15 January 1945. See also Craven and Cate, *Matterhorn to Nagasaki*, 165–75.

113 An overview is in Marc Jacobsen, "Winston Churchill and the Third Front," *Journal of Strategic Studies* 14:3, 337–62. A more detailed examination is in John Ehrman, *Grand Strategy* V (London: HMSO, 1956), Chs. 11–12.

114 See Raymond Callahan and Daniel Marston, *The 1945 Burma Campaign and the Transformation of the Indian Army* (Lawrence, KS: University Press of Kansas, 2021).

115 Callahan, *Burma*, 141 and 163.

Conclusion

In the end, treating China as a Great Power became less a means of grand strategy and more a political end in and of itself. Even before the war, the United States wanted to support China as a bulwark against Japan. Loans and China's inclusion as one of the first Lend-Lease recipients underscored this burgeoning American plan to use China as a means of grand strategy. Indeed, as war became inevitable, the United States had only China, to be used in some undefined way, and the Pacific Fleet, as the primary means of its grand strategy.

After Pearl Harbor, and the loss of its primary offensive tool against Japan, the United States moved quickly to define China's role in overall grand strategy against Japan. The US – at Roosevelt's insistence – worked with Chiang to create a China Theatre and named a prominent American general – at the Generalissimo's insistence – to lead an American mission and serve as his chief of staff. Moreover, Roosevelt enjoyed a lively personal correspondence with Chiang and sent him personal representatives to highlight the strong relationship between the two countries, as well as show China and the world that the United States viewed China as a Great Power.

Underscoring this was China's place relative to Great Britain. Certainly, there could be no equal to the "Grand Alliance" that emerged between the United States and Britain relative to the war against Germany. For the war in Asia, however, the Americans made it clear from the start that China was the main ally and all Allied efforts should go toward supporting it. The United States dictated a strategy that centred on Burma as China's strategic rear area. Without its clearance, as US and Chinese logic went, then China would be of no use in the war. Indeed, it could become a liability. The British, no fan of China or its supposed capabilities, fought against the China strategy in favour of their own preferred strategy. The US attitude and treatment of China shone through most clearly in these Allied discussions. As Roosevelt, Churchill, and the CCS negotiated with, threatened and bribed each other to achieve their preferred strategic directions, it was the American view of China that triumphed.

Finally, however, China lost its privileged place. The message from Roosevelt to Chiang on Stilwell's relief was not a message between equals but one from a frustrated father to a petulant child. By that point, the war's broader direction, as well as the tumult of the Chiang-Stilwell relationship, and the related tyrannies of distance and logistics, forced the United States to adopt a different grand strategy. China still had a role to play, though an ancillary one, holding down hundreds of thousands of Japanese troops. But as the American drive toward Japan intensified, China became nothing more than a strategic and political legacy. That legacy, however, augured China's potential as a strong postwar ally. Wartime agreements, declarations, emissaries, and strategic discussions helped build this potential, and it was this potential that prevented the United States from abandoning China. Indeed, the postwar period saw the United States experience even more intense struggles with and about China, as it attempted to prevent civil war while also grooming it as an ally. Underscoring this postwar situation was the American attempt to win the Pacific War by treating China as a Great Power.

Karl Hack
Grand Strategy and Its Layers: Britain and Southeast Asia, 1946–1954

This chapter starts with an apparent paradox. In 1942, Singapore fell, and Britain was humiliated, after plans to defend it and Malaya by holding a "Songkhla line" in southern Thailand proved abortive. "Operation Matador," which called for forces to rush across the border and seize a narrow defensive line across the Kra Isthmus, was never launched. Yet almost identical British plans emerged over 1950–1953. How could that be?

What might the answer tell us about British strategy for Asia and about strategy and "grand strategy" more generally? This chapter argues that the answer is to be found in the layered, pluralistic nature of "grand strategy" as an orchestrating force. Grand strategy for Britain consisted of orchestrating multiple subordinate strategies and instruments, for different functions (notably military, foreign policy, and colonial) and varied regions. Southeast Asian regional strategy was in turn formed by coordinating several sub-strands: historical "lessons"; planning apparatus in London and Singapore; global strategy, regional strategy; and finally force availability and posture (intended and actual). Within each of these strands there was a hierarchy. Global strategies set broad constraints, within which regional strategies had to nest, and then local dispositions and plans in turn. Taking these layers and ingredients together, the similarities and contrasts between the resulting dispositions and plans in 1942 and the 1950s – particularly the resurrection of Songkhla planning – start to make more sense, or at least to seem less nonsensical.

In turn, this suggests that existing definitions of "grand strategy" – and articulations of it as DIME (Diplomatic, Intelligence, Military and Economic) and other acronyms – might need to be more aware of both "historical lessons," and the assumed common sense those feed into calculations, and interactions between the global, regional and local layers.[1] It also suggests that "Grand Strategy," for some powers and periods at least, can be located as much in overlapping

---

[1] See US Joint Doctrine Note 1–18, Strategy, 25 April 2018: https://www.jcs.mil/Portals/36/Documents/Doctrine/jdn_jg/jdn1_18.pdf?ver=2018104125115004391540 and the conclusion to this chapter.

Note on sources: unless otherwise stated references are from the National Archives United Kingdom (NAUK).

https://doi.org/10.1515/9783110718713-009

networks of key central and regional actors and the evolving core of their thinking, as in any specific top level actors, principles or machinery.[2] As the Introduction suggests, national-level planning could be held captive by memory and regional circumstance. In this case at least, grand strategic limitations programmed in disaster in 1941–42, and then memory of that disaster helped to shape strategy long into the future.

Songkhla Plans in 1941 and 1950–1957

Plan Matador of 1941 aimed to hold any Japanese landward attack on the Singapore naval base (which faced the Malayan mainland across the narrow Johor Strait) as far from the base as possible. Defending the base near the base was out of the question, since that might make it vulnerable to aircraft and artillery, and allow the attacker to interdict naval and air reinforcements. The latter were crucial, since British strategy rested on holding on long enough for Malaya to receive reinforcements. Hard-pressed in Europe and the Mediterranean, this allowed Britain to concentrate resources on other threats unless and until Malaya was in imminent danger, if not actually attacked. The "period before relief" (before a main fleet could arrive from elsewhere) gradually increased from 42 days to over 180 by September 1939 and became indeterminate after mid-1940.

A defensive line in central Malaya, one of the few places where there was a good east-west road, would still offer insufficient depth of defence. As the peninsula bulged here to its widest, around 320km (200 miles) across, it would also suffer from a long lateral communication line over the mountain spine that dissected the territory. The border with Thailand was also unsuitable, given it snaked 595km over mountain and jungle. By contrast, South Thailand's plains offered a 100km front with good lateral communications. This would screen Malaya's excellent west coast road system, and the northern airfields through which air reinforcements could be flown via India and Burma.[3]

There were three main flaws with the position in 1941. First, the need to wait for reinforcements of ships, aircraft, and tanks meant forward defenders

---

[2] This is echoed by the 'perceptual factors' and emphasis on responding to exigencies rather than shaping them per se of Thierry Balzacq, Peter Dombrowski, and Simon Reich, "Comparative Grand Strategy: A Framework and Cases," Oxford Scholarship Online, July 2019: DOI: 10.1093/oso/9780198840848.001.0001.

[3] 1951 BDCC(FE) reasons for a Songkhla position echoed Matador's rationale: DEFE11/42, BDCC(FE) to COS, SEACOS 235, 27 September 1951.

risked being outgunned even if they were not outflanked by landings elsewhere.[4] Second, the enemy's air and sea supremacy meant it could choose where to land, so defending forces had to be widely dispersed. Third, the position needed to be prepared at least 24 hours before invasion and ideally at least three days, but there was likely to be reluctance to violate Thai neutrality unless attack was certain. It was almost inevitable that British representatives in Thailand would argue against occupation before any Japanese arrived on Thai soil, and that local representatives would want clear prior approval from London.

This last flaw, the difficulty of launching a pre-emptive occupation, was potentially crippling. How could a commander-in-chief be sure the Japanese ships spotted near the Gulf of Siam on 6 December were going to enter it, let alone invade Thailand and Malaya? What if they provoked Britain into violating Thai neutrality, so opening Thailand to Japanese influence without an invasion? In the event, the commander-in-chief ordered troops to be made ready but then waited for confirmation that the ships were part of an invasion fleet. By the afternoon of 7 December, further sightings of Japanese vessels brought him to the cusp of launching Matador.[5] But the Japanese forestalled this by landing in southern Thailand and northeast Malaya early on 8 December local time (7 December in London and Washington). From southern Thailand they made a sprint to Malaya's northwest border. Once there, they used superiority in aircraft, tanks and tactics to launch a blitzkrieg down Malaya's west coast. Singapore surrendered on 15 February, after a mere 70 days of battle.[6]

The map below shows the intended position of Operation Matador's defensive line – except the map this is based on does not date to 1941 and was not for Matador. It is adapted from a map appended to planning papers from a decade later, in 1951–1953.[7] The original was drawn up to illustrate what ultimately became Plans Warrior, Irony and Ringlet. Warrior envisaged the Songkhla [Singora] position being seized in global war and held by forces already in Malaya, or

---

[4] PREM3/168/3, General Wavell's report, Operations in Malaya and Singapore, 8 September 1942. Matador, "without denying the enemy in any appreciable degree . . . [gave] every possibility of losing an entire brigade."

[5] Major-General S. Woodburn Kirby, *The War Against Japan, Vol. I, The Loss of Singapore* (London: HMSO, 1957 [reprinted Uckfield: Naval and Military Press, 2004]), 173–86.

[6] Karl Hack and Kevin Blackburn, *Did Singapore Have to Fall?* (London: Routledge, 2004), 39–55. For Matador as promising, Ong Chit Chung, *Operation Matador* (Singapore: Times Academic Press, 1997).

[7] DEFE5/44, COS(52)72, 29 January 1952, Defence of Malaya, Background. COS(51)686 ordered BDCC(FE) to draw up plans for holding the Kra Isthmus in global war, the BDCC submitting a first paper in July 1951.

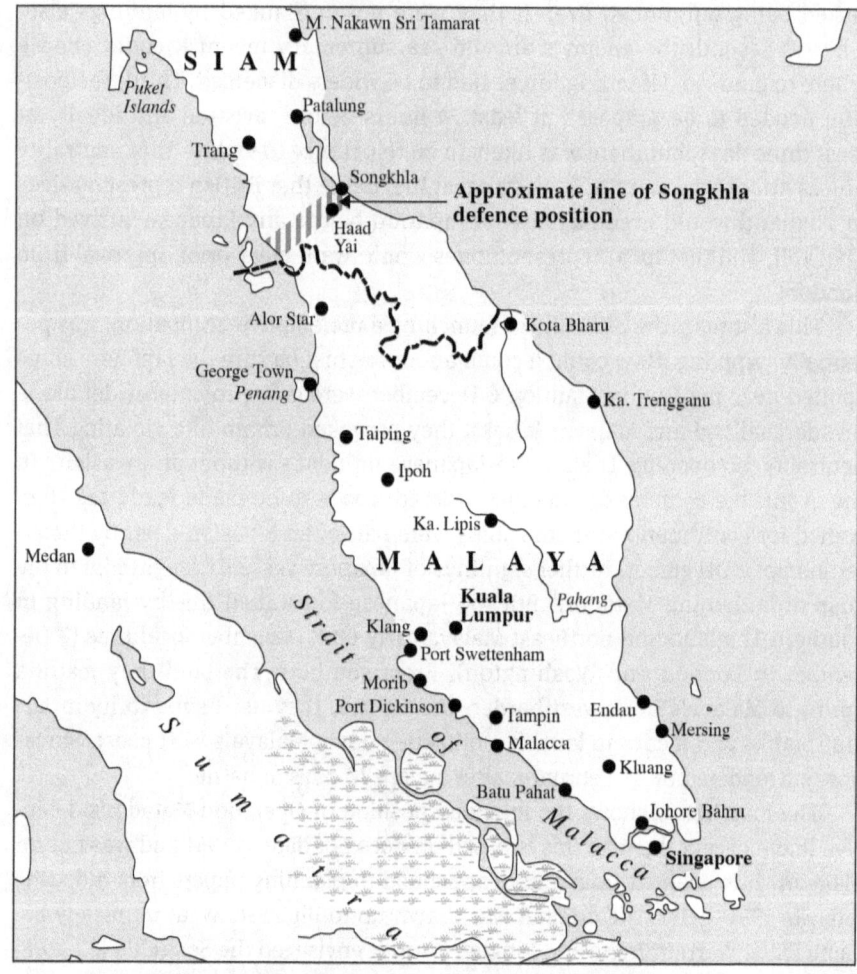

Map 6.1: The Songkhla Position in the 1950s.
Source: Karl Hack, adapted from NAUK, DEFE5/44, COS(53)99, 17 February 1953, Appendix B.

those left after some had been withdrawn for a life-and-death struggle in other theatres. The British Defence Coordination Committee (Far East) (BDCC(FE)) in Singapore even proposed they be allowed to proceed within 24 hours of sending "an emergency codeword telegram," unless explicitly countermanded.

In 1953, the British Defence Committee was reminded that, should Tonkin (northern Indochina) fall, Cabinet might have to decide whether to invade southern Thailand at short notice. The difficulty of that decision would depend on whether Chinese forces openly attacked Indochina, or communists gained control of Thailand by increments and without an overt communist Chinese march south.[8] By 1954–1955, plans called for two Special Air Service (SAS) squadrons to seize the position against little opposition when Thailand looked like falling or had just done so (whether by invasion or coup). That would pave the way for a brigade, and for the four months development needed prior to any significant attack. Ultimately, a division would be concentrated there, against communist forces that could reach 200,000 after D+4 months. Further reinforcement would depend on availability of Australian and New Zealand divisions. Irony, for limited war, was similar, but offered hope of keeping most forces in theatre. Ringlet covered a situation short of limited war, when Thailand was about to fall under communist influence, or had just done so.[9]

From 1955 there was a Commonwealth Far East Strategic Reserve (CSR) in Malaya, available for the early part of these operations. It combined Australian and New Zealand forces with British and Gurkha units (in Malaya since 1946). The CSR gained an Australian (1955 onwards) and later a New Zealand (1958) infantry battalion, multinational supporting arms, and a New Zealand SAS Squadron was available from 1955–1958. In addition, in 1954 Britain asked Australia (later New Zealand too) to switch priority for wartime reinforcement from the Middle East to Southeast Asia. That meant the position could now be reinforced by up to five divisions (three Australian, one British and one New Zealand).

Even after the American-backed Southeast Asia Treaty Organisation (SEATO) was formed in September 1954, Songkhla planning continued. With SEATO offering an American-backed guarantee to the "designated" Indochina states (Cambodia, Laos, and South Vietnam), which were forbidden by the July 1954 Geneva Agreements from joining it, British planners thought SEATO made the position more sustainable. In global and possibly in limited war involving China, American planners had also become increasingly determined that nuclear weapons should be used to blunt any major Chinese attack, by hitting bases and logistics at source. Following the Korean War and then the July 1953 armistice there, they were reluctant to commit again to large-scale conflict with China, without that added element of atomic warfare. Under Eisenhower, there was also a move in 1953 towards assuming that nuclear power, with the hydrogen bomb now also available, should be used in global war, and would quickly blunt any attack on Europe and the Middle East. American action might, therefore, reduce the residual threat to Malaya from any Chinese southward thrust. In more limited war or when Thailand had

---

[8] DEFE5/44, COS(53)99, 17 February 1953, Defence of Malaya, Recommendations; DEFE11/42, GHQ Farelf to MOD, SEACOS 142, 18 December 1950.
[9] DEFE5/54, COS(54)294, 7 September 1954.

simply dissolved into a pro-communist position internally, it was easier to imagine Britain, Australia and New Zealand finding the requisite resources anyway.

The Songkhla plans only ceased to be seen as practical in the late 1950s, as the United States became more directly involved in supporting South Vietnam, and as Australia fell in line with American insistence that the defensive focus must be on Indochina. After all, Australia's forward commitment was as much about cementing its Australia-New Zealand-United States (ANZUS) and wider relationship with the US as about any particular place. In addition, the advent of Malayan independence, on 31 August 1957, saw a local government committed to forging closer ties with Asian neighbours. A compromise had to be found that assured Britain could support SEATO, but allowed Malaya to say its bases could not be used without permission – that compromise being the British right to withdraw forces to Singapore and deploy them from there.

Plan Hermes, as the latest version of Warrior was renamed by late 1954, was now deemed politically and militarily impractical. Attention shifted to getting inner circle "Four Power" (US, Britain, Australia and New Zealand) planning so as to understand how British action could support SEATO, and what role its V-bombers and nuclear interdiction in Indochina and even the Kra might play in war.[10] By 1956, Britain was eager that, even after Malayan independence, it should retain the ability to deploy nuclear-capable bombers from Singapore. This would allow it to claim a cheap contribution to SEATO, even as it hoped to scale down forces in the area over 1957–1962.[11] The idea of being able to send up to three nuclear-capable V-bomber squadrons emerged in 1956. By 1957, this was being used to assuage Australian doubts about plans to reduce British military presence in the Malayan area.[12]

In 1957, a request was made to extend Tengah airfield in Singapore to 9,000 feet (2,700m) to allow bombers to hit targets in the Red River Delta, North Vietnam, and in South China, and the British told SEATO in March 1957 they would despatch squadrons if needed.[13] The first two Valiant bombers visited Tengah in October 1957, with regular detachments afterwards, and plans to

---

10 AIR20/10113, Hermes, eg HQ Far East Air Force to Air Ministry, Cinc22, received 6 December 1957 for VCAS.
11 PREM11/2641.
12 Ibid.
13 DEFE7/688 (22) Minute by Gough for Cole, 7 January 1958. In DC(56)18 (retained) the COS argued eastern nuclear capability was essential to retain SEATO and ANZAM credibility. DEFE7/688 (4), G. Whitturch to D.R. Serpell, 6 November 1957, for targets. DEFE7/688 (11), Minute by V.H. Cole, 22 November 1957. AIR20/10314. DEFE13/228, Memorandum to Cabinet members of 25 February 1956. Karl Hack, *Defence and Decolonisation in Southeast Asia: Britain, Malaya and Singapore, 1941 to 1968* (Richmond: Curzon, 2001), 206–10.

have nuclear weapons available by 1960 and a specialist store around 1961–1962. The plan to reinforce the east with nuclear bombers echoed prewar emphasis on just-in-time despatch of critical reinforcements. Until around 1962, it mainly consisted of flying nuclear weapons out on the planes concerned in an emergency, though there was some carrier-based nuclear capacity from around 1960.[14] Authorisation to store nuclear weapons locally at Singapore came in August 1962.[15] If Songkhla planning was an odd echo of 1941, the emerging determination to claim nuclear capability suggests a strained attempt to maintain credibility with Australia and the United States as Britain withdrew forces. Arguably, the detonation by China of a nuclear weapon in 1964 then sounded the death knell for such nuclear-based planning against China.

So until 1956–1957 the main British approach fixated on a defence just north of Malaya, rather than a regional one with allies, or one limited to Malaya. This contrasted with the 1950 views of some Malay Sultans (heads of the nine Malay States of the Federation of Malaya). In May 1950, they expressed their version of a domino theory, writing that they feared if Indochina fell, up to 40,000 armed communists could seize power in Thailand within 48 hours. Their proposed reaction was inward-looking. "With the use of bulldozers, a clearance a quarter of a mile wide . . . coast to coast [at the border]. Electric wire fencing, a permanent military garrison and mobile patrols should then enable the army to carry out a thorough sweep from the north of Malaya southward" with no back door through which "bandits" (Malayan communist-led guerrillas) might escape.[16] So the British and the Malay Sultans agreed Chinese-dominated Malayan insurgents needed to be isolated from communist expansion southward, but came to very different conclusions about how.

In summary, from 1950–1957 Britain planned for a Songkhla operation as its backstop should Indochina or Thailand, or both, fall. What combination of military, regional, and colonial strategies, combined with geography and events, led British planning back to this position – despite it having proved abortive in December 1941, and despite planners believing the real key to defending Malaya, and Southeast Asia as a whole, lay in Tonkin?

---

14 DEFE7/668, Air Ministry Works Overseas.
15 DEFE7/688 (68) and (98). DEFE5/102, 21 April 1960, Control of Nuclear Weapons. AIR23/9589. David Lee, *Eastward: A History of the RAF in the Far East* (London: HMSO, 1984). Matthew Jones, "Up the Garden Path? Britain's Nuclear History in the Far East, 1945–1962," *The International History Review* 25, 2 (2003), 306–33; Richard Moore, "Where her Majesty's Weapons Were," *Journal of the Atomic Scientists* 57, 1 (2001), 58–64.
16 CO717/197/4, Record of a meeting with the Sultans of Pahang and Perak, 15 May 1950, and Memorandum from Sultans of Johore, Pahang and Perak for James Griffiths' visit.

Military Strategy (with An Interlude on Colonial Strategy)

Key shapers of Britain's postwar military strategy for Southeast Asia included the strategic "lessons" derived from 1942, regional strategy-making machinery, resource limitations and force posture, and Britain's military, foreign and colonial strategies. In each case, local decisions had to nest in prior regional strategy, and the regional in global strategy.

First, there were the supposed lessons of the fall of Singapore, which coalesced over 1942–1946. What *could* have been deduced was that the United Kingdom could not defend the Malayan area by itself in global war conditions, or when there was major war in other theatres. After all, the British did not send Malaya the 500-plus aircraft planners originally forecast as required to meet any Japanese attack, nor the 300-plus total revised down to appear more realistic. They also repeatedly extended the period before relief, and did not send tanks before the Japanese attack began. But perhaps that was too pessimistic a lesson to seem useful.[17]

Instead, two military conclusions emerged over 1942–1946. The first was that the ideal defence was regional. If Indochina fell – as it had fallen under Japanese military control in July 1941 – the rest of Southeast Asia would be vulnerable. After all, Japanese attacks on Thailand and northeast Malaya were launched by ships and aircraft coming from Indochina. The second conclusion was that not launching Matador was an error that deprived Malaya of an adequate forward defensive line, and a way of meeting the enemy on the beaches. The rapid Thai accommodation to Japanese demands after 8 December 1941 also contributed to the belief that "the Siamese character is to bend like a reed to the prevailing wind."[18] That was consolidated by Thailand's actions in 1941–1942, and by its elite machinations of the 1940s and 1950s. To Britain, it seemed that military and civil elites with shallow democratic roots jockeyed for power. In the early 1950s, the belief was that if communism took control of Indochina, Thailand would probably fall under its influence within a short time.[19]

The lessons of Singapore's fall fed into the machinery designed for the postwar world. Britain was determined that planning should be done in broad regional terms, and that Malaya should replace a soon-to-be independent India as its main eastern military bastion, base, and location for a regional strategic

---

17 Hack and Blackburn, 48–55.
18 FO371/101172, Wallinger, Bangkok, 16 March 1952; and Wallinger to Eden, 16 April 1954.
19 Hack, *Defence and Decolonisation*, 33–55.

reserve. These conclusions in turn helped to shape planning machinery and intended force posture.

To ensure broad regional planning, the BDCC(FE) was established in Singapore from 1946. As Map 6.2 below shows, its planning area stretched from the western borders of India to Hawaii in the Pacific, and from China to what would become Indonesia. In this schema, Hong Kong was a marginal outpost to a Singapore-centred system. India was a desired ally, and Nepal the source of a continuing stream of Gurkha recruits. The BDCC(FE) was served by a plethora of committees including a local Joint Intelligence Committee (Far East). It was chaired by the Commissioner-General for Southeast Asia in Singapore, the experienced and initially influential ex-Labour Minister Malcolm MacDonald, whose relaxed informality and openness went down well regionally, and included the regional commanders-in-chief for the main three services.

MacDonald's post was in turn an amalgamation of two prior ones: the Governor-General for the Malayan area (MacDonald's post of 1946–1948) charged with bringing Britain's Southeast Asian territories (the Federation of Malaya, the colonies of Singapore, Sarawak, and North Borneo, and protectorate of Brunei) closer together; and a Foreign Office Special Commissioner concerned mainly with food shortages and brokering peace between Indonesian Republicans and Dutch in the "Netherlands East Indies."

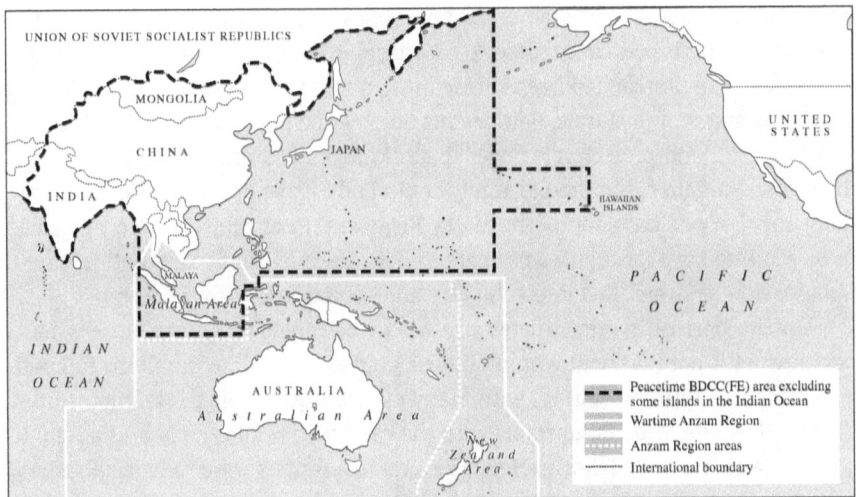

The BDCC and ANZAM areas in the early 1950s

Map 6.2: BDCC(FE), Malayan and ANZAM (Australia, New Zealand and Malaya) Planning Areas. Source: Karl Hack, adapted from an original in the NAUK, DEFE11/97.

In theory, the BDCC(FE) was supposed to have a regional strategic reserve in Malaya. This was to be a mixed British-Gurkha division, the latter to be reformed after the Gurkhas were divided between Britain and India ahead of August 1947. With Singapore's naval base, airfields, and logistics facilities at its disposal, Britain hoped it could use the reserve across the BDCC(FE) area in support of regional influence, especially if other returning colonial powers made timely concessions to nationalists and so forged new partnerships with them. By contrast, the internal and border defence of Malaya could over time fall to locally raised units. With MacDonald supposed to encourage gradual alignment (and ultimate fusion) of Malaya and Singapore, local forces were initially split by function: the Colony of Singapore getting the Royal Malayan Naval service; the Federation of Malaya a revived Malay Regiment.

Here it is worth making a brief detour to sketch in the colonial element of British strategy. At the "grand," central level, the lesson taken from 1942–1946 was threefold. First, a weakened Britain needed to rely on the Dominions as main support areas in their regions, where they would provide logistic, manufacturing, and support services.[20] They would share in or lead regional planning, in partnership with Britain. Second, India would become independent and must be courted as a new Dominion and possible military partner, which put a high premium on Britain being visibly committed to accelerated progress towards self-government more generally.[21] Third, the old trusteeship model by which Britain provided defence and an iron framework for different communities to coexist and develop in peace was insufficient. It had contributed to catastrophic defeat in Malaya. Britain's prewar Malayan territories had been divided into a mosaic of nine Sultanates (five in a loose federation), the Straits Settlements Colony (the ports of Singapore, Penang, and Malacca), and protectorates over three Borneo territories. The latter included the Brunei Sultanate, the Brooke family-controlled Sarawak, and the North Borneo Company. Bar one battalion of the Malay Regiment, local subjects were viewed as to be protected, rather than as partners in defence, and the fiercely anti-Japanese Chinese were only enrolled into voluntary and special forces from December 1941.

For the postwar world, trusteeship would be replaced by forging new partnerships with populations, who would be guided slowly but surely to full self-government within the empire, with many eventually attaining Dominion status. That is, they would be large states with the capacity for autonomy and ability to contribute to imperial defence. Hence several federations were to be established, including in the Caribbean and Central Africa, and fragmented territories such as

---

20 CAB133/86, PMM(46)1, 26 April 1946, COS Report on British Commonwealth Defence.
21 PREM8/743 Defence (Organisation) for 1947–1948.

Map 6.3: British Malaya and Its Administrative Divisions in 1941.
Source: Karl Hack (maps 1–3 use old Malayan spelling, eg Johore not Johor).

Nigeria kept as single entities. At the regional level, a new Federation of Malaya would be kept separate from Singapore (whose mainly Chinese population might otherwise make Malaya's Malays nervous). But in the long term the two should unite, initially as a pair and ultimately more widely with Borneo territories. That might produce a broader Dominion of Southeast Asia. This was a long-term, multi-decade if not multi-generational plan to turn microstates and passive subjects into partners, capable of strengthening rather than sapping British worldwide power. For this vision to come to fruition, small units had to coalesce into larger states, and subjects had to change into independent peoples freely associating with a British-led Commonwealth as *primus inter pares* (first among equals) and font of technological and diplomatic leadership. Thus the grand strategy for colonies set the tone for the regional one, and the regional approach in turn provided a frame for military planning.[22]

Returning to military planning, the proposed force posture and use of the strategic reserve were frustrated by events, namely the Malayan Emergency. Britain had provided training to Malayan Communist Party (MCP)-led anti-Japanese guerrillas in the war. Then tensions simmered between the MCP and government from 1945–1948, as the government resisted MCP attempts to control unions and push for faster reform. For instance, the MCP joined in broad protests against a British retreat in early 1948 from an original Malayan Union and generous citizenship for non-Malays, to a Federation with limited non-Malay citizenship. Faced with widespread Malay anger at the Union, Britain decided to take a step back, and work to persuade rather than force the Malays towards a broader, more inclusive "Malayan" citizenship and future.

The mainly Chinese MCP viewed that retreat as a step back to what they saw as feudalism and away from ethnic equality. They also fiercely opposed the separation of Singapore. With their protests against that separation and the new Federation ineffective, and growing tensions over MCP-led strikes and tightening restrictions on unions, they felt room for legal action was narrowing. As a result, March and May 1948 decisions committed them to gradually scale up violence, with a view to reaching full revolutionary war around September. The administration reacted to the resulting killings of blacklegs, Guomindang supporters, and then British plantation managers by declaring a state of Emergency in June 1948.

At that point there were 10 battalions in Malaya (13 with Singapore included), but many were understrength or undertrained. The proposed British-Gurkha strategic reserve was still aspiration rather than reality and some Gurkha

---

22 Hack, *Defence and Decolonisation*, 35–55.

battalions only just forming. As the Emergency deteriorated, all existing units were committed to it, and reinforcements rushed in, until in 1952 total army forces in Malaya (British and local) reached 40,000. At times, Hong Kong's already small garrison was reduced as units were moved from there to Malaya, despite the possibility of tension with Hong Kong's new communist neighbour. Around 23–25 British battalions and equivalent units were maintained in Malaya for several years from 1950, and only in the latter part of the conflict were some withdrawn from Emergency duties. So, despite a gradual decline in insurgents from a peak of around 8,000 in early 1951, to an average of 3,400 in 1954, and then just 1,830 in August 1957, force posture for the period consisted in Britain committing far greater numbers than intended, in return for which a small strategic reserve only began to coalesce from 1955.[23] Indeed, in 1948–1950 reinforcing Malaya drained UK forces so much that there was scarcely a reserve in the United Kingdom itself. Malaya's dollar earnings from rubber and tin, and its status as a "live" front in the Cold War, ensured it got priority for peacetime reinforcements in these critical years.

The silver lining to this cloud-strewn scenario was gradual victory over Malayan insurgency, and increases in local forces. The former was secured first by resettlement of Chinese squatters into "New Villages" and protection of other rural dwellers, and secondly by building upon that base control of space and people. From 1952–1953 the British then developed ever-more-refined big operations aimed at breaking MCP committees in one area after another, by a sophisticated combination of arrests, turning suppliers to provide information, and food and supply control to squeeze the insurgents, so forcing them out into killing grounds or inducing surrenders. All the while, recruitment of local forces accelerated, so that as early as 1954 Malaya had seven Malay Regiment battalions, and was starting to raise a multiracial Federation Regiment and supporting arms.

So strategic planning had to accommodate the harsh reality that the division-strong strategic reserve envisaged in 1946 never developed. Indeed, Britain was constantly looking for ways to reduce its own forces, bloated as they were by the needs of the Emergency. There was constant tension between the need to defend Malaya as a major live front in the Cold War, and the desire to draw down forces so some could return to the United Kingdom. Other commitments

---

[23] AIR20/10377, Director of Operations (Malaya), *Review of the Emergency in Malaya from June 1948 to August 1957*. Karl Hack, " 'Iron Claws on Malaya': The Historiography of the Malayan Emergency," *Journal of Southeast Asian Studies* 30, 1 (1999), 99–125; and "The Malayan Emergency as Counter-Insurgency Paradigm," *Journal of Strategic Studies*, 32, 3 (2009), 383–414.

periodically increased that tension, such as Egyptian nationalist pressure on British bases around the Suez Canal. By gradually substituting local and Commonwealth battalions (African, Fijian, Australian, and New Zealand) for British ones, the United Kingdom got the British-Gurkha share of forces committed to the Emergency back down to about 13 battalions by 1956.[24]

Planning against any regional deterioration therefore had to take cognisance of the real, as opposed to planned, force posture, and in addition had to mesh with plans for global and regional war. Global war plans went even further in restricting force availability for Southeast Asia than in 1941. Rather than envisaging Singapore being reinforced if attacked, as 1941 plans had, in the late 1940s they envisaged sending forces from there to the Middle East at the onset of global war, in a kind of "minor flotilla from Singapore" strategy.[25]

This fitted a multi-pillar view of postwar global strategy that consolidated over 1946–1948. First, a weakened Britain must fight any major war with the United States, encourage a Western European connection, and allow key Dominions such as Australia to act as "main support areas" (MSAs) in their regions. Second, with atomic power now crucial, British Empire and Middle East airbases were vital to enable bombers to strike deep into the Soviet Union, in order to blunt its thrust into Europe.[26] Even in limited war, the Middle East would remain a vital screen for oil and Africa. It became one of the initial "three pillars" of defence (UK, Middle East, Commonwealth communications), only falling from first to second priority for UK reinforcements in 1950, after the advent of NATO. Third, that meant Australian and New Zealand wartime reinforcements should again go to the Middle East, something they accepted in principle in 1949, though in reality Australia continued to plan for reinforcing *either* the Middle East or Asia in war. Britain also encouraged Australia and New Zealand to station some forces in the Middle East in peacetime, for the experience, to pre-entangle them in area defence, and as a Cold War contribution. By the early 1950s, both had aircraft stationed in the Mediterranean (Australian fighter aircraft in Malta 1952–1954, New Zealand fighter aircraft in Cyprus 1952–1955). Fourth, their status as MSAs and the need to give them confidence to send forces to the Middle East argued for giving Dominions, especially Australia, a prominent say in regional planning. The ANZUS agreement of 1951–1952 helped, by giving an apparent guarantee

---

[24] PREM1406, Memorandum by the Colonial Office on Security Situation in the Federation of Malaya, April 1949, and Note to PM (Colonial Secretary), 9 August 1951.
[25] DEFE6/11, JP(49)134(F), Plan Galloper, 1 March 1950; CO537/6264, JP(50)47(F), Strategy and Current Defence Policy in SEA and the FE, 6 April 1950.
[26] CAB131/4, DO(47)23, 7 March 1947, Memo by the COS, Defence of the Commonwealth.

their homelands would not be left unprotected if many of their forces went west. It also redoubled British desire (hurt by exclusion from ANZUS) to get meaningful regional military planning going in the area in the hope of using it to squirrel their way into American planning, and made Australia feel that serious ANZAM planning might increase its weight with the United States, and so get better access to US thinking.

Australia took up the running in suggesting planning for the waters stretching from Malaya into the Pacific back in 1948, with this dubbed the ANZAM (Australia, New Zealand, and Malayan) Area. ANZAM was initially part of the bigger planning framework for keeping Commonwealth sea and air communications going in war, intended to involve occasional planners' meetings and a naval focus. By February 1951, the United States recognised it as a planning area.[27]

Initially, planning for a Kra operation was presented as an additional reason Australasian forces could be sent to the Middle East in war. Provided the Kra position was held, Malaya could be insulated from infiltration, while the full weight of southward attack would not be felt at the Kra for nine months. Meanwhile there would be a US naval screen. Besides, neither the Soviet Union nor China were major naval powers, as Japan had been, so the threat to Australia was lower than in 1941.

Over 1952–1953, however, global planning, a shift in focus in the Cold War, and Australian attitudes, shifted in ways which ultimately undermined the Middle East emphasis. From 1952, British global war planning upgraded the impact of atomic bombing on any Soviet attack, and downgraded the likelihood of global war for as long as the significant American nuclear lead persisted. This reflected ballooning American nuclear stockpiles, and the expected arrival of the hydrogen bomb (first tested by the United States in November 1952). The decisive period in global war would now last weeks, against the months major Australasian reinforcement to the Middle East would take. In these circumstances, the Cold War was becoming a relatively greater priority than global war. Meanwhile, focus in the Cold War shifted eastwards.[28]

This shift was driven by the communist-led revolts in Southeast Asian countries from 1948, the Korean War of 1950–1953, and the deterioration in the French position in Indochina over 1950–1953. The latter saw Vietminh forces (with equipment flowing over the border from China from early 1950) cement their hold on the north of the country and then bleed over into Laos. Laos, in

---

27 Hack, *Defence and Decolonisation*, 75–78.
28 CAB131/12, D(52)41, COS, 29 September 1952. DEFE5/41, COS(52)514, 2 October 1952. DEFE32/2, COS meeting, 31 March 1952.

turn, could form a land bridge to Thailand's northeast, where Thai communists might join hands with them. Over this period, anxiety that France would be pushed out of Tonkin, if not withdraw altogether, increased, especially from 1952. Concern peaked from mid-1953, with the Korean Armistice and then proposals for a discussion of Korea at a Geneva conference in 1954. The fear was that Korean stasis might allow increased Chinese aid to Southeast Asia. Southeast Asia was seen as the Soviet Union's "proxy front" in the Cold War, with any defeat there likely to weaken the West before a major war could break out, if not presage gradual Cold War defeat without major war.

Any observer might have thought Britain would be inclined to put resources into Indochina at this point, given one of the key lessons of 1942 was that Southeast Asia had to be defended as a unit, with a forward line in Tonkin ahead of the area's crucial "rice bowls" in Thailand and Burma. In addition, from the outbreak of regional communist-inspired revolts in 1948, Malcolm MacDonald and the BDCC(FE) argued that communism might topple Southeast Asian countries like a row of dominoes, aided perhaps by their domestic Chinese minorities. These arguments were among several factors that helped cement US views of Southeast Asia over 1949–1950.[29] That view of a row of dominoes, with Tonkin the lead one, had been a constant since. But Britain had consistently refused to commit significant resources to the region beyond its own colonial territories. Discussions in mid to late 1953 continued to make it clear Britain should not risk any commitment to Indochina which might become the thin end of the wedge, and yet would be a drop in an American ocean of military and financial assistance to the French. Even requests for up to 40 transport aircraft to alleviate the pressure on the northwest went unheeded.[30]

Instead, British planners encouraged the French and Americans to make even greater efforts. The French did that in late 1953 by occupying Dien Bien Phu, a position sitting across Vietminh communications from northwestern Indochina into Laos. They hoped this might disrupt such movements, if not draw the Vietminh out to be defeated in the open. Meanwhile, British activity shifted in three ways in mid to late 1953. First, the BDCC(FE) continued Kra planning and warned they might have to ask for emergency authorisation to invade Thailand should that country slide towards communism. Second, by June 1953 the British planners became determined that the looming Korean armistice and so drawdown of Commonwealth forces there should facilitate more Australian

---

[29] Wen Qing-Ngoei, *Arc of Containment: Britain, the United States and Anticommunism in Southeast Asia* (Singapore: ISEAS, 2019), 5–9, 33–55 on MacDonald hammering this home with Americans and regional anti-Chinese sentiment fuelling regional anticommunism.
[30] CAB131/13, D(53)7, Minute 4, Southeast Asia, 24 April 1953.

forces going to Malaya (where it had sent aircraft from 1950), and the long-delayed establishment of a strategic reserve. For the latter, the aim had now shrunk to a brigade, and this was to be a Commonwealth brigade rather than the British-Gurkha division previously envisaged.[31] Third, when advised by officials that Australia would not commit more to Southeast Asia in peace while still bound to reinforce the Middle East in war, in October 1953 the COS accepted that Australia (but not yet New Zealand) should concentrate all its efforts on Southeast Asia.

By January 1954, the BDCC(FE) had endorsed this new priority for Australian forces, that they be committed to Southeast Asia in peace and wartime.[32] So by the start of the battle for Dien Bien Phu, in March 1954, it looked as if Britain might now be able to marshal resources for a more convincing Kra stand if needed. There were no longer plans to withdraw land forces from Malaya in global war, and in that and limited war a Commonwealth Far East Strategic Reserve (CSR) might soon be available to assist the position's seizure, with further reinforcements afterwards to hold it. There was also an American-led warning to China on 7 August 1953, that should major hostilities renew after any Korean Armistice, the United States and its allies would not be bound to restrict the response to the immediate area. To American planners, this was code for willingness to hit source Chinese airfields and logistics with nuclear power: something Britain soon feared the United States might do elsewhere as part of a desperate (and in British eyes almost inevitably futile) last-ditch attempt to save Dien Bien Phu.[33] From September 1954, there was also the possibility of any Chinese southward thrust tripping the American guarantee to the region contained in the Southeast Asia Collective Defence Treaty: which spawned SEATO. Even if the non-communist portion of Indochina south of the 17th parallel looked politically shaky, there was now more hope of American intervention *in extremis*.[34] So in the very worst regional scenarios it looked likely that any Chinese thrust south might be blunted long before it reached southern Thailand.

By now, East and Southeast Asia took priority over the Middle East in all conditions short of global war, since that was the live front. Losing there would, it was believed, significantly weaken the West at the onset of any

---

31 Hiroyuki Umetsu, "The Origins of the British Commonwealth Strategic Reserve," *Australian Journal of Politics and History* 50, 4 (2004), 509–25.
32 DEFE5/49, COS(53)501, Note of 8 October 1953, Australian and New Zealand Defence Contributions, as approved COS 6.10.53 for discussion with ANZ COS. DEFE11/97, (869), COS(53) 136, meeting of 1 December 1954. Hack, *Defence and Decolonisation*, 79–82.
33 Hack, *Defence and Decolonisation*, 70–72.
34 DEFE5/55, COS(54)345, 5 November 1954, Brief for C-in-C, Far East (Note by the Secretary).

limited or global war. This was the peak moment for the Kra plans. The main residual danger with the Songkhla Plan was that reinforcements might still be too slow to arrive, especially air reinforcements. In theory the Chinese airforce might concentrate up to 1,000 aircraft within a few months of overt attack, though it was hoped American actions would substantially reduce that. It therefore made sense to get additional Australian and New Zealand air as well as land elements into Malaya in peacetime, to ensure they could be brought to bear on time.

The fall of Dien Bien Phu in May 1954 and subsequent division of Indochina at the 17th parallel at the Geneva Conference in July 1954 merely confirmed that analysis. Even with the advent of SEATO, Britain could not be sure how far that body would develop into a credible organisation, and if so, when. Even if SEATO provided an effective deterrent to major Chinese incursion, it was not clear how effective it could be against subversion and outside aid.

Regional Strategy

In theory, British regional strategy – using diplomacy and assistance – should have offered an alternative stance. In practice, successive postwar visions for the region failed to come to fruition. The 1942 lesson here was that the region had to be seen as a unit and that sufficient political progress had to be achieved to make local populations active partners in defence, rather than passive recipients of protection. That crashed on the realities of the Indonesian war of independence of 1945–1949, and the French descent into the Indochinese war and foot-dragging over concessions. The 1945–1946 fantasy of Western cooperation with each other, as they slowly advanced colonial peoples to self-government and amiable postcolonial partnership, rapidly evaporated.[35]

The 1949 fantasy that replaced it was one of combining with newly independent powers, especially India, to deliver aid and assistance to the region. The hope was that this would help alleviate the social conditions on which communism fed, signal the West's genuine support for and partnership with emerging independent peoples, and so encourage the latter to align with the west at a diplomatic and military level as well as an economic one. The British recognised the French-backed Bao Dai government in Indochina in February 1950, but always

---

[35] FO371/63547, M. Dening, Note on Southeast Asia, 7 February 1947. NAA, A816/51, 11/301/698. Tilman Remme, *Britain and Regional Cooperation in Southeast Asia, 1945–1949* (London: Routledge, 1995).

felt the French were too slow to increase local political autonomy. The Dutch were pushed out of Indonesia in 1949, with a final agreement coming after a frustrating guerrilla war and American pressure. Britain therefore avoided more than minimal commitments to practical cooperation with other European powers in the wider region. The resources were not there to sustain more than minimal commitments, and they did not want to be tainted by support for fellow Western governments that, in their eyes and those of newly independent ex-colonies, appeared to be foot-dragging on concessions to nationalists.

At the same time, Britain hoped to keep a foot in the door in newly communist China, in the hope that Sino-Soviet differences would eventually emerge and these communist powers drift apart.[36] That might also make the Hong Kong colony's position less precarious. Britain was all too aware that it could not be defended against serious attack, instead keeping only enough forces there to deter any local communist official from independent action, and to manage its borders and internal security.[37] Britain duly increased the Hong Kong garrison to deter any over-adventurous local communist generals, and gave the new China de facto diplomatic recognition on 6 January 1950.

This fantasy also fell apart, if more slowly than the one about broad partnership between colonial and former colonial peoples and Western colonial powers.[38] First, a "Colombo Pact" was signed in 1950, with broad backing from Australia and Britain, and a broader Commonwealth membership that included India. India itself was kept in the Commonwealth despite becoming a Republic, by an agreement of April 1949 that recognised the Queen as the Head of the Commonwealth, but not necessarily of each individual country within it. By 1954, the United States, Thailand, Indonesia, Cambodia, and Laos were Colombo Plan members. But the financing available was limited and so the plan was unlikely to have broad impact. It did channel limited aid and technical assistance. But this had little if any effect on India and other powers' willingness to subscribe to Western diagnoses of the problems in Southeast Asia, to support the French or Bao Dai in Indochina, or to join military discussions. Instead, India gradually took up a position as an independent-minded middle power,

---

36 CAB129/CP(48)299, Recent Developments in the Civil War in China, Foreign Secretary, 9 December 1948.
37 CAB134/287, FE(O)(49)25(Revise), Draft memo by Colonial Secretary, 16 May 1949.
38 See also Robert McMahon, *The Limits of Empire: The United States and Southeast Asia since the Second World War* (New York: Columbia University Press, 1999), 43–69, 103.

that saw itself as able to deal with the West and communists alike and aspired to a degree of leadership among newly independent and neutral powers.[39]

Apart from the British-focused efforts, the Korean War made notions of China drifting away from the Soviet Union redundant in the short term at least. It also brought new pressures, such as the US desire that planning against any major new Chinese move should include strikes on China itself, possibly nuclear strikes, and pressure to block China from receiving rubber and other strategic exports from Malaya.

The first real indication that a partial thaw might be possible came with the Geneva Conference on Indochina in mid-1954, where China seemed eager for a solution, even if that meant the Vietminh getting less than they wished; and where the establishment of the International Control Commission for Vietnam, Cambodia, and Laos raised British hopes that critical areas could be neutralized or at least kept in precarious balance. In reality, that hope faded after Vietnam failed to hold the 1956 all-country elections the Geneva conference prescribed, and as the United States became more committed to the new Ngo Dinh Diem regime in the south from 1955 onwards. Nevertheless, the British hope that some areas could be kept from further conflagration persisted, with a last serious attempt at neutralization via an international conference on Laos in 1962.

Indochina Events and the Songkhla Position

Grand strategy for global and limited war, limited resources for anything in Southeast Asia beyond Malaya, and the difficulty in securing regional cooperation and goodwill between western powers and colonial peoples, had not in themselves been sufficient to resurrect Kra planning. Even the advent of the People's Republic of China, on 1 October 1949, did not achieve that. As we have seen, Britain's first response to the latter was to hope that if it kept a foot in the door it could bide its time until China's nationalist instincts and reconstruction needs softened its international stance. Perhaps, eventually, China might drift away from the Soviet Union. Cabinet even insisted that, should normal diplomatic

---

39 PREM8/1407, The Colombo Plan for Cooperative Economic Development in South and Southeast Asia. David Lowe, "Percy Spender and the Colombo Plan, 1950," *Australian Journal of Politics and History* 40, 2 (1994), 162–76. CAB134/288, FE(O)(49)81(Final), Southeast Asia – General, Brief for Commonwealth Conference by the Far East (Official) Committee, 15 December 1949. Hack, *Defence and Decolonisation*, 65–66. See also Chapter 8 by Andrea Benvenuti and Chapter 11 by Marek Rutkowski in this volume.

relations resume, Malaya must accept Chinese communist consuls. Understandably the authorities there, who were fighting the MCP, were horrified and complained vociferously before Korean War developments put the issue on the backburner.[40]

Even the early 1950 increase in Chinese aid to the Vietminh did not immediately change that diagnosis. Nor did the Chinese and Soviet recognition of the Democratic Republic of Vietnam in January 1950. Malcolm MacDonald hoped that the French experiment, in persuading the former emperor of Annam to re-emerge as prime minister of a local government with increased powers, might improve matters. MacDonald, whose congenial relations with Asian leaders predisposed him to over-optimism, gave the Bao Dai experiment a 50 percent chance of success, especially if the French could build up his prestige.[41] The French reorganised their territories into the "associated states" in 1949, with increased but still limited autonomy and with the "State of Vietnam" as one component. Bao Dai became premier of the latter. On 7 February 1950, Cabinet endorsed UK recognition of the Associated States of French Indochina, despite realising the Vietminh were still the most convincing nationalist force.[42]

What resurrected Kra planning was the gradual rise in Vietminh fortunes in Indochina, and belief that French defeat there could pave the way to rapid Thai collapse. A military takeover in Thailand in 1947, emergent leader Phibun Songkram's overt anti-communism (the Thais recognised the Associated States in February 1950), and limited American aid from 1950 did little to shake British fears that Thai politicians were elite opportunists with shallow popular roots. They even believed Phibun might turn communist in extremis, just as (in 1941) he had rapidly accommodated to the Japanese and then (in early 1942) declared war on Britain and then absorbed Malaya's most northern states. Meanwhile, ousted politicians included the left-leaning Pridi Phanomyong whose government had leaned towards the Vietminh, and there was a Thai Communist Party.[43] These fears about Thailand convinced Britain that Tonkin must be held as a forward screen. But from the start, the commanders-in-chief Far East were

---

40 FCO141/14394 and 14395.
41 Durham University, Malcolm MacDonald Papers, 20/9/3 ff, MacDonald to Foreign Office, 28 November 1949.
42 PREM8/1121, Indo-China, for Cabinet's 7 February 1950 decision.
43 DEFE5/24, COS(50)376, 23 September 1950, containing SEC(50)23 of 11 September1950, Defence of Malaya, by the Deputy Commissioner-General, Southeast Asia. Christopher Goscha, *Thailand and the Southeast Asian Networks of the Vietnamese Revolution, 1885–1954* (Richmond: Curzon, 1999). Eiji Murashima, "Thailand and Indochina, 1945–1950," *Journal of Asia-Pacific Studies* (Waseda University) 25 (December 2015): online at https://core.ac.uk/download/pdf/144455265.pdf .

less hopeful about the situation there than MacDonald. In late 1949, they discussed the possibility of British aid to the French if the Chinese attacked, concluding Britain could do little due to other commitments.

They also felt that the Chinese would not attack openly, but rather increase aid: "The French are thus fighting a war of attrition in which time is against them." There were already 50,000 metropolitan French troops, 20,000 Foreign Legion, and 50,000 Vietnamese. But arrayed against them were 86,000 regular and 90,000 militia, in 188 Vietminh battalions. Despite pessimism about French prospects, especially in north Vietnam, the British military believed continued French efforts were vital as a screen to British interests. They would also keep communist forces further away from the insurgents in Malaya for longer. So support of the French was vital, but that must stop short of committing resources given Britain's global and regional priorities.[44] In London, ministers decided as early as 16 December 1949 that Britain could not become directly involved in Indochina.[45]

The United States stepped in to offer the French aid in 1949 (shipments started to arrive from May 1950), solving that problem. That decision reflected the American NSC–68 grand strategy – which had emerged by April 1949 – with its conclusion that the communist world must be resisted not just by offshore island chains, but by denying it further gains on the Asian mainland; and the December 1949 appropriation of $75 million for the general China area (later extended to include Indochina).[46] By 1953, the United States was financing much of the Indochina war, while also trickling some assistance into Thailand.

Despite this ever-increasing flow of resources, French fortunes undulated, with bursts of hope successively punctured by further setbacks. In 1950, attempts to interdict Chinese supplies across the border resulted in catastrophic losses by isolated garrison forces when, in September 1950, the Vietminh drove the French from the strategically important Cao Bang ridge in northeast Indochina. They thus gained control of supply routes to China and much of northeast Tonkin. France

---

44 PREM8/1221, JP(49)162, Annex II, Threat to Indochina, late 1949 paper used in early 1950 discussions.
45 DEFE11/42, COS(50)426, 1 November 1950, the COS study on the BDCC's August 1950 paper. R. Ovendale, *The Foreign Policy of the British Labour Governments, 1945–1951* (Leicester: University Press, 1984), 127.
46 William Duiker, *US Containment Policy and the Conflict in Indochina* (Stanford CA: University Press, 1994), 61–98. Andrew Rotter, *Path to Vietnam: Origins of the American Commitment to Southeast Asia* (Ithaca NY: Cornell University Press, 1987), 2, *passim*. David L. Anderson, *Trapped by Success: The Eisenhower Administration and Vietnam, 1953–1961* (New York: Columbia University Press, 1993). Edward Cuddy, "Vietnam: Mr Johnson's War. Or Mr Eisenhower's," *The Review of Politics* 65, 4 (2003): 351–74.

continued to dominate the south, but French forces in Tonkin were left concentrated in the Red River Delta area around the cities of Hanoi and Haiphong.[47] Such defeats convinced the BDCC(FE) that Chinese support for the Vietminh would now flow freely, and that danger of French defeat in, or withdrawal from, Tonkin, was increasing. An Anglo-American defence of Tonkin remained their preference, but that might be impractical. Instead, these events triggered consideration of a Kra operation should Tonkin fall.

On 1 December 1950, the commanders-in-chief, Far East, warned the COS that "Chinese support of the present kind to the Viet Minh" might increase sufficiently to make the situation critical in the next two months, before French reinforcements arrived. In the same month, the BDCC(FE) accepted that the COS would not sanction British assistance of a defence of Tonkin, nor seeking any American guarantee of it. Winston Churchill also told colleagues in December that the Soviet Union was trying to entangle "democratic forces" in East Asia, and this was "a trap into which we must not fall."[48] In these circumstances, the BDCC(FE) told the COS that a Kra operation could become vital if Tonkin or Thailand fell, and that they would need a locally-based brigade to take the position.

In December 1950 the BDCC(FE) warned London: "The vital factor for . . . success . . . is the timing. The Communists as well as ourselves will realise that the Songkhla position is the key to the defence of Malaya. It was known to be this in 1941 and its importance has been argued in published books." London must act as soon as communist control of the Thai government seemed certain. Early action would boost morale in Malaya. "It would be a welcome indication of our determination to defend Malaya . . . and not as in 1942 to be driven from the country."[49] The COS authorised Songkhla planning on 22 December 1950, and detailed planning from January 1951, the Defence Committee endorsing this on 28 February 1951. But the Foreign Office remained cautious, recommending any operation be authorised, as in 1941, only to meet "a clear and imminent threat" to Malaya.[50] The Commander-in-Chief (Far East) issued directives for planning in January 1951, asking for plans for occupation against limited opposition after limited war broke out (Irony) or before (Ringlet). However determined Thai

---

47 Edgar O'Ballance, *Indochina War* (London: Faber, 1964), 113–39. DEFE11/42, COS(50)479, 18 November 1950. CO537/6328, BDCC telegram to COS, SEACOS 134, 1 December 1950.
48 FO800/462, Record of discussion, the Prime Minister, French Prime Minister and others, 21 December 1950.
49 DEFE11/42, GHQ Fareast to MOD, SEACOS 142, 18 December 1950. CO537/6328, BDCC telegrams to COS, SEACOS 134 and SEACOS 142, 1 and 18 December 1950.
50 CAB131/11, DO(51)16, Preparation for the Defence of Malaya, Note by COS, 21 February 1951. CAB131/10, DO(51)4, 28 February 1951, minute 1.

opposition was, it was anticipated that poor infrastructure (the lack of a main Bangkok to Haad Yai Road and so heavy reliance on 650km of single-track railway) would limit their effectiveness. Nevertheless, rapidity remained crucial, especially as the position needed to be fortified in depth, so it could not be outflanked.[51] Over 1951–1952, plans were developed for an initial brigade to seize the position, with up to three divisions ultimately required to hold off Chinese attack, should that develop.[52]

The urgency of Kra planning waxed and waned according to hopes for Indochina and international developments. Hence the January 1951 instructions to designate commanders followed an increase in Chinese intervention in Korea. In December 1950, the arrival in Indochina of the charismatic General Jean de Lattre de Tassigny gave new hope. He committed to defeating the Vietminh in the Muong region just west of the French-held Red River Delta and Hanoi, taking Hoa Binh as a focus for this. Was this the basis for a sustainable French forward movement back into the hinterland of Tonkin? But after he returned ill to Paris in January 1952 (soon to die), the Vietminh wore the French forward movement down with guerrilla tactics, forcing their withdrawal from Hoa Binh before the end of February.

During 1952, it became clear, therefore, that the French were not able to push the Vietminh back in any substantive way. In March 1952, Churchill told the Defence Committee there were solid reasons why the French should withdraw from Indochina and he believed they would. In the same month, Cabinet again discussed whether aid could be given to France, and again dismissed that as impractical. Instead, they supported the idea already being considered in case of an armistice in Korea, of a multinational joint warning to China about the consequences of any major escalation in fighting. A 16-nation warning concerning Korea was issued on 9 August 1953, after the armistice in Korea of July. But the idea of a similar warning over the consequences of major aggression in Southeast Asia was delayed by British nervousness about what any American response might involve, should the warning be ignored. Also in March 1952, Churchill told colleagues that "it would be silly to waste bombs in the vague inchoate mass of China and wrong to kill thousands of people to no purpose," while suggesting blockade might be worthwhile.[53] In joint planning discussions with the United States from 1952, Britain therefore wished not to give prior agreement that major Chinese action could result in widespread, and even nuclear, action against

---

51 DEFE11/43, Directive for the Defence of Malaya on the Kra Isthmus, CIC(51)1/1(P), C-I-C Far East for force commanders designate, 12 January 1951.
52 DEFE5/39, COS(52)303, Assessment of forces required for Songkhla, 10 June 1952.
53 CAB131/12, D(52)2nd meeting, minute 1, 9 March 1952.

China itself, and feared ineffectual use of nuclear power could weaken the Western position in the Cold War.[54] Into early 1954, the British felt any response should avoid the risk of tripping global war, of nuclear attacks failing in China's vast expanses, and of nuclear power appearing something the West used solely on Asians. They sought instead American assurances any response would be limited to attacks proximate or closely related to the battlefield. So as of early 1954, there was still no warning for Southeast Asia comparable to that for Korea.[55]

Meanwhile, by New Year 1953 British planners again thought the French were losing impetus, and that French worries about how to set up a European Defence Community (while constraining a rearming Germany) might encourage them to limit efforts in Indochina. The COS were told that if Tonkin fell, Siam would too "sooner or later," and if all Indochina fell "the fall of Siam (Thailand) to communism would be quick and certain." Thailand's fall to communism would lead to increased land and sea infiltration of Malaya and so improved insurgent morale there. It must therefore be taken as the trigger for Kra plans. Consideration could be given to consulting the Thais at the time, if it was believed they might support plans in order to give themselves "a convenient back door" to escape through. If they rebuffed an approach it must be taken by force. Even then the operation would require reinforcements of up to three brigades and more aircraft.[56] By April 1953, American frustration with the lack of progress in Indochina was rising. They were reportedly asking why they should continue funding unless the French "stopped sitting in Beau Geste forts on champagne cases."[57] In mid-1953, the French were seen as drifting towards collapse, especially if the Vietminh consolidated links they were making across the Tonkin border with Laotian communists, so opening up the route to Thailand. This was the point at which the BDCC(FE) warned London it might have to ask for authorization for a Songkhla occupation at short notice.

The French responded with another general and another plan. General Henri Navarre was appointed in May 1953. The "Navarre Plan" envisaged strengthening French and Vietnamese National Army forces, withdrawing isolated garrisons so as to consolidate, and a major offensive across the Red River Delta. The United

---

54 CAB131/12, 2nd DC meeting of 14 March 1952 on D(52)5. *FRUS, 1952–54*, Vol. XII, 1, 8–22. DEFE5/36, COS(52)64, 26 January 1952, Collective Measures against China, Brief for Sir William Elliot, approved 25 January 1952.
55 CAB131/14, D(54)8, Korea, Foreign Secretary, 1 February, D(54)5, 14 April 1954, minute 1. CAB131/13, D(53)57, COS, 30 November 1953.
56 DEFE5/44, COS(53)47, The Defence of Malaya in the Cold War, 23 January 1953. CAB131/13, D(53)1, Defence of Malaya, COS, 22 January 1953.
57 PREM11/645, Saigon to Foreign Office No 89, 24 April 1953.

States backed the plan with increased assistance. But Navarre also sought to interfere with Vietminh movement into Laos and draw them out to battle by garrisoning Dien Bien Phu in Tonkin's northwest. That ultimately proved fatal to the French empire in Asia. As the Vietminh besieged Dien Bien Phu's isolated garrison in early 1954, and pounded it with artillery from the hills around, the United States asked if allies might consider "concerted action" to save it. Britain feared, rightly or wrongly, that this could even include the use of tactical nuclear weapons, and could cause the abandonment or failure of the scheduled 1954 Geneva conference on Indochina.

This is not the place to rehearse the resulting crisis of April 1954, when US Secretary of State John Foster Dulles flew to London to demand allied help in "united action" to save Dien Bien Phu (following a 2 April French request for mass air support), and was rebuffed.[58] Even though his hints that its fall could scupper the European Defence Treaty, and that support might make the United States sympathetic to Britain's position in Egypt, fell on deaf ears, Foreign Secretary Anthony Eden was determined to refuse even moral support. From a British perspective, the request invoked their longstanding priorities of 1949–1953. The French should be kept fighting to defend the lead domino of Tonkin as long as possible, with American assistance, but Britain would not commit substantive resources, and did not want to risk wider war or further alienating China by drastic escalation there. As Churchill put it on 26 April: "The British people would not easily be influenced by what happened in the distant jungles of Southeast Asia," but would worry about dramatic action tripping wider war given a Sino-Soviet pact, and the possibility "of an assault by hydrogen bombs on these islands." The main American option might actually have been B–29 Superfortresses flying 2,000km from the Philippines to bomb Vietminh communications.[59] But the meeting of Churchill and Eisenhower at the Bermuda conference of December 1953 had already alerted the British to the emerging New Look American policy, with its higher reliance on nuclear power, including the assumption of its use against any major Chinese aggression in Korea or elsewhere in the East. So the "united action" suggestion heightened their gathering concerns. Besides which, Eden as Foreign Secretary was determined to make

---

[58] FO800/784 for March-May 1954 discussions.
[59] PREM11/645, Record of a Conversation at dinner at Chequers, Monday 26 April 1954, Note by General Brownjohn on "Air Support to French Forces" of 27 April, *passim*. John Prados, *Operation Vulture* (New York: Diversion Books, 2014).

the Geneva Conference succeed, ideally keeping the American idea of a coalition for "united action" on a back burner, with a view to creating defence planning or organisation for after Geneva.[60]

During 1953, Britain rejected sending even small amounts of equipment to Indochina in case it caused entanglement, and Churchill even questioned if a French withdrawal might help ease the way to a European Defence Treaty and German rearmament. Eden, meanwhile, saw the forthcoming Geneva Conference as a long-awaited chance to work towards normalising relations with China. Dien Bien Phu duly fell as the Geneva crisis conference on Indochina opened. With Eden helping to ease the way, the conference split Indochina at the 17th parallel, with an International Control Commission to supervise ceasefires and the prospect of unifying elections by 1956. The French subsequently withdrew, and in 1955 the United States committed to supporting the government in the south and its new leader, Ngo Dinh Diem.[61] In July 1954, meanwhile, MacDonald congratulated Eden on having begun the process of bringing China "into the comity of nations," and asserted that British influence could be crucial at a time many Asians felt the United States had acted with "immaturity" and feared another world war.[62]

Britain continued Kra planning throughout this, with attention to the need for radar and a jet-capable airfield in north Malaya in April 1954.[63] Even the signing of the Southeast Asia Collective Defence Treaty in September 1954 did not guarantee the survival of the new government of South Vietnam, or those in Laos and Cambodia. As SEATO emerged, its challenge would be to adapt to assist countries fighting subversion and guerrilla warfare, something to which it was never ideally suited. Nevertheless, it did provide a shield – in the form of a guarantee to defend members and the designated states in Indochina – behind which non-communist regimes were given time (and American aid) to fortify themselves against internal communist challenges.

The death of the Songkhla plans, in late 1957, was driven mainly by the combination of Malayan independence and the deepening American commitment to South Vietnam, and to consolidating the countries to Malaya's north. These developments intensified growing Australian doubts about the merit in

---

60 Matthew Jones, "US Nuclear Planning and 'Massive Retaliation' in East Asia, 1953–1955," *Journal of Cold War Studies* 10, 4 (2008), 37–65.
61 Hack, *Defence and Decolonisation*, 166–91.
62 DEFE11/102, MacDonald to Eden, Situation in Southeast Asia, 8 February 1955. PREM11/121, M1222, Success in Malaya, Field Marshal Montgomery, 2 January 1952.
63 DEFE5/52, CS(54)126, 20 April 1954, Request for Airfields, Air Ministry report on JIC(54)14.

Songkhla plans, now SEATO was a going concern.[64] By 1958, when deployment of nuclear-capable bombers to East Asia was approved in principle by the Defence Committee, the emphasis switched to playing an active part in SEATO discussions, and partly through that retaining influence and a restraining influence over US planning.[65] This was helped by the feeling there would be no Chinese overt attack southwards (hence Britain could promise nuclear contributions with little risk of being called to act), and the feeling from 1954 that the gradual increase in thermonuclear weapons was changing global war equations. Their greater power might rapidly minimise any threat to the Middle East in global war, or blunt any Chinese attack in Southeast Asia.[66]

Conclusion

Writing on grand strategy tends to emphasise how it aims to secure and advance a nation's core interests over time, sitting above more focussed strategies that target specific ends. It also tends to envisage grand strategy as manipulating multiple tools along various DIME (diplomatic, information, military and economic), MIDFIELD (military, information, diplomatic, financial, intelligence, economic, law and development) and other spectrums.[67] In the case of Britain and Southeast Asia, such acronyms and mnemonics capture both too much and too little. Too much, because Britain decided it did not have significant "E" (economic and equipment capacity) to use in the region, beyond providing for colonies and ex-colonial territories. In that sense, its toolset was more "DIM" than DIME. Too little, because the acronyms seem to miss important aspects out. Britain did employ multiple tools along the lines set out above, including the diplomacy of MacDonald, the semi-abortive attempts to construct a strategic reserve, and then a nuclear capacity to contribute to American plans and SEATO; but other aspects of strategy-making are important in any analysis of why grand strategy and planning turned out as it did.

---

64 DEFE11/100, 1152A, 17 November 1954, discussions between MacDonald and PM of Australia.
65 CAB131/19, D(58)8, 4 February 1958, The Deployment of V-Bombers . . . Far East. CAB131/18, D(57)26, 12 November 1957, Balanced Collective Forces, Minister of Defence Brief for PM-Eisenhower talks of October 1957. DEFE7/688, Mumford to Wolfe, 21 September 1959.
66 DEFE5/55 COS(54)335, Middle East War Planning Assumptions, 21 October 1954.
67 US Joint Doctrine Note 1–18, Strategy, 25 April 2018: https://www.jcs.mil/Portals/36/Documents/Doctrine/jdn_jg/jdn1_18.pdf?ver=2018-04-25-150439-540.

One is the layering of the global, regional, and local in each area of strategy, such that the global tended to frame possibilities quite severely. In the case of Southeast Asia, a significant increase in military resources (other than for the Malayan Emergency), only became possible after global strategy shifted in 1952–1953, in response to increasing Western nuclear capacity and its anticipated impact as a deterrent, and as a dampener on Soviet or Chinese thrusts should war break out. That shift, combined with repeated crises of confidence over the French position in Indochina, persuaded British planners to redirect Australian and then New Zealand efforts – both in Cold War and for reinforcement in limited and global war – away from the Middle East and towards Southeast Asia. In turn, that shift facilitated the construction of a CSR consisting of an infantry brigade and supporting elements.

Notwithstanding that shift, Britain's response to crises in Southeast Asia was so severely shaped by "lessons" learned from 1942, assumptions about Thai (in)capacity, geography, and severe resource limitations imposed by global strategy, that its response to tiresomely regular crises of confidence about French ability to hold Tonkin played out in repeating loops until 1954. A particular French defeat or fizzling out of the latest initiative would increase worries that Tonkin could fall and Thailand drift to communism, and British planners would decide they had severe doubts about French durability yet could offer no aid themselves, but that they should nevertheless encourage the French (with ever-more American money and equipment) to persevere. Each crisis boosted planning to seize the Songkhla position in an emergency, to seal Malaya off from communist infiltration, and to secure a viable defensive position: Malaya's "Thermopylae."

Even the crisis over Dien Bien Phu, with the garrison tottering under Vietminh onslaught in the leadup to the Geneva Conference, was a replay of this loop, now with an added dimension. The United States sought UK commitment (even if largely symbolic) to "united action" in order to snare a broader coalition and so persuade Congress. The United Kingdom refused, but saw the opportunity to resurrect the zombified remains of its 1949 vision for China: that China might be lured back into normal diplomatic relations based on national interest. The result of the Geneva Conference was, in a real sense, a temporary UK triumph, as Eden's middleman role facilitated a compromise based on partition of Indochina and a standoff in Cambodia and Laos and, even better, an International Control Commission to monitor the areas. Meanwhile, US determination to do something more did mature afterwards into SEATO, so providing confidence for non-communist Southeast Asian countries seeking to consolidate. The SEATO compromise, that it guaranteed prescribed Indochinese states which by the Geneva agreement could not be members, suited British grand strategy perfectly. It deterred overt aggression, promoted confidence, yet left open the possibility of neutralising much of Indochina.

Of course, the British vision of luring China back into the comity of nations, as MacDonald put it in mid-1954, gradually unwound as the United States replaced France as South Vietnam's main backer, the unifying elections in Indochina failed to take place in 1956, and finally from 1959 the Vietminh resumed pressure on the South. But even a slow unwinding was a sort of success: one which won time and facilitated British drawdown in the region.

What is clear is that tools of grand strategy are one thing. But Britain's "grand strategy" consisted of a series of strategies for separate military, diplomatic, colonial and other areas, and the way they interacted. These were generally not set out together in single papers, such as the American NSC-68. Even at this level of separate strands of "grand strategy," understanding why British strategy emerged as it did involves looking at the way "lesson-learning" was conducted across 1942–1946, in a way that embedded shaping assumptions. These included everything from assumptions about the way colonies needed to be reshaped to provide supportive partnerships from active and autonomous peoples in strong, enlarged states, through the value of particular areas (Tonkin, presented as Southeast Asia's key) and positions (Songkhla); to assumptions about key countries and elites (the Thais and Phibun Songkram). To ensure critical awareness at the moment of grand strategy making and remaking, policy makers and processes need acute self-awareness and reflectiveness about how such "lessons" came about: and so an ability to have them periodically and systematically revisited.

This example also shows that "grand strategy" can sometimes exist outside of overt "grand strategy" papers, and even outside thematic grand strategies (global and regional; military, colonial, economic etc), residing in the way these intertwine to define sometimes narrow possibilities. In the British case, individuals sometimes thought they were being original in pushing, say, a broader Federation of Malaysia in the early 1960s, when they were simply giving extra impetus to policies mandated by widely shared grand strategic assumptions such as those discussed above. The way these layers of strategy, and different areas of strategic concern, inter-related so as to create a relatively uncharted overall "grand strategy" or grand strategic nexus of thinking also explains how Britain ended up resurrecting plans to occupy the Songkhla position – plans strikingly similar to the one aborted in 1941.[68] Fittingly, the Anglo-Irish novelist J.G. Farrell narrates the

---

[68] Similarities extended to not having enough aircraft to match the key adversary (Chinese MIG–15s). DEFE5/49, COS(53)548, Action in the Event of Chinese Aggression . . . 4 November 1953.

confusion and indecision surrounding Matador in his satirical novel *The Singapore Grip* (1974). One chapter visits the night of 7 December 1941 through the minds of a multitude of characters, including the dreams of Commander-in-Chief Robert Brooke-Popham, the musings of Japanese "Private Kikuchi" on a landing craft off Kota Bharu, clutching *Read This Alone – and the War Can Be Won*, and the last moments before obliteration by Japanese bombs of a "Chinese wharf-coolie" in Chinatown. The operation that layers of British planning and strategy made so central to the defence of Malaya in 1941 and the 1950s had – cynics might think not before time – become the object of parody.[69]

---

[69] J.G. Farrell, *The Singapore Grip* (London: Weidenfeld & Nicolson, 2020 [first published 1978]), 235–48.

Section Three

S.R. Joey Long
Diplomacy, (Hot and Cold) War, and Grand Strategy, 1940–1954

Scholars who write about grand strategy engage the subject from three key perspectives. The first seeks to elucidate the domestic sources as well as the external determinants of a state's grand strategy, assessing the circumstances and conditions under which they change, and help shape a state's approach to issues and its interests over time. The second examines the institutions and personalities of a state; the manner and processes through which they formulate and pursue grand strategy; and the outcomes of their endeavours. The third is more policy-oriented, with analysts critiquing and generating for the state a range of proposals that will enable it to make and implement a prudent grand strategy. Whatever their approaches, all three fundamentally agree that grand strategy can be defined as a state's efforts to deploy all of its available means – non-violent and violent – to enhance and protect its peacetime and wartime ends and interests.[1]

The five essays in this section of the volume further agenda number two. They tackle the subject of grand strategy from the perspective of individuals in history, employing the diplomatic as well as cultural and informational resources of their states to pursue their governments' security interests and objectives, in peacetime and wartime. Jeremy A. Yellen examines the development of Japanese grand strategy, focusing on the roles that Japan's Cabinet, foreign ministers, and general staff played in formulating and advancing Tokyo's grand strategic objectives in Asia between 1931 and 1945. Andrea Benvenuti sets his sights on Prime Minister Jawaharlal Nehru's grand strategy between 1947 and 1954, with New Delhi keen to maintain stable relations with the communist powers and the United States so India could focus on economic development and state-building. Lauriane Simony investigates British grand strategy towards Burma between 1948 and 1955, and notes that British officials employed cultural and informational operations to preserve British influence in the country. S.R. Joey Long discusses the Eisenhower administration's grand strategy in Asia, its diplomats operating at the 1954 Geneva Conference to preserve US

---

[1] Rebecca Friedman Lissner, "What Is Grand Strategy? Sweeping a Conceptual Minefield," *Texas National Security Review* 2, 1 (November 2018), 52–73. See also Thierry Balzacq, Peter Dombrowski and Simon Reich, "Is Grand Strategy a Research Programme? A Review Essay," *Security Studies* 28, 1 (2019), 58–86.

influence and hold the line against communist expansion in the region. Marek W. Rutkowski also focuses on the 1954 conference, but his concerns are with India and its efforts to shape the future of Indochina along the lines that Delhi favoured. All of the chapters in this section, in sum, detail the acts that diplomats and policymakers undertook to further their governments' security objectives in Asia.

The chapters also offer insights into how the institutions in which the state actors operated facilitated or hindered their making and pursuit of grand strategy. They likewise highlight the roles that adversaries, allies, and other actors played in shaping the courses of action that policymakers took to accomplish their objectives. Enemies, friends, and the non-aligned could further undercut the ability of governments to achieve their policy aims or compel them to revise their goals and plans. Yellen contends that Japan was unable to effectively develop a coherent and functional grand strategy between 1931 and 1945. He attributes the Japanese shortcomings initially to the weak Cabinet oversight of the military. From 1937, however, the war in China compelled Tokyo to institute reforms that enabled the Cabinet and general staff to better align their interests, prosecute the war in Asia, and pursue the goal of dominating the region. Two leaders – Foreign Ministers Matsuoka Yosuke and Shigemitsu Mamoru – played pivotal roles in employing the liaison conferences to rally Japanese strategists to back, construct, and preserve the Greater East Asia Co-Prosperity Sphere. Even so, Japanese officials across the empire were unable to coordinate their efforts, resist the allied advance, and bring Matsuoka's and Shigemitsu's aspirations into being.

Like the Japanese, India's Nehru had his own vision of what constituted regional order. Benvenuti writes that Nehru sought to play his part in bringing about a region of states that respected each other's sovereign independence, worked to stabilize interstate relations, and kept Cold War politics at bay. The problem for Nehru, however, was that the Cold War powers had their own plans and might not share India's outlook for the region. Washington, in particular, baulked at Delhi's cultivation of relations with Beijing and Moscow – two states that Nehru thought were serious for the most part about adhering to their policy of peaceful coexistence. India, thus, had to engage the United States to keep Indo-American tensions from boiling over. While India-Soviet and India-US relations eventually stabilized, India-China relations swiftly unravelled in the early 1960s when their border dispute escalated into war. India, in the end, was unable to realize Nehru's "grand design."

Cold War competition likewise upset British objectives in Burma. Simony notes that British cultural diplomats did not have the Southeast Asian state to themselves. The Americans, Chinese, and Soviets ran their own cultural and information operations in Burma. Some of their activities even outshone the British efforts. Ultimately, the British found that they could not enhance their cultural influence in Burma. If the Americans, British, Chinese and Soviets wrestled with each other in Burma's cultural sphere, they also battled each other for the political spoils in Geneva in 1954. Long examines the Eisenhower administration's activities at the Geneva conference, and finds its aims and plans being reshaped and thwarted by its adversaries and allies. Its opponents maintained their unity of action and purpose, and parried the American attempt to divide them. American officials, meanwhile, were unable to overcome their differences with the British and French, and to work with them to deny the communists any gains. The Eisenhower government eventually had to revise its objectives, and pursue other ways to counter the communists in Korea and Indochina. Like Washington, New Delhi was unable to completely secure what it sought at Geneva. Rutkowski notes that India lobbied for and succeeded in gaining a mediatory role in the Indochina conflict. The Nehru government, however, could not bring into being his notion of the "Area of Peace" in Indochina – an area freed from Cold War contests and violence. Divisions among the Colombo powers ensured that India could not count on them to collectively promote Nehru's ideas. The Cold War powers also had other plans for Indochina. In sum, then, Rutkowski's chapter accentuates a similar point that the other four papers highlight: a state might be compelled by the counterforce exerted by adversaries and allies to revise its plans and adapt to new developments.

Finally, the five chapters in this section bring into sharp focus the point that the making and pursuit of grand strategy is not the preserve of the established powers. Less powerful actors could play their grand strategic games, and break or make a more powerful actor's plans. Yellen contends that a key reason Matsuoka's and Shigemitsu's initiatives fell through was because the Asian countries under Japanese domination resisted Tokyo's schemes. Benvenuti and Rutkowski show that India, arguably a potential but not yet a Great Power during the 1940s and 1950s, could make calculated moves to further its interests and obtain its place in the sun. Simony argues that the Burmese ultimately took what they wanted from the external actors' initiatives, and were able to fashion their own ways to develop their economy, educational system, and state. Long maintains that the South Koreans and Vietminh were able to play their games, and shape the proceedings and outcomes at Geneva. All told, the chapters in Section Three underscore the agency of less powerful actors in international politics, compellingly illustrating that their actions could shape the grand strategies of Great Powers and the course of history.

Jeremy A. Yellen
What Grand Strategy? Japan, 1931–1945

If ever there was a need for Japanese leaders competent enough to craft a grand strategy, it was during the tumultuous 1930s and 1940s. The global economic crash in 1929 hinted at the failure of liberal capitalism, and successive international crises pointed to the fragility of Anglo-American power. U.S. and British dominance in political-economic affairs appeared on the precipice of a sharp decline. Japan, conversely, was poised to become the leading power of Asia. Japanese political figures, intellectual leaders, and the mass media began to speak of a "great turning point" (*dai tenkanki*) in world history. At long last, Japan could shape its own destiny, gain a place of centrality in global history, and create a "new order" (*shinchitsujo*) for the region. Such dreams grew with Japan's expansion in Asia and reached their peak with the attempt to create the Greater East Asia Co-Prosperity Sphere in the early 1940s.[1]

Dreams and realities, however, are wholly different beasts. The leaders whose job it was to realize the sphere – and to craft a grand strategy to ensure it happened – were in many ways inadequate to the task. The failings of Japanese leadership could be seen in stark terms at a liaison conference between government and Imperial General Headquarters (IGHQ) in late February 1942, over two months after the outbreak of the Pacific War. At this meeting, Prime Minister Tōjō Hideki asked a shocking question. "What," he asked, "is the difference between the national defense sphere (*kokubōken*) and the co-prosperity sphere (*kyōeiken*)?" Even more astonishing than the question was the fact that nobody present could give a clear answer.[2] Cabinet Planning Board President Suzuki Teiichi further confused the issue when he replied that a resource sphere (*shigenken*) was "approximately the same thing as a co-prosperity sphere." The

---

[1] For extended treatment of the Greater East Asia Co-Prosperity Sphere, see Jeremy A. Yellen, *The Greater East Asia Co-Prosperity Sphere: When Total Empire Met Total War* (Ithaca and London: Cornell University Press, 2019); Kawanishi Kōsuke, *Teikoku Nihon no kakuchō to hōkai: "Dai Tōa Kyōeiken" e no rekishiteki tenkai* (Tokyo: Hōsei Daigaku Shuppankai, 2012); Adachi Hiroaki, *"Dai Tōa Kyōeiken" no keizai kōsō: Ken'nai sangyō to dai tōa kensetsu shingikai* (Tokyo: Yoshikawa Kōbunkan, 2013); Eizawa Kōji, *"Dai Tōa Kyōeiken" no shisō* (Tokyo: Kōdansha Gendai Shinsho, 1995); and Kobayashi Hideo, *"Dai Tōa Kyōeiken" no keisei to hōkai*, 2nd ed. (Tokyo: Ochanomizu Shobō, 2006).

[2] Kawanishi, *Teikoku Nihon no kakuchō to hōkai*, 7. See also Sugiyama Hajime, *Sugiyama memo: Daihon'ei seifu renraku kaigi tō hikki*, Vol. 2 (Tokyo: Hara Shobō, 1967), 41–44.

liaison conference ended with ended an agreement to study natural resources.³ In effect, the leaders tasked with creating the co-prosperity sphere called for more research on what Japan was already fighting a global war to achieve!

This shocking lack of understanding was all too common. It was once again betrayed at the meetings of the Greater East Asia Construction Council – an official deliberative body meant to establish a long-term plan to construct the co-prosperity sphere. On 11 March, 1942, Ōtani Kōzui, a committeeman tasked with drafting population policies, could not contain his dismay at being asked to help construct something that nobody understood. "From the start, the government has not given a clear definition of the Greater East Asia Co-Prosperity Sphere," he complained. If the government could not provide a convincing vision, how could he? Ōtani continued: "I find it extremely troubling that I am asked to state my views on it. I don't know where it is. Interpreting from a narrow sense, the Co-Prosperity Sphere is [composed of] Manchuria and China. But before we knew it, it had become a Co-Prosperity Sphere in Greater East Asia. I have absolutely no understanding of what Greater East Asia is."⁴

How could a Nation have a Grand Strategy if those Tasked with Planning were Confounded by such Basic Points?

Grand strategy must match ends with means. It blends vision with purposive action. This implies not only that a state or group has longer-term visions or objectives, but also that it has consistent tactics or strategies to meet those objectives. A highly articulated vision without tactics to achieve it thus cannot be called a grand strategy. Further, grand strategies at the state level must involve the coordination of a range of tools – diplomatic, military, economic, and informational – in a comprehensive manner.⁵ In this chapter, I define grand strategy in a way that aligns with the Introduction to this volume: grand strategies directly involve the summit of state authority and connect means and ends in geopolitics and statecraft. In all but the most authoritarian regimes and dictatorships, enacting a grand strategy also necessitates alliances between and coordination among the various policy elites. Disagreements over visions and tactics may be present,

---

3 *Sugiyama memo*, 2: 42–43.
4 Dai Tōa Kensetsu Shingikai, "Dai san bukai giji sokkiroku," March 1942, in Dai Kikakuin and Dai Tōa Kensetsu Shingikai, *Dai Tōa Kensetsu Shingikai kankei shiryō: sōkai, bukai, sokkiroku*, Vol. 2, Akashi Yōji and Ishii Hitoshi, eds. (Tokyo: Ryūkei Shosha, 1995), 16.
5 For more on grand strategy, see, for instance, John Collins, *Grand Strategy: Principles and Practices* (Annapolis: Naval Institute Press, 1973); Williamson Murray, Richard Hart Sinnreich, and James Lacey, eds., *The Shaping of Grand Strategy: Policy, Diplomacy, and War* (Cambridge: University Press, 2011); and John Lewis Gaddis, *On Grand Strategy* (New York: Penguin Press, 2018).

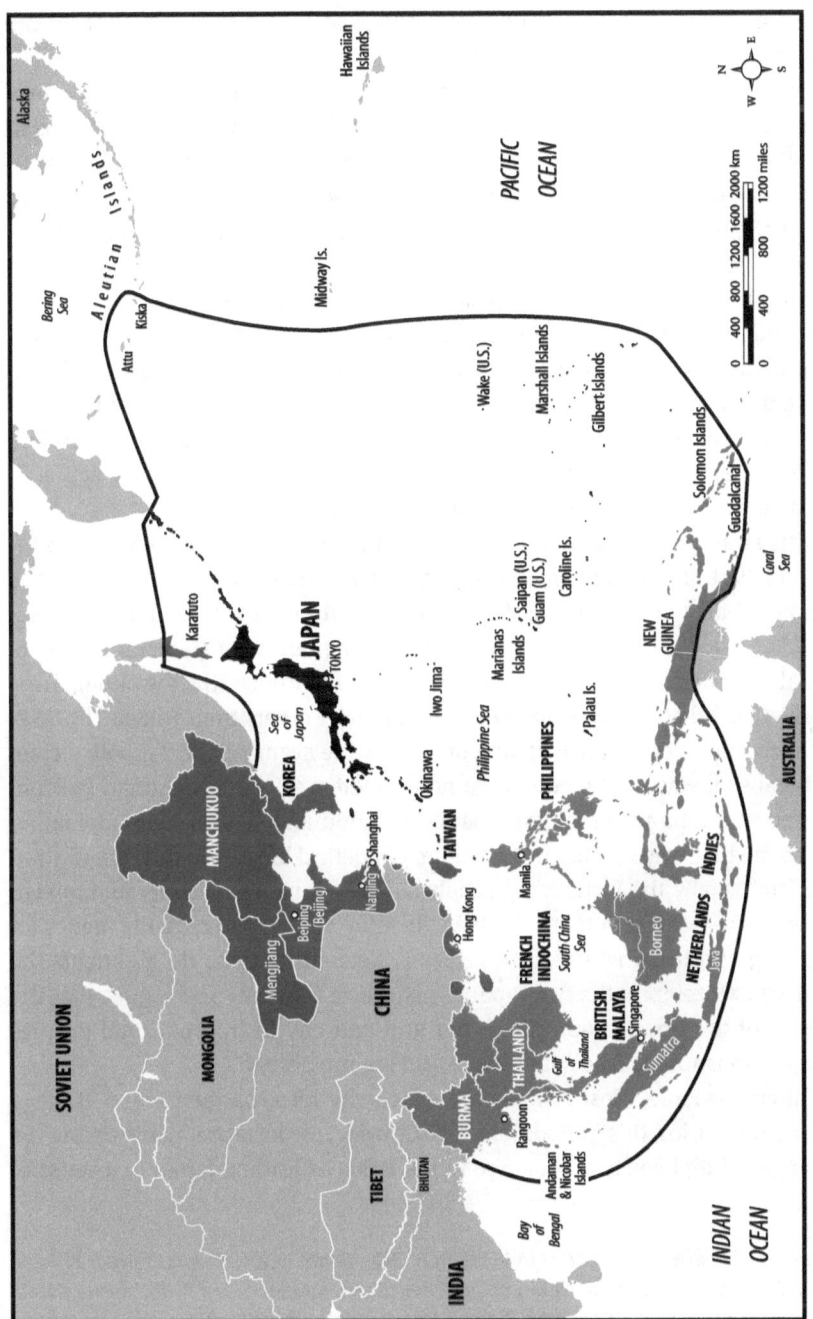

Map 7.1: The Empire of Japan in early 1942.

but any state that pursues a grand strategy must smooth over such disagreements to enact coordinated policies for the future.

Before 1931, Japan was guided by what might be thought of as a grand strategy of accommodation. Under the guidance of the Meiji oligarchs and other groups in the conservative ruling elite, Japan adapted to the existing international environment, adopting new practices that helped advanced national power and status. In the age of empire (1868–1919), Japan became a modern empire, and built its empire in a way that aligned its practices with those of the European colonial powers. In the interwar era of internationalism and imperial retreat (1919–1931), Japan embraced the "new diplomacy" advanced by U.S. President Woodrow Wilson and the new liberal internationalist norms of disarmament, peace, and conference diplomacy. Both periods witnessed severe disagreements about how best to achieve Japanese interests. Nonetheless, such disagreements were smoothed over by a conservative elite that recognized Japan was best served by acting in accordance with the "trends of the times."[6]

This strategy of accommodation ended in the wake of the Manchurian Incident of 1931. In September 1931, Japan took advantage of the collapse of the liberal-capitalist order to seize Manchuria and, ultimately, to establish the "independent" satellite regime of Manchukuo. Yet the seizure of Manchuria was not originally the desire of the Japanese government. Far from it, the Kwantung Army launched its full-scale invasion in defiance of direct orders from Tokyo. The takeover succeeded because it had support from wide segments of the policy elite, and because it was widely popular at home. Moreover, the Manchurian Incident occurred at a time when military insubordination and threats of assassination were so rife that they had become a feature of political life. Given this, grand strategy is not usually the focus when scholars debate Japanese security and foreign policies of the 1930s and 1940s. Perhaps the only author who cogently argues for something approaching a grand strategy is Kenneth B. Pyle. He highlights the "primacy of foreign policy" in Japanese strategic thought, and argues that the collapse of the liberal-capitalist order and anarchy in international politics led Japan to embrace fascism at home and empire abroad.[7]

Others disagree. Most scholarship rejects the idea that any grand strategy was at work during this period. James B. Crowley, for instance, understands the challenges of diplomacy and empire in the 1930s as leading Japan to a series of

---

[6] These trends have been outlined in Kenneth B. Pyle, *Japan Rising: The Resurgence of Japanese Power and Purpose* (New York: PublicAffairs, 2006); and Frederick R. Dickinson, *World War I and the Triumph of a New Japan* (Cambridge: University Press, 2013).

[7] Pyle, *Japan Rising*, Chapters 5 and 6. See also Kenneth B. Pyle, "Profound Forces in the Making of Modern Japan," *Journal of Japanese Studies* 23:2 (Summer 2006), 410–12.

security solutions: from the construction of an "independent" Manchukuo to the advancement of a Monroe Doctrine for Asia, broader encroachment into China and the South Seas, and the creation of a national defence state.[8] Yet, far from grand strategy, his work hints at the gradual, if messy, alignment of foreign and security policy aims among the policy elite. S.C.M. Paine is even more critical. Paine declares that leaders in the post-Meiji generation were wholly incapable of enacting a grand strategy, or even understanding its various components. Instead, "the military leaders who dominated the government applied operational military solutions to foreign policy problems." The army's strategy for Asia, Paine concludes, was "anything but grand."[9]

Grand strategy or grand absence? The truth is somewhere in between. Japan's ruling elite did have a consistent aim during the tumultuous 1930s and 1940s: to become Asia's leading power. But the system of policymaking in the 1930s and the independence of the military from cabinet control initially constrained the government's ability to coordinate military actions with state policy. This chapter argues that total war in China from July 1937 necessitated increased coordination between military and state officials, and made grand strategy possible in a way it had not been since the Manchurian Incident. Additionally, this chapter maintains that the increased coordination among elites culminated in two moments of what I call "inchoate grand strategy" to construct Japan's Greater East Asia Co-Prosperity Sphere – one guided by Foreign Minister Matsuoka Yōsuke in 1940–1941, the other led by Foreign Minister Shigemitsu Mamoru in 1943. To understand the processes that led to these inchoate grand strategies, we must first look at Japan's messy, shifting security strategies in China in the early 1930s.

Wanted: A China Policy

The years after the takeover of Manchuria were highly fluid and policymakers had difficulties forging comprehensive security strategies. Between 1933 and 1937, most important decisions were made by the five ministers conferences, or what historian James B. Crowley refers to as the "Inner Cabinet." This group consisted of the prime minister along with the foreign, army, navy, and finance

---

[8] James B. Crowley, *Japan's Quest for Autonomy: National Security and Foreign Policy, 1930–1938* (Princeton: University Press, 1966).
[9] S.C.M. Paine, *The Japanese Empire: Grand Strategy from the Meiji Restoration to the Pacific War* (Cambridge: University Press, 2017), 111, 121.

ministers, and they held regular meetings to discuss policy. As Crowley shows, the Inner Cabinet became the ultimate decision-making group in the Japanese government.[10] Yet, although the Inner Cabinet sought to promote regional hegemony, its efforts were inconsistent and did not always align either with the situation on the ground or with ideas emerging from the army general staff.

The difficulties of coordinating policymaking owed to the structure of Japan's political system. Although the Inner Cabinet was the main decision-making body, the military was in important respects independent from cabinet control. The cabinet, via the army and navy ministries, could only play a role in military administration, size, and budgets. Military operations were wholly outside the purview of the civilian government. That is, the military had what was known as the "independence of supreme command" (*tōsuiken dokuritsu*). Originally established in 1878 based off the Prussian military model, this ensured a system wherein the apparatus of supreme command – the general staff –was directly responsible to the emperor, not the prime minister or the cabinet. It created a complex system in which the cabinet made decisions concerning state or civil affairs, and the supreme command in the case of military affairs (see Figure 7.1).[11]

The independence of supreme command was not always a problem. In the Meiji period (1868–1912), Japan's elder statesmen – the Meiji oligarchs –had the standing and the flexibility to interpret it however they wished. As historian Tobe Ryōichi has noted, Prime Minister Katsura Tarō ignored the institution when it hindered his effectiveness as a leader. During the Russo-Japanese War, despite his role as prime minister, Katsura attended important meetings at the Imperial General Headquarters (IGHQ) and played a role in crafting Japan's wartime strategy.[12] Nonetheless, over time, the system ossified. By the 1930s, most of the elder statesmen had died off, and a generation of military leaders had grown up believing so wholeheartedly in the independence of supreme command that the navy could claim the government's decision to override the naval chief of staff's objections and to sign the London Naval Treaty constituted a usurpation of the prerogative of supreme command. After the Manchurian Incident, when the army became more active on the continent, it was not an institution that could be easily ignored. More pointedly, in the 1930s the indepen-

---

10 Crowley, 192.
11 See Hata Ikuhiko, *Nihon riku-kaigun sōgō jiten* (Tokyo: Tokyo Daigaku Shuppankai, 1991), 757.
12 Tobe Ryōichi, "Tojo Hideki as a War Leader," in Brian Bond and Kyoichi Ichikawa, eds, *British and Japanese Military Leadership in the Far Eastern War, 1941–1945* (London: Frank Cass, 2004), 27.

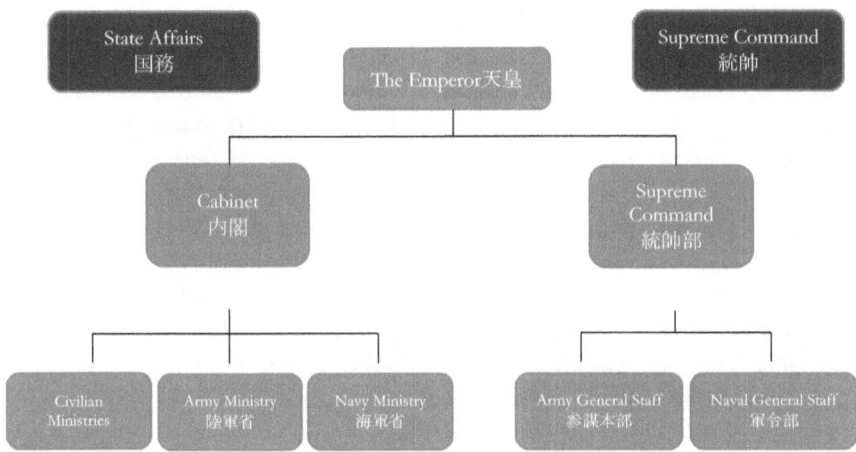

Figure 7.1: Japan's decision-making structure in the prewar and wartime era.

dence of supreme command contributed to the already huge difficulties the Inner Cabinet had in comprehensive and consistent policymaking.[13]

A perfect example can be found in Japan's China policy, which fluctuated in the years after the Manchurian Incident between efforts at rapprochement and designs to detach North China from the rest of the country. Rapprochement was the stated aim of the foreign ministry. Foreign Minister Hirota Kōki and his vice minister, Shigemitsu Mamoru, at first pursued rapprochement through what may best be described as a diplomacy of conciliation. Shigemitsu believed it was in Japan's interest to develop Manchukuo as an independent state, and that Japan could only do so through cooperation with Nationalist China and a commitment against intervening in Chinese affairs.[14] "The idea," Shigemitsu wrote, "was that Manchuria would be Manchukuo, and mainland China would be a new China, and we calculated that if we went with this policy we could resolve the Manchurian issue."[15] Hirota initially pursued this through a 22 January 1935 goodwill speech explaining Japan's

---

[13] This difficulty was compounded by increasing efforts by the general staff to intervene in policymaking, especially through appointments in the army ministry's bureau of military affairs. See Mori Yasuo, *Nihon rikugun to Nitchū sensō e no michi* (Tokyo: Minerva Shobō, 2010).

[14] Shigemitsu claims in his memoirs to have been responsible for creating measures for the emerging situation in China and Manchuria, and that he worked closely with Asian Bureau chiefs Tani Masayuki and Kuwashima Kazue. Shigemitsu Mamoru, *Gaikō kaisōroku* (Tokyo: Mainichi Shinbunsha, 1978), 149. This Hirota-Shigemitsu diplomacy is discussed in Arima Manabu, *Teikoku no Shōwa* (Tokyo: Kōdansha, 2010), 194–95.

[15] Shigemitsu, *Gaikō kaisōroku*, 149.

global diplomatic strategy. He called in this speech for thorough arms reductions and, more importantly, announced the "principles of no threat, no invasion" (*fukyōi, fushinryaku no gensoku*) of China.[16] So successful was this initial statement and the follow up diplomacy that the Chinese Nationalist government ordered newspapers against publishing anti-Japanese content, and even prohibited educational institutions from using anti-Japanese textbooks.[17]

Even as Hirota promoted this sober and restrained policy, Japanese field armies in China had already begun efforts to detach North China from the rest of the country. The Kwantung Army used incidents in Chahar and Rehe to expand Japanese interests and to augment the demilitarized area near Manchukuo. By May 1935, both the Kwantung Army and China Garrison Army had come to the decision that it was in Japan's interest to separate from China the five northern provinces of Hebei, Shandong, Shanxi, Chahar, and Suiyuan. Kwantung Army Commander Minami Jirō even dispatched Major General Doihara Kenji to Beijing [Beiping] in September 1935 to build an alliance for this five-province breakaway. The discrepancy between Foreign Minister Hirota's diplomacy of conciliation and army actions in North China made it appear as if Japan was engaging in a "dual diplomacy."[18] Political and military intrigues undermined efforts at restoring friendly relations and precipitated a hardline turn by Japan.

The Okada Keisuke cabinet confirmed this hawkish turn in early 1936. On 13 January, the cabinet adopted a policy document, "Outline of Measures to Deal with North China," that outlined Japan's ultimate goal as "self-government in the five provinces of North China." This scheme to create an autonomous North China, in fact, constituted a longer-term vision. In the short-term, the policy sought to ensure that the "Nanking government has no room to carry out anti-Japanese and anti-Manchukuo policies," and noted that Japan "take no measures to create an independent state like Manchukuo or to bring about the enlargement of Manchukuo."[19] Hard on the heels of this cabinet decision, on 21 January, Foreign Minister Hirota officially announced in the Imperial Diet his so-called Three Principles (*Hirota sangensoku*), which called on China to suppress anti-Japanese

---

[16] For Hirota's speech in the House of Peers, see "Gaimudaijin no enzetsu," 23 January 1935. *Teikoku gikai kaigiroku*, National Diet Library (henceforth TG-NDL), *Kanpō gōgai*, Kizokuin giji sokkiroku dai 2 gō, 6. Teikoku gikai kaigiroku database [http://teikokugikai-i.ndl.go.jp.] See also *Tōkyō Asahi shinbun*, evening edition, 23 January, 1936, 1.

[17] Tobe Ryōichi, "Nitchū sensō e no dōtei," in Hatano Sumio, Tobe Ryōichi, Matsumoto Takashi, Shōji Jun'ichirō, and Kawashima Shin, *Nitchū sensō: ketteiban* (Tokyo: Shinchōsha, 2018), 37.

[18] Crowley, 231.

[19] Gaimushō, *Nihon gaikō nenpyō narabini shuyō bunsho*, Vol. 2 (Tokyo: Hara Shobō, 1965–1966), 322–23.

activities, to recognize the existence of Manchukuo, and to form with Japan a united front against communism.[20] This represented a volte-face from Hirota's diplomacy of conciliation, and fostered a fear among Chinese diplomats that Japan might use it as pretext to foster autonomous movements.[21]

Yet even this new strategy was not long in force. By early 1937, after the Xi'an Incident and the formation of a united front in China against Japanese imperialism, there emerged in Tokyo an unexpected sense that tensions could only be resolved by practical policy. Upon forming a new cabinet in February 1937, retired General Hayashi Senjūrō noted his personal disdain for "pugnacious foreign policy."[22] His foreign minister, career diplomat Satō Naotake, also held moderate views and hoped to conduct equitable relations with China. Even the Army General Staff modified its hardline stance. When Major General Ishiwara Kanji assumed the directorship of the First Bureau (Operations), he issued new policy plans that rejected the schemes for creating an autonomous North China.[23] This is striking. Ishiwara, the driving force behind Japan's takeover of Manchuria in 1931, by 1937 was calling on the army to take a more conciliatory stance toward North China. The policy elite had thus swung back in favour of rapprochement with China.

This renewed strategy of rapprochement only lasted a matter of months – until shortly after Konoe Fumimaro formed his first cabinet in June 1937. Chinese newspapers initially held a degree of hope that Konoe would continue previous Foreign Minister Satō's diplomacy of reconciliation and equitable relations. But Konoe took a harder-line stance toward China than that practiced by his predecessor, and stated his desire to return to a policy based on Hirota's Three Principles. This, historian Furukawa Takahisa notes, was "a clear policy misstep" (*akiraka na shissei*), one that deepened the Japan-China conflict less than a month before the conflict turned hot.[24] Ultimately, a skirmish at the Marco Polo Bridge on the outskirts of Beijing in July 1937 started a chain reaction leading to

---

20 See Gaimushō, *Nihon gaikō nenpyō*, 2: 325–26; and "Hirota Kokumudaijin no enzetsu," 22 January, 1936. TG-NDL, *Kanpō gōgai*, Kizokuin giji sokkiroku dai 3 gō, 11–1. The three points were approved by the Inner Cabinet on 4 October 1935, and the Chinese Ambassador to Japan was informed of them on 10 November.
21 *FRUS, 1935, Volume 3: The Far East*, The Ambassador in China (Johnson) to the Secretary of State, 11 November 1935.
22 Quoted in Crowley, 316.
23 Iwatani Nobu, "The Marco Polo Bridge Incident: From the Signing of the Tanggu Truce to the Failure of the Trautmann Mediation Attempt," in Tsutsui Kiyotada, ed, *Fifteen Lectures on Showa Japan: Road to the Pacific War in Recent Historiography*, trans. Noda Makito and Paul Narum (Tokyo: Japan Publishing Industry Foundation for Culture, 2016), 146.
24 Furukawa Takahisa, *Konoe Fumimaro* (Tokyo: Yoshikawa Kōbunkan, 2015), 106–08.

a total war with China that the Japanese political and military establishments neither desired nor planned.

The years after the Manchurian Incident were thus bereft of grand strategy. Groups in control of the Japanese state could agree on ends, but not means. This owed in part to a changing geopolitical landscape. More importantly, it resulted from the structure of decision-making in Japan. The civilian government's inability to coordinate policymaking with the general staff meant that the Inner Cabinet was just as likely to respond to military moves by field armies in China as it was to lead them. Even cabinets led by former army generals often fell within a matter of months, and lacked the ability to guide national policy. All major groups in Japan may have desired to ensure hegemony in East Asia. But without robust mechanisms to harmonize elite interests, and with the swing of policy to and away from efforts at reconciliation, far-reaching tactics were impossible to implement.

Grand Strategy and the China War

Total war in China from July 1937, however, made grand strategy possible in a way it had not been since 1931. The war necessitated total coordination between civil and military affairs. But the independence of the supreme command and the long-held notion that military strategies and operations should always be independent of political issues restrained policymakers' abilities to form coordinated strategies. Japan's ruling elite resolved this problem by creating informal institutions of decision-making that began to provide the very coordination leadership lacking throughout the early 1930s, when Japan was not in a state of war.

In November 1937, when it was clear that the fighting in China would not be contained, Japan re-established the IGHQ as the highest body of the supreme command. Yet the IGHQ was a purely military institution designed to deal with military strategies and operations. Since military leaders in the 1930s fervently believed that the independence of supreme command must be preserved at all costs, only senior active-duty officers from the general staffs and the army and navy ministry could attend its meetings. The prime minister, foreign minister, and other civilian cabinet members were prohibited from involvement. This made it challenging to provide comprehensive leadership over the escalating war in China. Prime Minister Konoe tried to ensure that he could participate in IGHQ meetings, and even explored a cabinet reshuffle to create a war cabinet.[25]

---

[25] Ibid., 121.

Yet he was rebuffed. To ensure communication between civilian and military elites, Japan ultimately established informal liaison conferences between government and the Imperial General Headquarters (*Daihon'ei seifu renraku kaigi*), which were held at the imperial court.[26] These liaison conferences allowed leaders to coordinate on matters of joint importance in domestic and security affairs. The first liaison conferences were called irregularly, when policymakers had important matters to discuss, and constituted little more than simple organs that allowed the government and military to "liaise." Yet, following Konoe's January 1938 announcement (against the advice of the general staff) of Japan's refusal to deal with Chiang Kai-shek's Nationalist government, Japan held no liaison conferences for over two years. This owed to opposition among the general staff, which feared that they might be overruled by the civilian government.[27]

Over time, liaison conferences re-emerged, shifted in form, and gradually became something akin to a war cabinet. From November 1940, the government held regular liaison meetings (*Daihon'ei seifu renraku kondankai*) in the prime minister's office, beginning the process of institutionalising the meetings into the very workings of the political system. By the time of the third Konoe cabinet in July 1941, those liaison meetings (*renraku kondankai*) were replaced once again by liaison conferences (*renraku kaigi*), held every Tuesday and Friday in the imperial court. These conferences brought together the army and naval general staff chiefs (and the vice chiefs, from 1941), the premier, and the foreign, finance, army, and navy ministers. Depending on the issue discussed, liaison conferences were also open to such other ministers of state as the president of the cabinet planning board. When dealing with very important matters, the liaison conferences would be followed by imperial conferences, attended by the emperor.[28] Fifteen imperial conferences were held between 1938 and 1945 to ratify the decisions made at the earlier liaison conferences.

---

26 Bōeichō Bōei Kenshūjo, Senshishitsu, *Daihon'ei rikugunbu* Vol. 1 (Tokyo: Asagumo Shinbunsha, 1967), 495. Henceforth all books in this 10-volume series will be listed as *Daihon'ei rikugunbu*, followed by the volume number.
27 Moriyama Atsushi, *Nihon wa naze kaisen ni fumikitta no ka? "Ryōron heiki" to "hikettei"* (Tokyo: Shinchōsha, 2012), 20–21.
28 The emperor's role in policy decisions remains controversial. The most convincing take is that he did try to influence policy and made his thoughts known largely in informal ways, but "rarely displayed the type of leadership associated with strong wartime leaders." Edward J. Drea, *Japan's Imperial Army: Its Rise and Fall, 1853–1945* (Lawrence, KS: University Press of Kansas, 2009), 193–94.

Although they had no legal power to make decisions, the liaison conferences became the *de facto* decision-making body of wartime Japan, and were able to make critical decisions on "national policy." As Tōjō Hideki noted in his post-war interrogations, since the liaison conference was not an official decision-making body, cabinet members in theory could have disagreed with its "decisions." In practice, however, they generally "agreed and did not say anything."[29] Liaison conferences had become so important in policymaking that by June and July 1941, Foreign Minister Matsuoka Yōsuke attended all liaison conferences but missed most cabinet meetings.[30]

Liaison conferences could influence the fate of the empire, but they were complicated affairs. As political historian Moriyama Atsushi argues, liaison conference "decisions" were often ambiguous, could be interpreted in multiple ways, and failed to outline concrete policy measures. On the one hand, they tended to record conflicting opinions side by side (*ryōron heiki*), as epitomised by the famous 2 July 1941 decision both to "advance north" against the Soviet Union and "advance south" into Southeast Asia. On the other hand, liaison conferences also suffered from a culture of what Moriyama calls "non-decision" (*hikettei*), wherein major policy decisions could be postponed again and again.[31] This culture of ambiguous policymaking and "non-decision" owed to the fact that liaison conferences were governed by consensus, wherein discussions continued until the participants reached a unanimous agreement. Despite these problems, liaison conferences still served as a venue for leaders to assert their views, and come to agreements over matters of national interest. If one minister (or group of ministers) articulated a coherent vision and could either dominate liaison conferences or generate a consensus among the policy elite, then they could influence national policy. Thus, with the advent of liaison conferences grand strategy became possible once more – and would exist in inchoate form under the leadership of two foreign ministers: Matsuoka Yōsuke (1940–1941) and Shigemitsu Mamoru (1943–45).

---

29 International Military Tribunal for the Far East (IMTFE) documents, Interrogation of General Hideki Tojo, 14 March, 1946, 1410–1630 hours. National Archives of Japan, File 4A.18.242, Kyokutō kokusai gunji saiban kankei shiryō (Ei-bun) kyōjutsu chōsho – Tōjō Hideki, 225.
30 Ishii Akiho, *Ishii Akiho Taisa kaisōroku*, 135. National Institute of Defense Studies, Tokyo (henceforth NIDS), Chūō. Sensō shidō jūyō kokusaku bunsho 799.
31 Moriyama discusses the period between the second Konoe Cabinet in July 1940 and the outbreak of war in 1941. See Moriyama Atsushi, *Nichi-Bei kaisen no seiji katei* (Tokyo: Yoshikawa Kōbunkan, 1998); and Moriyama, *Nihon wa naze kaisen ni fumikittanoka*. With his second work, Moriyama subtly changed his notion of "non-decision" (非決定*hikettei*) to decision avoidance (*hikettei*, or 非(避)決定).

Matsuoka Yōsuke's Grand Design

The first inchoate grand strategy was the brainchild of Foreign Minister Matsuoka Yōsuke. Matsuoka not only had a creative vision to bring about Japanese hegemony in Asia, but also had a sense of tactics to bring his vision to fruition. Matsuoka, in short, had a grand strategy he wanted to implement, and he used his mastery over liaison conference meetings to ensure his ability to implement it.

Matsuoka's vision centred on the construction of Japan's Greater East Asia Co-Prosperity Sphere. He announced the sphere in an August 1940 radio address meant to explain Japanese foreign policy, and used the rest of his time as foreign minister to bring this vision to fruition. His desire to construct the co-prosperity sphere emerged from his understanding of international politics. Like many men of his era, Matsuoka believed that the world had irrevocably changed owing to the rise of Nazi Germany in Europe, the decline of British power, and the growth of Japanese power in Asia. He saw the international system as destined to break up into five blocs: the Western hemisphere led by the United States, Europe and North Africa under Germany and Italy, the British Empire, the Soviet Union, and East Asia under Japan. Yet he did not think this trend would automatically lead to future conflicts. Far from it, Matsuoka wrote in May 1940 – two months before becoming foreign minister – that Great Power rivalries were not inevitable, and "reasonable men" could avoid war. The keys to global peace were accepting and respecting pan-regional spheres of influence.[32] This idea formed the core of his vision for the Greater East Asia Co-Prosperity Sphere.

Upon becoming foreign minister in July 1940, Matsuoka began to construct the co-prosperity sphere through what I call "sphere of influence diplomacy."[33] Matsuoka pursued this diplomacy in two ways. First, he sought to use peaceful negotiations with French Indochina, Thailand, and the Netherlands Indies to build acceptance of Japan's regional leadership and gain economic benefits from resource-rich Southeast Asia. Second, and more important, he sought to gain Great Power acceptance and respect for Japan's regional spheres of influence. To this end, he signed the Tripartite Pact with Nazi Germany and Italy,

---

[32] Matsuoka Yōsuke, "Sekai daihenkyoku ni chokumen shite," *Taiheiyō*, Vol. 3, No. 5 (May 1940), 2–11.
[33] A fuller exploration of Matsuoka's diplomacy, and much of the material discussed below, can be found in Yellen, *The Greater East Asia Co-Prosperity Sphere*, 46–70; Kawanishi Kōsuke, *Dai Tōa Kyōeiken: Teikoku Nihon no Nanpō taiken* (Tokyo: Kōdansha, 2016), 26–70; and Mori Shigeki, "Matsuoka gaikō ni okeru tai Bei oyobi tai Ei saku: Nichi-Doku-I dōmei teiketsu zengo no kōsō to tenkai" in *Nihonshi kenkyū*, No. 421 (Sep. 1997), 35–62.

conducted a whirlwind tour of Europe in March and April 1941 that culminated in a nonaggression pact with the Soviet Union, and planned to hold broad-based discussions with the United States. As historian Kawanishi Kōsuke writes, the point of this was the creation of a global order where great powers "respect each other's co-prosperity spheres."[34]

In important ways, Matsuoka was successful in his efforts to realise his grand strategy. His Asian diplomacy met with two great successes. First, he negotiated an August 1940 agreement with Vichy France to recognize Japan's "preponderance of interest in economic and political spheres in the Far East." The agreement also ensured the "superior status" of Japanese nationals over those of any third power, and granted the Imperial Japanese Army (IJA) the right to station troops, transport war materiel, and use airfields in northern Indochina.[35] Matsuoka's foreign ministry followed up with a May 1941 agreement that gave Japan preferential amounts of rice, coal, tin, raw rubber, manganese, and other mineral products, and gave Japanese nationals equality of treatment as well as access to many professions prohibited to foreigners.

The second success, and one of Matsuoka's greatest triumphs as foreign minister, came with Japan's arbitration of the Thai-Indochina border dispute of 1940–41. The dispute began owing to French weakness, which Thailand used to reclaim from Indochina its "lost territories" of Luang Prabang and Pakse. This border dispute constituted the first major test for Matsuoka's attempt to realize the co-prosperity sphere. It also served as a test of Matsuoka's political acumen, as the Thai-Indochina crisis led to criticisms in the army general staff of his "lukewarm diplomacy". Not only did Matsuoka thwart those criticisms, he also worked against army staff efforts to advance into Southeast Asia and to forge a military alliance with Thailand.

It was Matsuoka's control over liaison meetings (*renraku kondankai*), in particular, that allowed his stewardship of Japanese foreign policy. Matsuoka found a close political ally in Army Minister Tōjō Hideki, who clamped down on the army and punished any commanders who engaged in opportunistic adventurism.[36] This, in turn, strengthened Matsuoka's control over foreign

---

34 Kawanishi, *Dai Tōa Kyōeiken*, 38–40.
35 Matsumoto Shun'ichi and Andō Yoshirō, eds., *Nihon gaikōshi 22: Nanshin mondai* (Tokyo: Kajima Kenkyūjo Shuppankai, 1973), 132–34.
36 Tōjō held Matsuoka in such high esteem (and saw him as such a close friend) that, during his postwar interrogations by the International Military Tribunal for the Far East, he always referred to Matsuoka as "Matsuoka-sensei." See National Archives of Japan, IMTFE File 4A–18–2420, 175, "Sugamo Prison Interview of Tojo," 4 March 1946.

affairs.³⁷ But more importantly, Matsuoka never backed down from a good fight. The liaison meetings, as one historian notes, "provided the arena in which he pit his views against those of army and navy leaders."³⁸ Matsuoka found himself pitted against general staff chief Sugiyama Hajime, a respected army elder and the mouthpiece of army demands.

Matsuoka defended his policymaking from Sugiyama's critiques through a mesmerizing combination of hawkish arguments, dovish counterarguments, and confusing non sequiturs. During some liaison meetings in January 1941, he championed policy so hawkish that it bewildered Sugiyama. At times, Matsuoka even called for a sneak attack on British territory and the capture of Singapore. Other times Matsuoka took a dovish tack, and appealed for peace and restraint lest Japan antagonise Britain and the United States. Sometimes, he even rattled on about the complexities of his diplomatic strategies. U.S. Ambassador to Japan Joseph C. Grew often noted Matsuoka's amazing loquacity, remarking in April 1941 that "it would take a superman to outtalk Matsuoka."³⁹ This loquacity, along with his tendency to grandstand and stubborn urge to have the final say, helped him keep his opponents off balance.⁴⁰

Sugiyama even tried to play the military's trump card: a direct appeal to the throne. Sugiyama met with the emperor on January 24, 1941, and advocated the general staff's desire to advance military interests into Indochina and to sign a military pact with Thailand. Had he received the emperor's approval, the army could have asserted the "independence of supreme command" to press forward with its own designs for Asia. But Matsuoka secretly met with the emperor before Sugiyama's audience, and convinced him to refuse the general staff's demands.⁴¹ Sugiyama left his meeting with the emperor red-faced and embarrassed – publicly humiliated by his rival.⁴²

Japan ultimately mediated the dispute, hammering out a middle-of-the-road agreement that was wholly acceptable to neither side and thus a good compromise. In return for its arbitration, Japan included a clause in the final

---

37 See David J. Lu, *Agony of Choice: Matsuoka Yōsuke and the Rise and Fall of the Japanese Empire, 1880–1946* (Lanham: Lexington Books, 2002), 185–87.
38 Kawanishi, *Dai Tōa Kyōeiken*, 49.
39 Joseph C. Grew, *Ten Years in Japan: A Contemporary Record Drawn from the Diaries and Private and Official Papers of Joseph C. Grew, United States Ambassador to Japan, 1932–1942* (New York: Simon and Schuster, 1944), 378.
40 Moriyama Atsushi also makes the trenchant observation that instead of focusing on Matsuoka's ever-changing, incoherent statements, we should look at what he was trying to achieve through them. See Moriyama, *Nihon wa naze kaisen ni fumikittanoka*, 44–45.
41 Yellen, *The Greater East Asia Co-Prosperity Sphere*, 53–54.
42 Tanemura Sakō, *Daihon'ei kimitsu nisshi* (Tokyo: Fuyō Shobō, 1979), 66–67.

agreement that forbade both Indochina and Thailand from entering into an agreement detrimental to Japanese interests. In this sense, the accord confirmed Japan as Southeast Asia's hegemonic power. The formal signing on 11 March 1941 was thus met with great fanfare and viewed as a "historic victory."[43] Even the army general staff gave grudging respect to Matsuoka's power politics. Firebrand Tanaka Shin'ichi, one of the three most influential staff officers in the army, saw the arbitration as "the first step to the establishment of Japan's leadership position in Thailand and French Indochina."[44]

At the same time he was trying to build the co-prosperity sphere, Matsuoka used great power diplomacy to seek recognition of Japan's expanded Asian interests. His Great Power diplomacy also had two great successes. His first, which he later came to see as his greatest failure, was the signing of the Tripartite Pact. Public excitement for the alliance had grown by June 1940, after the German war machine defeated France and became ascendant in Western Europe. At the same time, foreign ministry and some mid-level army elites also shouldered fears that Germany might claim political control over French and Dutch colonies in Asia. These fears, and a desire to keep Nazi Germany out of Japan's new order in Asia, committed elites in the foreign ministry to support a full alliance.[45] Matsuoka championed the closer relationship with Germany for similar ends. He sought German recognition of Japan's sphere of influence across Greater East Asia and, in return, he was prepared to recognize Nazi Germany's sphere of influence in Europe and North Africa. In signing the Tripartite Pact on 27 September 1940, he laid the groundwork for great power recognition of Japan's sphere of influence in Asia.

The other major success came with Matsuoka's famous whirlwind tour of Europe in March and April 1941, where he met with Hitler and Stalin and signed a nonaggression pact with the Soviet Union. Traditional scholarship argues that Matsuoka sought to create a four-power entente. This interpretation is open to debate, but it is clear that Matsuoka saw the European tour as an important part of his sphere of influence diplomacy.[46] In fact, Matsuoka sought

---

[43] *Tōkyō Asahi shinbun*, 11–12 March 1941.
[44] See NIDS, 11 March 1941 entry, Tanaka, *Dai Tōa Sensō e no zentei*, Vol. 1: *Futsuin-Tai funsō chōtei*: 77.
[45] For a full exploration of this, see Jeremy A. Yellen, "Into the Tiger's Den: Japan and the Tripartite Pact, 1940," *Journal of Contemporary History* 51:3 (July 2016), 555–76.
[46] For scholarship that questions the four-power entente ideal, see Miwa Munehiro, "Nichi-Doku-I Sangoku dōmei teiketsu toki ni okeru, Nichi-Doku-I-So kōsō e no gimon: Matsuoka kōsō-setsu e no gimon," *Nihon Daigaku seisan kōgakubu kenkyū hōkoku B*, Vol. 25, No. 1 (June 1992), 21–39.

from Moscow similar terms to what he hoped to achieve with Berlin and Washington: recognition of each power's sphere of interest. Japan's aims were summarised in a policy document, "Outline for Negotiations with Germany, Italy, and the Soviet Union," which was prepared by the foreign ministry on 6 January 1941 and adopted by a liaison meeting with only minor revisions on 3 February. It called for a world of four large spheres (Greater East Asia, Europe/Africa, the Americas, and the Soviet Union), and pressed for mutual recognition of each other's spheres of influence. "The Empire," it noted, "will consent to the Soviet position in Xinjiang and Outer Mongolia; the Soviet Union will consent to the Empire's position in North China and Mengjiang."[47] This was sphere of influence diplomacy writ large.

Moreover, Matsuoka believed that an accord with the Soviet Union would be a powerful diplomatic lever against Washington. As Matsuoka explained to his secretary before departing to Europe: "To shake hands with Germany is a temporary excuse to shake hands with the Soviet Union. But that hand shaking with the Soviet Union is also nothing more than an excuse to shake hands with the United States."[48]

It was in Moscow that Matsuoka had his greatest success. On 13 April 1941, he signed a five-year neutrality pact with the Soviet Union at the expense of Japan's concessions in North Sakhalin. The pact called for peaceful relations between the two powers, and neutrality should either country open hostilities against another power. More importantly, Matsuoka even received from Moscow an official statement confirming their respective spheres of influence. The Soviet Union pledged to respect the territorial integrity of Manchukuo, and Japan promised the same for the Mongolian People's Republic.[49]

Matsuoka had every right to be excited. The neutrality pact and its accompanying pledge validated his sphere of influence diplomacy, and may have convinced him that the world he sought to build was within his grasp. Matsuoka repeatedly toasted his diplomatic victory after signing the pact, and continued drinking when Stalin unexpectedly went to Moscow Station to bid him farewell. Matsuoka reportedly got so drunk that Stalin's entourage had to help him onto the train. His inebriation could be read metaphorically as well – Japan's foreign minister was so drunk off his diplomatic victories that he was ready to believe he could get Washington to fall in line and achieve his grand design.

---

[47] Bōeichō Bōei Kenshūjo, Senshishitsu, *Daihon'ei Rikugunbu Dai Tōa Sensō kaisen keii*, Vol. 3 (Tokyo: Asagumo Shinbunsha, 1973), 357–58. Henceforth cited as *Kaisen keii*.
[48] Quoted in Eri Hotta, *Japan 1941: Countdown to Infamy* (New York: Vintage Books, 2011), 59.
[49] *Kaisen keii*, 3: 416–17.

In the end, Matsuoka's grand strategy was undermined by developments in Asia and by his failed negotiations with the United States. On the one hand, Japan's negotiations with the Netherlands Indies ended in utter failure. Matsuoka had not taken centre stage in the talks. The negotiations nonetheless constituted a central part of his efforts to acquire natural resources and to secure recognition of the Netherlands Indies participation in Japan's Greater East Asia Co-Prosperity Sphere. By June 1941, however, it had become clear that the Netherlands Indies would neither provide the resources Japan demanded nor accept the notion of Japan as the region's leading power. With this failure, hotheaded staff officers in both branches of the military began to argue that it was time to forge "co-prosperity" through force of arms.

More importantly, Matsuoka's sphere of influence diplomacy (and his position as foreign minister) was undermined by developments in U.S.-Japan relations. Matsuoka had used his Moscow trip to lay the groundwork for negotiations with Washington. He visited U.S. Ambassador to the USSR Laurence Steinhardt to discuss his visions for an amicable settlement, in the hopes that the discussions would reach President Roosevelt's ear.[50] It was from those discussions that Matsuoka hoped to begin negotiations with Roosevelt. But when Matsuoka arrived at Dairen on 21 April 1941, he was shocked to learn that Japan had already opened exploratory talks with Washington. Over the next few days, he learned that the talks featured a "proposal for understanding" drafted by the so-called John Doe Associates.[51] Adding insult to injury, the proposal was tantamount to a complete reversal of Matsuoka's strategy. The proposal would have undermined the Tripartite Pact, which Matsuoka saw as a mainstay of his diplomacy. Moreover, it called for a Japanese withdrawal from China, and promised peaceful expansion in Southeast Asia in return for U.S. help in acquiring essential resources. The proposal thus handicapped Matsuoka's sphere of influence diplomacy.

Even if Matsuoka had gotten on board with the John Doe Associates' proposal, the negotiations with Washington still had little chance of success. But Matsuoka chose the worst possible way to respond to the new state of affairs. Instead of coopting the John Doe Associates' activities, Matsuoka sought to quash them. Instead of working within the confines of the Washington conversations,

---

50 Matsuoka's messages were suppressed by Secretary of State Cordell Hull. Roosevelt never saw them. Lu, *Agony of Choice*, 209.

51 For an engrossing history of this group and the exploratory conversations, see Robert J.C. Butow, *The John Doe Associates: Backdoor Diplomacy for Peace, 1941* (Stanford: University Press, 1974). See also Tsunoda Jun, "Confusion Arising from a Draft Understanding between Japan and the United States," in James William Morley, ed., *Japan's Road to the Pacific War: The Final Confrontation* (New York: Columbia University Press, 1994), 1–105.

Matsuoka subverted them to reaffirm his sphere of influence strategy. In the process, he reiterated Japan's commitment to the Axis pact and to the military occupation of China. This dogged commitment owed to Matsuoka's misreading of the Americans. Matsuoka believed that although they might preach pacifism and good relations, Americans responded to bravado and swagger. Talk tough, and Americans would come to terms with his sphere of influence diplomacy. This fundamental misinterpretation clouded Matsuoka's vision, and would spell the death knell of his grand design.

In the end, the impending failure of the Washington conversations, in addition to Matsuoka's hard-line response to the German-Soviet war, spelled Matsuoka's demise. The Konoe cabinet responded by ousting Matsuoka the only way it could: resigning *en masse*. On 16 July the cabinet resigned, and on the following day Konoe formed his third cabinet, with the lone change that Vice Admiral Toyoda Teijirō replaced Matsuoka as foreign minister. With this, Matsuoka's hard-nosed sphere of influence diplomacy, and his vision for the co-prosperity sphere, came to a crashing close. Thus ended the first moment of inchoate grand strategy in wartime Japan.

Shigemitsu Mamoru's Wilsonian Dreams

Two years after Matsuoka's grand design came crashing down, Japan had a second moment of inchoate grand strategy. This second moment, led by another foreign minister – Shigemitsu Mamoru – was no longer an attempt to construct the sphere via "sphere of influence" diplomacy. It was instead an attempt to shore up Japan's regional leadership through a return to liberal-internationalist principles. Shigemitsu's strategy emerged in the lead up to the Greater East Asia Conference of November 1943, wherein policy had to be totally remade owing to Japan's military decline. Thus, whereas the first moment of inchoate grand strategy under Matsuoka was a sign of Japanese strength, this second moment emerged from Japanese weakness.

The war, after all, was not going well for Japan. The Battle of Midway in June 1942 resulted in the loss of the four aircraft carriers that formed the core of the Imperial Japanese Navy's (IJN) power projection capabilities. Moreover, the six-month Guadalcanal campaign, which ended in a full-scale Japanese evacuation in February 1943, placed Japan on the defensive in the Pacific. Guadalcanal also weakened Japan's military power owing to its consistent attempts to reinforce failing defenders with fresh supplies and troops. A perhaps more powerful, psychological shock came in April 1943 when Admiral Yamamoto Isoroku, the architect of the surprise attack on Pearl Harbor, was shot down over Bougainville in the South Pacific. One could perceive the dismay of navy leader Yoshida Zengo, who called Yamamoto's death "an irrecoverable loss."[52]

The faltering advance in the Pacific was not the only source of concern. Japanese leaders also keenly perceived the deteriorating war situation in Europe. Ambassador to Nanjing Shigemitsu Mamoru, for instance, looked uneasily at Germany's faltering Atlantic submarine warfare and declining air superiority. He realised that a German defeat would allow the Allies to focus their military and technological might into the Asia-Pacific. Shigemitsu thus began publishing position papers highlighting the shared destiny of the Axis powers. He argued that German military difficulties "directly affect Japan's military affairs."[53] And Shigemitsu called for increased Axis cooperation to deal with the unfavourable war situation.

Shigemitsu became instrumental in rethinking Japan's wartime strategy. He drafted widely circulated position papers from 1942 that criticised the onesided, ham-fisted, military-first nature of Japan's war. Shigemitsu continually insisted that victory did not depend solely on fortunes met at the field of battle. "Military force," he asserted, "must be met with military force, and diplomacy must be countered with diplomacy."[54] He called for a revitalised diplomacy to counter the allied propaganda of the Atlantic Charter and to secure Asian support for the war effort. Smart foreign policy, he argued in mid-1942, "has the same effect as military affairs in deciding victory or defeat."[55]

Shigemitsu called for a sea change in Japanese policy. Victory in Asia depended on whether Japan could win the hearts and minds of occupied territories. But Shigemitsu criticised policymakers' tendency to pay mere lip service to Asian liberation while gearing Japan's war aims to securing autarky and regional hegemony. At a time when regional support was critical for the war effort, such a mindset was naïve at best, and dangerous at worst. Shigemitsu argued that Japan could only win hearts and minds by creating a nationalities policy of high ideals. He emphasized in his position papers the necessity of "establishing political equality among all nations." Maintaining dependencies or colonies in Greater East Asia would dampen any emergent spirit of cooperation. Japan instead had to support *actual* independence: Shigemitsu emphasised

---

52 Kensei Shiryōshitsu, National Diet Library, File 4–1, *Yoshida Zengo kankei monjo*.
53 Shigemitsu Mamoru, *Shigemitsu Mamoru: Gaikō ikenshoshū*, Vol. 2: *chū ka taishi, gaimudaijin jidai* (Tokyo: Gendai Shiryō Shuppan, 2007), 259.
54 Ibid., 302.
55 Ibid., 119.

that countries in Greater East Asia "must be given the authority of independence and autonomy that will allow them to manage their national affairs."[56]

These views do not imply that Shigemitsu was an anti-imperialist or an anticolonial advocate. Far from it, Shigemitsu was a consummate political realist who recognized the importance of power in international relations.[57] He had supported the Manchurian Incident in 1931 and the formation of Manchukuo. Moreover, while vice-foreign minister between May 1933 and April 1936, he pursued a policy of rapprochement toward China while also calling for something akin to an Asian Monroe doctrine, noting Japan's determination to maintain security in East Asia.[58] But by 1942, with Japan's empire teetering on the precipice of disaster, Shigemitsu had changed his tactics. He began to counsel a diplomacy of reconciliation, and saw an East Asian union as the "biggest weapon" in Japan's fight for Asia.

This was a call to arms for the foreign policy establishment, an appeal to wage a war of diplomacy. Superficial propaganda had done little to promote Japanese leadership, and could not bolster Japan's faltering international position. Shigemitsu wrote, "If we display a policy of aggression and exploitation abroad where we cry wine and sell vinegar, then our [vision] will be meaningless both during wartime and peacetime." Instead, Shigemitsu advocated pragmatic measures to promote Japan as the moral leader of Asia and to crush the Anglo-American propaganda of the Atlantic Charter. He argued that a voluntary union between East Asian states "will become during wartime the biggest weapon, and in the postwar era will become the greatest foundation of the empire's expansion."[59]

To enact this strategy and reassert Japan's moral leadership, Shigemitsu championed a New China Policy and a New Greater East Asia Policy. The New China Policy represented Shigemitsu's understanding that peace with Chiang Kai-shek's Nationalist regime was the precondition for peace in Asia. Thus, the policy called for the revision of the unequal treaties, respect for Chinese sovereignty, and the eventual withdrawal of troops from Chinese territory. This policy formed the basis for his New Greater East Asia Policy. Shigemitsu argued that extending independence and autonomy to former European colonies would set Japan apart from the Allied powers, which preached high ideals but controlled

---

56 Ibid., 268.
57 Shigemitsu Mamoru, *Shigemitsu Mamoru shuki*, Vol. 2 (Tokyo: Chuo Kōronsha, 1988), 335.
58 Usui Katsumi, "Gaimushō: hito to kikō," in Hosoya Chihiro, Saitō Makoto, Imai Sei'ichi, and Rōyama Michio, eds., *Nichi-Bei kankeishi: kaisen ni itaru 10-nen (1931–41-nen)*, Vol. 1: *seifu shunō to gaikō kikan* (Tokyo: Tōkyō Daigaku Shuppankai, 1971), 119–23.
59 Shigemitsu, *Gaikō ikenshoshū*, 2: 245–46.

far-flung empires. More importantly, these two policies represented the core of Shigemitsu's broader wish to bring about "the liberation and rebirth of Asia."[60]

Shigemitsu's ideas struck a chord with Prime Minister Tōjō and other leading policymakers. Facing a string of military failures, the High Command began to pine for diplomatic successes. Thus, from December 1942 Japan embarked on a new strategy that mirrored the very policies Shigemitsu advocated from his position as Ambassador to Nanjing. An imperial conference confirmed the decision to abolish the unequal treaties with the Chinese Nanjing Regime and forge a more equal partnership. After Japan had begun implementing this policy, Tōjō on 20 April 1943 invited Shigemitsu to join his administration as foreign minister. Shigemitsu agreed, after gaining Tōjō's consent to enact his strategy for Asia.[61] This overall strategy, approved at a series of liaison conferences in 1943, had four main components.

First, Japan enacted the New China Policy, which gave greater independence to Wang Jingwei's collaborationist Nanjing regime. Japan announced the end of extraterritorial rights and allowed the Nanjing regime to declare war on Britain and America, thus eliminating most vestiges of overt political control. This was part of a naïve attempt toward peace with Chiang Kai-shek. Japanese leaders believed that showing a new sincerity of intentions toward China would set the stage for peace talks with the Nationalist government in Chungking [Chongqing], to be initiated through the Nanjing government.[62] This was Shigemitsu's signature policy, and he helped implement it upon assuming the foreign ministry portfolio.

Second, Japan extended independence to other parts of the Greater East Asia Co-Prosperity Sphere. The willingness to do so predated Shigemitsu's return to Tokyo, but was also influenced by his position papers and his aggressive promotion of the New Greater East Asia Policy. On 21 January and again on 28 January 1943, Prime Minister Tōjō made statements in the Imperial Diet calling for the extension of independence to Burma and the Philippines.[63] A 10 March liaison conference followed up on this call, agreeing to grant independence to

---

60 Shigemitsu, *Shōwa no dōran*, Vol. 2 (Tokyo: Chūō Kōronsha, 1952): 171.
61 Shigemitsu, *Shigemitsu Mamoru shuki*, Vol. 1 (Tokyo: Chūō Kōronsha, 1986), 321–23, 328–29. See also Itō Takashi, Hirohashi Tadamitsu, and Katashima Norio, eds., *Tōjō naikaku sōridaijin kimitsu kiroku: Tōjō Hideki Taishō genkōroku* (Tokyo: Tokyo Daigaku Shuppankai, 1990), 175.
62 Akira Iriye, *Power and Culture: The Japanese-American War, 1941–1945* (Cambridge MA: Harvard University Press, 1981), 96–112.
63 *Daihon'ei rikugunbu*, 7: 361.

Burma and calling for the country's leadership under Ba Maw.⁶⁴ Shortly after, Japan decided to bestow independence to the Philippines – with Jose P. Laurel as President. A 31 May imperial conference solidified and endorsed these decisions. Burma and the Philippines received independence on 1 August and 14 October, respectively, and on 21 October Japan helped establish the Provisional Government of Free India (Azad Hind) under nationalist leader Subhas Chandra Bose.

One should be careful to avoid overstating the extent of this independence. This independence was part and parcel of what Prasenjit Duara calls the "new imperialism," wherein "sovereign" satellite regimes were controlled indirectly by Japan.⁶⁵ In this sense, neither Burma nor the Philippines gained true self-determination. Independence instead preserved Japanese leadership and control. Both regimes, in fact, signed agreements that gave the Japanese military wide leeway to intervene in their domestic affairs.⁶⁶ Japan could mark nearly all demands for aid, facilities, infrastructure, or territory as "military necessities," demands that neither government was able to refuse. Thus, Japan merely bestowed nominal independence to Burma and the Philippines, and further extended the Manchukuo model of semi-colonial governance to Southeast Asia. Nominal independence was a propagandistic means to highlight Japanese benevolence and to win new loyalties across the region.

Third, Japan launched a public relations campaign across Asia. Prime Minister Tōjō and other state officials made state visits to Manchukuo, the Philippines, Thailand, and Indonesia. No doubt these visits were seen as measures to build legitimacy and to demonstrate the power of Asia's new overlord. Tōjō's trip to the Philippines in May 1943 also provides a fascinating glimpse into the dynamics of empire that belied the benevolent image Japan sought to create. Japanese Consul Kihara gave a list of orders to Philippine Executive Commission Chairman Jorge Vargas in advance of Tōjō's visit. All residents were expected to wave Japanese flags and greet Tōjō with screams of *"Banzai!"* as the

---

64 *Sugiyama memo*, 2: 386–88; and TG-NDL, "Kanpō," *Gōgai*, 22 January 1942.
65 Prasenjit Duara, "The Imperialism of 'Free Nations': Japan, Manchukuo, and the History of the Present," in Ann Stoler, Carole McGranahan, and Peter Perdue, eds. *Imperial Formations* (SAR Press, 2007), 211–39. Hatano Sumio calls this type of "new imperialism" the "Manchukuo model" of "dependent independence." See Hatano Sumio, *Taiheiyō Sensō to Ajia gaikō* (Tokyo: Tokyo Daigaku Shuppankai, 1996), 103–04.
66 Bōeichō Bōei Kenshūjo, Senshishitsu, *Biruma kōryaku sakusen* (Tokyo: Asagumo Shinbunsha, 1967) 544–45; for the Philippine case, see "Memorandum on Questions between Japan and the Philippines arising from The Philippine Independence," October 1943. Taken from Teodoro A. Agoncillo, *The Fateful Years: Japan's Adventure in the Philippines* (Quezon City: R.P. Garcia Publishing Co., 1965), 977–82.

premier went past. Filipinos were also ordered to attend the ceremonies held at Luneta Park, and were instructed to wave Japanese flags to greet the visitors and to break out into applause after each speech. More than 400,000 Filipinos, young and old, braved the fierce summer sun to watch Tōjō speak. This left the Japanese premier trembling with excitement. After wearing himself out with bowing and saluting, Tōjō took on Hitler's affectations, walking through Luneta with his hand held high.[67]

Fourth, Japan held a "Greater East Asia Conference" and released a joint declaration outlining the principles behind Japan's reimagined new order. The Greater East Asia Conference and joint declaration were part of a charm offensive to build moral and political support for Japan's war. A liaison conference and an imperial conference on 26 and 31 May 1943 solidified the commitment to holding the conference, and a 2 October liaison conference formalised the conference details. Participation was limited to Asia's "independent" countries: Japan, Manchukuo, China, Thailand, Burma, and the Philippines.[68] The Provisional Government of Free India would attend as an observer. Moreover, the liaison conference outlined the purpose of the conference: delegates were to trumpet their "firm resolution to prosecute the war to a successful conclusion" as well as their support for the Greater East Asia Co-Prosperity Sphere.[69]

The decision to hold the conference represented an agreement between two visions of Japanese foreign policy. Prime Minister Tōjō and the supreme command saw the conference as a practical means of galvanizing Asian support for the war and undermining Allied morale. Foreign Minister Shigemitsu agreed with these goals, but also saw the conference as the first step toward the creation of a "Greater East Asia Confederation," a group of independent states that would provide for cooperation in the postwar international regime. Shigemitsu and other foreign ministry bureaucrats also hoped their idealistic joint declaration – modelled after the Atlantic Charter – would create a positive image of

---

67 See Teodoro A. Agoncillo, *The Burden of Proof: The Vargas-Laurel Collaboration Case* (Mandaluyong, Metro Manila: University of the Philippines Press, 1984), 48; and Armando J. Malay, *Occupied Philippines: The Role of Jorge B. Vargas During the Japanese Occupation* (Manila: Filipiniana Book Guild, 1967), 114–16.

68 *Daihon'ei rikugunbu*, 6: 536, 538. *Sugiyama memo*, 411, 414. Shigemitsu argued for limiting the conference to independent countries, as inviting representatives from all areas of the sphere might negatively impact Japan's relations with its "independent" partners. *Daihon'ei rikugunbu*, 7: 382.

69 *Sugiyama memo*, 2: 497–498.

Japan's war aims in Britain and America.[70] Although Japanese historians often highlight the differences between Tōjō and Shigemitsu, both leaders shared common goals. They sought to rally Asian nations to make war, and to convince Britain and America to make peace.

The Greater East Asia Conference formally convened at 10 a.m. on 5 November 1943. Each delegation filed into the Imperial Diet Building and took their seats. The delegations were headed by the following leaders: Prime Minister Tōjō, Japan; President of the Executive Yuan Wang Jingwei, the China Nanjing Regime; Prime Minister Zhang Jinghui, Manchukuo; Prime Minister Ba Maw, Burma; President Jose P. Laurel, the Republic of the Philippines; Deputy Prime Minister Prince Wan Waithayakon, Thailand; and Subhas Chandra Bose, the Provisional Government of Free India. The full attendance of the event was nothing short of miraculous. Both Ba Maw and Prince Wan's planes purportedly crashed on the way to Tokyo. And Prince Wan was hit by a 40-degree (Celsius) fever after arriving in Tokyo, but felt well enough to attend the afternoon session of the first day.

The climax of the conference came on 6 November, with the unanimous decision to approve the Greater East Asia Joint Declaration. This was what I refer to as Japan's Pacific Charter, meant in opposition to the Atlantic Charter. The Pacific Charter was defined by five main principles, drafted by the foreign ministry, that articulated the principles that would undergird the new order:

1. The countries of Greater East Asia through mutual cooperation will ensure the stability of their region and construct an order of common prosperity and well-being based upon justice.
2. The countries of Greater East Asia will ensure the fraternity of nations in their region, by respecting one another's sovereignty and independence and practicing mutual assistance and amity.
3. The countries of Greater East Asia by respecting one another's traditions and developing the creative faculties of each race, will enhance the culture and civilization of Greater East Asia.
4. The countries of Greater East Asia will endeavour to accelerate their economic development through close cooperation upon a basis of reciprocity and to promote thereby the general prosperity of their region.
5. The countries of Greater East Asia will cultivate friendly relations with all the countries of the world, and work for the abolition of racial discriminations,

---

[70] Yasuda Toshie. "Dai Tōa Kaigi to Dai Tōa Kyōdō Sengen o megutte," *Hōgaku kenkyū* 63:2 (February 1990), 373–74, 382; and Hatano Sumio, "Shigemitsu Mamoru to Dai Tōa Kyōdō Sengen," *Kokusai seiji* 109:5 (May 1995), 40, 42.

the promotion of cultural intercourse and the opening of resources throughout the world, and contribute thereby to the progress of mankind.[71]

The Pacific Charter's five principles represented Japan's answer to the Atlantic Charter. The drafters even referred to the Atlantic Charter when drawing up the document – hence the strong resemblance between the two charters. Both the Atlantic and Pacific Charters called for something akin to national self-determination or at least the autonomy of independent states. Both called for similar measures in the economic realm. Both sought to advance international cooperation for economic development, to promote economic prosperity, and to guarantee equal access to markets and resources. And both charters emphasised cooperative coexistence, peace, and prosperity.

There is good reason why foreign ministry officials referred to the Atlantic Charter when drafting the joint declaration. Japanese authorities had struggled to forge an ideology that would win the hearts and minds of political elites in the region. This resulted from longer-term trends in Japanese political culture. Foreign policy since the late Meiji period operated as a realist pursuit of national power. Ideology played a mostly negligible role in the attainment of empire. From the 1930s, however, pan-Asianism took a stronger foothold among Japanese political elites owing to Japan's intellectual and political revolt against the West. Japanese leaders used pan-Asianism as part of a propaganda campaign in support of war in China and the new order. But pan-Asianism never had a defined ideological program or systematic doctrine, and it lacked a positive programme that Japanese leaders could use to gain allegiance in the region.[72] The urgency of forging a compelling ideology – particularly as the war turned against Japan – led the drafters of the declaration (at least those in the Foreign Ministry) to liberal-internationalist language to resolve Japan's crisis of legitimacy. Borrowing Wilsonian language does not suggest, as Akira Iriye argues, a return to values held in the 1920s.[73] Instead, it reveals the pragmatism of Japanese elites, who utilised such values to rally Asian support for Japan's imperial project.

---

[71] The original draft can be found in Ministry of Greater East Asiatic Affairs, *Addresses Before the Assembly of Greater East Asiatic Nations* (Tokyo, 1943), 63–65.

[72] For excellent works on pan-Asianism, see Cemil Aydin, *The Politics of Anti-Westernism in Asia: Visions of World Order in Pan-Islamic and Pan-Asian Thought* (New York: Columbia University Press, 2007); Eri Hotta, *Pan-Asianism and Japan's War, 1931–1945* (New York: Palgrave Macmillan, 2007); and Matsu'ura Masataka "*Dai tōa sensō" wa naze okitanoka: pan-Ajia shugi no seijikeizaishi* (Tokyo: Nagoya Daigaku Shuppankai, 2010).

[73] Iriye, *Power and Culture*.

This pragmatic attitude led Tokyo to accept the greatest difference between the two documents: the clause abolishing racial discrimination. At its core, this clause is much more idealistic than the Atlantic Charter, which lacks similar provisions. But conflict within leadership circles over whether to include the clause reveals the pragmatism behind the use of such language. According to Lt. General and army ministry military affairs bureau chief Satō Kenryō, assistant secretaries in the foreign, army, and navy ministries initially opposed the racial equality clause, believing that it would prove an obstacle to reaching a separate peace with the Allied powers. Ultimately, however, they were convinced that the clause would "win public sentiment" and breed fear among the Allied powers that the war would devolve into a race war.[74] The lack of idealism behind this revolutionary clause is telling. Leaders enshrined it in the declaration to provide Japan with sufficient leverage to prosecute or end the war on favourable terms.

The Pacific Charter was more than mere propaganda – it was to be the blueprint for a new grand strategy of late wartime Japan. But it never forged a new reality for the region. Granted, independence was bestowed to the Philippines and Burma. Nonetheless, that independence never translated into absolute sovereignty nor did it guarantee freedom from Japanese interference.[75] Ultimately, both Philippine President Laurel and Burmese Prime Minister Ba Maw used the Pacific Charter to protest Japanese violations of local industry and national sovereignty. They pointed out that Japanese forces often prevented their regimes from safeguarding local interests or developing local industry, and highlighted that this contravened the spirit of the Pacific Charter.[76] But in both cases, there is no evidence that Japan made any efforts to resolve the matter to the satisfaction of its Southeast Asian partners.

In fact, Japanese military authorities made comments indicating an unabashed disdain for the Pacific Charter. In November 1944, Lt. General Kimura Heitarō, commander-in-chief of Japan's Burma Area Army, called on Burmese to "trust implicitly in Nippon's sincerity." He argued that full and complete independence would come sometime in the future. For the time being, he called on Burmese to understand that they would need to sacrifice for their future.

---

[74] Satō Kenryō, *Satō Kenryō no shōgen* (Tokyo: Fuyō Shobō, 1976), 437; Satō Kenryō, *Dai tōa sensō kaikoroku* (Tokyo: Tokuma Shoten, 1966), 319.
[75] Jeremy A. Yellen, "Wartime Wilsonianism and the Crisis of Empire, 1941–1943," *Modern Asian Studies* 53:4 (July 2019), 1305–08.
[76] See Jose P. Laurel Memorial Library, Manila, Jose P. Laurel Papers, Series 3: Japanese Occupation Papers, Box 7; and U Hla Pe, "U Hla Pe's Narrative of the Japanese Occupation of Burma," Data Paper Number 41, Southeast Asia Program, Cornell University, (March 1961), 59.

Burma, he argued, needed to go through "war time quasi-civil administration" before finally reaching a "normal peacetime form of government" after war's end.[77] Burmese would have to "trust implicitly" in Japan to practice what it preached. This highlights a view that Japanese army authorities largely viewed the Pacific Charter as worth less than the paper on which it was written – and suggests that any grand strategy concocted in the metropole did not imply its implementation across the region.

In the end, this second moment of inchoate grand strategy is best thought of as a head-birth. Granted, in some ways it was realized. Japan provided nominal independence and a level of autonomy to some Asian nations, and produced a Pacific Charter that in some ways was more liberal than the propaganda of Japan's enemies. Nonetheless, the strategy was impeded by problems of total war it was meant to resolve. The activities of Japanese forces across the region ensured that there would be a disconnect between the dreams of elites in Tokyo and the realities on the ground. Without the ability to distinguish local interests from official policy, and military operations from political expediency, the inchoate grand strategy advanced by Shigemitsu and others was more dream than reality. Moreover, this strategy would have further weakened the Japanese Empire had it survived the war. The advancement of independence, the pacts of alliance, and the Pacific Charter all gave subordinate countries a rhetorical means to protest the realities of their nominal independence, and gave other territories a means to demand independence and autonomy from Japan. This highlights a critical irony behind this new grand strategy. Although pursued in the service of empire, it would have ultimately hastened Japan's imperial demise.

Conclusions

Grand strategy was not totally foreign to the period of Japan's revolt against the old order. Granted, scholars are correct to note that the Manchurian Incident initially heralded the death of grand strategy. The first few years after the Manchurian Incident witnessed shifting, confused efforts to secure Japanese interests in North China. This owed in part to the inadequacies of the system of decision-making, particularly in the wake of the passing of Japan's elder statesmen. The dogged insistence on the independence of supreme command from political oversight led to spotty coordination between state and military elites. Things began to change, however, with the outbreak of the

---

77 BL, Burma Office Records, IOR: M/5/88, Asia, Pacific and Africa Collections.

total war in China in 1937 and the establishment of liaison conferences/meetings – Japan's *de facto* war cabinet. This made grand strategy possible once more. In the end, wartime Japan saw two moments of inchoate grand strategy to construct or to preserve the Greater East Asia Co-Prosperity Sphere.

Nonetheless, both inchoate grand strategies were never fully implemented, and were most striking for their weaknesses or absences. Matsuoka's was the grand strategy of a stargazer. He had a global vision that emerged during a time of Japanese strength. But enacting that vision required a string of improbable foreign policy successes that brooked no failure. Matsuoka even thought he could come to an accord with Washington through little more than swagger and bravado. His vision was thus as impractical as it was naïve. Conversely, Shigemitsu Mamoru's grand strategy epitomized Japanese weakness. He advanced a strategy of promoting independence, sovereignty, and cooperative regionalism to help Japan win through diplomacy instead of losing in battle. His ultimate goal was for Japan to survive the Pacific War with empire intact and regional leadership confirmed. But the disconnect between the vision in the metropole and the realities of a brutal war waged throughout the region ensured that Japan would remain unable to win the hearts and minds of peoples across Asia. Grand strategy would never be more than inchoate in nature, and never more than opportunistic efforts to realise leadership in the era after war's end.

What lessons do Japan's tumultuous decade and a half hold for grand strategy? If anything, the Japanese experience attests to the difficulties of forming cohesive and long-term strategies during times of war. Grand strategies require flexibility and coordination in the service of national goals. Although liaison conferences made policy coordination possible, Japan's ruling elite still lacked the flexibility to adapt to the emerging situation and the ability to coordinate policy measures with the state of affairs across the empire. In the process, grand strategy became episodic, undisciplined, and inefficient – never more than inchoate and opportunistic in nature. It was not until Japan re-emerged from its fiery defeat in World War II that a consistent, implementable grand strategy in Japan would be possible once more.

Andrea Benvenuti
Frustrating the Americans and Befriending the Communists: Nehru's Policy in the Early Asian Cold War, 1947–1954

On 25 June 1954, a chartered Air India Constellation aircraft carrying Chinese Premier Zhou Enlai landed at Delhi's Palam airport. To greet him on arrival was Prime Minister Jawaharlal Nehru, his ministers, and some members of the ruling Congress Party.[1] Over the next three days, the two leaders spent several hours together.[2] Though they had never met before, they struck a good personal rapport and shared similar views on a broad range of issues – from peaceful coexistence to American containment in Asia.[3] Zhou told Nehru that China embraced the Five Principles of peaceful coexistence and supported India's desire to "create a large area of peace" in Asia. Such an area of peace, Zhou claimed, "would be very beneficial" to both countries for it would "prevent US attempts to organise military blocs in this area." Nehru argued that India, too, was "totally opposed" to American plans to create a Southeast Asian collective defence system. He excoriated the United States for its exaggerated fear of communism. He also heaped scorn on American attempts "to build hundreds of bases around Russia and China." These attempts, Nehru argued, would only serve to create "an impression in the minds of Soviet Russia and China that they will be attacked." Unlike the Americans, he was unconcerned about "the attitude of great states like Soviet Russia and China" since communist revolutions, he maintained, could not be "exported." If anything, it was the activities of regional communist parties that troubled him. Such activities, he said, generated anxiety and stood in the way of good relations with communist countries. In response, Zhou volunteered, somewhat disingenuously, that "we must make efforts to remove such entirely groundless, baseless fear which exists in Asia."[4]

---

[1] NAUK, FO 371, 1122010, L10310/8, G.H. Middleton to Commonwealth Relations Office [CRO], despatch 56, 1 July 1954. See also NAA, A4231, 1954/New Delhi, Walter Crocker to Richard Casey, despatch 12, 30 June 1954.
[2] NAUK, FO 371, 1122010, L10310/8, Middleton to CRO, despatch 56, 1 July 1954.
[3] For the record of the Zhou-Nehru talks, S. Gopal, ed, *Selected Works of Jawaharlal Nehru* [SWJN], Second Series, Vol 26 (New Delhi: Nehru Memorial Fund, 1984–2015), 366–96 and 398–406.
[4] Ibid. See also Andrea Benvenuti, "Constructing Peaceful Coexistence: Nehru's Approach to Regional Security and India's Rapprochement with Communist China in the mid-1950s," *Diplomacy & Statecraft*, 31:1 (2020), 91–117.

https://doi.org/10.1515/9783110718713-012

Nehru liked what he heard. He hailed the talks as "a historic change in the relationship of forces in Asia" and a step forward towards peaceful coexistence.[5] He told British Foreign Secretary Anthony Eden that the visit had helped clear the air and improve mutual understanding.[6] In October 1954, Nehru reciprocated Zhou's visit by travelling to China. Nehru's trip was to herald the beginning of the remarkable, if short-lived, *Hindi Chini Bhai Bhai* (Indians and Chinese are brothers) moment in Sino-Indian relations.[7] In Beijing, Mao Zedong and Zhou Enlai went out of their way to reassure their Indian guest of China's peaceful intentions. It was, they argued, Washington's "aggressive" and "expansionist" behaviour – not China's policies – that "came in the way of peace."[8] Nehru was not as harsh as his hosts on the United States. However, he concurred with Zhou that if Washington opposed peaceful coexistence and wanted war, India and China should "isolate America diplomatically." A way, he emphasised, must be found "to create a situation in which America will feel isolated."[9] And, indeed, a way would be found in the weeks following Nehru's visit to China. Thanks to his support, China was invited to the April 1955 Afro-Asian Conference in Bandung. In Nehru's mind, such an initiative was intended to promote peaceful coexistence, entrench opposition to Cold War alliances and isolate the United States regionally.

The Americans followed Indian moves with some trepidation, for Nehru's policy promised to undercut their efforts to contain China. However, had they been privy to these discussions, the tenor of Nehru's remarks would have instilled even greater uneasiness in them. Over the years, Nehru had spared no criticism of American policy in Asia. Yet, his characterisation of the United States as the primary threat to regional stability would have gone beyond what they had come to expect from him. In the event, the Eisenhower administration did not have to wait long to get the first inklings of what Nehru had in mind. Nehru's championing of the Bandung conference was followed by another diplomatic coup. In June 1955, India's hitherto languishing ties with the Soviet Union received an unexpected boost following Nehru's visit to that country. A

---

[5] "Significance of Talks with Chou En-lai: Nehru's letter to C.C. Presidents," *Hindustan Times*, 8 July 1954.
[6] NAUK, FO371/1122010, L10310/4, Delhi to CRO, telegram 619, 28 June 1954.
[7] *Hindi Chini Bhai Bhai* stands for "Indians and Chinese are brothers" in Hindi.
[8] NAUK, PREM 11/916, Note on Visit to China and Indochina, 14 November 1954; Zhou Enlai and Nehru, first and second meeting, 19 and 20 October 1954, http://digitalarchive.wilsoncenter.org/document/121746 and http://digitalarchive.wilsoncenter.org/document/121747; Mao Zedong and Nehru, second meeting, 23 October 1954, http://digitalarchive.wilsoncenter.org/document/117815.
[9] Zhou Enlai and Nehru, first meeting, 19 October 1954, http://digitalarchive.wilsoncenter.org/document/121746.

few months later, in November 1955, Soviet leader Nikita Khrushchev returned the courtesy by undertaking a two-week tour of India. As to be expected, Khrushchev's trip generated anxiety in the United States.[10] Even though the administration ruled out the prospect of India moving into the communist orbit, the gulf dividing Washington and New Delhi appeared wider than ever.

Given that the United States and India were then, as now, the world's two largest democracies, how could their relations have drifted so far apart? More specifically, how could Nehru have come to view American containment as more threatening than Sino-Soviet communism? In answering these questions, this chapter aims to revisit Nehru's Cold War policy. While no Great Power, India was not an insignificant player in the Asia of the 1950s. True, actions by the United States, Soviet Union, and China, and their differing visions of regional order defined, above all, the regional Cold War. Yet Nehru's India carved an important niche for itself by giving a powerful voice to those nations of recent independence who either shunned or opposed Cold War alignments. The fact that New Delhi's regional influence declined dramatically following the disastrous 1962 border war with China should be no reason to neglect India's role in the early Cold War. And so, by relying on the available archival evidence and the most recent Cold War scholarship, this chapter aims to reassess a central aspect in Indian foreign policy – New Delhi's handling of its relations with the United States and the two communist powers – and to make an original contribution to the existing literature on India's foreign relations during the early Cold War – a still somewhat underexplored topic in contemporary international history.[11] In so doing, the chapter advances two key arguments. First, just like the United States, Soviet Union, and China, India, too, had its vision of regional order – or "grand design" – and a grand strategy to achieve it. Second, the extent to which Nehru's grand design and grand strategy differed from that of these Great Powers also shaped India's approach to them. In other words, Nehru's response to their Cold War strategies was directly proportional to how these strategies facilitated or hampered the pursuit of New Delhi's grand strategy. That Nehru, rightly or wrongly, came to see American containment as a more destabilising force than communism is no surprise. Paradoxical as this may have appeared to Western policymakers at the time, he considered American efforts to check

---

10 H.W. Brands, *The Spectre of Neutralism: The United States and the Emergence of the Third World* (New York: Oxford University Press, 1989), 119.
11 On India as a neglected Asian power in contemporary Cold War historiography see Arne Westad, "The Cold War: A World History," podcast available at http://www.lse.ac.uk/website-archive/newsAndMedia/videoAndAudio/channels/publicLecturesAndEvents/player.aspx?id=3961.

communist penetration in Asia not only aggressive but also inherently misguided given growing Sino-Soviet emphasis on peaceful coexistence in the mid-1950s. As he told US Secretary of State John Foster Dulles in 1956, American-led regional pacts "had done good to nobody . . . The only result was frightening the opposite party and encouraging it to create trouble."[12]

Both vision and strategy owed a lot to Nehru. From the grant of India's independence in 1947, Nehru emerged the uncontested maker of India's foreign policy until his death in 1964. Not only did he keep for himself the portfolio of external affairs throughout his long premiership, but he was also the Congress Party leader with the keenest interest in world affairs.[13] So dominant was his influence on foreign policy that, as one of his biographers put it, Indian diplomacy "could hardly have taken the course it did had Nehru not been at the helm in the early years of Indian independence."[14] His popularity among the Indian masses and Congress's electoral ascendancy in the early 1950s reinforced Nehru's remarkable influence on India's foreign policy.[15] "[T]he acid test of a policy," as Henry Kissinger once said, "is its ability to obtain domestic support. This has two aspects: the problem of legitimizing a policy *within* the government apparatus . . . and that of harmonizing it with the national experience."[16] Nehru enjoyed such support and, after Sardar Vallabhbhai Patel's death in December 1950, his influence on India's foreign policy grew stronger. Congress heavyweight and Interior Minister Patel had advocated a shift in India's external policies, arguing that India "must strengthen its military establishment if it is to effectively face its communist neighbour and that it cannot properly strengthen its military establishment without aid from West, particularly US."[17] Had his approach prevailed over Nehru's, Patel might have helped nudge India in a different direction. With his death, however, Nehru's line won the day.

---

12 NMML, Subimal Dutt Papers [SD], subject file 87, Note on Jawaharlal Nehru's conversation with Dulles on various international issues, 10 March 1956.
13 J.N. Dixit, *Makers of India's Foreign Policy: Raja Ram Mohun Roy to Yashwant Sinha* (New Delhi: HarperCollins India, 2004), 79–80.
14 B.R. Nanda, *Jawaharlal Nehru: Rebel and Statesman* (Oxford: University Press, 1999), 223.
15 Bipan Chandra, Mridula Mukherjee and Aditya Mukherjee, eds., *India Since Independence* (New Delhi: Penguin Books, 2008), 171.
16 Henry Kissinger, *Nuclear Weapons and Foreign Policy* (New York: Harper, 1957), 326.
17 *FRUS, 1950, The Near East, South Asia and Africa,* Vol. V, 1474–75.

Nehru's Grand Design

"At the stroke of the midnight hour, when the world sleeps, India will awake to life and freedom." With these evocative words delivered before an expectant Constituent Assembly on the eve of India's independence, Nehru welcomed the fulfilment of a life-long ambition. In his brief speech, the new Indian prime minister rejoiced at such a "bold advance." However, he also stressed the significant "responsibilities and burdens" – from nation-building to economic development – that awaited India's postcolonial leaders. Conscious that India could not overcome these challenges without external stability, Nehru pledged India's commitment to "furthering peace, freedom and democracy" in cooperation with other nations.[18] And so, in an attempt to insulate India from external threats and attend to its urgent domestic priorities, Nehru chose to pursue an activist foreign policy – one designed to shape India's external environment in accordance with what amounted to a veritable "grand design," the consolidation of a world of independent nations working together to promote peace, freedom and democracy. Nehru believed that its size, natural resources and geostrategic location accorded India an important role in world affairs. He defined such a role as that of a pacifier, mediator, and stabilizer. For Nehru, India's leadership was not to be based necessarily on economic or military power, but on its cultural and political influence in Asia.[19] In contrast to the more low-key regional approach pursued by his successors, Nehru's foreign policy was globalist in outlook. Furthermore, far from concentrating solely on the Indian Subcontinent, Nehru identified the whole of Asia as India's area of primary concern.[20] He had no narrow conception of India's role and interests in international affairs. In brief, he had an ambitious blueprint for a new regional (and global) order. However, as this chapter shows, such a blueprint was not necessarily in sync with the policies pursued by the region's major powers. The extent to which it accorded (or clashed) with alternative visions of regional order shaped India's attitude towards these powers.

The means through which he sought to achieve his vision of a safer and fairer regional (and global) order constituted Nehru's grand strategy. Although the study of grand strategy is an expanding field of scholarly enquiry, no single or univocal understanding of this concept exists. This chapter somewhat departs from Brian P. Farrell's definition of grand strategy in the Introduction to

---
[18] For Nehru's "tryst with destiny" speech see Jawaharlal Nehru, *India's Foreign Policy: Selected Speeches, September 1946-April 1961* (New Delhi: Government of India, 1961), 13–15.
[19] Dixit, *Makers of India's Foreign Policy*, 83–84.
[20] Zorawar Daulet Singh, *Power and Diplomacy: India's Foreign Policies During the Cold War* [Kindle book]: http://www.amazon.com.au.

this book and relies, instead, on a definition recently put forward by American historian Hal Brands. As Nehru was determined to avoid, as much as possible, the use of military force to pursue India's national interests, Brands's definition helps to better capture the nature of the Nehruvian grand strategy. According to Brands, grand strategy can be best described as a "conceptual framework that helps nations determine where they want to go and how they ought to get there; it is the theory, or logic, that guides leaders seeking security in a complex and insecure world." It is, in other words, "the intellectual architecture that gives form and structure to foreign policy." It can also be characterised as "a purposeful and coherent set of ideas about what a nation seeks to accomplish in the world, and how it should go about doing so."[21] In Nehru's case, such a grand strategy consisted of four interrelated elements.[22]

The first and arguably most important was non-alignment – the veritable organising principle that guided Indian policy during the Cold War. Often confused for neutrality or neutralism, the practice of non-alignment neither involved sitting on the fence nor avoiding taking sides in international disputes.[23] It rather meant that India was "unaligned" and "uncommitted to blocs."[24] By practising non-alignment, Nehru set out to achieve key national goals such as enhancing India's autonomy and national security, raising its prestige internationally, and advancing its economic interests. "While remaining quite apart from power blocs," Nehru once said, "we are in a far better position to cast our weight at the right moment in favour of peace, and meanwhile our relations can become as close as possible in the economic or other domain with such countries with whom we can easily develop them."[25] In any case, as he remarked on another occasion: "Even in accepting economic help or in getting

---

21 Hal Brands, *What Good Is Grand Strategy? Power and Purpose in American Statecraft from Harry S. Truman to George W. Bush* (New York: Cornell University Press, 2014), 3. For a brief examination of the concept of grand strategy see Rebecca Friedman Lissner, "What Is Grand Strategy? Sweeping a Conceptual Minefield," *Texas National Security Review* 2:1(2018), 53–73.
22 This section builds on S. Kalyanaraman, "Nehru's Advocacy of Internationalism and Indian Foreign Policy," in *India's Grand Strategy: History, Theory, Cases*, Kanti Bajpai et al, eds. (New Delhi: Routledge, 2014), 151–75, especially 168–72. For a brief examination of Nehru's grand strategy see also C. Christine Fair, "India," in *Comparative Grand Strategy: A Framework and Cases*, Thierry Balzacq et al, eds. (Oxford: University Press, 2019), 171–91.
23 For the concept of neutralism see Robert A. Scalapino, "Neutralism in Asia," *American Political Science Review*, 48:1(1954), 49.
24 Nehru cited in A. Appadorai and M.S. Rajan, *India's Foreign Policy and Relations* (New Delhi: South Asian Publishers, 1985), 86.
25 A. Appadorai, *Select Documents on India's Foreign Policy and Relations, 1947–1972, Volume I* (New Delhi: Oxford University Press, 1982), 14.

political help, it is not a wise policy to put all our eggs in one basket."[26] Moreover, India's refusal to join military alliances would "go farther in gaining security than almost anything else."[27] In this context, Nehru not only regarded non-alignment as "the best contribution that a weak, but supposedly powerful, India could make towards maintaining the balance of power between the Soviet and Western blocs." He also saw it as a necessary step to avoid giving the two communist land powers a pretext "to invade India alone or as part of a general attack against the non-communist world."[28] Lastly, he also viewed non-alignment as a means of taking the wind out of the sails of India's homegrown communists thanks to his government's accommodating attitude towards the Soviet Union and China.

Intimately linked to non-alignment was the second element of Nehru's grand strategy – his rejection of power politics, spheres of influence, and military power as the foundations of international life.[29] In 1954, he began to popularize the Five Principles of peaceful coexistence as the basis of a new approach to international relations.[30] The Five Principles were mutual respect for territorial integrity and sovereignty, non-aggression, non-interference in other nations' internal affairs, equality and mutual benefit, and peaceful coexistence. Although the Chinese communists had come up with them originally, Nehru made them his own, arguing that if Asian nations put these principles into practice, they could help create an "area of peace" – that is, a neutralized buffer between the two blocs – and make a contribution to "collective peace" in Asia.[31] As he warned the Afro-Asian leaders gathered in Bandung in April 1955, any step that reduced the "non-aligned area" was "dangerous" and likely to "lead to war."[32] It was also likely,

---

26 Nehru, *India's Foreign Policy*, 35.
27 Appadorai, *Documents on India's Foreign Policy*, 16.
28 Lorne J. Kavic, *India's Quest for Security: Defence Policies, 1947–1965* (Berkeley and Los Angeles: University of California Press: 1969), 40 and 208.
29 Appadorai and Rajan, *India's Foreign Policy*, 44–46, 51.
30 Benvenuti, "Constructing Peaceful Coexistence." See also NAA, A1838, 169/11/87 part 4, Commonwealth Prime Ministers' Conference 1955. Vol. II – Agenda Papers, Part A: Relations between India and China, undated.
31 The five principles of peaceful coexistence were a Chinese idea. See Zhou Enlai, *Selected Works of Zhou Enlai, Vol II* (Beijing: Foreign Languages Press, 1988) 128; Sarvepalli Gopal, *Jawaharlal Nehru: A Biography. Vol Two 1947–1956* [Kindle book]: http://www.amazon.com. For the five principles applied to Asia see Anton Harder, "Defining Independence in Cold War Asia: Sino-Indian Relations, 1949–1962" (unpublished PhD thesis, LSE, 2015), 131; see also Sulmaan Wasif Khan, "Cold War Cooperation: New Chinese Evidence on Jawaharlal Nehru's 1954 Visit to Beijing," *Cold War History*, 11:2(2011), 211–12.
32 Nehru cited in Charles Heimsath and Surjit Mansingh, *A Diplomatic History of Modern India* (Bombay: Allied Publishers, 1971), 64.

Nehru feared, to promote great power interference in the domestic affairs of the recently decolonised states.[33]

The third pillar of his grand strategy was the United Nations (UN). A strong supporter of the UN, Nehru believed it should provide the much-needed basis of a "world structure," which he called "One World." He was also of the opinion that the principles of its Charter should govern relations between states.[34] During the Nehru years, India was steadfast in its support of the UN as a "mechanism of peace" and "an instrument of negotiation and compromise."[35] India, in particular, played an active role in key UN proceedings and debates, such as the settlement of disputes involving the Great Powers, arms control and disarmament, anti-colonialism, human rights, and economic aid.[36]

The fourth component of Nehru's grand strategy was India's staunch and often vocal opposition to colonialism, imperialism, and racism, which he saw as harmful forces likely to generate instability and conflict. As he told his fellow countrymen soon after assuming the leadership of the Indian interim government in September 1946: "We believe that peace and freedom are indivisible and the denial of freedom anywhere must endanger freedom elsewhere and lead to conflict and war. We are particularly interested in the emancipation of colonial and dependent countries and peoples, and in the recognition in theory and practice of equal opportunities for all races."[37] Both within and without the UN, Nehru's India often acted as a catalyst against the preservation of European colonial rule in the Afro-Asian world.[38] Nehru's decision to convene an Asian Conference in New Delhi in 1949 to support the Dutch East Indies' emancipation from Dutch rule was a typical example of India's anti-colonial advocacy outside the UN.[39] Related to his opposition to colonialism, imperialism, and racism, was also Nehru's promotion of Afro-Asian solidarity. In his inaugural address to the March 1947 Asian Relations Conference in New Delhi, Nehru argued that Asians had for too long been "petitioners in Western courts and chancelleries." They should no longer be "the plaything of others," but "function effectively in the maintenance of peace."[40]

---

33 Amitav Acharya, *Whose Ideas Matter? Agency and Power in Asian Regionalism* (New York: Cornell University Press, 2009), 47.
34 Appadorai, *Documents on India's Foreign Policy*, 5; Nehru, *India's Foreign Policy*, 167.
35 Heimsath and Mansingh, *Diplomatic History*, 86 and 91.
36 Ibid, 85–115.
37 Appadorai and Rajan, *India's Foreign Policy*, 34. See also Nehru's speech to the Indian Council of World Affairs on 22 March 1949 in Nehru, *India's Foreign Policy*, 48.
38 On India's role in the UN see Mark Mazower, *Governing the World: The History of an Idea* [Kindle book]: http://www.amazon.com.au.
39 Appadorai and Rajan, *India's Foreign Policy*, 36.
40 Nehru, *India's Foreign Policy*, 86.

A few months later, in December 1947, he told the Constituent Assembly that "a new spirit in Asia was drawing Asiatic countries closer together in self-defence and promoting world peace."[41] By this, Nehru also meant that Asia's future should lay in the hands of Asians and that India did not look favourably on a continuing Western politico-military regional presence.[42]

From the preceding three paragraphs, Nehru's grand strategy clearly responded to an important domestic imperative – that of ensuring that, insulated from Cold War tensions, India could channel its resources towards fostering economic development and national cohesion, without which no grand design would be attainable in the long term.[43] These demanding tasks, coupled with India's financial limitations, required the Indian government to keep military spending low.[44] As a result, it was no accident that, following independence, India was severely constrained in what it could do to boost its poorly equipped, if large, armed forces. Due to fiscal stringency, the army's "effectiveness" was to "be subordinated to size" and its role essentially confined to maintaining internal security, guarding the frontiers, and defending the country against a minor power such as Pakistan. In time, India would develop not only a small navy capable of handling "any neighbouring country in the strategic arc from Suez to Singapore," but also a balanced air force able to deal with any neighbour except Red China.[45] In a nutshell, however, it was soft power, not hard power, that Nehru's grand strategy would rely upon.

Implementing the Vision

For all Nehru's best efforts, his grand strategy did not go uncontested. The spreading of Cold War tensions to Asia made it increasingly difficult for him to achieve it. Although a bamboo curtain did not descend across Asia until the outbreak of the Korean War in June 1950, Nehru already had a foretaste of what rapidly escalating bipolar tensions might hold for India. Both before and during

---

41 NAA, A1068, M47/9/1/2, Delhi to Department of External Affairs [DEA], cablegram 659, 5 December 1947.
42 On this point see, for instance, Anita Inder Singh, "Britain, India and the Asian Cold War, 1949–1954," in Anne Deighton, ed., *Britain and the First Cold War* (London: Macmillan, 1990), 229.
43 See, for instance, Sisir Gupta, *India and Regional Integration in Asia* (Bombay: Asian Publishing House, 1964), 10.
44 Kavic, *India's Quest*, 39.
45 Ibid, 211.

his visit to the United States in October-November 1949, he became the focus of growing American expectations as the symbol of a post-colonial Asia friendly to the West.[46] Despite its frustration with Nehru's non-alignment and his failure to draw any appreciable distinction between a democratic America and a totalitarian Soviet Union, the Truman administration was not blind to the positive role India could play in the Third World if only it displayed a more pro-Western attitude.[47] In talks with their Indian guest, American policymakers curiously refrained from canvassing any specific Indian contribution to the West's anti-communist effort, preferring, instead, to confine themselves to a broad examination of the international situation.[48] At the same time, however, they detected no desire, on Nehru's part, to take sides in the emerging Cold War. Nor did they sense any hardening of Nehru's attitude towards communism.[49] On the contrary, they gloomily concluded that "India was making no contribution to [the solution of] world problems, was unlikely to do so as long as the present policy persisted and that Nehru displayed little sense of the practical realms."[50]

Relations with the Soviet Union appeared to be even less promising. For all his desire to establish friendly ties, Nehru got very little out of Moscow.[51] In the late 1940s, the Kremlin's attitude towards India oscillated between coolness and hostility. Independent India's first ambassador to the Soviet Union (1947–1949), Vijayalakshmi Pandit, was treated, in the words of one of Nehru's advisers, "with polite indifference by the Soviet Foreign Office."[52] Pandit, who incidentally was Nehru's sister, complained to her brother of being left out in the cold, unable to make contact with the Soviet leadership and "exasperated" with Soviet bureaucracy.[53] Moscow's attitude, however, should not have come as a surprise. The Kremlin harboured a deep distrust of non-communist nationalist leaders such as

---

46 Robert J. McMahon, *The Cold War on the Periphery: The United States, India and Pakistan* (New York: Columbia University Press, 1994), 43–45, 50–52, 54–55; Srinath Raghavan, *Fierce Enigmas: A History of the United States in South Asia* [Kindle book]: http://www.amazon.com.au; Tanvi Madan, *Fateful Triangle: How China Shaped US-India Relations During the Cold War* [Kindle book]: http://www.amazon.com.au.
47 NAA, A3094, 2/3, Visit of Pandit Nehru to the United States, 22 November 1949; McMahon, *Cold War*, 40–44, 50–51; Madan, *Fateful Triangle*.
48 NAA, A3094, 2/3, Visit of Pandit Nehru to the United States, 22 November 1949.
49 McMahon, *Cold War*, 55–56.
50 US Ambassador in New Delhi Loy Henderson quoted in ibid, 58.
51 On Nehru's desire for friendly relations see *SWJN*, 1, 449.
52 Subimal Dutt, *With Nehru in the Foreign Office* (Calcutta: Minerva Associates Publications, 1977), 192.
53 Rakesh Ankit, "India-USSR, 1946–1949: A False Start?," in Madhavan K. Palat, ed, *India and the World in the First Half of the Twentieth Century* (New York: Routledge, 2018), 167–72.

Nehru. Guided by Andrei Zhdanov's 1947 "two-camp" doctrine, it viewed them as reactionaries and stooges of the West.[54] India's decision to remain in the British Commonwealth certainly did not help.[55] It reinforced Stalin's preconceived notion that the Indian government "was merely a tool of the 'Anglo-American imperialists'."[56] As Pandit alerted Nehru, the Soviet leadership was "not convinced of [India's] impartiality."[57]

A further obstacle to better relations was the attitude of the Communist Party of India (CPI). Following the enunciation of the Zhdanov line, the CPI denounced Nehru as a lackey of imperialism and resorted to armed struggle in an attempt to overthrow the Indian state. In 1948, it supported an armed peasant revolt in Telangana against the Nizam of Hyderabad. The following year, it launched a national railway strike with the deliberate intention of stirring up a nationwide uprising.[58] According to British sources, until 1951 the CPI "had little direct contact with Moscow."[59] Stalin, apparently, "saw little benefit to be gained from the fractious Indian Communist Party, which was prone to both leftist and rightist deviations."[60] In any case, as Charles Heimsath and Surjit Mansingh have observed, "the question of precisely the kind of influence that Moscow exerted over Indian communism was less important than the current Indian belief that the CPI was controlled by the Communist Party of the Soviet Union."[61]

---

54 Ted Hopf, *Reconstructing the Cold War: The Early Years, 1945–1958* (New York: Oxford University Press, 2012), 131; Vladimir Pechatnov, "Reflections on Soviet Foreign Policy, 1953–1964," in *Peaceful Coexistence? Soviet Union and Sweden in the Khrushchev Era*, Helene Carlbäck et al, eds., (Moscow: Centre for Baltic and East European Studies Södertörn University, 2010), 27.
55 For India's decision to remain in the Commonwealth see Michael Brecher, "India's Decision to Remain in the Commonwealth," *Journal of Commonwealth and Comparative Politics*, 12:1 (1974), 62–90.
56 Heimsath and Mansingh, *Diplomatic History*, 400; NAUK, FO 371/116667, NS10385/3, Indo-Soviet Relations, 1947–1957, 15 April 1955.
57 Pandit cited in Ankit, "India-USSR," 168.
58 Chandra et al, *India Since Independence*, 258.
59 NAUK, FO 371/116667, NS10385/3, Indo-Soviet Relations, 1947–1957, 15 April 1955.
60 K.P.S. Menon cited in Michele Louro, *Comrades Against Imperialism: Nehru, India and Interwar Internationalism. Global and International History* (Cambridge: University Press, 2018), 279.
61 Heimsath and Mansingh, *Diplomatic History*, 402. According to Christopher Andrew and Vasili Mitrokhin, in the early years of independence the Indian Intelligence Branch regularly intercepted correspondence directed from the Kremlin to the CPI. See Christopher Andrew and Vasili Mitrokhin, *The Mitrokhin Archive II: The KGB in the World* [Kindle book]: http://www.amazon.com.

With the outbreak of the Korean conflict, the Cold War extended to Asia. Washington's response to North Korea's attack on the South was robust. Suspecting that Moscow and Beijing were behind Kim Il Sung's assault, the Truman administration abandoned its earlier reluctance to get involved in Asia and moved to meet the communist challenge forcefully. Along with its decision to intervene in Korea, it took several important steps to contain regional communism, including an extensive programme of national rearmament, the development of a network of regional alliances, and the provision of military assistance to noncommunist Asian states.[62] While effective in deterring the Soviet Union and China from making major inroads in Asia, Washington's containment was likely to provide only a temporary inhibiting effect on communist hopes of expanding regional influence. By the early 1950s, with the Kremlin recognising China's leadership of the Asian revolutionary movement, Mao Zedong's radical credentials received a significant boost.[63] He viewed the encouragement of anti-imperialist regional revolutions and the sponsorship of local communist parties as "an ideological and political imperative."[64] In his view, only the radical transformation of world politics and the formation of friendly communist regimes on its periphery would allow China to consolidate its domestic revolution and enhance its external security.[65] Mao's support for North Korea's attack on the South, his decision to intervene militarily in the Korean conflict, and his willingness to offer economic and military assistance to the Vietminh in Indochina must be seen in this context.[66] At the same time, however, his desire to place China at the forefront of the Asian revolution, enhance its standing within the communist bloc, and bolster its regional strategic position was bound to put him on a collision course with the United States by heightening American concerns about China's militant regional role.

---

[62] Andrea Benvenuti, "US Diplomacy in Asia," in Andrew T.H. Tan, ed., *Handbook on the United States in Asia: Managing Hegemonic Decline, Retaining Influence in the Trump Era* (Cheltenham: Edward Elgar Publishing, 2018), 163–64.
[63] Zhihua Shen and Yafeng Xia, "Leadership Transfer in the Asian Revolution: Mao Zedong and the Asian Cominform," *Cold War History*, 14:2(2014), 212–213.
[64] Andrea Benvenuti, "US Relations with the PRC during the Cold War," in Andrew T.H. Tan, ed., *Handbook of US-China Relations* (Cheltenham: Edward Elgar Publishing, 2017), 48; Qiang Zhai, *China and the Vietnam Wars, 1950–1975* (Chapel Hill: University of North Carolina Press, 2000), 4; Jian Chen, *Mao's China and the Cold War* (Chapel Hill: University of North Carolina Press, 2001), 7.
[65] Benvenuti, "US Relations with the PRC," 48; Zhai, *China and the Vietnam Wars*, 4.
[66] Benvenuti, "US Relations with the PRC," 48; Fredrik Logevall, "The Indochina Wars and the Cold War, 1945–1975," in *The Cambridge History of the Cold War*. Vol. 2, Melvyn Leffler and Odd Arne Westad, eds., (Cambridge: University Press, 2010), 120.

Nehru reacted to deepening regional tensions with disquiet. His primary concern was that they would force Asian nations to take sides, thus increasing the risk of war. But he also worried that these tensions might have other unwelcome consequences, including the protraction of European colonial rule in Asia. Growing American support for the French military effort in Indochina alerted Nehru to the prospect of Cold War *realpolitik* providing a new lease of life to colonialism. Moreover, he could see how American aid to non-communist Asian states might give rise to Western neo-colonial domination of Asia by turning them into *de facto* American colonies.[67] As Nehru told Third World leaders gathered in Bandung in April 1955, he found it "intolerable" that Afro-Asian countries "should come out of bondage into freedom only to degrade themselves" by joining military pacts.[68] In brief, Cold War bipolarity was a threat to both his vision and grand strategy. Nehru's response was to try, if not to defuse, at least to reduce bipolar tensions. His policy of non-alignment appeared to be neatly tailored to this task, for non-aligned status conferred India the necessary credibility to mediate between the emerging blocs. Yet, as Nehru soon found out, his efforts to act as an intermediary between the Americans and the Chinese during the Korean War exposed him to criticism from both quarters and only partially allowed him to defuse tensions. The Americans, Russians, and Chinese all regarded non-alignment with a degree of suspicion.[69]

In this increasingly tense regional setting, three factors shaped India's attitude towards the United States, Soviet Union, and China: first, the role played by these powers in the emerging Cold War; second, the way in which they related to India and were prepared to heed its political and strategic concerns; and, third, the manner in which Nehru rationalized their roles in Asia. Paradoxically, far from perceiving Sino-Soviet communism as the key challenge to regional stability – and, hence, to his regional vision – he came to see Western policy in Asia as being increasingly at odds with India's grand strategy. Rightly or wrongly, he judged it more likely to create tensions – so much so that he appeared keener to restrain the exercise of American power than to contain regional communism.

---

67 That is, for instance, how Nehru viewed American plans to provide military aid to Pakistan. See A. Martin Wainwright, *Inheritance of Empire: Britain, India and the Balance of Power in Asia, 1938–55* (Westport CT: Praeger, 1994), 156–57.
68 Nehru cited in Acharya, *Whose Ideas*, 58.
69 Robert Barnes, "Between the Blocs: India, the United Nations and Ending the Korean War," *Journal of Korean Studies*, 18:2(2013), 263–86; Heimsath and Mansingh, *Diplomatic History*, 70–73; Madan, *Fateful Triangle*.

Before the Korean War, Washington showed limited interest in India, treating it as a marginal concern.[70] However, as American policymakers awoke to the perils of growing communist influence in Asia, India's strategic importance grew in their minds. Of particular concern was the possibility that intense anti-colonial feeling and widespread economic discontent in South and East Asia might provide fertile ground for communist expansion. As a result, they recognised the need to "exploit every opportunity to increase the 'present Western orientation' of South Asian countries by helping them to meet the minimum aspirations of their people and to maintain internal security."[71] Yet, for all its fresh emphasis on India being potentially a major "centre of non-communist strength in Asia,"[72] the Truman administration still envisaged no more than a limited American role in the Subcontinent. It still expected Britain – on the strength of its historical ties with South Asia – to carry the burden for the West there.[73] But as the Cold War descended on Asia, the Americans began to consider adopting a more proactive stance towards India, seeking to enlist its support and sympathy.[74] Not surprisingly, American policymakers felt that India, too, ought to be concerned about the expansionist nature of communism. Accordingly, they exerted increasing pressure on India to take a more sympathetic attitude towards the West.

To Washington's frustration, Nehru did not share its threat perceptions – or at least not to the same degree. The fact that India was a liberal democracy and Nehru was genuinely committed to the democratic method did not necessarily predispose him to follow Washington's lead. Contrary to the American view that both the Soviet and Chinese brands of communism were a serious threat to regional security, Nehru believed that neither of them posed an imminent danger to India. In 1952, he told the head of India's Intelligence Bureau, B.N. Mullik, that India did not share a common border with the Soviet Union and, in any case, he did not think Moscow "had any designs on India" despite the Soviet press's unfriendly attitude towards the Indian government. Unlike China, which Nehru regarded as a potentially aggressive and expansionist power, the Soviet Union "was not at all anxious to extend her territories any further." The government, Nehru

---

70 See McMahon, *Cold War*, 49; Andrew J. Rotter, *Comrades at Odds: The United States and India, 1947–1964* (Ithaca, NY: Cornell University Press, 2000), 54.
71 *FRUS, 1949, The Far East and Australasia, 1949*, Vol. 7, Part 2, doc. 387.
72 Ibid., doc. 386.
73 Paul McGarr, *The Cold War in South Asia: Britain, the United States and the Indian Subcontinent, 1945–1965* (Cambridge: University Press, 2013), 40–41; Anita Inder Singh, "Post-imperial British Attitudes to India," *Round Table*, 74:296 (1985), 369.
74 McGarr, *Cold War in South Asia*, 42–43.

told Mullik, should continue to keep an eye on "the developments in international communism" since they "had a direct bearing on the Indian Communist Party." But the fact remained that the Soviet Union did "not pose a danger of the type that China did." In fact, Nehru did not rule out the possibility that the Soviet Union and India might even be "allies one day against a common enemy."[75] In June 1954, Nehru further argued that

> the Soviet Power, however great it might be, cannot think in terms of coming down to India partly because of the tremendous difficulties due to the mountain ranges, etc, and partly because, in case of war, the real arenas of conflict will be elsewhere. Neither the Soviet group nor the Western group can afford to fritter their strength in India when they have to fight a life and death struggle elsewhere.[76]

In March 1951, Nehru told visiting US Assistant Secretary of State George McGhee that he "agreed Russia had aggressive and expansionist designs," but then he had blamed the West for it, arguing that "Russia is what she is today largely because of the way nations isolated her when young. Same mistake [is] being made today with China."[77] A few weeks earlier, he told US Ambassador Loy Henderson that "he was not convinced of inherent aggressiveness [of] international communism" and that it was India's policy to "endeavour [to] restore confidence and convince each side other had no aggressive intentions."[78]

Clearly, Nehru's approach to the Soviet Union was complex and somewhat ambiguous. Although he was no communist, he was not unsympathetic to the Soviet Union. As Michele Louro has recently shown, his worldview was "a blending of nationalism with socialism" and one "in which anti-imperialists including the Soviet Union and the colonies had collectively sought to challenge imperialism."[79] Hence, after the Second World War, Nehru "could not imagine the country as an imperialist power." American attempts to cast the Soviet Union as an imperialist or neo-imperialist power cut no ice with him. In fact, this type of argument was "a complete anathema to his conception of imperialism and anti-imperialism, born out of his interwar worldview and despite his own turbulent experiences with the post–1929 communist-run LAI [League Against Imperialism]."[80] Not only had he seen the Soviet Union as playing a major role in the struggle against imperialism in the 1930s, but, in *Glimpses*, he

---

75 B.N. Mullik, *My Years with Nehru, 1948–1964* (Bombay: Allied Publishers, 1972), 78–79 and 81.
76 *SWJN*, 26, 309.
77 NARACP, RG59, Central Decimal Files, box 2858, 611.91/3–1051, Henderson to Secretary of State, telegram 2374, 10 March 1951.
78 Ibid.
79 Louro, *Comrades Against Imperialism*, 279.
80 Ibid, 273 and 278.

also portrayed the Soviet Union and international communism as a symbol of hope for the anti-imperialist cause in the postwar world.[81]

In relation to China, too, Nehru exhibited a much less confrontational attitude than that displayed by American policymakers. Whereas the United States refused to recognise the People's Republic of China, India was one of the first non-communist nations to do so in December 1949. For all of India's accommodating attitude, New Delhi's relations with Beijing lacked warmth in the early 1950s.[82] Like its Soviet comrades, the Chinese communists treated India warily, believing it to be a stooge of the West.[83] Nehru, in turn, reacted with anxiety at the arrival of Chinese troops on the Indian-Tibetan border in October 1950.[84] Yet, he refused to view the re-imposition of Chinese authority over Tibet as an imminent strategic threat to India.[85] He was fully aware that confrontation with China would impose a huge financial and military burden on India.[86] In 1953, Nehru told a gathering of Indian Heads of Mission in West Asia that "those 3,000 miles or so of border all along China did not frighten him in the least but it did make one think intensely all the time. It created new problems, new burdens, new financial burdens, new military burdens . . . "[87] Furthermore, he knew that in the light of Pakistan's hostility towards India, he could not rule out the possibility of Sino-Indian tensions escalating into a two-front war involving India's two neighbours.[88] Nehru was, therefore, prepared to cut China

---

[81] Ibid, 187.
[82] François Joyaux, *La Chine et le Règlement du Premier Conflict d'Indochine: Genève 1954* [Kindle book]: http://www.amazon.fr.
[83] Ibid; Jian Chen, "Bridging Revolution and Decolonisation: The 'Bandung Discourse' in China's Early Cold War Experience," *The Chinese Historical Review*, 15:2(2008), 207fn2; Qiang Zhai, "Road to Bandung: China's Evolving Approach to De-Colonization," in Tomohiko Umaya, ed., *Comparing Modern Empires: Imperial Rule and Decolonization in the Changing World Order* (Hokkaido: Slavic-Eurasian Research Centre, Hokkaido University, 2018), 187–88.
[84] *FRUS, 1950, East Asia and the Pacific*, Vol. VI, 551; Heimsath and Mansingh, *Diplomatic History*, 188.
[85] NAA, A1838, 3107/40/147 part 1A, Delhi to DEA, cablegram 311, 31 October 1950.
[86] "Prime Minister Nehru's Note on China and Tibet dated 18 November 1950," in Durga Das, ed., *Sardar Patel Correspondence [henceforth SPC]*, Vol. 10 (Ahmedabad: Navajivan Publishing, 1974), 344.
[87] Extract from the Speech of Prime Minister to Heads of Indian Mission in West Asia, 27 March 1953, in Avtar Singh Bhasin, ed., *India-China Relations 1947–2000: A Documentary Study. Vol II* (New Delhi: Geetika Publishers), 913.
[88] Judith Brown, *Nehru: A Political Life* (New Haven CT: Yale University Press, 2003), 268; *SWJN*, 15/II, 542–47; see also *SPC, Vol 10*, 344.

some slack in the hope that a friendly approach could induce Beijing to moderate its revolutionary zeal and loosen its ties with Moscow.[89]

In 1951, he told the Americans it was "quite possible" that China might "develop into [an] explosive dangerous force." However, "there was," he believed, "at least a good chance that [the] future development of China [could] be guided into different channels." Therefore, "the best interests of India, the US and free world lay in a policy of keeping China's door open." In his view, the "world had nothing [to] lose and much [to] gain in any effort to split [China] and Russia, or if that [was] impossible at least to modify China's willingness [to] swallow [the Soviet] line completely."[90] Yet, in the presence of others, Nehru's assessment of the Chinese challenge was far less sanguine. As he told Mullik, "all through history China had been an aggressive country," which had now "acquired an aggressive political philosophy" and "was being governed by very aggressive leaders." As soon as she secured some economic and political stability, China "would try to extend her influence and leadership, if not political suzerainty, over Asia."[91] For the time being, however, Nehru was prepared to rule out any hostile Chinese move against India. His rationale was essentially twofold. First, a Chinese military offensive would inevitably bring other powers into the conflict.[92] Second, the inhospitable Himalayas would make any large-scale attack all but impossible.[93]

Peaceful Coexistence and Its Impact on India's Approach to the United States, Soviet Union and China

Although Nehru never regarded non-alignment as synonymous with neutrality,[94] India had hitherto remained broadly equidistant from the two blocs. India was indeed often critical of the United States and the West. Yet, for all its criticisms, India's continuing membership of the British Commonwealth and its economic links with the two Anglo-Saxon powers ensured that it maintained a working, if at times touchy, relationship with the West. More important, Nehru had not moved any

---

[89] Harder, "Defining Independence," 97 and 106.
[90] *FRUS, 1951, Asia and the Pacific*, Vol. VI, Part 1, doc. 488.
[91] Mullik, *My Years with Nehru*, 78.
[92] *SWJN*, 15/II, 342–47.
[93] *SWJN*, 26, 315; NAUK, FO 371/112196, DL1022/2, India's North-East Frontier Policy, 2 June 1954; McGarr, *Cold War in South Asia*, 39.
[94] See for instance NAA, A4231, 1955/New Delhi, Crocker to Casey, despatch 1, 5 January 1955.

closer to the communist bloc. As seen earlier, his friendly attitude towards China produced no breakthrough. Nor had he abandoned his "cautious and even cool" attitude towards the Soviet Union.[95] He had no compelling reason to do so. When India's new ambassador to the Soviet Union was finally able to see Stalin in mid-January 1950, there was no real meeting of minds between the two. To Radhakrishnan's exhortations that the Soviet Union take the lead in calling off the Cold War, Stalin replied that this "did *not* depend on him alone". When Radhakrishnan told him that Nehru "would be glad to visit Moscow," Stalin remained silent. When the Indian ambassador conveyed the Indian desire to see relations with the Soviet Union strengthened and stressed that "India's policy of neutrality was real and positive," the Soviet leader "seemed to approve." Yet, during the half-hour conversation, Stalin "seemed anxious to know if she was more or less independent than, say, Canada" and "if India was entitled to have her own army without any restriction and also if there was a navy."[96] Radhakrishnan's efforts to persuade the Kremlin that "Nehru was sincere in his policy of non-alignment" appeared eventually to pay off.[97] In 1951 Stalin told visiting CPI leaders that he could "not consider the government of Nehru to be a puppet."[98]

According to Subimal Dutt, Nehru's Foreign Secretary (1955–1961) and Ambassador to the Soviet Union (1961–1962), the first notable change in the Kremlin's attitude towards India took place in January 1952. In that month, the Soviet representative at the UN, Jacob Malik, who had, until then, refrained from taking a stand on the controversial Kashmir issue in the Security Council, castigated both the United States and Britain for their alleged attempts to turn the former princely state into an Anglo-American colony and a military base.[99] Around that time, the Soviet press also started expressing approval of "India's policy of promoting peace in the world."[100] In brief, even though Stalin had, by the early 1950s, toned down his negative view of India, India's relations with the Soviet Union had not gained much momentum. Since December 1950, a number of cultural missions had begun to travel in both directions, but that was as far as the two countries were prepared to go.[101] As K.P.S. Menon, one of

---

95 Heimsath and Mansingh, *Diplomatic History*, 400.
96 Record of the Conversation between I.V. Stalin and Sarvepalli Radhakrishnan, 15 January 1950, http://digitalarchive.wilsoncenter.org/document/119261.
97 Anthony R.H. Copley, "Radhakrishnan, Sir Sarvepalli (1888–1975)," *Oxford Dictionary of National Biography*, 6 January 2011, 2016, available at https://doi.org/10.1093/ref:odnb/31577.
98 Record of a conversation between Stalin and representatives of the Indian Communist Party, 9 February 1951, https://digitalarchive.wilsoncenter.org/document/113938.
99 Dutt, *With Nehru*, 193.
100 Ibid.
101 NAUK, FO 371/116667, NS10385/3, Indo-Soviet Relations, 1947–1957, 15 April 1955.

Nehru's closest advisers, pointed out years later, "all one could do was, to put it bluntly, to wait in patience for Stalin to pass."[102]

Stalin eventually died in March 1953. His death led to a significant reappraisal in Soviet foreign policy. Stalin's successors gradually discarded his "two-camps theory" and adopted a less confrontational approach to foreign affairs. By 1956, the Soviet Union under Nikita Khrushchev had made a full switch to "peaceful coexistence" as the guiding principle of Soviet foreign policy.[103] Needless to say, accommodation with the capitalist West did not amount, in Khrushchev's mind, to any fundamental change in Moscow's overall strategy. The Soviet Union was not yet ready to abandon its revolutionary mission and bury its rivalry with the West.[104] For the new Soviet leader, accommodation meant, more simply, that in future, bipolar competition would be essentially confined to the political, economic, and technological realms. And nowhere was this tactical change destined to manifest itself more clearly than in the Afro-Asian world, where Khrushchev was impatient to seize the political initiative and forge close links with local national-bourgeois movements.[105] As to be expected, given its acceptance of Moscow's ideological leadership, China, too, embraced peaceful coexistence.[106] Bloc loyalty was not Beijing's only reason for doing so. Mao was also aware that China's participation in the Korean conflict had not only been a huge drain on its resources, but also aroused the ire of Washington and worried its neighbours.[107] And so, he sought to shed China's aggressive image and replace its revolutionary radicalism, which had done so much to isolate China regionally, with peaceful coexistence.[108] By changing tactics, Mao also wanted to thwart

---

102 K.P.S. Menon, "India and the Soviet Union," in B.R. Nanda, ed., *Indian Foreign Policy: The Nehru Years* (Delhi: Vikas Publishing House, 1976), 136.
103 A.A. Fursenko and Timothy J. Naftali, *Khrushchev's Cold War: The Inside Story of an American Adversary* [Kindle book]: http://www.amazon.com.au; Vladislav Zubok and Constantine Pleshakov, *Inside the Kremlin's Cold War: From Stalin to Khrushchev* (Cambridge MA: Harvard University Press, 1996), 184.
104 Ibid, 175; William Taubman, *Khrushchev: The Man, His Era* (London: Free Press, 2003), 348.
105 Odd Arne Westad, *The Global Cold War: Third World Interventions and the Making of Our Times* (Cambridge: University Press, 2005), 67; Robert J. McMahon, "The Illusion of Vulnerability": American Reassessments of the Soviet Threat, 1955–1956," *International History Review*, 18:3 (1996), 601.
106 Jeremy Friedman, *Shadow Cold War: The Sino-Soviet Competition for the Third World* (Chapel Hill: University of North Carolina Press, 2015), 25.
107 Chen, "Bridging Revolution," 218.
108 Zhang, "Peaceful Coexistence," 513; Chen, "Bridging Revolution," 207–41.

American attempts to encircle China as well as reduce the West's politico-military presence in Asia.[109]

Nehru welcomed the Sino-Soviet shift towards peaceful coexistence for it promised, by reducing bipolar tensions, to usher in a new phase in the regional Cold War. It was, in other words, an opportunity not to be squandered. He knew, of course, that a mere relaxation of tensions would not be enough to make his grand design a reality. Still, he calculated that lower tensions might go some way in helping carry out his grand strategy by making it possible to create an "area of peace" (or more), thus improving India's strategic environment. He defined an area of peace as a zone characterized by the absence of conflict, and underpinned by a reciprocal commitment on the part of the Great Powers to underwrite peace and stability within that geographical space. In addition, the countries in such a space would not be aligned with either bloc.[110] As he further explained during the course of 1954–1955, he also expected these countries to adhere to the Five Principles because doing so would help "create an environment wherein it becomes a little more dangerous to the other party to break away from the pledges given."[111] In brief, his concept of areas of peace became an integral part of his grand strategy and, in his intentions, was to bring him closer to the achievement of his grand design.

Alas, in order to succeed, Nehru's concept required the United States and the two communist powers to stand by it. In the two years following Stalin's death, Nehru came to the conclusion that with the Soviet Union and China genuinely committed to peaceful coexistence, India should spare no effort to ensure that this positive trend in Soviet and Chinese foreign policy not be reversed. He drew encouragement from the two communist powers' behaviour at the 1954 Geneva Conference on Indochina. The role played by their representatives in securing a settlement to the Indochinese question reinforced in him the belief that Beijing and Moscow were interested in working out a *modus vivendi* with the West.[112] In recognition of their shift towards peaceful coexistence, Nehru moved to establish closer relations with the two communist powers. In December 1953, India and the Soviet Union agreed to a five-year trade and payments agreement which

---

[109] Chen, *Mao's China*; Gregg Brazinsky, *Winning the Third World: Sino-American Rivalry During the Cold War* (Chapel Hill: University of North Carolina Press, 2017), 76–78.
[110] Nehru, *India's Foreign Policy*, 67; Singh, *Power and Diplomacy*.
[111] Nehru cited in Nicholas Tarling, *Southeast Asia and the Great Powers* (New York: Routledge, 2011), 28.
[112] Gilles Boquérat, "India's Commitment to Peaceful Coexistence and the Settlement of the Indochina War," *Cold War History*, 5:2(2005), 217.

promised to increase bilateral trade.[113] Earlier in July, the Soviet Union decided to earmark 4 million rubles to the UN Expanded Programme of Technical Assistance for projects in developing countries.[114] No less important, as many as 14 Indian delegations, consisting of sportsmen, film artists, and industrialists, visited Moscow in the 18 months following Stalin's death.[115] At about the same time, India began negotiations with China aimed at reaching a settlement on "all matters pending between the two countries with regard to their relations in Tibet."[116]

As the Indian government moved to improve ties with the Soviet Union and China, its relations with the United States hit significant turbulence. Policymakers in New Delhi viewed the election of a new Republican administration with some concern given Eisenhower's strong anti-communist pronouncements during the 1952 presidential campaign.[117] Despite periodic disagreements with the previous administration, the Indian government had come to accept that "a coalition of liberal Democrats in Congress had consistently expressed strong support for India and had worked hard to gain more economic assistance for India."[118] However, as the Indians soon discovered, the Eisenhower administration was less inclined to pay attention to Indian sensibilities. First, it "reacted much more slowly" than Nehru would have wished to Moscow's shift towards peaceful coexistence.[119] Then, Washington stepped up support for the French war effort in Indochina – a step that deeply worried Nehru for its destabilising effects.[120] Next, it viewed his Five Principles and areas of peace with profound scepticism on the ground that India's policy would help the Chinese "lull other Asian nations into false sense security [regarding the] 'peaceful' nature their own intentions."[121] Finally, the American government considered, to Nehru's chagrin, the Geneva settlement on Indochina unfavourable to Western security interests.[122] For this reason, it did not endorse it, concluding that only through collective defence could the independence of South Vietnam, Laos and Cambodia, and the non-communist character of the rest of Southeast

---

113 NAUK, FO 371/116667, NS10385/3, Indo-Soviet Relations, 1947–1957, 15 April 1955.
114 Kaushik, *Soviet Relations*, 48–49.
115 Ibid, 48–49; see also Appadorai and Rajan, *India's Foreign Policy*, 264.
116 Bhasin, *India-China Relations*, 940–41 and 933–37.
117 McMahon, *Cold War*, 156.
118 Ibid, 155.
119 NAUK, FO371/123587, L10338/3, Escott Reid to Lester B. Pearson, telegram 817, 3 December 1955.
120 Boquérat, "India's Commitment to Peaceful Coexistence," 215–17.
121 *FRUS, 1955–1957, East Asian Security; Cambodia; Laos*, Vol. XXI, doc. 23.
122 For Nehru's deep disappointment see Boquérat, "India's Commitment to Peaceful Coexistence," 215–17.

Asia, be preserved. Sceptical that the Soviet Union and China would stick to both the spirit and letter of the Geneva accord, the Eisenhower Administration moved, in the second half of 1954, to establish a Western-led defence alliance in Southeast Asia.[123]

Washington's intention was to send a clear signal to the communist powers that further communist penetration in Indochina would be resisted.[124] Disappointingly for the Americans, British efforts to have India involved bore no fruit. The latter and most of its Colombo partners (Indonesia, Burma and Ceylon) chose not to join a Western-led defence pact.[125] Only Pakistan showed interest in the initiative, thus becoming one of the founding members of the Southeast Asian Treaty Organisation (SEATO). American and Western policymakers were not sure what to make of Karachi's support: some saw it as a welcome development that might help bring other neutrals around.[126] On the other hand, others remained lukewarm on Pakistan's participation, fearing that it might provoke Indian vocal opposition to the Western-led collective security pact without making any appreciable military contribution.[127]

Indeed, this turned out to be the case. Nehru interpreted American policy as the main obstacle to his plans. The issue of Pakistan no doubt played an important part in shaping Nehru's response to American moves. Pakistan's participation in SEATO came hot on the heels of Washington's decision in early 1954 to offer military aid to Pakistan in an attempt to secure its participation in the defence of the Middle East alongside Turkey, Iran, and Iraq.[128] Eisenhower's attempts to reassure Nehru that closer defence ties with Pakistan were not directed against India had no calming effect on him. He bitterly complained that

---

[123] For the origins of SEATO see Roger Dingman, "John Foster Dulles and the Creation of the Southeast Asia Treaty Organization in 1954," *International History Review*, 11:3(1989), 457–77.

[124] For the American rationale in greater detail see *FRUS, 1952–1954, East Asia and the Pacific*, Vol. XII, Part 2, doc. 267.

[125] Nabarun Roy, "Assuaging Cold War Anxieties: India and the Failure of SEATO," *Diplomacy & Statecraft*, 26:2 (2015), 322–40.

[126] NAUK, FO 371/111875, D1074/300, Pakistan and SEATO, Note by J.G. Tahourdin, 29 July 1954.

[127] On doubts about Pakistan's capacity to make a meaningful military contribution see Francine Frankel, *When Nehru Looked East: Origins of India-US Suspicion and India-China Rivalry* [Kindle book]: http://www.amazon.com.au.

[128] On the Mutual Defence Assistance Agreement, its origins, and rationale see Robert J. McMahon, "United States Cold War Strategy in South Asia: Making a Military Commitment to Pakistan, 1947–1954," *Journal of American History* 75:3(1988), 812–40; H.W. Brands, "India and Pakistan in American Strategic Planning, 1947–1954: The Commonwealth as Collaborator," *Journal of Imperial and Commonwealth History*, 15:1(1986), 47–50; McMahon, *Cold War*, Chs. 4 and 5.

Washington's support of Pakistan would give rise to a whole series of undesirable consequences for India. Not only would it bring the Cold War to India's doorstep and alter the Subcontinent's strategic balance, but it would also fuel tensions between India and Pakistan (and, quite possibly, between India's Hindus and Muslims as well) and increase the influence of the military within Pakistan.[129]

Still, Pakistan was not the only reason for Nehru's vehement opposition to American plans. As he told Burma's Prime Minister U Nu and the other leaders of the Colombo group on 31 July 1954, he found several faults with the American initiative. In a nutshell, Nehru believed a Western-led regional alliance to be neither "purely defensive" nor consistent with "the spirit of United Nations Charter." Moreover, "coming so soon after the Indochina settlement and embodying a reverse trend to peaceful approach, conciliation and an extension of the peace area in Southeast Asia," it was "calculated to affect the prospects of peace and stability in our area adversely rather than otherwise."[130] On 1 August 1954, Nehru elaborated on this point in a message to British Foreign Secretary Anthony Eden. Mincing no words, Nehru told Eden that Indian "participation in or our lending support to" such an arrangement was "not merely to abandon our well considered policies on international relations," but also "to help to extend the area of the Cold War with its attendant progressive armed preparedness and the psychosis of hatred and suspicion in this part of the world." This, Nehru added, might well render Southeast Asia "a potentially explosive theatre of the Cold War." India, therefore, would want no part in the establishment of a potentially destabilising military alliance. The only way forward, he told Eden, was a widespread acceptance of the Five Principles that India and China had agreed upon in April 1954. In urging Eden to reconsider London's commitment to a Southeast Asian military alliance, Nehru also raised the question of China's admission to the UN, arguing that Chinese membership would make a "great contribution to stability and peaceful progress in Asia."[131] Indeed, as one of his close advisers, T.N. Kaul, warned Nehru at the time, the creation of SEATO risked pushing China into "adopting an aggressive attitude" and "forming a counter-alliance" of its own. To avoid this, and to encourage China to allay its neighbours' fears that it harboured expansionist designs towards them, Kaul

---

129 *SWJN*, 24, 421 and 442; *FRUS, 1952–1954. African and South Asia*, Vol. XI, Part 2, doc. 1077.
130 *SWJN*, 26, 417–19. Nehru, incidentally, also referred to India's future role in the neutral Supervisory Commission on Indochina as one of the reasons why joining SEATO was out of the question.
131 *SWJN*, 26, 419.

suggested that India might consider supporting Indonesian calls for an Afro-Asian conference.[132]

Nehru had, until then, been rather unenthusiastic about the Indonesian idea. However, in late September, he came to the conclusion that, in the light of important regional developments (namely, the creation of SEATO and rising Sino-American tensions over Taiwan), the prospect of such a conference assumed "an added significance" and India would be ready to lend its support to it.[133] By the end of the year, Nehru fully supported convening an Afro-Asian conference and was instrumental in pushing for China's participation in it.[134] More to the point, such a conference had become "part of Nehru's strategy to offset US alliances by consolidating India's position with China."[135] This was no surprise. Throughout 1954, the Indian government rejected strategic cooperation with Washington and assumed a more assertively independent stance in foreign affairs.[136]

And the process was far from over. After Bandung, Nehru rapidly moved to improve relations with the Soviet Union. By 1954, the Soviet Union had already begun courting India.[137] In the summer of that year, Soviet Ambassador to India Mikhail Menshikov tentatively suggested that India and the Soviet Union make a formal commitment not "to participate in any coalition directed against the other" – an idea Nehru shot down quickly on the grounds that it would be tantamount to agreeing to a non-aggression pact and hence in breach of India's much cherished non-aligned stance.[138] Then, later that year, the Soviet Union offered to assist in building a large steel mill at Bhilai, then located in the state of Madhya Pradesh.[139] Next, in early June 1955, Nehru travelled to the Soviet Union where large crowds cheered him enthusiastically and the Soviet leadership received him warmly.[140] In his talks with Soviet leaders, Nehru contrasted "the many steps" taken by the Soviet Union "in the cause of peace to remove

---

132 NMML, Jawaharlal Nehru Papers [JN], file 285/I, T.N. Kaul to Nehru, 23 August 1954.
133 NMML, JN, 285/1, Note on Proposal to Hold an Afro-Asian Conference, 24 September 1954.
134 *SWJN*, 27, 107–12.
135 H.W. Brands, *India and the United States: The Cold Peace* (Boston: Twayne Publishers, 1990), 83.
136 Wainwright, *Inheritance of Empire*, 158–59.
137 McMahon, *Cold War*, 217.
138 *SWJN*, 26, 516–517; NMML, SD, 16, "Prime Minister's talks with Soviet leaders," note by K.P.S. Menon, 12 July 1955.
139 McMahon, *Cold War*, 271. An agreement between the Soviet Union and India was eventually reached in February 1955. See David C. Engerman, *The Price of Aid: The Economic Cold War in India* (Cambridge, MA: Harvard University Press, 2018), 122.
140 McGarr, *Cold War in South Asia*, 33; Appadorai and Rajan, *India's Foreign Policy*, 264.

fear and suspicion in the minds of other nations" with the Eisenhower Administration's regrettable tendency to "go about showing [its] muscles."[141] He learned of their desire for closer bilateral ties and secured their support for his Five Principles.[142] The joint communiqué, signed on 22 June, formalised Indian and Soviet support for the Five Principles as a means of allaying the fears of smaller nations, and affirmed their common belief that "states of different social structures could exist side by side in peace and work for the common good."[143] Nehru's party was said to have been "much impressed . . . at the complete lack of revolutionary fervour."[144] The Secretary General of the Indian Ministry of External Affairs, N.R. Pillai, drew the conclusion that the Soviet Union was no longer "suspicious" of India's "ability to act in an independent manner" and that, in fact, it now viewed its foreign policy as "the best guarantee for its security on its southeastern border."[145] For his part, Nehru returned to India "convinced that the Soviet people desired nothing more than peace."[146]

In November and December 1955, Khrushchev and Soviet Premier Nikolai Bulganin reciprocated Nehru's visit by touring India for nearly three weeks, meeting several leading local personalities, addressing large crowds and visiting ancient monuments, farms, big factories, and dams.[147] Wherever they went, the two Soviet leaders received an enthusiastic reception similar to the one given to Nehru a few months earlier in the Soviet Union.[148] The visit was not without its awkward moments, though. While his Soviet guests referred to India as an "ally" in public speeches and reiterated Moscow's desire to establish closer ties with India, Nehru stressed his continuing commitment to non-alignment and friendship towards the West.[149] At one time, he also questioned

---

141 *SWJN*, 29, 208 and 212. Extracts of these conversations are reproduced in *SWJN*, 29, 201–32.
142 Ibid., 209–10.
143 Ibid., 220fn 2.
144 NAUK, FO 371/123587, L10338/5, Bottomley to Golds, 1054/1/6/56, 12 January 1956; FO 371/123587, L10338/13, India: Indian Purchases of Military Equipment, SA14/7, 13 April 1956.
145 N.R. Pillai, *Visit to the Soviet Union: Some Impressions and Reflections* (New Delhi: Government of India 1955), 24, in NAUK, FO 371/123587, L10338/12.
146 Nehru cited in Dutt, *With Nehru*, 194.
147 *SWJN*, 31, 354 and 331–32; NAUK, FO 371/123587, L10338/7, India: Visit of Marshal Bulganin and Mr Khrushchev, SA/5/34/15, 23 January 1956.
148 *SWJN*, 31, 354.
149 NAUK, FO 371/123587, L10338/3, Reid to Pearson, telegram 817, 3 December 1955; L10338/7, India: Visit of Marshal Bulganin and Mr Khrushchev, SA/5/34/15, 23 January 1956.

the two leaders about Moscow's presumed links with the Indian communists, which they flatly denied.[150] For his part, Khrushchev indulged in some blunt and crude anti-Western remarks which annoyed his hosts.[151] On the whole, however, the visit went well. The British High Commission reported to London that Khrushchev and Bulganin had gone "a good way to destroying in the minds of large numbers of Indian people the old picture of Russia as a barbarous, dangerous northern bear" and "by their joviality and friendship and offers of aid" projected an image of the Soviet Union as "friendly," "progressive" and "peace-loving."[152] Khrushchev and Bulganin's support for a rising Asia, their denunciation of military alliances and their approval of India's "truly peace-loving" attitude pleased their hosts.[153] The talks laid the ground for closer collaboration between India and the Soviet Union.[154] The final communiqué highlighted a significant degree of convergence on peaceful coexistence, military alliances, and on China's admission to the UN.[155] The two governments agreed to boost their economic ties, although Soviet promises of substantial aid did not yet materialise.[156] The visit's outcome was enough to raise hopes in Moscow that the Soviet Union "could use India to move the 'correlation of forces' in the struggle with the United States decisively in Soviet favour."[157] In his memoirs, Khrushchev compared the degree of suspicion and reluctance with which, in 1955, the Afghan government received Soviet offers of economic aid with the total lack of mistrust on the part of the Nehru government.[158] For his part, Nehru drew the conclusion that the Soviet Union was serious about peaceful coexistence and that, by pursuing a policy of friendly cooperation with the Soviets, India could "help

---

150 *SWJN*, 31, 338–45.
151 NAUK, FO 371/123587, L10338/7, India: Visit of Marshal Bulganin and Mr Khrushchev, SA/5/34/15, 23 January 1956; L10338/1, Delhi to CRO, telegram 383, 28 December 1955.
152 NAUK, FO 371/123587, L10338/3, Reid to Pearson, telegram 817, 3 December 1955.
153 NAUK, FO 371/123587, L10338/1, Delhi to CRO, telegram 383, 28 December 1955.
154 Lengthy extracts of the conversations and other documents relating to the Khrushchev-Bulganin tour of India are reproduced at length in *SWJN*, 31, 299–365.
155 NAUK, FO 371/117299, L1632/33, Delhi to CRO, telegram 1453, 14 December 1955 and attachments; FO 371/123587, L10338/1, Delhi to CRO, telegram 383, 28 December 1955.
156 NAUK, FO 371/123587, L10338/7, India: Visit of Marshal Bulganin and Mr Khrushchev, SA/5/34/15, 23 January 1956; FO 371/117299, L1632/35, Delhi to CRO, telegram 1455, 14 December and Delhi to CRO, telegram 1474, 16 December 1955; Engerman, *Price*, 123.
157 Vojtech Mastny, "The Soviet Union's Partnership with India," *Journal of Cold War Studies*, 12:3(2010), 55.
158 Nikita Sergeevich Khrushchev and Strobe Talbott, *Khrushchev Remembers: The Last Testament* (London: Andre Deutsch, 1974), 301–02.

in the reconciliation of the Russians to the conditions in the non-communist world."[159] Moreover, he saw Soviet economic cooperation as instrumental in securing for India "a future that was industrial and self-sufficient but not Soviet."[160]

Although, quite inevitably, the warming of Indo-Soviet ties raised concerns in the United States,[161] neither Nehru nor Eisenhower were prepared to allow reciprocal disagreements to derail the overall relationship.[162] On the American side, there was a growing realisation that India was too important to let it drift towards the eastern bloc.[163] Dulles's visit to India in March 1956 helped the administration get a better appreciation of Nehru's concerns. Although his talks with Nehru were not all plain sailing, Dulles had the impression that the relationship was on the mend.[164] In any case, the administration began to soften its stance on non-alignment.[165] As for the Indian side, Western sources could, by the end of 1955, already detect that "Indian dislike of SEATO had cooled distinctly" given the fact that "SEATO had not been so provocative as they originally feared."[166] Quite significantly, Nehru was also unlikely to put at risk continuing American aid by antagonising Washington. His decision to turn down a Soviet offer to provide bombers to India must be seen in this context. Furthermore, Soviet repression in Hungary and Chinese actions in Tibet troubled him.[167] Nehru's visit to the United States in late 1956 helped improve the atmospherics of the relationship.[168]

And so, by the mid-1950s, both blocs came to view India's non-alignment "as a tolerable or even a beneficial state of affairs" and thus their approach to India changed accordingly to ensure "the preservation of its special relationship to both sides."[169] While Indo-American relations would not be free of

---

159 NAUK, FO 371/123587, L10338/11, Karachi to FO, telegram 394, 6 March 1956; L10338/13, India: Indian Purchases of Military Equipment, SA14/7, 13 April 1956.
160 Engerman, *Price*, 129.
161 See, for instance, *FRUS, 1955–1957, South Asia, Vol. VIII*, doc. 154; *FRUS, 1955–1957, Foreign Aid and Economic Defence Policy, Vol. X*, doc. 8; Brands, *Spectre*, 119; McMahon, *Cold War*, 218–20.
162 Raghavan, *Enigmas*; Brands, *Spectre*, 120–25.
163 On Eisenhower's view that India was too important to US interests in Asia to let it go see McMahon, *Cold War*, 221.
164 *FRUS, 1955–1957, Vol. VIII*, docs. 156–57; McMahon, *Cold War*, 225–26.
165 Raghavan, *Enigmas*.
166 NAUK, DO 35/5977, Macdonald to Laithwaite, 6 December 1955.
167 Brands, *Spectre*, 123–24; McMahon, *Cold War*, 226–27.
168 Raghavan, *Enigmas*.
169 Heimsath and Mansingh, *Diplomatic History*, 62–63.

hiccups, the frustration and even the acrimony experienced by both sides during 1954 and 1955 appeared to have subsided. As for the Soviet Union, its relations with India grew in significance in parallel with Khrushchev's increased interest in expanding Soviet political and economic influence in the Third World.[170] Between the late 1950s and mid-1960s, New Delhi received around 470 million rubles worth of Soviet largesse, thus making India the second largest recipient of Moscow's aid in Asia after Indonesia.[171] Initially conceived as an attempt by Khrushchev to seize opportunities accorded by emerging decolonisation to "break into the soft underbelly of imperialism" and "win the sympathies of the millions of peoples" in the Third World,[172] Moscow's politico-economic offensive soon assumed an anti-Chinese complexion. As the Soviet Union's relations with China unravelled in the late 1950s, a fierce rivalry developed between them for the hearts and minds of Asia – one that led Moscow to treble its financial and technical aid to developing countries by 1961.[173] Like Khrushchev, Nehru was soon forced to deal with an increasingly hostile China.[174] In the early 1960s, the rapid unravelling of his *Hindi-Chini Bhai Bhai* diplomacy turned China into a constant thorn in New Delhi's flesh, as well as a major long-standing roadblock to Nehru's grand design.

Conclusion

In May 1957, the British High Commissioner to New Delhi, Malcolm MacDonald, endeavoured to make sense of India's friendly attitude towards the Soviet Union and China, for the benefit of his superiors in London. In a passage worth quoting in full, he argued that

> If Mr Nehru is more afraid of Russia than of China in the short term, he is probably more afraid of China in the long term. He thinks that the Chinese Communist Revolution is by no means yet losing its original fanatical enthusiasm . . . They [Nehru and his colleagues]

---

170 Andreas Hilger, "Communism, Decolonisation and the Third World," in N. Naimark et al, eds., *The Cambridge History of Communism* (Cambridge: University Press, 2017), 325.
171 Ragna Boden, "Cold War Economics: Soviet Aid to Indonesia," *Journal of Cold War Studies*, 10:3(2008), 116–18 and 120. However, unlike Indonesia, India used Soviet aid mostly for economic ventures and not military purposes.
172 Georgy Mirsky cited in Vladislav M. Zubok, *A Failed Empire: The Soviet Union in the Cold War from Stalin to Gorbachev* (Chapel Hill: University of North Carolina Press, 2009), 139.
173 Friedman, *Shadow Cold War*, 30.
174 For a succinct account on the worsening of Sino-Indian relations see Srinath Raghavan, *War and Peace in Modern India* (London: Palgrave Macmillan, 2010), Chs. 7 and 8.

calculate that in any case the Chinese will be so occupied for the next ten or twenty years with the colossal task of creating modern satisfactory conditions in their own country that will not be seriously tempted to interfere in the affairs of their neighbours. By then Mr Nehru . . . expect[s] to have developed in India a democratic socialist society strong enough to withstand the claims of rival systems. And they [Nehru and his colleagues] trust that in the meantime the fanatical phase of Chinese communism like that of Russian communism, will have evolved into a more relaxed and liberal state animated by neighbourly friendship towards non-Communist peoples abroad. All this makes Mr Nehru want a decade of peace in which the process of strengthening democracy in India and of weakening Communist zeal in Russia and China can both have uninterrupted play.[175]

This was also why, throughout 1954 and 1955, Nehru was so eager to encourage Soviet and Chinese moves towards peaceful coexistence and, at the same time, so averse to embracing American containment. As mentioned above, the whole of Nehru's grand strategy was geared to ensure that a young and undeveloped nation, such as India, be able to focus on economic development and nation-building. Anything that turned it away from these crucial tasks was unwelcome to Nehru. And so, with communism under control domestically and the two communist powers intent, at least temporarily, on pursuing peaceful co-existence, Nehru had every reason to avoid doing anything that could upset what he regarded as positive trends in the communist world. If his efforts to seek an accommodation with the communists gave rise to American complaints, that was a price he was more than willing to pay. After all, he knew that, for all their alleged shortcomings, the Americans would put up with his barbs and go to great lengths to prevent mutual disagreements from causing long-lasting damage to the overall relationship.

---

[175] NAUK, DO 35/5977, MacDonald to CRO, 14 May 1957.

Lauriane Simony
The British Council and Its Rivals: Great Powers' Cultural Competition in Post-Independence Burma, 1948–1955

After the end of the Second World War, anti-British sentiment rose rapidly within the Burmese population. Under pressure from the Burmese nationalist movement, which united under the banner of the Anti-Fascist People's Freedom League (AFPFL) in 1945, British Prime Minister Clement Attlee's administration had no choice but to accelerate the process of independence: on 4 January 1948, Burma obtained its independence from the British Empire and became a republic. Although the transfer of power was in fact rather peaceful, Burma decided to leave the Commonwealth upon independence. Worried by Burma's radical rejection of the British connection, the Foreign Office (FO) thought it essential to find new ways of preserving Britain's "special relationship" with its former colony, especially in the context of the Cold War.[1] Indeed, as early as 1948, communist rebellions broke out throughout the country, threatening the stability of Burmese Prime Minister U Nu's newly established central government. In the broader Cold War context in Southeast Asia, the proclamation of the People's Republic of China in October 1949 and its ideological alignment with the Soviet Union meant that the "communist threat" was becoming more tangible in Burma, which shared a border with China. Examining British policy in Southeast Asia in the early Cold War, British historian Peter Lowe explained that Britain's "grand strategy" for post-independence Burma entailed supporting Burma's political development on democratic lines, eradicating communist movements inside the country, and encouraging Burma's alignment with the West on the international stage.[2] The interconnectedness between British strategies directed towards maintaining an influence in Burma after independence and those aimed at containing communism in the country underlines the links between processes of decolonization and Cold War challenges, put forward by several historians.[3]

---

[1] John Darwin, *Britain and Decolonization, The Retreat from Empire in the Postwar World* (New York: Palgrave Macmillan, 1988), 298.
[2] Peter Lowe, *Contending with Nationalism and Communism: British Policy Towards Southeast Asia* (Basingstoke: Palgrave Macmillan, 2009), 98.
[3] See Christopher E. Goscha and Christian F. Ostermann, eds., *Connecting Histories: Decolonization and the Cold War in Southeast Asia, 1945–1962* (Washington: Woodrow Wilson Center

To meet their objectives of preserving a connection with a former colony that expressed no desire to maintain it, and opposing communism inside and outside the country, British policymakers decided to supplement their political actions – such as providing financial or military assistance to Burma's government in order to help them push back the communist insurgents[4] – with cultural activities. As suggested in this book's Introduction, there were other methods besides military actions by which Great Powers intended to conduct their grand strategy, including soft power: this chapter argues that, from the 1940s, culture became an important aspect of British grand strategy towards Burma. Two years before independence, the Burma Office and the colonial administration on the ground oversaw the opening of a first British Council centre in Rangoon to further British interests in the post-independence period and encourage the development of new, informal relations between British and Burmese elites. Through the British Council, the British aimed to become more active in the educational and cultural fields in Burma: education and culture were considered strictly apolitical by British officials and, as such, less likely to be rejected by Burmese authorities. In a letter to Sir John Clague, adviser to the Secretary of State for Burma at the Burma Office, in which he detailed certain conditions attached to establishing a British Council centre in Burma, Arthur John Stanley White, secretary-general of the British Council, wrote: "Another rule which we find essential is that propaganda and politics must be rigorously eschewed." White here highlighted one of the main principles underlying British cultural action abroad – referred to as "propaganda" in the quote – namely that it had to be formally detached from the political sphere and therefore independent from the British government.[5]

In the first few years after independence, the British Council in Burma expanded and increasingly specialised in English language teaching. But FO and British Council officials were becoming aware of cultural competition from other great powers involved in the Cold War, namely the United States, the Soviet Union, and China, and this cultural competition on the ground came to reflect the broader strategies at play between the different actors in the Cold War. In the late 1940s, the Americans launched cultural activities of the same sort as the British: the United States Information Centre, located in Rangoon, offered English classes to the Burmese public but their superior financial means enabled them to

---

Press, 2009); Leslie James and Elisabeth Leake, eds., *Decolonization and the Cold War: Negotiating Independence* (London: Bloomsbury Academic, 2015).
4 See Matthew Foley, *The Cold War and National Assertion in Southeast Asia: Britain, the United States and Burma, 1948–1962* (London: Routledge, 2010), 3.
5 NAUK, BW 19/1, Arthur John Stanley White, secretary-general of the British Council, to Sir John Clague, adviser to the Secretary of State for Burma, Burma Office, 11 July 1944, 1.

carry out work on a much larger scale. Although the Americans were in fact advertising a similar model of Western democracy as the British, they remained Britain's rivals in the field of cultural relations in post-independence Burma. Moreover, in the early 1950s, the Soviets launched a Burma-Soviet Cultural Association, roughly at the same time as the first Chinese Cultural Mission was sent to Burma: unlike the British and the Americans, whose main focus was on education and English language teaching, the Soviets and Chinese preferred to showcase their respective cultures through large-scale exhibitions and performances.

As Soviet and Chinese cultural efforts were perceived by the British as obvious propaganda that needed to be countered, the British Council started spreading a much clearer anti-communist message in the mid-1950s. Although the British Council had been voluntarily maintained "at arm's length" to the British government, the publication of the Drogheda Report in 1954 redefined its goals in foreign countries, notably in the global fight against communism, and marked the formal recognition of culture as a major instrument of diplomacy, capable of furthering FO strategies.[6] In the 1950s, the British Council thus became an integral part of the coordinated effort by the FO to fight the Cold War in the cultural field. The Information Research Department was created in 1948 within the FO to conduct "offensive propaganda," ie to attack the communist model directly, in areas where the Soviet Union threatened British interests. This meant that what was known as "positive propaganda," ie the promotion of the British model abroad in order to discredit the communist model in an indirect way, was left to independent institutions such as the British Council.[7] This chapter focuses on this second aspect of British cultural strategy in the Cold War.

Based on British Council archives gathered at the National Archives in London, this chapter shows that British cultural efforts in Burma during the Cold War were increasingly superseded by cultural propaganda from other Great Powers involved in the conflict. While they implemented different strategies, the American, Chinese, and Soviet cultural missions in the country were clearly considered threats to Britain's "special relationship" with Burma in the cultural and educational fields. The communist powers, in particular, were accused of conducting an anti-Western propaganda offensive. Focusing on British policy-making in Burma after independence and underlining the divergences between

---

[6] NAUK, CAB 129/64/5, Overseas Information Services, *Report of the Drogheda Committee*, November 1953. The Drogheda Report was published as a White Paper in 1954; Cmd 9138, *Summary of the Report of the Independent Committee of Enquiry into the Overseas Information Service: The Drogheda Report* (London: HMSO, April 1954).

[7] Andrew Defty, *Britain, America and Anti-Communist Propaganda, 1945–1953: The Information Research Department* (London: Routledge, 2004), 65.

the United States and Britain's cultural strategies in the Cold War, this chapter builds on recent histories of the Cold War which challenge the traditional, bipolar vision of the experience as a conflict between the United States and the Soviet Union. In line with John Lewis Gaddis and Odd Arne Westad's works, this chapter also aims to emphasize Burmese agency in the process.[8] Far from being a mere pawn, subjected to external powers' prerogatives, evidence shows that Burma strove to extract itself from the Cold War competition by drawing from different models of development to build the state, while refusing to embrace one entirely. Highlighting the British authorities' illusory sense of grandeur, based on their belief that Britain was still part of the Big Three,[9] this chapter confronts the British objective to maintain a dominant position in the region with the reality of the other major powers' increasing weight in Southeast Asia. Notwithstanding a few recent publications on the Cold War analyzing the cultural dimension of the competition between the Great Powers, such as Gregg Brazinsky's book on the US-China rivalry in which a whole chapter is devoted to culture and propaganda, this aspect of Western and communist powers' competition for the informal control of former colonies remains understudied.[10] This chapter addresses that lack.

First, this chapter focuses on the development of British Council activities and examines the significance of English language teaching and culture within Britain's broader "grand strategy" in Burma, which aimed at diverting Burma from communism and encouraging a political development on Western democratic lines. It then studies the different cultural strategies implemented by the other Great Powers in Burma in the Cold War context, namely the United States, the Soviet Union, and China, from a British Council and FO perspective. Finally, based on analyzing original material from the archives of the Burmese Ministry of Education, it reflects on the extent to which Burma was indeed influenced by foreign cultural propaganda, and the ways in which the former British colony, in turn, tried to draw both from Britain and its "cultural rivals" to serve its own nation-building goals.

---

8 See John Lewis Gaddis, *We Now Know: Rethinking Cold War History* (Oxford: University Press, 1997) and Odd Arne Westad, *The Global Cold War: Third World Interventions and the Making of Our Times* (Cambridge: University Press, 2012). See also Robert J. McMahon, *The Limits of Empire: The United States and Asia Since World War II* (New York: Columbia University Press, 1999).
9 The "Big Three" refers to the three Allied powers that won the Second World War, namely Britain, the United States and the Soviet Union.
10 Gregg A. Brazinsky, *Winning the Third World: Sino-American Rivalry During the Cold War* (Chapel Hill: University of North Carolina Press, 2017), 132–65.

The Cultural Dimension of British Grand Strategy in Cold War Burma: Diverting Burma from Communism and Promoting a Western Model of Democracy

When Burma obtained its independence, Britain enjoyed a special position in the country as its main diplomatic, military, and economic partner. On the military side, the Britain-Burma Defence Agreement of August 1947 signed between the British government and Burma's provisional administration set up a British Services Mission whose goal was to provide military assistance to Burma in the form of supply of arms and military training. The mission enabled the British to maintain a military presence in the country after independence and made Burma closely dependent on the former colonial power for its defence. The Agreement stated: "The Government of Burma agree [. . .] to receive a Naval, Military and Air Force Mission from the United Kingdom Government and not from any Government outside the British Commonwealth."[11] Its explicit purpose was therefore to prevent Burma from forming military alliances with potential enemies of Britain after independence and ensure that Burma somehow remained in the British sphere of influence. In the economic field, Burma remained part of the sterling zone until 1966 and continued to rely largely on the British and Indian markets for its rice exports in the first few years after independence.[12] Moreover, several historians and political scientists, including French Burma specialist Renaud Egreteau, have underlined certain similarities between the British political system and the political system of independent Burma, to show that the AFPFL still considered Britain a major source of inspiration until the mid-1950s.[13] In 1947, the Burmese Constitution adopted a form of parliamentary democracy derived from the British model with a bicameral parliamentary system.[14] At the first general election in the country in 1951, the AFPFL kept its majority in Parliament and launched a vast programme of social reforms aimed to set up a welfare state in Burma. According to British historian Hugh Tinker, this programme, called the Pyidawtha Plan, presented many similarities with the British postwar Labour model

---

[11] Clement Attlee and Thakin Nu, *Britain-Burma Defence Agreement* (Rangoon: 29 August 1947).
[12] Foley, *The Cold War and National Assertion*, 41.
[13] Renaud Egreteau, *Histoire de la Birmanie Contemporaine: le pays des prétoriens* (Paris: Fayard, 2010), 134.
[14] *Constitution of the Union of Burma* (Rangoon: 24 September 1947).

of the Welfare State, as illustrated for example by 1954 laws enacting free access to medical care, clearly derived from the British National Health Service.[15]

Moreover, British officials also acknowledged that Burma represented one of the only Southeast Asian countries where the central government was in fact opposing communist insurgents within its borders. The FO's concern over a communist takeover in Burma – linked to the eruption in 1948 of quasi-simultaneous communist rebellions in Burma, Malaya, the Philippines and Indonesia, which seemed to give weight to British fears of a communist revolution in Southeast Asia in the broader Cold War context[16] – were somewhat qualified by the Burmese authorities' firm stance towards the rebels. The insurgency was led by two important figures of the nationalist movement for Burmese independence, Thakin Than Tun, leading the White Flag communist group, and Thakin Soe, at the head of the Red Flag communist faction, who both opposed the terms of independence contained in the October 1947 Treaty signed between the British and Burmese governments.[17] According to them, the treaty was largely responsible for perpetuating Burma's heavy dependence on Britain. The Burmese Army (or *Tatmadaw*) launched a counter-insurgency to quash the communist rebellions and restore political stability in the country and were supported in their endeavour, both militarily and financially, by the FO.[18] Offering financial support to the Burmese central government represented an important dimension of British grand strategy in Burma in the early Cold War: besides military support in the form of arms and training, encouraging the economic development of the country was perceived as an efficient way to earn the goodwill of the Burmese authorities. In June 1950, the British government, along with Commonwealth members (India, Pakistan, Sri Lanka, Australia and New Zealand), agreed on a £6 million loan to Burma, to support the counter-insurgency financially and help stabilize the regime.[19]

However, in the late 1940s and early 1950s, there were signs that Burma was increasingly looking towards the East for assistance. For the FO, the position of Prime Minister U Nu's government regarding communism remained unclear. On

---

[15] Hugh Tinker, *The Union of Burma, A Study of the First Years of Independence*, 2nd ed. (London: Oxford University Press, 1959), 213.
[16] Gaddis, *We Now Know*, 158.
[17] Clement Attlee and Thakin Nu, *Treaty Between the Government of the United Kingdom and the Provisional Government of Burma* (London: HMSO, 17 October 1947).
[18] NAUK, FO 800/441, memorandum on Burma, enclosed in telegram from Ernest Bevin, Foreign Secretary, to Clement Attlee, 25 April 1949.
[19] Foley, *The Cold War and National Assertion*, 35. In the end, Burma decided against resorting to this Commonwealth loan, mainly because of its political implications.

26 May 1948, U Nu announced his "Leftist Unity" programme, expressing a commitment to nationalisation and announcing his wish to develop political and economic relations with the Soviet Union. This was perceived by British officials as evidence of Burma embracing communism.[20] It also represented the first step in Burma's efforts to diversify its international partners and limit its political and economic dependence on Britain. Although most of the "Leftist Unity" programme was quickly set aside in favour of a much more moderate programme of social reforms, the Pyidawtha Plan, Burma did start developing diplomatic relations with the Soviet Union in 1951.[21] Additionally, in order to limit its military commitments to Britain, the Burmese government, under the influence of General Ne Win, head of the Burmese Armed Forces, announced its decision to put an end to the 1947 Defence Agreement in July 1953. In the economic field, Burma strove to expand its markets from the mid-1950s onwards: for instance, the Burmese government signed a series of barter deals with China and the Soviet Union in 1954 and 1955 to try to reduce its economic dependence on Britain and Commonwealth countries.[22] Diversifying its economic and political partners was also a way for Burma to express its refusal to be involved in the strategic alliances of the Cold War: the early 1950s marked Burma's increasing commitment to neutrality in the field of foreign policy, culminating with its role in organizing the Bandung Conference in April 1955.

The Burmese move to reject the "special relationship" shaped British policymaking in the post-independence period and accounts for the growing place of culture in British grand strategy towards Burma. Well aware of the nationalist atmosphere and strong anti-British sentiment within the Burmese population, British officials decided to rely on what they called "cultural propaganda" (which was simply synonymous with cultural promotion in the 1940s) to further their objectives.[23] Unlike the political, economic and military aspects of the two countries' relationship, culture appeared as a more "informal" way to maintain a connection – as opposed to the "formal" control the British imposed on Burma during the colonial period, in the words of British historian John Darwin[24] – and

---

[20] NAUK, FO 435/1, "Leftist Unity" programme, enclosed in a letter from James Bowker, British Ambassador to Burma, to Ernest Bevin, Foreign Secretary, 26 May 1948, in *British Documents on Foreign Affairs: Reports and Papers from the Foreign Office Confidential Print*, Anthony Best, ed. (Bethesda, Maryland: University Publications of America, 2001), Part IV, Series E, Vol. 7, 23–24.
[21] Chi-shad Liang, *Burma's Foreign Relations: Neutralism in Theory and Practice* (New York: Praeger, 1990), 176.
[22] Foley, *The Cold War and National Assertion*, 118–19.
[23] See for instance NAUK, BW 19/1, "Burma – British Cultural Propaganda" (1944–1946).
[24] Darwin, *Britain and Decolonization*, 244.

perhaps less likely to elicit Burmese authorities' suspicion or rejection. Indeed, as White explained: "Such cultural links between two countries tend to be of particular value when other links are diminishing because of political change."[25] In the tense political situation of the last years of colonial domination of Burma, the British Council could nurture "informal" links between the two countries to ensure a lasting British presence on Burmese territory after independence. It would also soften the blow of Burma's hasty emancipation from the British Empire.

The close cultural ties that Burma and Britain maintained were of course inherited from the colonial period. The English language in particular, being the language of the country's political and intellectual elite, needed to be protected after independence as the basis for projecting an entire cultural model and protecting British interests in Burma. Although the centrality and tremendous influence of English language teaching within British cultural diplomacy would only formally be acknowledged by the publication of the Drogheda Report in 1953–1954, it was already the preferred entryway into the establishment of cultural relations with Burma in the late 1940s. When the first British Council centre opened in Burma in 1946, two years before independence, under the direction of Representative J. Stewart Bingley, its initial activities targeted the English-speaking portion of the population. In a long letter detailing his first weeks in Burma, which in fact constituted the first report on British Council activities in the country, Bingley wrote: "Personally I think we could combine the cultural and social activities quite easily, although in the early stages no doubt the stress would be on the social activities. Introduction to the cultural side of our work would have to be done gradually."[26] The first British Council activities therefore aimed less at promoting British culture than encouraging social encounters between British colonial administrators and the Burmese elite, outside of the political sphere. The other professed aim of the British Council in its early years was to preserve an entire educational model inherited from the colonial period and try and shape the postcolonial educational institutions, such as the British-modelled Rangoon University or the Anglo-Vernacular schools, where the English language was still the medium of instruction.[27]

---

25 NAUK, BW 19/1, White to Clague, 11 July 1944, 1.
26 NAUK, BW 19/6, letter from J. Stewart Bingley to T.P. Tunnard-Moore, Director of the Department of Dominions and India of the British Council, 21 June 1946, 14–15.
27 BL, IOR/M/4/2408, memorandum on Burma's likely needs for the Education Department, enclosed in a letter from J.L. Leyden, Government of Burma, to H.F. Searle, Burma Office, 7 February 1945. During the colonial period, the "Government of Burma" referred to the British administration in Burma.

In post-independence Burma, as previously explained, the fear of a communist revolution largely influenced the direction of British Council activities under Bingley's successor, Representative J.E.V. Jenkins, who looked for efficient ways to spread the British democratic model through cultural events and English language teaching. It is not surprising that, in the early 1950s, the British Council's activities came to target young people in particular: one of the main objectives of British cultural promotion in Burma, which was also formalised by the publication of the Drogheda Report in the mid-1950s, was to shape an entire generation of young Burmese students, partly educated in the Western fashion and perhaps more inclined to conduct their political action in a democratic way. The British Council notably took advantage of the large educational reforms launched by the Burmese government in the early 1950s to get involved in the writing of school manuals used in Burmese schools and spread British political ideals. It relied on certain senior figures within the Ministry of Education, such as Director of Public Instruction U Kaung, to do so. U Kaung wanted to "[instil] in the Burmese minds the qualities that [would] make democracy work" and was for example instrumental in incorporating extracts from the British Council publication *British Life and Thought* in school manuals in Burma.[28]

University students, more specifically, were identified as the group of people most likely to be seduced by communism, and the Drogheda Report underlined "the degree to which the work of the Council was likely to lessen this danger."[29] In Burma, there was indeed a strong revolutionary tradition at the University of Rangoon and communism was very influential among students, especially those organised within the Rangoon University Students' Union. Consequently, the British Council strove to reinforce its presence in higher education by filling positions in the English Department of the University of Rangoon with professors sent from Britain. In 1950, the British Council sent its first English professor, Mr Morgan, to Burma and this "brought the British Council in close touch with many educational bodies in Rangoon." Morgan was for instance included in the organisation of the university examinations and came to occupy several administrative positions at the University of Rangoon.[30] He was quickly followed by several others. By the end of the 1950s, six British Council professors were installed in posts at the University of Rangoon and the newly established University of Mandalay.[31]

---

28 NAUK, BW 19/7, report by A.J.S. White, Controller of the Overseas Department of the British Council, 19 May 1952, 1.
29 NAUK, CAB 129/64/5, *Report of the Drogheda Committee*, 50.
30 NAUK, BW 19/7, Representative's annual report, 1950–1951, 2.
31 NAUK, BW 19/10, Representative's annual report, 1959–1960, 1.

The British Council also encouraged the development of academic exchanges between Britain and Burma by offering scholarships to Burmese students. Because British Council officials had no say in the selection of students sent to British universities, as the decision lay entirely with the Burmese government, they looked for alternative ways of "controlling" Burmese students. They focused on students once they arrived in Britain, through the Student Welfare Department of the British Council which offered culture classes to foreign students, emphasising the positive aspects of the British model, and working to integrate Burmese students into British society.[32] At the other end of the process, the British Council deemed it important to maintain a link with these Burmese students who were trained in British institutions, launching an association that enabled former British Council scholars to meet at social events. The British Council Scholars' Association sponsored talks by Burmese students to encourage them to share their views of British universities with the Burmese public and to accentuate the positive aspects of receiving a British education.[33] This particular attention given to those who benefited from the institution's scholarship scheme shows that the British Council largely relied on academic exchanges to further British influence in a former colony. The British Council directly included the local population in its promotion of the British model.

In the cultural field, the British Council relied on various types of media to promote British culture and deliver a pro-British message in Burma, as part of its "positive propaganda" effort. In the early part of the 1950s, a series of conferences by British academics or parliamentarians were organised by the British Council in Burma. The themes of the conferences were mainly chosen for their capacity to influence Burmese politicians during the period of state-building that marked the first few years after Burma gained independence. Two major topics of the British Council's cultural promotion stood out, namely the Welfare State in Britain and the form of government. Between 1949 and 1957, there was at least one conference on the subject of trade unions every year, which is somewhat telling at a time when Burmese authorities appeared to be hesitating between embracing the British left-wing, democratic model and the Soviet model, as illustrated by the successive launches of the "Leftist Unity" programme and the Pyidawtha Plan, in 1948 and 1951 respectively. It seemed to be in the interest of British policymakers, even under a Conservative government

---

32 See J. M. Lee, "Commonwealth Students in the United Kingdom, 1940–1960: Student Welfare and World Status," *Minerva* 44:1 (2006): 1–24.
33 NAUK, BW 19/7, Representative's annual report, 1951–1952, 2.

from 1951, to promote a non-revolutionary type of left-wing model to divert Burmese politicians from the lure of communism.

In January 1950, the Burmese Parliament received a British delegation composed of Labour MPs and peers. On this occasion, the British parliamentarians delivered several speeches discussing various aspects of the implementation of the postwar Welfare State in Britain and the British democratic model, in front of a large audience of Burmese university students and politicians. Labour MP James Haworth's conference, once again dealing with trade unions, was introduced with a speech from Rangoon mayor U Tun Tin, who shared his impressions about Britain's Trades Union Congress and welcomed the recent formation of an international organization of trade unions on democratic, non-revolutionary lines in 1949. His firm rejection of the communist-oriented World Federation of Trade Unions, coupled with Haworth's talk on the workings of British trade unions, was crucial at a time when the Burmese Trade Union Congress was heavily divided between its socialist members, close to the ruling AFPFL, and its more radical members wishing to join the World Federation of Trade Unions.[34]

The form of government was the other widely discussed subject. Ahead of the 1951 elections in Burma – the first democratic elections held in the country since independence – British Council Representative Jenkins organised several conferences on the British parliamentary model, and a projection of the British Council-produced film *General Election*, for the Burmese government. This 15-minute film, dealing with the electoral process in Britain, focuses on the transmission of a few key messages, such as the importance of multi-party politics in the organisation of democratic elections or the need to make one's voice heard by voting, even from a distance – the narrator evokes British soldiers, still based in Burma towards the end of the Second World War, who sent their ballots by post. Along with this hint at the Burmese military campaign, other elements of the film would have been particularly evocative to the Burmese public, such as the importance of young people's engagement in politics or the difficulties linked with accessing the polls in the countryside. The reference to the freedom of the press, in the end, sounds like a simplistic propaganda sentence: "In England, the freedom of the press holds good. There is no question of censorship or interference from outside."[35] Specifically designed for a foreign audience, the film *General Election* was typical of the British Council's "positive propaganda" in the early 1950s and represented a good example of British officials' use of culture to

---

34 NAUK, BW 19/6, introductory speech by U Tun Tin, Mayor of Rangoon, 18 January 1950, 2. He was referring to the International Confederation of Free Trade Unions, formed after a split with the World Federation of Trade Unions.
35 Ronald Riley, *General Election* (British Council Film, 1945).

promote non-revolutionary democratic values, as opposed to the Soviet model. According to Jenkins, the impact of the film on the democratic unfolding of the 1951 elections could not be denied: "The General Elections Commission undoubtedly planned its system for the recent general election on British lines as a direct result of information provided by this office, supported by the showing of the film *General Election*."[36]

At the same time that the British Council was orienting its strategy towards promoting a Western-type democratic model in Burma, new foreign cultural centres opened in Rangoon, led by the other major powers involved in the Cold War conflict in the region, and immediately perceived as cultural competition by both FO and British Council officials. In 1945, British Council reports had already been describing Americans and Chinese as potential cultural "rivals" in Burma after the war and underlined the importance of developing cultural activities in Burma at an early date: "[The Americans and the Chinese] will be planning to resume activity in the postwar period and British Council plans must be designed to make an appeal at least equal to these rivals in width and in depth."[37] This quote suggests that Burma's cultural field had to be conquered in the aftermath of the war; the prospect of increased rival cultural propaganda in the country also accounts for the early opening of a British Council centre in the latter part of the 1940s.

Cultural Competition in Burma in the Early Cold War: The British Council Versus American, Chinese and Soviet Cultural Missions

The United States launched cultural activities in Burma quite early on. As US activities sometimes encroached on the British Council's ground, for instance when Americans started offering English classes to the Burmese public, they were also considered as competition by the British institution. The report entitled "British Council Activities for Southeast Asia" previously mentioned already highlighted the "considerable" and "unique" position of American missionaries in Burma.[38] Founded by Adironam Judson in 1814, the first American Baptist mission had notably participated in the creation of the University of Rangoon in 1920. Adironam

---

[36] NAUK, BW 19/7, Representative's annual report, 1951–1952, 4.
[37] NAUK, BW 1/174, "British Council Activities for Southeast Asia," 1945, 4.
[38] Ibid.

Judson gave his name to Judson College, one of the two faculties in the university, and American missionaries taught at the University of Rangoon until independence.[39] After the war, the Americans resumed their cultural activities and were present in Burma before the British Council centre even opened. Upon arrival in the country, Bingley made several references to the United States Information Centre of Rangoon.

The United States Information Centre was part of the United States Information Service (USIS) and acted both as the information section of an embassy and a cultural organisation. Unlike the British Council whose missions were distinct from the Information Service of the British Embassy, the United States Information Agency was a federal agency directly dependent on the United States Department of State and therefore explicitly linked to American foreign policy objectives.[40] During the Cold War, it was a major propaganda agency, as historian Walter Hixson explained. All the cultural activities promoted by the United States Information Agency in the 1950s were supposed to meet three important policy objectives: denounce communism, glorify the capitalist system, and promote democracy.[41] Made up of a library and a reading room, the United States Information Centre in Burma was essentially used by students from the University of Rangoon. It also organized cultural events and American film projections were particularly popular. Although Bingley affirmed that this centre "would not compete with our activities," as it did not target the same public audience on the eve of independence, he regretted that "the US have something to show whereas we do not" in the cultural field, and the United States Information Centre's cultural events became incentives for the rapid development of similar activities by the British Council.[42]

Little interested in Burma before the late 1940s, the Americans turned their attention towards the country after the proclamation of the People's Republic of China in 1949. The increasing influence of communist China in the region led the United States, which had always considered Burma a "minor concern," to reconsider its general interests in Southeast Asia, and the strategic importance

---

[39] Kenton J. Clymer, *A Delicate Relationship, the United States and Burma/Myanmar since 1945* (Ithaca: Cornell University Press, 2015), 10–11.
[40] The United States Information Agency centralised all the cultural activities of USIS from 1953, although the acronym "USIS" continued to be used to refer to American cultural activities in foreign countries.
[41] Walter L. Hixson, *Parting the Curtain: Propaganda, Culture and the Cold War, 1945–1961* (New York: St Martin's Griffin, 1998), 122.
[42] NAUK, BW 19/6, letter from Bingley to Tunnard-Moore, 21 June 1946, 16.

of Burma in the Cold War conflict.[43] In the same way as the fear of communist expansion in Burma gave impetus to British cultural propaganda, US policymakers relied on the possibilities offered by culture and education in the global fight against communism and encouraged the development of academic ties with Burma. Scientific and academic exchanges, in particular, became some of the United States' favoured weapons during the Cold War. According to political scientist Joseph Nye, these "high culture contacts" largely increased American soft power by spreading the Western democratic model in areas the Soviet Union also coveted.[44] In 1947, the United States and Burma signed a Fulbright Agreement, establishing a US$3 million fund to be spent on academic exchanges.[45] It was one of the first Fulbright conventions established in the world.[46] Simultaneously, another organisation was founded, the Burma-America Cultural Institute, to offer English classes to the Burmese population. To Jenkins, this institute only copied British Council activities in the field of English language teaching and "produced nothing original."[47]

Historian Matthew Foley shows that, in the diplomatic arena, British policymakers' reactions towards the United States' renewed interest in Burma were somewhat mixed. He explained that "British officials watched the development of American interest in Burma, and in Southeast Asia as a whole, with a mixture of relief and trepidation."[48] Of course, the British government was counting on American help to limit communist influence in the region, which it deemed harmful to its own economic and political interests, and acknowledged their common membership in the Western bloc. But Britain also aspired to maintain its position as the main power in Southeast Asia and feared that American intervention in the region might endanger its "special relationship" with Burma. James Bowker, the first British ambassador to Burma, summarized the British position in these terms:

---

43 Matthew Foley, *The Cold War and National Assertion*, 77.
44 Joseph Nye, *Soft Power: The Means to Success in World Politics* (New York: PublicAffairs, 2004), 45.
45 United States Office of Public Affairs, Department of State, *Burma: Outlines of a New Nation* (Washington: US Government Printing Office, 1951), 8.
46 The Fulbright programme was founded in 1946 to promote "international good will through the exchange of students in the fields of education, culture and science"; United States Department of State, Bureau of Educational and Cultural Affairs, "The Fulbright Programme, the Early Years", accessed 19 June 2020, https://eca.state.gov/fulbright/about-fulbright/history/early-years.
47 NAUK, BW 19/7, Representative's annual report, 1952–1953, 3.
48 Foley, *The Cold War and National Assertion*, 88.

> While we should continue to encourage the Americans to take an active and positive interest in Burma we should disabuse them of any idea that we ourselves are no longer able to play a useful role here. We should on the contrary try to convince them of what I am sure is the truth, namely that our former associations with the Burmese and our policy of giving them their independence give us still a special position here which is not enjoyed by any other power.[49]

In other words, the FO hoped to rely on its diplomatic ally in the Cold War (and especially its large financial means), while influencing the American decision-making process regarding Burma. British authorities considered that the United States had neither Britain's prestige nor expertise in the country. Besides, even though Britain and the United States belonged to the same bloc in the Cold War, British and American policymaking regarding Burma differed on a number of issues. The British for instance condemned American clandestine actions in Burma in the early 1950s, aimed to support Guomindang troops that found refuge in northeastern Burma after the end of the Chinese civil war against Chinese communists. They feared this foreign intervention into Burmese domestic affairs might alienate the Burmese government from the Western bloc.

The diplomatic divergences between the two Western powers were reflected in the cultural field. British authorities' distrust of American ambitions that could jeopardize their dominant position in the region found an echo in British Council officials' suspicions towards the USIS' cultural effort in Burma. Successive British Council representatives were mostly concerned by the possibility that the United States might overtake them in the cultural field. While, in their reports, they presented the British Council as a model for other cultural ventures and insisted on their long-standing experience in Burma – which in fact may have been to the advantage of the Americans who did not share Britain's colonial past – they regretted the institution's restrained budget. In comparison, the USIS' budget was considerable. The representative reminded British Council staff in London that the amount of money spent by the United States on its library represented one and a half years of the British Council's total budget provision.[50] The USIS employed 35 people at the time; in comparison, until 1950, the British Council Representative was the only London-appointed official. Finally, Jenkins noted that the "premises [of the United States Information Centre] would contain the British Council's four times over."[51] For British officials, the American involvement in the cultural field therefore represented a

---

[49] NAUK, FO 371/83122, letter from James Bowker, British Ambassador to Burma, to Sir Robert Scott, Deputy Under-Secretary of State for Foreign Affairs, 2 March 1950.
[50] NAUK, BW 19/7, Representative's annual report, 1950–1951, 1.
[51] Ibid.

threat to British Council activities: "[the Americans] have now started functions on exactly similar lines to those we have been running for three and a half years and with their extra comfort and ability to spend money on those functions, this will undoubtedly affect our impoverished efforts adversely."[52]

To increase their cultural influence in Burma, the Americans relied on a large diversity of sources of funding. The important financial means of private American foundations such as the Fulbright Foundation or the Ford Foundation enabled many Burmese students to go to the United States. Interestingly, the private status of these foundations also helped them evade close Burmese government scrutiny. For example, Burmese officials did not consider the educational opportunities offered by the Fulbright Foundation, in contrast to the British Council, part of a foreign scholarship scheme. While the former establishment could select and fund its own Burmese scholars for further studies, therefore, the British Council could not.[53]

The diversity of actors driving the American cultural effort in Burma also helped shape the multidisciplinary nature of US cultural endeavours. Unlike the British Council, which mostly promoted cultural activities and English language classes in the early 1950s, an important part of the American cultural budget was spent on the scientific and technological fields, in keeping with large-scale American programmes of technical assistance to Southeast Asia launched in the early 1950s. The United States, for instance, financed the opening of an American Teaching Institute in 1951, offering classes in the humanities (language and literature), but also vocational training in various subjects such as cinema projection and librarianship. Unlike the British who focused on sending English professors to teach at the University of Rangoon, the Americans provided professors and free equipment for the Engineering Department of the university in the early 1950s.[54]

Therefore, the two Western powers' cultural promotion efforts differed in terms of means and strategies. The British Council preferred to showcase the "elite" aspects of British culture – what is commonly referred to as "high culture"[55] – by relying primarily on English literature. Every year, the British Council organized a Shakespeare-related event in Rangoon, in the form of conferences, exhibitions, radio programmes or plays. Historian James Lee Taylor analyzed

---

52 Ibid.
53 NAUK, BW 19/7, Representative's annual report, 1953–1954, 5.
54 NAUK, BW 19/7, Representative's annual report, 1951–1952, 3.
55 Joseph Nye makes a distinction between high culture and popular culture: the former term comprises literature, arts, and education, while the second refers to mass entertainment, such as the cinema; Nye, *Soft Power*, 11.

plays by Shakespeare that were produced abroad by the British Council, both in the context of decolonization and the Cold War, to show that the famous British playwright played a symbolic role. Considered by the British Council as the "exemplary figure of transnational high culture," Shakespeare was deemed capable of encouraging interactions between intellectual elites around the world.[56] Shakespeare, as well as British high culture generally speaking, were thus part of the elite-based strategy of the British Council, intended to penetrate the Burmese cultural scene from the top. American cultural propaganda relied on a combination of mass culture (with for instance Hollywood film projections) and elite culture – particularly through scientific and academic exchanges – to shape minds. According to political scientists Jean-Claude Allain and Robert Frank, the power of attraction of the American model and the success of its export abroad were precisely linked to its capacity to influence the lives of both the elites and the masses.[57]

The cinema, in particular, became one of the main tools of the American government's anti-communist campaign in Southeast Asia during the Cold War. The United States already wielded an important cultural influence in Burma thanks to the cinema before the Second World War; its film industry had a near-monopoly over the projection of entertainment films to the Burmese public in the country's main cities. After the war, the USIS continued to dominate the film sector. It produced and shot films directly on Burmese territory, most of the time to illustrate simple ideas about citizenship or democracy.[58] In the 1950s, the Americans intended to preserve their monopoly in the field of cinema. The USIS signed a series of long-term contracts with most cinemas in Rangoon to prevent the communist powers from showing their films to the Burmese public. To avoid being labelled as propaganda, American films were often projected in Burmese cinemas without mentioning they were "USIS" products.[59] British Council Representative H.T. Lawrence, who succeeded Jenkins in 1955, underlined the double reach of American cultural involvement in Burma, interweaving high and popular culture. Lawrence described, on the one hand, American action in the scientific field, with for instance the gift of a large technical library about nuclear power to the Burmese government, aimed at putting forward its peaceful uses – part of the "Atoms for Peace" programme launched

---

[56] James Lee Taylor, "Shakespeare, Decolonization and the Cold War" (PhD diss., The Open University, 2018), 31.
[57] Jean-Claude Allain and Robert Frank, "Les Composantes de la Puissance," in *Pour l'histoire des relations internationales*, Robert Frank ed. (Paris: PUF, 2012), 159.
[58] Nicholas Cull, *The Cold War and the United States Information Agency: American Propaganda and Public Diplomacy, 1945–1989* (Cambridge: University Press, 2008), 109.
[59] Brazinsky, 142–43.

by the Eisenhower administration in 1953.⁶⁰ On the other hand, he accentuated the tours undertaken by world-famous American dancers or singers such as Martha Graham, a figurehead of contemporary dance, in Burma in December 1955.⁶¹ Combining modern technical expertise (targeted at the Burmese scientific or intellectual community) with mass entertainment (which reached a larger audience), the Americans mounted a highly visible cultural offensive in Burma.

American cultural propaganda also aimed to persuade the Burmese public to embrace the American version of progress and modernity – something the British Council could not effectively compete against. Certain international events organised in Rangoon saw the participation of both the British Council and the USIS. Compared to the American exhibits, the outdated British installations in fact undercut their reputation. In January 1950, the two cultural organizations took part in an industrial exhibition in Rangoon. After the event, Representative Jenkins regrettably stated that the British section, consisting of only photographs of industrial objects, was "unconvincing and dull" in contrast to the "excellent" displays put up by the Americans.⁶² Jenkins praised the Americans' modern equipment, efficient lighting, and unequalled publicity techniques. But American competition provided an incentive for the British Council to enhance its efforts to promote the British cause. Jenkins asked the British Council in London to send him new objects or media that would give a more modern image of British culture, such as sports photographs or recently designed machines. He concluded by saying that "this was one occasion when the Americans could teach us something."⁶³

By the mid-1950s, American cultural activities had increased tremendously and largely overtaken British cultural efforts. In 1956, the British Council Representative remarked: "The Fulbright Foundation, the Ford Foundation, the USIS Library, the Asia Foundation have all flourished."⁶⁴ Even in sectors formerly dominated by the British, such as university exchanges – prestigious British universities such as the School of Oriental and African Studies and the London School of Economics had been the traditional academic partners of the University of Rangoon – the United States managed to gain ground. Burma specialist Hugh Tinker reveals that, in the mid-1950s, the number of Burmese students choosing to pursue their studies at a British university were fewer than those

---

60 Cull, 104.
61 NAUK, BW 19/7, Representative's annual report, 1955–1956, 1.
62 NAUK, BW 19/6, J.E.V. Jenkins, report on industrial exhibition, January 1950, 1–2.
63 Ibid, 2.
64 NAUK, BW 19/7, Representative's annual report, 1955–1956, 1.

choosing to study at an American university.⁶⁵ Looking at the broader picture, he nevertheless mocks American and British competition in post-independence Burma: "One absurd item is the small-scale rivalry between the representatives of Britain and the United States for the privilege of being 'top Power' in independent Burma."⁶⁶

Indeed, in the context of the early Cold War, the main threat to Britain's position in Burma came from the communist powers. Both the Soviet Union and China started developing diplomatic relations with Burma in the early 1950s. Encouraging the concurrent development of cultural ties with the country formed part of their broader strategy of wielding influence in the newly independent states of Asia. In 1950, China opened an embassy in Rangoon, and the first Chinese cultural mission was sent to Burma the following year. The Burma-China Friendship Association was also founded in late 1951, but its initial actions mostly concerned Burma's Chinese community. According to historian Gregg Brazinsky, the Chinese diaspora remained the main target of the Chinese government in the first few years after its proclamation, as it aimed at forging networks of support to the communist regime across Asia. In the 1950s, shows and cultural events specifically devised for the Chinese communities abroad were organised by China, such as in Rangoon in 1955.⁶⁷ The Soviet Union opened an embassy in Rangoon in 1951 and in the same year formed the Burma-Soviet Cultural Association. Although it was presented as being primarily a Burmese association, it was in fact an institution promoting Soviet cultural diplomacy in Burma.

An MI5 agent, posted in Rangoon between 1951 and 1954 to monitor communist insurgencies inside the country, reported on the establishment of Soviet and Chinese cultural missions in Burma, which he immediately described as propaganda "to strengthen and propagate the ideas of the left and to direct the attention of the Burmese public towards the communist countries and their achievements in the non-political sphere."⁶⁸ Even though these two cultural associations were not very active at first, the FO and British intelligence saw the

---

65 Tinker, *The Union of Burma*, 210.
66 Ibid, 369.
67 Brazinsky, 162.
68 NAUK, FO 371/101004, letter from the British Embassy in Rangoon (Chancery) to the Southeast [Asia?] Department of the Foreign Office, 30 January 1952, 1. Although it may seem odd that Burma should fall under MI5's responsibility, which normally deals with British territories and Commonwealth countries, it actually reflects the institutional gap in which Burma found itself, for British policymakers, in the first few years after independence, as a former colony that had left the Commonwealth; Calder Walton, *Empire of Secrets: British Intelligence, the Cold War and the Twilight of Empire* (London: HarperPress, 2013), 801.

emergence of such cultural centres as evidence of the Soviet Union and China trying to turn the attention of the Burmese public towards communist countries. Interestingly enough, the meaning of the term "propaganda," used in British Council papers to refer to Soviet and Chinese cultural activities in the 1950s, was very different from that of the British institution's "propaganda" of the late 1940s. Unlike the so-called apolitical "cultural propaganda" of the British Council, Soviet and Chinese "propaganda" were perceived as both explicitly political and potentially harmful.[69]

British policymakers were particularly worried about the formation of the Soviet cultural centre in Burma. There was a representative of VOKS, the Soviet Society of Cultural Relations with Foreign Countries (ie the Soviet propaganda body), on the Burma-Soviet Cultural Association's executive committee, and the FO regarded this as a "remarkable instance of direct foreign representation in an indigenous association."[70] Even if the Soviet Union wanted to give the illusion of a local organisation directed towards establishing cultural relations with Burma and promoting Burmese and Soviet friendship, this explicit connection between the local organisation and VOKS revealed that the association was in fact part of the propaganda offensive that the Soviet Union was developing in Burma and in other Southeast Asian countries. The constitution of the newly formed association, reproduced in the *Union Gazette* of 12 January 1952, insisted on the "positive" dimension of Soviet propaganda. The Burma-Soviet Cultural Association intended to promote Soviet culture in Burma, to encourage the development of academic partnerships between the two countries, and to set up a network of Soviet libraries.[71]

Despite FO concerns, the purpose of Soviet and Chinese cultural action in Burma in the early 1950s was in reality quite similar to that of the British Council, although communist propagandists did not adopt the same strategy. Both the Chinese and Soviet governments drew on media commonly associated with the cultural influence of their respective countries to promote their ideals. Chinese cultural propaganda heavily relied on arts and crafts, which were popular abroad. For example, China put together an important exhibition displaying Chinese pottery,

---

[69] On the semantic shift of "propaganda" in British Council papers, see Alice Byrne, "Propagande culturelle ou relations culturelles? La mission ambiguë du British Council, 1934–1954," *Transatlantica* 2 (2018): 1–15.
[70] NAUK, FO 371/101004, letter from the British Embassy to the Foreign Office, 30 January 1952, 1.
[71] NAUK, FO 371/101004, constitution of the Burma-Soviet Cultural Association in *Union Gazette* (12 January 1952).

porcelain and lacquerware at Rangoon City Hall in November 1954.[72] The Soviet Union opted for ballet and Russian classical music and organized several tours in Burma, culminating with enormous gala concerts including large numbers of dancers and musicians, such as in 1955.[73]

To illustrate the grandeur of the communist model of development, the communist governments' cultural strategy relied on transmitting a simple message. The Soviets and Chinese laid emphasis on large-scale performances and mass media, considered as much-too-obvious propaganda by British Council officials as opposed to the elite-based strategy of the British Council. In his annual report for 1951–1952, Jenkins depicted the first Chinese cultural mission with much contempt, stating that it consisted of 15 to 20 representatives from communist China "who sped about Rangoon in convoy in expensive-looking cars speaking in Chinese to anyone able and prepared to listen"; he also described the "so-called Exhibition of Chinese Art," which was, according to him, mainly composed of tacky propaganda photographs. Even so, this travelling exhibition, easily accessible to the spectator and devised for a large audience, appeared to have been well received by the Burmese public.[74] Although Chinese and Soviet cultural activities remained somewhat spotty in the early 1950s, they intensified their cultural offensive in Burma in the latter part of the 1950s. Cultural propaganda was a major part of the Chinese government's "People's Diplomacy," launched after the Korean War. According to American secret intelligence services, China sent more than 5,800 dancers, comedians, and artists to 33 countries in 1955.[75] The increase in the number of Chinese- and Soviet-financed cultural events also illustrated the diplomatic rapprochement between Burma and the two communist countries.

British Council reports show that this type of monumental propaganda, whose approach could be described as "positive" as it aimed at advertising the two countries' positive aspects, was accompanied by a much more "offensive" propaganda, in particular conducted by the Soviet Union. In the mid-1950s, the Soviet Union devised a new strategy which consisted of flooding the book market in Burma with cheap material in English. By circulating a large number of English-language classics with attractive covers for a small price, "frequently [. . .] chosen to reflect the less attractive side of British life and history," the Soviet Union wished to spread an anti-British discourse in Burma. In other words, they chose British tools to attack the British model.[76] The offensive side of Soviet

---

72 NAUK, BW 19/7, Representative's annual report, 1954–1955, 2.
73 NAUK, BW 19/7, Representative's annual report, 1955–1956, 2.
74 NAUK, BW 19/7, Representative's annual report, 1951–1952, 3.
75 Brazinsky, 134–35.
76 NAUK, BW 19/7, Representative's annual report, 1957–1958, 4.

propaganda, by directly attacking Britain, proved quite effective. Books imported from Britain were more expensive, difficult to access, and therefore less popular with the Burmese. The flooding of the book market with cheap books also represented unfair commercial competition for the British. Simultaneously, the Soviets pursued their "positive" propaganda efforts in the book sector. They sold so-called "happy books" in the country's bookshops, which painted a positive image of contemporary Russia. They likewise promoted Soviet scientific and medical books and accomplishments to Burma's intellectual and scientific community.[77] Indeed, in the latter part of the 1950s, the Soviet Union started to target the intellectual elite of the country and, much in the same way as the British Council at the time, the Soviet government championed academic exchanges between the two countries as a way to reinfore diplomatic links.

The Burmese Government's Observation Missions in the Field of Education: A "Synthesis" of Western and Eastern Educational Models

However, the Burmese government distrusted the external powers' involvement in the cultural field and looked for ways to limit their propaganda efforts.[78] Between 1951 and 1953, the Burmese government imposed a ban on all foreign cultural activities in the field of education. Foreign films and foreign magazines could no longer be used in schools, and access to schools by foreign teachers was heavily restricted. In 1953, the British Council Representative wrote: "We must report restrictions on all work in schools."[79] In spite of the British Council's numerous attempts to engage in talks with the Burmese Ministry of Foreign Affairs regarding the status of the institution – to show that the British Council was a "non-diplomatic cultural and educational body" that should not be included in such official censorship[80] – the ban was enforced equally on all foreign cultural missions and only lifted in the mid-1950s. For Jenkins, the British Council's cultural activities did not compare and should not be amalgamated with Soviet and Chinese propaganda, held entirely responsible for the implementation

---

77 NAUK, BW 19/13, "Propaganda in Burma," 11 March 1958, 1.
78 NADB, AG 12/9, Acc: 631, speech by U Thant at the Educational Conference of the Teachers Union of the City of New York (1948).
79 NAUK, BW 19/7, Representative's annual report, 1952–1953, 4.
80 Ibid.

of the ban: "The main reason is stated to be fear of propaganda work carried out by Chinese and Russian Embassies and any ban applying to them must apply to all."[81] This controversial decision underlined the Burmese government's desire to keep the ideological conflict of the Cold War at bay and presaged Burma's neutral position on the international stage in 1955.

Indeed, the Burmese government was well aware of the different Great Powers' ambitions in the broader Cold War context. Although evidence regarding Burmese reactions to these foreign cultural missions cannot be found in the Burmese government's official papers from the 1950s, the reports of Burmese educational missions sent to Western and Eastern bloc countries in the early independence era (when the AFPFL launched a series of large-scale reforms meant to shape the postcolonial state) reveal the Burmese authorities' views of their diplomatic and cultural relations with the different major powers. These reports in fact suggest that the Burmese government did not really mind foreign cultural rivalry in the country. It also sought to exploit the competition to further its more immediate objectives of nation-building. This meant borrowing from each educational model the aspects that seemed to fit the Burmese context best and refusing to embrace one entirely. This original material from Burmese archives, in particular the papers dealing with Burmese educational missions sent to communist countries, also challenges British discourses which continued, up until the 1960s, to put forward Britain's "special (cultural) relationship" with Burma, despite the much larger financial and human means deployed at that time by the other Great Powers involved in the Cold War conflict.

In the late 1940s and early 1950s, the Burmese Ministry of Education sent several small-scale missions to Britain and the United States, at a time when broad reforms were being implemented in the field of education. This section focuses on an important educational mission, composed of six Burmese officials, sent to several Western countries (Britain, Switzerland, the United States, Mexico, and Canada) in 1951 to observe and study two particular aspects of education: first, the use of school manuals, ahead of the production of Burmese language textbooks; second, the workings of technical and vocational education, before a similar system could be introduced in Burma. This mission had concrete purposes: learn from the West and undertake reforms in Burma – tasks that the members of the delegation pursued to modernize the Burmese education system in the early 1950s. The mission was based on "sampling," which gave an important leeway to the different governments of the countries that the delegation visited, free to choose the institutions they wanted to present to the

---

81 Ibid.

Burmese delegation. This of course gave them the possibility of putting forward the most positive aspects of their respective models. This method of sampling was accompanied by "friendly and informal discussions" with various actors from the educational world and the delegation brought back several documents from its mission, in particular Western reference books on education.[82]

If the important place of Britain on the mission schedule may seem surprising, at a time when Burma was trying to define its own model, sometimes in rejection of the practices imposed by the British in the colonial period (by attempting to "burmanize" education for instance), it was obvious, in the final report, that Western powers still constituted important references for the young nation looking to develop itself on a stable basis. Several recommendations formulated in the report thus came directly from what the delegation observed in Western countries, such as the creation of a centralized Ministry of Education overseeing all education-related matters, including vocational education.[83] Another government report, published later but referring to the 1951 observation mission, noted that this "very fruitful tour" was followed by concrete reforms in the sphere of education in Burma. The positions of Director of Technical Education and Director of Text-Book Procurement were created after the mission, within a much larger Ministry of Education than before.[84] Moreover, this visit enabled Western countries to advertise what they had to offer to the young nation. The report recommended, upon a suggestion by the receiving governments, that Burma employ foreign expertise (here meaning Western expertise) to develop technical education in the country and train Burmese engineers.[85] After visiting some Burmese students who were sent to a Western university, the delegation affirmed the high-quality training their citizens received: "The mission is glad to report that the Union has in these students now being trained abroad a body of young men and women who are burning with enthusiasm to serve their country."[86] The positive feedback of the delegation suggests that the Burmese authorities still valued, in the early 1950s, Western practices when they sought to fashion their own education policies and systems. The academic exchanges, in other words, furthered the Western strategy of influence.

---

[82] NADB, AG 3/13, Acc. 702, Burma educational observation and study mission, interim report, 19 May 1952, 2.
[83] Ibid, 13.
[84] NADB, AG 4/5 (21), Acc. 4262, "Progress in Education in the Union of Burma during Public Instruction," 1952–1953.
[85] NADB, AG 3/13, Acc. 702, interim report, 17.
[86] Ibid, 19.

However, in the second half of the 1950s, after the Bandung Conference which marked the symbolic emergence of Burma on the international stage and expressed the nation-state's desire to remain neutral in the Cold War, the Burmese government increasingly looked in new directions to continue reforming the educational field. A second, large-scale educational mission was organised by the Burmese Ministry of Education in September-October 1958 and sent, this time, to communist countries: the Soviet Union, China, and the Socialist Republic of Romania. There were other missions of enquiry into these countries in the previous years – a delegation went to the Soviet Union in October 1956, and another to China in May 1958 – but the September-October 1958 mission distinguished itself by its scope. It covered all levels of education, from pre-school education to university, and from general to technical education; it also focused on extra-curricular activities and youth organisations. Although the report published by the Burma delegation upon its return stated that it was purely an observation mission and that the Soviet Minister of Education had no intention of engaging in "propagandist exhibition or talk,"[87] the programme of the delegation's visit to the Soviet Union suggested otherwise. It is quite obvious that Soviet officials supervising the mission used the visit as a pretext to promote the communist model and emphasise the Soviet Union's technical prowess. The Burmese delegation was taken to a number of institutions or places that had little or no relevance to education, such as pavilions dedicated to nuclear power, modern machines, and spacecraft, at the agricultural and industrial exhibition of Moscow.[88]

Several points stand out in the report, notably the highly centralized and state-controlled system of education in the Soviet Union or the absence of tuition fees in primary, secondary, and higher education in China (as opposed to the semi-private models of education in Britain and the United States). Many issues dealt with during the observation mission in communist countries were of particular interest to the Burmese government, but did not resonate with officials in the Western countries that the Burmese previously visited. For instance, the Burmese delegation was interested in the medium of instruction in schools. While the British at the time insisted on the importance of maintaining good standards of teaching and learning English in Burma, the Burmese were struggling to impose a single language policy on the entire population, including the ethnic minorities, in an attempt to define Burmese identity. In that respect, the

---

87 NADB, 4/5 (21), Acc: 15297, report of the Burma education delegation to the Union of Soviet Socialist Republics, the People's Republics of Rumania and China, 1958.
88 Ibid, 6.

Chinese government, confronted with a similar challenge of unifying China linguistically in spite of the large diversity of minority languages spoken in the country, emerged as a more relevant model for the Burmese government. The report explained that "the linguistic problems of the Soviet Union and the People's [Republic of] China are of no small magnitude, but these problems have been solved [. . .] by throwing away the barren, narrow and poisonous parochial sentiments in the larger interest of the Union or Republic for harmony and solidarity."[89] The active promotion of the Burmese language, to the detriment of minority language teaching in schools, was derived from Chinese and Soviet policies of forced linguistic integration through the imposition of a single language – and would be reinforced after General Ne Win's military coup in 1962.

The report also highlighted the importance of foreign language teaching in school and at university – a field in which China and the Soviet Union had distinguished themselves. The Burmese delegation's visit gave the Chinese an opportunity to demonstrate their skills in the field of foreign language teaching. They asked Chinese students from the University of Peking who studied (and mastered!) Burmese, as well as Burmese students learning Chinese, to act as interpreters for the delegation. This strategic approach was a way for China to put forward what Burma could gain if the two countries continued to develop their academic partnerships. Just as in the early 1950s, after the Burmese delegation's educational mission sent to Western countries, the report published after the 1958 Eastern bloc mission had a direct and concrete influence on the implementation of reforms by the Burmese government. Burmese officials described with admiration the Institute of Foreign Languages of Peking and encouraged the Ministry of Education to open a similar school in Burma.[90] A few years later, Burma did open its own Institute of Foreign Languages, offering courses in Japanese, Russian, German and French.[91] English classes were conspicuous by their absence from the list and perhaps indicated that the Burmese government was increasingly leaving aside its traditional partners on the international stage.

In any case, the rejection of the old model of education imported into Burma by the British was explicit in the report. The delegation noted: "We should discard the practice of resorting to the old 'frame of reference' which has no relevance to our presentation situation."[92] On the opposite side of the British model, outdated and referring to "bygone colonial days," Burmese officials were seduced by the

---

89 Ibid, 70.
90 Ibid, 12, 69.
91 NAUK, BW 19/10, Representative's annual report, 1963–1964, 5.
92 NADB, 4/5 (21), Acc: 15297, report of the Burma education delegation, 69.

Chinese and Soviet models which "combine[d] studies with productive labour," that is to say associated more closely theory and practice, and appeared to be more in touch with the development and nation-building objectives that concerned Burma.[93] The Burmese delegation's report finally encouraged the Burmese government to move away from the Western model, so as to adopt "revolutionary thinking in education."[94] Towards the end of the 1950s, the "special relationship" between Burma and the former colonial power in the cultural field, put forward in British Council or FO papers, was perhaps not so "special" any more. On the contrary, in the latter part of the 1950s, the Burmese government increasingly looked for new models to shape its policies in the field of education.

Conclusions

In the late 1940s and early 1950s, because of Burma's increasing rejection of the British connection and the growing influence of communist powers in the country, British grand strategy in Burma relied more heavily on culture. To meet the FO's strategic objectives in both the post-independence and Cold War contexts, the British Council, whose first centre in Burma opened on the eve of independence, devised cultural activities deemed capable of promoting a Western-type democratic model in Burma and diverting Burmese politicians from the lure of communism. However, in spite of their strong belief that they were still Burma's top diplomatic and cultural partner in the early post-independence period, the British were in fact starting to lose ground to the other major powers involved in the Cold War conflict. Within the Western bloc, the Americans developed similar types of cultural action and language courses but benefited from more substantial funding than the British Council. Within the communist bloc, China and the Soviet Union devised different cultural strategies to promote their respective models, relying on large-scale performances and exhibitions to reach a larger, and perhaps less elitist, portion of the Burmese population; their cultural offensive intensified greatly in the latter part of the 1950s. Nevertheless, the Burmese government was well aware of the propaganda underlying such cultural activities sponsored by foreign powers and decided to take part in organizing the Bandung Conference in April 1955, to express its commitment to neutrality in the Cold War conflict.

---

93 Ibid.
94 Ibid.

From the mid-1950s, the Burmese government increasingly drew from different educational models and, by looking alternatively towards Western and Eastern countries, Burma attempted to manipulate the Cold War conflict to serve its own nation-building goals.[95] In 1957, the Director of the Far East Department of the British Council wrote that "assistance was received by Burma from a number of countries and cultural exchanges were arranged between communist and non-communist countries alike," to highlight Burma's refusal to favour one bloc over the other, and the Burmese government's strategy of accepting financial and educational aid from every country that offered it, without making any distinction between Western and communist states.[96]

---

95 Foley, *The Cold War and National Assertion*.
96 NAUK, BW 19/7, comment by the Director of the Far East Department, 21 May 1957.

S.R. Joey Long
Adversaries, Allies and the Shaping of US Grand Strategy: The Eisenhower Administration and the 1954 Geneva Conference

During the mid-1950s, officials from both sides of the Iron Curtain engaged each other to bring order to political developments in Asia. Meeting in Berlin between January and February 1954, policymakers from Britain, France, the Soviet Union, and the United States agreed to reconvene in Geneva in April to address the conflicts in Korea and Indochina. Geneva hosted not only the four major powers but also welcomed officials from Beijing. Representatives from the Democratic Republic of Korea and the Republic of Korea were present at the Korean leg of the conference. Officials from Cambodia, Laos, the Democratic Republic of Vietnam, and the State of Vietnam discussed Indochina. Meeting for close to three months, the delegates failed to resolve the Korean conflict. They halted, however, the fighting between the French and Vietminh in Indochina, and partitioned Vietnam along the 17th parallel. Undersecretary of State Walter Bedell Smith, who headed the American delegation in Geneva, thought the non-communists had denied the communists a victory in Korea.[1] On the Indochina question, he remarked that "the results are the best that could be expected in the circumstances."[2] US President Dwight Eisenhower agreed, recognizing that the Vietminh had militarily defeated the French.[3]

Scholars predominantly think that the Eisenhower administration erred in its approach to the Geneva Conference. They argue that US officials, especially Secretary of State John Foster Dulles and Assistant Secretary of State Walter S. Robertson, were obstructive at the proceedings, did not favour a negotiated settlement, and hoped the talks would end in failure. American diplomats refused to find common ground when they interacted with their adversaries. They alienated their allies who sought to find workable solutions to ostensibly intractable problems. They contributed in the main to the collapse of the Korean phase

---

[1] *FRUS, 1952–1954*, Vol. 16, Smith's Remarks, 23 June 1954, 393 [hereafter volume and page numbers].
[2] *FRUS, 1952–1954*, 16:1552.
[3] DDEL, Ann Whitman File, Administration Series, Folder: Gruenther, Alfred 1954 (3), Eisenhower to Alfred Gruenther, 19 July 1954.

of the conference. And they alienated many by their conduct during the Indochina chapter of the proceedings.[4] In contrast to the critics, some scholars laud the Eisenhower government's handling of the negotiations. They credit US officials, especially Smith, for adapting well to new developments, playing the hand they were dealt, and generating the most optimal conference outcomes.[5] Others argue the Eisenhower administration achieved short-term tactical success at Geneva, but imposed longer-run and problematic commitments on the United States towards Indochina.[6]

This chapter wades into that historiographical and historical debate by assessing the Eisenhower administration's endeavours to further US objectives at the Geneva Conference. It engages the historical episode from the perspective of grand strategy. Scholars who write about grand strategy predominantly

---

[4] For the Korean phase of the conference, see Yong-Pyo Hong, "Why Have Attempts to Settle Inter-Korean Conflict Failed?: Lessons for Peace Building in the Korean Peninsula," *The Korean Journal of International Relations* 48, 5 (2008), 141–42; and J.Y. Ra, "The Politics of Conference: The Political Conference on Korea in Geneva, 26 April–15 June 1954," *Journal of Contemporary History* 34, 3 (July 1999), 414–16. For the Indochinese phase of the conference, see David L. Anderson, *Trapped by Success: The Eisenhower Administration and Vietnam, 1953–1961* (New York: Columbia University Press, 1991), 41–64; Richard Immerman, "The United States and the Geneva Conference of 1954: A New Look," *Diplomatic History* 14 (1990), 494–516; Kathryn C. Statler, *Replacing France: The Origins of American Intervention in Vietnam* (Lexington, KY: The University Press of Kentucky, 2007), 85–114, 284–85; Kevin Ruane and Matthew Jones, *Anthony Eden, Anglo-American Relations and the 1954 Indochina Crisis* (London: Bloomsbury Academic, 2019); and James Waite, *The End of the First Indochina War: A Global History* (New York: Routledge, 2012).

[5] For the Korean phase, see H.W. Brands, "The Dwight D. Eisenhower Administration, Syngman Rhee, and the 'Other' Geneva Conference of 1954," *Pacific Historical Review* 56, 1 (1987), 59–85; and Sydney D. Bailey, *The Korean Armistice* (London: Palgrave Macmillan, 1992), 150–70, 207–08. For the Indochina phase, see H.W. Brands, *Cold Warriors: Eisenhower's Generation and American Foreign Policy* (New York: Columbia University Press, 1988), 71–92; D.K.R. Crosswell, *Beetle: The Life of General Walter Bedell Smith* (Lexington, KY: The University Press of Kentucky, 2010), 71–94; Fredrik Logevall, *Embers of War: The Fall of an Empire and the Making of America's Vietnam* (New York: Random House, 2012), 549–613; and Robert F. Randle, *Geneva 1954: The Settlement of the Indochinese War* (Princeton NJ: University Press, 1969), 555–57.

[6] George C. Herring, " 'A Good Stout Effort': John Foster Dulles and the Indochina Crisis, 1954–1955," in *John Foster Dulles and the Diplomacy of the Cold War* ed. Richard H. Immerman (Princeton NJ: University Press, 1990), 213–34; Gary R. Hess, "Redefining the American Position in Southeast Asia: The United States and the Geneva and Manila Conferences," in *Dien Bien Phu and the Crisis of Franco-American Relations, 1954–1955*, ed. Lawrence S. Kaplan et al (Wilmington, DE: Scholarly Resources Inc, 1990), 123–48; as well as Anderson and Statler's works cited above.

focus on statecraft and have proposed a number of definitions of the term.[7] Building on their scholarship and conforming to the ideas advanced in the Introduction of this book, this essay defines grand strategy as a process by which an actor – collectively those residing at the "summit of authority" or "summit of command" – identifies the ends, generates the means, deploys the limited resources, and employs multidimensional ways to further the objectives of its security policy. In other words, grand strategy entails the actor identifying what ends it seeks to achieve. It entails the actor using its limited resources to further its stated objectives. It entails the actor determining how to generate its preferred outcome – what actions need to be undertaken to achieve success.

Grand strategy also obliges the actor to deal with the means and ways its competitive adversaries, as well as those of its not always cooperative allies, employ to advance their objectives. The actor-adversary-ally relationship is ultimately dynamic and often unpredictable. That interaction creates a dynamic that could move developments in various trajectories. As Chief of the Prussian/German General Staff Helmuth von Moltke the Elder once indicated: " . . . no plan of operations extends with any certainty beyond the first contact with the main hostile force."[8] The same goes for plans derived from grand strategy. Studying history can help one gain insight into how actors in the past pursued their grand strategy against equally capable and forceful adversaries and allies.

Employing that understanding of grand strategy, this chapter assesses the Eisenhower government's endeavours to confront the communists at Geneva in 1954. More precisely, it evaluates the nature and quality of the Americans' interactions with their adversaries and allies as Washington sought to counter communist advances in Asia. Given that adversaries and allies can decisively shape an actor's pursuit of its grand strategy, it is necessary to ascertain the multinational challenges influencing US officials to act in Geneva and Washington.

This chapter argues that the Eisenhower administration's adversaries and allies did much to shape the manner in which Washington pursued its grand strategy in Asia in 1954. During the Korean phase of the Geneva Conference, a strong-willed Korean leader played a significant role in undermining the negotiations. During the Indochinese phase, adversaries and allies narrowed the range of options the Americans could pursue to achieve their objectives. The

---

[7] See Hal Brands, *What Good Is Grand Strategy? Power and Purpose in American Statecraft from Harry S. Truman to George W. Bush* (Ithaca, NY: Cornell University Press, 2014), 3; Paul Kennedy, "Grand Strategy in War and Peace: Toward a Broader Definition," in *Grand Strategies in War and Peace*, ed. Paul Kennedy (New Haven, CT: Yale University Press, 1991), 5.
[8] Daniel Hughes, ed., *Moltke on the Art of War: Selected Writings* (New York: Presidio Press, 2009), 92.

Geneva discussions ultimately left the Korean question unresolved and the stability of Indochina dependent on the willingness of the signatories to abide by the terms of the settlement. The whole episode underscores the challenges leaders confront in crafting and effecting a grand strategy. However lucid and sharp they articulate their strategic vision, and however well resourced and skilled they are in pursuing it, their adversaries and allies will have their say in the making and implementation of their grand strategy.

The rest of this chapter is divided into four sections. The first section considers the Eisenhower government's security concerns and grand strategy towards Asia and the Geneva Conference. It also reviews the interests of other actors concerned about developments in the region. The second gauges the US diplomatic manoeuvres during the Korean phase of the negotiations. The third examines the Indochina phase of the discussions. The chapter concludes by appraising Washington's moves during the conference and their outcomes.

Security Considerations and Grand Strategy

Assuming office in January 1953, Dwight Eisenhower and his administration officials took an active interest in developments in Asia. Their view of the region was not fundamentally different from that of the Harry Truman government. Like the Democrats, the Republican administration did not want an adversary to dominate and undermine US interests in Asia. They thought Beijing and Moscow cooperated to expand their influence in the region. The two appeared to be exploiting regional political uncertainties and anti-colonial conflicts to further the communist cause.[9] Washington had to respond.

The Eisenhower government regarded the markets and resources of Asia as vital American interests. It envisaged non-communist Asia and Europe as one interconnected political economic space, functioning to further Washington's global containment of Chinese and Soviet power. Southeast Asia's rich natural resources and dollar earnings underpinned Japan and Western Europe's industrial recovery. Southeast Asia's economic development would also benefit from the maintenance of strong economic links with non-communist Northeast Asia and Western Europe. If Washington did not resist communist aggression against the political economic order that it had helped establish in Asia, it could lose important allies and

---

9 Robert Ferrell, ed., *The Eisenhower Diaries* (New York: Norton, 1981), 223.

undermine its containment of the communist bloc.¹⁰ Likewise, the Americans were keen to ensure that France ratify the treaty establishing the European Defence Community – a supranational organization developed to militarily strengthen the security of Western Europe. They did not want developments in Indochina to undercut that endeavour in Europe.¹¹

Besides the broader political economic considerations, American strategists were determined to safeguard US access to the network of forward bases in Asia. These bases furnished Washington with defence in depth. If global war erupted with the communists, the Americans planned to fight their adversaries in the region. US naval forces stationed in other oceans would mass for a confrontation with the communists along the Asian coastline or in the Pacific Ocean. To sail a fleet from the Indian Ocean to the South China Sea, US strategists needed to ensure that American warships would not have to run a gauntlet of hostile forces lined along the Southeast Asian littoral. American officials thus paid attention to developments in Northeast and Southeast Asia, concerned that the fall of non-communist states to communism would undercut American military plans and threaten US long-term security.¹²

Finally, the Eisenhower administration was determined to uphold its repute and the credibility of US power. The Republicans had taken the Democrats to task for ostensibly losing China to communism. They now had to back their words with actions in Asia. Losing literally more ground to communists at Geneva could seriously damage the Republican presidency's domestic electoral appeal. If Washington failed to counter communist aggression in Asia, American officials further feared their foes, friends, and the non-aligned or undecided might think the United States unable or unwilling to confront the communists. A feeble US response could embolden the communists to intensify their offensives against the non-communist world. A weak American reaction could induce friends to review their relations with Washington and seek benefits elsewhere. Governments that were undecided might also align themselves with the communists rather than the American-led bloc to protect their interests. Entertaining such ideas, US policymakers resolved to stop communist gains in Asia. They

---

10 *FRUS, 1952–1954*, 12:368, NSC 5405, 16 January 1954; DDEL, WHOOSANSAR, NSC Series, Briefing Notes Subseries, Box 16, NSC Briefing Notes, 15 June 1959.
11 Logevall, *Embers of War*, 311–12.
12 DDEL, WHONSCSP, OCB Central File Series, Box 79, OCB 091.4 SEA (File #1) (8) [September 1953–July 1954], Special Report to NSC, 24 June 1954.

could not allow the communist powers to isolate and strategically disadvantage the United States.[13]

The Eisenhower administration, then, was in no mood to be equivocal about American intentions in Asia. US policymakers did not think it strategically prudent to be ambiguous either. They thought the Truman administration had done just that – be ambiguous. Secretary of State Dean Acheson seemingly encouraged communist aggression on the Korean peninsula when his public remarks in January 1950 suggested that Seoul was excluded from the American defensive perimeter in the Pacific. The Eisenhower government did not want to make the same mistake. As Dulles stated in a National Security Council meeting in March 1953: "There must be no repetition of the fuzzy situation in Korea in the spring of 1950, which constituted an invitation to the Soviets to move against South Korea." Washington must be firm in handling the communists. It should also "hold the vital outpost positions around the periphery of the Soviet bloc" and combat communist expansion. These "positions" included Indochina, Iran, Japan, South Asia, and Western Europe. Dulles "warned that the loss of any one of such positions would produce a chain reaction which would cost us the remainder." He did not see Moscow starting a general war to absorb them into the communist camp. He envisaged the Soviets employing other methods such as supporting "civil wars" to bring contested areas under their control. The United States should thwart their plans or lose the ability to extend and protect the boundaries of the so-called "free world" from communist machinations. Containing the communist advance, Washington could then apply "pressures . . . psychological or otherwise" to "force a collapse of the Kremlin regime or else transform the Soviet orbit from a union of satellites dedicated to aggression, into a coalition for defence only." Eisenhower agreed, endorsing Dulles's "warning against any relaxation of [US] pressure on the USSR."[14]

While American leaders concurred that the United States should sustain the fight against the communists, they did not rule out the employment of diplomacy as an instrument of statecraft to further their objectives in Asia. Diplomacy was one key component of NSC 162/2 – Eisenhower's "New Look" containment strategy. NSC 162/2 determined that US officials should not rule out negotiations with the communists to achieve "settlements . . . compatible with basic US security

---

[13] Ibid. See also Nancy Bernkopf Tucker, *The China Threat: Memories, Myths and Realities in the 1950s* (New York: Columbia University Press, 2012) on the political pressure that the China lobby and Republican right consistently put on the administration to be uncompromising towards China during the 1950s.

[14] *FRUS, 1952–1954*, 2:267–68, NSC Meeting, 31 March 1953; see also Richard H. Immerman, *Empire for Liberty: A History of American Imperialism from Benjamin Franklin to Paul Wolfowitz* (Princeton NJ: University Press, 2010), 163–95.

interests." The Eisenhower government understood the positive effects bilateral and multilateral talks with the communists could have on US relations with its allies and the non-aligned world. They could assure allies that Washington was not bent on starting a general war and compelling its friends to fight the communists. They could also correct the impression among the non-aligned that the United States was the actor that intensified global tensions.[15] Still, while expressing its willingness to negotiate with the communists, the Eisenhower administration maintained it would refuse to recognize the Chinese Communist Party as the legitimate authority in Beijing. It would not permit the Chinese regime to exploit the Geneva Conference to extend its influence across Asia.[16]

American participation in the 1954 Berlin talks stemmed from those considerations and principles. Convened to address European security matters, the conference also saw the four foreign ministers discuss the Korean and Indochinese questions. They agreed to hold talks in Geneva to resolve these conflicts. Following tough negotiations, especially between Dulles and Soviet Foreign Minister Vyacheslav Molotov, the diplomats agreed to invite Beijing to participate in the conference. The final communiqué, however, stated that the Chinese presence in Geneva did not imply US recognition of Beijing.[17]

In preparation for the talks in Switzerland, US policymakers detailed the outcomes they wished to achieve. State Department officials declared that US objectives were "to avoid communist control of the [Indochina] area and, as in the case of Korea, to secure the control of the entire area by indigenous non-communist elements capable of sustaining themselves against internal subversion."[18] Undersecretary Smith stated simply that the "sole objective is to negotiate a peaceful agreement for a unified independent Korea."[19] As regards Indochina, Secretary of Defence Charles Wilson endorsed the views of the Joint Chiefs of Staff, which asserted that "no solution to the Indochina problem short of victory is acceptable." If the outcome was "a negotiated settlement which fails to provide reasonably adequate assurance of the future political and territorial integrity of Indochina, the United States should decline to associate itself with such a settlement and should pursue, directly with the governments of the Associated States and with other Allies (notably the United Kingdom), ways and means of continuing the struggles against the Viet Minh in Indochina without participation of the

---

15 *FRUS, 1952–1954*, 2:1:584–88, NSC 162/2, 30 October 1953.
16 *FRUS, 1952–1954*, 7:1:993, Meeting Record, 8 February 1954.
17 *FRUS, 1952–1954*, 7:1205, Final Communique, 14 February 1954.
18 *FRUS, 1952–1954*, 16:437, Bonsal Memorandum, 8 March 1954.
19 *FRUS, 1952–1954*, 16:458, Smith to U.S. Embassy, Taipei, 13 March 1954.

French."[20] The most important US consideration, then, was that the conference should not furnish Washington with outcomes that undercut American political economic and security interests in Asia.

However clearly stated US objectives were, American diplomats had to confront diverse challenges. Washington's opponents and allies could prove equally uncompromising in the objectives they sought to advance at Geneva. The Soviets aimed to score political points against Washington by positioning themselves as champions of diplomacy rather than confrontation. The Chinese wanted a buffer between themselves and the Americans in Asia. The Koreans on the respective sides of the demilitarized zone sought to bring the whole peninsula under their respective control. The Vietminh wanted to translate its victories on the battlefield to political gains at the conference. The French sought an end to the war in Indochina – whether by choice or necessity. The British wanted to prevent the violence in Asia from escalating into a general war.[21] If the differing aspirations between the communist and non-communist camps were stark, America's allies could likewise choose courses of action deemed unacceptable to Washington.

There were also no guarantees that the assumptions underpinning the US approach to the conference were valid. One of them was the belief that the Americans might be able to drive a wedge between the Chinese and the Soviets.[22] If the communists stood unfazed, US diplomats might not be able to squeeze out any positive gains in Geneva. Whatever the case, the Eisenhower government planned to press its case in Switzerland. Its actions bring into sharp focus the challenges and difficulties of doing grand strategy. The unpredictable course of events that grand strategists seek to tame might prove utterly uncooperative. American officials responding to developments between April and July 1954 had their work cut out for them.

---

20 *FRUS, 1952–1954*, 16:478–79, Enclosure 2, 17 March 1954; Walton S. Moody, *History of the Joint Chiefs of Staff: The Joint Chiefs of Staff and the First Indochina War, 1947–1954* (Washington: Office of Joint History, Office of the Chairman of the Joint Chiefs of Staff, 2004), 156.
21 CWIHP, Draft Outlines for Soviet Delegation, 17 March 1954; Tao Wang, "Neutralizing Indochina: The 1954 Geneva Conference and China's Efforts to Isolate the United States," *Journal of Cold War Studies*, 19 (2017), 3–42; CWIHP, Zhou Enlai, "Preliminary Opinions on Geneva Conference," 2 March 1954; Kevin Ruane, "Anthony Eden, British Diplomacy and the Origins of the Geneva Conference of 1954," *The Historical Journal* 37 (1994), 153–72.
22 *FRUS, 1952–1954*, 14:296, Enclosure to NSC 166/1.

The Korean Phase

During the Korean phase of the conference, American officials found themselves in bed with an Asian leader who sought to reunify Korea. A fiercely anti-communist politician, a complex authoritarian figure, and an ambitious nationalist determined to bring the Korean peninsula under one (his) rule, South Korean President Syngman Rhee confounded the Eisenhower administration's attempts to make him conform to its approach to the conference.[23] Rhee conformed instead to his past behaviour. He was obstructive during the 1953 armistice negotiations. He attacked the Americans for pursuing talks with the communists. He informed Eisenhower his forces were prepared to fight the Chinese, North Koreans, and Soviets on their own if the Americans signed the armistice. Rhee further attempted to undermine the armistice discussions and provoke fresh fighting between the two sides.[24] Eisenhower was infuriated with the Korean president. But he did not remove or support Rhee's removal from power.[25] Washington accepted that Seoul did not have another tough anti-communist leader who could hold the South together and resist the North Koreans. It eventually pledged to negotiate a mutual defence treaty with the Rhee government – a pact signed on 1 October 1953. In return, Rhee agreed not to block the armistice agreement.[26]

Still, Rhee remained obstructive after the ceasefire came into effect on 27 July 1953. The armistice called for a political conference to be held before the end of October 1953 "to ensure the peaceful settlement of the Korean question." Rhee repeatedly undermined the endeavours to bring that conference and other preparatory talks into session. He also threatened to resume hostilities against the North. The US government had to restrain him, with Vice President Richard Nixon dispatched to Seoul in November 1953 to warn Rhee against unilaterally starting a war with the North.[27]

Rhee's pattern of behaviour saw no dramatic change after the four powers agreed in February 1954 to discuss Korea in Geneva. In fact, the president expressed

---

23 Stephen Jin-Woo Kim, *Master of Manipulation: Syngman Rhee and the Seoul-Washington Alliance 1953–1960* (Seoul: Yonsei University Press, 2001); Yong Ick Lew, *The Making of the First Korean President: Syngman Rhee's Quest for Independence* (Honolulu: University of Hawaii Press, 2013).
24 *FRUS, 1952–1954*, 15:2:1200–05, 150th NSC Meeting, 18 June 1953.
25 Ferrell, *Eisenhower Diaries*, 248.
26 Edward Keefer, "President Dwight D. Eisenhower and the End of the Korean War," *Diplomatic History*, 10 (1986), 267–89.
27 *FRUS, 1952–1954*, 15:2:1590–93, Dulles to Nixon, 4 November 1953.

regret that Washington endorsed the initiative.[28] In March 1954, Rhee's foreign minister, Pyun Yung Tai, wrote to Secretary of State Dulles, imploring the United States to support Seoul and fight the North if the Geneva negotiations collapsed. Only then would the Rhee government consider participating in the talks.[29] A week later, Rhee repeated the message in a letter to Eisenhower. He also asked the US president to help Seoul double the size of its military and arm it. "If either of the two proposals is accepted," Rhee stated, "we shall agree to participate in the Geneva Conference."[30]

Eisenhower deflected Rhee's attempt to trap Washington into making a commitment to help Seoul fight Pyongyang. He warned that the South risked being a pariah state if it refused to peacefully resolve the Korean question.[31] Rhee replied that the communists could not be trusted to conclude a fair and enforceable peace settlement.[32] With the conference scheduled to start on 26 April 1954, the Eisenhower administration recognized it needed to change Rhee's mind. It eventually dispatched General James Van Fleet, former commander of the US Eighth Army and United Nations (UN) Forces in Korea, to engage Rhee.[33] Rhee welcomed the visit, which also involved Van Fleet discussing the expansion of the South Korean military. Thus appeased, Rhee endorsed Seoul's involvement in Geneva.[34]

While US officials welcomed Rhee's decision, they were also determined to protect US interests in Korea. They did not want to be outmanoeuvred by the communists. They also did not want European allies to seek an unfavourable compromise with their adversaries. If Washington was compelled to withdraw its forces from Korea as part of a negotiated settlement, it would lose its access to bases in an important part of Northeast Asia. That outcome would undercut US security interests and standing in Asia.[35] Safeguarding US interests in Korea, obtaining a favourable result for Rhee, and painting the communists as the aggressors loomed as American diplomats' most critical objectives in Geneva.

---

28 *FRUS 1952–1954*, 16:19–20 and 24–25 respectively, Briggs to the Department of State (hereafter DOS), 20 February and 1 March 1954.
29 *FRUS, 1952–1954*, 16:29–32, Briggs to DOS, 6 March 1954.
30 Quoted in Tan Ze Hui Richmond, "Fighting Against Negotiation: Seoul, Washington, and the International Politics of Korean Unification" (BA thesis, National University of Singapore, 2019), 29.
31 *FRUS, 1952–1954*, 16:44–46, Dulles to Briggs, 20 March 1954.
32 *FRUS, 1952–1954*, 16:79–80, Briggs to DOS, 8 April 1954.
33 *FRUS 1952–1954*, 15:2:1785–88, 193rd NSC Meeting, 13 April 1954.
34 *FRUS, 1952–1954*, 16:111–13, Briggs to DOS, 18 April 1954.
35 *FRUS, 1952–1954*, 16:317–19, Arthur Dean Memorandum, 25 May 1954.

To further those ends, what the Americans generally pursued in April 1954 were rules for Korea's peaceful reunification. These involved, among other things, supervised elections exclusively in the North or across the peninsula, and whether the rules of the contest would be determined by the South Korean Constitution or a new political compact. The composition of the supervisory team – whether it comprised UN officers or representatives from neutral countries – also came under intense scrutiny. Rhee wanted elections to be held only in the North, with his government remaining in power. The Europeans sought to wipe the slate clean, with countrywide elections held to bring into power a popularly elected Korean government that possessed the political legitimacy to write a new constitution and rebuild Korea.[36] Several American officials supported a solution that retained the South Korean constitution, and the holding of countrywide legislative and presidential elections to determine the Koreans' political future. The proposal could potentially oust Rhee from power. US officials, nevertheless, decided they might have to accept that possible outcome. Undersecretary Smith, who led the negotiating team in Geneva, argued that if the UN forces had decisively defeated the communists, they could impose their will on their adversaries. But they did not. All sides thus had to compromise. As Smith wrote: "It is difficult to see how we can, with [a] straight face, join Rhee in seeking to impose terms of a conqueror – unconditional withdrawal [of] Chinese communist troops, surrender [of] North Korean Army to [the] ROK, leaving [the] ROK in military control of North Korea before elections and unification."[37]

Rhee, though, refused to remain silent as external powers attempted to determine his and his country's political fate. It made no sense to him to dissolve his presidency and run for elections he probably could not win in the North. He also thought he had compromised too much with the communists. He consequently pushed back when US Ambassador Ellis Briggs discussed the American proposals with him. Rhee demanded that Chinese forces withdraw from the peninsula and Pyongyang surrender its forces to Seoul before elections could be held.[38] He subsequently insisted again that Washington back his plans to attack the North.[39] Rhee clearly had no plans to endorse schemes that threatened his position.

Van Fleet supported Rhee. If the Eisenhower administration was compelled to choose between the Europeans and Rhee, he advised Washington to back

---

36 *FRUS 1952–1954*, 16:131–39, Van Hollen Memorandum, 24 April 1954.
37 *FRUS 1952–1954*, 16:249, Smith to US Embassy, Seoul, 11 May 1954.
38 *FRUS 1952–1954*, 16:205–07, Briggs to US Delegation, Geneva, 5 May 1954.
39 *FRUS, 1952–1954*, 16:215–17 and 239–41 respectively, Briggs to US Delegation, Geneva, 7 and 10 May 1954.

the South Korean. He argued that Rhee was the leader that could best confront communism in Korea. The South Korean had the gumption and resolve to stand up to the North. If Washington wished to preserve its interests in South Korea and prevent the communists from scoring any gains at Geneva, it would do best to support Rhee.[40]

Developments in Indochina strengthened the force of Van Fleet's arguments. The French position at Dien Bien Phu collapsed on 8 May 1954. The communist world appeared to have notched up another victory, inducing Dulles to think the US government might have overplayed its hand in agreeing to negotiate with the communists in Geneva. Following Van Fleet, he advised the American delegation in Switzerland to back the South Koreans even at the cost of alienating the Europeans. He refused to risk Rhee's political future, stating "it is one thing to gamble with something affecting one's own country but another thing to force a gamble on the government of the country which is itself at stake." US officials needed to stand behind Rhee. As Dulles elaborated to Smith: "I think it important that we basically follow a line which will keep the confidence of our anti-communist allies in Asia rather than seem to be working against them with a view to winning the favour of Western European countries which are not disposed to be very helpful to us in Asia."[41]

By 10 May, then, the Eisenhower government decided to back Rhee. The American decision occurred against the backdrop of significant US posturing at the negotiations. To present a united front against the communists, the Americans paid attention to details such as the conference seating plan. Dulles "stressed the importance of the representatives of the Republic of Korea sitting next to us." He insisted "we should take a strong line on this and should oppose any purely alphabetical seating arrangement which would make it impossible for us to sit next to them."[42] When the talks began on 26 April, Dulles also refused to shake hands with Chinese Foreign Minister Zhou Enlai, signalling Washington's uncompromising attitude toward China. The Eisenhower administration's call for the formation of military alliances in Northeast and Southeast Asia further rattled the Chinese.[43] If the initial US manoeuvres and tactics sought to rally the anti-communist camp against the communists and mobilize domestic US support for Washington's participation in the conference, the US moves from May 1954 reflected a further hardening of its posture in Geneva.

---

40 *FRUS 1952–1954*, 16:237–39, Briggs to DOS, 9 May 1954.
41 *FRUS, 1952–1954*, 16:243, Dulles to Smith, 10 May 1954.
42 *FRUS, 1952–1954*, 16:47, Memorandum of Conversation (hereafter Memcon), 25 March 1954.
43 Wang, "Neutralizing Indochina," 35.

During the meetings among the allied delegations in May, Smith stood with the South Koreans against the proposals raised by Belgian Foreign Minister Paul-Henri Spaak, British Foreign Secretary Anthony Eden, Canadian External Affairs Secretary Lester Pearson, and Philippine Foreign Secretary Carlos Garcia to break the impasse in the negotiations. The US delegates rebuffed their suggestions to hold countrywide elections or entertain communist concerns about the composition of the election supervisory teams. US officials, however, agreed to work with their colleagues to formulate "general principles" rather than specific solutions to address the Korean question.[44]

Even on that front, though, American officials found Rhee and Pyun restricting their capacity to be more conciliatory towards the other members of the allied working group. The South Koreans repeatedly rejected proposals that undercut the power of the Rhee regime or did not further their preferred outcomes, such as the complete withdrawal of Chinese communist forces from the North and the surrender of the North's army to the South.[45] By 19 May, American officials were voicing their frustrations with Rhee. Smith wrote to US diplomats in Seoul – Briggs and Dulles's Special Representative Arthur Dean – that Rhee's recalcitrance and rejection of a broadly supported proposal were becoming intolerable. He warned: "Unless we can do so by [the] next plenary [scheduled for 22 May], [the] situation [is] likely [to] deteriorate to [the] point where we will have abandon[ed] all hope [of] united support for [a] single proposal." The communists could exploit that development to score propaganda points.[46]

US military leaders also chimed in. General Earle Partridge, commander of the Far East Air Forces in Tokyo, argued Washington might have to "accept the status quo and work out the best solution possible under existing circumstances." Korea's reunification could only be achieved by force. Rhee would embrace that outcome. But Washington's allies and the American public would baulk at renewed bloodshed and hostilities. Partridge maintained that the US government should not embolden Rhee to attack the North. As Washington worked with Seoul to bring their defence treaty into effect, it should stipulate that American forces would be deployed only in the event that the North was the aggressor. In other words, the Americans should back Rhee's regime, but not give it a blank cheque to do whatever it wished.[47]

---

44 *FRUS 1952–1954*, 16:259–61 and 266–67 respectively, Smith to DOS, 13 and 14 May; 16:261, Smith to DOS, 13 May 1954.
45 See, for example, *FRUS, 1952–1954*, 16:279–81, Smith to Briggs and Dean, 18 May 1954.
46 *FRUS, 1952–1954*, 16:287, Smith to Briggs and Dean, 19 May 1954.
47 *FRUS, 1952–1954*, 16:297, Briggs to DOS, 20 May 1954.

With Rhee standing pat on his views, US officials accepted they had to review their approach to the Geneva negotiations.[48] On 22 May, Smith wrote to Washington, spelling out the delegation's intent to terminate the Korean phase of the proceedings. Smith indicated his team would look for the appropriate moment to make the move. The Americans sought to blame the communists for the failure of the talks. Smith stated he would wait for the communists to oppose a proposal and use it as a pretext to end the negotiations.[49] Deputy Undersecretary Robert Murphy endorsed the plan, proposing other measures US officials could pursue to trip up their adversaries. The US delegates could corner the communists to accept a UN role in the final settlement. They would attack the communists for defying international opinion if they refused.[50] Dulles agreed, stating that once the communists created an opening, he "would favor earliest termination [of the] Korean talks."[51]

Having decided on the outcome they wished to obtain, US diplomats pulled out all the stops to achieve it. They rejected the allied attempts to develop general principles on resolving the conflict.[52] They worked with the South Koreans to bring the bilateral defence pact into effect.[53] They opposed a Thai proposal to establish a separate group of representatives that would continue to sit and find ways to resolve the Korean question.[54] They essentially acceded to Rhee's views that a "clean break at Geneva with no leftovers and no cold salad gathering mould in [the] UN icebox is [the] least unproductive result likely to follow [the] conference deliberations."[55]

Two opportunities presented themselves to the American diplomats to make the clean break. At the 5 June plenary talks, Smith almost seized on the Chinese and North Korean delegations' biting criticisms of the allies to end the discussions. Molotov, however, appealed to the delegates to compromise.[56] Refusing to furnish the communists with a propaganda win and with Dulles' approval, Smith stayed his hand.[57] He then worked with the other allied delegates to upend Molotov's attempt to prolong the proceedings. He also convinced the

---

48 *FRUS 1952–1954*, 16:306–09, Briggs to DOS, 21 May 1954.
49 *FRUS, 1952–1954*, 16:314–15, Smith to DOS, 22 May 1954.
50 *FRUS, 1952–1954*, 16:326–27, Murphy to Smith, 31 May 1954.
51 *FRUS, 1952–1954*, 16:341, Dulles to Smith, 3 June 1954.
52 *FRUS, 1952–1954*, 16:333–34, Smith to DOS, 1 June 1954.
53 *FRUS, 1952–1954*, 16:320, Briggs to DOS, 26 May 1954.
54 *FRUS, 1952–1954*, 16:329–33, Memcon, 1 June 1954.
55 *FRUS, 1952–1954*, 16:336, Briggs to DOS, 1 June 1954.
56 *FRUS, 1952–1954*, 16:348–54, 13th Plenary Session, 5 June 1954.
57 *FRUS, 1952–1954*, 16:354–55 and 356–57 respectively, Smith to DOS, 6 June and Dulles to US Delegation, 7 June 1954.

group to back the American position.⁵⁸ At the 16 June plenary session, Smith made his move. When the communists proposed to establish an all-Korea body to administer elections on the peninsula, Smith and the other allied delegates chided them for their unwarranted criticisms and distrust of the UN. On behalf of the 16 allied delegations, Thai Foreign Minister Prince Wan Waithayakon read a statement, accusing the communists of undercutting the UN and undermining the possibility of free elections in Korea. Wan called for the negotiations to be terminated. There would be no final agreement on the Korean question. The talks had collapsed.⁵⁹

Partners, then, even materially weaker ones, want and usually have a say in their allies' making of strategy and tactics. A strong-willed actor like Rhee certainly wanted and had significant say in the Eisenhower administration's strategy and tactics at Geneva. He was obtuse. He was belligerent. And he was unbending in his attitude toward the conference and communists. He opposed any initiatives that threatened his political position. He wanted Korea reunified, but on his terms. He was also able to extract a mutual defence treaty from Washington – signed in October 1953, ratified in January 1954, effected in November 1954. He was, in other words, able to impose much of his will on the American negotiators, so much so that US officials had to act to manage him. The Americans not only arranged to hold all command authority of Korea-US alliance forces for operational reasons. They also did it to prevent Rhee and other likeminded South Korean leaders from undertaking unilateral aggressive actions against Pyongyang. The Americans did not want to be entrapped by Seoul to invade the North even if they had obtained a relatively favourable result for Rhee at the Geneva talks.

The Eisenhower administration, indeed, thought it had broadly achieved its objectives during the Korean phase of the conference. It thwarted the communists' endeavours to bring the whole peninsula under their control. It protected the Rhee regime. It preserved allied unity, despite finding ways to undermine the negotiations. Operating as a spoiler from late May 1954, the Eisenhower administration worked to ensure the collapse of the Korean talks. US officials then turned to a bilateral security arrangement and the propping up of an authoritarian anticommunist regime to further US interests in Asia. The Eisenhower government helped bring an end to large-scale armed violence in Korea. But it also left unresolved the Korean question – an armistice that continued to require significant numbers of American troops to police.

---

58 *FRUS, 1952–1954*, 16:357–58, Smith to DOS, 8 June; 16:360–61, Smith to DOS, 10 June 1954.
59 *FRUS, 1952–1954*, 16:376–85, 15th Plenary Session, 16 June 1954.

The Indochina Phase

If the conference on Korea shows that a materially weaker but assertive ally could have a significant voice in a stronger power's strategy, the Indochina episode illustrates that adversaries could also disrupt an actor's attempts to pursue and achieve its objectives. The communists did much to thwart Washington's endeavours to destroy the Vietminh, deny them any gains in Indochina, and bring about the conference's collapse. They exploited the allies' disagreements to outflank the Americans. Still, the communists did not achieve total victory. Despite its military achievements, the Vietminh obtained a settlement that enabled it to dominate only half of Vietnam.

Before the Indochina discussions started, the Eisenhower administration stated emphatically to Paris and London it would oppose any deal that enabled the communists to claim they had won a victory in Southeast Asia. Dulles also informed Foreign Ministers Anthony Eden and Georges Bidault that the US government did not think France should concede defeat. Bidault assured Dulles his government intended to seek an honourable solution to the conflict but without yielding to the Vietminh. Eden, however, did not appear to have the same resolve. Dulles noted that the British official encouraged France to swiftly end the conflict.[60] Indeed, Eden wanted to resolve the Indochina question diplomatically. He was circumspect about Dulles' plan to create an anti-communist coalition in Southeast Asia, believing it would escalate tensions and undercut the negotiations.[61] Until the outcome in Geneva became clearer, Eden thought Britain should not commit itself to the regional institution and become embroiled militarily in the Indochina conflict.[62]

As the delegates prepared to tackle Indochina in Geneva, the Eisenhower government pressed the point of non-compromise at its National Security Council meeting in May 1954. Eisenhower insisted the administration should not endorse a stop to the war against the Vietminh unless the delegates brokered a ceasefire acceptable to Washington and its allies. Any political agreement should also not dishearten Paris and cause it to reject the European Defence Community. The council agreed that Washington should continue to aid France's military efforts in

---

60 *FRUS 1952–1954*, 16:575–76 and 576–77 respectively, Dulles to DOS, 26 April and Dulles-Eden Meeting, 27 April 1954.
61 *FRUS, 1952–1954*, 16:623–24, Memcon, 30 April 1954.
62 NAUK, FO371/112058, Eden to Foreign Office (hereafter FO), 2 May 1954.

Indochina. It wanted the Vietminh's regular divisions destroyed. Washington would also work to establish a coalition to confront the communists in Southeast Asia.[63]

The communists, however, had no plans to back down from a confrontation with Washington. Indeed, the Chinese, Soviets, and Vietnamese comrades were more cohesive in their preparations for Geneva. They intended to dig in and obtain satisfactory outcomes at the conference. They also expressed their intent to further a common position.[64] The communists sought to consolidate the gains the Vietminh had obtained. China was particularly concerned about the Americans exploiting the conflict to establish a strong presence in Southeast Asia. Foreign Minister Zhou Enlai condemned the move. Characterizing Dulles' decision to leave the negotiations to Smith as Washington's facesaving attempt to participate in a conference it had failed to disrupt, Zhou looked to preserve communist interests in Geneva.[65]

Notwithstanding Zhou's criticism of the American move, Smith was arguably the best person Washington could have sent to Geneva. He was Eisenhower's chief of staff during the Second World War. He was brusque, but he got things done. He also had a keen mind. He had a knack for digesting a complicated brief, and deftly critiquing or explaining its contents. What he lacked in formal education, he picked up from reading books and people. He had dealt fairly with a long line of difficult personalities during the war – including Bernard Montgomery and George Patton. While he had a foul temper, aggravated by a duodenal ulcer, he demonstrated a remarkable ability to connect with his staff and foreign counterparts. Smith related well with British and French officials. He knew Molotov from his years serving as US ambassador to Moscow. Smith was not acquainted with Zhou, though that did not matter. Dulles instructed him to keep at bay the foreign minister of a state Washington refused to recognize.[66]

Smith understood the allies would negotiate from a position more of weakness than strength. The start of the Indochina discussions coincided with French forces capitulating to the Vietminh at Dien Bien Phu. The French

---

[63] *FRUS, 1952–1954*, 13:2:1509, 196th NSC Meeting, 8 May 1954; *FRUS, 1952–1954*, 16:631–32, Bonsal Memorandum, 30 April 1954.
[64] CWIHP, Molotov Journal, 6 March 1954. See also Shu Guang Zhang, "Constructing 'Peaceful Coexistence': China's Diplomacy toward the Geneva and Bandung Conferences, 1954–1955," *Cold War History* 7, 4 (November 2007), 515–17; and especially Pierre Asselin, "The Democratic Republic of Vietnam and the 1954 Geneva Conference: A revisionist critique," *Cold War History* 11, 2 (May 2011), 155–95, who dispel the consensus view that Hanoi had been unhappily compelled to follow the dictates of Beijing and Moscow.
[65] *CWIHP Bulletin* 16 (Fall 2007/Winter 2008), Zhou to Mao Zedong, 1 May 1954, 15–16.
[66] D.K.R. Croswell, *Beetle*; *FRUS, 1952–1954*, 16:778–79, Dulles to Smith, 12 May 1954.

surrender hardened the communists' resolve in Geneva. Yet it also strengthened the Eisenhower administration's determination to confront the communists. Dulles reminded Smith the delegation should not sanction any agreement that enabled the communists to claim victory. Smith supported the overall spirit of Dulles' approach. But he recognized Beijing and the communists could gain a lot at Geneva. Holding superior positions on the battlefield, they could drag the diplomatic process out, portray intransigent American officials as warmongers, and turn Asian and European opinion against the United States. He assured Dulles his delegation would find ways to undercut the communists. But Washington should be prepared for a stern reply from its adversaries.[67]

The communist delegates did respond sternly. In the plenary and private meetings, they stood their ground on a host of issues. They were determined to pack a committee observing a ceasefire with members that were either friendly or at least neutral to their cause.[68] They wanted the military issues and the political future of the Indochina states to be addressed concurrently rather than separately.[69] They parried any attempts by their adversaries to indict the Vietnamese communists for interfering in the affairs of Cambodia and Laos. And they acted to ensure Washington could find no legitimate reasons to intervene in Indochina.[70] The communists intended to exploit their military gains to wrest concessions from their opponents.

Smith confronted the communists when the negotiations began. He took the communist vitriol during the plenary sessions in his stride as he understood the delegates were playing to the gallery. As Smith indicated to Molotov in a private meeting on 10 May, the delegates had to appear tough against their adversaries.[71] When the delegates held their third restricted meeting on 19 May, it was clear to Smith that other moves were needed to prod the negotiations along. The Chinese and Vietminh representatives continued to take turns attacking France and its allies for preserving imperialism in Southeast Asia. They offered little to the allies.[72] Smith noted that the communists "appear confident and [are] in no hurry to get

---

[67] *FRUS, 1952–1954*, 16:731, Dulles to Smith, 8 May; 16:738, Smith to DOS, 9 May 1954.
[68] *CWIHP Bulletin* 16 (Fall 2007/Winter 2008), Zhou to Mao, 9 May, and CCP Central Committee (hereafter CCPCC) to Zhou, 9 May 1954, 17–18.
[69] NAUK, FO371/112065, Eden to FO, 14 May 1954.
[70] CWIHP, Minutes of Wang Jiaxiang, Pham Van Dong and Andrei Gromyko Meeting, 15 May 1954.
[71] *FRUS, 1952–1954*, 16:756, Smith-Molotov Meeting, 10 May 1954.
[72] CWIHP, Zhou to Mao, 17 May 1954.

down to business. They have a big fish on the hook," he added, "and intend to play it out."[73] The communist victories on the battlefield and low French morale gave the Vietminh confidence it could oust the French and dominate Indochina.

What Smith attempted to do was divide the communist house. He worked his charm on Molotov, assuring him that the Eisenhower administration was interested in peacefully resolving the conflict. Smith said Beijing seemed intent on pursuing its aggressive designs against Southeast Asia. If China continued to act in that manner, Smith warned Molotov that Washington would meet Chinese aggression with force. The Soviet official defended the Chinese, pointing out that Washington had repeatedly provoked Beijing. He added that China was ultimately interested in its domestic affairs and development. It was a fledgling nation-state surrounded and threatened by hostile powers. Smith interjected, arguing that if Washington was determined to crush China, it could have employed the full force of the American arsenal against Chinese forces in Korea. Yet Washington exercised restraint. Molotov appreciated Smith's candour, revealing that Moscow had likewise checked the Chinese in Korea. Still, he insisted that Washington's intimidating posture towards Beijing was counterproductive. The two officials eventually ended the conversation. Smith reported that Molotov was cordial throughout the exchange, but was not moved to give anything to the allies.[74]

At the 24 May restricted meeting, the communist delegations predictably insisted that the troubles in Cambodia, Laos, and Vietnam be collectively resolved. To Smith, the Vietminh seemed determined to consolidate its gains in Indochina. If it could not capture the whole area, it appeared to be seeking to take at least half of each state by negotiating for an agreement to partition each one.[75] In response, Eden proposed that all parties agree to a ceasefire and redeploy their forces to designated zones.[76] The Americans, however, rejected Eden's proposal. Dulles informed the National Security Council that the British plan would permit the communists to consolidate their positions and control significant parts of Indochina – an outcome he could not allow to occur. At the 27 May restricted session, Eden found himself the lone person on the allied side who supported a ceasefire. Smith backed Bidault who proposed that the belligerent parties negotiate the redeployment of forces on the battlefield first and that any solutions

---

[73] FRUS, 1952–1954, 16:856, Smith to DOS, 19 May; 16:865, Smith to Dulles, 20 May 1954.
[74] FRUS, 1952–1954, 16:895–99, Smith-Molotov Meeting, 22 May 1954.
[75] FRUS, 1952–1954, 16:911, Smith to DOS, 25 May 1954.
[76] NAUK, FO371/112067, Eden to FO, 26 May 1954.

arising from the negotiations should not undermine Vietnam's territorial integrity. Smith reported: "It was a day of complete frustration and we encountered absolute intransigence on [the] communist side."[77]

With reports indicating the allies were disunited in their negotiations with the communists, Smith had to front a press conference to reshape the narrative. He denied the allies were divided in Geneva. Insisting the American and British governments were fundamentally united in the aims they wanted to accomplish, Smith declared that Anglo-American relations were in excellent shape. The two allies merely differed on the "tactics and timing" of their approaches to counter the communists.[78]

Despite Smith's public spin, there was no hiding British frustrations when the American delegation upheld its position on Eden's ceasefire plan in the closed-door meetings on 28 and 29 May. Apart from the Americans, the other delegations essentially endorsed Eden's proposal. Smith refused. He declared he could not support any settlement that enabled the communists to control Indochina. Smith's pronouncement, made towards the end of the session, annoyed British officials. Eden and Minister of State for Foreign Affairs Lord Reading "gave a startling public exhibition of impatience and pique which included an irate aside by Reading, audible throughout [the] room to [the] effect [the] UK should withdraw its proposal."[79] Eden was upset because Smith gave him no forewarning about the US move. He assessed that "the Americans are mortally afraid of any agreement, however innocuous, reached with the communists."[80] The fissures in the allied camp caught Zhou's attention, strengthening his conviction that the communists should press home their advantage against their opponents.[81]

The developments in Geneva forced American officials to review their approach. Deputy Undersecretary Robert Murphy wrote to Dulles, commenting that the communists would likely profit from the conference. The British and French appeared intent on concluding the fight, and reaching a diplomatic settlement that enabled the communists to reap some gains. Murphy accordingly proposed that the US government dissociate itself from the negotiations.[82] Smith was equally apprehensive about the likely conference outcomes. He assessed that Vietnam would be partitioned and parts of Laos would likely be

---

77 *FRUS, 1952–1954*, 16:943, 199th NSC Meeting, 27 May; 16:947, Smith to DOS, 27 May 1954.
78 *FRUS, 1952–1954*, 16:951–52, Smith Press Briefing, 27 May 1954.
79 *FRUS, 1952–1954*, 16:974, Smith to DOS, 28/29 May 1954.
80 NAUK, FO371/112068, Eden to FO, 30 May 1954.
81 CWIHP, Zhou to Mao and CCPCC, 30 May 1954.
82 *FRUS, 1952–1954*, 16:991, Murphy to Dulles, 31 May 1954.

communist-controlled. The communists had expanded their influence in Indochina whether Washington liked it or not. Dulles agreed with Murphy that the conference was producing outcomes that the US government had to reject. He consequently instructed Smith to distance the United States from the proceedings. US delegates could offer advice, but not participate in shaping agreements they were obliged to accept.[83]

While the Americans altered their approach to the proceedings, the Vietminh continued to skirmish with and overcome French forces in the Red River Delta. By 7 June, Smith had come to a firmer view that Vietnam's partition along a line slightly north of Hue might "be the best we will be able to get, and that we well may get something worse." He wrote to Dulles that the outcome might upset American politicians and the voting public. US military officials, who argued that the delta was too strategically important to lose, would likewise protest. Unless Washington deployed its military to crush the Vietminh and probably fight the Chinese, Smith contended that partition was the most viable solution to contain further communist expansion in Southeast Asia.[84] Dulles affirmed the logic of his undersecretary's views, but reiterated that Washington did not wish to see Vietnam partitioned.[85]

The Eisenhower government's refusal to compromise upset the communists. Chinese Foreign Ministry official Wang Bingnan complained to his French counterpart, Jean Chauvel, about Smith's ostensible disinterest in whether or not the conference was making progress.[86] Wang also accused the Americans of trying to establish military bases in Cambodia and Laos – a charge Chauvel denied.[87] Molotov, too, protested. He told Smith directly that the allies were in denial with their attitudes and demands. He said the Vietminh should be "entitled to more than 50 percent of the spoils of war – even up to 75 percent."[88] He reiterated those views at the 8 and 10 June plenary sessions.[89]

The communists' stance induced the allies to review their negotiating tactics in mid-June. The Joseph Laniel government in France had also collapsed, replaced by the centre-left Pierre Mendès-France administration. On 12 June,

---

[83] *FRUS, 1952–1954*, 16:992–93, Smith to Dulles, 31 May; 16:994–95, Dulles to Smith via Murphy, 1 June 1954.
[84] *FRUS, 1952–1954*, 16:1014, Smith to DOS, 3 June; 16:1054–55, Smith to Dulles, 7 June 1954.
[85] *FRUS, 1952–1954*, 16:1056, Dulles to Smith, 7 June 1954.
[86] CWIHP, Minutes of Wang, Chauvel and Jacques Guillermaz Meeting, 6 June 1954.
[87] NAUK, FO371/112069, Reading to FO, 7 June 1954.
[88] *FRUS, 1952–1954*, 16:1060, Memcon, 7 June 1954.
[89] CWIHP, Zhou to Mao and CCPCC, 7 and 11 June 1954; *FRUS, 1952–1954*, 16:1072–74, 8th Plenary Session, 8 June 1954.

Smith told Eden it was time for the allies to shore up their military and political positions in Southeast Asia. Since May, American, Australian, British, French, and New Zealand military officials had explored plans to form a regional alliance. London hesitated to take more aggressive action and alienate Commonwealth partners such as India.[90] But it wanted to be included in the talks.[91] The first five-power meeting produced several agreements: Chinese forces had numerical superiority in the theatre of operations; the Soviets would likely intervene to help their allies; and the allies would consider employing conventional and nuclear weapons to fight the communists.[92] The five powers, however, differed on whether and when they should intervene militarily in Vietnam. The British, for one, were reluctant to upend the negotiations in Geneva, despite Smith warning Eden that the allies were emboldening the communists with their weak moves.[93]

Indeed, the communist delegates assessed they had several things going for them. First, the allies seemed disunited in purpose. France wanted to end the war. The United States aimed to contain the communist advance. And Britain sought responses that would not alienate its Commonwealth partners. Second, the allies appeared disunited in effort. Paris was under pressure to pull its troops from Indochina and make the negotiations work. Washington was disassociating itself from Geneva. And London favoured negotiation rather than war. Third, the allies were disunited in action. British and French diplomats continued to engage their communist counterparts in Geneva. US officials stood mostly aloof. Communist officials thus concluded that if they persisted in their negotiating tactics, they could achieve their objectives. If the talks collapsed, they could attribute it to American actions and score a propaganda victory. To put Washington on the defensive, the communist delegates agreed to yield on some issues. They would, however, work to obtain the conference's agreement on communist control of parts of Vietnam.[94]

Zhou presented the proposals to the conference delegates on 16 June. He called for a ceasefire; the withdrawal of foreign forces from Cambodia and Laos; a stop to foreign material and military support for the conflicts in Indochina; and international oversight of the ceasefire and resolution of political questions. Smith's rejoinder was that the ideas could be further discussed – a

---

90 *FRUS, 1952–1954*, 13:2:1533, Memcon, 11 May 1954.
91 *FRUS, 1952–1954*, 16:791–92, Smith to DOS, 13 May 1954.
92 *FRUS, 1952–1954*, 12:558–59, Five-Power Conference (3–11 June) Report, 11 June 1954.
93 *FRUS, 1952–1954*, 16:1062–64 and 1130 respectively, Dulles to US delegation, Geneva, 8 June, and Smith to DOS, 13 June 1954.
94 CWIHP, Zhou to Mao and CCPCC, 14 June, Zhou comments, 15 June 1954.

response that frustrated the communists.⁹⁵ Zhou privately told Eden that Smith's reply must have been motivated by American aspirations to establish military bases in Indochina. Still, Zhou appeared intent on continuing the negotiations. Molotov expressed similar views to Bidault. Both did not want the talks to collapse.⁹⁶

If the communists' intent was to signal to their adversaries that they wanted a diplomatic settlement, they largely succeeded in convincing Bidault and Eden of their aspirations.⁹⁷ Dulles remained doubtful. Zhou's schemes did not assuage his concerns. The communists in Cambodia and Laos would remain active, sustaining Vietminh influence in the two countries. Prohibited from intervening in Indochina, foreign forces would not be able to defend the area against the communists. Dulles remarked that any agreement reached in Geneva must not prevent Cambodia and Laos from participating in his proposed Southeast Asian regional alliance. He likewise expressed concern about the supervisory commission, which might not be sufficiently effective to check communist aggression.⁹⁸

To re-evaluate the American approach to the conference, Eisenhower recalled Smith to Washington in mid-June. Before leaving, Smith engaged Molotov in a blunt exchange of views. Molotov accused the Americans of undermining the negotiations. Smith replied that if foreign forces left and Vietminh insurgents remained in Cambodia and Laos, the two countries would remain politically unstable. He also criticized the Vietminh for wanting to dominate the delta. Molotov said France was the difficult party. It was in no position to demand the retention of the centre, southern, and parts of northern Vietnam. If Paris and its allies approached the negotiations from that unjustifiable standpoint, they could lose the whole of Vietnam. He maintained that both parties should work toward an acceptable agreement involving the country's partition. Instead of prolonging the war, American officials should help France accept the military realities and compromise. Countrywide elections would also resolve the temporary division of Vietnam. Smith ended the talk by reiterating his government's concerns. All told, the undersecretary assessed that the communist delegates intended to see the Vietminh dominate no less than half of Vietnam, and shape developments in Cambodia and Laos. Whether "through military conquest, French capitulation, or infiltration," it appeared their ultimate aim was to bring Indochina under communist domination.⁹⁹

---

95 *FRUS, 1952–1954*, 16:1158–60, 14th Restricted Session, 16 June 1954; NAUK, FO371/112073, Eden to FO, 16 June 1954.
96 *FRUS, 1952–1954*, 16:1170–74, Smith to DOS, 17 June 1954.
97 CWIHP, Zhou to Mao and CCPCC, 17 June 1954.
98 *FRUS, 1952–1954*, 16:1174–75, Dulles to Smith, 17 June 1954.
99 *FRUS, 1952–1954*, 16:1189–93, Smith-Molotov meeting, 18 June 1954.

Smith's evaluation of communist plans was not far off the mark. By mid-June, Zhou was prepared to lean on the Vietminh to pull its operators from Cambodia and Laos. He wrote to Mao that the communists should resolve the Vietnam question. They could attend to the other two Indochina states thereafter. Zhou reasoned that the move would stave off American military intervention in Indochina and bring the war to a close. With a strong presence in Vietnam, the communists could bide their time and expand their sway across Indochina later.[100] Beijing supported Zhou's view, agreeing China would restrain Vietminh military operations in the delta and keep France invested in a settlement.[101]

Mendès-France was invested in Geneva, aspiring to reach an agreement by 20 July. But he complained to British Ambassador Gladwyn Jebb that the Americans and Vietminh were not helping his cause. The former seemed unsupportive of any agreement. The latter did not wish to compromise. Mendès-France pledged that he would not undermine the Western alliance to resolve the conflict, but he might have to act in France's interest to get things done.[102]

In fact, Mendès-France was getting things done. His envoys continued to meet the communist delegates – sometimes in secret talks that raised the ire of Dulles who insisted on being apprised of the dealings.[103] The French had their reasons for keeping the meeting details confidential. They considered all possible solutions, including those the Americans opposed. Chauvel raised a number with Zhou on 22 June. One was a commission to supervise the ceasefire. Dulles had criticized its effectiveness. The Mendès-France government did not agree. The other was Zhou's 16 June proposals, which Chauvel welcomed.[104] On 23 June, Mendès-France conversed with Zhou personally, affirming what Chauvel conveyed to the Chinese official earlier. The prime minister agreed to work with the communist delegates to broker a deal.[105]

With the French pursuing a settlement with the communists, Smith commented on the development. Writing to Dulles, he argued that the Eisenhower administration might have to back the agreement. What Washington ultimately wished to achieve was a power balance favourable to the non-communist world. The Vietminh's military victories undermined that objective, but Washington could confine Vietminh influence to as small an area in Indochina as possible. Obtaining a respectable outcome in Geneva, US officials could help to enforce

---

100 CWIHP, Zhou to Mao and CCPCC, 19 June 1954.
101 CWIHP, CCPCC to Zhou, 20 June 1954.
102 NAUK, FO371/112074, Jebb to FO, 20 June 1954.
103 *FRUS, 1952–1954*, 16:1225, Dulles to US delegation, Geneva, 23 June 1954.
104 CWIHP, Minutes of Zhou and Chauvel Meeting, 22 June 1954.
105 CWIHP, Record of Zhou-Mendès-France Meeting, 23 June 1954.

the agreement's implementation. If Washington distanced itself from the Geneva process, it might alienate its allies and undercut its ability to further its long-term security objectives.[106] Eisenhower and Dulles, however, were unmoved. They feared the domestic political repercussions of endorsing a settlement that permitted communists to dominate Indochina. They hoped France could take a harder line against the Vietminh.[107]

Mendès-France assured the Americans his government intended to do that. If Vietnam had to be partitioned, he wanted the divide to be located slightly north of Dong Hoi – along the 18th parallel. Vietminh officials sought the 13th. Also under consideration was the date for the reunification election.[108] Competing against the communists would be a non-communist government that France would help build. An effective southern Vietnamese administration could eventually bring the whole of Vietnam under non-communist rule.[109] Mendès-France hoped either Dulles or Smith would return to Geneva to help him realize his plans. The secretary hesitated.[110] Eisenhower ultimately intervened, agreeing to send Dulles to Paris and Smith to Geneva. He did not want France to blame Washington for the collapse of the talks.[111]

While Washington made its moves, so did the communists. Chinese and Soviet leaders plotted to keep the Mendès-France government in the game and the hawks in the United States out. They agreed to offer Paris some concessions. One was the partition line.[112] Zhou advised Pham Van Dong, who led the Vietminh delegation, to accept the 16th parallel. The Americans could intervene if the Vietminh prolonged the war. A diplomatic settlement, however, would divide the allies. It would further enable the Vietminh to operate from the economically and numerically superior north, and bring the whole country eventually under its control.[113] Agreeing with Zhou, Dong informed Mendès-France he was prepared to accept the 16th parallel as the partition line. Mendès-France was caught off guard, but agreed to consider the offer.[114]

With the communists offering a deal, the ball was in the allies' court. Dulles met Eden and Mendès-France in Paris on 13 July. The French premier briefed

---

106 *FRUS, 1952–1954*, 13:2:1733–34, Smith to Dulles, 23 June 1954.
107 *FRUS, 1952–1954*, 16:1256–57, Dulles to US Embassy, Paris, 28 June 1954.
108 NAUK, FO371/112075, Jebb to FO, 30 June 1954.
109 *FRUS, 1952–1954*, 16:1251–52, Johnson to DOS, 26 June 1954.
110 *FRUS, 1952–1954*, 16:1309–11, Dulles to US Embassy, Paris, 8 July 1954.
111 *FRUS, 1952–1954*, 16:1333–34, Hagerty Diary, 11 July 1954.
112 CWIHP, Zhou to Mao and Ho Chi Minh, 11 July 1954.
113 CWIHP, Minutes of Dong, Zhou, and DRV and PRC Delegations Meeting, 12 July 1954.
114 *FRUS, 1952–1954*, 16:1368–69, Bonsal to DOS, 14 July 1954.

the two on his discussions with Dong, putting Dulles on the defensive. Eden thought the secretary "cut a sorry figure . . . in his attempts to explain why the Americans could not face the responsibilities of any Geneva decisions."[115] Sorry figure or not, Dulles told his counterparts the communists compromised to pit the Western allies against each other. For international security and domestic political reasons, the Eisenhower administration could not endorse any settlement that rewarded the communists for their bellicosity. Mendès-France said he understood. But he hoped Washington would at least unilaterally pronounce at the conference its intentions to act if the communists violated the terms of the agreement. Dulles agreed.[116]

Upon returning to Washington, Dulles briefed the National Security Council on the Paris meetings. He said the United States confronted a series of wicked dilemmas. If Washington officially endorsed a settlement, it would be accused of "guaranteeing Soviet conquests." If it rejected the negotiations, it would alienate France which sought to end the war. If it backed France too stridently, Paris might refuse to negotiate with the communists and seek American assistance to sustain the fight. If the Eisenhower government refused to back France militarily, it could critically undermine Franco-American relations. Those considerations compelled the US government to continue to participate, but not officially endorse, the outcomes of the Geneva Conference. More negotiations were expected, and Smith would return to Switzerland to help the French.[117]

If, in early 1954, the Eisenhower government thought it could use diplomatic means to bend the communists to conform to its will in Southeast Asia, it would by mid-1954 get more than it bargained for. Its foes stood united in pushing for outcomes they wanted. They eventually compromised, but looked likely to obtain the more populated and productive parts of Vietnam. Concerned about domestic public opinion, allied unity, and what the French might do, the Eisenhower administration now had to manage its involvement in the conference more delicately. It thus kept Smith on a tighter leash, with Dulles instructing the undersecretary on how he should handle matters in Geneva. Smith would operate as an interested party eager to help the allied camp obtain an honourable settlement. But he would not endorse or be responsible for any agreement. Smith should also not encourage the French to think that Washington would intervene militarily in Indochina if the talks collapsed.[118]

---

115 NAUK, FO371/112077, Eden to FO, 14 July 1954.
116 *FRUS, 1952–1954*, 16:1348–54, Memcon, 13 July 1954.
117 *FRUS, 1952–1954*, 13:2:1835–38, 206th NSC meeting, 15 July 1954.
118 *FRUS, 1952–1954*, 16:1390–91, Dulles to Smith, 16 July 1954.

Smith's return to Switzerland on 17 July induced the communist delegates to plan their next move. With the political questions largely addressed, their attention turned to the proposed Southeast Asian collective defence arrangement. Beijing was especially jittery, as the organization appeared to be targeted at China. Zhou stated that the communists should oppose the Eisenhower administration's attempt to recruit the Indochinese states into the group. Dong and Molotov agreed. The three planned to exploit Anglo-American differences to further their plans. London appeared to favour the Locarno form of security arrangement, where each signatory state would resolve their disputes peacefully and support each other against unprovoked external attacks. The Americans, conversely, seemed bent on establishing an alliance modelled on the North Atlantic Treaty Organization. The communists sought to drive a wedge between the two powers and undermine the proposed security institution.[119]

To that end, Zhou engaged Eden on 17 July. He said the proposed anti-communist alliance would escalate regional tensions. Eden replied that the institution, like the Sino-Soviet alliance, was a defensive organization. Zhou countered that Beijing's security relationship with Moscow was aimed at confronting potential Japanese militarism. He then highlighted Eden's Locarno idea, which seemed more benign than the anti-communist alliance. Eden explained that he hoped every signatory to a Geneva agreement would pledge to uphold the terms of the settlement and sustain peace in Southeast Asia. He envisaged the Colombo powers supporting his proposal too. Zhou replied that he harboured no concerns about Britain's plans. His unease arose from the allies' intentions to form a military bloc with Southeast Asian states – including those in Indochina. Eden replied the bloc would not be necessary if the Geneva talks succeeded.[120]

While Zhou obtained the assurances he wanted, Smith did not. The undersecretary proposed to Eden that they proclaim their plans to form the regional security grouping before the conference closed. Eden hesitated, falling back on his government's position that the talks should be given the chance to succeed.[121] On 18 July, however, he informed Smith that London would issue the declaration if the talks failed.[122]

As things turned out, the course of deliberations between 18 and 21 July saw the conference delegates reaching agreement on various issues. The State of Vietnam and the United States notably refused to endorse the conference declaration. Foreign Minister Tran Van Do attacked the partition of Vietnam

---

119 CWIHP, Memcon involving Dong, Molotov and Zhou, 16 July 1954.
120 CWIHP, Memcon, 17 July 1954; NAUK, FO371/112080, Allen to Paterson, 18 July 1954.
121 *FRUS, 1952–1954*, 16:1420–21, Smith to DOS, 17 July 1954.
122 *FRUS, 1952–1954*, 12:1:644–45, Smith to DOS, 19 July 1954.

while Smith announced the American intention to function merely as an interested party in the proceedings. Smith's declaration upset Eden. As the foreign secretary commented: "Since Dulles was at least as much responsible as we for the calling of the Geneva Conference and the present terms of reference, I find this attitude unreasonable."[123]

Yet the American play moved the British and French to push for a breakthrough in the negotiations. Between extending the war and pursuing a workable settlement, Eden sought the latter.[124] Mendès-France compromised despite recognizing that he had obtained a less militarily defensible partition line.[125] All told, the conference supported the agreement to cease hostilities in the three Indochina states; partition Vietnam along the 17th parallel; hold reunification elections in Vietnam in July 1956; and establish a commission comprising Canada, India, and Poland to supervise the implementation of the accords. Also included in the final agreement were statements declaring that while the Indochina states could obtain foreign assistance to defend themselves against external threats, they would not be formal members of any military alliance.[126]

The conference failed to fully live up to Washington's hopes. In his statement to the press, Eisenhower said he welcomed the end of the Indochina conflict. The agreement, however, had stipulations he did not support. The president did not publicly identify them but turning half of Vietnam over to the communists was one outcome his administration opposed.[127] Dulles publicly echoed Eisenhower's views. He was, however, candid in what he thought had undermined the allied efforts. The first was the minimal involvement of Cambodians, Laotians, and Vietnamese in the war against the communists. The second was the allied failure to establish the regional security organization. Dulles suggested the institution could have aided the allied efforts against the communists.[128] Finally, Smith accentuated the bad hand the allies were dealt. Without clear successes on the battlefield, the Geneva outcomes were "the best" the allied diplomats could obtain.[129]

The Eisenhower government, then, publicly attributed much of Geneva's shortcomings to the nature of the Indochina conflict and lack of battlefield

---

123 NAUK, FO371/112080, Eden to Churchill, 19 July 1954.
124 Ibid.
125 *FRUS, 1952–1954*, 16:1548–49, Gowen to DOS, 23 July 1954.
126 *FRUS, 1952–1954*, 16:1540–42, Final Declaration, 21 July 1954.
127 *FRUS, 1952–1954*, 16:1503, News Conference, 21 July 1954.
128 *FRUS, 1952–1954*, 16:1550–51, News Conference, 23 July 1954. The organization involving Australia, Britain, France, New Zealand, Pakistan, the Philippines, Thailand, and the United States was formed only in September 1954.
129 *FRUS, 1952–1954*, 16:1551–52, Smith Statement, 23 July 1954.

accomplishments. It was less direct in criticizing allied disunity, but American dissatisfaction with the British decision to wait until the end of the conference to declare their support for the regional security group was evident in private correspondence. Less mentioned privately and publicly, though, was the manner in which the communist bloc engaged its adversaries. The Chinese, Soviets and Vietminh were largely united in purpose, effort, and action in Geneva. They collectively acted to disrupt the allies' ability to counter their moves. While the Eisenhower administration could marshal the means and generate the ways to pursue its carefully formulated objectives in Geneva, it encountered crafty and trying opponents that were able to exploit the diplomatic and military opportunities to frustrate the Americans. Unable to outmanoeuvre their adversaries, US officials had to choose a course of action that ostensibly gave them more options to deal with the issues in Indochina after Geneva. In pursuing them, the Eisenhower administration would find itself dragged deeper into developments in Southeast Asia.

Conclusions

Adversaries and allies, then, exercised a significant influence on the way the Eisenhower administration pursued its grand strategy in Asia in 1954. While US officials could marshal the means and employ the ways to pursue the security objectives they formulated, they had to deal with competitive and forceful foes and friends who had the means and could find the ways to work for the ends they wished to achieve. The conference on Korea saw a strong-willed Korean leader endeavouring to bend American officials to his will. The conference on Indochina witnessed the US government's European allies narrow the range of options Washington could adopt to further its ends in Southeast Asia. The Indochina discussions found the communists assuming a united front, coordinating their diplomatic activities, and exploiting their military accomplishments in Indochina to frustrate allied attempts to thwart their plans. The products of that contest were unresolved issues on the Korean peninsula; an accord containing statements pledging that the signatories would peacefully resolve the political differences in Indochina; a partition line separating an ancient Southeast Asian society; a web of US-led bilateral and multilateral alliances shielding non-communist areas against perceived communist aggression; and a network of agreements binding the communist powers to help one another advance their aims in Asia. Infused into that regional arrangement, though, was profound wariness, as the Geneva Conference did not do a lot to build mutual trust among the delegates. As distrust turned into disappointment and aggression, the agreements struck in 1954 would eventually unravel and entangle the actors in another violent conflict in Indochina.

More broadly, the course and outcomes of the 1954 Geneva Conference bring to mind the notion that grand strategy should not be thought of simply as an ends, means, and ways equation or formula. It would be even more egregious if one were to think of grand strategy as one's ends, one's means and one's ways. Doing so marginalizes the competitive adversary as well as the amenable ally who have their own grand strategies to pursue. The person or state that is on the receiving end of one's grand strategy will invariably react. The person or state that reacts may derail or radically change one's capacity to deploy the means and ways to achieve one's ends. To appropriately formulate and implement a grand strategy, then, the grand strategist needs to make iterative refinements to one's assumptions and findings about the actor's, the foe's, and the friend's ends, means, and ways of doing things; the economic, international, and sociopolitical contexts in which the grand strategy is pursued; and the risks the actor, the ally, and the opponent are willing to bear to pursue various courses of action. In other words, to craft and implement an effective grand strategy, one should consider not only one's own ends, means, and ways, but also those of friend and foe. After all, if the sound of one hand clapping is soundless, it behooves the actor wishing to discern the sound to use at least two hands to clap.

Marek W. Rutkowski
Expanding the Area of Peace: India and the Geneva Conference of 1954

The Geneva Conference is a bit of a historical puzzle. Praised at the time for its achievement in ending the war in Indochina and bringing peace to the world for the first time since the Great War, it has rarely been studied on its own or given careful consideration by historians of the Cold War.[1] Perhaps it fell victim to the orthodox perspective of the Vietnam War, which emphasizes the inherent flaws of the Geneva framework and its inability to prevent the resumption of war. The partition of Vietnam along the 17th parallel at the Ben Hai River and the vague provision for unification through elections, which did not materialise in 1956, paved the way for the mounting of the communist subversion and increased American presence, ultimately resulting in the eruption of the Vietnam War in 1964. While it is hard to dispute such narrative in the context of Vietnam, it is unduly limiting to reduce the discussion on the Geneva Conference only to the fate of the settlement of the Indochina conflict. Held at the historical juncture of the Cold War and decolonization, it was the first international attempt to manage the future of Asia after the Second World War. A broader look at the Geneva deliberations can offer valuable insights into the power play, grand strategies, and conflicting visions of reordering the Asia Pacific that came into conflict and shaped the final settlement.

The Geneva Conference was unapologetically a Great Power conference. Chaired by British Foreign Secretary Anthony Eden and Soviet Foreign Minister Vyacheslav Molotov and including only the United States, France, and China as the other permanent members, it was held between 26 April and 20 July 1954 at the Palais des Nations in Geneva, to look for resolutions to the ongoing conflicts in Korea and Indochina. The gathering was only possible due to the renewed Soviet interest in negotiating with the West following Stalin's death in 1953. While the "Big Four" Berlin conference in early 1954 did not produce any results on European questions of Germany and Austria, the decision to host a conference on Asia with China's participation was a promising result demonstrating reduction of the Cold War tension. Several smaller players were invited

---

[1] Key existing accounts include: Robert F. Randle, *Geneva 1954: the Settlement of the Indochinese War* (Princeton: University Press, 1969); James Cable, *The Geneva Conference of 1954 on Indochina* (Houndmills: Macmillan, 1986) and James Waite, *The End of the First Indochina War: A Global History* (New York: Routledge, 2012).

to join the Korea and Indochina legs of the conference, including the Republic of Korea, Democratic People's Republic of Korea, State of Vietnam, and Democratic Republic of Vietnam.[2]

A few accounts have been published exploring the agenda and rationale of the major powers at Geneva that made the conference possible and shaped its outcomes. Kevin Ruane and Matthew Jones look at the role of Eden, the key architect of the Geneva settlement. Motivated by fear of a Cold War escalation in the thermonuclear age, they argue, Eden was able to bring the conference to a conclusion, even when it meant damaging the Anglo-American "special relationship."[3] In this volume, S.R. Joey Long looks at the grand strategy the Americans pursued in Asia at Geneva, and explores how influential allies and adversaries ultimately shaped and undercut it. Washington hoped to prevent the communist takeover of Indochina, he argues, but the efforts were frustrated by disunity among the allies and the strong united front of the opponents.[4] Qiang Zhai explores the Chinese approach, pointing to the skilful diplomacy of Foreign Minister Zhou Enlai whose main goal was the re-emergence of China on the international scene after years of isolation. Chen Jian, in turn, argues that the Geneva settlement was in China's best interest as Beijing was keen to focus on its domestic problems after the end of the Korean War, which was more important than the interests of the Vietnamese communist comrades.[5] The Soviets, Ilya Gaiduk argues, sought to eliminate the danger of the crisis in Southeast Asia expanding into a wider confrontation, and were keen to bring China out of international isolation.[6] The British, French, Soviets, and Chinese left Geneva satisfied with the outcome. The lengthy and costly war was over, the danger of escalation was averted, while the prestige of the conciliatory communists increased. The Americans, in turn, could not swallow the emergence of independent North Vietnam under communist leadership and dissociated themselves from the political provisions of the Geneva Accords. They turned to collective security instruments in the form of the Southeast Asia Treaty Organization (SEATO) to hold the line in the region.

---

[2] Kevin Ruane, "Anthony Eden, British Diplomacy and the Origins of the Geneva Conference of 1954," *The Historical Journal* 37, 1 (1994), 153–72.
[3] Kevin Ruane and Matthew Jones, *Anthony Eden, Anglo-American Relations and the 1954 Indochina Crisis* (London: Bloomsbury Publishing, 2019).
[4] Chapter 10 in this volume.
[5] Qiang Zhai, "China and the Geneva Conference of 1954," *The China Quarterly* 129, 129 (1992), 103–22; Chen Jian, "China and the Indochina Settlement at the Geneva Conference of 1954," in *The First Vietnam War: Colonial Conflict and Cold War Crisis*, eds. Mark Atwood Lawrence and Fredrik Logevall (Cambridge MA: Harvard University Press, 2007), 240–62.
[6] Ilya V. Gaiduk, *Confronting Vietnam: Soviet Policy Toward the Indochina Conflict, 1954–1963* (Stanford: University Press, 2003), 28–53.

The existing scholarship on the Geneva Conferences misses one important element: the Asian voices. While some discussion on Vietnamese and Korean agency has emerged,[7] the literature for the most part does not account for the role of India and the emerging Afro-Asian movement. This is an important oversight, as the documents of the time and even mainstream media reports show an explicit connection. A year before the historic Asian-African Conference took place in Bandung, the situation in Indochina was the key matter driving its precursor, the Colombo Conference, which, running concurrently with Geneva, brought together the leaders of India, Pakistan, Ceylon, Burma, and Indonesia to address regional security matters. Led by Indian Prime Minister Jawaharlal Nehru, the Colombo powers made conscious efforts to influence the deliberations at Geneva, emphasizing that the future of Asia should be decided with the involvement of Asian statesmen. Nehru himself used his influence with Eden and Zhou to direct the deliberations towards a non-aligned solution for Indochina along the lines of his envisioned Area of Peace in Southeast Asia, while his envoy and confidant V.K. Krishna Menon worked behind the scenes at Geneva.

It is therefore rather surprising that the literature dealing with the end of the First Indochina War pays comparatively little attention or explicitly disregards the Asian influence over the negotiated settlement achieved at Geneva. Robert Randle in his 600-page monograph *Geneva 1954* makes but a cursory mention of Asian players, though he acknowledges India as a participant of the conference through the mediatory role of Menon, and provides a limited analysis of New Delhi's policies.[8] British diplomat-turned-historian James Cable, in turn, focusing on the British role at Geneva, directly contests Nehru's alleged influence on Eden and, in a rather disparaging manner, brands Menon "an international busybody."[9] In a recent addition to the scholarship, James Waite revisits the topic using archival materials from the United Kingdom, France, the United States, Australia and New Zealand. Subtitled "A Global History," Waite's book, however, fails to account for the Asian dimension and offers a rather Eurocentric narrative.[10]

This chapter focuses on India and its activist policy at the time of the Geneva Conference. It revisits an old argument advanced by historian D.R. SarDesai in 1974 that "India literally forced itself upon the circle of countries ... that were

---

7 For example, Pierre Asselin, "The Democratic Republic of Vietnam and the 1954 Geneva Conference: A Revisionist Critique," *Cold War History* 11, 2 (2011), 155–95.
8 Randle, *Geneva 1954*.
9 Cable, *The Geneva Conference of 1954 on Indochina*.
10 Waite, *The End of the First Indochina War*.

determining the fate of Southeast Asia at the time."[11] I argue that India's strategic interests caused it to attempt to influence the future of Indochina along the lines of the concept of the Area of Peace and principles of non-alignment advocated by Nehru. The practical application of this policy was twofold. On the one hand, India presented itself as a leader of the Colombo powers, a voice of newly decolonized and neutralist Asia, foreshadowing the future Bandung challenge to the Western designs of the order in the Asia Pacific. On the other hand, Nehru had reservations about the extent of joint action that the Colombo powers should undertake and preferred to involve India in Great Power politics by engaging China, and directing Menon's diplomatic activity. The outcomes of these endeavours were, however, only partially successful. The declared neutralization of Laos and Cambodia realized in part India's hope for a non-aligned Southeast Asia, but a pact guaranteeing the outcomes that Nehru favoured was never adopted. Nevertheless, the provision for the unification of Vietnam, which India hoped to influence as the chair of the International Control Commission (ICC), was an encouraging development.[12]

The chapter is divided into four sections. The first explores the principles of Indian grand strategy, and their application to the context of Indochina and Geneva deliberations based on the concept of the Area of Peace. The second looks at the Colombo Conference and India's efforts to influence the Geneva Conference in concert with other Asian leaders, and through close correspondence with Anthony Eden. The third focuses on India-China big power diplomacy, which Zhou Enlai brought to the table at Geneva. The paper concludes with a discussion on the most tangible outcome of the Indian endeavours, the chairmanship of the ICC.

Nehruvian Grand Strategy and Southeast Asia

In keeping with the theme of this volume, the starting point of the discussion on India's approach to the Geneva Conference shall be defining the principles of New Delhi's grand strategy that guided its diplomatic initiatives. In doing so, this chapter uses a simplified definition of the term adopted by prominent India scholars. Grand strategy is defined as "the combination of national resources and

---

[11] D.R. SarDesai, "India: A Balancer Power?," in *Southeast Asia Under the New Balance of Power*, ed. Sudershan Chawla et al (New York: Praeger Publishers, 1974), 95.

[12] Ironically, it involved India in a long and frustrating engagement with Indochina until 1973, which became a burden once the hopes of unification did not materialize. See also Chapter 8 by Andrea Benvenuti in this volume.

capabilities – military, diplomatic, political, economic, cultural and moral – that are deployed in the service of national security."[13] Such framing closely reflects the parameters set in the Introduction to this volume, which views grand strategy as the art of relating means to ends with the direct involvement of the summit of authority. In the context of post-independence India, the summit of authority was clearly Prime Minister Nehru. What then can be defined as principles of India's national security under his leadership?

The discussion on India's foreign policy has to centre around Jawaharlal Nehru, the prime minister and foreign minister who was at the helm of the government from independence in 1947 to his death in 1964. Scholarly treatment of Nehru's foreign policy for a long time involved an idealism-versus-realism debate, with scholars arguing what was the key driving force behind his international initiatives.[14] A recent wave of archival-based scholarship on Indian foreign policy during the Cold War, however, aims to rescue the field from this longstanding debate by offering more nuanced approaches. Manu Baghavan emphasizes the ideals behind India's promotion of human rights and vision of a unified world, but points to Nehru's realist qualities as well.[15] Srinath Raghavan, in turn, situates India's first prime minister between the camps, as a realist in pursuit of national interests but informed by ideals.[16] This is also a stance adopted by Andrew B. Kennedy, who argues that Nehru's international efforts at transforming global norms and institutions were expressions of his moral principles, but also narrow national interests.[17] The present study takes the same approach. While Nehru's foreign policy principles in the context of Indochina were guided by ideals, they were implemented in the service of India's national interests and security – thus constituting India's grand strategy.

S. Kalyanaraman identifies five key elements of Nehruvian foreign policy: opposition to colonialism, imperialism, and racialism; non-alignment; an active

---

13 Kanti Bajpai et al, "Introduction: India's Grand Strategic Thought and Practice," in *India's Grand Strategy: History, Theory, Cases*, ed. Kanti Bajpai et al (London: Routledge, 2014), 1.
14 For a traditional argument for realism, see K. Subrahmanyam, "Nehru and the India-China Conflict of 1962," in *Indian Foreign Policy: The Nehru Years*, ed B.R. Nanda (New Delhi: Vikas, 1976), 102–30. For an example of an idealism argument, see T.T. Poulose, "India's Nuclear Policy," in *Perspectives of India's Nuclear Policy*, ed. T.T. Poulose (New Delhi: Young Asia Publications, 1978), 102.
15 Manu Baghavan, *Peacemakers: India and the Quest for One World* (New York: Palgrave Macmillan, 2013).
16 Srinath Raghavan, *War and Peace in Modern India* (Basingstoke: Palgrave Macmillan, 2010).
17 Andrew B. Kennedy, "Nehru's Foreign Policy: Realism and Idealism Conjoined," in *The Oxford Handbook of Indian Foreign Policy*, ed. David M. Malone et al (Oxford: Oxford University Press, 2015), 92–103.

mediatory role in time of conflicts; promotion of disarmament; and adoption of the Five Principles of Peaceful Co-existence (*Panchsheel*).[18] Three of these elements seem to have informed the Indian policymakers' approach to Indochina, with non-alignment wielding the most influence.

Arguably rooted in Nehru's understanding of the history of the Great War, non-alignment characterised India's foreign policy since independence in 1947. The Indian leader refused to align his newly independent country with any of the emerging Cold War blocs, securing more flexibility, but also earning scorn from both the United States and the Soviet Union.[19] Nehru believed that the decolonizing Third World should be free from Cold War entanglement as the Great Power rivalry could bring war and endanger the livelihood of young nations. In this context, the prolonged wars in Korea and Indochina worried the Indian leader. The growing support that communist China gave to the Vietminh and the American backing of France made Indochina a potentially explosive Cold War development, in a region proximate to Indian borders. Speaking in Parliament in early 1954, the prime minister commented about "the misfortune of Asia during the past some hundreds of years," as the victim of colonialism but also "the theatre of war for others and by others." Nehru hoped for peace to prevail in Asia and believed that the future of the continent "depend[ed] a good deal on what happen[ed] in Indochina or Korea."[20]

Nehru's solution to the problem was an expansion of non-alignment through the concept of the Area of Peace. It is hard to find a clear-cut definition of what exactly the Indian prime minister meant. He often mentioned the concept at the level of ideas, though one cannot find a document or pronouncement explaining how it should be attained. Krishna Menon explained, in a rather hazy way, that the Area of Peace was a kind of antidote to the bloc-divided world, a natural consequence of the Indian non-aligned policy, yet not a "Third Bloc."[21] In practical terms, the Area of Peace would then mean an area free from Great Power competition and removed from military blocs – in other words, a non-aligned group of states. Such a group was emerging, with Burma and Indonesia choosing to follow

---

[18] S. Kalyanaraman, "Nehru's Advocacy of Internationalism and Indian Foreign Policy," in *India's Grand Strategy*, 153–54.
[19] B.R. Nanda, *Jawaharlal Nehru: Rebel and Statesman* (Oxford: University Press, 1995), 223–49.
[20] India and International Situation, *Selected Works of Jawaharlal Nehru* (hereafter *SWJN*), Vol 25, ed. Ravinder Kumar and H.Y. Sharada Prasad (New Delhi: Jawaharlal Nehru Memorial Fund, 1999), 400–01.
[21] Michael Brecher, *India and World Politics: Krishna Menon's View of the World* (London: Oxford University Press, 1968), 8.

Nehru's approach to foreign affairs, and Ceylon and Pakistan at least temporarily drifting in the same direction. In Nehru's mind, adding Indochina to the Area of Peace would have done a great deal to lessen tensions and free Asia from the danger of the Cold War inadvertently becoming unbearably hot.

The other two elements of Nehruvian foreign policy applicable to the case of Indochina are anticolonialism and the willingness to perform mediatory roles in times of crisis. Nehru initially took a cautious approach to developments in Indochina after the start of the Franco-Vietminh war in 1946. If he could take a strong stand in support of Sukarno's Indonesia, including action in the United Nations and suspension of Dutch transit through Indian airspace, he was less forthcoming in his support of Ho Chi Minh's Democratic Republic of Vietnam (DRV). The prime minister forbade the deployment of Indian troops to Indochina in 1946 and criticized the French-sponsored government of former emperor Bao Dai at the Commonwealth Conference in Colombo in 1950, but was not ready to extend any tangible help to the DRV or even to officially recognise Ho's government.[22] According to Indian scholars A. Appadorai and M.S. Rajan, there were three main reasons for Nehru's approach to the problems in Indochina: the communist nature of the DRV, the emergence of an aggressive communist China, and the enduring existence of French enclaves in India.[23] Even if not unsympathetic to the nationalistic ambitions of Ho Chi Minh, Nehru was concerned about the communist advances in Asia. Indeed, he did not oppose the arrests of Indonesian communist leaders in 1946 and did not hesitate to supply Burma's U Nu with arms against the communists in 1948.[24] Moreover, the Soviet Union and the newly established People's Republic of China were hostile towards India, and the French were being obstructive in the final transfer of their colonial settlements in India to New Delhi. In these circumstances benevolent neutrality was the best India could offer to the DRV.

The circumstances changed with the improvement of Sino-Indian relations in the early 1950s, which culminated in the signing of the Agreement on Trade and Intercourse between Tibet and India in 1954. The agreement espoused the

---

[22] Ton That Thien, *India and Southeast Asia 1947–1960* (Geneva: Libraire Droz, 1963), 119–30. For an in-depth discussion on the recognition problem, see Christopher E. Goscha, "Choosing Between the Two Vietnams: 1950 and Southeast Asian Shift in the International System," in *Connecting Histories: Decolonization and the Cold War in Southeast Asia, 1945–1962*, ed. Christopher E. Goscha and Christian F. Ostermann (Washington: Woodrow Wilson Center Press, 2009), 218–29.
[23] A. Appadorai and M.S. Rajan, *India's Foreign Policy and Relations* (New Delhi: South Asian Publishers, 1988), 352.
[24] D.R. SarDesai, "India and Southeast Asia," in *Indian Foreign Policy: The Nehru Years*, ed B.R. Nanda (New Delhi: The Nehru Memorial Museum and Library, 1976), 83.

Five Principles of Peaceful Coexistence, which were to govern mutual relations. Relations with the Soviet Union similarly improved after Stalin's death.[25] India was ready to become more actively involved in Indochinese affairs after the Berlin Conference of Great Powers in early 1954 announced their plans to convene the Geneva Conference. Nehru did not wait long to take a stand in the new circumstances and start an active campaign to influence the situation based on his vision: advocating for ceasefire and decolonization and indirectly offering his mediatory services.

Four days after the Berlin resolution, on 22 February 1954, the prime minister appealed in the Indian Parliament "in all humility . . . to the powers to strive to have a ceasefire" in Indochina "without any party giving up its own position," since the matter was to be taken up by the upcoming conference.[26] Nehru was quick to point out, however, that India had "no desire to interfere or to shoulder any burden or responsibility in this connection."[27] Even with this qualification it is hard to consider the statement to be merely a wishful plea. Already on 20 February, the *Washington Post* reported that Krishna Menon, Indian delegate to the United Nations, "quietly started soundings" among delegates about the issue of ceasefire[28] in anticipation of what the *Manchester Guardian* termed a possible "Indian intervention."[29] Nehru himself cabled Indian Ambassadors in China and Soviet Union instructing them to find out "at [the] highest level what their reaction [was] to the proposal." The response of the Chinese Ambassador in New Delhi was reportedly "friendly but noncommittal."[30]

For a brief moment it seemed that the Indian proposal might carry the day when the French Parliament agreed to debate it on 5 March 1954. On 3 March 1954, it was announced that the French Cabinet would accept Nehru's proposal "if adequate guarantees can be obtained for the safety of the French expeditionary corps and for persons friendly to France."[31] This prompted even more optimistic reports by the *Times of India* speculating that the parliamentary debate in Paris "may well produce a bid from France for Indian services as a go-between." It is fair to assume that such speculations were not confined to press reporters only, for Krishna

---

25 Harish Kapur, "India and the Soviet Union," in *India's Foreign Relations During the Nehru Era*, ed. M.S. Rajan (Bombay: Asia Publishing House, 1976), 108–09.
26 Appeal for Ceasefire, 22 February 1954, *SWJN*, Vol. 25, 437.
27 Ibid.
28 "India Readies Indochina Truce Move," *Washington Post*, 21 February 1954, M1.
29 "Indian Intervention On Indochina?," *Manchester Guardian*, 22 February 1954, 1.
30 Cable to N. Raghavan, 25 February 1954, *SWJN*, Vol. 25, 438.
31 "Paris to Accept Nehru's Truce Plan If It Protects Indochina Allies," *Washington Post*, 4 March 1954, 1.

Menon "did not rule out a formal mediator's role" at the lunch by the UN Correspondents' Association on 4 March 1954.[32] French Prime Minister Joseph Laniel ultimately frustrated these hopes on 5 March 1954 by demanding the withdrawal of Vietminh forces from Laos and Cambodia as preconditions to a ceasefire.[33]

In fairness, France was not the only power unable to accept Nehru's ceasefire proposal. British Foreign Secretary Anthony Eden was "not very happy" about it and thought it difficult in a conflict without clear frontiers to ensure that non-communists would not be left at the mercy of the Vietminh.[34] In fact, the only endorsement came from Canadian Prime Minister Louis St Laurent, who was on an official visit in India at the time.[35] Nehru acknowledged as much in Parliament on 23 March 1954, admitting however that he felt "it has done some good, in the sense that there has been a good deal of consideration given to these problems and the possibilities of a ceasefire by the countries concerned."[36] It also established India as a potential player in the Indochina crisis in the wake of the Geneva Conference. The *Observer* noted on the 14 March 1954 that Nehru's ceasefire appeal was interpreted at the United Nations in New York as a bid for participation in the conference and approvingly admitted that "some kind of mediator would be necessary."[37] Nehru himself was careful to point out that India was "not looking for kudos nor . . . wish[ed] to interfere," but asserted that a "third party's advice may be beneficial." "So we gave a hint and will do so again if an opportunity arises," he added.[38] As it turned out, the upcoming Colombo Conference was to be the perfect opportunity for India, with the potential support of Burma, Pakistan, Ceylon, and Indonesia, to articulate its views on regional affairs.

The Colombo Conference: Bringing in the Asian Voice

The idea of the Colombo Conference first surfaced months before Geneva. It is tempting to put it in the sequence of Asian gatherings from the Asian Relations Conference in 1947 to the Bandung Conference in 1955. As much as Colombo

---

32 "India May Mediate in Indochina," *Times of India*, 6 March 1954, 1.
33 "French Ask Indochina Guarantees," *Washington Post*, 6 March 1954, 1.
34 Anthony Eden, *Full Circle: The Memoirs of Anthony Eden* (Boston: Houghton Mifflin, 1960), 101.
35 "Mr St Laurent Backs Mr Nehru's Appeal," *Times of India*, 25 February 1954, 1.
36 Issues in Foreign Policy, 23 March 1954, *SWJN*, Vol. 25, 382.
37 "India Ready to Mediate," *Observer*, 14 March 1954, 1.
38 Principles of Foreign Policy, 24 March 1954, *SWJN*, Vol. 25, 389.

was a precursor of the Bandung meeting, there is little evidence to link it directly with previous gatherings. Nehru spoke of Colombo as "[a] conference, which was the first of its kind," bringing together representatives of the five countries to address common problems.[39] When John Kotelawala, the new prime minister of Ceylon, proposed a periodic meeting of South Asian heads of government in December 1953, it was by no means obvious that the conference would take up the issue of Indochina. In fact, Kotelawala conceived of it as a meeting of neighbouring countries – India, Pakistan, Ceylon, and Burma – to discuss common problems without a specific agenda. "It was not our intention to be 'Pan-Asian'," he asserted.[40] However, visiting New Delhi in January 1954, Kotelawala proclaimed that "with the world divided into two camps, the emergence of an Asian bloc . . . may well be the only means of averting a third world war." When at Nehru's suggestion Indonesia became the fifth participant of the upcoming conference, the meeting ceased to be just a gathering of former South Asian British colonies and assumed a role of a conference of the non-aligned or "Asian Neutrals" as the Western press sometimes liked to refer to the group – in other words, Nehru's envisioned Area of Peace.[41]

The Indian prime minister made sure Indochina would be at the top of the Colombo agenda, presenting a new proposal on the issue on 24 April 1954. Speaking as usual in Parliament, Nehru explained at length the background of the conflict in Indochina. Building upon his earlier proposal, he presented an elaborate six-point programme for peace including: one, establishing a climate of peace, two, direct ceasefire negotiations between France and Vietminh, three, independence for Indochinese states, four, direct negotiations between interested parties, five, agreement on non-intervention, and six, good offices of the United Nations.[42] "The Big Powers at Geneva will undoubtedly watch the proceedings at Colombo with close interest," a journalist wrote in the *Times of India*. "Mr Nehru's latest declarations have presented the issues in a manner that cannot be ignored unless the Colombo meeting is to be no more than an amiable picnic," he added.[43] Branded "his 'third force' plan for peace in Indochina" by the *Washington Post*,[44] Nehru's proposal indeed became the basis for the Colombo discussion on the issue. The six points were, however, not accepted unanimously by the five leaders, and the meeting at times saw heated

---

39 "India and International Situation," 15 May 1954, *SWJN*, Vol. 25, 401.
40 J. Kotelawala, *An Asian Prime Minister's Story* (London: George G. Harrap, 1956), 117–18.
41 Robert Trumbull, "Dulles Pact Plan Opposed by India," *New York Times*, 16 April 1954, 2.
42 Proposals on Indochina, 24 April 1954, *SWJN*, Vol. 25, 439–44.
43 "Efforts For Peace in Indochina," *Times of India*, 26 April 1954, 1.
44 "Five-Nation Conference Opens Today in Ceylon," *Washington Post*, 28 April 1954, 5.

debate on the merits of Nehru's proposal. Daily news reports on quarrels between the prime ministers and extensive leaks of behind-close-door deliberations did not help to keep the inflated hopes high. "Colombo has not produced 'an Asian lead for Geneva'," dismissed the *New York Times* on 1 May 1954. "[A]ll it seems likely to produce is a rather nebulous statement."[45]

In fact, after a long discussion and a day's extension of the meeting, the conference finally agreed on a joint communiqué. In the end, all of Nehru's points were affirmed with the exception of the one on non-intervention, which was deeply opposed by Pakistan. Emphasizing the Indian desire for an immediate ceasefire, the Colombo communiqué contained, however, general statements about peace, and did not provide any specific plan or steps towards settlement of the Indochina conflict. Nehru was aware of this shortcoming and tried to influence his colleagues to issue more concrete plans. "The Geneva Conference . . . was eagerly awaiting . . . recommendations," he pointed out on 1 May, singling out the United Kingdom and France as the most eager to achieve settlement. He went on to suggest to his Asian counterparts that it was "their duty to make some concrete proposals for the solution of the problem rather than to pass vague and indefinite resolutions which would be of no help at all."[46] The *New York Times* commented, however, that in the end "Little Geneva" was able to "contribute little except to refer the issues to Geneva with its 'best wishes for success'."[47] Not all the comments were so critical. The *Times of India* emphasised that Colombo's support for Geneva should improve the chances of a negotiated settlement being brokered among the participants, while the *Manchester Guardian* praised the Colombo powers for overcoming their disagreements on key matters and uniting to support the Geneva negotiations. Prime Minister Nehru seemed also moderately satisfied. "Quite inevitably, there were somewhat different approaches to some of the problems," he reported in Parliament, adding however that the outcome was nearly identical to his six-point proposal. "It shows that sometimes, whatever differences there may be between us . . . there is a vast common ground in regard to which we think alike, and that is an important factor," Nehru asserted.[48]

While the press reports were overly optimistic before the Colombo Conference about its potential and possible role in Switzerland, the Western powers assembled at Geneva were worried about possible anti-Western pronouncements being issued from Colombo. British Foreign Secretary Anthony Eden told

---

45 Philip Deane, "No Asian Lead from Colombo," *Observer*, 2 May 1954, 1.
46 Drafting the Communiqué, 1 May 1954, *SWJN*, Vol. 25, 433–34.
47 "Indochina and Geneva," *New York Times*, 4 May 1954, 28.
48 India and International Situation, 15 May 1954, *SWJN*, Vol. 25, 401–04.

US Secretary of State John Foster Dulles on 30 April that he "had been working very hard" to avert any such possibility.[49] Indeed, Eden was the only one of the conference members to try to engage the Asian partners. Writing to Nehru, Kotelawala, and Pakistani Prime Minister Mohammed Ali in the wake of the Colombo gathering, Eden reassured them that the United Kingdom would not do anything at Geneva that "would conflict with the legitimate desires of Asian nations." Going a step further, he asked if the Asian powers would associate themselves with Geneva and guarantee the future settlement. Nehru replied on 4 May that "within the limits of our policy of non-alignment and our own resources, we would assist in promoting and maintaining a settlement in Indochina," committing India directly, for the first time, to upholding the Geneva settlement.[50]

It seems that little thought was given at Geneva to the outcomes and recommendations of the Colombo Conference, and Nehru's proposal on Indochina. Americans condemned it for leaning towards communist positions and overlooking safeguards demanded by the West, while the conference was still engaged in procedural debates.[51] Only Lester Pearson of Canada seemed interested. He "thought possibly there might be something in Nehru's proposals"[52] and Canada seemed particularly interested in the indication that India was willing "to share the responsibility for policing a ceasefire."[53] Indeed, already on 5 May 1954, Krishna Menon told Canadian Ambassador in India Escott Reid that New Delhi would agree to participate in a prospective control body in Indochina.[54]

Historian Cindy Ewing is the only scholar who makes a direct connection between the conferences in Geneva and Colombo based on extensive reading of archival documents. In a recent article she takes a broad look at the achievements of the Colombo powers and credits them with raising the issue of Asian representation in international negotiations, encouraging Asia's collective move towards multilateralism, and initiating a shift in Asian relations towards a more global orientation, culminating with the Bandung Conference in 1955. It is hard to

---

49 *FRUS, 1952–1954*, Vol. XVI, *The Geneva Conference*, Dulles-Eden Meeting, Geneva, 30 April 1954, 167.
50 Message to Anthony Eden, 4 May 1954, in *SWJN*, Vol 25, 436.
51 *FRUS 1952–1954*, Vol. XVI, Memorandum by the Adviser to the United States Delegation (Stelle) to the Special Adviser to the United States Delegation (Bowie), 30 April 1954, 638.
52 *FRUS 1952–1954*, Vol. XVI, Memorandum of Conversation by the Special Adviser to the United States Delegation (Merchant), 30 April 1954, 629.
53 *DCER*, Vol. 20, *1954*, Secretary of State for External Affairs to High Commissioner in India, 5 May 1954, 1666–67.
54 *DCER*, Vol. 20, High Commissioner in India to Secretary of State for External Affairs, 6 May 1954, 1671.

disagree with this appraisal. The Colombo Conference was a starting point of the Afro-Asian momentum and the Bandung challenge to the Western vision of order in Asia Pacific. Ewing, however, seems to slightly overstate the influence that Colombo had on Geneva. She convincingly argues that it "reinforced the impression that the [Colombo] group was the representative diplomatic force for Asia," but other tangible results were rather limited.[55] While Nehru spoke of "a unique event of historic significance,"[56] he was not initially in favour of expanding it into a broader conference, which, championed by Indonesian Prime Minister Ali Sastroamidjojo, became the Bandung Conference. With an absence of hard evidence, one can only speculate that the Indian prime minister was in part frustrated with the Colombo experience. He kept in close contact with his counterparts following the event, but turned down invitations to intervene more directly in the Geneva negotiations as a unified group. Instead, without consulting the other Colombo powers, Nehru met Chinese Foreign Minister Zhou Enlai in New Delhi on 21 June 1954 for a series of discussions, in which he emphasized the concept of the Area of Peace.

Sino-Indian Intervention at Geneva

As mentioned earlier, the improvements in Sino-Indian relations in the 1950s were one of the reasons that enabled Nehru to become more actively involved in advocating solutions for Indochina. Elsewhere in this volume, Andrea Benvenuti takes a closer look at the development of this relationship (Chapter 8). For the purpose of this chapter it suffices to say that China's endorsement of *Panchsheel* and acceptance that non-aligned states had roles to play in international affairs gave India hope that it was possible to expand the Area of Peace in Southeast Asia. Krishna Menon was at Geneva from 22 May 1954 and he invited Zhou Enlai to visit India during a break in the conference proceedings.

Nehru found the Chinese leader open, receptive and "Asia-conscious."[57] "If I may say so without conceit – of all these people in Southeast Asia, the Chinese and Indians are the most mature, individuals apart," Nehru told Zhou in the course of their conversations in New Delhi, using language that would

---

55 Cindy Ewing, "The Colombo Powers: Crafting Diplomacy in the Third World and Launching Afro-Asia at Bandung," *Cold War History*, 19:1 (2019), 1–19.
56 Ibid.
57 Message to V.K. Krishna Menon, 27 June 1954, in *SWJN*, Vol. 26, ed. Ravinder Kumar and H.Y. Sharada Prasad (New Delhi: Jawaharlal Nehru Memorial Fund, 2000), 410.

today raise many eyebrows.⁵⁸ The Indian leader was satisfied with this meeting of two aspiring powers. He played a role of mentor of a kind to Zhou, explaining to him the circumstances in various Asian countries. In exchange, Nehru was happy to find the Chinese receptive to his vision for the region. Already before the visit, China agreed on 19 June 1954 to the withdrawal of all foreign forces from Laos and Cambodia, as a concession towards the final settlement. Now Zhou proclaimed that Laos and Cambodia should become "Southeast Asia-type countries," his shorthand for non-aligned states.⁵⁹ This perfectly matched Nehru's concept of the Area of Peace and vindicated his political vision. Nehru wrote to Eden on 26 June 1954 that Zhou "laid stress on enlarging the Area of Peace in Southeast Asia."⁶⁰

The Chinese leader did something even more important. He accepted Nehru's position as his own and returned to Geneva advocating to implement the Area of Peace concept in Laos and Cambodia. Speaking to Eden on 17 July 1954, Zhou said that he and Nehru were "trying to create a peaceful region" in Southeast Asia.⁶¹ If Eden was in touch with Nehru since the Colombo Conference, after the New Delhi visit, it was Zhou who took the lead in bringing India's voice to the negotiating table at Geneva. The neutralization of Indochina was one of the matters; the other was the Eastern Locarno idea, a pact that could safeguard the security of the non-aligned region.

The problem of guaranteeing the settlement was one of the key issues discussed at Geneva. The Americans were preoccupied with the concept of collective defence for Southeast Asia, but the British, Anthony Eden in particular, advocated "a dual system of guarantees." The collective anti-communist defence agreement (SEATO) could be accompanied by a broader Locarno-type pact,⁶² whose signatories would pledge to act against future violations of the settlement.⁶³ It could include the Colombo powers and potentially the independent countries of Southeast Asia. India expressed an interest in the latter idea. In fact, Nehru might have indirectly suggested the very concept to Eden by emphasising the need for guarantees from both sides of the Cold War.⁶⁴ He also

---

58 Conversation with Zhou Enlai IV, 26 June 1954, in *SWJN*, Vol. 26, 395.
59 Conversation with Zhou Enlai I, 25 June 1954, in *SWJN*, Vol. 26, 370.
60 Message to Anthony Eden, 26 June 1954, in *SWJN*, Vol. 26, 355.
61 Minutes of Conversation between Zhou Enlai and Anthony Eden, 17 July 1954 [Excerpt], in *Cold War International History Project* [hereafter *CWIHP*] *Bulletin*, Issue 16, 66.
62 Reference to the treaties guaranteeing the western border of Germany in the interwar period, which were negotiated in Locarno in 1925.
63 Anthony Eden, *Full Circle*, 132–33.
64 Conversation with Zhou Enlai II, 25 June 1954, in *SWJN*, Vol. 26, 382n5.

reportedly mentioned the possibility of extending it to cover the whole of Southeast Asia,[65] clearly in line with the vision of the Area of Peace, and hoped the Commonwealth allies could support Eden's proposal. Canada, or at least its High Commissioner in India, Escott Reid, was indeed in favour of the Asian Locarno, and Reid took pains to reconfirm Indian support.[66] Nehru discussed the issue with Zhou Enlai and secured his concurrence that an agreement along these lines was desirable.[67] Both leaders, however, believed that it should be an alternative to SEATO and not a concurrent arrangement. It is worthwhile to quote at length Zhou's arguments presented to Eden on 17 July 1954 as they demonstrate the degree of alignment in Sino-Indian views, and the extent to which Zhou used Nehru to support his position:

> When I was in India, both Prime Minister Nehru and I thought highly of a Southeast Asian Locarno Pact [as] proposed by Mr Eden. I do not know if our interpretation is correct, but we thought that your proposal meant putting all the Southeast Asian states together to form a collective peace pact . . . Thus regional peace could be guaranteed, and it would include not only the two hostile sides, but also third-party states. This way we can experiment with peaceful coexistence in Southeast Asia.[68]

Unfortunately for Zhou and Nehru, Eden did not find support in the United States as "Locarno" turned out to be a dirty word for the Americans linked to the memory of appeasement. He also did not see any incompatibility between Locarno and "a NATO-style Southeast Asian pact." Zhou used Nehru's name once more to counter this argument:

> When I was in Delhi, I discussed this issue with Prime Minister Nehru from various perspectives . . . At that time we thought that Mr Eden was trying to counter a Southeast Asian defence pact with [the] Locarno [idea]. If the two were to exist at the same time, it would be unthinkable.[69]

In the end, the whole Locarno concept was dropped as the British did not wish to proceed without American support. Canadian High Commissioner Reid said bitterly that "the United States preferred a SEATO treaty without India and China to a Locarno-type treaty with India and China."[70]

---

65 *FRUS 1952–1954*, Vol. XVI, The United States Delegation to the Department of State, 11 May 1954, 769.
66 Escott Reid, *Envoy to Nehru* (Delhi: Oxford University Press, 1981), 74–75.
67 Conversation with Zhou Enlai V, 27 June 1954, in *SWJN*, Vol. 26, 401.
68 Minutes of Conversation between Zhou Enlai and Anthony Eden, 17 July 1954 [Excerpt], in *CWIHP Bulletin*, Issue 16, 66.
69 Ibid, 66–67.
70 Reid, *Envoy to Nehru*, 78.

The lack of a guarantee pact significantly undercut Nehru's diplomatic efforts, especially when the future of Vietnam remained unclear. But the Sino-Indian collusion of interests was an asset, which the Indian leader would try to cultivate. It is quite clear that Nehru felt comfortable discussing the big picture with a strong neighbour. "We are both big countries," he told Zhou, "actually strong and potentially strong or going to be strong."[71] Apart from talks about the regional arrangement, Zhou touched on the configuration of the International Control Commission, which was to be established at Geneva to supervise the future agreement. He told Nehru on 25 June 1954 that India would be named the chairman of the upcoming commission, while other member states had not yet been agreed on.[72] It was a tangible success of Nehru's diplomacy. India was the only ICC member equally acceptable to both sides of the Cold War divide and potentially able to use this position to influence the implementation of the future agreement along Nehru's vision.

India and the International Control Commission

If there was one practical effect of the Colombo Conference on the Geneva deliberations, it was Anthony Eden's conviction that the five Colombo powers would make a good supervisory group, neutral and acceptable to both sides of the Cold War. As early as 11 May 1954, the American delegation at Geneva reported to Washington about the British proposal to engage the Colombo powers as supervisors of the future settlement, with India and Pakistan providing the lion's share of troops and Ceylon, Burma, and Indonesia supplying token forces.[73] Interestingly, Nehru was perturbed to learn that a Reuters report publicly confirmed India's willingness to participate in the supervisory group on 17 May. He strongly reprimanded his Ambassador in Washington, G.L. Mehta, for letting the news out before the government had officially announced its decision.[74] As mentioned in an earlier section, India agreed to participate in principle "within the limits of our policy of nonalignment and ... [available] resources" already on 4 May.[75]

---

[71] Conversation with Zhou Enlai IV, 26 June 1954, in *SWJN*, Vol. 26, 394.
[72] Conversation with Zhou Enlai II, 25 June 1954, in *SWJN*, Vol. 26, 377.
[73] *FRUS 1952–1954*, Vol. XVI, The United States Delegation to the Department of State, 11 May 1954, 768–69.
[74] NMML, G.L. Mehta Papers, 3rd and 4th Instalment, Subject File No 1, Jawaharlal Nehru to G.L. Mehta, 17 May 1954.
[75] Message to Anthony Eden, 4 May 1954, in *SWJN*, Vol. 25, 435–36.

Still, the prime minister did not appreciate the media issuing proclamations while negotiations were ongoing.

Even though Nehru would not have acknowledged it openly, India clearly sought for itself a mediatory role in the Indochina conflict. With the arrival of Krishna Menon at Geneva on 22 May 1954, however, it became clear that India would seek this appointment on its own terms. The Colombo variant was not India's favourite, again pointing to the problematic relations among the Colombo powers. Initially en route to New York, Menon spent nearly three months in Switzerland engaging in numerous behind-the-scenes conversations with all the parties. "India has [a] new plan for Indochina?" the *Times of India* asked in large font on the front page the next day.[76] The American delegation, in turn, thought that Menon's presence at Geneva would result in a push for India's formal participation in the conference.[77] Neither seemed to have happened, but Menon proved to be a skilful negotiator and a useful go-between with a particular vision of India's supervisory role. Upon arriving in Switzerland, he confirmed India's willingness to participate in the commission overseeing the future settlement, suggesting however that it should be paired with Norway.[78] Talking to the American representative, Walter Bedell Smith, on 24 May, Menon mused about possible supervising powers, again favouring Norway, but rejecting Sweden as it ostensibly participated in NATO activities, and opposing Latin American countries due to their political association with the United States.[79] Interestingly, Canada was also discussed, but the Indian official believed, although "otherwise very good, [it] was probably out for the same reason."[80] Menon embarked on a mission to sell the India-Norway idea to the Soviets and Chinese, but apparently to no avail. On 31 May, the Soviets proposed their ideal configuration: India, Pakistan, Poland, and Czechoslovakia.[81] Accommodating the communist view, Menon started advocating inclusion of at least one country with relations to the Vietminh in the future commission.[82]

---

76 S. Mulgaokar, "India Has New Plan For Indochina?," *Times of India*, 23 May 1954, 1.
77 *FRUS 1952–1954*, Vol. XVI, The United States Delegation to the Department of State, 22 May 1954, 884.
78 *FRUS 1952–1954*, Vol. XVI, The United States Delegation to the Department of State, 24 May 1954, 913.
79 As much as this seems illogical since Norway is a founding NATO member and Sweden never joined the alliance, this is how the sources present Menon's views.
80 *FRUS 1952–1954*, Vol. XVI, Smith-Menon Meeting, Geneva, 24 May 1954, 914.
81 *FRUS 1952–1954*, Vol. XVI, The United States Delegation to the Department of State, 31 May 1954, 992–93.
82 *FRUS 1952–1954*, Vol. XVI, The United States Delegation to the Department of State, 8 June 1954, 1062.

Realising the difficulties in excluding communist participation in the supervisory group, the Western powers gradually agreed that the best possible outcome they could hope for would be the configuration involving the Colombo powers cherished by Eden, or a variant.[83] Weighing all the options available, Bedell Smith came to that conclusion on 30 May 1954:

> The communists will probably propose a counterpart of the NNSC [Commission in Korea], possibly offering India as a fifth. The British will probably propose India in association with a European country (Norway is India's choice). The communists would not accept Thailand or the Philippines, and India would not accept association with them . . . I am still of the opinion that the Colombo powers, in association with a neutral European nation of their selection, would be the best solution.[84]

When the British officially proposed the idea of deploying five Colombo powers to staff the commission on 8 June, they surely did not anticipate only lukewarm support from New Delhi. Replying to Eden, Nehru pointed to difficulties in relations between India and Pakistan and the need to wait for the "pattern emerging from Geneva" to be able to commit further.[85] Indeed, there seemed to have been a change of heart on this matter in New Delhi. It is true that Menon never suggested the Colombo option, although he did consider Burma as one possible supervisory power. Secretary General of the Ministry of External Affairs, N.R. Pillai, however, reportedly believed it was an interesting idea, only to backtrack on it later. Some British diplomats in India speculated that the change was a result of Menon's "guidance."[86]

G.L. Mehta in Washington had a hard time explaining to Canadian Ambassador Arnold Heeney, who considered the Colombo idea reasonable, why it was not acceptable to Delhi. Mehta's line that China and the Soviets would not accept Pakistan as a neutral power did not seem very convincing, since Moscow already included Pakistan in its configuration.[87] This was, however, the official Indian position, and Nehru used exactly the same argument in an internal correspondence to Menon, adding as another reason that he "foresaw difficulties in

---

[83] This was particularly the American position, but the British and French seemed in agreement. For example *FRUS 1952–1954*, Vol. XVI, Thirteenth Restricted Session on Indochina, Geneva, 14 June 1954, 1138–39.
[84] *FRUS 1952–1954*, Vol. XVI, The United States Delegation to the Department of State, 30 May 1954, 981–82.
[85] Message to Anthony Eden, 11 June 1954, in *SWJN*, Vol. 26, 345.
[86] *FRUS 1952–1954*, Vol. XVI, The Chargé in India (Mills) to the Department of State, 11 June 1954, 1120–21.
[87] NMML, G.L. Mehta Papers, 3rd and 4th Instalment, Subject File No 1, G.L. Mehta to Jawaharlal Nehru, 17 June 1954.

sharing responsibility with Pakistan."[88] India's reaction was not only surprising to the Geneva participants and the Western powers, but also to other Colombo countries. James Barrington, Burmese Ambassador to the United States, appreciated the Indian reasoning, but told Mehta that "the Colombo Conference countries could play a very great role in helping to arrive at a settlement."[89] Similarly, Indonesian Prime Minister Ali Sastroamidjojo thought that the idea of the Colombo powers as supervisors was an excellent compromise.[90] It turned out that the proposal was in any case unsatisfactory to the communist powers and therefore the discussions were put on hold. It is quite clear, however, that by this point India was more inclined to act unilaterally than to cooperate with the other Colombo powers in jointly lobbying Geneva for their inclusion in a supervisory commission.

The final configuration of the ICC was agreed upon on 19 July 1954. India was to be joined by communist Poland and anti-communist Canada in a setup that "seemed as obviously responsive to everyone's requirements as it was altogether unexpected."[91] The ultimate selection was a long-discussed combination of the Soviet and Eden's proposals. Moscow agreed to drop its 50–50 configuration, which allowed for an odd number of members in the commission,[92] and the West gradually accepted the possibility of complementing the Colombo countries with one communist and one anti-communist state.[93] The final tripartite configuration was suggested by the French. Tellingly, Menon approved of it, as the Chinese reported, "express[ing] satisfaction that it did not provide for the participation of Pakistan."[94] It is evident that India was chosen to chair the commission by virtue of its activist position towards the Indochina settlement. This selection was, however, also an appreciation of an independent Asian voice that was heard before and during the Geneva Conference. Even though this voice was not always united and Nehru himself did not see eye to eye with the other Colombo leaders, Asian opinion was able to ensure that the Indochina question would not be settled without Asian participation. Speaking in retrospect, Ceylon Prime Minister S.W.R.D. Bandaranaike expressed this sentiment:

---

88 Cable to V.K. Krishna Menon, 11 June 1954, in *SWJN*, Vol. 26, 346.
89 NMML, G.L. Mehta Papers, 3rd and 4th Instalment, Subject File No 1, G. L. Mehta to Jawaharlal Nehru, 21 June 1954.
90 To Ali Sastroamidjojo, 12 June 1954, in *SWJN*, Vol. 26, 349n12.
91 Cable, *The Geneva Conference*, 119.
92 Molotov at first suggested adding Indonesia to its initial proposal. See *FRUS 1952–1954*, Vol. XVI, The United States Delegation to the Department of State, 15 June 1954, 1153.
93 *FRUS 1952–1954*, Vol. XVI, Smith-Eden-Mendes-France Meeting, Geneva, 17 July 1954, 1406.
94 From the Journal of Molotov: Top Secret Memorandum of Conversation with Zhou Enlai and Pham Van Dong, 17 July 1954, in *CWIHP Bulletin*, Issue 16, 98.

"The world was trembling on the brink of war at that time and it was probably Sir Anthony Eden, assisted by countries such as India, who resolved that problem with some measure of success."[95]

The *Times of India* praised India's involvement on its front page on 22 July 1954 and asserted that "without her cooperation and active participation no lasting settlement could be achieved in Indochina."[96] The country was proud of its peacemaking role, which Indian Vice-President Sarvepalli Radhakrishnan unequivocally expressed to the Polish ambassador: "The world is looking at India; we will live up to expectations."[97]

Conclusions

India's pursuit of an independent vision of the future of Indochina and Southeast Asia was an important, if rarely acknowledged, undercurrent of the Geneva Conference. Guided by Nehruvian principles, India strived to influence the future of the proximate region along the principles of non-alignment. Nehru hoped for an expansion of the Area of Peace, a region of non-aligned states, safeguarded by a guarantee treaty. Such an arrangement would reduce the danger of a Cold War conflict escalating into a general war in Asia, and allow for newly decolonized states to preserve their sovereignty and independence. Nehru was here clearly guided by the principles of realism and idealism. His internationalist ideals caused him to speak on behalf of decolonized Asia, and against colonialism and foreign intervention. His realist considerations focused on preventing armed conflict and securing peace around India's borders. His intervention in Indochinese affairs was only possible due to the favourable diplomatic situation, especially India's improved relations with China and the Soviet Union. Abandoning his moderate position on Vietnam upheld since 1946, Nehru launched a series of initiatives directed firstly at a ceasefire and then at remodelling Indochina on his non-aligned vision.

Nehru used a variety of means to achieve his strategic goals. India was not invited to the Geneva Conference, but the Colombo Conference scheduled

---

[95] Prime Minister S.W.R.D. Bandaranaike's Views on the Commonwealth, 5 July 1956, in *Documents on Sri Lanka's Foreign Policy 1947–1965*, ed. Amal Jayawardane (Colombo: Regional Centre for Strategic Studies, 2005), 99.

[96] S. Mulgaokar, "Peace Comes at Last to War-Weary Indochina," 22 July 1954, *Times of India*, 1.

[97] Grudziński (New Delhi) to Słuczański (Warsaw), 26 July 1954, Archiwum Ministerstwa Spraw Zagranicznych [Polish Foreign Ministry Archive], Zespół Depesz [Collection of Dispatches] 6/77, Wiązka [Bundle] 39, Teczka [File] 487.

concurrently offered a platform for him to influence Geneva from afar. The Indian leader took the lead in convincing his counterparts to issue a strong and specific statement along the lines outlined in his six-point peace proposal. The Colombo Conference succeeded in making a strong claim for Asian participation in decisions pertaining to Asian security, and set a foundation for the future Afro-Asian movement and the Bandung challenge to the Western vision for Asia. However, from the practical point of view, Colombo did not make much impact at Geneva. The final communiqué was worded in general terms, and the lack of agreement among the Colombo powers was publicly exposed. Nehru then started distancing himself from the activity of the group and engaged in direct negotiations with Chinese Foreign Minister Zhou Enlai and, through Krishna Menon, with other participants at Geneva.

The Sino-Indian collusion of interests was perhaps the main factor leading to a partial realisation of Indian ideas. Zhou agreed to the neutralization of Laos and Cambodia, and strongly lobbied for the establishment of the Eastern Locarno arrangement with Anthony Eden. As Nehru had hoped, China was willing to abandon its expansionist policies in Southeast Asia for fear of American intervention. While the Eastern Locarno was not accepted due to American objections, India was generally satisfied with the Geneva Accords. Krishna Menon said on 29 July 1955 that "the agreement is only a beginning[,] [a]greement is not a conclusion, it's a path to solution."[98] India now had a tool to further influence the developments in the region through its chairmanship of the International Control Commission, a clear recognition of Nehru's activist approach.

Indeed, the Geneva Accords were not the end of India's efforts to promote the Area of Peace in Indochina. As the chair of the ICC, India took it upon itself to promote the reunification of Vietnam via elections in 1956, which Nehru believed was the key to resolving the conflict in Indochina. In retrospect, there is no doubt that these attempts failed and India's strategic interests in Indochina were not accomplished. Cambodia was arguably and tenuously part of the Area of Peace. Laos remained a conflict zone where communist and royalist forces fought each other, while Vietnam remained divided between two ideological camps supported respectively by the Cold War powers. The outcomes should, however, not cause one to overlook the important role that India played in advancing a regional solution at Geneva that would stabilize, albeit temporarily, the situation in Indochina, and secure its national interests.

---

98 "Geneva Negotiations First Since War to Succeed: Mr Krishna Menon's Views on Pact," 30 July 1954, *Times of India*, 7.

Coda

Brian P. Farrell
On Two Doorsteps: Middle Powers and Grand Strategy

One concept present in any discussion of Great Powers and grand strategy is the problem of the agency, and leverage, of powers that were not Great. The problems posed by so-called "Middle Powers" are particularly interesting: states strong enough to generate useful supporting power or present annoying obstacles, while not themselves capable of projecting sustained power, independently, beyond their own boundaries. This volume has already examined at least two such examples: postwar India, seeking a path to greater power, and the Republic of Korea. There was another. What made it even more interesting was that it was an outlier: of the West, yet not in it; in the region, yet not of it. This was Australia.

Paul Keating, Prime Minister of Australia from 1991 to 1996, captured one aspect of why Australia interests us here. In the aftermath of the 1975 repeal of the "White Australia" policy, Keating called for Australia to shift its focus to its own neighbourhood: to Asia, to become the "odd man in." Keating's challenge to Australia to rethink its identity provoked controversy at home and abroad. Less controversial was the repeated declaration by one of his predecessors, Robert Menzies, Prime Minister from 1939 to 1941, then again from 1949 to 1966, that Australia could always look for security from its relationships with "great and powerful friends," which was always understood to mean the British and, increasingly as the years wore on, the Americans. They both agreed with all their predecessors, of whatever political stripe, that Australia could not defend itself by itself against the most dangerous threats it might encounter. These prime ministerial musings frame the relevance of Australia to our discussion: location, identity, size, and choices.

Throughout the period we engage here, Australia remained a Western society, anchored within the "British world," which happened to be located a world away from "home," but right next door to Southeast Asia. The volatile region we identified as the Asia Pacific was on Australia's doorstep, and it was the only Western state which had to be existentially concerned with the order of the region. What London called the "Far East," Australians called the "Near North." Economically successful and dynamic, Australia became an important factor in British calculations, particularly when it came to grand strategy in Asia. Australia's decades of development as a new nation-state unfolded squarely within the period during which offshore Great Powers, fundamental to Australian security, sought to reorder this larger region. Australia was small enough to be dependent, but big enough to matter, and in a place that came to matter very much. What light can be shed then, on our larger problem, by a closer look at this state one level below Great Power status, one short distance removed from the heart of the region?

Peter Dean finds a great deal with which to illuminate our reflections. He situates Australia within a triangle that defined the grand strategies it could pursue: identity, location, and capability. The volatile relationship between these factors, influenced by choices Australians made about how to leverage or nudge them one way or another, tells us much about both how the problems of the region had wider consequences and how an interested but not mighty party could try to come to terms with them. Dean critiques a mixed record that included both success and shortfalls; but he also analyzes a trend, if fitful, towards an Australia developing the desire, and the ability, to press its own choices. Ultimately, however, he also argues that while 1954 was indeed a moment of great significance to this wider story, for Australia it was because it shone, too briefly, as a false dawn.

Peter Dean
Managing Great Power Allies: Australian Grand Strategy in Asia, 1900–1954

During the period from 1900 to 1954, Australia become a nation through the peaceful process of federation, fought in two world wars and a Cold War and, like most nations in the region, had to learn how to live in an Asia dominated by competing Great Powers. As the late and great strategic studies scholar Coral Bell once commented, Australia in Asia is a tale of the nation's ability to make its way in the world while "Living with giants."[1]

As a self-described middle power in Asia the Australian experience in this epoch provides a historical landscape that is full of insights. There are, however, a number of key issues that do work against the broad applicability in the search for lessons from this part of strategic history. Most significantly during this period Australia did not see itself as part of Asia: rather it sought security from Asia. In addition Australia's combination of geography and geopolitics is unique. Nevertheless, as Australia is an important player in the geopolitical landscape of Asia today, this epoch provides for a platform from which important observations about the Australian experience can be made.

While not a major power, Australia is a major global player. Its economy places it well within the G20 grouping of countries, it has played an outsized role in international multilateral diplomacy and it is the 13th largest global spender on defence, making it a significant regional military power. Furthermore, Australia's modern conception of its geography – the Indo-Pacific – places it, along with maritime Southeast Asia, on the hinge of the most significant strategic system in the world today. Thus the story of Australia's experience with Great Powers and grand strategy in Asia during this period remains highly relevant.

Any essay on grand strategy has to have a definitional anchor point. This chapter uses a definition of grand strategy provided by the American historian and strategic studies scholar Hal Brands. In his 2018 book *American Grand Strategy in the Age of Trump* Brands argues that:

> Grand strategy is frequently maligned by its distractors, in part because it is oversold by its advocates. Contrary to the common mystique, a grand strategy is neither a road map nor a cure-all for the complexity of global affairs. It is simply an integrated set of concepts that offers broad direction to statecraft. A grand strategy consists of considered assessments of

---

[1] Coral Bell, *Living with Giants: Finding Australia's place in a more complex world* (Canberra: The Australian Strategic Policy Institute, 2005).

the global environment, a country's core interests and objectives, the most important threats and opportunities and the ways finite resources can be deployed across key issues. These assesments constitute a conceptual framework that streers policy – the concrete initatives through which states engage the world.[2]

Map 12.1: Map of the Asia Pacific Region in the 21st Century.

---

[2] Hal Brands, *American Grand Strategy in the Age of Trump* (Washington DC: Brookings, 2018), 51. This approach broadly aligns to that provided in the Introduction to this volume, which notes that "it is frankly easier to define grand strategy as a concept, as something that

This understanding of grand strategy – as a set of concepts that provides broad direction to statecraft, based on some basic principles of a nation-state's circumstances – forms the foundation for this outline of the Australian experience from 1900 to 1954. In doing so, it rejects the idea that "Australia has traditionally done without a grand strategy, relying on Defence White Papers to set out a military strategy that is largely subordinate to the grand strategy of its great power ally."[3] Using the definition of grand strategy outlined above, this paper unpacks the context of Australian grand strategy from a collection of British colonies in 1900, amended by Federation as a Commonwealth in 1901, through to the signing of two key alliances: the ANZUS Treaty with the United States (1951), and the Manila Pact (1954) establishing SEATO.[4] Most significant: this era covers Australia's path of anchoring its security through a Great Power protector in Asia, from the United Kingdom to the United States. This was done in the face of two critical threats to Australia's strategic interests and objectives in Asia – militarist Japan during the Pacific War and Communist China in the early Cold War.

In assessing the arch of Australia's engagement with Great Powers in Asia during this period this chapter addresses two key questions: how did Australia, as a new nation in 1901, attempt to provide for its security during this period? What does this period reveal about the continuity and changes of Australia's approach to its grand strategy? In doing so it also draws inspiration from Michael J. Green's work *By More than Providence: Grand Strategy and American Power in the Asia Pacific Since 1783*. Like Green, this chapter addresses its key questions in the context of a number of central ideas: that grand strategy largely resides among an often close-knit group of elites; that it may never be clearly articulated; and that the best way to unpack and understand grand strategy is through the use of chronology (while trying to avoid falling prey to the notion of events being linear or that a nation's approach to strategy "progressed"). The major benefit for the use of chronology, as Green states, is that it provides for "thinking in time," thus allowing us to explore the evolution of a topic, so that we can extrapolate the key principles that guided, drove and influenced the nature and character of Australia's approach.[5]

---

exists and can be understood and applied, when the context is direct and clear." The fundamental aim of this chapter is to clarify the context of Australian grand strategy.
3 See Michael Wesley, "Australian Grand Strategy and the 2016 Defence White Paper," *Security Challenges*, 12:1 (2016), 19–30. This paper contests such an approach through the definition of grand strategy provided.
4 Australia-New Zealand-United States, ANZUS. Southeast Asia Treaty Organization, SEATO.
5 See Michael J. Green, *By More Than Providence: Grand Strategy and American Power in the Asia Pacific Since 1783* (New York: Colombia University Press, 2017).

Geopolitics: From Terra Australis to Federation

The key principles that drive grand strategy are a nation's geography, history, politics, identity, social interactions, population size, strategic weight and foreign relations. In applying the broadest possible brush to such an approach during this period it has been argued that Australia is a fundamentally "Western" country located at the bottom of Asia. In this assessment Samuel Huntington described Australia in his controversial 1995 work, *The Clash of Civilizations*, as a "torn country."[6]

Since European settlement/invasion, Australia has been a country of immigrants built on a foundation of British imperialism, Western liberal democracy and capitalist economics. Its national culture is – and was heavily during this period – infused with inherited British traditions and identity as part of the British Commonwealth, the Anglo-sphere and the "Western" world. Australia's social make-up, especially since the post-Second World War era, has evolved to become an exceptionally successful multicultural society. Its political system is based on a mashing together of British and American political traditions – often called a "Wash-minster" system. During the period in question it overwhelmingly identified itself as "British."[7]

A key overriding consideration in Australia's strategic history and grand strategy is its geography. As Immanuel Kant noted in the 1790s, geography is the very "foundation of history." Abraham Verghese argued that "Geography is destiny," while Robert Kaplan argued for the centrality of geography and geopolitics in understanding strategy and conflict.[8] Locally, one of the doyens of Australia strategic thinking, Professor Paul Dibb, has never failed to remind anyone with an interest in Australian defence policy that strategy always starts with a map of "one's country and its geopolitics."[9] There are many ways to look at Australia but almost all of them start with geography. From descriptions such as the "antipodes" and the "land down under," through discussions of its unique flora and fauna, to an acknowledgement of its status as the only "island

---

6 Samuel P. Huntington, *The Clash of Civilizations and the Remaking of World Order* (New York: Simon & Schuster, 1995), 151.
7 Neville Meaney, "Britishness and Australian identity: The problem of nationalism in Australian history and historiography," *Australian Historical Studies*, Vol 32, No 116, 76–90.
8 Robert Kaplan, *The Revenge of Geography: What the Map Tells Us About Coming Conflicts and the Battle Against Fate* (New York: Random House, 2013).
9 Paul Dibb, *Essays on Australian Defence*, Canberra Papers on Strategy and Defence No 161 (Canberra: ANU Press, 2005). See especially Chapter 3, "Does Asia Matter to Australia's Defence Policy?."

continent," it is impossible to escape the importance of a map to Australia's strategic past, present and future.[10]

Location reveals many things.[11] Australia's remote locality led to centuries of speculation and wonder in the ancient civilizations of the Mediterranean and Renaissance Europe. Legends from Greek and Roman times prophesied the existence of a southern mega continent.[12] But for centuries, *Terra Australis Incognita* ("the unknown great southern land") remained a mystery. During this period, its very existence in the "western world was denied though the Christian Church's insistence that the earth was flat [that] led to the complete eradication of all belief in a southern continent."[13] However, its reappearance in the fifteenth and early sixteenth century was driven by sea exploration that "confirmed the approximately spherical shape of the earth."[14] All such claims would have been news to the oldest continuous human civilization on earth – the Australian Aborigines.[15]

While European exploration was slow and largely confined to Western Australia in its early iterations, the Macassans of Sulawesi had been trading with the indigenous nations of northern Australia since the late seventeenth century.[16] It took until the epic journey to the Pacific Ocean of Captain James Cook, Royal Navy (RN), to map and chart the east coast of Australia. It took until 1788 before the First Fleet of British colonists arrived.

Debate is still ongoing in historical sources as to the reasons for British settlement of the antipodes. The main debate lies between a convict goal and the strategic importance of Australia. As Stuart Macintyre has noted, "the dispute over the motives for settlement is necessarily difficult to resolve because the

---

[10] Desmond Ball, Sheryn Lee, *Geography, Power, Strategy and Defence Policy: Essays in Honour of Paul Dibb* (Canberra: ANU Press, 2016).
[11] The argument in this section is derived directly from Peter J. Dean "Towards an Australian Marine Corps? Australian Land Power and the Battle between Geography and History," in *A New Strategic Environment and Roles of Ground Forces* (Tokyo: National Institute for Defence Studies, 2019), 29–44.
[12] W.J. Mills, "Terra Australis Incognita" in Andrew J. Hund, ed, *Antarctica and the arctic circle: a geographic encyclopaedia of the earth's polar regions* (Santa Barbara CA: ABC-CLIO, 2014).
[13] "Terra Australis Incognita," in I.C.B. Dear and Peter Kemp, *The Oxford Companion to Ships and the Sea*, 2nd ed. (Oxford: University Press, 2006).
[14] Ibid. For an outline of these views in relation to Australian history see Frank Welsh, *Great Southern Land: A New History of Australia* (London: Penguin Books, 2004), Ch 1.
[15] See for instance Geoffrey Blainey, *The Story of Australia's People: Vol. 1 The Rise and Fall of Ancient Australia* (Melbourne: Penguin, 2016).
[16] Marshall Clark and Sally K. May, eds., *Macassan History and Heritage: Journeys, Encounters and Influences* (Canberra: ANU Press, 2013).

official documentary record is so circumstantial."[17] The strategic significance of the Australian continent centres on the continuation of British maritime dominance, whereby this small island off the coast of Europe settled the great southern land as part of its grand strategic vision to maintain its pre-eminence as the world's great maritime power. Such a grand strategy view, based on assessing the British Empire at this time, favours the logic of the strong benefits to sea power to be derived from establishing a British colony in Australia. Great Britain was, as Andrew Lambert has argued, one of the true sea power states, able to project this sense of state strategy into a broad ranging national character.[18]

The strategic case is evident through the benefits that the settlement of Australia brought to the British Empire: expansion, maritime trade and natural resources.[19] In particular, Australia was seen as a source to secure and extend British maritime power by providing an additional "source of flax for canvas and ropes, and timber for mast and spars." In addition, despite its remote geographic location the South Pacific was the site of European expansion, and the colonization of Australia helped to secure Britain's place in the South Pacific in an increasingly frenetic scramble by European powers for overseas colonies.[20]

For the fledgling colonies in Australia, and later the nation after federation in 1901, the RN was the centrepiece of the defence of the Australian continent. The continent's regional security in Asia, and the broader Indo-Pacific, was guaranteed by the maintenance of Anglo-Saxon maritime supremacy in these regions. Unsurprisingly, the primary drivers for Australian (really local British) strategy during this period were the capabilities of the RN and its presence in the region.

A distinctive Australian commitment to this strategy occurred within 10 years of the Federation of the Commonwealth of Australia, with the formation of the Royal Australian Navy (RAN) fleet unit in 1911. The fleet unit's role was to

---

17 Stuart Macintyre, *A Concise History of Australia* (Melbourne: Cambridge University Press 2005), 29.
18 Andrew Lambert, *Seapower States: Maritime Culture, Continental Empires and the Conflict That Made the Modern World* (New Haven: Yale University Press, 2018).
19 Geoffrey Blainey, *The Tyranny of Distance: How Distance Shaped Australia's History* (Melbourne: Macmillan, 1968), 26–29.
20 G.J. Abbott, "The Botany Bay Decision," *Journal of Australian Studies*, 9:16, (1985); Blainey, *The Tyranny of Distance*, 29. See also Jeffery Grey, *Military History of Australia* (Melbourne: Cambridge University Press, 2008), 7–8; Greg Swindon, "Australian Naval Defence," in Craig Stockings and John Connor, eds., *Before the Anzac Dawn: A Military History of Australia before 1915* (Sydney: NewSouth, 2013), 125–26.

support the maintenance of the British maritime presence in the region.[21] The land defence of the continent was a second-tier priority, and was largely confined to the establishment of coastal defences and debates over the potential role for an expeditionary land force for the use of the British Empire, of up to six brigades of light horse and three of infantry, that "remained largely on paper."[22]

Thus from the time of European settlement, geography and British identity were *the* key driving forces in Australia strategy. These key factors were exacerbated by the vast land mass of the Australian continent – 7,741,220 sq km or 5 percent of the world's land mass – combined with an exceptionally small population (0.33 percent of the total world population in modern times);[23] its remoteness from its Great Power protector; its island status; and its position at the bottom of Asia with a land bridge that spans the Pacific and Indian Oceans. Taken together, this means that Australia's defence and strategic circumstances are unique. This combination of identity and geography formed the key foundational drivers for Australia's approach to grand strategy, which has been shaped from colonial times by the "ideas of weakness, vulnerability and isolation."[24]

Early Approaches to Australian Strategy

The ideas of "weakness, vulnerability and isolation" fostered a dependency from the eighteenth to early twentieth centuries on an external Great Power for protection. This became more acute at the end of the nineteenth century and the Australian colonies made a concerted effort to influence British imperial policy. This endeavour was focused around regional security through the idea of "British hegemony" across Australia's northern approaches in the South Pacific.[25] Australia strongly favoured an approach to geopolitics and regional

---

21 David Steven ed. *The Royal Australian Navy*, Vol. III, *The Australian Centenary History of Defence* (Melbourne: Oxford University Press, 2000), 5–26.
22 Grey, *Military History of Australia*, 71. For a broad overview see David Horner, "The Army, the Navy and the Defence of Australia and the Empire, 1919–1939," in Peter Dennis ed., *Armies and Maritime Strategy: 2013 Chief of Army History Conference* (Canberra: Big Sky Publishing, 2014), 119–20.
23 This has been consistent since the 1950s. See https://www.worldometers.info/world-population/australia-population/.
24 Hugh White, "Defence Policy," in Brian Galligan and Winsome Roberts, *The Oxford Companion to Australian Politics* (Melbourne: Oxford University Press, 2007), 150–53.
25 Neville Meaney, *The Search for Security in the Pacific, 1901–1914: History of Australian defence and foreign policy 1901–1923* (Sydney: University Press, 2009), Vol. 1, 10.

ordering in the Asia Pacific that was dominated by an external Anglo-Saxon Great Power. Influencing and leveraging its major power protector's strategy in the South Pacific and Southeast Asia for its own strategic interests thus became a core plank of Australia's grand strategy.

From its earliest origins, the difficultly of nestling Australia's strategic interests inside that of a geographically remote global power protector was at the forefront of Australia's policymakers' minds. In the late nineteenth and early twentieth centuries, Australian strategy was institutionally affixed inside British imperial policy. During this period, the Australian colonies, and later Commonwealth after 1901, lacked their own foreign affairs representatives. The Australian policy elite's dissatisfaction with this British monopoly on foreign affairs was soon palpable. With "geo-politics . . . the determining condition of Australian nationalism" coupled with the distance from London, the local political complaint, around the formation of a Commonwealth of Australia, was framed around the slogan of "a continent for a nation and a nation for a continent." This placed grand strategy at the forefront of the formation of the Australian nation-state.

Foreign affairs, immigration, trade, and defence issues were thus some of the key drivers for the establishment of the federation of the Australian colonies in 1901. Section 51 of the Australian Constitution,[26] outlining "Legislative powers of the Parliament," starts with "(i) trade and commerce with other countries." Key areas of the constitution include "(vi) the naval and military defence of the Commonwealth"; "(xxvii) immigration and emigration"; (xxix) and (xxx) on "external affairs" and "the relations of the Commonwealth with the islands of the Pacific"; "(xxxii) the control of railways with respect to transport for the naval and military purposes of the Commonwealth."[27]

One of the first bills brought before the new parliament on 23 December 1901 was the "Immigration Restriction Act." Commonly known as the White Australia Policy, this Act reiterated Australia's sense of itself as "British and white" and highlighted the underlying fears of being overwhelmed by the large, populous nations to Australia's north. In particular, this was couched in the terms of anti-Chinese racism and fears of China's rise as a major power. Fear for Australian security also came from concerns over European colonialism in the South Pacific. This sentiment drove the Australian colonies to push hard in the late nineteenth century for Britain to occupy all of the key islands of the South Pacific, to form a northern shield for Australia and to cement British dominance

---

[26] *The Australian Constitution*, https://www.aph.gov.au/about_parliament/senate/powers_practice_n_procedures/constitution, viewed 9 February 2021.
[27] Ibid.

of the region. Continuity with this strategic approach became the focus of the early post-Federation governments in Australia from 1901 to 1905.

The year 1905, though, brought a sudden and radical change to Australia's strategic position in Asia. The rise of an Asian Great Power in the form of Japan through its victory in the Russo-Japanese War of 1904–1905, coupled with the British withdrawal of battleships from the China Station, meant that for the first time Australia felt a primary threat to its territory.[28] The pre-existence of the Anglo-Japanese Alliance, concluded in 1902, failed to mollify Australia's anxiety. However, as Neville Meaney noted, "for the most part Britain ignored Australia's overtures until World War I and this led to a greater push for more 'independence' in Australia's approach to its foreign and defence policy."[29]

The first significant move by Australia in relation to balancing its defence posture with some independence was a call by Prime Minister Alfred Deakin to another Anglo-Saxon maritime power with interests in the Asia Pacific. Deakin wrote to US President Theodore Roosevelt on 24 January 1908 asking him to include Australia as a destination for the global cruise of the US Navy's (USN) "Great White Fleet," a move the British government opposed.[30] This was followed up by moves to establish a greater Australian naval capability. At the 1909 Imperial Conference, it was decided to deploy to Australian waters a naval unit consisting of at least a battle cruiser, three second class cruisers, six destroyers, three submarines, and a number of auxiliaries. The first units arrived in 1910 and in 1911 the Royal Australian Navy was born.[31]

The RAN and Australia's focus on its strategic concerns in the South Pacific featured prominently in the Australian Commonwealth's first major military action. Little known, even in Australia, are the operations to capture the German colonies in the Pacific in 1914. On 6 August 1914, just days after declaring war on Germany, Britain requested that Australia "as a great and urgent imperial service" seize and destroy the German wireless stations in the Southwest Pacific that were supporting Vice Admiral Graf von Spee's East Asiatic Squadron.[32] The Australian government agreed and in less than two weeks raised, equipped and

---

28 Stevens, *The Royal Australian Navy*, 14.
29 Meaney *The Search for Security in the Pacific, 1901–1914*, 12.
30 "Deakin's Great White Gamble," Museum of Australian Democracy, https://www.moadoph.gov.au/blog/deakin-s-great-white-gamble/#, accessed 9 February 2021.
31 Stevens, *The Royal Australian Navy*, 14.
32 C.E.W. Bean, *Anzac to Amiens: A Shorter History of the Australian Fighting Services in the First World War* (Canberra: Australian War Memorial, 1968), 31.

despatched an expeditionary force of 1,500 men for overseas service.[33] Designated the Australian Naval and Military Expeditionary Force, Australia's first amphibious force landed near Rabaul, the capital of German New Guinea, on 11 September 1914. Facing only limited resistance, it located and captured the wireless station. Surrender terms were signed within the week.[34]

The operation to capture German New Guinea provided for an improved sense of security to Australia in the Pacific and a culminating point to its strategic approach of the preceding decades. This operation served both an Imperial Defence requirement and also a significant regional defence requirement for Australia. Thus Australia was able to find synergy between imperial strategy and its regional strategic interests – the key goal in Australia's grand strategy.

With the defeat of the East Asiatic Squadron on 8 December 1914 at the Battle of the Falkland Islands,[35] the global strength of the RN coupled with the maintenance of the Anglo-Japanese Alliance meant that Australia's regional security was assured. As such, Australia was able to shift its military focus during the rest of the Great War to concentrate on raising, training, and deploying an expeditionary land force overseas, to support British imperial strategy. Thus Australia was able to successfully balance its imperial commitments with its emerging local defence needs in the period 1901–1918.

However, it was evident that the tensions between London and Canberra over regional security issues in Asia were to be ongoing. Issues of critical importance to Australia received scant attention in Whitehall. This led to fissures at the Paris Peace Conference as the Australian Prime Minister, Billy Hughes, sought to defy many of US President Woodrow Wilson's proposals. Furthermore, the gap between Canberra and London on strategic issues in the interwar period continued to grow. While 1915–1918 saw Australia's strategic focus concentrated on supporting the British Empire in the Middle East and Europe, from the end of the Great War Australian strategic focus returned to Asia and the

---

33 Ross Mallett, "The Preparation and Deployment of the Australian Naval and Military Expeditionary Force," in *Battles Near and Far: A Century of Overseas Deployment*, Peter Dennis and Jeffrey Grey eds. (Canberra: Army History Unit, 2005), 24.

34 S.S. Mackenzie, *The Australians at Rabaul: The Capture and Administration of the German Possessions in the Southern Pacific*, The Official History of Australia in the War of 1914–1918, Vol. 10 (Sydney: Angus & Robertson, 1937), 73–74.

35 Battle of the Falkland Islands was fought between the RN and Imperial German Navy on 8 December 1914 in the South Atlantic. It resulted in the destruction of the Imperial German Navy's East Asia squadron, their only permanent overseas naval formation, under the command of Admiral Graf Maximilian von Spee. This meant that the threat from German naval ships in the India, Pacific and Atlantic Oceans was reduced to commerce raiding by armed merchant ships and later U-boats.

South Pacific. During this time, the rise of Japan as a major power in Asia provided the only apparent direct threat to Australian security.[36]

Particularly concerning to Australia were some of the key territorial outcomes of the Paris Peace Conference. Japanese control of the former German Pacific colonies in the Mariana, Caroline and Marshall Islands cemented their "domination of the central and western Pacific."[37] These moves, coupled with the 1921 League of Nations mandate granted to Australia to administer German New Guinea, made Australia and Japan very uncomfortable neighbours in the Southwest Pacific. The consequences of these moves were a radically altered strategic position for Australia. It also had a major impact on the strategic calculations in the Pacific of another emerging Great Power – the United States.

The Interwar Period and the Second World War

The story of Australian grand strategy in the period 1919–1941 is one of failing to deal with the changing power dynamics of Asia.[38] Most significantly, while Australia recognised the emergence of an Asian Great Power in Japan and the threat that this posed to Australia's interests and territorial integrity in the region in the 1930s and 1940s, it failed miserably to deal with the declining power of its Great Power protector – the United Kingdom [UK] – while also failing to recognize and engage adequately with the rise of another Anglo-Saxon maritime power in the region – the United States.

These failures to adjust its grand strategy in Asia ultimately left Australia vulnerable to Japanese expansionist policies. The decline was rather rapid. The Washington Naval Conference of 1922 saw the end of the Anglo-Japanese Alliance, something both Australia and New Zealand fought hard to retain.[39] The Chanak Crisis of 1922 served to undermine the Australian government's faith in

---

36 David Day, *The Politics of War* (Sydney: Harper Collins, 2003), 1.
37 John McCarthy, *Australia and Imperial Defence 1918–1939: A Study in Air and Sea Power* (St Lucia: University of Queensland Press, 1976), 7.
38 This section is derived from Peter J. Dean, *MacArthur's Coalition: United States and Australian Operations in the Southwest Pacific 1942–1945* (Lawrence: University Press of Kansas), 11–28.
39 Timothy D. Saxon, "Anglo-Japanese Naval Ccooperation, 1914–1918," *Naval War College Review*, 53:1 (2000), 88–92. Saxon notes that neither the British or the United States were willing to continue close cooperation with the Japanese after the Great War. For a discussion of the Anglo-Japanese Alliance, the British government's changing policy towards Japan, and its misinformation to the Australian government during this time, see D.K. Dignan, "Australia and British Relations with Japan, 1914–1921," *Australian Outlook*, 21:2 (1967), 135–49.

the international postwar push for peace and disarmament.[40] After Chanak there was growing recognition that the Washington Agreements provided little real security for Australia.

Australia's response was to double down on its traditional approach to security. When Prime Minister Stanley Bruce went to the 1923 Imperial Conference he was resolved to ensure measures were in place to secure a strong British naval presence in the Pacific.[41] At the end of the conference it was agreed that while each part of the Empire was primarily responsible for its own local defence, in the Pacific a naval base would be built at Singapore to service the British battle fleet, thereby providing a deterrent to Japanese aggression.[42] While on the surface this looked like a triumph for Australia's grand strategic approach, it actually did little to account for the shifting power dynamics of the region or the relative, and real, decline of British power in the Asia Pacific.

Under the terms of this agreement Australia was responsible for the protection of maritime trade in the Australian region, and financial support was pledged for the construction of the Singapore base. At the time, this base was viewed by the British Chiefs of Staff as one of the "keystones on which the survival of the British Commonwealth of Nations would depend."[43] The Singapore Strategy, as it became known, thus came to form the very foundation of Australian defence policy throughout the interwar period.[44] This was despite the fact that it was never adequately revealed how the base in Singapore, some 6,200km by air from Sydney, and even further from the far reaches of the Southwest Pacific, would provide protection for the eastern seaboard of Australia, or the region, from Japanese naval aggression.

---

40 The crisis was a war scare in September 1922 between the the UK and Turkey over Turkey's attempts to reassert control of occupied and neutral territories after the defeat of the Ottoman Empire in the First World War. Turkish troops marched against British and French positions in the Dardanelles neutral zone. War was avoided through a negotiated settlement that gave Turkey the territory it wanted.

41 Paul Hasluck, *The Government and the People, 1939–1941*, Series 4, Vol. 1, *Australia in the War of 1939–1945* (Canberra: Australian War Memorial, 1952), 16.

42 Malcolm H. Murfett, "The Singapore Strategy," in *Between Empire and Nation: Australia's External Relations from Federation to the Second World War*, Carl Bridge and Bernard Attard eds. (Victoria: Australian Scholarly Publishing, 2000), 188–204. See also John J. Dedman, "Defence Policy Decisions Before Pearl Harbor," *Australian Journal of Politics and History*, 13:3 (December 1967), 331.

43 "Review of Imperial Defence by the Chiefs of Staff Sub-Committee of the Committee of Imperial Defence, 22 February 1937," as quoted in John McCarthy, "Singapore and Australian Defence 1921–1942," *Australian Outlook*, 25:2 (1971), 165.

44 Horner, *High Command*, 2. See also John Gooch, "The Politics of Strategy: Great Britain, Australia and the War against Japan 1939–1945," *War in History*, 10:4 (2003), 425–26.

Most significantly, the plan never adequately accounted for how the British were going to be able to actually deploy a fleet at Singapore in the first place.

A more realistic appraisal of the Singapore Strategy, one based on recognition of strategic geography and the decline of British maritime power, meant the naval enclave at Singapore, on the eastern edge of Asia, looked more like a base to bottle up Japanese power in the Pacific and deny their fleet access to the Indian Ocean. Its prospects as a base from which to project waning British power into the Southwest Pacific reduced as every year of the 1920s and 1930s passed. Compounding the problems of the Singapore Strategy were recurring delays in the construction of the naval base. Yet despite all these issues, the Singapore Strategy's position as the basis of Australian defence policy became an "article of faith that was not to be questioned."[45]

It is not like the shortcomings of the Singapore Strategy were not debated in Australia. However, by the onset of the Great Depression the self-delusion in Australia's grand strategy was well entrenched in government and policy circles. Despite the grievous shortcomings in this approach Australian governments, of both major political affiliations, remained committed to the strategy during the inter-war period for five major reasons:
- Prohibitive cost of self-defence;
- Long-term dependency on its Great Power protector – Britain;
- False perception of itself as the jewel in the crown of the British Empire (which in reality were India and the Middle East);
- Stilted nationalism and its continued attachment to Britain; and
- Economic reliance on the Empire.[46]

Dependence on Britain economically, along with imperial loyalty, gave successive Australian governments a rationale for a reduction in spending on defence far below levels that its military advisers thought wise. Instead of seeing the Singapore Strategy as requiring Australia to invest in defence capability, especially as Imperial Defence was centred on self-reliance in a constituent country's immediate region, Australia saw this strategic approach as a way to outsource its defence to the RN. This led to massive cutbacks in defence spending after the signing of the Washington Naval Treaty in 1922.[47] Such cutbacks were further

---
[45] Jeffrey Grey, *The Australian Army: A History* (Melbourne: Oxford University Press, 2006), 82.
[46] See Augustine Meaher IV, *The Road to Singapore* (Melbourne: Australian Scholarly Publishing, 2010).
[47] Albert Palazzo, "The Overlooked Mission: Australia and Home Defence," in *Australia 1942: In the Shadow of War*, Peter J. Dean ed. (Melbourne: Cambridge University Press, 2013), 57.

entrenched after the onset of the Great Depression in 1929. By the mid-1930s when this policy approach was changed, Australia was hamstrung by its inability to independently produce modern military equipment, especially cutting-edge aircraft and mechanized land forces, as global rearmament placed enormous constraints on the international arms market, restricting Australia's ability to procure arms from overseas.[48]

Australian governments had also assessed that it was more likely that other dominions within the Empire would be in the front line of any future conflict, abdicating the need for a heightened regional security posture. At the same time, the poor state of Australia's defences meant that if the continent was threatened the country would have to rely upon Britain in any case. Furthermore, faith in the Empire remained widespread in the community and political circles.[49]

To make matters worse, the Australian relationship with the other rising Great Power in Asia in this period, the United States, was massively underdeveloped. If a key plank of Australia's grand strategy was reliance on a largely white Anglo-Saxon power maintaining maritime hegemony in Asia, loyalty to the British Empire blinded it to the obvious benefits of much closer defence ties with the United States.

Despite the success of the two USN fleet visits to Australia in the interwar period, for most of the 1920s and 1930s "Australian strategic culture had little to do with the United States."[50] In fact, Australia had gone out of its way in the early 1930s to economically alienate the United States. Australia's 1936 Trade Diversion Policy, which protected and promoted trade within the British Empire, led to a downgrading of Australia's "most favoured nation" status in the United States.[51] These measures reinforced the maxim that Australia, rightly or wrongly, looked to Britain not just for its defence, but also for its economic prosperity.[52]

Meanwhile the fissures deep inside the Australian-British relationship regarding their approach to Asia soon started to boil over. By the mid-1930s,

---

[48] See Hasluck, Ch. 2 – "Between the Two Wars, 1918–1938."
[49] For details of Australia's history and relationship with Britain after the Great War see Gavin Souter, *Lion and Kangaroo: The Initiation of Australia* (Melbourne: Text Publishing, 2001).
[50] Peter Edwards, *Permanent Friends? Historical Reflections on the Australian-American Alliance* (Sydney: Lowy Insitute, 2005) 8.
[51] Lloyd G. Churchward, *Australia and America, 1788–1972: An Alternative History* (Sydney: Alternative, 1979), 134. These measures were ended in 1938.
[52] Edwards, *Permanent Friends?*, 8.

differences in strategic policy between London and Canberra over Asia led Prime Minister Joseph Lyon to raise with US President Franklin D. Roosevelt in 1935 the idea of a Pacific Pact between the two countries. This was later expanded at the 1937 Imperial Conference into an idea of a broader Pacific conference of nations. Australia, however, was a small player among the Great Powers, in an Asian strategic environment in flux and buffered by the winds of a global economic depression. Lyon got a "polite reaction" at the conference but British support was eventually forthcoming. Once the idea was expanded, the reaction from Pacific nations was mixed. The Chinese were enthusiastic, Soviets interested, the United States cautious, and the Japanese dead opposed. London soon went cold on the idea and it was eventually killed off by the Japanese invasion of China in July.[53]

In the end, as the 1930s drew to a close, Australia was slow to abandon its interwar policies in order to meet the changing strategic circumstances in the Asia Pacific.[54] In 1939, after the outbreak of the Second World War, Australia decided to send a large number of troops, naval forces and aircrew to the Middle East and Europe. It was believed that Australian security in the Asia Pacific would continue to be guaranteed by the British presence in Singapore. Australia clung to its faith in the Empire and only slowly came to accept the reality of British weakness in the Asia Pacific.

The Pacific War

By the second half of 1941, Australia could not ignore Japanese moves in Asia and it responded with a range of initiatives that reaffirmed its grand strategy. As part of its commitment to Imperial Defence, it maintained its forces in Europe and the Middle East while also sending reinforcements to Singapore and Malaya. With an eye to its local defence requirements, reinforcements also went to New Britain and Australia's island possessions to its north. The Curtin government heightened home defences and tried to coordinate defence planning with the US, British, and Dutch forces in the Pacific. However, as David Stevens has argued, "firmly tied to the imperial view of the world, the Australians had little previous experience to call upon [to negotiate defence agreements

---

53 Norman Harper, A *Great and Powerful Friend: A Study of Australian Americans Relations Between 1900 and 1975* (St Lucia: University of Queensland Press, 1987), 86–87.
54 Roger Bell, *Unequal Allies: Australian-American Relations and the Pacific War* (Victoria: Melbourne University Press, 1977), 11.

with the major powers] and for the most part remained only concerned observers."⁵⁵ Australia's difficulties were exacerbated by the United States' refusal to give Australia, Britain or the Netherlands an explicit commitment of military assistance against Japan in the Pacific until the outbreak of war on 7 December 1941.⁵⁶

Despite its efforts, when the Pacific War started Australia was far from prepared. Home defence capabilities remained limited and the bulk of Australia's capable military formations remained in the Middle East. The sudden Japanese advance and the collapse of the British forces at Singapore saw Australia's defensive plans fall apart. This catastrophe spurred a complete reappraisal of Australia's strategic approach. As David Horner has noted:

> One positive outcome from Australia's involvement in these [early] ill-fated campaigns [in Southeast Asia] was that for the first time Australia became properly aware of the strategic importance of the region. Thousands of Australians had lived and worked in the region and they knew that after the war Australia would not be able to ignore the region. It was a true turning point in Australia's appreciation of these nearby lands.⁵⁷

Australia's lifeline came in the form of the other great Anglo-Saxon maritime power in the Asia Pacific, the United States. The decision by Admiral Ernest J. King, Chief of Naval Operations USN, to prioritise the defence of Hawaii and the sea lines of communication to Australia and New Zealand, in the face of the Japanese onslaught, brought Australia firmly into the US strategic orbit. This decision was followed by the US Joint Chiefs of Staff commitment to defending Australia by establishing in April 1942 a new theatre, the Southwest Pacific Area, based in Australia and under the command of General Douglas MacArthur.

While this move helped to secure the Australian continent, and shift Australia's alliance focus, at least temporarily, to the new coalition with the United States, it was soon evident that Australia's control over its strategic destiny was strictly limited. As the machinery for running a truly global war was established in 1942, the Australian government was not represented in any of the major Allied grand strategy decision-making bodies. Australia was given a position on the Pacific War Council but it quickly became clear that this body had little to no influence.⁵⁸

---

55 David Stevens, "The Royal Australian Navy and the Strategy for Australia's Defence, 1921–1942," in Stevens ed., *In Search of a Maritime Strategy*, 81.
56 Bell, *Unequal Allies*. 10.
57 David Horner, "Australia 1942: A Pivotal Year," in Peter J. Dean, ed., *Australia 1942: In the Shadow of War* (Melbourne: Cambridge University Press, 2013), 18.
58 For details, see Christopher Thorne, *Allies of a Kind: the United States, Britain and the War Against Japan, 1941–1945* (New York: American Council of Learned Societies, 1978).

Realising its lack of institutional influence inside the senior Allied command organisation, the Australian government, led by Prime Minister John Curtin, hoped to use MacArthur to obtain more Allied resources for operations in the Australian area. During 1942 and 1943, the Australian government formed a synergistic relationship with MacArthur through a coincidence of strategic interests between the Australian government and the Southwest Pacific Area's Commander-in-Chief. This provided a firm foundation for Australian strategy from April 1942 to November 1943. However, what the Australian government did not fully realise was the temporary nature of its relationship with MacArthur. Imbued with a false sense of fidelity based on MacArthur's self-serving platitudes and charm, the Curtin and later Chifley governments only grasped far too late MacArthur's Machiavellian approach to strategy in the Pacific War. Between 1944 and 1945, as Australian and MacArthur's interests diverged, the setting of Australian strategy became strained, and the true extent of the limitations of its wartime coalition with the United States was revealed.

The Pacific War taught Australia a number of important lessons, such as the stark display of declining British power; the limitations for a middle power in accessing the global strategy of its major power allies; the difficulties of exerting strategic influence through regional combatant commanders; and a healthy scepticism of US interests in Asia vis-à-vis Australian strategic interests. Significantly, while the historical focus is often placed on Australia's process of "turning to America" (announced in early 1942), it was a strategic shift, that, as historian James Curran accurately points out, was always anchored in the notion of defending the British Empire.[59]

The limitations of Australia's wartime relationship with the United States were evident from early on in the relationship. The day after the Japanese midget submarine raid on Sydney Harbour in June 1942, MacArthur met Curtin and declared that:

> Australia was part of the British Empire and it was related to Britain and the other dominions by ties of blood, sentiment and allegiance to the Crown. *The United States* was an ally whose aim was to win the war, and it *has no sovereign interest in the integrity of Australia* . . . In view of the strategical importance of Australia in a war with Japan, this course of military action would probably be followed *irrespective of the American relationship to the people who might be occupying Australia.*[60]

---

[59] James Curran, *Curtin's Empire* (Melbourne: Cambridge University Press, 2012).
[60] NAA, A5954 1/1, Minutes of Prime Minister's War Conference (PWC), Melbourne, 1 June 1942; PWC Minutes, No 1 of 8 April 1942 to No 69 of 14 January 1943, and No 78 and 79 of 17 March 1943 (emphasis added).

MacArthur was entirely consistent with this approach throughout the Pacific War and it was naive of members of the Australian government to ignore the clarity he provided at this time. It meant that by the end of the Second World War, the path to the ANZUS Treaty in 1951 was not certain. Furthermore at the end of the war the United States refused an Australian overture to maintain the naval base at Manus Island in the South Pacific, a decision reversed in 2018 in the face of a different rising Asian Great Power.[61] Overall though, 1941–1945 had, yet again, revealed Australia's difficulties in aligning its strategic interests, priorities and objectives in the South Pacific and Southeast Asia with that of Britain and the United States – this time in the face of major war with a revisionist Asian power.

Diplomacy and the United Nations

Feeling abandoned by Britain in 1942 and with the limitations of the US wartime coalition readily apparent by 1944, Australia next turned to the international system to help provide for its security. During the war, Australia greatly expanded its capabilities in both diplomacy and defence strategy. This expanded ability paved the way to craft its foreign and defence policies in more independent ways.

Australia was a firm supporter of the Atlantic Charter signed in 1941. Thereafter it entered into its first major independent bilateral strategic partnership when it established the ANZAC Conference with New Zealand in 1944 to help inform their views of the postwar world in the South Pacific – much to the chagrin of the British and Americans. In the immediate postwar period, Australia emerged as a firm advocate of multilateralism – a core tenet of its grand strategy that remains to this day. Australia eagerly supported the establishment of the United Nations, securing a place on the Executive Committee, and in 1948 was elected to the presidency of the General Assembly; Dr Herbert Evatt presided over the third session of the General Assembly as president in 1948–1949.[62] In a foretaste of things to come, Australia led a strong middle power coalition for

---

[61] Ben Wan Beng Ho, "The Strategic Significance of Manus Island for the US Navy," *Proceedings*, Vol 144/12/1, 390, United States Naval Institute, 2018. https://www.usni.org/magazines/proceedings/2018/december/strategic-significance-manus-island-us-navy.
[62] "Australia and the United Nations," National Library of Australia, https://www.nla.gov.au/research-guides/united-nations/australia-and-the-united-nations, accessed 12 April 2021.

the establishment of the Charter of Human Rights, the Genocide Convention, and the establishment of the International Human Rights Court.[63]

However, while Australia remained committed to global moves for peace and security and was a strong advocate of regional and global multilateralism, in the postwar period it was soon apparent that the collective security system being developed through the United Nations was not adequate. Australian defence policy would therefore always be a hedge against the potential failure of the liberal international system. From a defence policy perspective, it was clear that Australia could not defend itself unaided against a major power in Asia and a more independent and globally active diplomacy must be only one arm of its grand strategy. Its direct defence and security in Asia was, therefore, again intrinsically linked to the British Empire; for although Australia also saw American assistance in the region as essential, it placed no reliance on this assistance being forthcoming, given the experience of relations with the United States in, and between, the two world wars.[64]

The Cold War

At the end of the Second World War, Australia still had to solve the same basic strategic problem: how to defend a thinly populated continent, off the archipelago of Southeast Asia, far removed from its allied Great Power(s)? While the removal of the threat of direct invasion or the establishment of an illiberal great power with regional hegemony inimical to Australia's interest was now seen as redundant with the defeat of Japan, as the Cold War dawned Australia again found itself in a difficult strategic position.[65]

While reassured by the role of the United States in Asia, Australia was also concerned about the level of US commitment to the defence of Southeast Asia, the South Pacific, and the Australian continent, i.e. Australia's regional interests. It also had to enter into a new phase of Great Power relations – juggling a balancing act between its desire for a strategic partnership with the United States, while providing continued fealty to the British Commonwealth with

---

[63] Ibid.
[64] "An Appreciation of the Strategical Position of Australia, February 1946," in Stephan Frühling, ed., *A History of Australian Strategic Policy Since 1945* (Canberra: Defence Publishing Service, 2009), 58.
[65] The material for this section is based on material in Peter J. Dean and Tristan Moss, eds., *Fighting Australia's Cold War: The nexus of strategy and operations in a multipolar Asia, 1945–1965* (Canberra, Australian National Univerity Press, 2021).

whom it had, once again, anchored its strategic posture. As late as 1965, not long before the British announcement of their strategic retrenchment "East of Suez," leading Australian military commentator T.B. Millar was calling the ANZUS Treaty incomplete and arguing for a move from a trilateral defence treaty between the United States, Australia and New Zealand to a quadrilateral treaty with the inclusion of Britain.[66]

At the start of the Cold War, two things became clear to Australian strategists: first, that the "West" was locked in an existential strategic competition with communism and second, given the distance between Central Europe and the South Pacific, Australia and its regional surrounds would not be at the epicentre of this competition. As such, initial strategic thinking in Australia fell along rather traditional lines, with consideration for the deployment of a third Australian Imperial Force to the Middle East in the event of the Cold War turning hot. This was predicated on the idea that any land-based threat to Southeast Asia would develop only with extended warning time and therefore, in the early stages of any third world war, an Australian commitment to the Middle East "would have a beneficial effect out of all proportion to their size."[67]

The risks and threats to Australia's regional security, however, were not to be diminished by its geographical remoteness from Europe, and the pressures being asserted in the regional security environment soon saw the global focus to Australian strategic planning come unstuck. Considerations for a commitment to the Middle East were, in 1950, signed off by the Australian Council of Defence only "four days before the North Korean surprise attack that began the Korea War."[68] Australia soon found itself engaged in that conflict, enabled by its ongoing military presence in Japan alongside the United States and Britain.

Australia was deeply engaged in the occupation of Japan through the British Commonwealth Occupation Force (BCOF), which saw some 16,000 Australians serve in-country, "and throughout its existence BCOF was always commanded by an Australian officer."[69] This meant that Australian aircraft, army units and ships were all stationed "not far away" from the new conflict zone on the Korean Peninsula. However, as the Australian official historian Robert O'Neill noted,

---

66 T.B. Millar, *Australia's Defence* (Melbourne: University Press, 1965), 80.
67 NAA, A816, 14/301/781, Defence Committee, "The Basic Objectives of British Commonwealth Defence Policy and General Strategy," 1950.
68 Frühling, *A History of Australian Strategic Policy Since 1945*, 13.
69 "British Commonwealth Occupation Force 1945–1952," Australian War Memorial, accessed 14 April 2021, https://www.awm.gov.au/articles/atwar/bcof.

these forces "were not in any way ready . . . to be committed to combat operations at short notice. Rather they were preparing for withdrawal to Australia."[70] Their unpreparedness did not stop the Australian government from its strategic commitments; two RAN ships were made available to the US-led United Nations Command (UNC) on 29 June and a Royal Australian Air Force (RAAF) squadron was offered the next day. Army forces were soon mobilised from BCOF and Australia and by the end of combat operations "over 17,000 Australians served during the Korean War, of which 340 were killed and over 1,216 wounded [while] . . . a further 29 had become prisoners of war."[71] Australian forces remained on the peninsula until 1957. Australia's presence in Korea is ongoing. As Bill Paterson, a former Australian Ambassador to the Republic of Korea, has noted:

> Since 2010, Australia has led the UNC (Rear), located in Japan, and has assigned officers, currently around six, to the UNC headquarters in Korea. From 2014, it also assigned an embedded star-ranked officer to the United States Forces Korea, and has regularly sent personnel to major exercises on the peninsula. Australia has been one of the most active, sometimes the most active, participant in this continuing arrangement . . . It would be reasonable to conclude from this that Australia is one of the Republic of Korea's closest defence partners.[72]

The most significant strategic outcome for Australia linked to the Korean War was the signing of the ANZUS Treaty in 1951. While Australian land forces fought the war as part of a British Commonwealth Brigade, and later Commonwealth Division, Australia used the onset of the conflict to leverage its engagement with the United States. Australia announced its decision to join the conflict independently of Britain and organised to do so in order to make its announcement to the US before Britain did.

The onset of the war also made it more urgent to sign a formal peace treaty with Japan. The price of such an agreement, Australia made clear, was a mutual defence treaty with the United States. As W. David McIntyre argued, the story of ANZUS is the story of how "two small countries persuaded a very large one to join it in a military alliance which the latter did not really want."[73] Australia

---

70 Robert O'Neill, *Australia in the Korean War 1950–1953*, Vol. II *Combat Operations* (Canberra: Australia War Memorial, 1985), 3.
71 "Korean War, 1950–1953," Australian War Memorial, accessed 14 April 2021, https://www.awm.gov.au/articles/atwar/korea.
72 Bill Paterson, "Australia and South Korea can and should have closer defence ties," *The Strategist*, Australian Strategic Policy Institute, 20 August 2020 https://www.aspistrategist.org.au/australia-and-south-korea-can-and-should-have-closer-defence-tiesoul/, accessed 18 April 2021.
73 W. David McIntyre, *Background to the ANZUS Pact: Policy-Making, Strategy and Diplomacy, 1945–1955*, (Canterbury: University Press, 1995), 1.

and New Zealand managed to secure something rather less than the Washington Treaty that established the North Atlantic Treaty Organization (NATO) – mainly no automatic defence agreement. The US military made sure there was no joint planning or command arrangements and while the US Joint Chiefs of Staff agreed to staff talks, their chairman, General Omar Bradley, expressed the hope that the Australians "will get tired of hanging around [in Hawaii] with nothing to do."[74]

The other significant move with the United States in the 1950s was the formation of the Radford-Collins Agreement between the US and Australian navies. This formalized the geographic and organizational separation of peacetime surveillance and wartime protection of shipping between the British Commonwealth's engagement in Southeast Asia and US efforts in the Pacific. Once again, the Australians had sought joint planning arrangements, and once again were rebuffed.[75]

In Southeast Asia, Australia's position at the crossroads of the Indian and Pacific Oceans, and at the anchor point of the Southeast Asian archipelago, meant that postwar decolonization was occurring on Australia's front doorstep. These pivotal events in regional reordering, along with Australia's newfound diplomatic and military role in Asia, meant that its engagement with this region from the end of the Second World War provided for some significant strategic changes. The RAN was busy on Cold War operational deployments in Southeast Asia from the 1950s through to 1972, while the RAAF and Australian Army were involved in various operational deployments. Australia's military forces were constantly on operations in this period, many of which involved conflict. This meant a significant portion of Australia's Cold War in Asia was decidedly "hot."[76]

Initially, Australia was engaged in the Malayan Emergency. From 1950, the RAAF was involved in "cargo runs, troop movements, and paratroop and leaflet drops in Malaya," as well as bombing operations. In 1955, Australia committed ground troops with the arrival of 2nd Battalion, Royal Australian Regiment. Thereafter Australia maintained one infantry battalion in Malaya on Emergency operations through 1959. As the Emergency wound down, Australia's commitment

---

[74] Henry Brands Jr, "From ANZUS to SEATO: United States Strategic Policy Towards Australia and New Zealand, 1952–1954," *International History Review*, Vol. 9, No. 2, May 1987, 254.

[75] Andrew Brown, "The History of the Radford-Collins Agreement," Royal Australian Navy, Sea Power Centre, http://www.navy.gov.au/history/feature-histories/history-radford-collins-agreement, accessed 16 April 2021.

[76] For details of Australia's engagement in Southeast Asia during this time see Peter Edwards, *Crisis and Commitments: The Politics and Diplomacy of Australia's Involvement in Southeast Asian Conflicts 1948–1965* (Sydney: Allen & Unwin, 1992).

became a core part of its engagement with the Commonwealth Far East Strategic Reserve – a combined force of troops, aircraft and ships from Britain, New Zealand, and Australia, based in Malaya and Singapore. The Far East Strategic Reserve was a key part of the shift in the focus of Australian defence planning in the Cold War from the Middle East to the ANZAM (Australia, New Zealand, and Malaya) region in Southeast Asia, which had started as early as 1952.[77]

With this change Australia became a leading force with its major power allies in pushing for the maintenance of the British Commonwealth's positions in Malaya in the event of a global war. In 1953, Australia hosted Field Marshal Sir John Harding, Chief of the Imperial General Staff, and during the staff talks in October it was agreed that "Australia's primary objective in global war would . . . be the security of Malaya."[78] As Field Marshal Bernard Montgomery had noted, "so long as we held Malaya, we retain control of SE Asia and we block the direct land approaches to Australia and New Zealand."[79] Thus, as David Horner has argued, "the British agreement to the downplaying of the Middle East was a major success for the Australian Defence Committee."[80] In essence, Australia achieved a major strategic objective: keeping one of its major power allies focused on Australia's key strategic interests in Southeast Asia.

The other key prong of Australia's grand strategy in this period – the engagement in Australia's core strategic areas of its other major power ally – was not so successful. In the 1950s, the US Joint Chiefs of Staff proved ever resistant to any commitment in Southeast Asia. In the event of a global war with communism erupting in Asia, the US preferred direct naval and air strikes on the Chinese mainland and a naval blockade. Thus the 1952 Five Power talks between the United States, Britain, France, Australia, and New Zealand could not agree on strategy for Southeast Asia, though they all agreed on the region's importance.[81]

---

[77] NAA, A1209, 1957/4152, Defence Committee, "Strategic Basis of Australian Defence Policy," 8 January 1953.
[78] David Horner, *Defence Supremo: Sir Frederick Shedden and the Making of Australian Defence Policy*, (Sydney: Allen & Unwin, 2000), 311.
[79] Field Marshal Bernard L. Montgomery, Memo, 15 October 1953, as quoted in Horner, *Defence Supremo*, 213.
[80] Ibid.
[81] David Lee, "Australia and allied strategy in the Far East, 1952–1957," *Journal of Strategic Studies*, Vol 16:4 (1993), 514–16.

1954 and the False Summit of Australia's Strategy in Asia

Strategic uncertainty as to the outcome of the Cold War in Southeast Asia took a turn for the worse in 1954 with the defeat of the French in Indochina. Debate swung back and forth between the United States and Britain over defensive options in Southeast Asia. In April 1954, the United States raised the idea of what later became the Southeast Asia Treaty Organization (SEATO), despite differences in opinion between the Pentagon, which endorsed the idea, and the State Department, which remained more reticent. However, by May 1954 US Secretary of State John Foster Dulles argued that the US should "not abandon the idea of a NATO-type defence [agreement] in Southeast Asia."[82]

At this moment, it seemed like Australia's grand strategic objectives with its Great Power allies had been met. Britain had agreed to support the Australian position in ANZAM through the Far East Strategic Reserve and in the event of the Cold War turning into outright war, Malaya would be maintained as a key defensive position in a global conflict. SEATO held out the promise to bring a reluctant United States more directly into the defence of Southeast Asia.

June 1954 proved to be the high point of Australia's strategic engagement with the Great Powers in Asia during this period. Japan had been defeated and ANZUS, despite its shortcomings, provided a defensive shield in case of any bid by China to overturn the regional order by force. Australia fought alongside Britain and the United States in the Korean War, shoring up its position as a reliable and effective alliance partner. In the face of rising communist aggression in Asia, Commonwealth defensive arrangements allowed Australia, with British support, to focus on the defence of Malaya and Southeast Asia even in the face of a global hot war. Now, with the fall of Indochina and the signing of the Geneva Accords, the rise of SEATO brought the promise of direct military and strategic planning with the United States, and direct US engagement in the defence of Southeast Asia and Australia's core strategic interests.

The culmination of Australia's grand strategy ambitions with its Great Power allies proved, however, to be rather fleeting. While SEATO was the regional hope for a multilateral alliance network in Asia to replicate the success of NATO in Europe, it never lived up to this promise and proved to be largely ineffectual. At the heart of SEATO lay a number of fundamental differences with NATO, the two most significant being the lack of an Article 5 provision like NATO, where an attack on one member of NATO is an attack on all of its members, and the fact that

---

82 Ibid, 518.

most countries in SEATO (United States, Britain, France, Pakistan, Australia, New Zealand, Philippines, and Thailand) were not part of Southeast Asia. This meant that in many senses SEATO was not unlike Voltaire's characterization of the Holy Roman Empire, which he saw as neither Holy nor Roman, nor in fact an Empire. SEATO was not really an alliance, was not really Southeast Asian, and in the end not much of an organization. Its failures led US diplomat James Cable to call SEATO "a fig leaf for the nakedness of American policy."[83]

Despite its flaws, Australia at first persisted with its initial faith in SEATO. The 1956 Strategic Basis of Australian Defence Policy noted that SEATO was the "most effective and economic method of ensuring Australia's security."[84] However, by the next strategic assessment in 1959 SEATO was seen as a weak organization, with unrealistic assumptions about military planning. By then it was clear that British power in Asia was in serious decline, making ANZAM of "limited value." This Australian strategic assessment noted that "potentially ANZUS is the most effective treaty to which Australia is a partner" and that Australia's contribution to a major war in Southeast Asia was contingent on US participation.[85] Australia's optimism in 1954 was dashed and the future was set. By the middle of the next decade Australia had pointedly turned from Britain to the United States as its Great Power protector and entered into a land war in South Vietnam, alongside the US and without Britain. Britain would soon announce its withdrawal from the region and thereafter its decision to join the European Common Market.

Conclusion

This chapter asked two key questions about Australia's approach to grand strategy from 1900 to 1954: how did Australia, as a new nation in 1901, attempt to provide for its security during this period? And what does this period reveal about the continuity and changes of Australia's approach to its grand strategy? This chapter used a high-level narrative to unpack Australia's approach to grand strategy in this period. It reveals both a high level of continuity and considerable change: one could argue, in the vein of the great strategist Karl von Clausewitz, that Australia had a nature and a character to its grand strategy in this period.

---

83 Kevin Ruane and Matthew Jones, *Anthony Eden, Anglo-American Relations and the 1954 Indochina Crisis* (London: Bloomsbury, 2019), 231.
84 NAA, A1838, TS677/1A ANNEX, Strategic basis of Australian defence policy, 1956.
85 NAA: A2031, April 1959, Strategic basis of Australian defence policy, 1959.

The nature of Australian grand strategy was fixed in its approach to the use of a Great Power protector in Asia. This Great Power protector was personified by a Western, democratic maritime power that, preferably, exercised hegemony – or at least maritime dominance – over Asia. This approach was supported by Australian policy elites and enacted by its governments, who all decided that, given Australia's geographic location, geopolitics, demographics, social and cultural make-up, strategic interests and its relative strategic size and weight, it was unable to provide for its security unaided. The risk that this approach entailed was one of geography, distance, and interests.

This combination of Australia's geography and history led to a rather unique set of strategic drivers. Throughout Australian history, this combination of location at the bottom of Asia combined with a reliance on a great and powerful ally located on the other side of the globe resulted in a relatively high degree of continuity in national security strategy. Captured as a whole, this was personified by an "enduring sense of historical anxiety about Australia's perceived security vulnerabilities" in the world, that led to a sense of "pessimism and uncertainly." In addressing these issues, Australian grand strategy has thus been largely based on:

- An alliance with a Great Power – first Britain and then the United States;
- The promotion of a local defence capability aimed at deterring conventional threats from Asia (mainly through the development of naval and air forces);
- A state-based focus for national security policymaking;
- A "realist" (pragmatic) tradition in foreign policy;
- From the post-Second World War era, an active bilateral and multilateral approach to diplomacy;
- A liberal internationalist approach to this diplomacy.[86]

The dominant theme in this approach has been Australia's relationship with its "great and powerful friends." Throughout this period, Australia struggled to align its strategic interests and objectives in Southeast Asia and the South Pacific with its major power allies. It was dogged in its pursuit of this alignment (as it is to this day), with various degrees of success. On one level, the main debate in Australian grand strategy during this period was about dependence versus independence in its alliance arrangements – both in military capability

---

[86] Andrew O'Neil, "Conceptualising Future Security Threats to Australia's Security," *Australian Journal of Political Science*, 46:1 (March 2011), 19–21; Michael Wesley, "The Rich Tradition of Australian Realism," *Australian Journal of Politics and History*, 55:3, 324–26; Alex Burns and Ben Eltham, "Australia's Strategic Culture: Constraints and Opportunities in Security Policymaking," *Contemporary Security Policy*, 35:2 (August 2014), 187–91.

terms and foreign policy, with respect to Australia's Great Power allies. A consistent strain of development of this time was Australia's continual grappling with how to exert more "independence" from its major patron.

The character of this approach was reflected in the changing circumstances, actors, threats, and the international environment of the Asia Pacific that the country has faced. One of the key elements of the changing character of Australia's grand strategic approach (which is also a key continuity) has been the debate that continually revolves around how it calibrates this Great Power relationship, and the degree to which it can or must show self-reliance inside this major power alliance framework. This is one of the most enduring debates among strategic elites in Australia.

During this period, Australia moved from being a collection of colonies in the British Empire to a nation-state that saw itself as a key part, as well as an enthusiastic supporter of, Imperial Defence. During the post-Great War period, faced with the threat of Japan, Australia grappled with its increasing differences with London over the direction of Empire strategic policy in Asia. The war in the Pacific from 1941 exposed British weakness and drove Australia into a coalition with another major Western maritime power in Asia – the United States. But the war also fully exposed the limitations of a middle power like Australia to influence the grand strategy of the Allies, dominated by the United States and Britain. It also drove home the importance of accessing and influencing strategic decisions made in Washington, as opposed to those of the US strategic commander in a local theatre. It reiterated the need to balance local defence capabilities alongside its Great Power allies – something abrogated in the inter-war period.

In the Cold War era, Australia expanded its range of approaches to grand strategy. During the Second World War and the period immediately after, it developed two key capabilities, an independent (from the British Foreign Office) diplomatic corps and a more robust defence force. This allowed Australia to pursue an ambitious programme of liberal internationalism in support of the postwar liberal order and multilateralism, as well as developing a more robust ability to provide for local conventional defence deterrent that could also be deployed overseas in support of its Great Power ally, and its interests in Asia.

In many senses, after a brief moment of potential triumph in mid-1954, the end of this period saw Australia back where it started – desperate for its Great Power protector to have a military presence in the regions of greatest importance to Australia: the South Pacific and Southeast Asia. In its search for security in the Pacific, Australia had mixed results. In 1914–1918, it was able to align its interests in Asia with those of Britain. It failed miserably to deal with the shifting regional order in Asia doing the inter-war period and its fidelity to the Empire restricted its ability to forge a deep relationship with the United States. It was moderately successful in the Pacific War. It managed to forge a successful partnership with the United States in 1942 to provide for its security in the face of an existential threat. Thereafter it struggled to exert influence on US strategy in the Pacific and later the British return to the Pacific in 1945. During the early Cold War it was successful in aligning British interest with its own in Southeast Asia, but failed to secure the support of the United States, upon whom its future security now seemed to depend.

The years 1900 to 1954 were a journey from British colonialism in the South Pacific to US imperialism in Southeast Asia – and in both of these endeavours, Australia's ambitions for strategic security were thwarted. A decade on from 1954 the United States committed troops to the defence of Southeast Asia and was in the end humiliated in the process. Its retreat in 1969 through the proclamation of the Nixon Doctrine, as well as the British commitment to withdraw from East of Suez, forced Australia yet again to re-assess its role in Asia – but this time, to start seeking security with, rather than from, Asia.

Brian P. Farrell
Reflections: Making Sense of and Shaping Order in the Asia-Pacific 1900–1954

For nearly the whole period we focused on in this volume – from 1900 through 1954 give or take either way – China was not a Great Power. Yet, as one chapter noted was done by President Franklin Delano Roosevelt (FDR), we treated it as though it always had to be seen as something more than a "Middle Power." For FDR, this was aspirational, to try to reorder a new region using China as a fulcrum.[1] It was not aspirational for us, but we also saw the central fact of the geopolitics of time and place: whatever it was at any given time, China was the fulcrum. What happened in 1900–1901 cemented an accomplished fact. The fading of the Qing as a power guaranteed there would be no serious Asian pushback to the expansion of Western power in Southeast Asia – a term not then even in use for a region not then even defined – and opened up mainland East Asia to reordering. In retrospect it became obvious how tightly entangled the two areas were, something now topical again due to the PRC decision to resurrect the old Qing claim that the South China Seas are Chinese territorial waters. Nor was that claim ever completely buried; the spurious Nine Dash Line Map that expresses this claim dates back to a 1935 assertion by the Republic of China, revived postwar, then adopted by the PRC from 1952; the problem as a whole stemmed directly from the Qing agreement to cede suzerainty over Vietnam to France, in 1885.[2] Chinese weakness and the assertion of Western power obscured this continuity: the condition of China remained the defining factor in shaping the larger region from Vladivostok to Rangoon. The military defeat of the Qing in 1900 and the Protocol imposed on them in 1901 were intended not only to make sense of this new condition, but also henceforth to regulate efforts by the various Great Powers to reorder the region. These were now the "rules of the road."

The principal story of this time and place from the Boxer Protocol to the outbreak of the Pacific War was the challenge that emerged within these new agreements: how could the Great Powers manage three things at the same time without resorting to major war: the globalization of a new China, the rising ambitions of Japan, and the increasing importance of the USA? Over time the

---
1 See Chapter 5 in this volume.
2 Wu Shicun, *Solving Disputes for Regional Cooperation and Development in the South China Sea: A Chinese Perspective* (Oxford: Chandos Publishing, 2013).

Chinese made it clear that theirs would in the end be the principal voice in their own transformation. But this dragged on a painfully long time, generated much confusion, and triggered more dangerous confrontations. Notwithstanding the Great War and the Russian Revolution, the greatest of these became in time a head-on collision: between a USA determined that in the end no one state would became a hegemonic defining power in the region, and the ultimate Japanese decision to try to become just that. This led to the fusion of two great struggles: the Japanese drive to establish dominance on the Chinese mainland, the Second Sino-Japanese War; and the American-led effort to prevent this, the Pacific War.

We proposed that grand strategy, the process by which a power organizes and applies its strength to achieve its goals, was the most useful vantage point from which to try to understand this experience of Great Powers and reordering the region. In his own magisterial contribution to the iconic British Official History of the Second World War subseries titled *Grand Strategy*, Michael Howard began Chapter I with the following declaration:

> Grand strategy in the first half of the twentieth century consisted basically in the mobilization and deployment of national resources of wealth, manpower and industrial capacity, together with the enlistment of those of allied and, when feasible, of neutral powers, for the purpose of achieving the goals of national policy in wartime.[3]

This definition fit only one of our chapters: number five, discussing Allied grand strategy for the Pacific War against Japan, with particular reference to China and Southeast Asia. Elements of it applied to nearly all our other studies, but only one saw the hand fit the glove. Why therefore did a focus on grand strategy prove so useful? Because the concept itself, with sincere respect to Michael Howard, was more constant, more flexible, and more multifaceted, in Asia, during the first half of the twentieth century (and likely everywhere, all the time). There proved to be neither need nor utility to restrict its operation to "wartime."

We did not set out to theorize grand strategy, although we consulted many studies that tried to do so.[4] We affirmed our own suspicion: it was and is too elastic a concept to be reliably theorized. Instead we approached it from a

---

[3] Michael Howard, *Grand Strategy, Vol. IV, August 1942 – September 1943* (London: HMSO, 1972), 1.
[4] Two of note include Christopher Coker, *The Improbable War: China, the United States, and the Logic of Great Power Conflict* (NY: Oxford University Press, 2015), and Matthew Kroenig, *The Return of Great Power Rivalry* (Oxford: University Press, 2020).

different direction. Rather than seeking to uncover a tightly woven underlying connecting pattern – such as the score of a symphony – we explored a variety of situations that related in some way to our central question and problem, to see whether we would find in variety what others sought in coherence: fundamental defining connections. This volume produced a jazz score, not a symphony – one that combines a steady and discernible rhythm section with connected, but strikingly diverse, individual riffs. The conclusions come from the combination of rhythm and riff.

The USA experienced stark and fundamental change in this experience. It went from looking for ways to exert influence within China without a grand strategy to waging total war in order to prevent someone else from doing so, then trying to reorder a region as the new global leading power. Japan went from exploring ways to work within agreed rules of the road to hedging its bets against their failing, then moving in new directions, then rolling the dice to try to fundamentally reorder the region by exerting its own national power. The British went from trying to gradually and peacefully revise the rules of the road – while holding what they had for as long as they could – to trying to guide the new leading power towards what remained their own constant goal: to manage change with as little violence as possible; it must thus be admitted that the Pacific War marked, for them, fundamental failure, and thus new challenges. Those new challenges arose in such diverse situations as trying to retain influence through soft power in a former colony, or trying to retain leverage within a military alliance to retain wider influence in the wider region. Whether it was through the agency of a determined individual leader trying to assert the influence of his own emerging state, or a weaker power trying to play off rival Great Powers against each other to its own benefit, or a neighbor seeking its own identity by trying to define its relationships to both the region and the Great Powers, we encountered different experiences and expressions of grand strategy that connected to our larger problem: reordering a region that ultimately revolved around China, rewriting the rules of the road.

The Geneva Conference and Agreements of 1954 may or may not have amounted to the end of an era. For at least some, and in some ways, they clearly did: re-emergence of a China no longer a divided and stymied power; demarcation of the battle line in Northeast Asia and the terms and conditions by which it would continue in Southeast Asia; moments for reflection that they posed to such interested parties as the UK, India, and Australia. But in the end they certainly form a useful vantage point from which to pull together our jazz score: our exploration of grand strategy in order to understand the experience of Great Powers trying to reorder this region. Excepting Japan, they were all there in 1954. They all pursued an agenda, employed a grand strategy. What they did amounted to more than an episode, if perhaps less than a turning point. What emerged could not have happened without them. But none of them achieved what they wanted. Nor did anything later unfold as they wished. In that respect we see our cardinal point as well and truly made. In this part of the world, for this half century, the singular reality was that nothing could be reordered without China or the Great Powers being at the heart of it; but neither China nor the Great Powers could ultimately prevail either. China's situation made this time and place singular. But Clausewitzian friction, as always, drove the "rules of the road."

Index

ABDACOM 154, 155, 157, 160
Acheson, Dean 314
Afghanistan 276
Africa 71, 159, 192, 194, 196
airbases 88, 196, 209
aircraft 165
– bombers 196, 208, 210, 277
– fighters 196
– ground attack 135
– reconnaissance 135
– transport 157, 198
aircraft carriers 136, 145
Akyab 159, 166, 169
Alaska 105
alliances 85, 102, 154
aluminium 67, 68
American Asiatic Association 24, 25, 29, 47
American China Development Company 27–29, 31
amphibious operations 94, 97, 98, 111, 167, 171, 173, 175
Amur River 116
Anakim, war plan 158, 159, 162, 164, 165
Andaman islands 170
Anglo-Japanese Alliance 116, 147, 374, 375
anti-aircraft artillery 103
Anti-Fascist People's Freedom League 281, 285, 291, 303
ANZAC conference, 1944 382
ANZAM area 191, 197, 387, 388, 389
ANZUS Pact, 1951 188, 196, 197, 367, 382, 384–86, 388, 389
Arakan 159, 167, 172
Araki Sadao 73
Arcadia conference, 1941–42 154, 162
Area of Peace, concept 251, 342, 348, 359
Argentina 71
armoured cars 135
Army War College, USA 94, 95
Arnold, Henry "Hap" 163
artillery 103, 135, 138, 142, 143
Asian Relations conference, 1947 347
Assam 160, 166
assassinations 17, 56, 73–75, 224

Atlantic Charter 240, 244, 246, 247, 382
Attlee, Clement 281
Auchinleck, Claude 167
Australia 5, 71, 201, 363, 365, 368, 395
– Aborigines 369
– Army/land forces 196, 371, 384–86
– and Cold War 187–89, 196, 197, 199, 200, 210, 211, 286, 383–88, 391, 392
– Constitution of 372
– Council of Defence 384
– Naval and Military Expeditionary Force 373, 374
– Federation of 367, 370–72
– foreign policy 363, 376, 379, 382, 391
– grand strategy 363, 367, 371–79, 381, 383, 384, 386–91
– and Second World War 160, 165, 179, 379–82, 391, 392
– and SEATO 330, 367, 388, 389
– Trade Diversion Policy 378
– and USA 373, 375, 378–92
– White Australia Policy 363, 372
Austria 99
Austria-Hungary 1, 4

Baldwin, Stanley 124
Balfour, Arthur 125
Ba Maw 243, 245, 247
Bamboo curtain 259
Bandaranaike, S.W.R.D. 357, 358
Bandung conference, 1955 252, 257, 263, 274, 287, 305, 307, 340, 347, 350, 351
Bangkok 159, 175
banking, banks 20, 22, 26–28, 32–34, 37–39, 43
Bank of Japan 2, 58, 59
Banque D'Orsay 33
Banque de L'Indochine 43
Bao Dai 200, 201, 203, 355
Batam island 68
battlecruisers, battleships 373
bauxite 67, 68, 72, 76
Beatty, David 127
Beijing 27, 118, 125

https://doi.org/10.1515/9783110718713-019

– Soviet legation 139
Belgium 1, 27, 32
Bell, Coral 365
Bengal, Bay of 158, 160, 162–64, 170, 173, 175
Ben Hai River 339
Berlin conference, 1954 309, 315, 339, 346
Bidault, Georges 324, 327, 331
Bingley, J. Stewart 288, 293
Bintan island 67, 68
blockade 129, 148, 387
Bluykher, Vasily Konstantinovitch 121, 122
bombing, strategic 165, 168, 169, 171, 173–78
books 293, 301–04
Borneo 165, 179, 194
Borodin, Mikhail Markovich 121, 122, 140
Bose, Subhas Chandra 243
Boxer Protocol, 1901 1, 2, 5, 35, 125, 393
Boxer Rebellion, 1900 1, 35, 115
boycotts 34, 122, 148
Bradley, Omar 386
Brands, Hal 256, 365
Bridgestone 64, 65
Briggs, Ellis 319, 321
Britain-Burma Defence Agreement, 1947 285
British Army 194, 195
– and China 113, 125, 128, 129, 134, 135, 138, 147
– Durham Light Infantry 143, 145
– Fourteenth (14th) Army 179
– General Staff 113, 147, 387
– Gloucestershire Regiment 142, 145
– Gurkhas 187, 191, 192, 194, 196, 199
– Special Air Service 187
British Commonwealth Occupation Force (Japan) 384, 385
British Council 282–84, 288–93, 295–98, 300–02, 307, 308
British Empire 3, 106
– East of Suez, concept 384, 389, 392
– economic interests of 4, 5, 26, 27, 131, 370
– influence of 4, 5
– Imperial conferences 373, 376, 379
– Imperial defence, Asia 113, 124, 126–30, 134–38, 140, 141, 147–50, 187–92, 199–201, 203, 204

– Imperial defence, policy 113, 124, 196, 199–201, 371–74, 377, 389
– Imperial defence, strategy 187–92, 196, 376
British government
– British Defence Coordinating Committee Far East 186, 191, 192, 198, 199, 205, 207
– Burma Office 282
– Cabinet 124–26, 128–30, 134, 137, 138, 149, 186, 202, 203, 206
– Chiefs of Staff 125, 127–30, 137, 138, 140, 149, 157, 158, 162, 167, 174, 179, 199, 207, 376
– Commissioner General for Southeast Asia 191
– Committee of Imperial Defence 125, 137
– Defence Committee 186, 205, 206, 210
– Foreign Office 125, 126, 128–30, 132, 137, 146, 147, 205, 281–84, 286, 295, 299, 300
– Information Research Department 283
– Joint Intelligence Committee 191
– Joint Planning Staff 158, 165, 167
– Joint Staff Mission 163
– War Office 135, 143
British Malaya 68, 72, 76, 77, 192, 193
Brooke, Alan 162, 172, 174
Brooke-Popham, Robert 213
Bruce, Stanley 376
Brunei 191, 192
Bryan, William Jennings 46
Buccaneer, plan 170–77
Bulganin, Nikolai 275, 276
Burma 4, 217, 242–45, 247, 248
– and Cold War 198, 218, 219, 272, 281–84, 287, 293–95, 299, 301–08, 340, 344, 347, 348, 354
– defence of 285, 286
– foreign policy 287
– Ministry of Education 284, 289, 303–05
– Ministry of Foreign Affairs 302
– in Second World War 154, 156–62, 164–76, 178, 179, 184
Burma-China Friendship Association 299
Burma Road 156, 158, 160, 162, 165, 166, 168, 170, 172, 179

Burma-Soviet Cultural Association 283, 299, 300
Butler, Smedley 145, 146

Cable, James 389
Cairo 171, 175
Cairo conference, 1943 171–73, 175, 177
Cairo Declaration, 1943 171, 175
Cambodia 187, 201, 209, 211, 309, 326, 327, 330, 331, 336, 342, 347, 352, 359
cameras 64–66
Canada 303, 336, 350, 353, 355, 357
Cannibal, operation 159, 165
Canon 64, 66
Caribbean 29, 33, 34, 42, 88, 102, 192
Caroline islands 91, 375
casualties 90, 99, 385
Ceylon 272, 340, 345, 347, 348, 354
– (see also Sri Lanka)
Chahar 228
Chamber of Commerce, USA 21, 25, 31
Chamberlain, Austen 125, 130, 140, 147
Chanak Crisis, 1922 375, 376
Chang Tso-lin 139
Chapei 143
Charter of Human Rights 383
Chauvel, Jean 329, 332
Chen, Eugene 140, 141
Chennault, Claire 153, 159, 163, 164, 166, 176, 177
Chiang Kai-shek
– and grand strategy 154, 156, 159–61, 163, 170–73, 175
– and Guomindang 139–41, 147
– as military leader 139, 155, 178
– and Shanghai 82
– and USA 154, 159, 172, 180
Chifley, Ben 381
Chin Hills 159
Chindits 167, 169
China 5, 9, 19–21, 54, 84, 114, 116, 393, 396
– China market, the 20, 22, 23, 25–30, 34, 35, 47, 86
– Communist Party of 121, 139, 140, 142
– Concessions, foreign 28, 115, 117, 121, 125, 132
– Consular courts in 131

– extraterritoriality in 117, 119, 121, 131, 163, 242
– foreign residents in 122, 127, 137, 138, 145
– geopolitical influence 1–4, 6, 139
– loans to 43, 44, 46
– missionaries in 25, 35, 132
– nationalism in 117, 118, 121–24, 127, 130, 146–50
– railways in 26–28, 36, 43, 44, 133
– spheres of influence in 27, 31, 123
– and Second World War 82, 151, 160–63, 165–71, 173–78
– Settlements, foreign 115, 117, 132
– tariffs and 119, 126
– treaty ports in 131–33
– treaty rights and 118, 125, 128, 131, 134, 145
– treaty system and 1, 31, 114, 115–19, 127, 130–32, 140, 141, 150
– unequal treaties and 1, 115, 131
China Eastern Railway 38
China, Qing 1, 16, 34, 115, 131, 393
China, Republican 5, 46, 115, 116
– foreign policy 116, 119, 228, 393
– National Revolution of 121
– United Front in 121, 123, 139
– warlords (*tuchuns*) 118, 119, 123, 136–39
China, People's Republic of 1, 7, 395
– and Cold War 186, 187, 189, 197, 198, 200, 202, 204, 262, 269, 306, 346, 352
– foreign policy 1, 2, 203, 299–301, 393
– Geneva Conference and 1, 2, 202, 325, 326, 332, 335
– and India 252, 257
– Korean War and 1, 206, 262, 319
Chindits 167, 170, 172
Chinese Civil War
– 1927–37 82, 140
– 1937–49 295
Chinese Cultural Mission, Burma 283
Chinese (Imperial) Maritime Customs Service 30, 131
Christmas Memorandum, the 126, 127, 138, 146
Chungking 156, 173
Churchill, Winston Spencer 125
– and China 130, 157

– and grand strategy 130, 154, 157, 165, 167, 168, 170, 172–74, 179, 205, 206, 208, 209
cinema (films) 291, 292, 296, 297, 302
Clague, John 282
Clary, Clarence 29
Clausewitz, Karl von 389, 396
Cleveland, Grover 20
coal 40, 234
Cold War, the 5, 7, 196–98, 218, 219, 251, 253, 259, 274, 282, 286, 339, 344
Colombo 345
Colombo conference, 1954 340, 347–51, 358–59
Colombo Plan 201
Colombo powers 219, 273, 340, 342, 354–57
Combined Chiefs of Staff, the 154, 160, 162, 166, 168, 172, 174
Comintern, the 121, 139, 140
commandos 175
Commonwealth, British 194, 201, 267, 281, 286, 345
– Brigade, Korean War 385
– Division, Korean War 385
– Strategic Reserve Far East 187, 190, 191, 199, 211, 387, 388
communism, communists 194, 197, 198, 203, 205, 207, 211, 229, 251, 257, 286, 291, 384
Conger, E.H. 28
consortiums, international 33, 34, 42–44, 46
consortiums, national 2, 32, 48
Cook, James 369
cotton 30, 31, 63, 71, 75, 76
cruisers 55, 104, 125, 136, 137, 145, 373
culture 217–19, 268, 271, 282–84, 287, 288, 290, 292–307
Culverin, plan 167–70, 172
Currie, Lachlin 160, 161
Curtin, John 379, 381
Cyprus 196
Czechoslovakia 355

Dalian (Dairen) 238
Day, William 28
Deakin, Alfred 373

Dean, Arthur 321
decolonization 5, 200, 201, 258, 263, 271, 284, 306, 307, 339, 358
Democratic Party, USA 312, 313
Denby, Charles 20, 27, 28
destroyers 55, 137, 373
Deutsche-Asiatische Bank 43
Dibb, Paul 368
Dien Bien Phu 198–200, 208, 209, 211, 320, 325
Dill, John 163
DIME, model 10, 81, 114, 148, 183, 210
diplomacy
– applied 11, 16, 32, 33, 141, 147, 149, 206, 207, 227, 228, 241, 297, 299, 304, 314, 324
– defined 9, 210, 217, 219, 233, 311
– summit 163, 172, 237, 328, 339
Dog, plan 107, 109
domino theory 189, 198
Drogheda Report 288, 289
Drum, Hugh 155
Dulles, John Foster 208, 254, 277, 309
– diplomacy 315, 320, 322, 324–26, 334
– and grand strategy 314, 320, 326, 327, 329, 331, 333, 334, 336, 388
Duncan, John 135, 142, 143
Dunlap, Robert H. 96
Dutt, Subimal 268

economics 9–11, 15–17, 32, 49, 50, 54
Eden, Anthony
– at Geneva Conference, 1954 209, 211, 328, 331, 333–36, 339, 340, 358, 349, 350
– and Nehru 252, 273, 342, 347, 350
– and SEATO 330, 335, 352, 353
– and Vietnam War 208, 324, 327, 354
education 282–84, 288–90, 294, 296, 302–08
Egypt 70, 71, 196, 208
Eisenhower, Dwight D. 277
– and Cold War 252, 271, 272
– and Geneva Conference, 1954 309, 331, 336
– and Korean War 317, 318
– and grand strategy 187, 208, 217, 312, 314, 333

elections 291
Ellis, Earl "Pete" 89, 91, 96
Eureka conference, 1943 174
Europe 67, 384
European Common Market 389
European Defence Community 207, 208, 313, 324
Evatt, Herbert 382
exports 60, 63, 68–71, 93, 202, 285

Falkland Islands, battle of, 1914 374
Farrell, J.G. 212, 213
First National Bank 43
Five Power Talks, 1952 387
Five Power Treaty, 1922 55
Five Principles, the 251
Fleet, James Van 318–20
Flying Tigers, the 153
Foord, John 24, 25, 29, 30, 35
Ford Foundation 296, 298
Foster, John 34
Four Policemen, concept 172
Four Power Declaration, 1943 171, 172
Four Power Treaty, 1922
Fourth (4th) May Movement 117
France 3, 22, 54, 102
– and China 1
– fall of, 1940 4
– grand strategy 330
– as Great Power 4, 204, 207, 387, 389
– and Shanghai 142
– Vichy regime 234
– and Vietnam 197, 198, 204, 325, 326, 329, 331, 346, 347, 357
Franco-Chinese War 115, 393
French Indochina 1, 83, 188, 189, 200, 233
– Associated States of 187
Fuji Film 64, 65
Fulbright Agreements 294
Fulbright Foundation 296, 298

G20, the 365
Garcia, Carlos 321
General Electric 64
Geneva Agreements, 1954 11, 202, 211, 359, 388, 395

Geneva Conference, 1954 1, 2, 198, 200, 202, 208, 209, 211, 217, 219, 309, 311, 349, 350
– disputes 320–23, 326–32, 334, 335, 337, 355
– objectives 315, 316, 318–20, 324, 325, 330–32, 334, 335, 339, 340
– outcomes 311, 323, 324, 335–40, 342, 357, 359, 388, 395
Geneva Final Declaration, 1954 1, 2
Genocide Convention, the 383
genro 36, 224, 226
geography 34, 136, 363, 365, 368, 369, 371, 386, 390
geopolitics 1–6, 9, 11, 15, 45, 81, 115, 124, 365, 368, 371, 372
Germany 4, 22, 54, 102, 233, 236, 237, 240
– and China 1, 26, 32
– East Asiatic Squadron 373, 374
gold standard, the 55–57, 59
Gort, John 143
Goto Shinpei 40, 44
Graham, Martha 298
grand strategy 2, 5
– applied 130, 134, 136–38, 140, 142, 145, 148, 150, 189, 190, 192, 194, 196, 200, 205, 210–12, 239, 247–49, 282, 284, 287, 307, 389–91, 396
– definitions, scholars 6, 7–11, 15, 19–21, 32, 34, 48, 82, 84–87, 114, 123, 124, 126, 183, 184, 210, 212, 217–19, 222, 224, 225, 230, 232, 249, 253, 255, 256, 282, 311, 338, 342, 343, 364–67, 390, 394, 395
– historiography 7, 9, 10, 19, 85–87, 152, 217, 219, 224, 225, 232, 255, 256, 281, 309, 310, 340, 341, 365–67, 394
Great Britain. See United Kingdom.
Great Depression, the 5, 16, 17, 49, 54, 56, 59, 81, 92, 377, 378
Great Kanto Earthquake, 1923 55
Great Powers 1, 8, 15, 114, 339
– agency of 2, 4–6, 9, 11, 81, 363, 364, 396
– definitions of 3, 4, 6, 253
– limitations of 2, 4–6, 396
Great War, the 5, 6, 16, 50, 55, 90, 116, 373, 374, 394

Greater East Asia Confederation 244
Greater East Asia Conference, 1943 239, 244, 245
Greater East Asia Co-Prosperity Sphere 218, 221, 222, 225, 233, 238, 242, 244, 249
Greater East Asia Joint Declaration (Pacific Charter) 244–48
Green, Michael J. 85, 86, 367
Grew, Joseph C. 235
Griscom, Lloyd C. 22, 23, 31
Guam 86, 88, 101, 109
Guangdong 118, 157
Guangzhou 122, 132, 137
Guomindang, the 118, 134, 137, 149, 194, 295
– factionalism 120, 136, 138–41
– grand strategy 121, 123, 129, 138, 141
– and Japan 138, 149, 228
– organization 120, 121, 139
– and Soviet Union 120, 121, 138–40

Hai River 125
Haiphong 160, 205
Halifax 94
Hamaguchi Osachi 54–56
Hankou 27, 132
– Incident, 1927 123, 124, 126, 128, 136, 139–41
Hanoi 160, 205, 206
Hanyang 123
Harding, John 387
Harriman, Edward H. 22, 23, 35–39, 44, 47
Haw Par Villa 3
Hawaii 30, 87
Hay, John Milton 29–31, 34
Hayashi Senjuro 73, 229
heavy industry 17, 64, 65, 68–72, 75–77
Hebei 228
Heeney, Arnold 356
Henderson, Loy 265
Hepburn, Arthur J. 101
Hermes, plan 188
Higgins, Andrew Jackson 98, 102
Himalayas 265, 267
Hindi-Chini Bhai Bhai 252, 278
Hippisly, Alfred 30
Hirota Koki 227–29

Hitachi 64
Hitler, Adolf 99, 236, 244
Holcomb, Thomas 89, 92, 94, 95, 97, 105, 106, 108, 109
Holland. See Netherlands.
Hong Kong 82, 113, 122, 132, 136, 173, 191, 195, 201
Hong Kong and Shanghai Banking Corporation 33, 43, 56
Hopkins, Harry 177
Hoover, Herbert 93
Howard, Michael 394
Huangpu River 131, 142, 143
Hue 329
Hughes, William Morris "Billy" 374
Hukuang 43, 44, 46
Hump, the 157–59, 161, 163–66, 170, 172, 173, 175, 177
Hungary 277

Ichi-Go, operation 177, 178
immigration 34, 35
Imperial Japanese Army 65, 74, 248
– Burma Area Army 247
– China Garrison Army 228
– General Staff 226, 229, 231, 234, 235
– Kodo faction 73
– Kwantung Army 49, 56, 149, 224, 228
– Toseiha faction 73
Imperial Japanese Navy 65–67, 149, 239, 240, 381
– battleship *Musashi* 66, 67
– battleship *Yamato* 66
– Betty bomber 66
– Nell bomber 65
– Zero fighter 65, 66, 68
Imphal, battle of, 1944 179
imports 63, 68, 72, 76
India 70, 217, 395
– and Cold War 218, 252, 253, 259, 263, 272, 286, 336, 340–42, 345, 346, 354, 357, 359
– Communist Party of 257, 261, 265, 276
– Congress Party of 251, 254
– foreign policy 201, 202, 218, 254, 263, 271, 343, 355, 357
– Free India 243, 244

Index — 403

– and imperial defence 134, 190–92
– non-alignment 202, 342
– and Second World War 154, 156, 158, 159, 164, 177, 184
– Viceroy of 167
Indian Army 134, 167, 179
– Fourteenth (14th) Army 179
– GHQ India 154, 164, 167
Indian Ocean 313, 377, 386
Indonesia 201, 272, 274, 340, 344, 347, 348, 354, 357
– Independence War 191, 200, 201, 243, 258, 345
Inoue Junnosuke 54–56
intelligence, military 10, 130, 136, 138–40, 148, 149
International Banking Corporation 33
International Control Commission 203, 342, 354, 355, 357, 359
International Human Rights Court 383
international relations
– middle powers 5, 11, 219, 363, 365, 381, 382
– theory 9
investors, investments 16
Inukai Tsuyoshi 57
Iran 272, 314
Iraq 272
iron 40, 64, 72, 76, 77
Iron Curtain, the 309
Irony, plan 185, 187, 205
Ishiwara Kanji 56, 229
isolationism 81, 90, 92, 93, 98, 102
Italy 1, 4, 173, 233
Iwo Jima, battle of, 1945

Japan 2–4, 19, 20, 22, 25, 31, 36, 217, 395
– and China 1, 32, 116, 117, 119, 131, 134, 146, 147, 149, 225, 227–29, 242, 244
– and Cold War 314, 335, 384
– domestic politics of 16, 17, 36, 37, 49, 55–57, 64, 74–76, 146, 224
– foreign policy of 17, 44, 50, 75–77, 146, 147, 149, 224, 237, 240, 241, 243, 246
– and Great Depression 16, 17, 49, 50, 54, 57, 59, 60, 63, 64, 75, 92
– imperial conferences 231, 243

– Imperial Diet 228, 242
– Imperial General Headquarters 221, 226, 230, 231
– imperialism of 16, 17, 93, 116, 149, 221–23, 228, 229, 242, 243, 245, 373, 375, 394
– independence of supreme command 226, 227, 230, 235, 248
– Inner Cabinet 225–27, 230
– liaison conferences 221, 222, 231, 232, 234, 235, 242, 248
– and Manchuria 36, 37, 44, 149
– Meiji government 36, 224, 226
– militarism in 16, 74, 75, 77, 93
– and Shanghai 129, 134, 136, 145
– Showa Depression 54–56, 59, 76
– Showa Financial Crisis 146
– war plans 100
Jenkins, J.E.V. 291, 292, 294, 295, 297, 301, 302
Jinan 147
John Doe Associates 238
Johor 186
Johor Straits 184

Kaneko Kentaro 37
Kant, Immanuel 368
Karachi 272
Katsura-Harriman Agreement 36
Kaul, T.N. 273
Keating, Paul 363
Kellogg, Frank 145, 146
Kennan, George 85
Kennedy, Paul 10, 15
Keynes, John Maynard 17, 59, 60
Khrushchev, Nikita 253, 269, 275, 276
Kim Il Sung 262
Kimura Heitaro 247, 248
King, Ernest J. 162, 174, 380
Kissinger, Henry 254
Knox, Philander 42–45
Komura Jutaro 37
Konoe Fumimaro 229–31, 239
Korea (see also North and South Korea) 1, 23, 25, 32, 67, 71, 165, 262
Korean War, 1950–53 1, 197–99, 202, 206, 259, 262, 263, 356, 384

– controversies 314, 317, 323, 337
Kotelawala, John 348, 350
Kra Isthmus 83, 188, 197, 198
Kuhn, Loeb & Company 22, 43

Lampson, Miles 129, 130, 137
landing craft 98, 101, 102, 106, 174, 175
language 282–84, 288, 289, 296, 305, 306
Laos 201, 209, 309, 330, 331
– and Geneva Agreements 187, 202, 211, 328, 342, 352, 359
– and Vietnam War 197, 198, 208, 326, 327, 336, 347
Large Policy, the 28–30, 33
Latin America 30, 70, 96
de Lattre de Tassigny, Jean 206
Laurel, Jose P. 245, 247
League of Nations 76, 93, 118, 130, 149
– Mandates 375
Leahy, William D. 166, 174
Ledo 166
Lejeune, John A. 89, 90, 92, 94
Lend-Lease 151, 153, 180
liberal internationalism 5, 224, 239, 246, 358, 383, 390
Linlithgow, Lord (Victor Hope) 167
Lippmann, Walter 151
Lloyd George, David 142, 143
loans 175–77, 180, 286
Locarno Agreements, 1925 335
– Eastern Locarno concept 335, 352, 353, 359
Lodge, Henry Cabot 29, 30
logistics 88, 157, 158, 159, 162, 164, 166, 169, 170, 173, 175, 178, 179
London 58, 363
London Naval Conference, 1930 55
– Naval Treaty, 1930 56, 226
London School of Economics 298
Long Range Penetration Groups. See Chindits.
Lukouchiao 27
lumber 28
Luneta Park 244
Luttwak, Edward 85, 86
Lyon, Joseph 379

MacArthur, Douglas 103, 380–82
MacDonald, Malcolm 191, 192, 198, 203, 204, 209–12, 278, 279
machine guns 103, 142
Madison Project, database 49, 54
Magruder, John 145
Mahan, Alfred Thayer 21, 29, 30
Malacca (Melaka) 192
Malay Regiment 192, 195
Malaya
– and Cold War 83, 185, 186, 188, 190, 195, 197, 199, 202, 205, 207, 211, 387, 388
– Federation of 189, 191, 192, 194
– Malay States 193
– Unfederated States 192, 193
Malayan Communist Party 194, 195, 203
Malayan Emergency 83, 194–96, 203, 204, 386
Malayan Union 194
Malik, Jacob 268
Manchester Guardian 346, 349
Manchukuo 68, 70, 71, 93, 224, 225, 227–29, 237, 244, 245
Manchuria 19, 23, 25–27, 32, 35, 37, 116, 175
– Neutralization Scheme, 1909 42–46, 48
Manchurian Incident, 1931 49, 50, 56, 59, 60, 63, 65, 75–>77, 224, 248
Mandalay 289
Mao Zedong 252, 262, 269, 332
Marianas islands 91, 100, 375
Marshall, George C. 104, 105, 111, 153–56, 160, 162, 164, 169, 174
Marshall islands 91, 100, 375
Matador, plan 83, 183–85, 186, 190, 213
Matsuoka, Yosuke 218
– and diplomacy 233–36, 238, 239
– and grand strategy 225, 232–37, 239, 249
– and Soviet Union 236, 237
– and USA 237–39
Matsushita (Panasonic) 64
McGhee, George 265
McKinley, William 16, 28, 29, 47
Meaney, Neville 373
Mediterranean Sea 135, 184, 196, 369
Mehta, G.L. 354, 356
Mendès-France, Pierre 329, 332–34, 336
Menon, K.P.S. 268, 269

Menon, V.K. Krishna 340, 344, 346, 347, 350, 351, 355–57, 359
Menzies, Robert 363
Mexico 303
Micronesia 100
Middle East 167, 187, 196, 197, 199, 272, 374, 379, 384, 387
Midway island 101, 109
military education 93, 94
military manuals 94, 96, 101
Millar, T.B. 384
Mindanao 165
mines, mining 28, 40
Minseito, party 54, 55, 57
Mitsubishi 56, 64, 65
Mitsui 56
Mituchi Chuzo 55
Moltke, Helmuth von 311
Molotov, Vyacheslav 315, 322, 326, 327, 331, 335, 339
Mongolia 23, 237
Montgomery, Bernard Law 325, 387
Morgan, J.P. 22, 43, 47
Morocco 164
Moscow 171, 305
Moulmein 159
Mountbatten, Louis 168, 170–74
Mukden 23, 37, 40, 47
Mullik, B.N. 264, 265, 267
Munich Agreement, 1938 99
Muroto Typhoon, 1934 60, 74
Murphy, Robert 322, 328, 329
Myitkyina 178

Nagata Tetsuzan 73
Nanjing 132
– incident, 1927 137–41
– massacre, 1937 99
National Association of Manufacturers (USA) 21
National City Bank 43, 56
National Revolutionary Army, China 121, 129, 136, 137, 142, 149
– and Second World War 156
nationalism 5, 9, 37, 286
naval bases 91, 376, 382
Navarre, Henri 207, 208

Navy League (USA) 21
Ne Win 287, 306
Nehru, Jawaharlal 254
– Area of Peace concept 219, 251, 257, 270, 340, 344, 345, 351–53, 358
– and China 251, 252, 263–67, 273, 274, 278, 279
– Five Principles 251, 257, 270, 273, 275, 276, 344, 346, 351
– foreign policy 254, 255, 258, 259, 270, 343, 345–49, 351
– Geneva Conference 270, 340, 342, 350, 356, 359
– and grand strategy 217, 218, 255, 256–59, 270, 279
– and non-alignment 252, 256, 257, 264, 267, 274, 275, 340, 344, 352, 358
– and USSR 251, 252, 260, 261, 264–68, 274–77, 279
– and USA 251–54, 260, 263–65, 272, 273, 275, 277, 279
– and Zhou Enlai 351–54, 359
Nepal 191
Netherlands, The 1
Netherlands East Indies (also Dutch) 67, 68, 70–72, 76, 77, 160, 191, 233, 238
Neutrality Acts, USA 1935–37, 98
New Britain 160
New Deal, the 54
New Guinea 160, 165, 374, 375
New Look strategy 208, 314
New Villages 195
New York 28, 54, 56
– Wall Street 58
New York Times 349
New Zealand 196, 286
– and ANZUS 188, 384, 386, 389
– and Cold War 187, 188, 197, 199, 211, 387
– and Commonwealth Strategic Reserve 187
– and grand strategy 188, 197, 199, 200, 211, 375, 387
– and SEATO 330, 389
Ngo Dinh Diem 202, 209
Nichi Nichi Shimbun 44
Nikon 64
Nine-Dash Line 393
Nine Power Treaty, 1922 119, 120, 153

Nippon Steel 68
Nissan 64
Nixon, Richard 317
Nixon Doctrine 392
North Atlantic Treaty Organization 196, 335, 386, 388
North Borneo 191, 192
North China Daily News 134n.29
North Korea (Democratic People's Republic of Korea) 309, 319, 340
North Vietnam (Democratic Republic of Vietnam) 188, 203, 309, 340
Northeast Asia 1, 16, 19, 20, 313, 318, 395
Northern Expedition, 1926–28 121–23, 129, 134, 136, 138–40, 142, 147
Norway 355, 356
Nova Scotia 94
Nye, Joseph 294
Nine-Power Treaty, 1922 126
nuclear war 187–89, 196, 197, 199, 202, 206–08, 210, 330
nuclear weapons 187, 189, 197, 208, 210

Observer, the 347
official histories 10, 153, 384, 394
oil 72, 76, 165, 196
Okada Keisuke 228
Okura Company 40
Olney, Richard 20, 27
Olympus 64, 65
Open Door policy 16, 25, 30–35, 39–45, 86, 119, 151, 153
Opium Wars 115
optical industry, instruments 64
Orange, plan 87–89, 91, 95, 99, 100, 102
Osaka 54
Overlord, operation 174–76

Pacific Mail Steamship Company 22
Pacific Ocean 376, 377, 386
Pacific War. See Second World War.
Pacific War Council 380
Pakistan 259, 266, 272, 273, 286, 345, 347–49, 354–57, 389
Palestine Revolt, 1936–39 113
pan-Asianism 246, 348
Panama 34

Panama Canal 102
Pandit, Vijayalakshmi 261
Paris Peace Conference, 1919 5, 116, 374, 375
Partridge, Earle 321
Patel, Sardar Vallabhbhai 254
Patton, George S. Jr. 94, 325
peaceful coexistence policy 251, 254, 257, 269
Pearl River 136
Pearson, Lester B. 321, 350
Peking Agreement, 1905 39
Penang 192
People's Liberation Army 83
Persia 23, 31
Pham Van Dong 333, 335
Phibun Songkram 203, 212
Philippines 356
– annexation of 16, 29, 35, 86
– defence of 88, 101, 103, 389
– and Japan 70, 71, 242–45, 247
– and USA 20, 25, 34, 39, 176
Pillai, N.R. 275, 356
Poland 336, 355, 357, 358
Portal, Charles 175
ports 28, 132, 133
Portsmouth, Treaty of, 1905 32, 35, 36, 48
Pridi Phanomyong 203
propaganda 121, 122, 245–48, 283, 284, 287, 291–94, 297–303, 305
public opinion 36, 291
Pyidawtha Plan 287, 290
Pyongyang 319
Pyun Yung Tai 321

Quadrant conference, 1943 168, 170
Quebec
– conference, 1943 168, 170
– conference, 1944 179
Qing. See China.
Qingdao 116

Rabaul 374
racism 34, 247, 258, 372
Radford-Collins Agreement 386
Radhakrishnan, Sarvepalli 268, 358
radio 296, 373, 374

railways 36-38, 42, 261
Rainbow, plans 102, 105, 106
Ramgarh 157, 159, 177
Ramree Island 166, 169
Rangoon 1, 158, 159, 179, 282, 297-99, 301, 393
Rangoon University 288, 289, 292, 293, 296
Ransome, Arthur 143n.43
Reading, Lord (Gerald Isaacs) 328
realism, realpolitik 263, 358, 390
Red River 188, 206, 207, 329
Rehe 228
Reid, Escott 350, 353
Republican Party, USA 81, 312, 313
Reuters 354
Syngman Rhee 317-23, 337
rice 56, 234, 285
Ringlet, plan 185, 187, 205
riots 36, 122
Robertson, Walter S. 309
Rockhill, William Woodvale 22, 30
Roebling, Daniel 98, 102
Roosevelt, Franklin Delano 95, 97, 105, 379
 – and Chiang Kai-shek 154, 155, 159, 161, 164, 170, 171, 173, 175-78, 180
 – and China 153, 159, 163, 393
 – and grand strategy 105, 108, 159, 161-64, 170, 175-77
Roosevelt, Samuel 36, 37
Roosevelt, Theodore 16, 19, 23, 29, 31, 35, 39, 47, 48, 373
Royal Air Force
 – and China 135
 – and Malaya 188
 – V bombers 188, 189
Royal Australian Air Force 196, 199, 385, 386
Royal Australian Navy 370, 371, 373, 385, 386
Royal Australian Regiment 386
Royal Malayan Naval Service 192
Royal Marines 90, 123
Royal Navy 131
 – and Australia 369, 370, 373, 374, 377
 – British Pacific Fleet 179
 – China Station 125, 126, 128, 131, 135-37, 145, 148, 149, 373
 – HMS *Prince of Wales* 66

 – HMS *Repulse* 66
 – and Singapore 376, 377
 – and USA 179
rubber 64, 72, 76, 195, 202, 234
Rural Relief Package 59, 64, 73, 74
Russia 1, 3, 4, 19, 20, 22, 31, 32, 38
Russian Revolution 116, 394
Russo-Japanese War, 1904-05 22, 26, 31, 35-37, 226, 373

St. Laurent, Louis 347
San Francisco 58
San Francisco Conference, 1945 5
Sarawak 191
Sato Kenryo 247
Schiff, Jacob 2, 35, 47
School of Oriental and African Studies 298
seapower 4, 21, 165, 170, 370
Second World War, the 5, 7, 8, 15, 50, 54, 77, 180
 – in Central Pacific 83, 110, 111, 176, 180
 – China Theatre 82, 83, 155, 156, 177
 – conferences in 154, 161, 162, 166, 168, 171, 172
 – in Europe 77, 105, 108, 239, 240, 379
 – Germany First strategy 107
 – Guadalcanal, battle, 1942-43 110, 239
 – Iwo Jima, battle of, 1945 111
 – Malayan campaign 83, 183-85, 190, 213, 379, 380
 – in Mediterranean 173, 379, 380
 – Midway, battle of, 1942 110, 239
 – Okinawa, battle of, 1945 111
 – Pacific War 76, 83, 379-81, 394
 – Pearl Harbor, battle of, 1941 82, 110, 152, 153, 239, 240
 – Pelelieu, battle of, 1944 111
 – Saipan, battle of, 1944 111
 – in Southeast Asia 82, 83, 110, 152, 156-59, 164, 167, 177, 179, 185
 – in Southwest Pacific 83, 380, 381
 – Tarawa, battle of, 1943 111
 – war plans in 106, 107, 174, 175, 184, 185, 379
Seiyukai, party 55
Selective Service Act, 1940-41 109
self-determination 118

Seoul 319
Sextant conference, 1943 171–73
Shakespeare, William 296, 297
Shandong 27, 116, 117, 119, 228
Shanghai 173
– battle of, 1932 113, 149
– battle of, 1937 82, 113, 150
– Cordon Line 135, 141, 142
– Defence Force 82, 113, 134–36, 140, 142, 143, 145, 147–49
– economy of 132
– French Concession 132
– importance of 129–32, 134, 139, 141, 148
– incident, 1927 82, 113, 128, 129, 134–36, 139, 140, 142–45, 147, 150
– industry 122, 132
– International Settlement 128, 132, 140, 141, 143, 145
– naval landing parties 142
– North Railway Station 143
– Operation N 143, 144, 145
– organized crime 140
– White Terror, 1927 140
Shanghailanders 133, 134, 145
Shanghai Municipal Council 132, 134, 142
Shanghai Municipal Police 122, 134
Shanghai Volunteer Corps 134, 142
Shanxi 228
Sherman, John 27, 29
Shibaura Seisakujo 64, 66
Shidehara Kijuro 146
Shigemitsu Mamoru 218
– and China 227, 241, 242
– and diplomacy 240, 241
– and grand strategy 225, 239, 240, 242, 244, 245, 248, 249
shipbuilding 64, 65
Sicily 166
silk 63, 64, 75
Singapore 3, 54, 165, 179, 191, 192, 194
– and Cold War 83, 186, 188, 189, 259
– fall of 1942 83, 183–85, 190, 380
– naval base 376
Singapore Strategy 83, 184, 376, 377, 379
Sinic World Order 2
Sino-Japanese War, First, 1894–95 16, 26, 115

Sino-Japanese War, Second, 1937–45 5, 77, 99, 229, 230, 394
Smith, Holland M. 106, 108
Smith, Walter Bedell 309, 315, 319–23, 325–36, 355
Somervell, Brehon 163
Sodomei 72
soft power 9, 294
Songkhla Line 83, 183, 185–89, 200, 202, 203, 205–07, 209, 212
South Africa 71
South China Sea 157, 165, 179, 313, 393
South Korea (Republic of Korea) 309, 317–19, 340
South Manchuria Railway 36–38, 40
South Vietnam (Republic of Vietnam) 83, 187, 209
Southeast Asia 1, 2, 76, 77, 189, 313, 353, 363, 382–84, 386, 393, 395
Southeast Asia Command 167–71
Southeast Asia Treaty Organization 277, 352, 353
– founding of 83, 199, 200, 211, 273, 274, 330, 335, 337, 340
– members 272, 330, 389
– war plans 187, 188, 209–11, 388
Southwest Pacific 375–77
Soviet Union See USSR.
soy beans 70
Spaak, Paul-Henri 321
Spain 1
Spanish-American War, 1898–99 16, 19, 20, 29, 86
Spee, Graf von 373
Sri Lanka (see also Ceylon) 286
Stalin, Joseph 174–76, 236, 261, 268, 269, 339, 346
Stark, Harold R. 104–07
steel 68, 70
Steinhardt, Laurence 238
Stilwell, Joseph 152, 155
– and Chiang Kai-shek 156, 161, 163, 164, 177, 178
– and China 156, 172, 180
– and grand strategy 157, 160, 161, 166, 169, 173
Stimson, Henry 155

Straight, Willard 22, 23, 37–41, 43, 45, 47
Straits Settlements 192, 193
strikes 122, 194, 261
students 289, 290, 298
submarines 55, 240, 373
Suez Canal 196, 259
Sugiyama Hajime 235
Suiyuan 228
Sukarno 345
Sulawesi 369
Sumatra 164, 165, 167, 179
Sumitomo 56, 68
Sun Yat-sen 118, 120–22, 139
Suzuki Teiichi 221
Swanson, Claude 101
Sweden 355
Switzerland 303
Sydney 376, 381
Symbol conference, 1943 161–63

Taft, William Howard 19, 39–45, 47, 48
Taiping Rebellion 115
Taiwan 67, 71, 274
Takahashi Korekiyo 17, 22, 55, 58
– Economics of 57, 59, 60, 63–65, 70, 72–77
– importance of 17, 57, 72, 73, 75
– as Prime Minister 72
– relations with army 72–74
Tanaka Giichi 55, 146, 147
Tanaka Shin'ichi 236
tanks 135, 184
Tatmadaw 286
Tehran 173, 174
Ten Year Rule 149
Tengah 188
Terror, War on 7, 86
Thai-Indochina border dispute, 1940–41 234–36
Thailand
– and Cold War 184–87, 189, 198, 199, 203, 205–07, 211, 212, 356, 389
– and Japan 71, 233–35, 243–45
– and Second World War 157, 190
Thakin Soe 286
Thakin Tun Tan 286
Tianjin 125, 132
Tibet 23, 266, 277, 345

Times of India 347, 348, 355, 358
tin 72, 76, 195, 234
Tojo Hideki 221, 232, 234, 242–45
Tokyo (Edo) 54, 58
Tonkin 186, 189, 198, 203–07, 211, 212
Torch, operation 159, 161
Toshiba 64
Toyo Rayon 64, 65
Toyoda 64
Toyoda Teijiro 239
trade 16, 22, 25, 28, 30, 40, 69, 70, 369, 370
training, military and naval 88
Tran Van Do 335
Trans-Siberian Railway 36
Trident conference, 1943 166, 167
Tripartite Pact, 1940 233, 236
Truman, Harry S. 260, 262
Turkey 23, 31, 71, 272
Twenty-One Demands, 1915 116
Tyrwhitt, Reginald 128–30, 137, 138

U-Go, operation 177, 179
U Kaung 289
U Nu 273, 286, 287, 345
unemployment 92, 98
Union of Soviet Socialist Republics (USSR) 3, 4, 54
– and Cold War 196–98, 205, 252, 253, 260, 261, 268, 269, 275, 276, 278, 301, 302, 305, 306
– foreign aid 271, 276–78
– foreign policy of 203, 271, 299, 301
– and Geneva Conference, 1954 325, 327, 331, 357
– and Guomindang 120–22, 138, 139
– and Second World War 171
unions, labour 72, 139, 140, 290, 291
United Kingdom (UK) 395
– and China 1, 27, 114, 124, 126, 127, 130, 132, 133, 142, 146, 147, 149, 163, 202
– and Cold War 183, 196, 198, 202, 205, 206, 210, 251, 283, 295, 354
– defence policy 114, 330
– economy 57, 70, 71
– and Empire/Commonwealth 195–97, 281, 389, 392

– foreign policy 44, 45, 126, 128, 129, 142, 143, 147, 150, 194, 200–02, 209, 217, 294, 327, 328, 356
– and Japan 77, 128, 129, 147, 148
United Nations 258, 271, 347, 383
– Charter 273
– General Assembly 38
– Security Council 268
United States of America (USA) 3, 7, 8
– and China 1, 20, 29, 30, 34, 131, 145, 152, 153, 169, 176, 177, 180, 199, 202, 314
– and Cold War 187, 197–99, 204, 207–09, 252, 253, 260, 262, 264, 271, 277, 293, 297, 312, 314
– defence policy 90, 92, 102, 105, 272, 313, 315, 321, 330, 387
– economy 16, 54
– elections 42, 46, 95, 271
– foreign policy 5, 16, 19–26, 28–35, 39–42, 46–48, 86, 201, 209, 219, 292, 350, 353
– Geneva Conference, 1954 310, 311, 314–16, 318–20, 322–24, 328, 329, 332, 334, 335
– grand strategy, Second World War 152, 153, 156, 180, 181, 379–81
– and Japan 31, 34, 39, 40, 42, 86, 87, 394
– nuclear strategy 187, 189, 208
– and Pacific War 176, 179–81
– public opinion 19, 24, 34, 35, 90, 98, 109, 313, 333, 334
– and South Korea 317–23
– and South Vietnam 271
US Air Force
– Far East Air Force 321
US Army 90
– China Air Task Force 159
– 8th Army 318
– and grand strategy 86, 102, 107
– Merrill's Marauders 169
– 10th Air Force 163
– 14th Air Force 177
US government
– Congress 24, 30, 33, 45, 92, 95, 102
– US Information Agency 293
– US Information Service 293, 295, 297, 298
– Joint Chiefs of Staff 157, 160, 162, 165, 175, 176, 315, 380, 387

– National Security Council 314, 324, 327, 334
– State Department 22, 23, 27, 30, 31, 37, 41, 45, 388
– War Department 155–57, 177
US Marine Corps 81, 90, 145
– Advanced Base Brigade 8, 90
– Advanced Base School 8, 88
– defence battalions 103, 104, 106, 109, 110
– doctrine 81, 86, 88–92, 96, 97, 107, 110, 111
– equipment 86, 103, 104, 106
– Fleet Marine Force 94, 96, 97, 107
– and grand strategy 82, 86–88, 90, 94, 97, 101, 103, 107, 111, 112
– and Great War 89, 90
– Marine Corps Schools 96, 97
– mobilization 107, 109
– operations
– training 90, 97, 98, 103, 105, 106–08
– war plans 91, 100, 103, 107, 109
US Navy 81, 88, 90, 104, 145, 373, 378
– doctrine 101
– and grand strategy 86–88, 99, 101, 103, 106, 107, 313
– Pacific Fleet 180
– US Fleet 88, 103
– war plans 87, 88, 99–101, 103, 107

Versailles, Treaty of, 1919 5
Vietminh 197, 198, 202–04, 206–08, 212, 262, 309, 315, 325–27, 329, 347, 355
Vietnam (see also North and South Vietnam and French Indochina)
– Geneva Conference and 1, 187, 202, 324–40
– partition of 199, 200, 209, 309, 328, 329, 329, 333, 336, 337, 339, 359
Vietnam, State of 309, 335, 340
Vietnam War, American 86, 202, 338, 339, 389, 392
Vietnam War, French
– and Cold War 1, 83, 197, 198, 203, 208, 315, 316, 324, 325, 341, 344–48
– campaigns 197, 198, 204, 206–08, 320
– termination 200, 309, 330, 336, 388
Vinson, Carl 95

Vladivostok 1, 2, 39, 393
VOKS 300
Voltaire 389

Wakatsuki Reijiro 56, 57, 146
Wake Island 86, 101, 109, 110
Wan Waithayakon 245, 323
Wang Bingnan 329
Wang Jingwei 242, 245
Warrior, plan 185, 188
Washington 2, 58, 166, 354
Washington Conference, 1921–22 5, 118, 151, 375
– Agreements 119, 125, 376
– and China 118, 119
– negotiations 118, 119
– repercussions 120, 127, 149, 150
– System 5, 124, 149
– Treaties 119, 120, 377
Washington Post 346, 348
Wavell, Archibald 154, 157–59, 164, 165, 167, 185
Wedemeyer, Al 169, 178
Weigley, Russell F. 111
Westminster/Whitehall 58, 170, 374
Whampoa Military Academy 121
Wheeler, Raymond 170
White, Arthur J.S. 282, 287

Williams, Clarence Stewart 89
Wilson, Charles 315
Wilson, Huntington 41, 45
Wilson, Woodrow 16, 19, 46–48, 95, 117, 224, 374
Wingate, Orde 167, 168, 170
Wuhan 123, 138, 140
Wusong Creek 143

Xi'an Incident, 1936 229
Xinhai Revolution, 1911 46, 115, 118
Xinjiang 116

Yamamoto Isoroku 240
Yangtze River 27, 82, 122, 123, 131, 136, 137, 139
Yen Bloc, the 71, 72, 76
Yokohama Specie Bank 39, 58
Yunnan 156, 166

Zhadanov, Andre 261
Zhou Enlai 1
– and Cold War 251, 252
– and foreign policy 251, 257, 352
– at Geneva Conference, 1954 320, 325, 330–33, 335, 342, 353, 359
– and Nehru 251, 252, 351–54

www.ingramcontent.com/pod-product-compliance
Lightning Source LLC
Chambersburg PA
CBHW031749220426

43662CB00007B/333